NICOLAS
CAGE

THE UNAUTHORISED BIOGRAPHY

IAN MARKHAM-SMITH AND LIZ HODGSON

BLAKE

Published by Blake Publishing Ltd,
3 Bramber Court, 2 Bramber Road,
London W14 9PB, England

First published in paperback 2001

ISBN 1 85782 396 6

British Library Cataloguing-in-Publication Data:

A catalogue record for this book is
available from the British Library

Typeset by □

Printed in Great Britain by
Creative Print and Design (Wales),
Ebbw Vale, Gwent.

1 3 5 7 9 10 8 6 4 2

© Text copyright Ian Markham-Smith and Liz Hodgson 2001

ACKNOWLEDGEMENTS

Many people offered their generous assistance towards this book, some asking not to be identified by name. We would like to thank first of all, our friend and publisher, John Blake, for his continued encouragement and support. Also, we would like to thank his staff and especially Adam Parfitt and Rosie Ries.

In addition, our thanks go to Alan Aldaya, Albert Coombes, Rosalia de Guzman, Robert J Harbottle, Wade P Huie III, David A Jones, Barry Kernan, Patrick McQuaid, John Polsue, Jack Roth, Murray Rudomin and Jack Warford. And we are especially grateful to the wonderful and diligent staff at the Margaret Herrick Library of the Academy of Motion Picture Arts and Sciences.

Ian Markham-Smith
Liz Hodgson

CONTENTS

PROLOGUE

For Nicolas Cage, one of the finest cinema actors alive today, acting is not a drug that gives him a high, it is the medication that keeps him alive. In a career that has spanned more than 20 years, he has been making movies since he was just 17 and has become one of the most prolific Hollywood film stars of our time. Unlike many actors, he easily moves from one genre to another, whether that be daring art house films, crowd pleasing action blockbusters or tear-jerking romances.

'I've always seen acting as medicine,' he admits. 'When I first saw James Dean in *East of Eden*, that scene where he wants to give his father all the money, and his father gives it back, saying, "I don't want it," and he's weeping and weeping — well, it just ripped my heart clean out. I felt so, so sad. And it was at that point that I thought, well, that's what I want to do. That's what I want to say. I think audiences can relate to having problems in their homes and schools and lives, so I wanted to rip the mask off the superhero and get in closer to the community."

Ironic that this should come from an actor who for many years longed to play the ultimate superhero — Superman — although that dream turned into a nightmare and, unlike Superman, never took flight.

However, the star got over his disappointment playing a very different kind of super hero, an ordinary man who found love under extraordinary circumstances.

With his starring role in the movie version of author Louis de Bernières smash hit novel *Captain Corelli's Mandolin* Nicolas strives to touch every film fan's heart as he stretches himself yet again to play the music loving, bon-vivant Italian army officer who finds romance on an idyllic Greek island in the midst of World War II.

He confesses, 'When I first read the script, I was very emotional. I don't know why, I was moved by the story's romantic aspects. It seemed to me to be unlike anything I'd done before. I've normally avoided period pictures. I've felt inherently I was a contemporary personality. So I didn't know if I would be anachronistic or not. That had something to do with it, the challenge of wanting to try it.'

De Bernières' book found a worldwide audience with sales of more than 1.5 million and despite changes to the original story the movie *Captain Corelli's*

Mandolin exposes even more people to the wonders of his story of love and loyalty.

Ironically, there are many things about the star's character which can also be found in Corelli's. Like the lusty captain, the actor has an awareness of music and also found romance on the beautiful Ionian isle of Cephalonia.

Although his father, August Coppola, is an academic, Nick — as he is known to his family, friends and legion of fans around the world — comes from a long line of talented people. His uncle is *Godfather* trilogy and *Apocalypse Now* movie maker Francis Coppola, his aunt is actress Talia Shire and his grandfather was composer Carmine Coppola. His mother, Joy Vogelsang, was a dancer.

In fact, it was an awareness of his Uncle Francis' riches that ignited his ambitions. He says, 'It was kind of like this golden key that made me want to go out and get some of that for myself.' And Nick was attracted to Corelli partly because of his own musical heritage.

Nevertheless, wanting to distance himself from the Coppola family, and the baggage that brought with it in Hollywood, he changed his name to Cage, after one of his comic book heroes.

Under his new name, he established himself as an adolescent idol in *Valley Girl*, before moving on to roles in mainstream movies such as *The Cotton Club* and *Peggy Sue Got Married*. But he came into his own playing a string of weird and way out characters in quirky films like the Coen brother's cult hit *Raising Arizona*, opposite Cher in *Moonstruck*, *Vampire's Kiss* — in which he genuinely ate a live cockroach — and David Lynch's bizarre *Wild at Heart*. No sooner had he done that than he changed direction to make a series of light-hearted comedies including *Honeymoon in Vegas*, *Guarding Tess* and *It Could Happen to You*.

But it was memorable performances as a vicious killer in *Kiss of Death* and then a tragic drunk in *Leaving Las Vegas*, for which he won a Best Actor Oscar in 1996, that gained him respect as an actor's actor.

However, ever the Hollywood chameleon, he was not prepared to rest on his laurels and get typecast. In spite of his Academy Award, he set out to confirm himself as a highly popular action adventure actor in a string of blockbuster hits, *The Rock* with Sean Connery, *Con Air* and opposite John Travolta in *Face/Off*.

The critics were amazed that this newly established 'serious' actor would take the shoot-'em-up route. But his immediate post-Oscar choices were arguably his smartest decisions. Most actors use their Academy Award to make their small personal dream project but Nick used his to become a true international movie star, voted by the American magazine Entertainment Weekly as one of Hollywood's 25 Greatest Actors.

He also made his deliberate and calculated move on his terms. He says, 'I thought, how can I switch to mainstream movies and preserve some dignity and integrity?'

He managed it very successfully and justified his decision saying, 'I don't think it's crap to go to a movie and get your mind off your problems. If you just wanna get stupid, that's not crap. Why not see if it's possible to give all the explosions and whatever it is that stimulates people and gets their minds off their problems — which I think is cogent and nothing to be ashamed of. We're in the entertainment industry. It's not just putting on a beret and smoking a Gitane and saying, "I'm only going to do foreign films because I'm erudite and I'm so cool." I don't buy that. I think it's a matter of doing every kind of movie you can possibly do."

Since then he has changed direction yet again to star in the romantic drama

City of Angels; Brian De Palma's conspiracy mystery *Snake Eyes*; the dark detective thriller *8MM*; with his ex-wife, actress Patricia Arquette, in Martin Scorsese's *Bringing Out the Dead*; in yet another adventure epic, the critically bashed but highly popular *Gone in 60 Seconds*; the quirky romantic comedy, *The Family Man*; and in the expansive World War II epics *Captain Corelli's Mandolin* and *Windtalkers*.

All this from a man who was all but edited out of his first film, *Fast Times at Ridgemont High*, and whose looks were once compared to those of a basset hound.

'Even though he doesn't have a face like Robert Redford, he has a face that women are attracted to,' explained Mike Fenton, a veteran casting director who cast Nick in three of his early movies. 'The adulation, the money and the fame that he receives is the icing on the cake. But when one looks at his face, one knows he's having a great time even if he is in pain. Nicolas loves acting.'

Although he has a reputation for pushing himself to extremes and going over the top in his approach to his varied roles, Nick always attempts to humanise even his most outrageous characters, to bring an 'Everyman' quality to his performances to which his audiences can relate; indeed, critics have often picked up on the universal appeal he instills even in unpleasant personalities.

Nick's first acting experience came when he was growing up in suburban Long Beach, California, when he and his brothers put on back-yard shows for neighbourhood children, and he was first immortalised on film when his brother Christopher was given a Super-8 cine camera. After his parents divorced when he was 12, he moved with his father to Beverly Hills to enable him to attend the famous Beverly Hills High School, where he won a role in a school production of *Oklahoma*. When he was not cast in the following year's production of West Side Story he left school in disgust and started acting professionally.

The West Side Story disappointment was not the only misfortune he suffered at school. Despite his famous name his family was far from rich and he felt intimidated by his wealthier classmates — so intimidated he did not even date. After leaving school, however, his love life blossomed and he had relationships with a string of actresses. He was briefly engaged to Jenny Wright of *St Elmo's Fire* and had a long love affair with *The Doors* actress Christina Fulton, who bore him a son, Weston. A two-year relationship with model Kristen Zang followed.

But his most enduring love was to be with *Lost Highway* star Patricia Arquette. He proposed to her when they first met and pursued her so ardently she was scared off. Eight years later, by this time also the parent of a son, she proposed out of the blue, and they wed in 1995. But their relationship remained one of the most unconventional in Hollywood and after five bizarre years, during which they maintained separate homes, they finally divorced just months before the release of *Captain Corelli's Mandolin*. Ironically, while he was shooting that movie Nick fell for the charms of his beautiful Spanish co-star, the lovely Penélope Cruz, who had previously starred with Nick's wife in *The Hi-Lo Country*.

Nick now owns a string of magnificent homes in California and, along with the property, he has collected performance cars, Lamborghinis, Ferraris, Porsches, pop and classic artworks and vintage comic books.

He earned a reputation as a selfish, wild-man actor in his early days, bragging about going into the movies for sex, smashing up a trailer and petulantly refusing to do publicity for his movies. His image was further compounded by Nick eating a live cockroach on the film *Vampire's Kiss*, and invoking the spirit of Elvis Presley throughout his work.

But as he matured he became increasingly recognised, by film-makers, critics and the public alike, as an actor who could turn his talent to every movie genre, every type of part. Yet despite his professional success and the fame and fortune it has brought him, his most important role, though one that he accepted reluctantly at first, is being a father to his son Weston.

In the role he plays in *Captain Corelli's Mandolin*, Nick was able to display the passions that are hidden deep inside of him that make him such a great father and movie actor.

CHAPTER ONE
FROM LONG BEACH TO
BEVERLY HILLS HIGH

The skinny kid in jeans, cowboy boots and shades swaggered up to the bigger boys sitting at the back of the bus. Chewing his gum he drawled, 'I'm Roy Richards, Nicky Coppola's cousin, and if you screw with him again I'm gonna kick your ass.'

The older lads were stunned into silence as young Roy got off the school bus and walked away. What they could not tell from his back as he sauntered off was that a big grin had brightened up his solemn-looking face and that, in a way, a star had been born.

This was the defining moment that set 10-year-old Nicolas Coppola on the winding path that would propel him from a troubled childhood to a successful acting career that would see him win an Academy Award under his new name — Nicolas Cage. The imaginative child, who had long staged puppet shows for his brothers at home, realised with this public performance that he could transform himself into a new persona, convincing even people who knew him to accept him as someone else.

The school bus confrontation in the middle-class city of Long Beach in southern California had its roots in young Nick's love of bizarre practical jokes, a forerunner of the image he would later cultivate with wacky film roles.

An earlier prank that went wrong ended with him being thrown out of his first junior school and sent to a tougher environment where he was bullied mercilessly. That was the catalyst for him dressing up in his big brother's clothes, slicking back his hair with gel and confronting his enemies as Roy Richards.

Years later, he recalled, 'I was expelled from regular elementary school for being a prankster. Once, the kids all brought lunch to class and I said I'd bring egg salad sandwiches. I went to Farmers' Market and bought five cans of fried grasshoppers and crushed 'em up, put 'em in the egg salad and watched everybody eat them. They'd go, "Oh! There's an antenna in there!" Well, I got caught and expelled and I went to a very rough school — a juvenile delinquents' school. And I used to get beat up on the back of the bus because there were these three big guys who commandeered the back seat. They were 12 or 13.'

As well as hitting Nick, one of the lads used to demand that he hand over chocolate bars from his lunch box, and that upset him even more than the beatings, prompting him to adopt the disguise.

'They bought it,' he recalled gleefully. 'That was really my first experience in acting. And I think I knew then that I could make people believe I was somebody else. But I couldn't be threatening or intimidating as me — I had to think I was somebody else in order to get there.'

Inspired by his first success, he used the same tactic on another occasion.

'There was another neighbourhood bully who was always beating me and my older brothers up,' he said. 'One day I became the Incredible Hulk. I took off my shirt and screamed as loud as I could and chased him. I was just a skinny little runt of a kid but he ran off.'

Nicolas Coppola was not supposed to grow up to be an actor, or the kind of class clown who could be expelled before even reaching his teens. He was the youngest of August and Joy's three sons, and was exposed to the arts from an early age, his father hoping he would become a writer. But very early on it was clear he had a flair for the dramatic, starting with an allergy to his mother's milk and not being expected to live.

When Nick was older, his parents told him about his health problems and he recalled, 'I think everyone was concerned that as an infant I wasn't going to live. I always had this image of doctors putting these sharp objects in my head and in my face. The way my mother described it, it sure seemed a lot more intrusive than your standard allergy test today. So I don't know what it was, really.'

Nick was born on 7 January 1964, and when he was just four days old his father declared that his new son already had his own unique outlook on the world. August, who had also established the characters of his other sons, Marc and Christopher, four days after their birth, announced, 'Nick opened his eyes and had a peculiar, quizzical look that gave him a sense that the world was a strange place and he was taking it all in, in a very strange way. He was the only child I ever felt I had to introduce myself to. He looked like an alien.'

The Coppola family lived what appeared to be a normal, middle-class existence on Hackett Avenue, a tree-lined street near California State University, Long Beach. August, the oldest of three children of a second-generation Italian immigrant, was regarded as the genius of the family. He had a PhD in Comparative Literature and worked as a literature professor at the university. August's pay packet had to be stretched to make ends meet for his growing family, but the boys never felt deprived. Nor, when they were very young, did they have any reason to feel significantly worse off than their cousins, Gian Carlo and Roman, whose father, August's younger brother Francis, was a journeyman film-maker who had directed his first feature film, *Dementia 13*, for horror-meister Roger Corman, the summer before Nick was born.

August shouldered much of the burden of bringing up the boys, encouraging them to read and watch art films when their school friends were watching Walt Disney cartoons. It also fell to him to comfort young Nick when his over-active imagination generated bizarre recurring nightmares which he can still remember.

'At four, I used to have this terrible nightmare that I was on the toilet and this giant blonde woman in a gold bikini would reach into the bathroom window like King Kong and pluck me off the toilet seat and laugh at me,' he said. 'My father would come into my room when I was screaming and say, "Think of the white horse. The white horse will come and take your bad dreams away." And it did. I would meditate on the white horse. I would visualise it in the black.

'I remember another one, too: a clown scaling down a building like Spiderman. I knew he was coming and I would look out the window and he would look up and smile at me as he was coming. These and other dreams pervaded my childhood. I was scared of many things.

'And I used to have nightmares that my mother's head was attached to a cockroach's body and she was living in the garage. That really freaked me out. So I was always horrified of bugs.'

Ironically, as he grew older, one of Nick's favourite books was Franz Kafka's *Metamorphosis*, about a man who wakes up one morning to discover that he has been transformed into a giant beetle.

Looking back over his childhood, Nick believes the seeds of his desire to act were sown because he was frequently left to his own devices, while his father was at work and his mother was so often distracted.

'Since I was six, I had invented an imaginary world where I could go and be these other characters,' he said. 'That's probably where I started acting. I remember sitting on the living room floor and there was our 1969 television set, it was this beautiful little Zenith TV that was wood and had an oval screen. I would just sit there trying to work out how to get inside the TV — to become one of those characters in the TV. I had a very active imagination, and it was my protector in that I think I had a wonderful childhood.'

When Nick was only seven and in elementary school, he won a school talent contest singing The Beatles' 'Yellow Submarine' in a peculiar high-pitched voice. Looking back years later, he recalled, 'I had this voice, my mother called it the bottle voice. It was a wonderful feeling. Girls were screaming. I felt like a rock star at age seven.'

Some 25 years later, remembering the hours he spent in front of that television, he asked his maternal grandmother, Louise Vogelsang, if she had any idea where it might be. Much to his delight, she found it stored in her garage, and he installed it in his apartment in downtown Los Angeles.

'Because of my father's creative encouragement, I invented a fantasy world for myself,' Nick continued. 'Whether it was dreaming of being an astronaut or playing with my toys and puppet shows, I lived in a make-believe world of my own. I remember when I was nine or ten and crazy about comic books I came up with a comic-book alter-ego. I called myself "The Spirit" and I would put on this white T-shirt with a black "S" on it, a white fedora hat and a white cape and I'd strap a boomerang to my chest. Every night at about 2.00am, I would climb out of my window and patrol the alley behind my house, looking for evil-doers with my boomerang.

'Then I thought I was Evel Knievel! I saw George Hamilton play him in the movie and I remember thinking how cool he was, the way he would rev his bike, adjust the chain, wipe the grease off his boot — all in slow motion — then do the ultimate jump over 20 vans. That changed my life. From then on I started jumping over beer kegs on my bicycle. But that wasn't enough. So one day I made a big hoop out of cardboard and doused it in kerosene, and I announced to the whole neighbourhood that I was going to jump through this hoop of fire. Word quickly got out and all these kids started paying me money to watch me do it. But when the big day came, and all these kids were gathered around, my dad found out and shut the whole thing down.'

Despite his cycling ambitions, Nick was always more of a creative character than an active one. He recalled, 'Sports caused me a great deal of difficulty in school. My nightmare was that moment of "Who's going to get picked for the team?" My father wasn't the kind of guy that you played ball with. My brothers and I weren't really into sports. We were into creating.

'My brother got his first camera when he was 11 and we were always making Super-8 films and putting on shows. Christopher and I would play the Addams Family in this thing we did called *The Great Séance*. We'd invite the kids on our street to come over at around 9.00pm for the show and we'd rig up ghosts made out of plastic bags. We'd have all these different spook shows going and we even put on puppet shows.'

Christopher Coppola, now a movie director, added, 'We were doing pretty bizarre little films. And everybody always thought that Nick was going to be an actor, because he just had a presence.'

One special favourite, he recalled, was a tale of passion under the big top, called *The Unknown Circus*. Christopher said, 'My brother played the jealous clown who kills the tightrope walker for stealing his girlfriend!'

One of those early Super 8 films shows a young Nicolas Cage wearing a cape and tee-shirt with a Superman 'S' on the front, flexing his puny muscles and hurling himself at the wall of a barn. Superman was to become a motif for him in his adult film career, and for years he dreamed of playing the Man of Steel on the big screen.

Christopher was actually the first person to direct Nick, even before he got a camera. He said, 'We started holding these séances for neighbourhood kids when I was nine and Nick was seven. They were pretty great, actually. I put together the music and script. And I had a firm hand on it. I would direct the action and Nick would hide in the closet and be the actor. At the right moment, he would make weird noises.'

Although there would later be tension between uncle and nephew, Francis Coppola also recognised the potential in young Nick, saying, 'Nicolas was always fascinating to watch, even when he was little. At school, he was the heart of fascinating routines. He would repeat the same phrase again and again; each time it would become more hilarious.'

Years later, after he won his Oscar for *Leaving Las Vegas*, old neighbours remembered Nick as a creative, if somewhat eccentric, child.

'Nicky and his brother Christopher were always trying to get the other kids on the streets to come over to their house by putting on plays and holding séances, things like that and their parents didn't discourage them,' recalled Marlene Smith, a neighbour whose son Kent went to Tincher Elementary School with Nick. 'He was very animated as a child. He was unusual but he was real sweet. You just never knew what he was going to do next. I remember times when he would dress up like Dracula and run around the neighbourhood.'

Another neighbour, Brenda Chappell, also remembered young Nick's Dracula obsession, because he planted a love-bite on her five-year-old daughter, Renée.

'He put a hickey on my daughter's neck playing Dracula,' she said. 'I told him he'd better stop sucking on her neck or I'd knock his head off. I was happy when he won the Oscar, though. How many people know an Oscar winner who put a hickey on their daughter's neck?'

Nick was obviously conscious from an early age that his family was not well off, because he often tried to make money from his madcap escapades, like the Evel Knievel stunt that never got off the ground. Once, he and Christopher tried to charge their friends two cents each to watch one of their performances, but they were forced to cut their prices.

Brenda Chappell recalled, 'None of the kids had two cents so nobody went. So about half-an-hour later, Nicky and his brother came back, saying the price was now one cent. A lot of the kids went then. It's amazing when you think that he was once acting for a bunch of kids for a penny each. Now he's a big star, making millions of dollars.'

From the time Nick was six, his mother was frequently in hospital. It is a subject he finds painful to talk about, though he also notes, with some surprise, that he came through the experience remarkably unscathed for a sensitive soul.

'My mother was away a lot of the time. It left me to create an imaginary world in my playing. I was always creating roles. I was alone a lot but I enjoyed playing.

'My mother was — is — a very gentle person, a very fragile person, with an immense ability to show love but without having had a chance to express fully who she was as a talent. I think she was ultimately frustrated because she should have been expressing herself in an art form and she wasn't.

In fact, Nick later discovered that he was affected by his mother's illness. When he was in his thirties he read an article about schizophrenics and their children and realised it applied to him.

'The offspring tend to become over-achievers and they become this super-vigilant, over-achiever type of personality,' he said. 'I've actually got a label. I'm a "superfrenetic".' Superfrenetics — the offspring of schizophrenics — are rare. Charlie Chaplin was a superfrenetic. I finally found something I was comfortable with.'

To add to his worries prompted by his mother's illness, the young Nick had to live with the suspicion that he might actually be the son, not of August Coppola, but of actor Robert Mitchum, a suspicion bolstered by the similarities in their drooping eyes and hangdog expressions. He is convinced that the suspicion caused friction between him and his father, even after his mother confessed she had lied about having an affair.

Nick explained, 'They were fighting and she just said it to him, "Nicky's not your child!" There's a beautiful old picture of Robert Mitchum and it says, "To Joy, love and kisses, Bob." Obviously nothing happened; she was just a young lady in a dance group and Robert Mitchum was around, and she got an autographed picture. The fact is, if you looked at a picture of my dad and you look at me, it's obvious that I'm his son. But it was always there.

'I never knew there was this question until my mother, in the hospital, told me about it. She apologised. She admitted to me that she told him that in the heat of anger. I'm sure she doesn't feel good about it, but you know how people say things in arguments. But there's always been an edge from my father toward me, and that must be the reason. My dad always used to bring him up.'

Perhaps surprisingly, despite the tension, Nick started watching Robert Mitchum movies and became a huge fan.

Not all of his young memories of his mother are sad, of course. He said, 'If I look at home movies of when I was two years old, I can see that she was a very caring mother, the way she touched me. I remember one birthday party when I got scared by all the candles. I tried to run away and she turned me back. It was very beautiful.'

There were not too many home movies around, however. As Nick noted, 'One of the reasons why I think I became a film actor is by the time I came around, the home movie camera was not out as much. There were all these pictures of Marc and of Christopher but there were very few of me.'

As his mother's health deteriorated, the fortunes of his Uncle Francis were on the rise. Francis Ford Coppola won his first Oscar, writing the screenplay for *Patton* in 1970 and two years later picked up two more of the golden statues, for Best Director and Best Screenplay for *The Godfather*. His new-found success and growing fortune prompted tension between him and his older brother, who had always been regarded as the family star. But that did not stop August sending his sons to northern California where Francis lived, first to San Francisco, then to the wine country of the Napa Valley.

Nick recalled: 'I had really terrific summers with my cousins. Those are the best memories I have. I was always up to something, playing jokes. I got into trouble once for setting a firecracker off in my cousins' room.'

But he also remembers the rivalry between his father and uncle, and that it was expressed sometimes in petty ways. For example, he and his brothers were forbidden to wear *Godfather* T-shirts Francis sent them, and when August sneaked him in to see the film, when he was 10, he told Nick, 'Don't tell your uncle we went to see the movie.'

Nick said, 'There was a tension that went both ways. My uncle was always talking about my father's good looks and how outstanding he was at school, and how he was being groomed for something at the UN. There was always competitive pressure and it goes back to Italy, I guess.'

At the time, however, Nick was more concerned about the surprising effects *The Godfather* had on him than worrying about the relationship between August and Francis.

He laughed, 'I went to see *The Godfather* and there was that scene where Al Pacino kisses that beautiful Sicilian woman and she takes her bra off. I remember I was feeling new things. It really turned me on.'

He also recalled a youthful crush on Barbara Eden, star of the sitcom *I Dream of Jeannie*, in which she wore a daring (for the time) midriff-baring slave costume to play a genie in a bottle released by a young astronaut played by Larry Hagman, who would go on to find fame as JR Ewing in *Dallas*.

Although Nick and his father have not always got on, as a young boy he hero-worshipped him. 'My father looks a lot like Sean Connery,' he said. 'When my dad took me to see *Dr No* at the drive-in, I imagined myself as James Bond's son. Dad's one of the most remarkable characters anybody's going to meet. He intimidates my friends. For starters, he's an imposing-looking figure — white sideburns, a combination of Sean Connery and Beethoven. My father was very academic and very intelligent and for a while I idolised him. I wanted to be accepted and listen to the classical music and show him I had his tastes. There was always that desire to be recognised by my father as an intellectual.

'He had this very professorial air about him, but he always approached things with a great deal of creativity. My father was always doing things to encourage our imaginations. I remember one time I was upset about breaking a little Pinocchio toy that I owned. So my father planted Pinocchio's head in the garden and told me to water it. A couple of days later a great big plant-like thing had grown in its place. I ran out and opened it and it was a giant wooden Pinocchio that my father had placed there. I kept it and I still have it. After that I started planting all my hot-wheel cars with the hope that one of them would blossom into a real car but it never quite worked the same!'

The Disney film of *Pinocchio* also had a profound effect on Nick, and when he grew up he looked upon it as a parable for dealing with his profession.

'You can go a certain way and get totally taken off the path and find yourself being charmed by the sly fox. And, being an innocent, I think that happens to every young actor. They find themselves in a situation and somebody comes along and seduces them with drugs or promises. So, I mean, it's an interesting movie to watch for what *not* to do, especially if you choose the actor's life. You know, "An actor's life for me, hi diddley dee ..." '

Not all the films Nick watched as a child were as straightforward as Disney cartoons or the tongue-in-cheek action of James Bond. He went on, 'When I was a kid the other kids were seeing Disney and my father was showing me movies like Fellini's *Juliet of the Spirits*. This was before video so he would take us to the art-house cinemas. I saw *Citizen Kane*, and that's when I discovered Max Schreck and *Nosferatu* and *Dr Caligari*, which gave me nightmares. It is weird but I didn't think it was weird because as a kid you think it's like what everybody is doing.'

However, he admitted that some of the weirdness rubbed off and he always felt that he should be different from his friends — physically different. 'I was always shocked when I went to the doctor's office and they did my X-ray and didn't find that I had eight more ribs than I should have or that my blood was green,' he joked.

Nick was also very proud of an unusual exhibition his father designed for a San Francisco museum, to encourage people to explore all their senses. He bragged, 'My father created the Tactile Dome in San Francisco's Exploratorium. You crawl in total darkness and feel your way through sponges and netting and you fall into two tons of birdseed or land on a waterbed. But we were going through this exhibition when we were like six, and it scared the shit out of me. Looking at it now, it's brilliant. Disneyland wanted him to do one, but he wouldn't because he wanted it to be free.

'My father sometimes took things a little far, however. I remember one Thanksgiving we didn't eat because my father came home with a box of crayons and a bunch of paper plates and said, "OK guys, for our Thanksgiving we're going to draw our dinner." It was kind of funny and interesting — but, hey, we were hungry!'

In his adult life, Nick has had a series of unusual pets, and his passion for animals was also evident from his youngest days. Neighbour Pat Parris said, 'Once, when he was about five years old he came over just to talk about his previous life as a butterfly. I'd ask him questions and he'd make things up as he went. He did a pretty good job of it, too. Another time he started telling me about whales. I wasn't paying much attention and I think he got a little mad. He went over to his house and came back with a book to show me what he was talking about.'

He was fond of flora as well as fauna, and once told a story about feeling so sorry for a dying Christmas tree that, inspired by *Frankenstein*, he tried to save it by sewing and taping its trunk to a live tree. 'I felt so bad about the Christmas tree that I killed another tree trying to bring it back to life,' he said.

Nick's life took a dramatic turn when he was 12. After 16 years of struggle, August finally realised his marriage was over and Nick and his brothers were put in the awkward position of appearing before a judge to talk about who should have custody over them.

'When they split up, I was relieved,' Nick admitted years later. 'It was uncomfortable though. I had to sit down and talk with the judge. I went in and smiled the whole way through the meeting. That was a sad day because my mother obviously wasn't able to raise us, yet she still tried to be strong and have dignity and she wanted custody.'

August, however, was awarded custody of the boys.

It was not only Nick's family life that changed. Academic August, concerned about Nick's education, decided that the state school system in Long Beach was not good enough. He moved the family to San Francisco, where Nick was briefly enrolled in Japanese classes to expand his horizons — with somewhat mixed results. The first time he practised his new-found language skills in public was during a visit to Francis Ford Coppola's family. The film-maker was entertaining a potential investor and asked his nephew to break the ice with a Japanese greeting. Nick remembered with a grin, 'You know, it was like a big moment that one of the family was going to say something in Japanese to this Japanese businessman. So I looked at him, and I said, "Yasai." The Japanese guy says, "That's great. You know, most people say, 'Hello,' most people say, 'Good evening.' No one's ever said, 'Vegetable' to me before as a greeting." '

Unable to afford private school fees, August set his sights on one of the best public schools in the country, Beverly Hills High. That meant another move, this time to Beverly Hills, because demand for places at the school is so high that it only accepts students who actually live within the limits of the tiny city, and employs special inspectors to track down people who lie about their addresses to get their children in.

Nick looks back on his life in Long Beach with affection. He said, 'I think Long Beach is kind of a wonderful place to grow up in because it has a little bit of both. It has a sense of a city but at the same time it's more rural, or suburban, so you don't feel overloaded by the traffic or the sounds and bells and whistles of city life. I seem to always remember the light falling in Long Beach in a way that made everything glow, especially as a child playing in the back yard.'

The Coppola family moved to Hamilton Drive, just two streets from the eastern limits of the city and Nick duly enrolled at Beverly Hills High, *alma mater* of a host of actors, including Rob Reiner, Richard Chamberlain, Richard Dreyfuss, David Schwimmer, Betty White, Jamie Lee Curtis and Carrie Fisher. Nick's classmates included future actor Crispin Glover, who would achieve cult status with his role in *Back to the Future* and co-star with Nick in *Wild at Heart*, and singer-songwriter Maria McKee, a member of the popular California band Lone Justice in the 1980s and who now has a solo career.

He hated school right from the start, even though he was a bright pupil, because he was acutely aware of his family's relative poverty compared to most of the other kids living in million-dollar mansions.

'I didn't like high school,' he admitted. 'Frankly, I was a nerd and I didn't fit in. In high school I was always labelled the outsider or the weirdo. I went to Beverly Hills High but I hate saying that because it suggests that I came from a rich family. The truth is that my father was supporting three children on a teacher's wages. We didn't have any money. We lived right where it says, 'YOU ARE NOW ENTERING BEVERLY HILLS'. Going to a school like Beverly Hills High

School, where all the kids have money, and they're driving to school in Porsches and Ferraris and I'm taking the RTD bus, and I can't ask a girl out on a date because I'd have to ask her to take the bus with me — well, it was frustrating, to say the least. None of the pretty girls wanted to go out with me. They didn't want to ride the fucking bus with me!

'It angered me that I couldn't ask the girls out because I didn't have a fancy car. And so I was frustrated by that. I suppose that must have had more to do with my anger than anything else. I think the ultimate thing that angers any young man is sort of unrequited love or not getting the girl.'

At first, however, he flourished in the classroom. His first-year English teacher, Roberta Beatty, recalled, 'When we did group projects in class, he would elect to do them by himself and his work was the envy of the entire class. He was very intelligent and talented.'

School friends knew he was unhappy, however, and sensed he had great things in store. Maria McKee, who had a number-one hit in Britain with *Show Me Heaven*, the theme song from Tom Cruise's film *Days of Thunder*, recalled, 'Crispin, Nick and me — we were all misfits there. I just assumed we were all destined for something. I really believed in Nick and Crispin.' And John Prince, a writer and director who was a few years older than Nick and was therefore in a different class, pointed out, 'Everyone knew Nick Cage was going to be someone special. He did *Hamlet* as if it was solving geometry problems.'

Visits to Uncle Francis and his cousins, while enjoyable, only made him feel worse, and he somewhat shamefacedly admits that he was jealous because they were better off.

'They had things,' he said, 'Material things. My father's not a capitalist, he's a thinker. He's the kind of person who, if he invented a dental drill, he wouldn't ask to be paid for it. He'd provide it for the people. I feel silly sometimes that I had this driving need to make money. My uncle was always very generous, but at the same time I knew the things my cousins had were not the things that I had. It kind of motivated me to go out there and get them for myself.

'I've had a strange relationship with money, because I've seen it from an early age and seen the powerful effects of money. And even when I was a little child, spending summers at Francis' grand old Victorian house, the beautiful architecture and the smells of the old wood, I had a motivation to go out and get it for myself.

'I didn't know much about my uncle other than he was a very affectionate guy. He would come over and drink red wine and have goat's cheese. Food is a major bonding force in my Italian family. Then, as I got older, there was the visceral frustration of noticing material things that I didn't have. I would visit my cousins and my uncle in Lake Tahoe and they would have speedboats, yachts, big Victorian mansions and supercool electric walkie-talkies, and I was still flying my 25-cent balsa-wood gliders. I ultimately think it made me hungry. I went into a kind of Heathcliff mode where I wanted to claim my own stake in the material world. That was a motivation to become an actor.'

During one of Nick's holidays, he was driving with his brother, uncle and cousin Roman and heard a song which was to become a triumphal anthem for him — the Beatles' 'Baby, You're a Rich Man'.

'I first became aware of the power of that song when my Uncle Francis was driving in his car over the Golden Gate Bridge,' Nick remembered. 'I was in the back seat with my cousin Roman and my brother Christopher and he was listening to that album and that song came on. The words "How does it feel to be one of the beautiful people?" came on, and I was thinking, yeah, he really deserves to listen to this, doesn't he? The sun was really bright, the light was clear, everything was blue and I was 13 and very aware of his success and his accomplishments and starting to get a little intimidated by him. He was right at the height of *The Godfather Part II*. I was thinking about when I could have the right to listen to that song.'

Six years later, after the successful release of *Valley Girl*, Nick was to remember that moment and claim the song as his own.

When Nick was 15 and his older brothers had left home, August sent him to live with his uncle's family for a year while he was travelling. It is a period Nick looks back on with mixed feelings, but remembers that it fixed his path to becoming an actor when he entered the American Conservatory Theater in San Francisco for a summer acting course. Although he later confessed to suffering from stage fright, he was hooked.

His formal education was not so successful, however, and although he could hardly believe it, he actually missed Beverly Hills High.

'I was in ninth grade, getting straight 'A's, really excited about school,' he told the *New York Times*, on one of the rare occasions he did not dismiss his years there. 'Then I was put into this little country school. I went suddenly from being the cool guy to the geek. My grades went from straight 'A's to straight 'F's. I went from a public school to a private high school run by the Christian Brothers in Napa Valley and I was getting religion rammed down my throat. I thought it was dogmatic and unfair and said so. I said religion was only good for inspiration and works of art.'

His stay at the Coppolas' Napa Valley winery home, and his growing maturity, helped him gain a better understanding of his famous uncle and the tensions that often accompany creativity. 'Francis is a powerful man who enjoys his position,' he said. 'There's a strange mixture of pride and competition that I sometimes feel in the family. Very intense. It's a family rich in the sense of passion and feeling. We come from a long line of robbers and highwaymen in Italy, you know — killers, even. It's loaded with grudges and passion. There is also a lot of creativity. My family has always been very competitive. I mean, there's been a competitive edge on Francis' side ever since I can remember — any creative individual can fluctuate between being a very warm man to kind of dark.'

One of the most striking memories of this time of his life is the occasion he believes he just might have seen a ghost. He said, 'I was living in the attic and there were bats there in between the walls. You could hear them scratching and the place smelled of guano. One night I was not asleep yet but the door in front of my bed opened and there was this pitch-black silhouette of a woman with big hair. I thought it was my aunt coming in to say good night. So I said, "Good night," and it didn't say anything. Then it moved towards me and my body froze up and I let out this bloodcurdling scream and threw my pillow. Then it disappeared. Now, am I saying I saw a ghost? I still don't know. But I saw something that freaked me out.'

His cousin Sofia also remembers him and his cousin Roman getting up to mischief. She recalled, 'They exploded a blender! I think my mother made them save up their money and buy a new one. They were always doing things like that. It was fun to be around Nick. He was a hot disco king in high school. He also used to tell me ghost stories that were really scary.'

More scary than any ghost story, however, was the day on a later visit to the Napa Valley when he and Roman stumbled into a nest of rattlesnakes and thought they were going to die. Instead, one of the snakes met a grisly end as Nick became an action hero for the first time and killed it.

Referring to it as one of the most terrifying moments of his entire life, he said, 'I was once surrounded by rattlesnakes in a rattlesnake patch with my cousin Roman when we were 16 or 17. We were fishing in the Napa Valley and walked right into it. There was a huge one coiled in front of us. A bigger one, to the left, was uncoiled, so I knew he wasn't a problem. We had to go over the coiled one, so we felt trapped and paralysed with fear. There was nowhere to run, we were surrounded. I saw this pole with a nail through it and I knew that I had to do something, so I grabbed the pole and pounded the snake. Then it came up and started rattling and was about to strike. Roman was just standing there watching me. I killed it, but felt bad about it. I felt anything you kill you've got to eat, so I took it home, cut the poison glands out, took the rattles off and cooked it.'

Looking back on his time in Napa, Nick realised it had had a huge impact on his future career. He said, 'I was in this wonderful house with wonderfully generous people, but it wasn't my stuff, it wasn't my house. I didn't know why I was there. I was frustrated beyond belief. And at that point it was like a golden key was given to me. Because I said, "You know what? I am going to get back, I am going to get even somehow." I said I was going to buy a big house in San Francisco where they used to have a house — and I did. Francis was more of an inspiration than a teacher. He had a lot of neat stuff and I was always trying to figure out a way to get all that neat stuff. I think that's why I went into acting.'

Nick found another inspirational model, one who has motivated many an idealistic young actor — James Dean in *East of Eden*. He was so stirred by the latter-day Cain and Abel story that he switched his affection from comedy to drama, saying, 'I used to be very silly when I was a kid and that was usually how I made friends. I really loved comedy; it was always the most natural thing for me to do. For the longest time I was a fanatic about Jerry Lewis. Then, when I was about 15, I remember seeing an Elia Kazan movie and saying, "Wait a minute, that's the stuff I want to do. I want to do something dramatic. I want to really make people feel something." I saw *East of Eden*, where James Dean works so hard to get the money for his father and is rejected — that scene broke my heart. It still does. I was so moved by it that I said, "That's what I want to do. I want to be able to do that."

'The way Kazan portrayed that situation, of a son wanting the love from the authoritarian, paternal figure in a family so desperately, it clicked. Until then I was a fan of comedy, comedy, comedy, but that affected me more profoundly than anything I'd ever seen.'

Elia Kazan is the legendary director who made *A Streetcar Named Desire* and *On the Waterfront*, but who was scorned in Hollywood for years for 'naming names' of former Communist colleagues during the anti-red witchhunt of the 1950s.

When he returned home to his father in Beverly Hills, Nick joined the high school Drama Society. However, he did not tell his father about his ultimate ambitions, preferring to let him think he was following August's preferred path.

'When I was 15 I told my father I had decided to become a writer,' he said. 'That made him very happy. He had really hoped I would become a writer some day. He encouraged me to write all the time. He would give me great books to read, like *Siddhartha* or *Brave New World* and get me to write a missing chapter. He would say, "I want you to pretend you're inside the book and I want you to use the characters and the situations and write a chapter that doesn't exist." '

Nick was still trying to live up to his father's ambitions, despite his ambivalence towards him. And years later he remembered that his father's musical passions affected him in a similar way to his literary ones. He said, 'I discovered rock 'n' roll fairly late in life. My father, being a Professor of Comparative Literature, was always listening to Wagner and stuff like that, and because I wanted very much to be like my father I listened to it, too. I felt kind of sinful if I listened to rock 'n' roll music. Other kids were talking about Kiss and I was talking about classical music since I was seven. I guess they thought it was kind of bizarre. I said that's what I wanted to be, a writer, to impress him, but I wasn't being honest with myself. Now, whenever I do write and finish a story or a painting, I feel very satisfied because I know I've done it for the right reasons.'

Bizarrely, Nick claims he once convinced his father he was a secret songwriter. British-born singer-songwriter Joe Jackson had had a big hit in the United States with his single 'Is She Really Going Out with Him?' from his first album, *Look Sharp*, and Nick told August he had written it.

'I lied,' he confessed years later. 'There's a reason why I did that. My father, like anybody, has more than one side. He was very into the creative stuff but he could also be verbally abusive. I needed to believe he believed in me. And if he believed that I wrote that song, then he must have thought I was special. And if he thought I was special, then I could have the courage to get on with what I wanted to do with my life.'

At other times, Nick toyed with the idea of becoming a scientist or an astronomer, and he claims that once, when he was in hospital suffering from hepatitis, he fantasised about turning his back on his old life and joining the merchant marine, a fantasy that would recur when his early film career was not going well.

By this time, Nick was getting rave reviews for his performances at school. His former music teacher, Joel Pressman, vividly recalled Nick returning to school after his stint at the American Conservatory Theater, 'He became the focal point of every scene.' Pressman also remembered that today's multi-millionaire, award-winning star, was facing hard financial times as a youth. 'I remember he had trouble paying for a pair of dress shoes to wear with his madrigal singer's costume,' he said.

Nick's ambitions were revealed one night when he returned home late after staying on to audition for a role in a school production of *Oklahoma* to find his father in a foul temper.

'The dishes weren't washed and my father let me know it,' he said. 'He's like, "There's a million dishes in there. You'd better wash the dishes. Nicholas, you are never going to be an actor, so don't even try." It was the one time I stood up to my father. I just lost it. I blew up at him. I started yelling and screaming and all this rage came pouring out of me. I said, "You're wrong. I am going to be an actor. You are going to wish you hadn't said that to me." Years later, we had a drink together and he said, "I told you that so you would prove me wrong," but I don't believe him.'

Nick won the part of Judd Fry in the school's 1981 production of *Oklahoma* and that led to his breakthrough, although he was nervous at the thought of performing at first. He recalled, 'I was terrified because I wasn't a singer and I had to sing the song "Poor Judd is Dead." '

Drama teacher John Ingle, who went on to win a role in the long-running daytime soap opera *General Hospital*, helped him overcome his stage-fright. He said, 'We gave him voice lessons and he learned to sing. The fellow who played Curly used to stand behind him in rehearsals and would almost sing into his back so he would get the pitch right by vibrations.'

Nick continued to make Super 8 movies directed by his brother Christopher. In one, Nick played a Roman prince — clad in a white, off-the-shoulder toga — who loved his father because he believed he had saved Rome by slaying dragons. Then he learned from the Gods that his father was living a lie, and that he was actually a traitor who had killed the real dragon-slayer. The prince confronted the father angrily, and the older man fell on his sword.

In 1981 he and his Beverly Hills High classmates made an ambitious student film, *The Sniper*, in which Nick starred as one of two brothers pitted against each other in war. The film, a joint production of the drama and media departments, won him his first Best Actor award.

In his acceptance speech Nick, wearing a short-sleeved black tee-shirt over a long-sleeved white one, said, 'I would like to say I had a good time working with Larry and with everybody else in *The Sniper*, and I think it's great that finally the drama department and the media department are coming together. So thank you very much.'

Thanks to his roles in *Oklahoma* and *The Sniper*, Nick was cast for a part in a pilot for a proposed American television series, *The Best of Times*, and started pumping iron for his role as a surfer and bodybuilder. The pilot, which also starred class mate Crispin Glover, was a flop, but at least he had made a start. And for once in his life he had money burning a hole in his pocket. So he did what every red-blooded, 16-year-old American boy dreams of doing and bought a sports car. This led to yet more friction between him and his father, which is very easy to understand from Nick's point of view.

'When I was 16 I got my first car, which was a Triumph Spitfire,' he said. 'I got $5,000 for this small part in a crummy TV series. That surprised everyone because I'd kept it to myself what I was up to. It wasn't very good but I felt proud of it because it was something that happened of its own accord. It wasn't exactly a good show. I can only thank God it didn't get picked up. And I took half of the money and bought this car and my father wouldn't let me drive it. I used to sit in that car and imagine I was driving to the beach. And then my father would drive it with my stepmother at the time and I would be filled with jealousy — why can't I drive my yellow Triumph Spitfire that I spent every dime on? I bought it with my own money but had to watch him and my stepmother driving it. Finally I got it registered and then the car didn't work. It was always breaking down and I was always dragging it into the shop.'

That automobile fuelled a lifelong passion for fast, flashy sports cars. But while he took great care of his Spitfire and kept it for years, he was much more cavalier with his next purchase, a battered old Camaro. Old school pal Tony Darren remembered, 'He would floor it and he'd run into trash cans and have them flying off the roof. Just anything to create some kind of havoc.'

In 1999, Nick was astonished to find that his old yellow Spitfire was still on the road and promptly bought it. 'I wanted it to know it didn't get the best of me!' he quipped.

After his success in *Oklahoma* and the excitement of his first professional acting part, however dismal the show had turned out to be, Nick was bitterly disappointed not to be chosen for a role in a school production of *West Side Story*. He decided there and then he had had enough of formal education at the age of 17.

Surprisingly, his father backed his decision to leave school without formally graduating. Nick has always been at pains, however, to point out that he was not just a teenage drop-out but took a special exam, the General Equivalency Diploma, which shows that a student who could not complete their education for whatever reason would have been capable of graduating and going on to further education.

'I didn't drop out of high school,' he insisted. 'I took the proficiency exam and got out on that. I was only going there to be in the plays and when they didn't work, I got out. I just wasn't inspired to learn in the classroom. The only reason I was going to school was because the Performing Arts Department was so excellent. My father didn't really feel that was so terrible. He felt the educational system was so out of whack that you could get more out of experiencing life than going to high school.'

But before he left the shelter of school, he had to go through an all-important American rite of passage — the High School Prom. Proms, or end-of-term dances, are formal affairs which are often criticised for encouraging teenage greed and extravagance. Girls compete for the most elaborate outfits and boys squeeze uncomfortably into rented dinner jackets. Despite the advances of feminism, the boy is supposed to pick up the bill for transport to and from the dance and to present his date with flowers. Given his financial standing compared to many of his classmates, this presented quite a problem for Nick.

'I remember my prom night was a complete disaster,' he said wryly. 'I had a date. My grandmother had given my brothers and me savings bonds. One brother cashed his bonds and got a stereo system. My other brother bought a used car. I cashed my bonds and rented a tuxedo and limousine so I could take this beautiful girl to the prom. We're at the prom and I kissed her. When she responded, I was so nervous that my stomach got really nauseous and I said, "Excuse me," and just threw up on the street, all over my shoes and my rented tux. The limo driver wouldn't let me back into the limousine because there was vomit on my shoes. He split and I had to walk home. That was my prom night.'

As if that was not humiliating enough, Nick once told this story with a different twist. Writing about a cross-country trip for *Details* magazine, when Rick James' song 'Super Freak' came on the radio, he reflected, 'This song automatically brings me back to the frustration I felt in high school. Whenever I hear it, I get a warm knot in my throat and think about all the rejections I got from girls when I asked them to the school dances. This is an important point. Had the girls in high school not minded that I didn't have a car and could only take the bus, had Suzanne not left me standing at the prom with vomit on my shoes to take a limo, I might not have turned into the flagrant commitment-phobe that I am.'

So at 17, Nicholas Coppola was ready to make his mark on the acting world. He found himself an agent, Ilene Feldman, and set about searching for work. He later admitted that his motivations were not purely about art. 'Sex was also a motivation,' he laughed, a remark that would later come back to haunt him.

Years later, reflecting on his unusual childhood, he concluded that, while it was difficult for his father to cope with his mother's illness and their divorce, Nick escaped the traumas relatively unscathed and even gained from them.

'It was really hard on him,' he said of August. 'I think he got angry. It's an impossible situation, as anybody should know. I wouldn't change it for anything in one way; I think it made my life rich and gave me a depth of emotion ... it's like a blessing in disguise. I gained something from it. It gave me an insight and a sensitivity that I don't think I would have had.'

But he added, 'My childhood was, objectively, very difficult. If I really analysed my childhood, I would have some difficulty with some of the stuff that went on, but I think I had some kind of guardian angel protecting me, because no matter how bizarre something got, I was always able to look at it like it wasn't that strange.'

CHAPTER TWO

VALLEY HIGH

Despite the tensions between August and Francis Ford Coppola, and young Nick's ambivalence towards the northern Californian branch of his family, the Coppolas were always a tight-knit clan. While Francis was the obvious superstar once he started collecting Oscars and nominations, he was not alone in his artistic tendencies.

The original immigrants to the United States, Augustino and Maria Coppola, had moved from a small town called Bernalda, in the heel of Italy, to New York City. They had seven sons, one of whom, Carmine, won a scholarship to the prestigious Juilliard School, one of America's leading music colleges. There, Carmine, a gifted flautist, palled up with another first-generation Italian–American, who took him home to meet his family. Carmine promptly fell in love with his friend's sister, Italia Pennino, whose father had been a pianist, playwright and songwriter in his native Italy, and who was the earliest importer of Italian films to the United States.

After graduating, Carmine found a job in the orchestra at Radio City Music Hall in New York. Soon after Italia bore their first child, August, in 1934, he moved to Detroit, Michigan, working for the Detroit Symphony Orchestra, and Francis was born there in 1939. While in Detroit, Carmine was also the official arranger for the *Ford Sunday Evening Hour* radio musical show, a connection which accounted for Francis' unusual middle name of Ford. The car manufacturing giant's name was pervasive in Motor City; by coincidence, Francis was born at the Ford Hospital. The family moved back to New York in the early 1940s and Carmine worked as first flautist for the National Broadcast Corporation's orchestra, which was headed by the legendary Italian conductor Arturo Toscanini. His third child, daughter Talia, was born in New York in 1946.

After leaving NBC, he had a variety of jobs, including arranging music for the Rockettes dancers at Radio City, devising the score for the Paramount film *The Stars are Singing* and conducting travelling productions of musicals.

Although the children were exposed to music and the arts from their youngest days, Carmine did not want them to follow in his footsteps. He hoped August would grow up to be a doctor and Francis an engineer. Instead, August went the academic route and Francis, after flirting with music and mastering the tuba, won a drama scholarship to Hofstra University on Long Island, where August had done his first degree. After Hofstra, Francis enrolled in the graduate film school at the University of California, Los Angeles.

Talia also won a drama scholarship, to Yale, where she met her first husband, composer David Shire. By coincidence, both Francis and Talia started their professional careers thanks to horror director Roger Corman. Francis became a kind of jack-of-all-trades — general assistant, script doctor, special effects editor, second unit director and dialogue director on films such as *The Tower of London*, starring Vincent Price, *The Terror*, with Boris Karloff and Jack Nicholson, and a Russian film called *Battle beyond the Sun*, before directing his first feature film, *Dementia 13*, which he also wrote, for Corman. Talia made her first film, an apocalyptic story about a gas leak at an Alaskan defence station which wipes out everyone over 30, called *Gas-s-s-s*, for Corman in 1970.

Brother and sister joined forces for the first time on *The Godfather*, with Talia playing the part of Connie, whose wedding is the opening scene of the film. Ironically, Francis did not want to hire her but was overruled by Robert Evans and *Godfather* author Mario Puzo, both of whom were production executives on the picture.

After the runaway success of *The Godfather*, which won three of the ten Academy Awards for which it was nominated, Coppola films became family affairs. Talia was nominated as Best Supporting Actress for once again playing Connie in *The Godfather Part II*, and Carmine won the Oscar for best musical score. For *The Cotton Club*, Francis' sons Gian Carlo and Roman, then 20 and 18, worked as production assistants.

With this family background, nothing could have been more natural for young Nicolas Coppola than to appeal to his director uncle to give him a break. As a cocky 15-year-old, Nick recalled asking for a screen test. He was driving with Francis who was trying to cast a film called *The Escape Artist*. Nick told his uncle, 'Well, if you want to see acting, give me a screen test — I'll show you acting.' It didn't happen, but two years later Coppola decided to give his nephew a chance when he was in pre-production for *The Outsiders*. Rejected for a second time by his uncle after that reading, Nick instead auditioned for a high school flick, *Fast Times at Ridgemont High*, which starred members of the newly named Brat Pack.

As Nicolas Coppola, he tried out for the role of Brad but lost it to Judge Reinhold, who had previously made *Stripes* with Bill Murray. Instead, he was cast as 'Brad's buddy', was listed in 20th place on the cast list, and was not mentioned at all in reviews or newspaper cast lists, which generally note only the handful of leading players. He was not the only prospective star to be ignored in the ensemble cast, however. Eric Stoltz, who went on to star with Cher in *Mask*, and future *ER* heart-throb Anthony Edwards were also in the film, both listed simply as 'Stoner bud'.

Fast Times at Ridgemont High is a celebration of teenage sex, drugs and rock 'n' roll, written by 24-year-old *Rolling Stone* journalist Cameron Crowe, who had actually moved back in with his parents and gone to a high school in the beach community of Redondo Beach, California, for a year, posing as a teenager to do his research. He turned his experiences into a book in 1981 and Universal Pictures snapped it up as a film before the first page was even written. Crowe, who let four teachers in on the ruse, resisted the temptation to turn himself into the star; rather he tried to offer an accurate portrayal of the teenagers of the day, all raging hormones and insecurities.

The film starred Sean Penn, already tipped for stardom after his performance in the military school film *Taps*, Jennifer Jason Leigh, who appeared in the television film about anorexia, *The Best Little Girl in the World*, and Reinhold.

Made by first-time director Amy Heckerling, it follows the exploits of six teenagers through one year at the fictional Ridgemont High, set in the northern suburbs of Los Angeles. Stacy Hamilton, a 15-year-old eager to lose her virginity, played by Jennifer Jason Leigh, is coached in sexual behaviour — including how to perform oral sex on a carrot — by the older, more sophisticated and experienced Linda Barrett, played by model-turned-actress Phoebe Cates. The two girls have part-time jobs as waitresses in a suburban shopping mall. Stacy's elder brother Brad (Judge Reinhold) works part time with Nick at a burger joint in the same mall and is despondent when he is sacked for being rude to a customer. Then there is Mark Ratner (played by Brian Backer), a shy nerd who works at the mall's cinema complex, who wants to date Stacy. He asks his best friend, the extrovert and confident Mike Damone (played by Robert Romanus), for advice. He is, however, terrified of Stacy's sexual keenness and flees in panic. Determined to try sex, she turns to Mike, who deflowers her in a joyless encounter in a baseball dugout. She becomes pregnant and has an abortion.

Sean Penn as Jeff Spicoli is the total misfit, a surfer dude who has been stoned for years and who thinks nothing of ordering pizza to be delivered to his desk, then appearing astonished when the history teacher confiscates it. The same history teacher (played by *My Favourite Martian* star Ray Walston) later turns up at Jeff's house on the night of a school dance to coach him for an upcoming test.

The shoot was not a happy time for Nick. Although he was delighted to be making a real movie, he was acutely conscious of the Coppola name and his lack of experience. The other actors, with the careless cruelty of teenagers, sensed his insecurity and made life even more uncomfortable for him.

Years later he acknowledged, 'My fellow actors didn't accept me. They said I was there because of Francis Coppola. These actors know who they are. I felt I had to work twice as hard as the next guy to prove myself. I felt the burden of being his nephew. On the set, the actors would congregate outside my trailer and recite a version of Robert Duvall's line from *Apocalypse Now*, "I love the smell of napalm in the morning." But they said, "I love the smell of Nicolas in the morning." It was psychologically hard. No matter how good you are, you feel you're not good enough. So I really had something to prove.

'I would watch Sean Penn and try to get ideas. I was pretty much the nerd to everyone — people would ask me to be removed from their eye line. I was the brunt of jokes because my name was still Coppola.'

Despite that trauma, however, he was determined not to be discouraged. He went on, 'See, I knew something that no one else could possibly know. I knew I had wanted to act long before I knew anything else, long before I knew who Francis was. I knew it as a 6-year-old boy sitting on the rug in my living room, fantasising about how I could get inside the TV and be one of those people. It was a coincidence that my uncle was a great director.'

Judge Reinhold, who would later star with Nick in *Zandalee*, recalled years later that Nick was already deeply focused on his career. He said, 'Once I had Nick in my living room. He was maybe 17 years old and he's asking me if I think he has a shot at an acting career. And I didn't really know.'

Although the film was aimed at a teenage, high school market, it hit a major snag on the way to being released. The Motion Picture Association of America, the board which issues the all-important age ratings, gave it an X, meaning that not only would viewers under 18 be banned from seeing it, mainstream cinemas would not even show it because of the association of X-ratings and pornography. The MPAA objected to the dugout sex scene and another in a swimming pool cabana which featured a full-frontal view of naked Mike.

Universal agreed to trim the scenes to get the rating reduced to R, much to the disgust of Jennifer Jason Leigh, who said the cut scene actually showed the two teenagers were not really ready for uncommitted sex. She said at the time, 'What happens is I take the boy into the pool house. It's pretty obvious what Stacy wants to do — she's so hungry for affection. We start to kiss. I say, "Why don't you take off your clothes?" He says, "You first." So we finally take off our clothes at the same time. We kiss and lie down on a couch. We go through a lot of, "Wait, no. Wait, no." It's sad the middle of the scene was cut because the characters aren't ready for sex. It isn't what either of them thought it would be. The unedited scene was honest.'

However, the censored version was released, and even then, technically teenagers under 17 had to be accompanied by an adult over 21.

Overall, the film was well received by the critics, as a witty and accurate portrait of teenage life at the beginning of the 1980s. It even sparked a six-week television series called *Fast Times* in which Ray Walston reprised his role as Mr Hand. But young Nicolas Coppola did not get a mention.

In fact, he was so despondent that his lines ended up on the cutting-room floor that he decided the closest he was likely to get to the big screen was working in a cinema. 'I sold popcorn at the Fairfax Theatre concession stand,' he laughed. 'I was trying to figure out how to get from the concession stand to the screen. I had an ambition to be watched.'

Between his rejection for *The Outsiders* and disappointment over *Fast Times*, for a while Nicolas thought he had made the wrong career choice. He recalled, 'I'd reached a point in the Hollywood rejection system most actors go through, where I got pretty down on myself. So I thought, Well, I'll try this one more time, but if it doesn't work I'm going to get on a boat and write. I was pretty certain that I was going to join the merchant marines and get on a boat and do the Melville thing.'

Paradoxically, help came from an unexpected source, Francis Coppola, who had decided to follow *The Outsiders* with *Rumble Fish*. Both films were based on gritty novels about teenage life by SE (Susie) Hinton and were enormously popular among young readers. He made the pictures back to back in Tulsa, Oklahoma, first shooting *The Outsiders* which starred Matt Dillon, C Thomas Howell, Ralph Macchio, Patrick Swayze, Diane Lane, Tom Cruise, Emilio Estevez, Rob Lowe, Tom Waits and Leif Garret, all members of the up-and-coming Brat Pack whose future careers would, of course, lead them to very different fortunes. Dillon, Lane and Waits stayed on in Tulsa to make *Rumble Fish*, while Cruise passed on the offer of a role. Those who stayed were joined by Mickey Rourke, Dennis Hopper, Vincent Spano, Chris Penn and Laurence Fishburne, as well as Nick, working for his Uncle Francis for the first time.

He was overwhelmed to win the role as Smokey, which was completely unexpected. He was at a loose end when Coppola was finalising casting for the film, and his uncle asked for his assistance.

'I got a call to go in and read for the other actors auditioning,' he said. 'I would play the other characters while they did their auditions. I was just helping out, feeding lines to aspiring actors. I was there reading with Mickey Rourke and Matt Dillon. The minute it wasn't me auditioning, I began to show them something. The next day I found I had a part in *Rumble Fish* and I changed my name from Coppola, for obvious reasons. I was totally surprised that I got cast. Didn't expect it at all. It was weird. It really blew my mind.'

Nick chose the name Cage after much soul searching. 'I wanted to make it on my own, not trade on the family name,' he explained. 'At first, there was a lot of pressure for me, going to auditions with that name. I used to go to an office and talk about Francis for a few hours and I know that it did colour people's perception of my work. It was obvious that people were thinking about 20 years of someone else's history. I wanted to be able to go into an office and just do what I had to do. I wanted to be given a fair shot as an actor, to be taken seriously. So I took the name Cage and the first audition I did under that name was the best audition I'd ever done. That told me I'd done the right thing.

'Some of the names I was entertaining were so ridiculous,' he laughed. 'Nick Faust, Nick Mascalzone — my grandmother used to call me that; it means "bad boy" ... I even tried my favourite colour at the time, Nicolas Blue.'

As he discussed possibilities with his other grandmother, Louise Vogelsang — known by her nickname, Divi — Vogel was also in the running for a while. He finally settled on Cage because of his admiration of two very diverse characters, experimental composer John Cage and the comic-book character Luke Cage, a black superhero.

He also said he dropped the 'h' from Nicholas, but in fact he was actually christened Nicolas, and he kept his middle name of Kim.

Rumble Fish, a dark drama — literally as well as figuratively being shot mainly at night and in black and white — is the coming-of-age story of Rusty-James (Matt Dillon), a teenager living in the shadow of his legendary brother, onetime gang leader Motorcycle Boy, played by Mickey Rourke, who has drifted away to California, leaving his brother in virtual limbo. Motorcycle Boy is obsessed by the fish of the title, a Siamese fighting fish which is so ferocious it will attack any other fish put in its tank, even its own reflection. The brilliant orange fish in a local pet store are the only thing shown in colour in the movie. Rusty-James is constantly in trouble, being expelled from school and beaten up by thugs, as well as being dumped by his girlfriend, Patty, played by Diane Lane, when Motorcycle Boy reappears to help him, only to end up being shot after he breaks into the pet shop to steal the fish to release them into the local river. The film is so loaded with symbolism — the fish themselves, which would actually have died if they were released into fresh water; Dennis Hopper as the drunken father of Rusty-James and Motorcycle Boy and a mean cop, played by William Smith, showing the young that adults cannot be trusted; and a scene in which Rusty-James has an out-of-body experience after he is beaten up — that the story is completely overshadowed by the imagery.

Nick's character, Smokey, is Rusty-James' best friend. But he was not the only family connection to the film; in her screen début, his cousin, Sofia Coppola, played Diane Lane's character's younger sister.

Again, it was not an easy shoot for Nick. Although he had changed his name, everyone knew who he was and he was acutely aware of his lack of experience compared to his co-stars. He said: 'They seemed to know some secret that I didn't. I didn't know where they got their fire. So I locked myself up in my room and read books on Japanese management systems, because I thought my character would probably grow up to be a businessman.'

And Coppola made no concessions to family connections. 'Once Francis made me do 42 takes — a scene looking at a watch — and I've never had to do 42 takes again in my whole career,' he said at the end of 1995 looking back on making the movie. 'I know that was like some kind of strange trial that I had to go through.'

The next year, he again hinted to *Movieline* magazine that Coppola was being deliberately harsh. 'I still don't know what the reason for that was,' he went on, referring again to the watch incident. 'My first two takes were the best. I got a phone call after that movie from my father who said, "You're too restrained as an actor and I'm getting this from a very high level. I don't think you have what it takes." I thought, Who the hell's he been talking to? I guess people in my family were not impressed with the character.'

All the same, looking back on his first real part, he said later, 'That was pretty high pressure. Here I was, the nephew of the director, without any work under my belt to speak of, and that made the other actors nervous. I was an easy target. I felt this pressure to pull it off. I had a lot of pressure, being a family member, the other actors thinking I didn't really have the goods, as if they felt I wasn't an actor but was being granted a favour by the family. Young actors can be very cruel. When I look back, I think it was one of the better things I've done.'

Rumble Fish, with the tense relationship between two brothers at its heart, is dedicated to August Coppola, whom Francis called 'my first and best teacher'. According to Francis Coppola's biographer, Peter Cowie, the film was a kind of exorcism of the relationship between the two.

And August said the film, 'marks the closing of a phase — so there is regret. There's a recognition of the fact that, OK, I was the one he looked up to, but that he achieved things in the eyes of the world and of the others around him. The dedication was a recognition of my importance in his life, both good and bad. It's a poignant film in that Francis has often had regrets, because I was supposed, in his mind, to achieve what he achieved. Our family was consecrated to success.'

Nick was still ambivalent about his relationship with Coppola. He acknowledged that his uncle opened doors for him, but was also acutely conscious that he had to prove himself perhaps more than other young actors. He said, 'There are two sides to the coin. There's the side of it that you might get tossed a ball but then you have to run with it. If you don't, then you're going to be shot down. The attention can be so extreme in cases like that to see what the person will do, that if you don't come through, people are quick to point the finger and say, "Well, you're not really anything, nepotism got you where you are." I was quite tense when we made that movie. I felt a lot of prejudice from the other actors, that I didn't belong there. So it was kind of hard to relax.'

The critics were divided in their views of the film, which opened at the New York Film Festival in October 1983. Some dismissed it as pretentious and over-the-top, although generally agreeing it was beautifully made, while others hailed it as Coppola's finest work to date.

Sheila Benson, influential film critic of the *Los Angeles Times*, wrote, 'It isn't the story that fascinates Coppola, but the ways he can tell it. If you could divorce yourself from the fact that this frail story isn't worth one per cent of the invention being lavished on it, you could have a lovely time in all this gorgeous sound and music, which signify so little. The visual effects and the cinematography are sumptuous. It's difficult to talk about performances, since they are almost buried under this frenzy of style.' She went on, 'Nicolas Cage has, oddly enough, less chance to show what he can do than he did in *Valley Girl*.' The cult hit *Valley Girl*, made after *Rumble Fish*, was released before it in the United States.

Andrew Sarris said in *Village Voice*, 'In attempting an aura of psychological mystery, Coppola succeeds only in overloading his *mise-en-scène* with pretentious obfuscation and literally foggy mysticism.'

In *Newsweek*, Jack Kroll wrote, '*Rumble Fish* is a brilliant tone poem of this inner exile: the soundtrack and music (by Stewart Copeland of the Police) heaves and hisses, whistles and wails like our country giving birth to a monstrous mutation of city and nature. Stephen H Burum's dazzling black-and-white photography turns Tulsa into a city vibrating with fatality.'

A reviewer in *Daily Variety* said the film was, 'Overwrought and over thought,' but praised the acting. It said, 'Dillon and Rourke turn in good performances as does Dennis Hopper as their drunken father and Diane Lane as Dillon's dumped-on girlfriend. Diana Scarwid is unfortunately underused as an addict hung up on Rourke. Nicolas Cage is a strong presence with a small part that's potentially more interesting than the brothers, but never pursued.'

Bill Krohn in *Box Office* wrote, 'This is Coppola's best film since *Godfather II*.' But he added, 'Distrust of Coppola among many critics could keep *Rumble Fish* from crossing over to the wider audience Universal was aiming for when they opened the picture at the New York Film Festival.'

Despite his insecurity in the face of more experienced actors, during the making of *Rumble Fish* Nick called the star Matt Dillon an 'airhead', an expression he lived to regret. Years later, he pointed out that one of the major disadvantages of being thrust into the limelight at a young age is that it is very hard to live down youthful indiscretions as your fame grows.

'I don't think of Matt Dillon as an airhead now,' he ruefully told *Movieline* in 1996. 'The funny thing about growing up in movies is when you start acting at 17, you say things sometimes like a 17-year-old and those things come back to haunt you when you're 32. People have to be allowed to grow.'

It was not only his professional indiscretions that made him blush as he matured and looked back on his youth. 'You have to remember I started acting when I was 17, and the hormones were going crazy,' he told *Details* magazine four years earlier. 'I assumed that if I was an actor I would meet more girls. And I did, and I paid for it. My *naïveté* was often abused. I though that someone was interested in me, my soul or my thoughts, and I didn't want to admit that it was something else. As I got older and drove the sports car and had the high school prom queen, those things became boring. It's the immigrant's dream. I was always attracted to American symbols like the strong blonde. I wanted the girl I couldn't have. That was 11 years ago and I'm not putting it down — it doesn't matter what compels you to do or create.'

One searing memory is of the night his teenage hormones got the better of him in the landmark Los Angeles Jewish deli, Canter's.

'The ketchup bottle happened when I was 18 and I had just met this beautiful woman,' he said. 'And she was older than me and was like a young Grace Kelly. She gave me an education in the dark side of life. Here I was, still young, still very domestic, and she was making me watch movies like *The Story of O*. One night we went to Canter's Deli and I said, "What if we do something really dangerous right now? Do you want me to heighten the moment? To feel excitement?" And she said, "Yeah," and I said, "I'm gonna take the volume right up." And she said, "Yeah," and I took the ketchup bottle and threw it across the room and it smashed against the wall. Then all these cooks came out with their knives and started chasing me, and I was banned from Canter's for two years. But she was laughing hysterically and it was a thrill and that was the last time I did anything like that. It was about a young man learning techniques of excitement.

'I was doing all sorts of crazy things like that at the time. I guess it was part of growing up. The stupid thing is, the girl was impressed!'

When his banishment from Canter's, a place which was to have a profound influence on his later life, was over, the owners realised that wiping ketchup from the wall was a small price to pay for the publicity. Nick laughed, 'They got so much press from the story that I've got my own chair to sit in and have lunch.'

After shooting *Rumble Fish,* the newly christened Nicolas Cage needed to find another film. His agent, Ilene Feldman, got him an audition with respected documentary director Martha Coolidge, who was about to make her first feature film, another teen-themed picture. Feldman sent her a photograph of her client and she was delighted to see someone who broke the mould of the finely chiselled, handsome hunks who had already read for the part. 'Bring me boys who have depth,' Coolidge said excitedly. 'Bring me someone who looks like this!' Feldman said, 'She had no idea who he was, only that he had a small part in *Rumble Fish*.'

That audition convinced Nick that changing his name had been absolutely the right decision. Without the albatross of the Coppola image to worry about, he could simply concentrate on convincing her that he could do the job. He was, however, gracious enough to acknowledge that acting in a Francis Coppola film, whatever his name, was a boost to any young actor's career.

'That was the first film where I didn't have to talk about 20 years of Francis and I could concentrate on the scene,' he said. 'It turned out to be the right choice. I got the role just like that. Martha Coolidge later said she didn't know I was related to Francis and that if she had known it would have coloured her perception of me. But the fact that I was in *Rumble Fish* had a lot to do with me getting it, so in that way Francis really helped me. He gave me some cachet.'

His family were not altogether pleased about his new identity. His grandmother, Italia Coppola, called his decision to become Nicolas Cage 'a stupid, dumb decision'. His uncle Francis sent him a tongue-in-cheek telegram of congratulation signed 'Francis Cage', but after Nick won his *Leaving Las Vegas* Oscar, he said, 'My thought then, as now, is that he is a Coppola and we are proud of him and wish his name was still Coppola.'

Years later, Nick disclosed, 'My great-great-grandfather came to America from Italy and, you know, we were paupers struggling; and then my grandfather, Carmine, developed a talent, which was to play the flute. Carmine married my grandmother, who was a songwriter's daughter and that began this sort of illustrious life in the arts. With that is a certain kind of competition and pride and a thick kind of passion that, I guess, by changing my name I ended.'

Nick's role in Coolidge's film, *Valley Girl*, was the lead, Randy, a prototype punk Romeo in a leather jacket who wins the heart of a twin-set-and-pearls, squeaky-clean Juliet, a girl from a different world.

In 1982, avant-garde musician Frank Zappa had a cult hit with the satirical song *Valley Girls*, which poked fun at shopaholic teenage girls living in the suburban San Fernando Valley, north of the Santa Monica Mountains in Los Angeles. His then 14-year-old daughter, Moon Unit — who would later appear in the television series *Fast Times* — did killer imitations of 'Val-speak', the peculiar coded language in which the height of praise was 'tubular' and something totally disgusting was 'grody to the max'. Valley girls were perceived as air-headed clones with surgically perfected teeth and noses, driving from shopping mall to shopping mall in their parents' BMWs, comparing prices on designer labels and gossiping about their boyfriends. The Valley, a sprawling mass of single-storey houses with swimming pools in what used to be groves of orange and walnut trees, had long been disparaged as boring and terminally middle-class by residents of Los Angeles' 'West Side', which includes areas like Hollywood, Beverly Hills and Santa Monica, even though it is, in fact, home to major movie studios like Universal, Warner Bros and Disney, and is the pornographic film-making capital of the world.

This was the setting for *Valley Girl*, in which Deborah Foreman plays Julie, the Val who dared to break the rules for love.

As the film begins, Julie is splitting up from her clean-cut surfer boyfriend, Tommy, much to the horror of her girlfriends who think they are a perfect couple. Randy and a friend gatecrash a party to laugh at the Valley denizens, and he and Julie hit it off immediately. He introduces her to the joys of punk clubs on the West Side, where nose-studs and multi-coloured hair are more common than the cultured pearls and coiffed hairdos of the Valley. But at the instigation of her friends she drops him and returns to Tommy, at which point Randy begins a determined pursuit, sleeping outside her window, pretending to be a ticket-taker at the local cinema, masquerading as a waiter at a drive-through fast-food joint. Finally, Randy gatecrashes Julie's high school prom, where she and Tommy were due to be crowned king and queen, beats up Tommy and escorts Julie out of the school gym where the dance is being held and whisks her away in a rented limousine.

Perhaps because of the freedom his new-found anonymity gave him, Nick indulged in what was to be one of many quirks he brought to his screen characters. In Randy's first scene he was walking along the beach while, unknown to him, Julie and her friends are swooning over his 'totally awesome' physique. For the scene, Nick, who has always been noted for his remarkably hirsute body, shaved his chest-hair into a Superman-style 'V' shape.

An old school friend from his Beverly Hills High days noticed a personal mannerism she remembered. 'If you watch *Valley Girl* again, you'll notice Randy will have one shirt sleeve up and one down,' the girl, identified only as Lisa, told an Internet fan site. 'Nicolas did this in real life. He never had a reason for it. Just liked to be different.'

She added, 'I call him Nicolas because that's what he went by in high school. One day, I asked Nicolas for a nickel and he said to me, "I'm sorry, but I'm NICKEL LESS." I think that is so funny. That shows you the kind of witty guy he was.'

He generally enjoyed making the film, which took him back to many of the same Valley locations where *Fast Times* had been shot, notably the now-closed Sherman Oaks Galleria, the shopping mall which was the high altar of Vals in the

1980s and 1990s. 'The frustration that I felt in high school went right into the character of Randy in *Valley Girl*,' he said.

But if he enjoyed playing Randy, he could not say the same about his leading lady. 'I didn't like working with Deborah Foreman,' he said, 'because just before doing a scene, some guy would walk in.' He went on to imply that some flirting would go on.

Overall, his affection for the film was a lasting one, however. In 1990, seven years after he had made the movie, he told *American Film* magazine, 'It's still one of my favourite movies, actually, because it was a situation I'd gone through in high school. I was taking the bus there and other guys were driving Porsches. If there was a beautiful girl and I wanted to take her out, I couldn't do it, she just wouldn't go for it. I think that movie was about not listening to your friends, that it's just you and me.'

Martha Coolidge herself was also impressed with Nick's work. A few years after working with her, Nick recalled, 'She sent me a note that I've never forgotten. It read, "Your character is sad but not defeated." '

The movie, which had a budget of just $2.5 million, got better reviews in the western United States than on the east coast, and Nick, who had top billing, was singled out for praise in his first starring role.

Before it was released or reviewed, however, *Valley Girl* ran into a legal problem. Frank Zappa and his Pumpko Industries company sued the film-makers, claiming that using the name *Valley Girl* comprised false designation of origin, unfair competition and dilution of trademark, and he therefore demanded $100,000 damages. The suit alleged that long before plans for the film were announced, Pumpko had applied to register the expression 'Valley Girl' as a trademark and had signed a number of merchandising deals. Pumpko also wanted an injunction to stop the film's producers, Valley 9000 Productions Inc., from using the name and asked them to hand over the screenplay and other production documents.

Valley 9000 Productions immediately fought back, saying, 'The motion picture *Valley Girl* is an aptly titled teenage love story based on a copyrighted story. It is about a boy from Hollywood who falls in love with a well-to-do girl from the Valley, and the problems which ensue. The *Valley Girl* picture has no connection with the Zappa song. In any event, it is also Valley 9000's belief that the expression "valley girl" is a generic term and cannot be copyrighted. We believe the lawsuit filed is absolutely without merit.'

The lawsuit was settled but it was not the last legal run-in for the film. More than a year after it was released, director Coolidge, actress Lee Purcell (who played Julie's friend Beth), Colleen Camp (who played her ageing-hippy, health-food-store-running mother) and cinematographer Fred Elms sued Valley 9000, Atlantic Releasing, which distributed the movie, and two principals of the companies, alleging they had not been paid their promised share of the profits.

According to the suit, Coolidge was entitled to six points — six per cent of net profits from the film — Purcell and Camp half a point each and Elms one point. They claimed the film had grossed some $17 million by October 1983 and sought damages of $5 million.

When the film, which was completed in the autumn of 1982, was released in March the following year, Nick was quite justifiably pleased with the critics' reviews and his first leading role.

'What saves *Valley Girl* from lethal doses of "tubular fer sures" is Randy's breath of punk air, replete with its inbred distaste for any and everything Valleyish,' said Joseph Eckdahl in *The Hollywood Reporter*.

Sheila Benson, of the *Los Angeles Times*, called Nick 'a great discovery'. She added, 'With his sleepy eyes under their down-slanted eyebrows, Cage has a vague Peter Townshend look and an appeal that is part strength, part sensitivity, part romantic impetuousness. By turns comic, shattered, resourceful and genuinely love-struck, he is the reason we care while watching this amiable sociological study that drops Juliet among the Vals and Romeo at Hollywood High.'

Janet Maslin wrote in the *New York Times*, 'On the West Coast, where they know about such things, *Valley Girl* may conceivably strike a funnier and a more familiar chord than it does in New York. As played by Deborah Foreman, Julie is pretty, conventional and a little dull; certainly she's far too passive to carry the movie. Of her suitors, only Nicolas Cage as the downtown type (he likes louder music than his suburban counterparts and knows more people who put coloured rinses in their hair) has any vitality.'

Nick was delighted at his new-found success but also recalled his ambivalent feelings about the Coppola family's wealth in his childhood days, and his reaction to the song 'Baby, You're A Rich Man'. He said, 'Maybe I jumped the gun but when *Valley Girl* came out and was a hit, I got in my yellow Triumph Spitfire, put the top down, drove down Sunset Boulevard, put the cassette into the tape recorder, pressed play and just savoured every word.'

The film had a big impact on young Nick's burgeoning career. Shortly after the movie was released, Irene Feldman, his agent, said, 'It seems that he's being brought up for every project that is coming around these days. Since *Valley Girl*, there's been a tremendous change.'

Even more importantly, though, he was also convinced that *Valley Girl* had finally persuaded his father that he had a future in acting. 'I guess he thought I was too restrained in *Rumble Fish*,' he said. 'For *Valley Girl*, I had a new name. I opened the door and I did what I wanted to do and I didn't have the pressure of the family on me. I think my father learned a lot about me when he saw *Valley Girl*. He actually saw a lot more of me than he knew was there before.'

In his youthful arrogance, he also felt compelled to brag about his success to his Uncle Francis. He recalled, 'I was intimidated by my uncle when I began to understand what the word "godfather" meant — when I saw the way people treated him. It stopped being intimidating when I heard a line that James Joyce supposedly once said to Henrik Ibsen, "You were great, but I hold the mantle now." I heard that line first at Francis' house. My father was there and Francis was talking about Ibsen and Joyce and he said that line and then said, "I never understood what Joyce meant by that, but now I get it." So years later, when *Valley Girl* came out, I was sitting at his house and he was lighting a cigar by the fireplace and I just said it, "You were great, Francis, but I hold the mantle now." He got upset and flustered. His face got red, his voice got high, he got very upset. He said, "What are you talking about?" I don't know why I said it. It was more of a joke than anything. I would be lying if I didn't say that there is a fundamental competitive edge among the men in my family!'

However, Francis was actually impressed by his nephew's showing in *Valley Girl* and did not let his irritation cloud his judgement.

Nick recalled with delight, 'Francis saw the movie and called. I could hear the excitement in his voice. He wanted me to be in his next two movies.'

CHAPTER THREE

THE FAMILY BUSINESS

Francis Coppola was as good as his word. In a world which is notoriously fickle when it comes to making and breaking promises, he did indeed hire his nephew for his next two mainstream films, *The Cotton Club* and *Peggy Sue Got Married*. Although, between the pair, Coppola did make two other movies, there was clearly no place for Nick in either. He was executive producer of *Mishima: A Life in Four Chapters*, the story of Japanese novelist and self-styled Samurai Yukio Mishima, who committed suicide in the most grisly fashion after a failed attempt to overthrow the Japanese Government, by disembowelling himself as a follower cut off his head.

The film-maker followed that with a totally different but equally bizarre film, *Captain Eo*, directing pop singer Michael Jackson as the title character in a George Lucas-produced 3-D extravaganza for Disney. The high-volume, high-energy film showed at Disney theme parks around the world for more than 10 years before closing in 1997.

Following the success of *Valley Girl*, Nick discovered that his portrayal of Randy had been a hit with film-makers as well as viewers. His unconventional looks and his performance as a rough-edged youth won him a role in *Racing with the Moon*, a period piece about two young men's final weeks in their northern California hometown before joining up to serve in World War II.

Richard Benjamin, a former actor who had just directed his first feature film, *My Favourite Year*, with Peter O'Toole, cast Nick as Nicky, the best friend and foil to the leading character, Henry 'Hopper' Nash. He said: 'His looks are not television looks but they are movie looks. Look at Bogart. Look at Cagney. They weren't conventionally handsome either.'

Like *The Cotton Club*, *Racing with the Moon* had a chequered history. It started off at MGM/UA studios under producers Alain Bernheim and John Kohn, with director Richard Benjamin at the helm. At the time, the President of MGM/UA was David Begelman, a veteran talent agent-turned-studio head who had transformed the fortunes of then-ailing Columbia Pictures thanks to hits like *Funny Lady*, *Tommy*, *Shampoo*, *The Way We Were* and *Close Encounters of the Third Kind*. In

33

four years he reduced the studio's debts from $225 million to $60 million. But he left Columbia under a cloud after he forged the signature of Oscar-winning actor Cliff Robertson to cash a $10,000 cheque the studio had made out to the movie star. An investigation revealed he had actually embezzled more than $60,000. He pleaded no contest to three counts of forging cheques and was sentenced to community service.

Begelman had personally approved the script of *Racing with the Moon*, by young writer Steve Kloves. But when a best-selling book about the cheque scandal, *Indecent Exposure: A True Story of Hollywood and Wall Street*, re-opened old wounds and he was forced out of MGM/UA, his film project was ejected with him.

Bernheim shopped the script of *Racing with the Moon* around other studios and eventually, in late 1982, he took it to Sherry Lansing, President of 20th Century Fox and the first woman ever to head a major studio. She loved it and bought it within days. 'It called up a world as we'd all like it to be — clean, wholesome and innocent,' she said of the story. 'I cared about the people and when I came to the end of the script I didn't want to leave them.' Unfortunately for the film, however, also within days she announced that she was leaving Fox to become an independent producer at Paramount Pictures, in partnership with Stanley Jaffe, who had won a Best Picture Oscar for *Kramer v Kramer*.

Fox decided to go with the picture all the same, and it was set to roll in the spring of 1983 with a budget of $6 million and strict instructions to Benjamin to bring the film in on schedule. However, the producers sensed that the Fox executives' hearts were not in the project. They had kept in touch with Lansing and, two weeks before shooting was due to start, they formally asked Fox if they could take the project elsewhere. Lansing showed Jaffe the script and he was as enthusiastic as she had been from the start.

So just 10 days before the film was set to roll in Mendocino, on the northern Californian coast, it moved studios yet again, to Paramount.

Surprisingly for Hollywood, Fox did not take out any insurance by staking a claim for a cut of the box office if the film turned out to be a big hit, though Paramount, which upped the budget, did have to pay them back what they had already spent in pre-production. On the other hand, as strange as it might seem in the circumstances, MGM/UA had kept a small stake in the film.

The whole production team were delighted at the way things had turned out. '20th was very nice about it,' Lansing said at the time.

Producer Bernheim laughed that during the handover period, 'For a while, we kept both our 20th and Paramount parking stickers on our cars.' He added, 'Paramount gave us an extra week to prepare. They allotted Dick four more days to shoot and raised the budget from $6 million to $6.5 million. On a period film, even that little bit extra helps.'

The brief delay was actually beneficial because the weather improved. Benjamin said, 'If we had started when we were supposed to for Fox, we would have been four days behind in the first six days — because of rain at Mendocino.'

The change of studio also helped to iron out the last problem facing the production; casting Sean Penn, then 22, the producers' first choice for the lead character of Hopper. The threat of an actors' strike was hovering over Hollywood and Paramount was anxious to start filming promptly. At the same time, Penn was committed to the full run of the Broadway play *Slab Boys*, co-starring with Kevin Bacon. The solution was simple, if somewhat brutal. By coincidence, Paramount was one of the backers of the play. By an even bigger coincidence, director Herbert Ross wanted Kevin Bacon to star in the film *Footloose* — for Paramount. So Paramount simply withdrew their backing of the play and it promptly closed, freeing the two young actors for the movie roles.

'He's a rough kid, not a pretty boy, and that's exactly what this role required,' said screenplay writer Kloves, explaining why the production team were so keen to have Penn, who had won praise for his work on *Taps*, *Fast Times at Ridgemont High* and *Bad Boys*, for the role.

The third lead was Elizabeth McGovern, also 22 at the time, who had been nominated for an Oscar for *Ragtime* as well as appearing in the much-honoured *Ordinary People*.

Racing with the Moon tells the story of how Sean Penn's and Nicolas Cage's characters, best friends growing up in a small, seaside town, have enlisted in the Marines and are waiting to be called up to fight. The film, set in 1942, shows their last six weeks of innocent — and not so innocent — youth, working as pin-setters in the local bowling alley. Their biggest thrill in this small-town existence is chasing freight trains. Hopper (Penn) falls for the new girl in town, Caddie, played by McGovern. She works as a cashier in the cinema, but because she lives in a big house on the other side of the tracks he thinks she is rich; in fact, she is the daughter of the housekeeper. Nicky (Nick), meanwhile, is dating Sally, played by Suzanne Adkinson, who falls pregnant. Nicky asks Caddie for money for an abortion, despite Hopper's objections, and she tries to steal jewellery from her boss's daughter, who catches her in the act, but agrees to help out when she learns the reason for the theft. Hopper and Caddie accompany Nicky and Sally to a sleazy abortionist, and in the tension of the evening they all quarrel and Caddie admits she is poor. Naturally, before the boys go off to war, all four are reconciled.

The film was shot on schedule in eight weeks, on location in Mendocino, and on sound stages at the Paramount lot in Hollywood. Soundstage 16 became home to a lovingly re-created bowling alley, with 1940s-era lanes being shipped in from a US naval base at San Clemente, near San Diego.

Nick incorporated one of his personal quirks into the film. He has always been a devoted fan of comic books, and decided that his character of Nicky would harbour the same passion, reading at work whenever he had nothing to do. Unfortunately, on one occasion Nick became so absorbed reading his superhero stories that he ended up with a bowling ball smashing into his foot.

Journalist Michael London, who visited the set during production, recalled, 'Penn had brought McGovern to the bowling alley on a date. Cage was in his usual position behind the pins, perched on a low metal bar in a grease-stained T-shirt. In his hand was a 1942 comic book that his character would use for amusement between balls. The script called for Penn's first toss to be a gutter ball. Instead, his shot headed down the middle of the alley. In the next take, Penn's roll hit the gutter properly. McGovern followed with a strong throw down the middle of the lane. In the meantime, however, Cage, who was supposed to be reading his comic book, had become a little too engrossed; his right foot was unintentionally dangling close to the floor. McGovern's ball crashed though the pins and nailed him.

'Cage howled in surprise. The cameras stopped rolling. Penn, hands on hips, shook his head down the alley at his compatriate. "I'm involved," Cage muttered, pointing sheepishly at the comic book. "What?" yelled Penn. "I'M INVOLVED!" Cage bellowed back.'

In another incident, Nick's injuries were self-inflicted when, much to the horror of his director, he slashed his arm as the cameras rolled. 'I was really into breaking the fourth wall,' he explained. 'I was looking for hyper-realism, that kind of visceral aura. And I took out a pocket knife and basically cut my arm open. I wanted the blood to flow on film. And Richard said, "Wrong movie, Nick, let's cool it." He didn't like the idea at all.'

London was lucky to be able to witness even an event as innocuous as the bowling alley scene when he was trying to write his major feature for the *Los Angeles Times*. The three young stars were temperamental and refused to co-operate with the publicity machine which is so important to the marketing of films. Nick and Penn refused to speak to him at all, while McGovern gave a reluctant interview in the presence of the film's publicist, but refused to discuss working with Penn, admitting he had sworn her to secrecy. Even so, Penn was so annoyed that she had spoken at all that he shook her trailer during the interview, giving the impression that there was an earthquake.

The reason for his annoyance — and his ban on her speaking about him — became clear later. Like so many leading men and women, Penn and McGovern fell for each other during the shoot, and by the time the film was released, in March 1984, they were engaged. Reluctant to talk about their relationship, they extended their apparent vow of silence to include doing publicity for the film, and Nick joined them. Normally when a movie is about to be released, the actors make the rounds of television talk shows and meet journalists for one-on-one interviews or round-table discussions.

As well as the romantic pairing, Nick and Penn became firm friends, despite Nick's awe of him the first time they had acted together in *Fast Times*. He recalled, 'I remember Sean saying, "The nerd from *Fast Times* can actually act," and we became friends. There's one shot where Sean and I are standing in front of an oncoming train and have to jump out of the way at the right time. We got into this stand-off — who was going to jump first? It was good-natured but definitely a macho, boys'-day-out attitude between us.'

Nick, Penn and McGovern did agree to speak briefly to the *New York Times* when the film was in post-production in November 1983. Nick, described as the most high-spirited of the three leads, seemed bemused by his burgeoning career. 'I had this dream of six years of studying before I started working,' he said. 'Instead, I've done three films in a year. It's scary but exciting.' Penn refused to discuss his approach to the film, while McGovern said her character reminded her of her mother.

At the time, Penn was very much a rising star and the producers assumed he would be at the centre of the eventual marketing campaign. Co-producer Kohn said, 'In advertising the film, the emphasis will be on the love story. Also, there is a lot of heat on Sean Penn right now. He is always mentioned prominently in stories about young, up-and-coming actors. So I'm sure part of the promotional campaign will centre on him.'

But publicising *Racing with the Moon* at the time of its release was largely left to Lansing, who had, fortunately, been on the set every day during production.

She must have been gritting her teeth when she told the *Los Angeles Times*, 'These particular performers feel that they fulfil their obligation to a film when they leave the set. I'm eternally grateful for the performances that they delivered and for creating something I care about so passionately. But it's terribly frustrating and it puts me in a very uncomfortable position as far as creating an awareness of this film. Let's face it, Stanley Jaffe and Sherry Lansing are not Elizabeth McGovern and Sean Penn. When it comes to selling the movie, I respect their integrity but I disagree with their position. I honestly believe that your job doesn't end until the movie's on the last screen in the smallest city.'

She was still bitter about Penn's behaviour two years later when she told the doyen of Hollywood gossip columnists, *Daily Variety*'s Army Archerd, 'He was clearly non-co-operative from the time the picture was completed until the time it went into release. The man didn't speak to anyone. His career will be over if he doesn't change. He's very talented but he's self-destructive. He was brilliant in our picture and we desperately needed him to help sell it.'

Penn and McGovern turned down the cover of *People* magazine in exchange for a 10-minute telephone interview, because they believed — probably quite correctly — that they would be asked questions about their own relationship and forthcoming marriage. McGovern relented slightly, agreeing to another *New York Times* interview which also mentioned a Broadway production she was doing, as well as *Life* magazine and an appearance on the *Today Show*.

Lansing appeared on key television shows like *The CBS Morning News*, *Good Morning America* and the *Today Show*, and talked to the *Wall Street Journal* and *Vogue* magazine. The film's publicist, Marion Billings, said wryly, 'Sherry has suddenly emerged as the star.' Industry analysts estimated that the stars' refusal to do publicity reduced the opening weekend box office take by 30 per cent.

Nick's agent, Irene Feldman, told the *Los Angeles Times* why he was reluctant to give interviews. 'Nick just wants to work,' she said. 'To Nick, acting is just a job. He wants to do his best. If people want to write about his work on screen, he thinks that's fine. He just doesn't want to explain himself.'

She added that since his success in *Valley Girl*, both demand for his services and his pay packet had increased. 'Since *Valley Girl,* there's been a tremendous change,' she said. 'He doesn't acknowledge any of this new popularity. He's still insecure about readings.'

Nick also touched on his opposition to the publicity treadmill, when he addressed a group of students at the University of California, Los Angeles, saying, 'I'm reluctant to do interviews because they always ask you about your family and whatnot, and that's something I don't think should be talked about, really.'

The critics, unconcerned about the row over publicity, generally liked the film and had lots of praise for Nick.

Kirk Ellis wrote in *The Hollywood Reporter*, 'Of the two, the boozing, thick-skinned Nicky (Nicolas Cage) is clearly the ringleader. Cage nicely counterpoints Penn with an unfettered rowdiness, surely one of the most engaging louts in recent memory.'

The reviewer in *Motion Picture Product Digest* said: 'In this case, the three leading actors aren't just good, they're extraordinary. Sean Penn plays Hopper; he's a moody, intense young actor who can suddenly display a facetious side without faltering a whit. Elizabeth McGovern is Caddie; she's fresh and winsome and endows this life-affirming young female with considerable charm. Nicolas Cage is the mixed-up Nicky; volatile and earthy, the actor turns here the difficult trick of keeping a basically unsympathetic character likeable. Major stardom could be in store for all three.'

Sheila Benson in the *Los Angeles Times* wrote, 'Sean Penn is breathtakingly good as this utterly decent boy, who grows up before our eyes, and Elizabeth McGovern's unshy deliciousness is at its most radiant. Nicolas Cage, in what seems on the surface to be a less sympathetic role, is splendid.'

Cosmopolitan described Nick as 'impeccable as Penn's rampageous, incipiently alcoholic chum.' While Pauline Kael, one of the United State's most influential critics, wrote in *The New Yorker*, 'As the kind of jerk that it's easy to have a sentimental attachment to, Nicolas Cage makes the most of his sheik's dimples, his hound-dog eyes and his ace comedy timing.'

Others were less enthusiastic about the film as a whole, but still singled Nick out for praise.

Daily Variety said: 'Clearly, the story is hardly earth-shaking and, if anything, edges dangerously toward the bland for considerable stretches. This is such a white bread world that Cage's turbulent, urban-type character seems at times like an unnatural element; why does only he speak like a character out of *Mean Streets*?'

Peter Rainer in the *Los Angeles Herald Examiner* disliked the film overall, dismissing it as 'intentionally dated'. He wrote, 'Even though Sean Penn doesn't really move like a '40s character — his swagger is too hip-urban — he draws you into Hopper's head. Nicolas Cage is even more anachronistic in this rural '40s setting than Penn, but he's eminently watchable. He may appear to be a refugee from a Scorcese film (*Mean Dirt Roads?*) but his droopy glare and rebel-without-a-cause hip-swivel give the movie some punch. The script doesn't give Cage and Penn enough to do together but both actors are such intuitive performers that they make their partnership work anyway.'

Stephen Schiff in *Vanity Fair* found Nick 'a little wobbly' but added, 'But Cage has a great bit, singing "Tangerine" and romancing his broomstick. And he knows how to balance his loud-mouth bravado with the stricken, hound-dog quality in his eyes.'

Nick himself, in hindsight, dismissed the film a couple of years later. 'Everybody said it was a nice little movie,' he told *Cable Guide* magazine. 'I didn't like it myself. I felt it was a Hallmark card, to tell you the truth. I would have made it a little more dangerous. I would have made my character a circus clown going to war.'

During the filming of *Racing*, Nick forged what was to be a lengthy friendship with Sean Penn, though one which was to end acrimoniously in 1999. After the shoot, he palled up with another talented young man, the guitar player from a band called Kids. His name was Johnny Depp, and his biggest career achievement had been opening for bands like Iggy and the Stooges and the B52s in his native Florida.

Nick recalled, 'I met Johnny Depp playing Monopoly. I'd been seeing his ex-girlfriend. At first we didn't like each other but then we did and I told him he should be an actor. He has that thing that some people are just born with. I told him, "You should be in movies. You have a certain charisma that would be good." He said, "No, I can't act." Then he met my agent and the rest is history.'

Nick also introduced him to director Wes Craven, who was then casting the original *A Nightmare on Elm Street*. Depp got the part of big-haired preppie Glen, doomed to be eaten by his own bed. The two remained firm friends, partying together when they were not making films, and doing crazy stunts like dangling upside down from the fifth-floor car park at the Beverly Centre shopping mall. Nick made just one mistake in telling his tale about Depp; the girlfriend he mentioned was actually Depp's ex-wife, Lori Allison.

After *Racing with the Moon*, Nick moved on to a film beset with its own, very different problems — *The Cotton Club*.

The Cotton Club had a long and twisting road to the screen, and few people involved with it escaped unscathed. Financial and personal battles overshadowed the film to the extent that a movie with a mesmerising premise and big name stars ended up as a mess — a truly spectacular mess — but not one that many lovers of spectacles bothered to see.

It started auspiciously. As Executive Vice-President of Paramount Pictures in the 1970s, Robert Evans had optioned *The Godfather* for $5,000, approved the choice of Francis Coppola as director and supervised the picture. Coppola later said that there had been friction on the set and that Evans did not want Marlon Brando or Al Pacino in the movie, even though Brando went on to win the Best Actor Oscar and Pacino was nominated as Best Supporting Actor. It seemed unlikely either man would want to work with the other again, and as things turned out it was a bad move on both parts.

Evans, a flamboyant character once married to *Love Story* actress Ali MacGraw, left Paramount to become an independent producer, making such hits as *Chinatown*, *The Marathon Man* and *Urban Cowboy*.

In 1979, the same agent who had sold him *The Godfather* sent him *The Cotton Club*, the riveting tale of black entertainers and white gangsters in a prohibition-era Harlem nightclub, and he bought it for $350,000. The real Cotton Club in the 1920s and 1930s was a club where black artists performed for white audiences in a world controlled by mobsters, where fortunes were being made in black-market booze and illegal gambling. Duke Ellington was the house bandleader for a while, broadcasting a nightly radio show from the stage. He was followed by Cab Calloway, and guest performers included Bessie Smith, Josephine Baker and Lena Horne. New York glitterati, including Fred Astaire, Charlie Chaplin, Fanny Brice and Irving Berlin, thrilled to rub shoulders with gangsters like Legs Diamond and Lucky Luciano.

'Gangsters, music and pussy,' said Evans. 'How could I lose?' How wrong could he be? No studio was interested in making a 'black' movie. And it did not help his chances of finding backing that he had pleaded guilty to cocaine possession in July 1980.

However, in 1981, things began to roll. By coincidence, he met Melissa Prophet, a young actress who had had a bit part in his 1979 film *The Players*, and she told him that Arab arms dealer Adnan Khashoggi had befriended her and offered to finance a film for her. She introduced the two and Khashoggi agreed to put in $12 million to develop the book as a picture. Evans called in Mario Puzo, author of *The Godfather*, to write the script. However, Khashoggi hated his first draft and backed out of the deal. With Puzo on board, three studios became interested in financing, but Evans refused all offers and announced that he would raise the financing himself and direct the film.

Sylvester Stallone agreed to star for $2 million but Evans fired him when he upped his price to $4 million. He then courted Richard Pryor, but again baulked at his demand for $4 million. Even without a star, however, he was able to sell the project at the Cannes Film Festival, picking up guarantees of US$8 million from overseas distributors.

Eventually, after a convoluted search, Evans found backing from two Las Vegas casino owners, brothers Ed and Fred Doumani and their partner, insurance magnate

Victor Sayyah. He assured them he could make the film for $20 million, mentioned his $8 million in guarantees from Cannes and told them he had a domestic advertising and distribution deal with Orion Pictures worth $10 million.

He was courting Richard Gere, a big star thanks to *An Officer and a Gentleman*, but he, too, hated Puzo's script.

Then, in February 1983, Evans contacted Coppola and asked him to rewrite the screenplay. Coppola was in deep financial trouble. He had financed his 1979 movie *Apocalypse Now* himself and had used the profit to set up his own film company, Zoetrope Studios. But his ambitious and extravagant *One from the Heart* had cost $27 million to make and grossed only $1.2 million at the box office. He had also self-financed *The Outsiders* and *Rumble Fish* but they were never likely to make a dent in his $20 million debt. His studio was up for sale and creditors had a lien on his beloved Napa mansion. So he jumped at the chance of picking up a quick $500,000 for a rewrite.

Coppola wasted no time and handed in his first draft 22 days later. However, the Doumanis weren't impressed by the script and suspended financing. Evans was back to worse than square one because, by this time, he had scouted out locations in New York and started a million-dollar re-creation of the Cotton Club itself. He was already spending $140,000 a week on pre-production and was frantic for money.

He was therefore delighted to meet a wealthy widow, who called herself Elaine Jacobs, who in turn introduced him to vaudeville producer Roy Radin. Radin concocted an elaborate and dubious-sounding scheme to get $35 million in backing from the Puerto Rican Government. Then, on 13 May, Radin disappeared after a meeting with Jacobs. His decomposed body was found a month later in a canyon north of Los Angeles. He had been shot 13 times in the head and had a stick of dynamite stuffed in his mouth. Police investigating the murder interviewed Evans for four hours, but decided that he was not involved.

Finally, by early June, Coppola had rewritten the script sufficiently to satisfy the Doumani brothers and Sayyah. Evans had had second thoughts about directing and asked Coppola to take over the job. He agreed — for an extra $2.5 million, a cut of the gross takings and absolute authority over the final cut.

By this time, song-and-dance man Gregory Hines had been cast, and the storyline was to centre on the fates of two stars, one white, one black — Gere as cornet player Dixie Dwyer and Hines as hoofer Sandman Williams — both with troublesome younger brothers. Shooting was due to start in August 1983 and Coppola set about completing his cast. With echoes of their time together on *The Godfather*, he and Evans rowed over cast members — Evans objected to Fred Gwynne playing a mobster on the grounds that he was best remembered as Herman from the Gothic television series *The Munsters*. Determined not to relive the rows of the earlier film, Coppola threatened to walk off the production unless he was given a free hand. Evans capitulated and stayed away from the set.

Gwynne was hired, along with Diane Lane, Bob Hoskins and Lisa Persky. And Coppola made the set a family affair, casting his nephew Nick as Vincent Dwyer, his daughter Sofia as a child in a street scene, Nick's older brother Marc in a cameo role as Ted Husing and hiring his son Gian Carlo as second unit director. He also took on Gregory Hines' brother Maurice, also a dancer, to play his brother in the film, and gave his daughter, Daria, a part as a child. Even Hines' ex-wife had a bit part, and his father became a consultant to the film.

But it was far from being a game of happy families. Novelist William Kennedy was brought in to help rewrite the script yet again, and when shooting started on 22 August there still wasn't a completed draft. Richard Gere did not turn up for the first day's shooting. He stayed away for a week as rumours swirled that the film was going to be cancelled altogether. After a week with no leading man, Evans met Gere's lawyer and renegotiated his deal. On top of his already agreed $1.5 million fee with an extra $125,000 a week if the shoot went beyond the end of October, he swapped his 10 per cent cut of the film's gross for an additional $1.5 million in salary and agreed to start work the following Monday.

The finances were running completely out of control and it was plain that the original $20 million budget was a gross underestimate. Running costs were at least $1.2 million a week, on top of what had already been spent.

Six weeks into the shoot, Coppola had not been paid at all and his creditors were making more and more urgent demands. His American Express card was cancelled, he was terrified he was about to lose his home and Marlon Brando hit him with a lawsuit complaining he was owed money for his work on *Apocalypse Now*. He was under constant pressure to cut costs, and his temper was so frayed that on one occasion he slammed his desk so hard that his hand needed X-rays because he thought he had broken bones. On another occasion, he kicked a hole through his office door. One Monday in October, he had had enough. He hopped on a Concorde to London, looking for work. The Doumanis agreed to start paying him, but when he arrived back on the set on Wednesday morning he discovered that the cash to pay the cast and crew had not been delivered and they all went on strike, on union orders. The film, which was due to end in October, went on until Christmas and even then actors were called back for reshoots.

This was the atmosphere for Nick's first encounter with big-budget, big-name movie-making, and he was shell-shocked.

His character of musician Dwyer's younger brother was described by *The Hollywood Reporter* as a thinly disguised synthesis of real-life 1920s' mobster Vincent 'Mad Dog' Coll and legendary actor George Raft. When Dixie Dwyer saves racketeer, beer baron and psychopathic nightclub owner Dutch Schultz (another real character from that era, played by James Remar) from an assassination attempt, Schultz declares his eternal gratitude and hires him to play at Harlem parties. He also hires Vincent to act as debt-collector and general enforcer.

The film mixes real and fictitious characters from the shady world of the Jazz Age, with historic figures like Cotton Club owner Owney Madden, played by Bob Hoskins, gangster Charles 'Lucky' Luciano, played by Joe Dallesandro, and singer Cab Calloway, played by Larry Marshall, playing alongside creations like the singing and dancing brothers Sandman and Clay Williams, played by the Hines brothers.

In the real world of the Cotton Club, mobster Big Frenchy Demange, who ran the club's night-to-night operations, was kidnapped by a renegade member of the Schultz gang, 'Mad Dog' Coll, and held for ransom. In the film, however, it is Vincent who seizes Frenchy, played by Fred Gwynne, and holds him hostage.

Nick said at the time, 'The names have been changed to protect the guilty, and sharpen the plot. But, otherwise, my character bears a close resemblance to the real Coll. When "Mad Dog" poached on Dutch Schultz's turf and kidnapped Frenchy, he signed his own death warrant. The top gangsters in New York put up a $50,000 kitty as the price on Coll's head. Unfortunately, in the gang war that followed, and again this becomes a story point in the movie, an innocent child was killed. Now, there were gangsters who were willing to knock off Coll just for the hell of it. He was finally gunned down in a phone booth on 23rd Street.'

In the movie version, Dixie, by this time a Hollywood star and Mafia front-man, acts as a go-between to ransom Frenchy and tries to get Vincent out of danger; Vincent still ends up being shot.

From day one, *The Cotton Club* was not a happy shoot, and Nick shared the general misery. By the time the film was finished, it had gone through 30 versions of the script, and Coppola frequently improvised as he went along. Nick was originally meant to work on the film for just three weeks but ended up staying on the shoot for six months, having to pass up other projects, which added to his frustration.

Because he had expected it to be a short shoot, Nick toyed with the idea of 'method acting' — staying in character off camera, even when he went back to his hotel at night. But when he realised he was in for the long haul, he decided to play it day by day.

Even so, a combination of youthful hormones and anger at not knowing what was happening from day to day took its toll and he became a brooding bad boy, on one occasion smashing up his trailer on the set and on another wrecking his hotel room. He has had the good grace to be embarrassed by his behaviour as he has grown older, and admits his aggression was partly put on.

'I was very frustrated on *Cotton Club*,' he said. 'I was slated for three weeks of work. I was there for six months, in costume, in make-up, on the set, in case Francis got an idea that would involve my character. Meanwhile, I'm getting offers for starring roles in other movies and I can't do them. So my behaviour, all the acting out, came from frustration. I was young.'

He later recalled, 'I couldn't really be a madman for the six months I was filming because I'd be in jail by now. I tried it for the first three weeks. I tried to instill some horror in people, but again, that was during that time when I was still experimenting with those ideas.

'I was behaving like a guy who listened to early Who music and wanted to be a rebel, a punk rocker, an outlaw of some sort, and didn't really know how to act. I don't need to do that now but, because I went through that period, it still comes back to bite at me sometimes.

'Because I started acting at 17 I had an adolescent energy that was geared toward punk rock or that rebellious rock 'n' roll image. I had heard tall tales about idols and icons I admired and bought into the lore. I'm 19 or something and I wanted to get stories out there about me. I was playing the most feared gangster in Harlem. I wanted to live the part. It was more of a self-created thing than an outpouring of tension. I was trying to create a mythology about myself. But I quickly learned that you can't have a life if you live the part.'

On one occasion, he took his bizarre behaviour public, much to the amazement of passers-by. Walking through New York, he came across a man selling remote-controlled model cars in the street. He started chasing them and stomping on them, almost causing a riot because the terrified onlookers thought he was psychotic. Once he calmed down he apologised and paid for the damage he had caused.

Looking back on his image as an off-kilter character drawn to weird roles and bizarre behaviour, in 1990 he told the English newspaper the *People,* 'My trouble was that I used to submerge myself in a role. It was exhausting. I remember when I was with Richard Gere in *The Cotton Club*. He told me, "If you keep on acting like this, you only have three more films in you." I was so gung-ho. I was ripping apart my trailer, trashing my hotel room, walking on set and calling everyone "nigger" so they would all hate me. It was all aimed at getting a good performance. But now I think that manners and being polite are important. It is a waste of energy on the set.'

Nick made no secret of his unhappiness with *The Cotton Club*. After finishing the film but before its release, he told a gathering of students at the University of California, Los Angeles, that it had been plagued with in-house fighting between Evans and Coppola and money problems, and was the worst picture he had ever been in. 'The whole production seemed so dishonest that I wondered how anything good could come out of it,' he said.

As the production rolled to an end, the bitterness between Coppola and Evans continued. Evans was ordered out of the movie in December 1983 by the Doumanis and Orion, who threatened to pull all extra financing if he did not go. The following June, the squabble ended up in Federal Court, with Evans, Coppola, Ed Doumani, Sayyah and Orion's Executive Vice-President William Bernstein bitterly recounting their versions of what had gone on during filming. Evans was reinstated as producer, allowing him to negotiate for distribution rights, but was banned from taking part in any aspect of post-production. By this time, the estimates of the final budget ranged from $47 to $58 million, meaning the film would have to gross $150 million to break even.

Eventually, five years after Evans optioned the book, the film opened in December 1984. Nick's principal recollection of the première was playing a joke on singer-songwriter Carly Simon, who wrote 'You're So Vain'. He said, 'I took a programme, rolled it up, put it to her ear and whispered, "Clouds in my coffee". She whipped her head around, snarled, and I looked at my friend like he did it.'

The reviews, not surprisingly, focused as much on the background of the movie and the constant rows as on the film itself. While they praised some of the spectacle and the look of the film, they generally decided the movie simply did not go anywhere. Too many characters, too much plot and no full production numbers to showcase the Hines brothers' talents were frequent complaints. The critics were not particularly impressed by Nick either.

The reviewer in the trade newspaper *Daily Variety* said, 'The arrival of a new film by Francis Coppola brings with it the anticipation of greatness. His latest, *The Cotton Club*, certainly isn't in the same league as his best pictures but neither is it on the grim order of such recent efforts as *One from the Heart* and *Rumble Fish*. Generally speaking, *The Cotton Club* serves up more entertainment highs than lows.'

But while Gwynne, Hoskins, Remar, Hines and Lonette McKee, as Gregory Hines' love interest, were singled out for praise, Nick's character was dismissed as 'a trigger-happy gunman'.

Arthur Knight in *The Hollywood Reporter* said, 'Francis Ford Coppola's costly, trouble-plagued *The Cotton Club*, has to go down in film history as the first all-talking, all-singing, all-dancing gangster extravaganza ever made.'

While also praising Hoskins, Remar and Gwynne, he found the relationship between the dancing Williams brothers unbelievable. Knight added, 'The relationship between Gere and his "Mad Dog" brother (Nicolas Cage) is only less tenuous. A cornet player who likes to jam after hours with black musicians (Gere performs his own cornet solos — and creditably), he accidentally falls into the good graces of Dutch Schultz, who hires him to look after his girl (Diane Lane) and run after his laundry. Cage uses his brother's connection to get on Schultz's payroll, then tries to shake down underground boss Madden by kidnapping his henchman,

Frenchy, after a shoot-out on the Harlem streets that leaves five children dead. Blood may be thicker than water, but why Gere — the film's only relatively good guy — continues to intercede on his brother's behalf is never adequately explained.'

Peter Rainer, of the long gone *Los Angeles Herald Examiner*, said, 'It moves along at a rapid clip and the sound track and the glitzy production design are fairly effective camouflage. But on a conceptual level the movie is a mess. It's footage in search of a subject. The movie's real subject is gangsters and they're about as believable as the play-act hoods in a Roger Corman cheapie. Only *Cotton Club*, budgeted at close to $50 million, isn't cheap.'

Even when the film was finally released, its troubles were far from over. Actress Susan Mechsner threatened to sue Coppola for leaving most of her role as a cigarette girl on the cutting-room floor.

Then Joey Cusamano, a reputed associate of mobster Antony Spilotro, a Las Vegas mob boss, who was sent on to the set to act as line producer and keep an eye on production by Ed Doumani, was jailed for four years for racketeering. The case had nothing to do with the film — it was an insurance fraud — but Coppola wrote to the Las Vegas court as a character witness, praising him as a 'useful and productive member of the staff'.

The Cotton Club died at the box office, grossing less than $26 million dollars, and disappeared to become a video curiosity. But the dramas surrounding it were still not over. In 1990 three men and a woman were charged with the murder of Roy Radin. The woman was called Karen Greenberger, but in fact she was the woman who had been introduced to Evans as Elaine Jacobs. A self-confessed cocaine dealer, she denied allegations that she set up the murder because Radin was trying to cut her out of an agreed $50,000 finder's fee for linking him up with Evans. She was alleged to have hired the three men (William Mentzer, one of her lovers, Alex Marti and Robert Lowe, all former bodyguards of Larry Flynt, publisher of the porn magazine *Hustler*) to do the killing. The prosecution claimed Lowe was driving Radin and Greenberger in a limousine when Mentzer and Marti got in. Greenberger then got out, and they drove Radin to his death.

Sheriffs' investigators had all but given up on the case when they were contacted by Flynt's brother-in-law, William Rider, who said Mentzer and Marti had told him about the killings and that he had secretly recorded a conversation with Lowe in which he claimed Greenberger and Evans had financed the hit.

Evans was called to give evidence at the preliminary hearing but refused to testify, citing his fifth amendment rights against self-incrimination. He was never directly implicated in the murder, however, but said he would only give evidence at the full trial if he was granted immunity from prosecution. All four of the accused were convicted in 1991 — Greenberger and Lowe of second degree murder and kidnapping, and Mentzer and Marti of first degree murder, and were all sentenced to life in prison.

After months of frustration on *The Cotton Club* playing Vincent Dwyer, Nick made a radical change of direction, taking on a tormented character in what was undoubtedly his best and most rewarding performance at that point in his career.

In *Birdy* he played Al Columbato, a physically scarred and battered Vietnam War veteran summoned from the hospital patching up his body in the hope of helping to cure the more destructive mental scars of his best friend, Birdy, played by Matthew Modine. It was set against the backdrop of a more modern conflict than *Racing with the Moon*, the Vietnam War, although the book on which the film is based was also originally set in World War II. The story is the account, simultaneously grim and surreal, of the two boys' upbringings in lower-middle-class Philadelphia and the effects the war has had upon them. Modine's character is so-called because of his obsessive fantasy that he wants to be — and thinks he is — a bird. He loves birds, whether wild pigeons or pet canaries, and dreams about making love to them, especially his favourite canary, Perta. Trying to infect his more down-to-earth friend Al with his enthusiasm, he makes elaborate feathered costumes in which they attempt, unsuccessfully, to fly. The horrors of his war experience make him retreat into himself and further away from reality; he perches naked on the foot of his bed, like a bird, and refuses to speak. Hospital staff, in a desperate bid to recall him to normality, recruit Al, who is healing from his own wounds, to help. The film is told mainly through a series of flashbacks, showing Birdy's increasing obsession, while in the hospital scenes Al tries desperately to keep the psychiatrists from realising the background to Birdy's near-catatonic state.

The $12 million film was directed by British film-maker Alan Parker, who had made *Midnight Express* and *Fame*. Once again, Nick got the part thanks to his change of name. It was a challenging role because he carried much of the dialogue in the hospital scenes, when Birdy was virtually mute. He had to visualise himself as a wounded soldier with a hideously scarred face, suppressing his own terrors to help his friend.

'Alan Parker said he wouldn't have cast me in *Birdy* if he had known I was a Coppola,' said Nick. 'I don't really know why — probably because it's a competitive circle and who wants another great director's name on their movie?

'I was terrified of the role of Al, because it was like nothing I'd ever done before, and I didn't know how to get to the places the role was asking me to go emotionally. With a couple of those monologues — like at the end when Al says, "I'm going to sit in this room for ever" — how does somebody really come to that decision and mean it? I didn't know if I wanted to feel that way or could feel that way.'

Parker made Nick and Modine get to know each other in preparation, which did not altogether please Nick. He said, 'It's always difficult when a director says, "Hey, you two guys get together and become best friends." I can't say that we hit it off right away but at the end I would say Matthew was what you call a true friend. Still, I always find it funny when people say, "You two get together." I mean, do you have to fall in love with a person to play a love scene? That's why they call it acting.'

Getting to know Modine was not the only preparation Nick did, however. He deliberately lost weight, because he thought his character would probably have difficulty eating because of his smashed-up face and mouth. And, despite his disillusionment over his three-week attempt at method acting during *The Cotton Club*, he refused to remove the bandages swathing his face.

'I could have taken those bandages off, but I didn't,' he told the *New York Times*. 'I left them on for five weeks. I slept in them. I'd wake myself up in the middle of the night and say, "Don't sleep on that side; that's the side that was hurt." '

Actually, Nick was exaggerating when he claimed he slept in his bandages. They were put on fresh every day for the hospital scenes, but he did wear them away from the set. He explained, 'The only person involved with the film who saw my face was the woman who put the bandages on in the morning. I kept the bandages on during lunch and that made it hard to eat. I lost 15 pounds. I focused all my worries on the left side of my face. I'd wake up in the middle of the night and catch myself sleeping on that side. I don't know why I got so far into it. People on the set would look at each other and say, "Nicky's going through some weird method stuff." I guess I was just so worried that I felt I had to put myself through something drastic. I don't know whether it helped, but it was certainly one of the less fun experiences I've had acting.'

Another movie myth that surrounded *Birdy* — a myth destined to grow bigger and more dramatic over the years — was that to get into his character Nick had two teeth pulled out without any anaesthetic.

Nick said in another interview, '*Birdy* was part of a stage that I went through in terms of experimenting with some of the more physical sacrifices required to shoot the character, such as wearing the bandages off-screen or pulling the teeth out. I think that I did it because I was so impressed with stories I'd heard about great actors who sat on a block of ice so they could feel cold in a scene, or stayed up all night so they could be tired in a scene. I just wanted to try that approach at least once. It was exhausting and now I'm not sure how necessary that approach is to arrive at the depth of the character.

'I felt a little guilty about playing a guy who was in Vietnam, never having experienced anything like that. So I guess I became slightly masochistic and took it out on myself, to try to put myself through some sort of pain, to feel somewhat of a connection — even if it was only one per cent. But it didn't happen. How can you possibly know what Vietnam was like?'

It was the sober and restrained *New York Times* that started, again clearly at Nick's instigation, the legend — one of the biggest fables about his preparation for this role — that he had had two of his front teeth extracted. 'I wanted to look like I was hit by a bomb,' he said the week the film was released. 'It gave me a feeling of something I had lost. I felt this was a once-in-a-lifetime part and it deserved that much.'

He confessed the truth about the teeth to the British magazine *Time Out* a few years later, saying, 'I had to get the teeth extracted on account of there being baby teeth with adult teeth impacted. I mean, this whole kinda self-masochistic, acting experiment stuff is just not true. To tell you the truth, at that time I was fairly naïve in film acting. I didn't know how to look at it objectively, what would work, what wouldn't work. I just had this mountain of work in front of me, this big task, and I had to deliver. And the amount of lines Al had, I was just concerned about learning them and worrying whether I could emote. So much of my part was monologue and it kinda took all of my downtime away.'

But the myth has proved to be much more enduring than the truth. By 1992, *Cosmopolitan* was claiming he had had his wisdom teeth extracted without anaesthetic 'to approximate the pain of the wounded soldier'. The *Los Angeles Times* repeated this version a couple of years later. In 1995, *Rolling Stone* magazine had a variation on the theme: 'As a shellshocked Vietnam vet in *Birdy,* Cage took the occasion to have his still-intact wisdom teeth pulled (not, per the legend, having other ones knocked out).'

Once again Nick tried to set the record straight, admitting in the *Daily Telegraph Magazine* the following year that he had exaggerated the teeth story deliberately. He told the publication, 'I was struggling as a young actor to know how to hit the notes. I remember I never took the bandages off when I did *Birdy*. I kept them on and I thought, if I pull my teeth and I'll feel the pain it will be some kind of constant reminder that I had a bomb go off in my face. That kind of thing was good for me to try — but you grow past that.'

Still, *People* magazine wrote, 'To feel the pain of the Vietnam vet he played in 1984's *Birdy*, he had his wisdom teeth extracted without Novocain.'

Nick explained all, again, to *Playboy* in 1996. He said, 'I didn't need to pull my teeth out then. Medically I did — my baby teeth weren't coming out — but I didn't need to do it while I was making the movie. I thought it would be a way to connect with some kind of physical pain. I don't know what I was doing. I found myself, at 19, in a demanding role without proper training. I would cut my script up into a million pieces and tape monologues all over my hotel room walls, so that wherever I looked I saw my lines. I kept on the facial bandages I wore for that role, which was more interesting than pulling the teeth because of the reaction in public places. The way teenage girls would look at me and laugh. I thought, what if I really were bandaged up? What would that reaction do to me? Of course, the dentist did use Novocain. But it still was painful when the Novocain wore off. But I admit I did things for effect that I wouldn't do now. I no longer need to live my part when I'm not in front of the camera.'

But if he tried to correct the misapprehensions about the teeth, he reiterated the exaggerations about the bandages in *Entertainment Weekly*. He told the magazine, 'You know, pulling your teeth out is not living the part of a Vietnam veteran, but in my 19-year-old brain I was trying to do whatever I could. I'd get out of bed in the morning with bandages still on my face because I never took them off. I was trying to lose all this weight. I really beat myself up for that part. And when I saw the movie I thought, well, gosh, I didn't give it enough thought or shadings. At the time I referred to it as emotional vomit. But I look at it now and I feel better about it.'

If shooting the hospital scenes was gruelling, so were the flashbacks. The production used 80 canaries and 80 pigeons, trained by Gary Gero, Mark Jackson, Gwen Jackson and Larry Paine, along with a seagull, a tropical hornbill, a cat and 18 dogs.

Among the most graphic scenes was one where Al and Birdy free a truckload of stray and stolen dogs on the point of being delivered to a brutal-looking slaughterhouse, and another where a cat grabs Birdy's beloved Perta and he has to prise her from its jaws before it can kill her.

Director Parker admitted that the animal scenes were difficult — especially since he is not very keen on birds. He said, 'The slaughterhouse shooting was less than pleasurable. We borrowed dead horses from the local abattoir and the smell and the flies were awful. I had insisted on real butchers for authenticity, and they happily chopped up the chunks of beef and goats, quite unperturbed by our squeamishness. By the end of the day, there were 20 more vegetarians on the crew. One of the handicaps I had been working under, I must confess, is that I don't like birds very much.' Referring to a scene in the film, he went on, 'One at a time is OK by me, but in Mrs Prevost's porch aviary there were 150 of them. I started directing everyone through earphones while perched outside in the rain on a stepladder. It was hopeless and I eventually had to go inside and brave the birds. Funny how you forget your fears when you have to get a shot!'

The animal scenes caused a flap over the release of *Birdy*, when the American Humane Association complained that it had not been notified about the film in advance, or even invited to a screening of the completed movie. Normally, the AHA reviews scripts of mainstream films shot in the United States which use animals, and monitors production. Any production company which has a standard agreement with the Screen Actors Guild is required to co-operate with the AHA. Trainer Gary Gero had invited the AHA to the location shoot in Philadelphia, but the organisers said that was not a formal invitation, as required by the Guild agreement.

The AHA does not judge the content of a film, purely the treatment of animals involved in making it. So they had no objection to the scenes involving animals which were already dead, even though it was distasteful to see what appeared to be dead dogs — actually goats — being hacked to pieces.

But one scene which initially concerned them involved a pouter pigeon whose chest was puffed up with air, but that was given the all-clear once they learned that the blowing was done by an expert and that the bird did not suffer at all. Parker explained, 'Mr Tate, one of the characters on the porch, blew into a show pigeon to stuff up its breast. I had seen it once before on a documentary, and this elderly gentleman had come from New Jersey especially to perform the grisly task.'

The AHA was also worried about the scene in which Birdy wrestled with a cat, which required several takes. Carmelita Pope, director of the AHA's Hollywood office, said she was alarmed because the bird was seen to wriggle after Birdy rescued it. She explained, 'A sedated bird is very dangerous. But an already dead canary was given a loose mount. It was not stuffed tightly so the head still had some mobility.'

After an investigation, they announced that the film was 'believed acceptable'. The AHA's top rating is simply 'acceptable', but that is given only when they have been able to monitor the actual production. 'We were not eyewitnesses,' said Pope. 'But from what we've been able to learn, it seems to be all right.'

The film opened to rave reviews.

Jack Kroll in *Newsweek* said, '*Birdy* is one of the best films about young people to arrive in a long time. And Matthew Modine and Nicolas Cage, the two young actors who play the heroes, give marvellous performances that call for a team nomination for Academy Awards. It's impossible to separate them in their portraits of Al (Cage) and Birdy (Modine), the kids trapped in the junk-strewn Philly streets. Cage and Modine create a friendship that's as sweet, sad and crazy as the movies have shown us.'

In the now defunct *Los Angeles Herald Examiner* David Chute wrote: 'The dingbat Birdy retreats into fantasies of feathered flight, and his more stable chum Al struggles to snap him out of it. This kind of all-out devotion to a friend hasn't been celebrated convincingly in movies for some time, and it's surprisingly refreshing. Parker builds the movie around his two talented co-stars and lets them cook.'

'Mr Modine's performance is exceptionally sweet and graceful. Mr Cage captures Al's urgency and frustration. Together, these actors work miracles with what might have been unworkable,' wrote Janet Maslin in the *New York Times*.

In the *Los Angeles Times,* Sheila Benson wrote, 'To call Alan Parker's *Birdy* the season's high-risk movie is wild understatement. It attempts the almost impossible, to change an almost surreal novel's interior monologues and descriptions into vibrant screen action. And through an inventive adaptation and the passion and precision of Matthew Modine's and Nicolas Cage's beautifully sustained performances, it may well have succeeded. It becomes impossible to think of Cage or Modine separately, but to regard them together as two of America's most strongly promising young actors, connected by a particular inner sweetness both contain.'

And Julie Salamon wrote in the *Wall Street Journal*, 'Mr Cage, who has played variations on callow youth in *Rumble Fish*, *Racing with the Moon* and *The Cotton Club*, does his best work here. We watch him lose his swagger, painfully.'

Sadly, however, given the favourable reviews, *Birdy* did not fly at the box office. It was released in late December in just three cinemas in Los Angeles, New York and Toronto, to make it eligible for Academy Award nominations, but it was totally overlooked by Oscar voters and cinema-goers alike. By March, when it was re-released into more markets, it had grossed just half a million dollars.

The second release was no more successful. Under the headline CAGE ASIDE, BIRDY JUST DOESN'T FLY, Gene Siskel, one of America's most prominent and well-respected critics, wrote: 'Our heart at the end of the film does go out to Al, who selflessly tried to nurse Birdy back to health after he has fallen mute in a hellish hospital that could have existed in the middle of Parker's horror show film, *Midnight Express*. Thanks to Cage's performance, we realise that Al's a very decent guy and what happened to him in Vietnam shouldn't happen to anyone. And Al, bless him, doesn't employ a birdlike defence like Birdy. And even though Cage is given one painfully obvious, heartfelt speech after another to deliver to Birdy in the hospital, we still are moved by Al's predicament.'

However, it must have been a consolation to all concerned that *Birdy* won the Jury prize and a 12-minute ovation at the Cannes Film Festival that year.

Nick looked back philosophically on the film, and chalked it up to experience. 'I really think that the first five or six movies were an education for me, a learning process. I started early and that's how I taught myself, through trial and error. With *Birdy*, I was just open emotionally and let whatever happened happen.'

After the physical and psychological challenges of *Birdy*, Nick moved immediately on to very different material, the period piece *The Boy in Blue*. He plays Ned Hanlan, a real-life Canadian superstar of the late 19th century, thanks to his prowess as a rower. He learns his skills moonlighting as a booze smuggler, rowing to escape from Canadian coastguards when he offloads his moonshine on the shores of Lake Ontario. He is spotted by crooked trainer Bill, played by David Naughton, and is dazzled by Margaret, played by Cynthia Dale, the stuck-up daughter of manipulative Colonel Knox, played by Christopher Plummer. The film re-creates Hanlan's most famous races, the Philadelphia Centennial in 1876, which he won, the Boston Regatta, from which he was disqualified for unsportsmanlike behaviour, and the world championships on the River Thames, where he triumphantly regained his crown.

Nick had just one day's break between finishing the Parker film and starting work on location on *The Boy in Blue* just outside Montreal. This presented a clear logistical problem; as Al, Nick was a stone underweight and deliberately out of shape, but to play Ned he had to be a super-fit athlete.

He threw himself into mental and physical preparations wholeheartedly, working out with coach Atalibio Magione, an Olympic sculling champion, and learning how to handle a shallow-bottomed racing shell. He regained the 15 pounds he had lost in 10 days and started bulking up muscles which would be shown to good effect on screen for the first time.

'I can't explain how painful it was,' he said. 'For the first three days, I couldn't stand up. I was a skinny bag of bones when I started this film. I was a wreck right after *Birdy*. I was 15 pounds underweight and I limped. I had a week to become one of the world's greatest athletes. One of the reasons I really wanted to do it was that I needed a crash course to get me out of that guy in *Birdy*. That was an emotionally draining experience; I don't think I'll play another guy who thinks he's going crazy for a long time.'

To his credit, he quickly became an expert sculler and was able to row all his own races.

While working on the film, Nick was diplomatic, saying, 'I'm really happy with Ned. He's the most basic character I have ever played. He's a young man from a very poor background — he was working as a fisherman — who finds himself through betting and racing thrown into a very élite society. He falls in love with a wealthy girl, there's all this money going around, and I think he loses a little bit of what's there, in himself. Toward the end of the film, he begins to understand that it's not the money he's rowing for. Here are all these people from his home town, Toronto, cheering him on even after he has lost the race, and he realises this is what he must row for — he finds himself again.'

But a few years later, he called the movie a 'travesty', and admitted to *Us* magazine that he was so miserable making the film that he seriously thought about injuring himself to get out of finishing it.

'It was probably the first time I learned about disappointment and failure,' he said. 'There were times when I debated putting my hand in a trunk and smashing the lid down and breaking my hand so I wouldn't have to finish the movie. I had my shirt off a lot, it was this beefcake thing. I was young. I thought, Oh, this is what you're supposed to do. And then I said, "Hold everything. I don't wanna do this." '

He hinted that *The Boy in Blue* contributed to his weird characterisation in his next film, *Peggy Sue Got Married*, adding, 'So I went as far in the opposite direction as I could.'

Another reaction to the film was his decision, on Hallowe'en 1984, to get a tattoo — a fluorescent lizard on his back. 'At first it was just a lizard,' he recalled. 'But after I went home I thought, this is too serious and pretentious. So I went back and gave him a top hat and a cane. It was a stupid rationalisation — like I will never have to take my shirt off again in a movie — at a time when I felt like I could have fallen into the trap of being the beefcake hunk bullshit.'

He later claimed it was also a rite of passage, proving to himself and his father that he was his own man. 'I remember the look on my father's face when he first saw it — he just went white,' Nick said. 'But it was kind of a pleasing moment for me. I was claiming my own body and my own right as a man over myself in a circumstance where my father would see it. He went, "Oh my God." It was a good moment. Like a metamorphosis. I had sort of broken away and become a man, which is an interesting thing about tattoos. In African cultures they have things like tattoos and scarification, where you go from boyhood to manhood. There is nothing like that in American culture except maybe a barmitzvah. It always boggled me that I got one but then I started to realise what it was — I was trying to show that I'd become an adult. I think if I'd had a barmitzvah I wouldn't have gotten a tattoo.'

Filming of *The Boy in Blue* wrapped in October 1984 but it was not released until early 1986, to complete critical indifference, and was a total box-office flop.

The reviewer in *Variety* wrote, 'Subject matter and star attraction of Nicolas Cage may spark initial interest, but a host of weak reviews and poor word-of-mouth make box-office future look dim. Cage is too lunky and too much of a Yankee for the victorious oarsman's role here, although he looks great throughout the pic. His personality is all brawn. Kudos to Cage, though, for doing his own rowing and giving some credence to the action scenes.'

David Chute wrote in the *Los Angeles Herald Examiner*, 'Cage's Hanlan, with his surreal, dinner-plate pecs, represents the common "Johns" in symbolic showdowns with the smug Harvard boys who dominate the sport. Plus he wrestles with his under-developed conscience.'

In the *New York Times,* Nina Darnton said, 'For the most part, the performances are no more exciting than the script. Nicolas Cage (who gave an interesting performance as the Vietnam veteran in *Birdy*) and Cynthia Dale both seem to suffer from the same problem; they are playing a quality rather than a character — she, some sort of an aristocrat, and he, an untutored, boorish sort of lout with a good heart. But neither actor infused the role with the kind of professional detail that would make the characters come alive and we are left with an outer shell that, in both cases, seems phony.'

At least the *Los Angeles Times* liked Nick. Michael Wilmington wrote, '*The Boy in Blue* is such an old-fashioned movie that, after a while, its predictability becomes almost endearing, like a limping white elephant from the dead past, when movies failed in a big way. Cage makes Ned — the natural man breaking through all the starchy, arch formality — fairly compelling and engaging. Like Sean Penn, Matt Dillon or Emilio Estevez, Cage has developed such presence at such a young age that he occasionally puts you off (particularly when he gapes, stares and gulps) but he can also be fantastic — as in *Birdy* or *The Cotton Club*, though not always here.'

Nick took the criticism philosophically. He shrugged, 'The movies that I made that were mistakes, I always learned something from.'

CHAPTER FOUR

PEGGY SUE GOES POKEY

By the time Nick made *Peggy Sue Got Married*, his third film for Francis, he had broadened his acting experience considerably, winning praise for his role as a tortured Vietnam War veteran in *Birdy* and as a soon-to-be GI about to fight in World War II in *Racing with the Moon*. He had also made the yet-unreleased period piece *The Boy in Blue*, which marked the first but by no means the last time he had to do serious weight training to develop a set of bulging muscles.

His personal life was blossoming, too. After his lean high school years when he never got the girl, he now had a fiancée, actress Jenny Wright, who appeared in *The Wild Life*, written by *Fast Times* writer Cameron Crowe, and *St Elmo's Fire* with Rob Lowe. By coincidence, when Nick was shooting *Peggy Sue* in northern California, she was making *Valentino Returns* in Stockton, a city in central California, so they were able to see each other on days off.

In *Peggy Sue,* Nick plays Charlie Bodell, a wannabe rock 'n' roller in the late 1950s whose musical ambitions are sacrificed on the altar of commerce as he goes into the family business selling electrical appliances. As he starts settling into middle age, the sole remnant of his showbusiness ambition is his appearance as an embarrassingly brash television advertiser for his products. He is on the point of being divorced because of his womanising ways. His wife, the Peggy Sue of the title, is played by Kathleen Turner, who, when they started filming, was 31 years old to Nick's 21, although he turned 22 by the time the movie was finished because they had to reshoot the ending. Her character is the high school prom queen who had married Charlie when they both had stars in their eyes and who then spent about 20 years becoming gradually disillusioned. If the ten-year age gap between the two stars seems odd for high school sweethearts, it was completely calculated; the plot hinged on Peggy Sue being transported back to her teenage years and deciding whether to make different choices the second time around, and Coppola thought the age spread would help Kathleen be more convincing as a teenager and Nick more believable as a 40-something.

He said, 'Nick is a very different actor from Kathleen. He lives the character on and off the screen, trying to squeeze out any bit of real human stuff that he can use in the most honest way. If we'd cast a contemporary of Kathleen's, the two wouldn't have been believable at the younger age. By having that strain in the relationship, my hope was that they would both be forced to reach.'

The film was originally due to star Debra Winger, with Penny Marshall directing, but they both left after a row over the script, and the film was sent to Coppola shortly after he finished *The Cotton Club*.

He, in turn, sent the script to Kathleen Turner. She had already signed to make *The Jewel of the Nile*, the sequel to her romp with Michael Douglas, *Romancing the Stone*, but was intrigued by the plot and agreed to meet the director to discuss it.

She recalled, 'We sat down in an office and after a few minutes Francis said, "Let's get out of here." We took a ride on the Ventura Freeway and he started singing old songs. I was having such a good time and said I was very interested in *Peggy Sue* but I was already committed to *The Jewel of the Nile*. He said he would wait. I was thrilled.'

Next, he turned to Nick, who insisted at first he was not interested. But his uncle persisted saying that the film would be reminiscent of *Our Town*, a story by Thornton Wilder about idyllic small-town life in an earlier age. Nick reconsidered, but imposed a bizarre condition for taking the part.

'I did not want to do *Peggy Sue Got Married*,' he recalled years later. 'I turned it down three times. Francis said, "I really need you to be in the movie." I read the script, which was a perfectly romantic film, but the character he wanted me to play was boring. He was the babe to Kathleen Turner's starring role. Just like women don't want to play the babe in movies, I didn't want to be Kathleen Turner's babe. I just wanted to play a character. So I thought, How can I make this guy really far out? I asked Francis about it on the phone and he said, "Absolutely." I said, "I want to go really far out." He asked, "How far do you want to go?" '

Coppola must have been astonished by his demand. Recalling a claymation character from a popular children's television series of his childhood days, *The Gumby Show*, Nick announced that he wanted to give his character the distinctive voice of Pokey. Pokey was not even a person, but a talking horse!

Nick elaborated, 'I said, "I want to talk like Pokey," because, to me, it was funny. And also, it was the way a lot of guys in high school sounded before their voices changed — they always had this high-sounding voice that would crack. When I see the movie now I'm really happy I did that. I really am.

'Pete Townshend once said that sometimes a bad sound can actually be more interesting to listen to than a good sound, and that made sense to me in some way.'

He explained how the idea came to him. He said, 'I was channel surfing and I heard that voice. It stuck with me. I never felt my voice had any character to it on its own merit. So I was always trying to experiment. My character was an adult who goes back to high school, when guys' voices haven't necessarily changed yet. It actually had a point which was that I wanted the character to be the teenager who was always struggling with his changing voice, rather than some kind of jock stud. Also, Francis was doing a story about a woman who goes back in time to visit her dream. He painted the trees and the sidewalks. Why can't actors bend things a little bit, too? He said, "We'll see what happens in rehearsals." '

What happened in rehearsals, when Nick broke out what he called his 'helium voice' for the first time, was chaos. Everybody hated it, especially Turner.

He recalled, 'I was doing this way-out voice and people were rolling their eyes, saying, "What the hell is going on?" It was fairly shocking to people. Kathleen Turner came over and said, "You know, film is a permanent record. Be careful what you do." '

He later confessed that he had wanted to try a more surreal style, and picked Charlie Bodell as his experiment. 'I was an arrogant young man who knew that great artists were always put down for taking chances, so I thought, I have to do something where they're going to put me down or I'm not doing anything of quality,' Nick said. 'I saw Francis being very adventuresome, getting surreal. I thought, Why can't actors do that? I had licence to do whatever I want, because in dreams, you can get as abstract as you want.'

After a two-week rehearsal period the cameras rolled on 19 August 1985. The shoot finished on time and on budget in the third week of October. The small town of Petaluma, north of San Francisco and near the Napa Valley, had a suitable feel of Americana, while the High School at nearby Santa Rosa was perfect for the all-important prom scenes.

Compared to the endless delays and rows on *The Cotton Club,* it was a quick and efficient shoot. But there was, nevertheless, a lot of friction on the set, largely because of Nick.

He said, 'On *Peggy Sue Got Married* there was a great deal of improvising and rewriting. The character I played needed that kind of attention. The script had geared him to be the romantic leading man, who I think everyone has seen before. I'm interested in paradoxes. There needs to be a certain dichotomy of character. Someone loaded with braggadocio but, underneath it, the need for attention. In the rehearsals we were able to make adjustments. I added lines like, "I've got the hair, I've got the eyes, I've got the teeth," which is a pretty pathetic thing to say and it shows my character's insecurity.'

He worked at his singing for the film, because he thought it would add to the poignancy of Bodell's plight, having to give up his dreams to follow in his father's footsteps into electrical goods if it was something he was good at. He also suggested Bodell would be even more unhappy if he had traded his dreams for singing advertising jingles.

'Well, that concept ended up on the cutting-room floor,' he laughed. 'I think everybody felt nobody wanted such a person with Kathleen Turner.

'She did not like me very much and you can't blame her. She was supposed to be with someone written as a suave and romantic young leading man. I turned the character into a cross between a nutty professor and Jerry Lewis. It really freaked her out. It was another example of a character who had to get out because he was haunting me. I had to make it real. I was basically working without regard for anyone in the movie, just doing whatever I wanted and hijacking the movie, for better or worse. I would probably have got fired from some movies in similar circumstances but Francis stuck with me. I have no doubt that if anybody else had been directing that movie I would have been fired. Kathleen basically said, "Horrible, terrible." She gave me the full ice treatment. I thought it would be entertaining to everyone. Then I began to see that it wasn't.

'It was a shock to Kathleen Turner, I guess. It was like she wouldn't be in love with a guy who is that ridiculous. I don't think she blamed me after she saw the movie but while we were making it she was, you know, "What are you doing? You're ruining the movie." I was reading books on the painter Edvard Munch then, how everyone hated his works. So I thought I had to be met with opposition, because I had this arrogant, headstrong attitude at 22.'

Nick did, in fact, come perilously close to being fired because of his performance, and was saved only by family loyalty, and Francis' love of Italian cooking. During the darkest days of *The Cotton Club,* he had headed to the kitchen in his trailer to ease his frustrations, and the cast and crew would enjoy tantalising scents of garlic and pasta wafting out. Now he picked up his pans and spoons again to save Nick's bacon.

Nick explained, 'I know the TriStar people had gotten on the Lear jet to talk about removing me; they said, "This is not cutting it." But Francis cooked everyone a big spaghetti dinner. I didn't know that he was going to have to fight for me. I was just enjoying what I had stumbled upon. I would definitely have done it that way, no matter who was the director. It was a close call. Francis did stand by me on that performance. He knew I was going to do something way out and I really laugh when I see it. A lot of people have accused me of destroying the whole movie, but I think not. I thought, if Francis is going to paint the sidewalk pink and the trees yellow, why can't I have these big goofy teeth and gawky gestures and things that are a little bit larger than life? At least it struck a chord. Whether they hated it or loved it, I think they're gonna remember it.'

He was also philosophical about what would have happened if he had been fired. 'Well, I would've had to wait for another opportunity and try again,' Nick shrugged. 'Because it had to come out somewhere. *Peggy Sue* was another learning experience for me, a whole different movie. It didn't require so much of the darker side of human nature or the strain of emotion. It's lighter. That's basically why I did the film — because I could bring a different paint brush to the canvas. I like to believe that not only are the characters variables but that the approach should be variable too. When you start at an early age and you don't have a lot of life experience to draw on, you're sort of put in a position where you've got to try everything — it's part of experimenting and growing. One national magazine called it the world's worst performance. I thought that was good. It means they got it on some level. I struck a chord.'

Francis was not the only person to resort to cookery, though. Nick finally fulfilled a childhood dream and bought himself a child's play oven and taught himself to bake, because filming in a small town deprived him of all-night restaurants when the fancy took him. He said, 'It was a time when I was wearing pyjamas to bed so that I could roll out at 2.00 am and go to Denny's and have steak and eggs and roll back into bed. I was bored and I needed distractions so I went to Toys 'R' Us because I never got an E-Z Bake oven as a child. I always thought they were really cool but I don't think my father knew to buy me one 'cause they were sort of for girls — but I wanted one, deeply. I thought the way the cakes came out with the chocolate icing looked really tasty.'

On a personal note, however, *Peggy Sue* was good to Nick. An unknown actor with a goofy face was cast as one of Charlie Bodell's classmates, Walter Getz — now superstar Jim Carrey. The two quickly struck up a friendship which has endured ever since. When they were not needed on the set, they hung out together at their hotel, making videotapes of hotel room-service staff. Later, a rumour spread that they had actually abducted one of the staff for a film. Nick laughed this off, saying, 'That story was blown out of proportion. We were young and fooling around and the guy knew we were joking.'

Remembering the madness of those days, on another occasion he said, 'I used to wake up every morning and just say, "Fuck the world." That was like the first thing that came out of my mouth.' He also said, 'I'd go to work and put my sunglasses on and I'd stay in my trailer and know that everybody wanted to fire me, and I almost got energy from that.'

Carrey agreed, 'When we first hung out he was a little crazy, a little frivolous — raw emotion coming out everywhere, with a lot of anger. He was occasionally embarrassing to be around.' A decade after they first worked together, Carrey, the star of such hits as *The Mask*, *The Truman Show* and *Liar Liar*, recalled, 'Nick was just a little bit dangerous to be around. He was just expressing himself. He'd stare at someone in a really weird way, just to see what the reaction was. And I said, "Well, what are you being a psycho for?" But he's matured. He's gotten sophisticated about it now.'

Looking back on those early days, Carrey still admires Nick's courage on *Peggy Sue* — and Coppola's for backing him up. He said, 'He was the first guy I saw in a really big-money situation still experimenting, still going, "I'm gonna take huge risks with this." A lot of people felt he ruined *Peggy Sue* by talking like Pokey through the whole movie. Francis' take on it was, when Brando came to *The Godfather* they said he was making fun of the movie and they wanted him out. It turned out to be a classic. You just don't know. It takes huge guts for a film-maker like Francis Coppola to go, "I don't know." He believes in giving actors enough rope to swing to the next tree or hang themselves. And Nick was an incredibly brave artist.'

Despite the quick shoot, the film's opening was delayed several months because Coppola wanted to shoot a new ending — a happy one. Nick preferred the first version, but had no say in the matter.

By the time the film opened, at the end of the New York Film Festival on 5 October, 1986, Kathleen Turner had learned to put a brave face on her conflicts with Nick during the shoot. She said, 'I think that casting Nicolas opened up whole new possibilities. What Nick has done is brought in a lot of different colours and unexpected reaction without violating the character. I think that it's a more interesting story because of him.'

Between finishing the film and its opening, however, real life overshadowed the world of movies for the Coppola family. Francis' son Gian Carlo was killed in a boating accident off the coast of Maryland. Gian Carlo, 22, was out with his friend Griffin O'Neal, son of *Love Story* star Ryan, in a 14-foot runabout which slammed at full throttle into a line towing a disabled boat. He was thrown backwards on the deck, suffered massive head injuries and was pronounced dead in hospital. Griffin O'Neal, who has spent a year in a drug and delinquency treatment programme in Hawaii, and who had been arrested three days before the accident for reckless driving and carrying a concealed knife, told police that Gian Carlo had been piloting the boat, but witnesses said he had not. After a grand jury investigation, O'Neal was charged with 'boat manslaughter'. He was acquitted of manslaughter after a three-day trial, but put on probation for 18 months for negligence.

The death of his cousin, childhood friend and sometime workmate hit Nick hard. He said, 'Nothing prepared me for that. Shakespeare wrote tragedies and they had a medicinal purpose I think, along with an artistic purpose.' This was a theme to which he would return when he made *Leaving Las Vegas*.

Peggy Sue was popular and successful, but most reviewers agreed that was no thanks to Nick. They overwhelmingly hated the voice and the affectations, and questioned why Turner's character would ever have fallen for Bodell in the first place, never mind marrying him all over again, knowing what she was letting herself in for. Several of the critics pointedly commented that Nick was Coppola's nephew — so much for escaping from the mantle of the family name.

'Cage is almost a caricature of the primping, self-centred immature high school jerk who is really insecure deep down,' said the reviewer for *Daily Variety*. 'His character becomes exaggerated as the film progresses, giving a good clue to his future notoriety as an obnoxious TV appliance pitchman. He is strangely unintelligible at times but the dialogue isn't missed.'

The *Wall Street Journal*'s Julie Salamon called it a 'marvellous picture' but added, 'There is one casting glitch. Mr Coppola must have a blind spot for his nephew Nicolas Cage, whose Charlie is a wart on this otherwise lovely movie. Whenever Mr Cage appears on screen you cringe, particularly when the young actor plays the adult Charlie, looking like a poorly wired robot. As the callow Charlie he's tolerable, but he's best when he's safely off-screen.'

New York Times reviewer Vincent Canby was less keen. He wrote, 'Most of the time *Peggy Sue Got Married* is either underdeveloped or simply not thought through. Of more crucial importance is the lack of any sense of rapport between Miss Turner and Mr Cage. As the teenage Charlie, he's a charmless creep and, as the older man, in gross make-up, he looks like Peter Cushing playing Dr Frankenstein in a Hammer horror film.'

'Nicolas Cage's performance is the weirdest thing in the film,' wrote Peter Rainer in the *Los Angeles Herald Examiner*. 'It's a real movie wrecker. No doubt Coppola encouraged Cage to primp and ham in order to differentiate himself from Turner's work; you don't work up something this bizarre without a lot of encouragement from your director. Cage's Charlie is meant to be a touching doofus, a hood who realises that, in Peggy Sue, he's latched on to the best thing he'll ever have. But he's such a goofball cartoon that he throws the whole movie clear out of whack whenever he puts his pompadour into frame. It's easy to see why Charlie was smitten by her, but it's not clear what Peggy Sue would have seen in Charlie as a teenager.'

Said David Edelstein in *Village Voice*, 'Cage is like both halves of Jerry Lewis' nutty professor fighting it out in one body so that he's always striking poses and then obliterating them with a high, strangled sigh of embarrassment. On its own terms, the performance is daft and endearing, but it's a hollow stunt — weirdness for weirdness' sake, *Peggy Sue* be damned. Cage never inhabits the same universe as Turner, who has to fire herself up over him in a void. That takes its toll on her work, too. Coppola (Cage's uncle) should never have let it happen.'

New York magazine liked Charlie but hated Nick, 'The role works even though Nicolas Cage has been miscast and gives a strangely unappealing performance,' wrote the publication's reviewer. 'He's heavy-lidded and hangdog, with a toothy grin and a high, light voice that shades off into nasality, and you think that his Charlie isn't attractive enough to be Peggy Sue's mate.'

Jimmy Summers wrote in *Box Office*, '*Peggy Sue Got Married* is an imperfect but terrific movie. Yes, the imperfections include a performance by Nicolas Cage that is horrendously off-the-mark. What Nicolas Cage has attempted must be considered a failure, if not an embarrassment. For some reason he plays Charlie as a cartoon, with nasal voice and exaggerated mannerisms. Sometimes it's funny and sometimes it's annoying but it's always inappropriate for the movie's style. And, unfortunately, Charlie is at the centre of the movie's final minutes and his bizarre performance throws the scene off-kilter. His Uncle Francis should have told him to knock it off and play the character straight.'

However, *Ms* magazine, perhaps because of its younger outlook and leadership, loved him. Reviewer Susan Dworkin wrote, 'The casting of Nicolas Cage as Charlie is inspired. Alternately idiotic and charming, he blows Peggy Sue away all over again. (Cage is Coppola's nephew but charges of nepotism are misplaced here.)'

And Michael Rechtshaffen wrote in *The Hollywood Reporter*, '*Peggy Sue Got Married* is an instant classic, a delightful adult fairy tale with an '80s sensibility that stands an excellent chance of becoming Coppola's biggest commercial hit since *The Godfather*. Turner, who seems to get better and better with every role she takes, approaches perfection here as the world-weary Peggy Sue Bodell, Walking Anachronism. Nicolas Cage, meanwhile, adds some admirable character work to his repertoire, as Peggy's intense husband-to-be, a man who aspired to become the next Fabian, but is destined to become Crazy Charlie, with the lowest prices in town."

The film even prompted a serious opinion piece by science fiction writer Isaac Asimov in the *New York Times*, dismissing the romantic idea of travelling back in time and arguing that, even if it was possible, it would inevitably be disappointing.

Perhaps surprisingly, Nick loved the bad reviews and looks back on the movie with fond memories. 'It was an important film to me,' he said. 'It was at that time that I began to re-evaluate the kind of style I wanted to choose as an actor. That was when I began to realise that I could be a little more off-kilter and try something less naturalistic, more abstract. It sort of refurbished my whole interest in what I was doing.

'I had more courage then than I do now. I was a very young man and I felt I could do anything I wanted. In fact, I felt a need to do something outrageous in order to be considered an actor of consequence. I really felt then that to be considered worthy, you had to be slammed by the critics. I would have been miserable if I had not gotten bad reviews. I kept a notebook at the time with all the horrible reviews in it. I felt that if they hated me I would be around for a long time. It had to do with one of Machiavelli's theories. Now, of course, I don't feel the same way. I don't mind nice reviews at all.'

Looking back on the film in 1996, he said, 'I had a strong-willed way of looking at things. I guess you could say I was confident.' He added, 'I wanted to change acting. I was reading books about how people were lambasted for their art. I welcomed the idea of bad reviews because that would mean I was doing something that challenged the critics. I thought I could change acting, which isn't my goal any more. But at that time I was headstrong. I was happy with the results of the movie. A lot of my friends who didn't like it at first now like it. It did well. Kathleen Turner got an Academy Award nomination and it made a lot of money. But I was lambasted by the critics. I was the wart on an otherwise beautiful movie. Francis blamed me; he hasn't asked me to work with him since. I wanted to be in *The Godfather, Part III*. I thought that I would be a more logical choice as James Caan's son than Andy Garcia.'

However, Nick remains profoundly grateful to his uncle for the three films he made with him, whatever the tensions that have grown between them.

'I love Francis and his movies,' he said. 'I would have liked to have been in any of them. I think Francis likes to work in chaos, lotta different things happening at once and a certain amount of panic. The ultimate working situation for me is one where the director does have a strong vision but he gives room for creative input, because otherwise I feel like a marionette. Acting in itself is a silly thing in some ways.

'Sometimes I ask him questions about people he's worked with. Once I asked him about auditions because I was having trouble with readings. He reminded me that the reading is not a finished product and that has always calmed me down. He told me how Brando used to like to work with the artificial elements around him on films like *Mutiny on the Bounty*, where he requested a block of ice to sit on. I've learned so much from him, and he's given me opportunities to work that have been terrific.'

Even after his acclaimed performances in *Moonstruck* and *Raising Arizona,* he still looked back on *Peggy Sue*, scathing reviews and all, as the favourite film of his early career.

In 1988, he told the *Los Angeles Times*, 'I'd never deny that working with Francis hasn't been a great help to me because I've learned a great deal from him. He's one of the few directors around who enjoys making unpredictable choices and I like to experiment, too, so we work well together. Working with him on *Peggy Sue Got Married* was the most satisfying thing I've done as an actor and I consider it my best performance by far.'

Working with Francis Coppola in three movies was the first of many trilogies that Nick would encounter during his career. But this one was more colourful than many of the others to come.

CHAPTER FIVE

CHER JOY

Strapped snugly into his car seat, the baby gurgled happily, completely oblivious to the motor-biking thug bearing down on him, ready to scoop him up from where he sat in the middle of the road. A baby exposed to constant danger from bungling kidnappers and inept robbers does not sound like the central joke of a comedy. But that was the premise of Nick's movie after *Peggy Sue Got Married*, with Nick playing a career criminal who found an unlikely, totally devoted wife, in the shape of the policewoman who took his mug shot every time he was arrested.

Raising Arizona was the widely anticipated second movie from a pair of young film-making brothers, Joel and Ethan Coen. Their first effort, *Blood Simple*, was an intensely violent yet hilarious, low-budget thriller and morality tale, released in 1985 to become an instant cult classic.

Cinema fans expecting more of the same were in for a big surprise. The new film was a dark-yet-sweet comedy about theft, kidnapping and family life, with firepower and explosions thrown in for good measure. Nick's character Hi is a goofy, recidivist petty crook who specialises in targeting convenience stores like 7-Elevens; Holly Hunter played Edwina, the cop who books him into prison so many times they fall in love and marry. When she learns she cannot have children, and they can't adopt because of his long prison record, they decide to steal one — not just any old baby, but one of the famed Arizona Quins, arguing that their parents, furniture magnate Nathan Arizona and his wife, Florence, will hardly miss one. The baby, Nathan Jr, is kidnapped again, by a pair of escaped convicts, before being snatched by the Mad Biker of the Apocalypse, and smiles serenely as he is placed in constant danger, always being rescued at the last minute.

Although he is an incorrigible thief, and a pretty simple one, Hi, who narrates the film in a bemused tone, is also a kind-hearted, well-meaning soul who loves his wife dearly, and who offers a kind of trailer-trash version of southern hospitality to visitors, including the convicts and their super-fertile, partner-swapping neighbours, played by Sam McMurray and Frances McDormand (who would later become Joel Coen's wife).

61

Nick knew he wanted the part as soon as he read the script, but it took a hard sell to the Coen brothers to get the role. Although he then had eight films under his belt, with *The Boy in Blue* and *Peggy Sue* still not released, he did not fit their image of Hi at all, because they felt he was 'too urban' to play a country-hayseed character with a Texas twang. Nick was devastated, and determined to prove them wrong.

He said, 'When I read *Raising Arizona* I knew it was a film I really wanted to do. The script was incredible, one of the best I'd ever read. I loved Hi. He has a rhythm all his own. He has dignity and an integrity that is kind of goofy but that I found very moving. But after I met with Ethan and Joel Coen, they told my agent they couldn't see me in the role at all. I wanted the part but I'd played mostly big city characters so Joel and Ethan hadn't really seen anything that would suggest I could play Hi McDonnough. I was very disheartened. I felt so close to this character that I decided I just wouldn't take no for an answer. I knew I could do it and I wouldn't let it go, so I spoke to them on the phone a couple of times to let me read. Finally, they agreed to let me fly to New York and test for the part, and everything went well. I got the part.'

Casting Hi was actually a minor problem for the Coen brothers, who co-wrote their script over four months while locked up in their office in Manhattan. With baby quins forming a crucial part of the plot, finding the right babies was a nightmare. Under American law, infants can only appear on camera for short stretches at a time, so it is usual to have two or three similar tots playing each role. The Coens auditioned around 400 babies before selecting 15 who looked broadly the same for the quins' big scene, in which they run rings round a hapless Hi who is trying to decide which one of them to snatch from their parents' mansion. However, most unusually, they opted for just one, eight-month-old TJ Kuhn, son of a Phoenix detention officer and his nursing assistant wife, to play Nathan Arizona Jr in the rest of the film. 'It was a risk,' said Executive Producer Jim Jacks. 'But it paid off. TJ did just what he was supposed to do. He appeared to be smarter than any adult in the movie. Nathan Jr is supposed to be having the time of his life and he's not the least flustered by anything that goes on. So we wanted a baby who would go through anything and still look happy. We realised that was asking a lot from one infant, so we had planned to look for twins. We figured twins would allow us to keep working if one was getting cranky.'

Joel Coen added, 'Babies have about a 20-minute attention span and then they get cranky and you have to put in another child. The biggest problem we encountered turned out to be emotional. We had to fire one of the 15.' The baby's crime: he had learned to walk during filming!

They extended the baby motif in casting John Goodman and William Forsythe as the escaped convicts, Gale and Evelle Snopes, and even managed to convey images of a messy childbirth in their escape, when they tunnelled their way through heaving, gooey mud before emerging into fresh air. 'Bill looked like he was studying to be John,' said Joel. 'And they both had these faces — they looked like grown-up babies. We just decided on the spot to continue the baby theme.'

The Coen brothers, who have since made films like *Barton Fink* and *Fargo*, which won them Oscars for Best Original Screenplay and a Best Actress award for Joel's wife McDormand — ironically enough, presented to her by the previous year's Best Actor winner, Nicolas Cage — are deadly serious about their work, but not necessarily about discussing it.

So Joel, who directed the film, described the premise of the film in a rather tongue-in-cheek fashion. He said, 'It's sort of a love story that lets us examine the question of parenting. It has all the basic elements of popular contemporary moviemaking — babies, Harley Davidsons and high explosives. This movie is about parenting and neither of us is a parent. But we're not really intimately acquainted with murder, either, and we made a movie about killing people. Nick's character is caught in an internal struggle. He's being torn in two different directions. On the one side is his desire to settle down and have a family. On the other side is his inclination to respond to the call of the wild.'

Producer Ethan added, 'This one is totally the opposite of *Blood Simple*. We didn't want to do another scary movie. We've already gotten that out of our system. We wanted to try something with a faster pace and a lighter tone. We were ready to do something different. Hi is a thinker. He struggles with the grand issues. He just has an irrepressible urge to hold up convenience stores.'

The film was financed, for $6 million, by Ted and Jim Pedas, who owned the Washington Circle Theaters chain of cinemas in the Washington DC area. It was the first of a four-picture deal with the Coen brothers, an arrangement which they much preferred as it gave them independence from the whims of a big Hollywood studio. The director of photography was Barry Sonnenfeld, a former porn photographer who had worked with them on *Blood Simple* and who would go on to direct such hits as the second *Jurassic Park* movie, *The Lost World,* and *Men in Black.*

It was shot in just 12 weeks in Scottsdale, Arizona, and the Coens quickly realised they need not have worried about Nick's accent. He explained, 'To convince them that getting an accent was really a technical thing like fixing a car — you know, buy a book, you can do it — I worked with a vocal coach and went to Houston to listen. It was a question of getting the accent down. The narration was an important part of it. I wasn't sure how to do it without betraying too much of the character's insides.'

Nick continued to rave about the script, both during filming and afterwards, and said it made the movie much easier to shoot than other pictures, like *The Cotton Club,* where the script was altered constantly during filming, or even *Peggy Sue,* which was a quick shoot but then had the ending altered. And he revealed that he had shown the script to his Uncle Francis, who also loved it. Nick laughed, 'He said, "It looks great but where is all this stuff coming from?" I told the Coens and they laughed. We knew we were on to something.'

And he reiterated, 'It was just a luxury to read. It didn't need anything altering. It would just play. The first contact I had with the film was through the script, and I was sold as soon as I read it. I was impressed with it because it required no adjustments. It was terrific to finally find one like that. In this picture, we're all just trying to make the most out of what's on paper. We don't do a lot of improvising. Sometimes when you improvise it seems funny at first but in the overview it's only distracting. In this case, we're hardly doing any improvisation because the screenplay is so reliable.

'I don't find gag lines particularly funny. Humour has to come out of the attitudes of the characters. It's character and attitude that make me laugh, not jokes. This script is funny because you can see something very human in the way these people think and behave. I liked lines that Hi had like, "I don't mean to sound superior," you know. He had a lot of hospitality towards people but in his marriage he was always in the dog house, couldn't really move without getting barked at. He's a very unusual guy. He plays by his own rules but he's got a lot of integrity.'

Nick also compared his own personal life to Hi's, telling Carrie Rickey of the *Knight Ridder News Service,* 'I don't see my character as a family man, exactly. I see him as someone who isn't a family man trying to be one. In my own life, I haven't really decided to settle down. Being on location all the time makes it hard to be a family man.'

In fact, Nick looked as if he was indeed thinking about settling down. By the beginning of 1986, home for him and his fiancée Jenny Wright was an apartment in Hollywood, which they shared with Lewis, a Burmese cat and a pet octopus called Cool, one of many unusual marine creatures he would own over the years. He filled it with art deco paintings and furniture. He led a generally quiet life, despite the reputation he was to earn as a wild man — he once allegedly roughed up a photographer at a Hard Rock Café charity fundraiser, smashing his flashgun. The snapper demanded $100 for repairs but had to be satisfied with $95 when Nick emptied his pockets in front of a security guard.

This, and his sporadic outbursts of vandalism during the making of *The Cotton Club,* were Nick's only recorded instances of 'wild' behaviour when he won the role of Hi.

Despite welcoming the straightforward shoot and lack of improvisation, Nick did, however, add something of his own personality to what the brothers had written. According to co-star Holly Hunter, he suggested that his character and biker Randall 'Tex' Cobb, played by Leonard Smalls, should have a kind of psychic connection, by having matching tattoos of Woody Woodpecker. Years later, he told *Movieline* that just as he had sought inspiration from a cartoon character for the voice of Charlie Bodell in *Peggy Sue,* he had gone to the same kind of source for Hi McDonnough.

'I based him on Woody Woodpecker, yeah,' Nick said. 'It's fun and ultimately funny to do that. Comic books and cartoons have had a lot of influence in my life. I'm like a sponge. I could see a commercial on TV and get an idea, just the delivery somebody gave will stay in my head and I will spew it back out. What leaves an impression on me is probably what people respond to as being weird.'

In another interview, Nick revealed some of the other techniques he applied to the role. 'I looked at silent films and tried to copy some of the movement,' he said. 'I would ask to see the story boards — that way I could start looking at the camera angles as they were drawn and I could figure out how to kind of give my body a heightened, almost surreal movement within the frame. And I had this little tooth rigged to come out of my mouth so when Tex Cobb hit me I could spit the tooth in his face. It was the only movie where I ever got that technical.'

There was friction on the set at first, however. Perhaps because of their relative inexperience in moviemaking, the Coens did not let their cast review the film while it was being made, by watching the daily rushes, as is the norm, and Nick found himself arguing with them. 'Telling an actor he can't monitor his performance is like telling a painter to paint his canvas without looking at it,' he said. 'I had to argue quite a bit with Joel. After three weeks he relented, but by then it was too late. I was losing my concentration because of the arguments.' Ironically, he was particularly concerned to check that his Texas accent was constant because the Coens had been so worried about it.

However, once that difficulty was ironed out, Nick enjoyed the filming. He said, 'I don't approach comedy differently to drama. Comedy may give you more room to expand but it's all acting. The big difference between the Coens and all the other directors I've worked with is that the age gap is closer. We grew up with the same TV references. So when they gave me direction, it wasn't all involved. They could just say, "A little more Charles Nelson Reilly, please." ' Charles Nelson Reilly was a popular host of children's television and game shows when Nick was growing up.

The film-makers, for their part, had nothing put praise for Nick. Executive Producer Jim Jacks said, 'Nicolas was great. It's important in the movie for the audience to understand that this guy has a good heart and he's only doing what he does because he loves his wife. He has to be sympathetic for the comedy to work. Nick gets that across. He has instant likeability that lets you know he's not dangerous.'

Joel Coen added, 'We hired people who we thought were going to be likeable, and non-threatening as far as the baby was concerned.'

Raising Arizona was completed by August 1986 but not released in the United States until the following February. Nick, whose life was overshadowed by the tragedy of his cousin Gian Carlo's death for the rest of 1986, was happy to promote the film when it opened but was spared one indignity. 20th Century Fox, who distributed the movie, came up with the marketing ploy of having Nick and Holly Hunter pose for publicity pictures wearing disposable nappies as bandit-style masks. Fortunately for them, the Coen brothers were so horrified by the idea that they flew from New York to Los Angeles to argue, successfully, against the campaign.

Nick described the film as 'a first of its kind. It was one of those wonderful times where you had an especially gifted crew and a lot of creative energy on the set. There was this feeling that we were doing something original.'

He said he was looking forward to playing similar roles in the future. 'I don't really like to limit myself to reality,' he told the London *Evening Standard*. 'I've found myself doing that in the past but lately my taste has changed for these broader characters, I have more fun and also I think they are rarely done. The state of acting around the world is naturalism but I am enjoying these other performances like Dennis Hopper in *Blue Velvet* and Eric Roberts in *Star 80*. To me, that's brave and reminiscent of actors like James Cagney who were large and dynamic. I think that some of that dynamic acting has been lost on account of going for reality.'

Raising Arizona was launched with a star-studded advance screening, which Nick attended along with Mel Gibson, *The Big Chill* star JoBeth Williams, Susan Ruttan, Richard Dysart and Corbin Bernsen, all three then starring in the red-hot television series *LA Law*, and Justine Bateman of *Family Ties*, as well as the Coens and 20th Century Fox President Leonard Goldberg. Actress Amy Irving also attended, and said her then-husband, Steven Spielberg, was looking forward to seeing the movie.

The film opened to decidedly mixed reviews but it quickly became a sleeper hit and grossed $21 million, an eminently respectable figure for a movie with a $6 million budget.

Sheila Benson in the *Los Angeles Times* hated it. She thought it was horribly condescending to the low-life characters and felt sorry for Nick. 'The amazing thing about *Raising Arizona* is how it can move so fast, be so loud and remain so relentlessly boring at the same time,' she said. 'It comes swathed in a caul of superiority towards its characters, just plain folks. Nicolas Cage has crammed every inch of sweet earnestness into Hi and that is the sole quality that makes the character work. (You get the feeling that he might not have known the Coens' view of his character, might have believed the laughter was going to be with him, not at him.)'

Peter Rainer in the then *Los Angeles Herald Examiner* also loathed the film. He wrote, '*Raising Arizona* is a nutso yuppie comedy crossed with *Mad Max* with a little David Byrne thrown in. I don't mean that as an endorsement, exactly. It's a lampoon and the jokiness has a superior, derisive edge; the Coens turn their little people into Sunbelt loonies. Nicolas Cage is still doing his clunky lunkhead number from *Peggy Sue Got Married*, although he's toned it down. (At least you can hear him this time.) His mopiness can be touching but he wears out his charm. And Holly Hunter doesn't really connect with him; it's a mismatch that never matches up.'

The entertainment industry trade newspapers had more mixed feelings. *Daily Variety* did not really know what to make of the movie. '*Raising Arizona* may not be everyone's cup of tea but it's fresh enough to find a faithful following with the right handling,' wrote the reviewer, adding, 'Cage and Hunter are fine as the couple at sea in the desert.'

Bill Desowitz in *The Hollywood Reporter* loved the beginning and end of the film, but found the middle weak. However, he said, 'In what may be described as bravura farce, the film opens with a dizzying pre-credit sequence introducing us to the protagonists, superbly played by Nicolas Cage and Holly Hunter (a pair right out of Looney Tunes). Cage, who narrates with tongue held firmly in cheek (a terrific parody of *Bonnie and Clyde*), is a habitual two-bit criminal who lands in prison time and again, seeking a sense of communal belonging.'

Vincent Canby of the *New York Times* thought the idea was terrific but that neither the Coens nor the cast quite pulled it off. He wrote, 'Mr Cage and Miss Hunter, who should carry the movie, go at their roles with a tenacity that the film itself never makes adequate use of. They less often prompt spontaneous pleasure than the recognition that they're supposed to be funnier and more endearing than they manage to be. Raising Arizona may well be a comedy that's more entertaining to read than to see.'

'The Coens aren't yet expert directors of acting, and Cage is a hound dog who could use a trainer,' wrote Stephen Schiff in *Vanity Fair*. 'He's fine, even touching, in the quiet scenes, but he gnashes his way through the action stuff, squinting, shuddering and popping his eyes.' But he loved the film overall, calling it 'a rumbunctiously charming comedy'. And in marked contrast to Peter Rainer, he said, 'This isn't a parody; the humour comes from the characters, not from the redneck kitsch.'

Time magazine also loved it. Reviewer Richard Corliss wrote, 'Every character, great or small (and truth to tell, they're all small), has the juice of comic originality in him.'

And in *Screen International* the reviewer said, 'The pace may flag from time to time. But *Raising Arizona* is so slick, solidly built and downright funny, with great performances all round (and from Cage in particular), that it promises to be the surprise box-office hit of the European summer.'

Film reviewers were not the only critics of *Raising Arizona*, however. The residents of the state of Arizona were not amused by their portrayal as a bunch of bumbling rednecks. Scottsdale Mayor Herb Drinkwater complained, 'There was no redeeming social value to it. How do people even think to write something like that? It certainly isn't the image Arizona wants to project.' But co-producer Mark Silverman responded, 'It pokes gentle fun at humankind and our foibles. It wasn't the intent to ridicule Arizonans.'

Nick agreed, telling *Time Out*, 'It's an Arizona of the mind. It's kinda like the image of quintessential America, the way people would imagine it to be. But you see, why I say quintessential is it's the whole idea of what America should be like in the south west, because in Arizona they don't sound like that. It has the look of Arizona and the accent of Houston, Texas.'

A few weeks after the film opened, a group of parents, social workers and clergy in Seattle claimed the film encouraged child abuse and launched protests outside cinemas showing it. 'It encourages people to view children as objects and, in that way, encourages child abuse, child neglect and kidnap,' said Mike Zink, pastor of Family Life Centres in Seattle. He and his followers picketed the Alderwood Mall Grand Cinemas carrying banners reading 'BIG BUCKS IN BABY ABUSE'. But there were no indications that the protests had any effect on ticket sales.

After finishing work on the film, Nick decided to get himself into shape. Instead of joining one of the many up-market, air-conditioned gyms dotted around southern California, he took up boxing at the tough, no-frills Main Street Gym in downtown Los Angeles. Four times a week he headed for the seedy section of the city to improve his skills.

'I was afraid of going down and having the shit kicked out of me,' he confessed to writer Vanda Krefit at the time. 'And I wanted to confront that fear. The trainer didn't throw me in the ring right away. He let me box with the bag and skip rope. I'm not very good at it and I feel really stupid next to these other guys who can hit the bag at 100 miles per hour. But the situation is a challenge. It gives me something to aspire to.'

But if his physique was improving, the same could not be said for his personal life; he and Jenny were rumoured to have set a wedding date in October 1986, but instead, decided to split up.

He admitted that he was having difficulties with real-life romance, and disclosed that potential girlfriends were sometimes put off when he took them home and they came face-to-face with his pets, which by this time included sharks, eels, stingrays and the octopus. He said, 'The girls generally don't like the eels, so I often lock them in the men's room before a date arrives.'

Acknowledging the difficulties two young actors could face maintaining a close relationship, he told the London *Evening Standard*, 'I think that if I am with somebody who is an actor then a deal has to be made that when they are working I don't work and vice versa, so that you are there for them. But that's a very big demand to make on somebody if they get a great job. It's really a question of how much you want to commit and I think at my age I would find it a little unfair to be telling someone they can't work.'

While he was heartbroken over his split from Jenny, he put his sorrow to good use in his next film, in which he played another bizarre character tormented by love — Ronny Cammareri, the passionate, one-armed Italian baker who wooed an older widow to the strains of Puccini in what would become his first unquestionable, bona fide smash hit, *Moonstruck*.

'I wanted to express this pure love,' he said a couple of years after the movie was made. 'I had just broken up and I had a lot of emotion. I had gotten over it but it made me want to do something with the experience. It was almost a love letter in a way. I was talking to Cher and kind of hoping that Jenny would be out there somewhere, hearing it or seeing it. It gave me a chance to express feelings that coincided with my own.'

When he made *Moonstruck*, Nick was 23, playing a 30-year-old to Cher's 37-year-old Loretta Castorini; Cher was actually 40. Loretta is dowdy and older than her years, with greying hair and a sad expression. She has just accepted a marriage proposal from the kind-hearted but earnest and dull Johnny Cammareri, played by Danny Aiello, even though she does not love him, because she wants children before it is too late. She superstitiously believes her first marriage was doomed because she had a civil wedding and her father did not give her away. Her husband was knocked over by a bus and killed. Once she accepts Johnny's proposal, he is summoned to Italy to visit his mother, who is dying, and he asks her to contact his younger brother, Ronny, to invite him to the wedding to appease the bad blood that has kept them apart for five years. Ronny blames his brother for an accident that cost him his arm; he wears a fake, wooden limb. Loretta reluctantly agrees — and, predictably, sparks fly as soon as they meet.

Nick had played a romantic lead with an older leading lady in *Peggy Sue Got Married*, which would not have been regarded as a good advert for his abilities for most people. But his tortuous portrayal of Charlie Bodell struck a chord with Cher, and she lobbied director Norman Jewison to cast him.

Nick has always confessed he was bemused by her choice, although he was not surprised at being cast to play a character older than himself. He said, 'I used to go for the parts in the John Hughes movies but they never came through. They always felt I looked too old. Cher is one of the few people who appreciated and understood my work in *Peggy Sue* and it was largely on account of her that Jewison met with me.' John Hughes is the director who made such teen classics as *16 Candles*, *Pretty in Pink* and *The Breakfast Club*.

'I never really understood why Cher wanted to work with me after seeing me in *Peggy Sue*,' Nick admitted. 'I mean, I wasn't playing the kind of character that would suggest the Italian leading man for Cher in *Moonstruck*. When I asked her what it was about my performance in *Peggy Sue* that influenced her decision, she said it was like watching a two-hour car accident. She said she had just recovered from a car accident when she saw *Peggy Sue Got Married*.'

On another occasion he said, 'Cher was amazing that way. She saw something that nobody else saw. You wouldn't think of the guy who was sort of Jerry Lewis on acid as a romantic, powerful lead.' He added, 'Cher was a real champion for me. I had done *Peggy Sue* where I got slammed by the critics — slammed — which I was quite happy about, really, because I wanted to do something that would shake people up for some reason. But Cher saw that movie and she really wanted me for *Moonstruck*.'

Jewison agreed that Nick could bring the right mix of intensity and humour to the role. His reputation as an off-kilter character was also appealing to the director, who had no regrets about his choice. He said, 'It showed a tremendous amount of courage. He has a clear idea of who he is. Ronny Cammareri was the most difficult part in *Moonstruck*. He was obviously disturbed. He was a tormented character. But there's something kind of tormented about Nick. He has this lost, soulful look. The eyes of a poet.

'Cher and I both admired Nicolas' work in *Peggy Sue Got Married*. But the main reason she felt he was right for the part is because, like the character of Ronny, Nicolas struck her as a tormented soul. Nicolas did have a darker interpretation of Ronny than I did but we both agreed that a poetic quality was central to the character. When Ronny is first introduced in the film he's in a basement slaving over hot ovens and he almost has the quality of a young Lord Byron. Then, as the film progresses, Nicolas blossoms into a classic romantic leading man, and I think this is the first film where he's come off this way. There's one sequence in particular that's a sort of blue-collar re-creation of *Romeo and Juliet* where Nicolas has the gangling, vulnerable appeal of a young Jimmy Stewart.'

Even though Jewison wanted Nick, it was not a foregone conclusion. Nick was asked to do a screen test and fully understood why. 'MGM wanted to make sure I hadn't been to the imaginarium too many times,' he joked. 'When I say "imaginarium", I mean a place where ideas have feathers on them. They wanted to make sure I wasn't going to turn the part into something that wasn't on the paper.'

Italian family life was at the heart of the film, and Jewison worked hard to create a family atmosphere on his New York set and locations. He said, 'We rehearsed the film much as you would a play. I took a studio on lower Broadway in New York and the whole cast worked together for about two weeks. If one of the actors in the film was also doing a play across town, then someone else would read their lines while they were gone. At one point, Cher might be reading the dialogue of her mother in the film while someone else would be reading Cher's lines. In time, everyone knew not only their own lines but the lines of everyone else. This created a family-like atmosphere, which was very important to the film. I wanted to get to the point where all of the members of the cast talked alike, because that's the way families are in real life. Most of us talk like our parents talk, and like our brothers and sisters talk.'

One of the main 'characters' in the film is the huge harvest moon hanging over the East River, casting a bewitching spell over the intertwined characters. Not only are Ronny and Loretta cheating on his brother and her fiancé by falling in love, Loretta's father, Cosmo, played by Vincent Gardenia, is having an affair and her mother Rose, played by Olympia Dukakis, kisses another man.

Said Jewison, 'And all of this seems to be out of the characters' control. They're all affected by *la luna* — there's a full moon hanging over Manhattan and Brooklyn.' The Canadian director, who owned a cattle farm near Toronto, was not joking. He added, 'I'm a farmer so I know the moon affects cattle. And I think the moon affects humans to a greater extent than most of us realise.'

Perhaps because he used the exaggerated moon to such good effect, even to the point of choosing Dean Martin singing 'Amore' — 'When the moon hits your eye like a big pizza pie, that's *amore*' — as the theme song, Jewison let Nick employ a conceit of his own, echoing one of his beloved silent movies.

Nick said, 'I was still borrowing from the more heightened gestures of the silent movie days. If you look at *Metropolis*, there's a shot of the scientist who invents the technology to create the robot woman — he shows off the robot hand that he invented. He has it raised up and I told Norman Jewison that I really wanted to approximate that shot. He thought it was nuts but he went for it — so I could pull the glove off and show the wooden hand.'

The then young actor was enchanted by the romance of the film. He told the *Los Angeles Times*, 'I was attracted to the romantic element in *Moonstruck* because I think I am a romantic. There haven't been that many great romantic films — *The Graduate* and *Wuthering Heights* come to mind — and I think we need more of them. I am drawn to the romantic film. It's a very powerful emotion. The movies that have really affected me are romantic movies, mostly from another era, like *Wuthering Heights*. Even though romance isn't always a fun thing to go through, the things men and women experience through each other are utterly mystical and illusive. Ultimately, *Moonstruck* is a happy family film for an ensemble of actors rather than a purely romantic movie and I think it frustrated Norman that I leaned towards interpreting it as a desperately romantic *Beauty and the Beast* fable. I didn't change my character from the way it was written but I did try to play up the wolfish part of Ronny's personality. Hopefully, this movie will make people want to fall in love again, want to be with each other, want to work it out. It could be a medicine for couples that are falling apart. They would see *Moonstruck* and say, "See? It's all right to be angry with one another, it's all right to argue." Love is not just holding hands.'

As an opera fan in real life, he also enjoyed the importance of opera in the film — the actual scenes from *La Bohème* and the internal structure of the film. He said, 'I liked the project because there were two monologues that I thought had operatic builds. Rhythms are important to an actor. I envy painters like Picasso who can distort their lines. I think, why can't actors do that? A lot of people think realism is the highest form of acting. I'm not convinced. I kind of want to do something new. I don't know exactly what it is. I'm keeping an open mind.'

Nick had been a great fan of the *Sonny and Cher Show* as a kid, and recalled dreaming of having a Sonny-style moustache when he grew up, so he was thrilled to be working with Cher. 'She is a very easy-going, youthful person with a lot of spirit,' he told *People* magazine. 'Cher is about 16 years older than me but you would never know it. I have liked her since the TV days of *Sonny and Cher*. When I heard she wanted to work with me I was excited. I had plenty of imaginary fantasies about her. It was sort of about me remembering Cher in a sexy dress when I was six years old, getting turned on and carrying that into the movie. It was like cultivating the imagination and letting it fly. I didn't want to get involved with her for real. I wanted to imagine those things so that when we got to that first kiss, all those thoughts were coming out. And I think it worked ... I liked kissing her.

'That first kiss on screen was the very first kiss that existed between us. I refused to rehearse it. I wanted it jam-packed with energy. I think it was worth just cultivating the imagination. That was a *great* kiss. But my shaving, or lack of it, made her face raw after a while. It scraped off her make-up and irritated her skin.'

And he confessed to *Playboy*, 'There was an incredible amount of pressure to have a certain amount of male power with her. I remember thinking, I'm going to imagine what it will be like to kiss her. When we did kiss, there was a lot of power there. She's obviously a passionate woman.'

Cher was equally complimentary about him. She said, 'You see him thinking a lot. He thinks deep thoughts. Or — I don't know if they're actually deep thoughts but he's deep into thinking them. He gives into them like they're deep.'

The bakery scenes in the film were set in a real bakery, owned by Argentinian immigrant Gilberto Godoy, in Brooklyn. He featured in the film and also became a star. He had to join the Screen Actor's Guild because he had one speaking line, when Loretta arrived at the shop looking for her fiancé's brother, and he says, 'Ronny, someone's looking for you over here.'

Godoy had bought the shop from the Cammareri family, who had owned it for three generations and still lived above the shop, and Jewison changed the name of the original screen baking family, Paolo, to Cammareri, in their honour.

'Wherever I can, I like to cast people who do the same job in real life,' Jewison said. 'An actor baking bread is not the same as a baker baking bread.' The bakery had never been modernised since it opened around 1920, and that was a large part of the appeal for Jewison. 'It has one of the few coal-fired ovens left in the city,' he said. 'Heat and humidity are always there. And bread is always rising and there is an incredible smell. It helps the actors to be in a real environment.'

Godoy was far from being in awe of stars and movie-makers. He had never heard of Jewison when he was first approached, and when he was told that Jewison had made *F.I.S.T.* with Sylvester Stallone, he simply asked, 'Who is Sylvester Stallone?' When he agreed to let the cameras in for the three-day shoot, he also refused to close down his business, which made about 5,000 loaves a day.

'It was hysterical,' said Jewison. 'We had trucks, lights, cameras, Cher — and the poor guy was still baking.'

Godoy added, 'To make a movie is not a big deal. The movie stars made more mistakes than me. People rave about Cher. Listen, she went up and down the stairs for three days. She never did it right. With my part, we did it, one, two, three.'

Cast and crew tucked into bread, biscuits and cheesecake throughout the time they were there, prompting Godoy's wife, Nelida, to say of Cher, 'How does she have that figure? She started with little pieces of bread and then she went for the loaves.'

Godoy himself became an instant celebrity, with Manhattanites flocking across the river to Brooklyn to buy his bread and agents offering to put him in commercials.

Moonstruck opened in December 1987 in a handful of cinemas so that it would be eligible for consideration for the Academy Awards the following March. As it happened, it was nominated for Best Picture but lost to *The Last Emperor*. However, Cher won the Best Actress statuette, Olympia Dukakis was named Best Supporting Actress and John Patrick Shanley won for Best Original Screenplay. Nick also had his moment at the Oscars — presenting Sean Connery with the Best Supporting Actor award for his role in *The Untouchables*. The film also garnered Nick his first award nomination, for a Golden Globe as Best Actor in a comedy or musical, but he lost to Paul Hogan for *Crocodile Dundee*.

Nick later admitted he felt a little cheated. He said, 'My only disappointment was that some of my best work was cut by the director. Norman Jewison took me out for dinner afterwards and said he had to cut some of my scenes because they overshadowed the star. I don't know. On the one hand, if he had kept them in, maybe I would have gotten an Oscar nomination, too.' But he added diplomatically, 'You have to understand — this man is the conductor and he's trying to make the orchestra work.'

Most reviewers were in no doubt that the orchestra gave a bravura performance. In *The Hollywood Reporter*, Michael Rechtshaffen wrote, 'A romantic comedy that doesn't skimp in either department, Jewison's celebration of The Family, as captured by the pen of screenwriter John Patrick Shanley, expertly weaves the spell of a Capra or a Lubitsch.' He praised the entire cast for their sterling work, adding, 'And, of course, Nicolas Cage in the most appealing performance of his career.'

Daily Variety also loved his performance. Their reviewer said, 'Cage's Ronny is a brooding, vital, angry, barely contained force haunted by his past. He explains to the stunned Loretta how he lost his hand five years previously, in an accident he still blames on Johnny, and that his fiancée left him a short time afterwards.

'In Shanley's gorgeously written ensuing scene, the two adjourn to Ronny's apartment above his bakery and begin to talk about one another's lives. The different reactions of two people who see a second chance at true love staring them in the face is the theme of the rest of the film.'

Sheila Benson of the *Los Angeles Times* wrote, 'Even before we find out that Nicolas Cage is Ronny, an impassioned baker with a wooden hand and a soul as hot as his furnaces, we know that Mr Johnny had better not dally long in Palermo. The lupine Ronny's more civilised side is his passion for opera, and in the film's great Cinderella moment, he lures Loretta to *La Bohéme*. Cage attacks the role of Ronny with a nice balance between unbridled romanticism and tongue-in-cheek seriousness; he's marvellous.'

'*Moonstruck* is a delightful surprise,' wrote David Ansen in *Newsweek*. 'Who'd have thought that a cast including Cher, Nicolas Cage, Vincent Gardenia, Olympia Dukakis and Danny Aiello — actors whose combined potential for mannerism and excess could blow every fuse in Manhattan — would be fashioned into such an engaging and compatible ensemble. Cage makes his lunatic ardour as irresistible to the audience as it is to Loretta.'

The reviewer for *Village Voice* said, '*Moonstruck* is a gloriously foolish little movie, a sitcom infused with the rapturous passion of opera. Cage was dopey and affecting in *Peggy Sue Got Married,* but he didn't fit in with the rest of the actors' realism. Here, as in *Raising Arizona*, his stop-the-movie-I-want-to-smoulder routine has a bonkers integrity. Most actors would have played Ronny as a firebrand, but Cage's rhythms are more zonked and his heavy-lidded, cow eyes suggest tender infatuation with his own inner torment. (He has so much self-love that there's plenty left for the audience.)'

The *New Yorker* agreed, 'Cage is a wonderful romantic clown: he's slack-jawed and Neanderthal and passionate. He may be the only young actor who can look stupefied while he smoulders. And no one can yearn like Cage: his head empties out — there's nothing there but sheep-eyed yearning. Looking as if he's in a sick trance, the baker tells Loretta he's in love with her; she has just been to bed with him but when she hears this she slaps him two quick whacks and says, "Snap out of it." '

Not everyone raved quite so much. Deborah Kunk of the *Los Angeles Herald Examiner,* for one, was much less impressed. She wrote, 'In all, the acting talent gathered around the two lovers is nearly enough to swamp their efforts. Cher comes off much better, and she is especially fine at the beginning as a tempestuous Italian Donna. The equally nice-looking Nicolas Cage is the cast's weakest link. Those around him create exaggerated ensemble characters that work, while he, as the leading man, sometimes postures.'

Janet Maslin in *The New York Times* agreed, 'Johnny goes to Italy to see his dying mother and instructs Loretta to find his brother Ronny. This turns out to be Nicolas Cage, who has a role so awful it's hard to know who to blame. Ronny is a slob. He works stoking the oven in a bakery (as he describes the job it's "Sweat and sweat and sweat and shove this stinkin' dough out of this hot hole in the wall!"). Ronny is also missing a hand, which he lost when Johnny came to see him years earlier and Ronny, lost in conversation, forgot to keep an eye on the bread slicer. It's impossible to tell whether this is supposed to be funny, but the film does carry a "Mr Cage's Hand Design" credit for Eion Sprott.'

William Quinn in the *Daily Bruin,* the newspaper of the University of California, Los Angeles, said, 'Here, Cage's disfigurement is no satisfying symbol or metaphor — meaning organic as well as explanatory — rather merely a gimmick.'

In *The Christian Science Monitor,* David Sterritt wrote, 'Mr Cage, for instance, gets too carried away when his hot-headed character flies off the handle with rage.'

On a brighter note, at least as far as the stars were concerned, *The New Republic* hated the film as a whole but added, 'Two cheery notes: Nicolas Cage, as the erring brother, shows surprising signs of life; and Cher, as the erring fiancée, confounds those who swore she was a remote-controlled robot.'

With the release of *Moonstruck* Nick progressed from being a film actor to a star, a genuine heart-throb, much to his initial bemusement. 'I feel like there's a big wet fish slapping itself against the inside of my heart right now,' he told the *Los Angeles Times* shortly after the film opened nationwide. 'Things have changed quite a bit in the past few weeks and I don't know what to make of all the attention the film is receiving. I'm grateful that people seem to like the film, but the whole thing's a little bizarre.'

Cher was gracious about her co-star, telling the same paper, 'I don't know if Nicky will ever be a huge mainstream actor because he's so daring. He takes unbelievable chances as an actor and personally I think he's crazy — sometimes he was a blast on the set, other days I'd get real peeved at him. He's usually fun to be around, though, because he's very funny. And, of course, he's got those great eyes. Every time I got angry with him I'd just look in his eyes. In fact, I don't think I ever saw any other part of Nicky except his eyes because that's what I liked about him.'

Nick came clean about the real reason behind his reluctance to grant interviews to promote his films in the past — he was too nervous. He went on, 'I've never had an aversion to doing press so much as I haven't known how to do it. There's a technique involved that I still don't understand and if you do it wrong, you saddle yourself with misconceptions you'll spend years trying to shake. I also believe that an actor is someone you see playing a character and there's a danger in revealing too much about yourself because that gets in the way of whatever illusion you're trying to create on film. If you give away your tricks you lose the illusion. I don't discuss my acting technique. It's kind of like *The Wizard of Oz.* If you pull the curtain off, you just see a little man talking through a megaphone.'

Moonstruck has continued to be a popular video rental, and in 1999 was named the 13th most romantic film of all time by *Movieline* magazine.

Years after he had made the movie, however, Nick was to confess that he was very uncertain about his performance as Ronny. 'At the time, I was ashamed of being in *Moonstruck*,' he admitted. 'Although I now think it's a terrific film, at the time it wasn't me. When I made it, I wasn't at all sure if I did a good job or not; it was the first film I featured in that attracted a mature audience. Now I look back on it and think, God, I was starring opposite Cher, I was 23 and doing romantic scenes with her. I was about the same age as Eric Stoltz, who played her son in *Mask*! Now I look back and feel really proud of *Moonstruck*, and I received the best compliment ever when Elia Kazan said he liked it.' Nick has always admired controversial movie-maker Kazan and has often referred to him.

Even at the time *Moonstruck* was released, Nick admitted he had a bit of an ulterior motive in making his most mainstream film to date. He told the *Los Angeles Times*, 'One of the reasons I did *Moonstruck* was because I thought it would allow me to take more of a chance with my next film, which is a low-budget black comedy called *Vampire's Kiss* that hardly has mass commercial appeal written all over it. I play a man who's insane and thinks he's a vampire. Everyone told me not to do it but the script grabbed me by the collar and screamed, "If you don't do this movie you're a coward." I figure that in order to succeed in the film business you can't be afraid to roll the dice. And as long as I'm betting, I want to bet everything I've got.'

Vampire's Kiss was finished before *Moonstruck* opened, and Nick decided to take some time to relax. He enrolled in a wine-tasting course at UCLA — the University of California, Los Angeles — perhaps to enjoy better his Uncle Francis' Neibaum-Coppola wines.

He explained his decision to the newspaper *USA Today,* saying, 'It was just my 24th birthday and it was the first real birthday that I've had where I felt a sense of accomplishment. I was always in sort of a race before, but now I feel I can kind of slow down and feel good about it.'

Nick did not realise just how much relaxation he was in for. Despite the worldwide success of *Moonstruck,* both in critical and financial terms, Hollywood did not come knocking at his door for 18 months. It took a far-from-mainstream movie to kick-start his career.

'What's funny is that after *Moonstruck* was released, I didn't work for ages!' he recalled. 'And after *Vampire's Kiss* — a small-budget, off-the-wall movie — I found myself working with David Lynch.'

CHAPTER SIX
COCKROACH CUISINE

With bulging eyes and his body shaking, Nick stalked the filthy creature scuttling over the cooker of a New York apartment. He grabbed the giant cockroach, gulped — and ate it. This was no fake insect, made out of chocolate perhaps, or a last-minute substitution of a model for the real thing. The biggest acting feat in this scene was Nick steeling himself not to gag as the creature slipped down.

The same was not true of the audience. Not many people saw *Vampire's Kiss* during its brief theatrical release — but that scene must have provoked the biggest collective retch since Linda Blair spewed pea soup in *The Exorcist*.

Although he was sickened at the time, and continues to be revolted by the memory of that day, Nick has no regrets because he knows those few seconds burned irrevocably into film-goers' memories and that for evermore people would remember them and shudder.

'That scene will be remembered long after the movie is forgotten,' he said.

In *Vampire's Kiss,* Nick plays Peter Loew, a young Manhattan literary agent, a bad-tempered yuppie who mercilessly and brutally badgers his hapless secretary, Alva, played by Maria Conchita Alonso, in part because of frustration over his inability to find a steady girlfriend. Like many young professional New Yorkers, he is in therapy, but his psychiatrist, Dr Glazer, played by Elizabeth Ashley, cannot explain why he is turned on by the bat that has taken to flying into his apartment, driving women away but leaving him with erotic dreams. Then he meets Rachel, a beautiful and mysterious woman played by Jennifer Beals, who bites his neck and draws blood when they have sex. He becomes convinced she is a vampire and that she has made him her victim. The movie is a portrait of his disintegration into madness as he becomes more and more convinced he has become a vampire, too.

He affects mannerisms like wearing sunglasses by day, sleeping under a couch he has converted into a coffin and, notoriously, eating the roach. Paradoxically, his character is so obnoxious to start with, his colleagues do not notice the gradual changes in his demeanour. Only poor Alva realises how much he has deteriorated — he ends up raping her — and nobody takes any notice of her; all yuppie bosses in

1980s New York are supposed to be mean and crazy.

The film, by British director Robert Bierman, who had earlier made the television film *Apology* with Lesley Ann Warren, is ambiguous as to whether Rachel really was one of the undead, but there is no doubt that Peter believes it.

Fresh from his romantic turn in *Moonstruck*, Nick threw himself into his new role with characteristic enthusiasm — hence the cockroach scene, which he dreamed up himself. Just as he predicted, that scene took on a life of its own, overshadowing every other aspect of making the movie. He lost a battle with Bierman to have a live bat flitting through the set of his apartment but prevailed with the insect.

'I was sort of in an irate state during the making of that film,' he told *GQ* after its release. 'It was pretty hard to live with the character. I became obsessed with it and I wanted everyone else to care as much as I cared. I went beyond the call of duty. I wanted there to be a moment of something so real, a special moment in the film which would really shock. When I saw the film with an audience the reaction was so intense. All I had done was eat a cockroach!'

A later scene had his character catching a pigeon to eat, and Nick explained the reasoning behind his idea. 'The script said it was supposed to be a raw egg,' he said. 'But it didn't make sense to me that my character would eat a raw egg. He thinks he's a vampire. He's trying to graduate up the food chain from pistachio to cockroach to pigeon to person. I wanted to tie in the Renfield thing — the assistant to Dracula who eats bugs. It was a slow progression for my character; ultimately he bites a girl's neck and drinks her blood.

'So I said I wanted to eat a cockroach. And everyone went, "You've got to be crazy!" And I said, "Yes, I know what you mean." And they wrangled up these New York cockroaches. And the day arrived when I had to do it and I saw the bug when I walked on the set and its legs were kicking and it looked huge! I was going to say, "Guys, I can't do it." But I thought that would be a cop-out because I'd set it up. I put the cockroach close to me and every muscle in my body said, "Don't do it!" It was that unnerving. But I did it and I couldn't sleep for three nights. It was soft, not crunchy — just a nightmare. I actually have a fear of bugs, particularly cockroaches, and I had to disinfect my mouth with 100-proof vodka. In a sense, I was facing my devil. It makes me sick just thinking about it.'

To his horror, Nick then had to do it all again, because of what he later claimed was spite on the part of the director. He said, 'Robert Bierman had a bone up his butt about me because we were arguing. He got even with me by making me do it twice and then using the first take. We actually got along at the end of the picture.'

Vampire's Kiss made only $600,000 at the box office but is still a staple at video stores. Nick is convinced he knows why — the cockroach.

'To this day people ask me about the fucking cockroach,' he told *Entertainment Weekly* magazine. 'It was disgusting. I knew that if I ate the bug, you and I would still be talking about it today. People wouldn't forget that. It had to be real, I wanted everyone to know that the bug went into my mouth. The fact that it was real created this super-visceral experience.

'I'm sure that's the reason the movie has stayed on the video-store shelves for so long. I hope there are other reasons — I think it's a good movie — but people want to see the movie in which the guy eats a real bug. The fact is, I'm not sure I like being associated with cockroaches. I'm not that wild about them. Yet cockroaches and I have become linked. My manager threw a birthday party for me once and there was a giant cake in the shape of a fucking cockroach.'

Although Nick was to do his share of big-budget films with millions spent on special effects, he also pointed out that this was a stunt which had immense visual and emotional impact and did not cost a penny. Even though the cockroach was and still is the defining moment of the movie, and Nick was quite right that interviewers continue to be fascinated by it, he contributed more than that to the development of Loew's character. Once again he delved into his childhood memories of eerie, flickering black-and-white silent movies and realised he had a perfect opportunity to re-create something of their atmosphere on the modern screen.

'I was about 24 then and I was really into German expressionistic acting, people like Max Schreck, Emil Jannings and Conrad Veidt,' he told Lawrence Grobel of *Movieline* magazine. 'I saw their movies when I was eight because my dad would play them on a projector for a class he taught at Cal State Long Beach. I would see *The Cabinet of Dr Caligari* or *Nosferatu* and freak out, really get nightmares over them — well, you can imagine the effect they had on me. They were much more horrifying than anything today, claustrophobic and really spooky. The problem was how to make a modern movie with some German expressionistic acting. The only way to do it was to play a man who's going nuts, who thinks he's a vampire, with his shoulders going up and eyes bulging. I saw an opportunity to say, "Well, this man is insane, and so I have a right to do what I want; I can use some of those old German facial expressions and hand gestures and combine it with sound." That's why I was so excited about it.

'There was quite a bit of nervous tension on the set, because nobody had an idea which direction I was going to go. I choreographed more or less everything. But the director stood by it, though we had a few run-ins. No one had eaten a cockroach before and if I did it we could save the movie money because it would get the same reaction as a bus blowing up for a million dollars; because I knew that you and I would be sitting and talking about it ten years later. I wanted to do something that was punk, if you will. I had heroes in music like The Who, who smashed their guitars. I wanted to have that rock 'n' roll sensibility, a mini shock wave. It gave me nightmares. I wasn't able to eat food for a couple of days. If I think too much about it, it really makes me ill. You know, the animal rights people called when they heard I did that.'

Despite his genuine love of animals and his collection of pets which might make some people squirm almost as much as a scavenging insect, Nick had no concerns about the fate of the creature in question. So he was astonished to hear he could face prosecution for inflicting 'needless pain' on the bug. He recalled, 'There was a backlash from the animal rights people. I finally called one of them and said, "Do you have a can of Raid?" When she said, "Yes," I said, "Well then, what's the problem?" '

Vampire's Kiss may have seemed an odd choice for Nick after *Moonstruck*, almost a regression to his earlier, quirky films, but he loved the project from the start. He was less than happy with some of the decisions that were made once it was finished — especially the editing and the video promotions — and swore he would never eat another cockroach, but he had no regrets. It was the beginning of a pattern for him; taking advantage of the substantial salaries and increased power he got from a high-profile, bigger budget film to work for next to nothing on something unusual because he could afford to.

'It wasn't a practical choice to make, but it was an honest choice,' he said of *Vampire's Kiss*. 'After *Moonstruck*, I thought, OK, now I'm going to do the movie I care about, *Vampire's Kiss*, this angry little avant-garde movie, wanting to create this character that was more shocking and would get back to that younger, angrier audience. It was more punky. It appealed to kids of my age. Not many people saw it.

'Everyone from my agent to my lawyer and my publicist said about *Vampire's Kiss*, "*This is a mistake*." I even got talked out of it once. But the script haunted me. I kept on seeing the character of Peter Loew and thought about all the things I could do with him. With this insane character, I had the chance to realise all sorts of wonderful dreams.'

While he had fantasised about kissing Cher and enjoyed the moment when his dreams came true, the crucial kiss with Beals in this movie was a very different matter. Nick said, 'I did not know much about Jennifer and did not spend much time with her away from filming. But she did bite me pretty hard and there were bruises on my neck. I remember being a little afraid of it and thinking my neck was really going to start spurting blood. Some girl was massaging my foot off-camera — working yoga on my feet — during the scene. I was trying to get in to the sexuality of it all, despite the fact that Jennifer was starting to hurt my neck.'

Nick was proud of his work in the movie, even though many people found the character's descent into insanity disturbing, a response he rejected. He said, 'The funny thing is that if you study how insane people are in reality and then bring this to a film, people think you're going over the top. I've seen people in New York standing and talking to a wall and that's how the character is at the end of the movie. It really does happen like that. Maybe it's the idea that people don't want to be reminded of, or they want to escape and everyone has to be pretty and perfect and show the world what they are supposed to be like. But to me, that's an illusion.

'I'm very happy with that movie, only because I shouldn't have done it and I did it anyway. You know, that character meant a lot to me. I sort of incorporated my father and mother into the role and wanted to take a chance with it. Against everybody's wishes I turned him into a maniac with plastic fangs. OK, it wasn't a career move, but I'm glad I did it.'

He was not, however, glad about the way the production company, Hemdale, treated the finished product. He complained, 'Some of my work in *Vampire's Kiss* should not have been cut. It was unfair. I was the driving force of that movie. And it was some of the best work that I have ever done.'

This was not simply an actor bitching about losing time on the screen. Pauline Kael, who wrote for the *New Yorker* magazine and was probably the most influential film critic in the United States at the time, tended to agree with him. She said, 'The Hemdale people who backed the film made cuts — especially in Loew's sessions with his therapist — and, from reports of people who saw the director's version, key material was removed.' *New York Post* writer David Edelstein, who saw an earlier version of the film, also said that the emotional roots of Peter's disintegration were made clearer before the cuts.

Hemdale found it difficult to get a distribution deal for the film. It was entered into the Boston Film Festival in September 1988 to try to spark more interest. But the main response was a less-than-flattering review in *Weekly Variety*: 'Other than as a cult item at midnight, this confused picture has limited commercial possibilities due to a muddled script and another eccentric performance from Nicolas Cage.'

Producer Barbara Zitwer complained bitterly that Hemdale, and in particular company boss John Daly, were dragging their feet in getting the film released. It had been due to open on 29 July 1988, but by October it had still not been released. 'At the last minute, John Daly blocked it,' she complained. 'Now Daly won't tell me if the movie will ever be released.'

Daly countered, 'We don't have a date but it will be released. We've been going through a mental exercise deciding whether to go into distribution. Zitwer has probably shown it to her friends and is anxious for it to come out, but there is no point in bringing it out for just a week.'

The film was finally released in June 1989, to some surprisingly good reviews, especially for Nick's performance. Unfortunately, the subject matter clearly did not appeal to the American viewing public and it closed after six weeks.

Kevin Thomas of the *Los Angeles Times* had nothing but praise. 'In bringing Joseph Minion's mine-strewn script to the screen, British director Robert Bierman, in his theatrical feature début, and his protean star Nicolas Cage, never falter,' he wrote. 'The result is a sleek, outrageous dark comedy that's all the funnier for constantly teetering on the brink of sheer tastelessness and silliness. Never before has so much been demanded of him [Cage]. He must seem at once hatefully obnoxious yet pathetic in his progressive deterioration. Above all, he must always seem funny. Were he not, the film would be just too repellently venomous to contemplate. But Cage carries everything with a manic intensity that plays with throwaway ease but must have required the utmost energy and concentration — not to mention spontaneity.'

In the *Wall Street Journal*, Julie Salamon said, 'He's never been stranger or more flamboyant than he is in *Vampire's Kiss*. This time his contortions work, perhaps because here he is a one-man show. Mr Cage pulls off a delirious comic stunt as the foppish, irritable literary agent who becomes convinced he's a vampire. It's all very weird and quite amusing.'

The *New Yorker* loved both the film and Nick. Their reviewer wrote: 'Whether taken as a straight horror film or as a psychological nightmare with erotic overtones, *Vampire's Kiss* mixes fable and satire in startling and satisfying ways. The more horrifying and tragic Peter's situation, the wilder and funnier the working out becomes. Cage, with his light, hoarse voice and whipped-dog eyes, has been almost too strange for some of the ordinary-man heroes he has played. But as an urban swinger convinced that he requires, very late at night, a neck to bite, he's inspired.'

Andy Klein of the *Los Angeles Herald Examiner* wrote, 'For pure weirdness, *Vampire's Kiss* is without rival. It's also just about the most interesting film of the year so far. Cage plays his character insanely over the top from nearly the first scene. Cage delivers a remarkable portrayal of a completely obnoxious jerk. He's so offensive from the start that no one really notices his transformation, not even when he starts skulking around New York wearing cheap plastic fangs, his shoulders hunched in imitation of *Nosferatu*'s Max Schreck.'

Box Office recognised that the film would attract a limited audience, but loved it. Their reviewer wrote, 'This demented comedy comes up with an original take on the overly-familiar tale and the results, while not for everyone, are super. The actor infuses Peter with an uncut awfulness which is at first hard to take but which simply becomes funnier and funnier as the self-absorbed agent becomes ever more deranged.'

Pauline Kael in the *New Yorker* was not satisfied with the film as a whole, but compared Nick's approach to the way Robert De Niro gained weight for *Raging*

Bull. She said, 'In his own daring, light-headed way, he's a prodigy. He does some of the way-out stuff that you love actors in silent movies for doing and he makes it work with sound. This is somewhere between a horror picture and a black comedy. This daring kid starts over the top and just keeps going. He's airily amazing. At Loew's maddest, Cage's head is held back on his neckless body and his eyes bulge out like loose marbles. And this apparition is somehow a plausible part of the singles nightlife and the Manhattan street world.'

On the other side of the country, the critic for *Los Angeles Weekly* shared her opinion. The review read, 'As his state of mind deteriorates, so do his shoulders, which recede into memories. If you stick with Cage, his performance eventually establishes its own truth. He takes on a supernatural believability and makes the nostril-dilating and eye-popping work. Loew is weird even before his transformation begins. He speaks in a demented low-brow's idea of a British accent. Cage is a magnetic, resourceful presence. More to the point, he's an absolutely fearless actor.

'There's no ambiguity in Cage's performance whatsoever. The same thing, however, can't be said of *Vampire's Kiss*, a fantasy-or-reality tale that's more confusing than a trick mirror with a crack up the middle.'

Even reviewers who absolutely hated the film recognised Nick's talents. 'Whatever do director Robert Bierman and writer Joseph Minion intend here? A metaphor for AIDS?' asked Kirk Honeycutt in *The Hollywood Reporter*. 'For searching for love in all the wrong places? Does anyone care? What keeps the film afloat is Cage's manic energy. What Cage does here is not exactly acting but it is a performance. Leaping on to office desks, bugging his eyes out, trotting along city streets in the stiff slouch of one experiencing withdrawal symptoms, Cage struggles valiantly to give the tired vampire film an unpredictable spontaneity.'

In the trendy New York magazine *Village Voice,* Stuart Klawans said, 'Here is the movie that asks the question: Is there any difference between a vampire and a sexually aroused yuppie? Cage brings to the role the dumbfounded stare he used to such advantage in *Raising Arizona* plus a heretofore unseen talent for middle–class sleaze.'

BY Randall, in its Los Angeles counterpart, *Village View*, wrote, '*Vampire's Kiss* arrives as one of the most repellent and reprehensible examples of this blood-sucking boom. Meant as a black comedy, the story covers overly familiar territory but with a huge streak of misogyny thrown in as supposed fun. If in the past you've found Cage too mannered, wait until you get a load of his scenery-chewing affectations here, which would be in keeping if the film was consistent in its tone. *Vampire's Kiss* tries to have it both ways though, as a black comedy and a straight thriller, and winds up muddled mayhem. This film doesn't deserve an audience, it deserves a huge stake through its sick little heart.'

Nevertheless, *Movieline* named his performance one of the ten best by an actor under 30, and called Nick 'Our designated madman. Indeed, he is the madness in whatever is left of the Method these days.'

Vampire's Kiss also increased his award profile, when he tied for Best Actor with Michael Gambon of *The Cook, The Thief, His Wife and Her Lover* at the Catalonian International Film Festival in Spain. He was also nominated as Best Actor by Independent Feature Project West.

Years later, after Nick won his Oscar, *Entertainment Weekly* ran a retrospective of his career and pointed out that if the film did not work it was by no means Nick's

fault. The magazine said, 'He's at his most manic in the bizarre
and-miss comedy that doesn't quite manage to sell its hyster
misogynist premise. Cage plays a New York literary agent w
during sex by a mysterious woman who is at the very l
convinced that she's undead and he's been infected. He tak
to work, terrorising his secretary even more than usual an
sleazeball who has stumbled upon an excellent excuse for his ൦ഺ.
movie together as best he can. More important, he nails down his unique app.
to acting, managing to be simultaneously stylised and naturalistic.'

As Peter Loew sank to the depths of madness he went out shopping for kitschy
toy fangs. Nick was horrified that Hemdale focused on this aspect when the video
was released. He complained, 'The most frustrating thing about this film was the
studio's marketing tactics of the video. The jacket looks like a schlock vampire
movie, with me in a cape and stupid fangs like *Love at First Bite*. That's not what the
movie's about. It's much more complicated, it's about a man losing his mind. I never
once wore a cape in the movie. Big business marketed it as some schlock vampire
movie, some supernatural piece of shit! For a while there, I felt like I couldn't win. I
pour my heart into this and they put me in that stupid cape. What I gotta do? When
that video came out, it really hurt me.'

After his revelation during his publicity work for *Moonstruck* that he was shy
about interviews, Nick was in full-on weird mode when he did a 20-questions
interview with *Playboy* magazine to promote *Vampire's Kiss* — and managed to
discuss just about everything but the film in question.

Interviewer Robert Crane revealed, 'Cage reacted to being interviewed as
most people react to having dental work done. Unaccustomed to self-promotion, he
paced the floor like an inmate on death row, constantly running his fingers through
his shock of unruly hair. Yet he was very cordial.'

He was also very flip when he was asked about his love life. 'I don't know
anything about *amore*,' he said. 'I think I do have a romantic tendency in my life. I
do like women. I'm totally mystified by women. If I were to become a woman for a
day, the first thing I would do is masturbate. Cupid came around once or twice last
year but I didn't exactly get stung — you know what I mean.'

When asked what he would say to a woman if he could not perform sexually
with her, he announced, 'I don't have that problem. Maybe I'd look her in the eye
and say, "I dig affection, baby, but not while I'm driving." '

While he had a quick response to the three signs that a woman was interested
in him, 'When they pop their gum; when they arch their back; when they shout my
name and applaud ...' he appeared thrown when he was asked what Cher was like in
bed, stammering, 'Uh, oh, wow. Um. Cherilyn. Well, there's, I mean, are you
talking about the visual image? I'm sure she's great.'

On a more serious, but still bizarre, note, he revealed that he had considered a
nose job because he had breathing problems, but decided against it. 'I like the fact
that I have a nose problem,' he claimed. 'I know it bothers some of my friends. I've
recently investigated the possibility of getting it fixed. Some girl told me the other
day, "I'm a big fan but if you'd like a piece of advice, keep your mouth shut. Your
mouth is always open." I said, "It's because I can't breathe. I have to breathe through
my mouth." I've grown fond of my nose problem, my sniffle. I find it a youthful
thing. I don't like it when people say, "Smile" or "Cheer up." It's a real cheap line.
I'm feeling good. I'm feeling real grateful for everything. It's a solid time in my life.

ople say I look sad, they're wrong.'

though *Vampire's Kiss* was not released until more than a year after it was completed, and fared badly at the box office, it had a better fate than two other films made immediately before and after it, *Never on Tuesday* and *Time to Kill*.

Never on Tuesday is a silly road romp directed by then 20-year-old Adam Rifkin, a film-school reject who nevertheless went on to become a successful scriptwriter with *Mousehunt* and *Small Soldiers*.

It stars newcomers Peter Berg and Andrew Lauer as a pair of dozy Ohioans heading for California. They manage to crash into the only car they had seen for hours, driven by a beautiful photographer, played by Claudia Christian. Stranded in the desert, the boys are convinced their luck is in — until the photographer, the Tuesday of the title, announces she is a lesbian. That does not stop them fantasising about the possibilities of the situation, however.

Nick has an uncredited part as 'Man in Red Sports Car', one of a handful of trendy young guest stars who stop by the unfortunate threesome but do not help them. For his brief appearance, Nick wore a Pinocchio-style extra-long nose.

Other uncredited actors were Cary Elwes, Emilio Estevez, Gilbert Gottfried, Judd Nelson and Charlie Sheen.

The film languished unreleased before going straight to video in 1989, picking up a couple of reviews. *Los Angeles Weekly* pulled no punches, saying, 'It's not surprising that, as per his bio, 20-year-old Rifkin was not accepted into University of Southern California film school. This inane tale of two students who crash into a gorgeous photographer's car on their drive to California is proof that untalented teenagers should not be allowed to direct feature films, no matter who they know. The cameo presence of Judd Nelson and a couple of Sheen kids, instead of legitimising this waste of celluloid, serves to indicate their own sophomorism — something we've long suspected.'

Daily Variety was slightly kinder. It wrote, 'The talent and beauty of Claudia Christian is showcased in *Never on Tuesday*, an unreleased 1987 vanity production that should give Paramount Home Video sleeper possibilities due to the presence of several big-name guest stars. Rifkin manages to create some variety (and wish-fulfilment sexiness) with frequent fantasy sequences, but it is the periodic visits of quirky, uncredited cameo performers that keep the film going.'

After making the film, all three leads went on to become television stars; Peter Berg as Dr Billy Kronk in the hospital drama *Chicago Hope*, Andy Lauer as Charlie the messenger in the sitcom *Caroline in the City,* and Claudia Christian as Lt Commander Susan Ivanova in the sci-fi drama *Babylon 5*.

Time to Kill, also known as *The Short Cut* and *Tempo di uccidere* in Italy, was an Italian–French production starring Nick as Enrico Silvestri, an Italian lieutenant serving in pre-World War II Ethiopia — although it was actually shot in Kenya, Zimbabwe and Spain. The short cut of the title refers to an ominous walk Enrico takes by himself because his tooth aches so much, and he is too impatient to wait for a ride to get to a dentist. He meets a beautiful local girl, Mariam, played by French actress Patrice Flora Praxo, bathing nude in a lake. In what seems almost a dream sequence, they make love and end up spending the night together. During the night he hears a noise, which he thinks is an animal, shoots at it, and in a bizarre twist of fate, the bullet ricochets and seriously wounds the girl. The story is told largely in flashback, with Enrico describing events to his best friend, Mario, played by Ricky Tognazzi, and later to Mariam's father. It is not until late in the film that he reveals he had killed the girl to end her agony, and hidden the body. Consumed by guilt, he becomes obsessed with the idea that she was a leper and that he had been infected and would take the disease home to his wife and child.

Eventually, Mariam's father convinces him the girl was healthy and forgives him, and he is able to return home.

The film was well received at the Venice Film Festival in 1989. *Variety* said, 'The interior drama of a soldier who believes he's been infected with a disease in Africa is soberly lensed with no bow to touristic exoticism, yet *The Short Cut* has an inner tension that grabs hold. Cage gives the lieutenant a dull irritability and thoughtless presumption that keeps the viewer at a distance from the character — in this case, the right distance.'

Like *Never on Tuesday*, in the United States *Time to Kill* was released on straight to video.

Nick took advantage of the lull in his career while he was waiting for the release of *Vampire's Kiss* to get around to changing his name legally from Coppola to Cage. That involved placing a formal notice in the *Los Angeles Daily Journal*, a legal newspaper, for four weeks, announcing his intention and calling for anyone who objected to the change to appear in Los Angeles Superior Court for a hearing on 4 August 1989.

In his one-page petition, in which he listed his grandmother, Louise Vogelsang, as his nearest living relative, even though obviously both his parents were alive, he stated as his reason for the name change, 'I am a professional actor. All businesses are carried out under my stage name, CAGE. At this point I'm known by CAGE; having two names makes it hard on me.'

Nick did not explain why he chose that particular time to formalise his name, and has in fact claimed since then that he never did change it legally.

A few days after a judge rubber-stamped his name change petition, Nick went in front of the cameras in what was to be a pivotal film for his career, *Wild at Heart*. But before the controversial David Lynch film was released, Nick once again put on a military uniform, playing a pilot in the action-thriller *Fire Birds*. Although he filmed *Wild at Heart* first, it was released in the United States after *Fire Birds*.

Unusually, the inspiration for *Fire Birds* came not from a conventional film-maker but from three military men, retired US Army Lieutenants Colonel John K Swensson and Step Tyner, and retired US Marine Captain Dale Dye, who had worked as a technical adviser on the Vietnam War film *Platoon*. They approached producer Arnold Kopelson, who had won the Best Picture Oscar for *Platoon*, with the suggestion that he should make a film that would do for the American Army what Tom Cruise's *Top Gun* had done for the Navy, with the AH-64 Gunship helicopter, known as the Apache, as one of the stars. Ironically, Nick was later said to have turned down a role in *Top Gun* because he thought it was too right wing.

Kopelson spent two years developing the script with production partner Keith Barish. They hired British director David Green to make his first Hollywood film, and William Badalato as producer. They had full co-operation from the US Army and the Department of Defense, as well as private sector defence companies like Honeywell, General Dynamics, McDonnell Douglas and Bell Helicopter. One of their chief military liaisons was General Maxwell R Thurman, who led the US invasion of Panama to arrest Central American strongman Manuel Noriega.

The story centres on a secret US mission infiltrating a hostile Latin American country to combat drug lords, using the $10 million high-tech Apaches, equipped with laser-guided missiles, 70mm rockets and a 30mm automatic chain-gun and capable of flying and hunting their prey even in the dark or bad weather.

The principals had no hesitation in hiring Nick to play Chief Warrant Officer II Jake Preston when they learned he was looking for a change of image and would welcome being cast in a role both active and romantic. He also, quite frankly, needed the money. As he explained, 'It was as unlikely for me as you could get, but I was challenged by it and the people involved wanted to work with me. I like to keep myself off-guard with the choices I make. There is a kid inside me who likes helicopters and fireworks. And film is a big-business industry and this game needed to be played to secure that I continue to work. They made a deal that was respectable and made me feel good and got me out of some debts that I was severely into with the house. But this straightforward American hero was a challenge. I was at a place where I was starting to think that I should try to do something more mainstream just to ensure that I could get another job. It wasn't really true to my instincts.'

Director Green said, 'Nicolas Cage was a great idea for the part of Jake Preston. What I wanted from him was a very straightforward American hero-type of guy who goes out to beat the drug lords and overcomes his own problems and prejudices along the way. Cage did this extremely well.' Producer Badalato added, 'He managed to create a very realistic character, very serious and yet sympathetic. As a pilot his character is beyond any sort of criticism. It's his private life that gets in the way in this story.'

Tommy Lee Jones was a unanimous choice to play Preston's mentor, Brad Little, but Green had to fight to cast Sean Young as a female pilot and Preston's old flame, Chief Warrant Officer II Billie Lee Guthrie. He explained, 'When I thought about who to cast, Sean Young seemed the obvious choice. She's very attractive and also looks like she could fly a helicopter. She had to look very feminine on the ground and be very "pilot-like" in the air. To be honest, there was some opposition to her. I believe there were rumours about her not being the easiest actress to work with. I can only tell you what my experience was. She was very responsive and worked very hard. I fought for her because she's one of only a few actresses who could be believable as a pilot and also as a woman.'

In fact, Young had been involved in a bizarre row with actor James Woods a couple of years earlier, in which he sued her for allegedly trying to put a curse on him and his then fiancée. In the end, however, she was the one who won damages. She had also lost the role of Vicki Vale in *Batman* to Kim Basinger after she broke her arm in a horse-riding stunt accident. Her part ended up going to singer-turned-sometime actress Madonna, who did end up having a passionate affair with Beatty.

Nick did not enjoy working with Young. Once the film was released, he said, 'How can I describe her? Put it this way — the chemistry was not there. I guess in one movie she's good and another she's the opposite. Everyone warned me about it but I am not the kind to go on gossip. I just thought she was a good actress and wanted to knock heads with her to see how it went.'

The movie was shot on location in Texas and Arizona, with real military hardware, including the Apaches, as props. To help them give more convincing performances as pilots, Nick and Young had flying lessons in the flight simulator used to train real Apache pilots. Nick found the experience of grappling with cockpit controls and weaponry, while watching out for enemy activity in the simulated landscape below, bewildering.

'The simulator is almost more difficult to fly than the actual Apache,' he said. 'I don't know if I even got it to hover off the ground. I kept crashing and tilting the machine, like in an arcade game.'

For Nick, the best part of making the film was hanging out at a club called Maggie Mae's in Austin, Texas, with the military advisers who were coaching him in his role. On a return visit two years later, he recalled, 'I met a few great guys who were training me for the role, Chief Warrant Officers EJ Mikeska and Bill Lee. They brought me here and though it's been a couple of years I was hoping I might run into them again.' By coincidence, he did bump into them and they ended up in a strip club celebrating a going-away party for some other troops.

The film got a real-life boost before it was ever released, thanks to the televised invasion of Panama in December 1989, which resulted in Noriega being taken to the United States, where he was tried for drug trafficking and racketeering and was sentenced to 40 years in prison.

Kopelson said, 'I was terribly excited to see General Maxwell Thurman on my television set one morning during the routine coverage of the invasion of Panama. This man was the mentor of our film and here he was in real life, Apaches and all, going after Manuel Noriega, reputedly involved in a major drug cartel in Latin America. It was like seeing a trailer for our film.'

However, the coincidence of life imitating art did not help the film at the box office.

Daily Variety seemed to be alone in enjoying it. Their reviewer wrote, 'Canny casting against type defuses some of the gung-ho militarism of this enjoyable, old-fashioned aerial adventure. Camaraderie and rat-a-tat-tat dialogue among stars Nicolas Cage, Sean Young and Tommy Lee Jones may have started out as fun, à la Howard Hawks' classic *Only Angels Have Wings,* but emerges at times as a satire of the genre. Cage is fascinating to watch, allowed to explode occasionally from his tightly clamped shell.'

In the *Washington Post,* however, Hal Hinson dismissed it as a 'jingoistic 'copter adventure'. He wrote, 'It's more video game than motion picture — the first coin-operated movie. Ultimately, Cage wins the battle by virtue of sheer florid excess. What we're seeing here from this bonkers star isn't anything we haven't seen before, say in *Vampire's Kiss* or, to a lesser degree, in *Moonstruck,* but that doesn't make it any less nuts. With his sleepy eyelids and Modigliani face, Cage looks more like a cartoon wolf than a conventional leading man. Cage is a magnetic presence, for sure, but little things — like making an actual connection with his co-star — are beyond him.'

The *Hollywood Reporter* enjoyed the flying scenes and praised Tommy Lee Jones but hated everything else. Duane Byrge wrote, 'Cage's uncharismatic performance as the ace pilot, while properly hyperkinetic, never sets off any sparks — no magic swagger here. But in Cage's defence, the character as written is a dullard.'

'*Fire Birds* is such a shameless steal of *Top Gun* that the writers must've used tracing paper to concoct the screenplay,' scoffed Robert Morris in *Village View.* 'What in the world made good actors like Nicolas Cage, Tommy Lee Jones and Sean Young agree to take part in such garbage?'

Vincent Canby of the *New York Times* commented, '*Fire Birds* has one director, two writers and many laughs, all of them unintentional. Responsible for a lot of these is Mr Cage. Mr Cage simply won't quit. He never listens to or sees anybody else in a scene, being too busy monitoring his own utterly mysterious, attention-getting responses.'

In the *Los Angeles Times,* Michael Wilmington wrote, 'Lean, mean, clean and empty-hearted, *Fire Birds* is a video-game recruiting poster with a bomb ticking inside — a bomb that never goes off. The people who made this movie probably wouldn't be insulted if you told them they were trying a blatant *Top Gun* knock-off. They might smile and say anxiously, "Yeah! Yeah! Did we make it?" '

'I'd like to believe it's self-sabotage and not mere ineptitude that gives Cage's every line a near-psychotic edge,' Manohla Dargis wrote in *Village Voice*. 'Aviator sunglasses and faded 501s do not make Cage into Cruise and, repackaged as a romantic lead, Francis' nephew is nothing short of laughable.'

The film was renamed *Wings of the Apache* when it was released in Britain, but that did not help to sell it. However, Nick did not seem to be concerned. He had banked the money from the film and was basking in praise for a very different project.

Just before *Fire Birds* was released in America, the movie he had made for David Lynch, *Wild at Heart*, was booed at the Cannes film festival for the violence that threatened to earn it an X-rating, but it went on to win the Palme d'Or, the most prestigious award of the festival, and Nick's career switched back into top gear.

CHAPTER SEVEN

KING OF HIS CASTLES

Home life is extremely important to Nick, and in this, as in the roles he chooses, there are no half measures. From his humble beginnings in a modest suburban house in Long Beach, he has gone on to build a collection of houses, splitting his time between them. True to the spirit of his yellow Triumph Spitfire, he has built up an even more impressive assortment of performance cars. As his fortunes have risen, he has also developed an interest in a variety of artworks. In addition, over the years he has collected a motley menagerie of exotic pets.

Like many young actors, however, he started out in an apartment in the heart of Hollywood — Hollywood Boulevard, to be precise, saying he liked the 'carnival atmosphere'. Although Hollywood sounds glamorous to people who have never visited, only the name retained any real glamour by the early 1980s when he took up residence there. Tourists flocked to see the Walk of Fame, where celebrity names emblazoned in bronze stars line the Boulevard of Broken Dreams, and they came to Mann's Chinese Theater, home to a host of hand- and footprints embedded in the concrete of the forecourt. But many of the once-luxurious buildings were run-down and Hollywood was also home to muggers, pickpockets, junkies and hookers.

Nick's first flat was unremarkable and sparsely furnished, though it was full of books. He had started collecting art deco pieces and paintings — and pets. He called his two-and-a-half-foot-long monitor lizard Smokey, after his character in *Rumble Fish*, his baby octopus Cool and his Burmese cat Lewis. However, the sharks which inhabited two huge glass tanks went without names. He admitted he could not resist aquatic creatures. 'I like setting up aquariums,' he said. 'I'll go to the fish store and get an eel or a stingray or a horseshoe crab. I like bizarre-looking animals, things that are different.'

By 1984, he was living with actress Jenny Wright, a New Yorker, who had, by coincidence, worked with *Birdy* director Alan Parker before Nick, when she appeared in *The Wall*, based on the album by Pink Floyd, playing a groupie in pursuit of Bob Geldof. Unlike Nick, she was trained in acting, having attended the renowned Lee Strasberg Acting Institute in Manhattan when she was 16, and starting her career on the stage. She had also appeared in *The World According to Garp* and *St Elmo's Fire*.

Wright, who was a year older than Nick, had a common interest in exotic pets, in her case, lizards. She had two, one named Gazela and the other was, she said, 'too horrible to name'.

It was love at first sight when she met Nick at a friend's house in 1984. After they started dating, she confessed, 'I knew that he was the guy for me. He's a real traditional boyfriend. We might as well be married, the way we are. We're real true.'

Nick was less forthcoming, however, telling the *Los Angeles Times* that she was merely 'an actress friend'. Nevertheless, they planned to marry in October 1986, but broke up instead.

He subsequently moved to a much more impressive apartment building, the El Royale complex on North Rossmore Place in Hancock Park, one of the older suburbs of Los Angeles, south of Hollywood proper and an enclave of magnificent mansions in a variety of styles ranging from Spanish to mock English Tudor. By the end of the '90s, residents included actor Kiefer Sutherland and husband-and-wife movie stars Melanie Griffith and Antonio Banderas, in an enormous mansion which had been a notorious speakeasy during Prohibition. Rossmore Place backed on to the Wilshire Country Club and was convenient for Paramount Studios, Farmer's Market, which is a Los Angeles landmark for shopping and eating, and the La Brea Tar Pits, where the remains of prehistoric mammoths and other animals are preserved and which is one of Nick's favourite hangouts. His maternal grandmother used to live in the same area and, devoted grandson that he was, he was a frequent visitor to her home.

Legend had it that George Raft once painted a caricature in the El Royale's lift shaft, and that Bing Crosby had a flat there for his own private purposes. Mae West had lived over the road, at number 570, for decades.

Nick also met a new girlfriend, another actress, Christina Fulton — who also goes by the name Kristina — and she moved in with him.

At the beginning of 1989, they moved from their apartment at the El Royale complex to a bigger penthouse flat, number 1001, and the rent was increased by $1,000 a month, to $3,500. Nick and Christina both signed the lease. When they moved in he redecorated, putting in new carpets and wallpaper and installing shutters on the bedroom windows for $8,000. He also paid a $7,000 security deposit.

Although Nick has often admitted to a fear of heights, he enjoyed the sweeping views over Hollywood from the balcony of his 12th-floor penthouse, smog permitting. His furnishing style was eclectic, even bizarre. In one room he hung thick curtains to keep out the sunlight, preferring to illuminate it with a carved chandelier. Other lighting was provided by art deco lamps. Ruby red oriental rugs covered the parquet floor. A stuffed boar's head was mounted over one doorway and a giant model of a bumblebee also found a home there. In the hallway hung a neon sign reading, 'Rocket to Los Angeles'. There was room for more serious art too; a lithograph by Marc Chagall hung on one wall. There was also a family portrait of the Coppola family, including a youthful Nick before he changed his name, and a portrait of Elvis Presley. His library had grown to include a complete, leather-bound set of *Encyclopaedia Britannica*. Among other sound systems he had an old gramophone which played 78rpm records, on which he could listen to ancient recordings of Caruso.

By the end of the 1980s, Lewis had been joined by another cat, and the sharks had departed, giving way to small fish for a while. 'I do watch the cats,' he told an interviewer enigmatically. 'And some of what they do stays in my mind and appears later. Especially when they have sex.'

Equally enigmatically, he talked about moving from the apartment complex. 'They don't like my lifestyle,' he said. In preparation for the move, he bought a little house for $725,000 on Woking Way in the suburb of Los Feliz, near Hollywood, though he continued living at El Royale.

In 1990, he bought not one but two houses, one in San Francisco, the other in Los Angeles. Both were at the same time unique but wonderfully representative of their respective cities. The San Francisco house, which he bought first, was the fulfilment of a long-held dream. In 1988, when he had achieved a measure of critical acclaim thanks to *Moonstruck* and *Raising Arizona*, he wistfully told the *San Francisco Examiner*: 'I'm doing OK financially but I can't afford a palatial house yet, and I'm not into being a starving artist. I would like to have enough money to buy a Lamborghini Countache and maybe a place in San Francisco.'

The property he ended up with was a grey, clapboard Victorian house, vaguely reminiscent of the house in *The Addams Family*, on Franklin Street in Pacific Heights, one of the city's ritziest areas. It had once belonged to Werner Erhard, a used-car-salesman-turned-self-help guru who ran enormously popular and controversial weekend seminars in the 1970s, encouraging adherents like Diana Ross, John Denver and producer Peter Guber to 'get their heads straight' and take control of their lives. One of his followers in the 1970s was a young costume designer and former window dresser at Macy's department store called Joel Schumacher. He credits two weekend sessions with giving him the drive to break into directing films like *The Client, A Time to Kill* and two *Batman* films — and, later, the dark Nick Cage drama *8MM*. The upstairs study of Nick's new house was still home to a motorised, leather reclining chair which once belonged to Erhard, who was driven into exile in 1991 because of rows with the American tax man and an assortment of lawsuits.

'I used to spend my summers with my uncle and aunt and my cousins in San Francisco — some of the happiest days of my childhood,' Nick later told *USA Today*. 'So I bought this little Victorian house the first time I made any money.'

The Los Angeles house was a castle, built in 1928 in the Los Feliz area, where ironically, Madonna would buy her own castle a few years later. He paid about $1.5 million for the bizarre building on Tryon Road, which nestles in a hillside near the fabled Hollywood sign and had 5,367 square feet of living space. It had 11 rooms in all, including three bedrooms, four bathrooms and a shower room and maid's quarters. It sits on a third of an acre of land. The house had been completely gutted by fire and refurbished in the mid 1980s, and had steep walls, rounded turrets and massive stone steps leading up to the front door. It stood on a promontory with panoramic views over the city and the mountains. Every room had a view, even the white-tiled master bathroom.

'It was built in 1928 and it's trying to look like it was built in 1465,' laughed Nick. 'And it doesn't quite pull it off. So there's a sort of faux thing happening which I really like.'

By a strange coincidence, the previous occupant was called Peter Laslow, a very similar name to Nick's *Vampire's Kiss* character, Peter Loew, and as soon as his *Wild at Heart* director David Lynch saw it, he joked that it must once have been a vampire's lair.

'That's another one of those little tears in the envelope of time and space that I don't know how to deal with and I'm not going to address too much,' Nick recalled.

Nick set about imposing his personal style on both houses. A 6ft-tall sculpture of a winged Balinese God stood inside the massive front door of the castle to greet guests. Over the years, he built up a collection of stuffed, mounted and hanging insects, including beautifully back-lit butterflies. One report at the time of his purchase claimed he also had a human skull called Vincent and a preserved dead bat among the decorations. A myth has also grown about the headboard and bedside tables in the master bedroom — they were allegedly decorated with various insects as well as a giant cockroach, in memory of the bug he swallowed in *Vampire's Kiss*.

This is a myth, like the stories of him having his teeth pulled for *Birdy*, that he tries to repel. 'It is not a cockroach,' he patiently told *GQ* in 1997. 'Cockroaches live in the sewers and all the creepy, dirty places. It's a beetle. Beetles live in the forests and are very different to cockroaches. I have the Titanus Giganteus, which is the largest of all beetles, in the headboard, and on the end tables I have the Rhinoceros beetles.'

He did, however, admit that another vampire, Dracula, was part of the inspiration for his décor. Somewhat tongue-in-cheek, he said, 'Much of my lifestyle is modelled after him. I don't drink blood, but otherwise ... I just admire the sensibility. The Gothic décor of my home is inspired by it. To me, Dracula is love in exile.' He added, 'Bizarre stuff seems to appeal to me. I'm much more at home in a creepy environment than a pristine one.'

Nick favoured massive, heavy furniture and tiger- and leopard-print rugs, and described the ambience as 'Elvis Presley-slash-Hieronymus Bosch-slash-Liberace'. The living room was papered with maroon brocade and a candy-apple-red grand piano took pride of place. The master bedroom featured a black marble fireplace and purple velvet curtains, and lighting came from heavy chandeliers, some fashioned from antlers.

He also looked nostalgically back to his childhood, with a three-foot-tall model of Pinocchio and a picture of him at three, with his father, standing next to the same Pinocchio at Christmas. Later, when he became a father, he had a portrait of his son over the mantelpiece. He pointed out the striking family similarities — and bragged about his son's martial arts abilities — to *Vanity Fair* magazine writer Cathy Horyn. 'That's Weston,' he said. 'Oh boy, look at this. This is me when I was three with my father. I look like my dad and Weston looks like me. This is the board Weston broke in Tae Kwon Do class.' At the time, five-year-old Weston was about to get his orange belt.

That year, 1996, Nick displayed the Academy Award and other honours he won for *Leaving Las Vegas* on top of his television.

After living there for a few years, however, Nick changed his mind about the dazzling white stucco walls of his castle and announced plans — never fulfilled — to buy a European castle, or at least the stonework from a European castle to reface the building completely. 'I just don't like stucco,' he told Lucy Kaylin, of *GQ* magazine. 'I don't like that prefab, cottage cheese spray-on crap and my house has that now, unfortunately. And I've tried to sandblast it off; I've tried to put a night-growing creeper around it and nothing works. So it's just time to bring over a castle and start over.'

In the end, however, he contented himself with expanding the house, adding two bedrooms and a bathroom and redesigning the interior to include a circular library, a wine cellar and, when he succumbed to the cigar-smoking craze of the mid-1990s, a humidor. In 1999, he put it on the market for $2.2 million and sold it for about $1.5 million, the same as he paid for it.

In San Francisco, he installed specially-commissioned stained-glass windows featuring nature scenes, making them, to all intents and purposes, opaque. He explained, 'It's the opposite of a view. I think of it as a womb, an inner sanctum of not being able to look out but being totally inside a world that is completely my own that I can escape to. It's the Edgar Allen Poe in me. I love sea creatures and I love animals in the jungles, so I had the stained glass designed after that.'

Gargoyles, griffins and gilded swans all formed part of the decoration and, in keeping with his fascination with things Japanese, he kept a Samurai sword on top of a cabinet. He painted the wooden exterior a dense black, adding to the Addams Family image.

Originally, he had a small fireplace in the living room with a warrior's face superimposed over it, but he replaced that with a massive heart-shaped dragon with fire spouting out of its mouth.

People who had worked with him were not surprised by his oddball choices. His *Raising Arizona* director Joel Coen said: 'He's a little Addams Family. He likes to promote that image, anyway. He's a strange guy.'

'A little eccentric,' added Norman Jewison, director of *Moonstruck*. 'He'll try anything. There are no rules for him.'

Fashion stylist André Leon Talley, who worked with him on a 1998 *Vogue* photo-shoot, raved about his castle and his wardrobes. 'So unusual in a man!' he gushed. 'Hadn't seen anything so impressive since Jackie O's! Everything is beautifully racked: blue by blue, beige by beige.' As for the castle, he said, 'It's a postmodern mix out of D'Annunzio by Edward Scissorhands. It's all him, not some LA decorator.'

Although Nick bought the San Francisco house first because of his fond memories of the City by the Bay, at the time he said he actually preferred Los Angeles. 'I like that it's an automotive city,' he said. 'I like the wide-open space. I don't feel oppressed here.'

A couple of years later, after the Los Angeles riots raged through the city, following the acquittal of four white policemen over the videotaped beating of black motorist Rodney King, when talking about his homes he appeared to be changing his mind, saying, 'I also have a place in San Francisco that I want to get up to more often. LA is my home but it's getting worse. It's really getting bad. It's very scary, the crime. It's becoming pretty intense. I hear gunshots from my window. The whole Rodney King episode, that upset a lot of people and understandably so.'

After he was married he contradicted himself, telling Fred Schruers, of *Rolling Stone* magazine that the Pacific Heights house has been intended as his main home base. 'This was the first place I bought with some idea that I was actually going to live here — because I'm a family man I try to set up different worlds. I always fight with this feeling of being trapped, of being stuck in one place. It's kind of like I'm a shark, and I've got to move or I'll die. I think that comes from starting in acting at 17, living my life in hotels, then finding myself back at home, thinking, well, now what do I do; where do I go? Always wanting to keep moving.'

In a similar vein in 1996, he admitted to Steve Daly of *Entertainment Weekly* that he was thinking about making a move from California and buying a home on the East Coast. He said, 'I've been looking at places in New York. The idea of a foot culture, that you are going to observe more people, to me is food, you know, for acting. The idea of not having to rely on a car and not to be in that space bubble, seems pretty attractive to me right now. It's just that I'm 32 and I've been here all my life and I think I need to have a change. I need to meet different people, get different stimulus. I think I can get that in Manhattan. I just have to convince everybody to go there with me. Let's just say that moving won't be easy to do. It might take a little time.'

By 1998, he was looking still further afield. He told Lesley O'Toole of London's *Evening Standard*, 'When the kids are older, I'd like to move and go to New York or London. I love London, especially Notting Hill Gate and Portobello Road. I'd really like to spend a Christmas there soon.'

While Nick enjoyed his early taste of domesticity with his first purchases, his life with Christina had deteriorated. She became pregnant and the couple split up because Nick did not see marriage in his future. 'I'm about to be a dad and I'm fearing that my life as a debauched playboy is over,' he said. 'It's weird. This is the time to be debauched, isn't it? At 26, isn't it?'

He promptly began dating model Lisa Stothard, who accompanied him to the opening of his new film *Wild at Heart* and to London for the British première of *Vampire's Kiss*. Lisa later became an actress, with roles in *Dumb and Dumber* and *Gia*.

While he was in London, he refused to discuss his forthcoming fatherhood and told writer Garth Pearce, 'Maybe I'm doomed to bachelorhood for the rest of my life. A long-term relationship is a lot of work and very disappointing. I had one once. But we are not together now. Girlfriends react very differently to what goes with the job of acting, especially the love scenes. Some get jealous, others get turned on. And sometimes they don't comment at all. Yet I am not a person who wants to be a bachelor forever. It's just that my circumstances are not very pro-marriage.'

Surprisingly, only a few days after he returned to Hollywood, he took Christina as his date to the opening of *Rocky V*, which co-starred his aunt, Talia Shire. Only days before the birth of their son, Weston Coppola Cage, he was spotted in an all-night supermarket buying six cartons of chocolate ice-cream and four kinds of chocolate-chip cookies, telling insomniac shoppers that his girlfriend had woken up with chocolate cravings.

After Weston's birth, Nick said, 'I'm happy to be a dad but if I marry and settle down I'm going to be a frustrated 40-year-old. Love can make you crazy, happy, jealous — and can even make you kill someone.'

For a while, Nick and Christina seemed to have reached a compromise on parenthood. They were living back together as a couple, and when Nick went on a cross-country drive to New Orleans with a friend to write about the experience for an American magazine, the morning they set off he described a dream Christina had had the previous night, and wrote in the diary he kept of the trip, 'I miss my son.' He was also said to be furiously jealous because Christina had won a part in the film *The Doors* and the star, Val Kilmer, who played Jim Morrison, kept chatting to her.

Yet only a few weeks later, things once again turned sour between the two.

Christina told friends he had thrown her and Weston out of the castle with nothing but the clothes they were wearing and was refusing to support either of them. 'Christina is practically broke and Nick hasn't given her a dime,' a pal told *Globe* magazine. 'She can't raise their baby alone and she wants Nick to help financially.'

Spurned Christina filed a paternity suit in Los Angeles Superior Court saying, 'This is normal procedure to get the right amount of child support.'

Her lawyer, Ronald Anteau, added, 'There was a child conceived of this relationship. Since the couple is no longer together, the child has certain rights to establish a parental relationship. There is also the case of equal custody and support.'

By coincidence, at the same time as Christina Fulton was trying to establish paternity, she and Nick were brought together in another LA Superior Court case. They were accused of trashing the penthouse flat they had shared at El Royale during a fight and were sued for breach of contract, negligence and waste.

'On or about 26 June 1989, defendant Cage and defendant Fulton were involved in an altercation in Apartment 1001,' the suit alleged. 'As a result of such altercation, Apartment 1001 and Apartment 801 of the premises was severely damaged, including but not limited to flooding, bloodstains, damage to cabinets, tile counters, floors and walls.'

Nick and Christina moved out shortly afterwards and the landlords claimed that when they regained possession of the flat they discovered still more damage.

This time, the suit alleged, there had been 'damage to flooring from leaking shark tanks; damage to flooring throughout the apartment from cat faeces and cat litter; holes in the walls; French doors broken and off hinges; and damage to the refrigerator and kitchen appliances. Defendants have further breached the contract by failing to pay for the damage to the premises upon plaintiff's repeated demands for payment.'

The landlords, a property company called Mar-Scott Properties, also claimed that, apart from repairing the damage, they were unable to rent the flat for two months. They demanded about $15,000 in damages, plus legal fees.

But a bemused Nick claimed that he had been constantly harassed by the complex manager, who regularly tried to get money from him. He said, 'I don't know of any $15,000 in damage unless it was there when I moved in.' He insisted that he had always taken care to maintain his aquariums and that they had not had any leaks, and that not only were his two cats clean, he added, 'I change their litter boxes myself.'

Both Nick and Christina vigorously denied the charges. But the case worked its way through the Los Angeles Superior Court system until all parties were ordered to attend a mandatory settlement conference, in March 1992, to try to thrash out a deal without going to trial. However, the day before the conference they settled out of court, without disclosing any of the details.

Nick enjoyed being a homeowner, even though he admitted he was hopelessly impractical as a man about the house. 'I can't even fix the toilet when it overflows,' he said. 'I can't even use a plunger. I'm pathetic around the house. It's more about laziness.' So when he had a sudden urge to buy a third place, he didn't hesitate.

'I was driving late one night in my car,' he recalled. 'It was raining and I felt like going downtown. At night, LA becomes ... like Gotham. Totally empty. So I checked into a hotel and I thought, tomorrow I'm going to look for an apartment.'

Although it is home to City Hall, the courthouse, a major theatre complex and a number of hotels, downtown Los Angeles is far from an attractive place. It is home to the city's skid row, and homeless beggars doss down on the streets. During the day, it is full of workers who commute to the high-rise office buildings, but at night it is a virtual ghost town. There are a few blocks of luxury apartments, but they have heavy security, and after dark residents drive even a couple of blocks to a restaurant.

It is also a heavily Hispanic part of the city, with historic Olvera Street, the site of the original Mexican settlement of the City of Our Lady of the Angels, just to the north. In parts, more Spanish than English is spoken, and many cinemas screen Spanish films.

So the idea of being an anonymous 'Gringo' in a totally different world from his movie star existence appealed to Nick immensely. And, once again, he was lucky enough to find a place upon which he could put his unique stamp.

The 12th-floor penthouse he bought was actually three apartments knocked into one. It had once been the headquarters of the city's Department of Water and Power and still had an East Coast, clubby, masculine atmosphere. The walls were panelled with mahogany and had wooden pillars, and he chose big leather couches and heavy chairs to enhance the image. He also installed a grand piano, though he cannot play. The bedroom, in contrast, had a tiger-print motif.

'I've always been attracted to areas where most people don't like to go,' he said. 'I can walk around and it's completely anonymous. I can get a chicken taco or something and sit there in the market and imagine I'm in South America somewhere. It's like going to another country without going to the airport.'

Nick later used the apartment as a kind of office, often conducting interviews there rather than at home and, after his marriage, he and Patricia Arquette used it for throwing parties. He did not appear to have become any more domesticated over the years, however. When he let reporter Mary Roach spend the night there in 1997, because the parking lot where she had left her car was closed, she reported that the sole contents of the kitchen in the mauve-painted, fake-leopard-carpeted flat were a bottle of Glenlivet single malt whisky, Hershey's chocolate sauce and Pam cooking spray. She also noticed that the bathroom contained Phytorhum shampoo for 'lifeless' hair.

His next purchase was in complete contrast — a Cape Cod-style five-bedroom house on the beach in Malibu. He paid $3.6 million for the 3,000 square foot house in late 1996. It stands on an acre of land next to the Pacific Ocean, and has a creek running through the garden into the sea. It is approached by a cobbled driveway and, even though it is on the beach, also has a swimming pool.

Nick said, 'I think having different environments is better, rather than having one huge, you know, space that you reside in all the time. I think it's more interesting to have smaller spaces that you can explore and feel like different people.'

In early 1998, he extended his property empire still further, buying an English country house-style mansion with 33 rooms, including nine bedrooms and nine bathrooms, from singer Tom Jones and prepared to move there from the castle about a year later, after doing some renovations. He paid nearly $7 million for the 13,000 square foot house, which was built in 1940 and refurbished in the 1950s. Jones had originally bought it from Dean Martin. It is situated on an acre of land on Copa de Oro Road in Bel Air, one of Los Angeles' most exclusive suburbs, and has a separate guest house and a gym, as well as a private jogging path.

But Nick failed in another real estate venture he considered that year. Nick was one of a number of San Francisco high rollers who were interested in buying a 1.1 acre vacant lot with a spectacular view of the Golden Gate Bridge and the San Francisco Bay. It had once been a school, but had been abandoned for 25 years. Nick and *Nash Bridges* star Don Johnson were said to be among the people who had paid a deposit of $650,000 each just for the privilege of placing a sealed bid on the property. The L-shaped lot was the last bit of undeveloped land in the exclusive Pacific Heights area. In the end, however, the winner was property developer Mitch Menaged, owner of Historic San Francisco Homes, who planned to build several houses on the site. He paid $13.65 million, a record for San Francisco.

Nick did, however, buy a house for his mother, Joy, in San Francisco, again in Pacific Heights. Her health was failing again and he found a luxury retirement complex that could offer her round-the-clock assistance if she needed it, for a service fee of $4,000 a month.

'It's heartbreaking for him that his mom needs 24-hour care,' a friend told the *National Enquirer* newspaper. 'He's vowed that his mom get only the best. That's why he's moving her into one of the city's most exclusive retirement homes. Nick doesn't care what it costs.'

On his visits to San Francisco, Nick started making a point of taking Joy for drives and out to dinner at her favourite Italian restaurant, and he personally picked up prescriptions for her at the local chemist.

As Nick's pay for films went up, he began collecting an assortment of art for all his houses — all part of what *Details* magazine would later describe as 'morgue chic'. By far his favourite painter is Robert Williams, whose works are mainly weird and often brutal cartoons. Williams, who describes himself as a 'show-off' cartoonist, did the album cover for Guns N' Roses album *Appetite for Destruction*. His paintings are caricatures of horror, frequently portraying families about to face hideous nightmares. One, entitled 'While Travelling Near or Travelling Far, Keep Your Hands Inside the Car', shows a 1940s-style family out for a drive along a deserted road through a pine forest, unaware that around the corner lurks a green, hairy monster bedecked with knives, including one stuck up his rear end, and carrying a sack full of bloody, hacked-off limbs. It has subtitles including 'The Tale of the Roadside Arm Whacker Who Keeps His Cutlery "Where the Sun Don't Shine" and Whose Knives Stink So Bad That All Will Know Your Fate By the Smell Of Your Stump'. Another, 'Impervious to Chaos', shows a family saying Grace before dinner, the family cat curled up at their feet, with hellfire and monsters lurking under the floorboards. On the other hand, one of the Williams pictures hanging on Nick's wall is a gentler portrait of a Hindu goddess.

Nick said: 'I wanted to make the castle look Gothic Hot Rod. So I combined art which is by more underground artists, like Robert Williams and Anthony Ausgang, with a kind of Gothic feeling which I've always admired since I saw Jean Cocteau's *Beauty and the Beast*. That was my dream as a child — to live in the Beast's castle.'

On one occasion, the *Los Angeles Times* quoted him as saying, 'I used to collect really violent Robert Williams paintings but now I just like a simple Japanese print of a pear. The beauty of a pear; the simplicity of an Eames chair. I love glass, the fire, the colour of blown glass.' Nick was subsequently quick to fire off a letter confirming that he still loved Williams. He said, 'As a collector, I am always expanding my viewpoints but that in no way reflects negatively on any works in my existing collection, especially those by Robert Williams, who is my favourite artist. I treasure his work and consider him to be one of the most important painters of the 20th century.'

In his downtown penthouse, he has another Williams painting, 'The Four Seasons as Seen Through the Eyes of Jessica's Sock Monkey'; a work by artist Chaz Bojorquez made up of words like 'crack', 'tagging', 'police', 'swat', 'lapd', 'quality', 'abuse', 'cholo', 'aids', 'driveby', 'chp', 'system' and 'justice'; plus two guns, carefully mounted behind glass, that were commissioned for him for *Face/Off*. These are among very few movie mementoes he has kept. He regrets not saving the wooden hand from *Moonstruck*, and while he has no remorse about having made a gift of his trademark snakeskin jacket to Laura Dern at the end of the *Wild at Heart* shoot, he theorised, 'I just don't keep stuff from movies. It's almost like I'm trying to shed their skins.'

His other favourite collectibles include Italian Murano glass and works by Anthony Ausgang, a conceptual artist who creates limited edition posters and photographs and one-off pieces, often painted on doors of 1950s cars, as well as classic comic books. He built up a considerable collection of different sizes and scales of model trains, especially those designed by Raymond Loewy. He added to his collection a four-inch piece of rock from Mars, authenticated by NASA, which he bought at a Los Angeles auction for $45,000.

As his fortunes, both professionally and financially, continued to rise in the 1990s, he refused to let himself spend for the sake of spending. By the time he signed for *The Rock,* his fee had risen to $4 million. But he thought art prices were over-inflated and complained, 'It's the most expensive commodity and I really can't collect it any more. I was really into underground art and that was OK, but then that has become really expensive.'

The night he won his Oscar for *Leaving Las Vegas,* he planned to treat himself to something special. He said, 'There's a glass man named Chihuly. I love his work. After I won, I went to the Governor's ball because I really wanted to meet him. I said, "Mr Chihuly, I'm Nick Cage and I'm a glasshead and I love your ..." And then I was hurt. Because Mr Chihuly kind of went off, shouting, "Mr Trump! Mr Donald Trump!" I thought, ah, man. Well that saves me about $20,000. You know, it hurt me.'

In the living room of the Los Feliz castle, he had a collection of framed covers from comic book first editions, including the first *Superman* comic. He was unapologetic at keeping what some people might regard as kids' comics. 'The Greeks had their mythology and this is ours,' he said. 'Mickey Mouse and Batman and Superman and Coca Cola — they're our pride. The story of Batman is a modern myth.' He also collects more adult cartoon books, featuring gritty crime and Japanese erotica. He said, 'There's one I like called *Hard Boiled* by Frank Miller and Geoff Darrow. It's very intense with highly detailed drawings. I also like some of the erotic comics. There's a lot to be said for these Japanese cartoons of girls doing sexy things.' His favourite is one called *Legend of the Overfiend*. He said, 'It's operatic. It's not something you'd want your kids to look at but it's wonderful.'

Far from being snobbish about his collections, Nick dismisses himself as not being an expert but enjoying what he has. He said, 'I don't pretend to be a connoisseur. I would call myself an enthusiast. I'm passionate about adventure, about the beauty of an old train. I don't have much freedom. I don't have much time. I've been working since I was 17 and I'm very thankful for that. But I've always had an obligation. And sometimes the only way I can feel free is in the mobility I get when I spend money. I'll say, "I will have that bottle of wine,' or 'I will go to San Francisco — now." It has to happen in small doses because, beyond that, I'm spoken for.'

As important to Nick as the art works on his walls and in his rooms is his collection of cars. His 1967 Chevrolet Corvette is called the 'Blue Shark'. Nick laughed, 'It even has the gills. I bought the Corvette with money from *Vampire's*

Kiss. I do like to go out and get something that will remind me of the work.'

Over the years he has shelled out for two Lamborghinis, a Ferrari, a Porsche, a Bentley, a Mercedes — and a truck. While early in his career he denied claims that he hung out on a motorbike with bad boy actor Mickey Rourke, he did own a Ducati motorcycle and dressed up in black leather to ride round the city anonymously. 'This whole motorcycle thing — this has gotten out of hand,' he complained to the *Los Angeles Times* as long ago as 1988. 'Two years ago, I was feeling restless and I happened to see *Easy Rider* and thought, yeah, I have to get a motorcycle. As it happened, a lot of other people had the same idea at the same time, so I got lumped in with the whole Hollywood entertainers' motorcycle club. I know Mickey Rourke and I like Mickey Rourke, but I've never once ridden motorcycles with him. These stories of us roaring up to after-hours clubs are a complete fabrication. I don't belong to any social clubs.'

He drove the truck for a while because he thought his Mercedes was too conservative for a cool young movie star. He said, 'I put it somewhere, the way people put away their Rembrandts, because they're so popular. You know, there's a sort of rebelliousness for me driving that car at my age. I once saw Iggy Pop at a strip club wearing a gold Rolex. There he was, one of my idols — he was such a rebel and explorer — wearing a gold Rolex, and I thought it was such a statement, like, 'I can walk in your world but maybe you can't walk in mine.' It's like Pete Townshend driving a Lincoln Continental when he was smashing guitars. He was driving the car his parents were supposed to be driving.'

But he soon tired of the big sports utility vehicle and got back behind the wheel of his beloved sports cars. He admitted, 'I go for cars. The cars I go for are the ones I've always dreamed about. Italian cars; Ferraris, Lamborghinis. I have a lot of Italian furniture. I love Italian wine, I love Italian clothes. Forget the fashion or the status crap — I don't buy into that. But I do think there's an incredible amount of creativity coming out of that country. To me, a hand-made car is a work of art. It's a rolling sculpture. It's like you can drive a Picasso. The Lamborghini is like a triple espresso. It's like a bull, which is its symbol. You can't go anywhere without the police stopping you. You don't have to be moving. They'll stop you just because you're in that car. They will give you a ticket when the guy in the AMC Pacer is doing 100 and you're doing 35. They resent it. So I rarely drive it; only very late at night.'

In 1997, he bought a Lamborghini Miura SVJ once owned by the Shah of Iran for $450,000, twice the estimated price. It was one of 10 luxury cars once owned by the deposed leader which were confiscated by the Islamic revolutionary regime, who overthrew the Shah, and judged to be too decadent to be handed over to government service like the rest of his fleet. It was built in 1971, the first of only four SVJs ever built, and had just 1,879 miles on the clock when Nick, in a phone call from the west coast of America, made his winning bid to the London auction house Brooks Europe, which was overseeing the sale in Switzerland. It was the most expensive car sold at auction in Europe so far that year. The metallic burgundy car was sold by an unidentified Middle Eastern businessman, who was the previous owner.

If that was very much a collector's item, his black 1994 Lamborghini was definitely for driving. He said enthusiastically, 'What I like about this car is the way it sounds. It has this nice, low animal roar. And then on top of that, high-pitched jet whining sounds.'

He later owned a 1938 Bugatti Atlante coupé, which he showed at several Concours D'Élegance competitions for rare and classic cars in 1999 and 2000, an enthusiasm he shared with collectors like talk show hosts Jay Leno and David Letterman and fashion designer Ralph Lauren.

He confessed an ambition to design a sports car of his own, with a stained-glass, illuminated glove compartment.

Nick made no bones about enjoying having money to spend on his passions. He said, 'These actors work all their lives and start to make money and say, "I'm not really into it, the money's no big deal." I think about the guy who's out there struggling for his next dime, listening to the actor saying his millions are no big deal and the guy says, "Fuck you." I agree. Fuck him. I admit I like having the ability to buy these cars. The money also allows me to make low-budget movies for no pay, and it may allow me to branch out and try other things.'

As eclectic as his car collection is the menagerie, with its emphasis on sea creatures, reptiles and invertebrates.

When Weston was young, Nick got another octopus, saying, 'It's for Weston. Weston likes animals. I do, too. I like octopuses. I can't help it.' He also had a boa constrictor and an Indian reticulated python, which he occasionally wore around his neck when he took his son out for a drive.

In 1994, he bought the ultra-trendy pet of the 1990s, a pot-bellied pig, called Lucy, who caused a drama, according to *Star* magazine, when she fell from a pet-sitter's balcony and smashed two teeth.

Nick had got rid of his sharks in the early 1990s, although he always maintained aquariums in the houses in Los Angeles and San Francisco. He complained that he had been travelling so much for work the few fish he had left were strangers. 'That's what happens when you're away so long,' he lamented. 'I hardly know these guys.'

Towards the end of the decade, however, the snakes were joined by an 8ft monitor lizard called Dr Sheen, who had a specialist vet, Dr Ken Harkewicz, and a variety of fish, including 18in-long salt-water sharks. Unlike the lizard, however, Nick did not give them names. 'They're just beautiful and they don't seem unhappy, either,' he said. 'They seem like they're OK with the surroundings. I just think they don't have a relationship with people, so to speak. They're in their own world. I can't really see saying, "Here, Skippy," to a shark. I think that nothing would be the result. Certain animals just really couldn't give a damn about us and I don't think that naming them would in any way suit them. And it's rather condescending.'

He was fond of the creatures, though, and was horrified when reporter Mary Roach confessed during an interview that she had flushed her fish down the toilet when she was 14, because she was fed up with cleaning out their aquarium. He said in horror, 'You flushed your fish down the toilet? It isn't the best thing to do to your animals, is it? I mean, you could have returned them to the pet store, probably.' But he did add reflectively, 'Who am I to judge? We all do things we wish we hadn't done.'

Although he said he did not believe in relationships with fish, for a while he carried a photograph of a shark in his wallet where other men might carry pictures of their girlfriend. He once, bizarrely, claimed that he had had a relationship with a praying mantis! 'Her name was Gwendolyn and we met in Canada,' he said. 'She used to sit on my finger and I'd take her up to flies and wasps and she'd just pluck 'em out of the air and eat them. I don't know if she had any awareness of me, but we seemed to have a relationship. I let her go when I came back here. Praying mantises don't bother me — you can see the pupils in their eyes and they're very intelligent-looking for a bug.'

After they were married, Patricia did not share his fondness for the lumbering lizard, partly because of the freezer full of dead rats that made up his diet. She told chat-show host Rosie O'Donnell, 'It's got a whole habitat built for it with a pool and everything and we're building a big climbing area for him. It's about as big as me. It can take hold of your forearm. It's something I stay far away from.'

By 1997, the Cage/Arquette household included a grass-munching Chocolate Millipede, prompting a London Zoo insect expert to comment to the *Sunday Times*, 'I see no reason why they should not make good pets, but care is needed because some millipedes release a staining acid for defence and if they're lactating they can actually squirt.'

Alas, by the time he offered this advice, the millipede was dead. It had been a gift from talk-show host Jay Leno, and the next time Patricia appeared on his programme, she revealed, 'Last time I was here on your show you gave me this millipede and when I looked at it it had this little scab on its back. And I thought maybe it was some discolouration or something. I took it home. I fed it. I cut it some grass. I made it an environment and everything. It died the next day. It was a little sad.'

They also had dogs, a Chinese crown-crested hairless called Rascal and a dachshund called Dasha, which Nick had given Patricia as a Valentine's Day gift in 1998. 'Patricia's always liked the name Dashenka Dachshund, so Dasha is short for Dashenka,' he said. 'It's the nickname of a name that doesn't exist.'

One pet was destined not to be — an injured sea-bird chick Nick tried desperately to rescue. He said, 'A baby loon was abandoned in front of my house at the beach. It was covered in tar. I put it in my pool and it just dove down under the water — it was like God's art. It became the most elegant seal and then it came back up and it was happy for a minute. I called the animal rescue agency and they said to get it out of the pool because the chlorine was no good for feathers. So I put it in the bath tub, which was too cold and it was shivering. I finally got it to the pet hospital. By then, I was attached to the bird. Loons in China are pets, and I had this poetic fantasy of having this loon as a pet. The hospital made it clear to me that if they couldn't cure it to send it back to the wild, they would put it to sleep. I asked if I could have it as a pet and they said they weren't allowed. I left, but kept thinking, I don't know who these people are. What if they put it to sleep because it's a baby? So I went back at 11.00pm and told them that if they couldn't help the bird, then don't put it down, call me, I'd like to take care of it. He said they wouldn't put it down. I called them at seven the next morning and they said they put the bird in the incubator and tried to feed it, but it died.'

CHAPTER EIGHT
FRENCH KISS

Some 300 passengers listened in shock at the ominous words coming over the public address system: 'Ladies and gentlemen, this is your Captain speaking. I'm not feeling too good and I'm afraid I'm losing control of the plane. Please bear with me.' Some passengers were rigid with shock, others started screaming. A priest crossed himself and a teary wife kissed her husband goodbye.

Then the captain of USAir flight 103 from Los Angeles to San Francisco stormed furiously out of the cockpit, red-faced but suffering from no more than extreme anger, and wagged his finger at the man behind the microphone — Nicolas Cage.

'Not cool,' he said. 'Extremely uncool. Not funny. Not fucking funny.'

A chastened Nick returned to his seat for the rest of the uneventful journey, only to be greeted by the police when the plane landed, to be questioned about interfering with the flight. He was even hauled off to the airport jail to be lectured on the possible consequences of air piracy, before being set free with a warning.

He explained, 'I was with some friends and we were sort of goofing off. I'd had a few drinks and wanted to liven up the flight. And I was always that guy who had to go one up on everybody. Just go a little bit further. I grabbed the PA and told everybody that I was the Captain and that the plane was losing altitude. I didn't realise everyone could hear me. But they could. Everyone started freaking out. I thought it was a scream. I was greeted by three policemen at the gate. They asked me some questions and I admitted all of it, that we were just having some fun and that we're sorry. I apologised and was then taken to the airport jail where I had a very nice talking to. Now I fear divine retribution — and a real accident — whenever I fly.'

One of the passengers, Madelaine Jenner, said the whole plane had been taken in by the hoax. Jenner, who was 15 years old when Nick pulled his stunt, said, 'We thought it was the end. We thought we were going to crash. We were scared to death.'

Nick thought it was hilarious at the time. But nine years later, he told *Empire* magazine's Adam Smith, 'Well, that was a disastrous thing that I did which I regret to this day. This happened years ago. If it happened today, I'm sure I would be in jail.'

Irresponsible though his actions were, he had an explanation if not an excuse for playing wild at heart. After a dry spell following *Moonstruck*, with the dismal *Never on Tuesday* and the odd and overly-moralistic *Time to Kill* both languishing in video stores, he had just triumphed in his latest movie, *Wild at Heart*, a quirky, ultra-violent black comedy from director David Lynch. The film, threatened with an X-rating for violence, graphic sex and strong language, had won the prestigious Palme d'Or at the Cannes Film Festival — and won Nick some of the best reviews he had ever had. So his high spirits, though misdirected, were understandable.

In *Wild at Heart*, Lynch's long-awaited sequel to his darkly sexual exploration of American suburbia, *Blue Velvet*, Nick plays Sailor Ripley, a sweet-natured killer consumed by passion for his young lover, Lula Pace Fortune, played by Laura Dern. They are on the run from a host of horrors, past and present, a pair of white-trash low-lifes who have a charming, disarming innocence as they chain-smoke, talk dirty, have passionate sex — and blow people up.

The film was based on a then-unpublished novel by writer Barry Gifford, a former *Rolling Stone* magazine rock journalist based in Berkeley, California, who had published novels, poetry, a biography of Jack Kerouac and a book about horse racing. In April 1989, he showed the novel to a friend, Monty Montgomery, who loved it and optioned it for a movie which he planned to direct. He, in turn, showed it to Lynch, then heavily involved in the first episodes of the cult television show *Twin Peaks*, suggesting he might like to produce it. Lynch, who had also directed *Eraserhead*, *The Elephant Man* and *Dune*, instantly fell for the characters of Sailor and Lula, suggested that he direct it and Montgomery become the producer, and hammered out a first draft in six days. He made the original story, mainly told in conversations between the lovers, darker and more violent, and introduced a host of exaggerated, near-fantasy characters.

He then had to find the perfect pair to play the lovers, who were already vivid in his imagination. Nick had been keeping a low profile — not deliberately, but because he did not have anything out in the cinemas. Then *Vampire's Kiss* opened and Lynch was determined to have him for the role of Sailor. He said, 'I knew that Nicolas was Sailor — a rebel, very much in love with his girl, who finds himself in the wrong place at the wrong time too often. Nick's got nerve. It's amazing how much courage it takes to say certain things and he's got that courage. Sailor's a weird man. That's why I wanted Nick. He's a jazz musician of actors. He's always got a very interesting, strange slant. And he's completely unafraid.'

The two men were nodding acquaintances, if not friends. They were both regulars at Musso and Frank Grill, a legendary Hollywood restaurant which opened in 1919 and has scarcely changed since. It specialises in old-fashioned steaks and chops and the bartenders mix mean martinis. Tables are set in red vinyl booths, or solo diners can sit at the counter. Both men usually chose the counter. Lynch said, 'I like to stare at the chimney above the grill. It reminds me of old Hollywood and Nick is a Hollywood type of guy.'

Nick recalled their first meeting.

'When I first met him in a restaurant in downtown LA, I heard someone call, "Nick, Nick" in this voice that sounded exactly like James Stewart and I was quite taken aback when I realised it was David Lynch,' he said. 'About a month later, I found out I was working with him on *Wild at Heart*. He'd told me he'd seen me once before — in Thrifty's — and I was buying ... er ... actually I was buying ... er ... those things, you know ... those things that women need every now and then. Yes, tampons. I was buying tampons for my girlfriend and David saw me. So he'd always say, "Hey! We shop at the same store, you and I. We both go to Thrifty's." ' Thrifty was a chain of drug stores that sold a wide variety of household goods as well as prescription medicines.

Lynch also wanted Laura Dern, who had co-starred for him in *Blue Velvet*, to be his Lula 'with every fibre of my body'.

He introduced Nick to Dern and while they were talking, a famous old cinema, the Pan Pacific, burned down a few blocks away. Lynch saw that as an omen, since fire was to be a recurring theme in his movie. 'The film has a lot to do with fire so that was kind of interesting,' he said. 'I sat opposite Nick and Laura and the whole time I'm sitting there I'm thinking how both of them have this same quality of being beautiful and not beautiful, intelligent and yet so understanding of ordinary life.'

Lynch already knew he was going to ask his stars to perform extremely sexually explicit scenes and wanted them to be totally comfortable together before they started taking their clothes off in front of the cameras. He suggested they went away together for a few days to get to know each other before the filming started in August in Los Angeles. That suggestion, and the sizzling sex performances the pair pulled off on the film, quickly sparked suggestions that they had become lovers.

'We went on a road trip from Los Angeles to Las Vegas, about 300 miles, before we started filming, just to get to know each other,' explained Nick. 'The sex in the film is very intimate so it was important to be with someone I genuinely liked. We had a great trip, a real crazy time.'

Dern added, 'I know it's an unusual way to get to know your leading man but it worked. We had to be in sync. So we spent many hours in the car driving through the desert. We got bored and sweaty but we got to know each other.'

They maintained, however, that they were no more than good friends. Nick told English interviewers when he was promoting the film, 'For the record, we're good friends and that's it. Lovers we're not. Just the fact that I really liked her and we were able to cultivate our imaginations made it work. We're dealing with a movie here that is extremely sexual and you can imagine the stories that generates. The sex is hot and hard — but that's OK, it's loving too. Why can't people accept that things can be both at once? Laura was a joy to work with. She is so positive you can't feel really down when she's around. I would have done anything to help her get the part together and she'd have done the same for me. As far as my love-life goes, my relationships have always been tumultuous, kind of unstable. Love is a very interesting emotion. It can make you crazy, it can make you happy, it can make you jealous, it can make you want to kill someone, it can make you want to cook for somebody. It inspires all sorts of feelings. I've been drawn to romantic films which allow me to be free with the things that I do and also to purge some of the things that I feel. Love in general inspires me.'

Nick, who had just learned from Christina that he was about to be a father, went on, 'I certainly don't think it's a requirement to have an affair to make it work. Wondering what it would be like is more exciting than knowing. Like with Cher on *Moonstruck* — I didn't want to kiss her until the time I did have to kiss her in the film. And it really worked. It was exciting. I put every thought that I had about it into it. In fact, if I was going to have an affair with a lady, I would do it at the end of the shoot. It would be more meaningful if it had nothing to do with the movie. I would get nauseated thinking, well, we're going to fuck because it's going to help the character. But I really don't like working without some attachment to somebody. It's all the trials and tribulations that get me wanting to do something.'

As Sailor, Nick plays a character who can rip a man to death with his bare hands, as he does at the beginning of *Wild at Heart*, killing the hit-man sent in by his girlfriend's obsessive mother, Marietta (played by Diane Ladd, Laura Dern's real mother from her marriage to actor Bruce Dern). She wants Sailor dead because he had rejected her sexual advances. He serves two years for manslaughter before being released on parole and his girl, Lula, is waiting for him. Marietta still wants him done away with, in part because she suspects he might have been a witness the night she had her husband set on fire. The lovers flee on an odyssey that turns out to be part *Wizard of Oz* and part *Bonnie and Clyde*, and Marietta orders her boyfriend, private detective Johnnie Farragut, played by Harry Dean Stanton, to track them down. When he fails, she calls in a former lover, mobster Marcello Santos, played by JE Freeman. Sailor and Lula travel across the southern states and in flashbacks and present time the audience is introduced to a host of obscure, sometimes menacing figures.

In sequences that could be real or dream-like, characters like Lula's cockroach- and Christmas-obsessed cousin Dell, played by Crispin Glover, and her incestuous Uncle Pooch, played by Marvin Kaplan, flit across the screen. Willem Dafoe plays a brooding, dark angel, Bobby Peru, who has his head blown off in one climactic scene, accompanied by *Blue Velvet* star Isabella Rossellini — Lynch's real-life girlfriend — as his lover. Sailor is a low-key reincarnation of Elvis, Lula is undoubtedly a trailer park heroine; but they love each other with an endearing passion, even during the film's most violent moments.

Nick said, 'For me, this is a love story. *The Wizard of Oz* is in there somewhere, but this film is about getting to that place with your baby where no one can touch you. Lula is all that matters to Sailor. I had a hankering to portray this sort of character who would do just about anything for the woman he loves. She's more important than any country, any battle — more important than anything in the world. There's also a danger to Sailor. He's capable of killing a man with his bare hands, but he's also a good guy. There's just that edge ... It's hard for me to analyse Sailor. I don't know what I did to get there. I've often played roles that were very large and sort of manic and I wondered how I could be that ludicrous but in a very contained way. Sailor is a lot more sedate than I've been in a while in a film — he's a strong character who doesn't need to rant and rave to get attention. The challenge is to be mega-cool in a way that will be totally absurd.

'It's a road picture in the sense that the two lovers on the run are a perfect formula for meeting interesting characters. With David's imagination those characters on the road get pretty extraordinary. It's like love in hell. I felt at home with David directing and in lots of ways I wasn't trying so hard as I have in the past because I trusted him. Working with David was very liberating. His set is the most open and relaxed I've been on. A lot more natural flow. And Laura as an actress is very bold and free-spirited and she can play off anything. I don't think she is the kind of actress who could ever be stumped. Her reactive ability is pretty amazing. If I want to go to Jupiter she'll match that and take it to Saturn. She's out there and can keep up with anything and throw some curveballs back. It makes for an exciting combination.

'I've followed his movies ever since I saw *Eraserhead* and I've seen all of them. I was a big fan of Lynch, so when I started working with him I was a little bit nervous. And he put me right at ease, and I discovered him to be very light on his feet. He's like a magician. He believes in cultivating the accidents and his set is a very playful set and there's not a lot of pressure. It's demanding but it's open to free-flowing thoughts and I trust his judgement, so it was a luxury because I was able to go out of control as an actor and let him sculpt.

'With David directing, I knew that I would have the ability to go out there. This is what making movies is supposed to be like. David is the kind of guy that, no matter how late it is, if it gets to be four in the morning or if it gets really cold, he'll come out and say, "Are you ready to have some more fun?" I really admire that. I think that's why so many spontaneous things happen in his movies. I've been starting to try and use that positive attitude in my life.'

It was not only Lynch who recognised Sailor in Nick; *Wild at Heart* author Gifford also said, 'I do think the choice of Nick was inspired. I knew he had real affection for the character.'

The shoot, which reunited many crew members from *Blue Velvet* as well as Rossellini and Dern, was a happy one. It started in August 1989 and took eight weeks in Los Angeles and then a move to New Orleans for shooting in the French Quarter, especially the restaurant Café du Monde. Lynch threw in unexpected surreal moments to increase the sense of unreality in the already bizarre plot — like rounding up 60 New Orleans locals, many of them dossers at a flea-pit hotel where Sailor and Lula were staying, to cheer as they drove away in their Thunderbird convertible; or adding a glimpse of three fat, naked women shooting a porn movie in the courtyard of an apartment complex.

The friendship between Nick and Dern flourished during the shoot. They called each other nicknames — he was Rattlesnake and she was Shadow Fire. Dern called Nick 'an action cat on the move', and laughed, 'We got under each other's skins forever during filming. Every day was a journey to Disneyland. He's the rattlesnake king of the universe'.

Nick responded, 'Laura is a passionate person who is totally endearing. In the movie, we enjoy turning each other on.'

That was probably just as well given the amount of sex in the film. Nick said it was easy shooting even the strongest love scenes with Dern because of their friendship. 'Laura is such a likeable person that she's fun to be around and you like being with her,' he explained. 'The last thing you want to do is to be around somebody you can't stand and jump into a bed and wrestle with them. The fact that she's such a sweet personality made it so much easier. I think the sex in the movie is my favourite thing in the film because it's so pure. When I watch it I don't feel I'm spying on these people. I feel like I'm celebrating with them. Sex has been exploited and presented in the most tacky ways in the past. To be able to present it in a way that's thoughtful and meaningful is a good thing.'

Despite their ease with each other and in front of the cameras, there were a few sticky moments. In one rehearsal, when Lula was licking the crotch of Sailor's pants, Nick laughed, 'What kind of rating are we going to get?' It was a prescient question, because the American censors were very concerned about the finished product. Laura blushed and said, 'This is sooo embarrassing.'

But Laura went from having a sudden flush to turning woozy when Lynch asked her to smoke four cigarettes at once in one deep inhalation. Laura passed clean out. When she came to, she saw the worried director standing over her asking, 'Tidbit! Are you all right?'

Other ad-libbed moments were much more light-hearted. In one romantic scene, the lovers drove off into the sunset and kept going even after Lynch called 'Cut.'

'For a moment, we thought we might never stop,' Dern admitted. 'There's that side of Nick that's spontaneous, an openness for adventure that's sad and heroic. I respect it a lot.'

For Nick, who called the lovers 'Elvis and Marilyn on the road to hell', the potentially most embarrassing part of the production was having to sing two songs by Elvis Presley. In fact, with Lynch's encouragement, he played Sailor as a freaky reincarnation of The King. Lula delivered the line that summed up the movie, 'The whole world's wild at heart and weird on top,' and Nick's portrayal, as he himself admitted, fell decidedly into the realms of the weird.

Two months before he was cast as Sailor, Nick fell in love with a garish snakeskin jacket and had to buy it. 'I knew I was going to wear it in some movie,' he recalled. The jacket became his trademark in *Wild at Heart*, heightening the Elvis impression.

'Deciding to play him as Elvis was a weird thing to do because at that time it was considered taboo to use imitation,' Nick said later. 'In the book *An Actor Prepares* by Stanislavski, it says that the worst thing an actor can do is to copy another performer.'

Konstantin Stanislavski, who died in 1938 aged 75, was a Russian actor, director and drama coach whose teaching on acting is still considered standard practice in much Western training.

'I had always believed that,' Nick went on, 'but then with *Wild at Heart*, I thought, maybe it's time to try something else. I used to call that my Andy Warhol period because I would take the icon of Elvis the way Warhol would and try to put something on top of it and filter it in some way. I was taking the biggest American icon, Elvis, and trying to do an impersonation. You know how Warhol would take these fantastic icons like Muhammad Ali or Marilyn Monroe and do that with them? I was going to try to do that with acting. David Lynch, being such an intense Presley fan, saw it as an opportunity to get as close to casting his hero as he was ever going to get. This was the kind of movie I wish Elvis had made.'

Nick also said, 'There were really two Elvises, pre-army and post-army. Something happened to change him. What I liked about *Wild at Heart* was how it enabled me to adopt the essence of Elvis which is the next best thing to him being alive. I am an Elvis fan, I admit, but I'm more taken with the myth of Elvis than the actual man and his music.'

As the film progressed, the director decided to take the Elvis image even further by having Nick croon some of his music. Nick remembered, 'When Lynch told me that I was going to sing a couple of Presley tunes I started adopting more and more of Presley's mannerisms and he gave me the green light on that. At that time, the previous work that I'd done was absurd in a way that was large, and very abstract, and I was becoming curious about how I could be absurd and subtle. Well, Elvis has been ripped off so much, and he's so tired as a character rip-off, that it's like a joke that loses its humour, then starts it again by the sheer repetition of it. And I thought, if I can adopt Elvis' mannerisms and put a true heart behind it, Sailor's heart, then I would be killing two birds with one stone. I would be absurd and I would also be providing a tone to the film.'

He lip-synched a lush rendition of 'Love Me' to his own pre-recorded voice in a scene shot in a country and western club in North Hollywood, but meant to be set in North Carolina. The extras were primed to swoon and scream, but according to writer Ralph Rugoff who watched the scene, a genuine sensation of awe hushed the set when Nick grabbed the microphone.

'Without coaching from their director, the extras go wild, mobbing Cage for autographs when he finishes his steamy, hip-grinding number,' he said. 'An assistant director has to shoo them away. Lynch beams with pleasure throughout the entire performance, looking very much like someone lost in a happy daydream.'

Nick later confessed: 'It was horrifying for me to sing two Elvis songs in *Wild at Heart*. When you have one of the greatest directors in the world telling you that you're gonna do a couple of Elvis numbers, and what's more, you're gonna sound just like Elvis, that's a lot of pressure. Thank God, you know, they souped up my voice a little.'

When filming was over, Nick, Dern and Lynch were unstinting in their praise for each other. Nick recalled how he planned his every move in *Vampire's Kiss* and pointed out the differences from the new film. He said, 'With *Wild at Heart*, being that I trusted Laura and David so much, I could let my guard down and be more spontaneous, free-flowing. I wasn't blocked into anything at all. Sailor is like an old Corvette in a snakeskin jacket. He breaks down, he starts up, he breaks down. When he's driving, he drives fast and he drives cool, but he needs a tune-up. And even though he would beg and steal — like in that Elvis song — even though he killed a man, he did it because of love. He felt he was doing the right thing even though it was pretty screwed up. There's not a lot of rationality between his instincts and his actions.'

He explained, 'Sailor is a romantic. I wanted that. I wanted the love story aspect of *Wild at Heart* to be strong, to have a pure love in this hellish world that they're surrounded with. So did David. Actually, David's one of the warmest people I've ever met. I think he has that poetry inside of him that believes in true love and some of the more delicate things in life. And he's rooting for them to survive.

'David is like a criminal director. He's not concerned with Establishment laws and rules. He just does what he does — and it's honest. He's constantly sculpting and fishing. A scene can turn into a comedy or into heavy horror in a fraction of a second. He's very much a sculptor, a spontaneous sculptor. When you talk about various levels in acting, the same is true with David in *Wild at Heart*. It's a very universal film, operating on different levels. It operates on a comedic level. It operates on a real level. And also on that absurdist level. Like, there's this gritty road movie, this gritty love story on the road, emanating through a *Wizard of Oz* tonality, which gives it more texture and colour.

'The funny thing is, the less literal route is the more truthful way, I think. Because you get at what's beneath the surface. There are flashes that happen in people's brains that are real, and people do not want to put them out. I guess that's where a signature would come from, to allow yourself to put those flashes out there and not edit yourself or hold back.'

In turn, Lynch said, 'There's a lot of things that made Nick unique. His way of delivering lines, his look. He's got an ability to do real heavy things and goofy things. His attitude encouraged me to think of things for him to do, because he's so good at going to strange places. You give him an idea and he grabs on to it like crazy. He's like a wild dog on a leash. I used to believe that if an actor changed even a little apostrophe or something, I'd go nuts. But after a while, everybody — the prop man — could come up with a great idea because he's tuned into the picture now and into the world. So the ideas are based on the truth of the rules of the world. And when Nick and Laura caught the drift of Sailor and Lula, their ad-libbing is Sailor and Lula. It's like music to my ears to hear Sailor and Lula talking. Why am I going to tell them anything? That's Sailor and Lula there.'

Dern said of Nick, 'He has this giant heart. For the first time, it was exposed. He was Nicolas more than we've ever seen.'

Lynch took advantage of having two young, adventurous actors working with him to make an even more bizarre and surreal piece immediately after *Wild at Heart*. With composer Angelo Badalamenti, who wrote the' score of *Wild at Heart*, Lynch also wrote a multimedia piece, *Industrial Symphony Number 1: The Dream of the Broken Hearted*. It was a dreamscape drama starring Nick as Heartbreaking Man and Dern as Heartbroken Woman. Julee Cruise, a Lynch favourite who would appear in *Twin Peaks*, played the oddly-named Dreamself of the Heartbroken Woman, a character who floated through the air over an industrial wasteland, all the time singing ballads of love. It was broadcast as a 50-minute television special and released on video. A musical version was also performed by the Brooklyn Academy of Music.

Wild at Heart was entered into the prestigious Cannes Film Festival in May 1990 in anticipation of its American release. Before Cannes, an early cut was presented to the Motion Picture Association of America for classification. Meyer Gottlieb, President of the releasing company Samuel Goldwyn, said it had been presented for 'informational purposes only and guidance from the board', and that it would be formally rated after the festival. However, an MPAA spokeswoman, while refusing to comment on the classification, insisted, 'You can only submit a film for rating purposes.' In the previous month, the ratings board had hit three films with an X: *The Cook, The Thief, His Wife and Her Lover, Wild Orchid* and *Tie Me Up! Tie Me Down!*. The first two were released without certificates, but were also cut to make the R rating for the home video market. *Tie Me Up!* was released as an X and is now reclassified as NC-17, which replaced X.

Lynch did decide to make some cuts, however, when 70 members of a test audience of 300 walked out during a particularly gruesome torture scene. He explained, 'I'm not looking to disturb people so much that they turn on the film. A film can't be for everybody. But when you get this group of 300 people and you feel the film break for everybody, then you know you're doing something wrong.'

The film was finally completed only a day before its world première at Cannes and ran ten minutes short of the time advertised in the show programme. By this time, Lynch was being celebrated not just for his films but for his new, must-see cult television series, *Twin Peaks*, which had been launched in the United States a month earlier. Throughout the festival, crowds thronged the American Pavilion on Thursday nights to watch new episodes, and Lynch was so hot that even though the first screening of *Wild at Heart* was scheduled for the uncivilised hour of 8.30am, more than 1,000 people had crammed into the Grand Auditorium Lumière by eight o'clock.

The film was greeted with cheers of appreciation and howls of derision by the stunned audience.

Lynch admitted in a press conference later, 'It's not a movie for everyone.' And he acknowledged that he would have to make cuts because he was contractually obliged to bring in an R-rated movie for America. 'This is the version that will be shown in Europe,' he said. 'But we're going to have a few problems in the US for sure. I don't know why it is, but the ratings board has been getting very conservative lately. There will be some changes we have to make. We're upset about having to cut scenes to get an R rating. But there's not a whole lot we can do about it.'

Nick, harking back to his appreciation of terrible reviews for *Peggy Sue Got Married*, added, 'It was good that they booed. That means the movie affected them. There will be a lot of controversy and that will be good for us.' He then whisked Dern off to the casino, where they won $1,000.

The Hollywood trade newspapers sent reviewers to Cannes, and they raved about the film. Robert Osborne wrote in *The Hollywood Reporter*, 'Love it or hate it, no one's going to doze during David Lynch's *Wild at Heart*. It's the movie equivalent of a hell-bent, fast-forward locomotive, without breaks but with a wildly imaginative engineer in charge. Cage is superb as Sailor; the role is a skintight fit and allows the actor to give a wonderfully amusing and animalistic interpretation of Southern dawg.'

The critic for *Daily Variety* was even more enthusiastic, though the review warned that the film would have serious problems getting less than an X rating without cuts. It read, 'Joltingly violent, wickedly funny and rivetingly erotic, David Lynch's *Wild at Heart* is a roller-coaster to redemption through an American gothic heart of darkness. Cage, who has overacted in other roles, can't possibly do so in the anything-goes Lynchian universe. He's born to the role of the rock 'n' roll macho man Sailor, a tough guy with a tender heart who never had any parental guidance. Lynch does a lot more than suggest their molten sexual bond. Although it's life-affirming and crucial to establishing their relationship, it's unlikely that Cage and Dern's transfixing love-making scenes will survive the censors' scissors in the US.'

The film was the surprise winner of the coveted Palme d'Or, the festival's top award. Nick, Dern, Ladd, Dafoe and Rossellini were there to hear the announcement by Jury President Bernardo Bertolucci, who directed *The Last Emperor* and *Last Tango in Paris*, and watch Lynch receive the award from Anthony Quinn. *Daddy Nostalgia*, starring Dirk Bogard, Clint Eastwood's *White Hunter, Black Heart* and *New Wave* from Jean-Luc Godard had been considered the front-runners.

The crowd was not as enthusiastic about the prize as they had been about the première itself. Influential American critic Roger Ebert led about half the audience in booing the decision. Lynch did not care. He said, 'It's a true dream come true.'

He discovered an added benefit of winning once he returned to the United States. Winning the Palme d'Or seemed to have softened the censors' stance towards the film and the only change he had to make was to add smoke and fire to about 25 frames to conceal the most graphic parts of a shooting and decapitation scene.

Nick was left with one particularly indelible memory of the festival, the night he attended a formal banquet at the Carlton Hotel and was seated with Gilles Jacob, the festival President. Looking back a couple of years later, he said, 'There was a big banquet with, like, 400 people all dressed to the nines in tuxes and evening gowns. I was sitting there with David and Laura Dern, and the President of the festival and his wife. The President's wife said, "Would you please sing 'Love Me Tender' to me?" And I just went white and started trembling. David was like, "Nickster, buddy, man, ya jump up on that table and ya sing to her, now." So I did jump up on the table and in this quavering, eggshell voice, sang "Love Me Tender" to her with sweat drenching my forehead, like Albert Brooks in that movie *Broadcast News*. Then I got back down and was met with fairly courteous applause. It was one of the most terrifying things I've ever had to do and probably the most embarrassing. But there was no other thing that could be done. It had to be done. So I did it.'

Being part of the success of *Wild at Heart* must also have cheered Nick up over the terrible reviews for *Fire Birds*, which opened a few days after the prize-giving.

The film's American première, on 13 August 1990, was held at Universal City and followed by a star-studded party at the trendy Arena nightclub in Hollywood. Nick was accompanied by girlfriend Lisa Stothard and his parents, Joy and August. Laura Dern was with her then love, director Renny Harlin, and her mother. Other guests included Steve Martin and Victoria Tennant, who were married at the time, Dweezil Zappa, Corbin Bernsen and Amanda Pays, Rebecca de Mornay, Harry Hamlin and Nicolette Sheridan, Kelly Emberg and Jennifer Tilly.

The entertainment included a fire-eater and a woman snake-charmer. Film fans wore black, the women in ultra-mini skirts and stilettoes. Lynch was delighted with the response. He said, 'I didn't get to talk to everybody at the screening. I kind of left fast but I could feel the audience was with this film. A couple of critics are not going to dig it but the reaction seemed to be good.'

Lynch was right in his prediction. Some critics raved, some ranted. Others were bemused by the whole mad mix. But most agreed with Lynch that Nick was Sailor.

'Nicholas Cage may be the most high-flying actor in the movies right now,' said Peter Rainer in the *Los Angeles Times.* 'He's the perfect performer for Lynch because, like the director, he doesn't censor his wildest intuitions and so his performance has the expressionist unpredictability of a dream. *Wild at Heart* is a comedy of a very special sort. The violence in it, like the sentimentality, is so over-the-top that sometimes the only sane response is a cackle — it's the only way to defuse the horror.'

Ella Taylor wrote in *Los Angeles Weekly*, 'On *Wild at Heart,* David Lynch lets out a yelp of joy. *Wild at Heart* is about white trash, and God knows it's not a sympathetic or generous reading of their hi-tack world, a diabolical comic book filled with hoods, whores and voodoo operators all drawn with an overkill that rushes between the hilarious and the horrific. But it's Cage who turns *Wild at Heart* into Lynch's funniest film yet. Lynch's comedy is at its deadpan best when he steals the clichés of everyday life and plugs them into ridiculous contexts. Wearing a snakeskin jacket that's "a symbol of my individuality and my belief in personal freedom", Cage is at once a shambling lummox with an uncertain IQ and a sultry sexpot who can sing the whole Presley repertoire and lets his willing Lula have it at any and every opportunity.'

'It's the old fun-house principle,' analysed Vincent Canby in the *New York Times.* 'Nightmares are made real. Without moving, one seems to plummet through pitch darkness. The response in a fun-house is a pleasurably scary physical sensation. The Lynch films go several steps further; nothing in life is fixed. All reality is relative. Mr Cage is not always an easy actor to accommodate. He tends to go over the edge. Here, however, he has a role that perfectly fits him, like the Elvis-inspired snakeskin jacket he wears (and which Sailor says symbolises his individuality). This time it's the director, not Mr Cage, who gets out of hand.'

Marilyn Moss said in *Box Office*, '*Wild at Heart* takes off in a blaze and barely slows down, except for a few dragging moments near its conclusion. Trailing the path of two young lovers on the run, the film's most bewitching moments are those when Lynch plummets both these lovers and the audience into unexpected moments of horror and outrageous comedy.'

In *Village View*, Jeff Schwager called it an 'insubstantial exercise in style', saying, 'The surfaces of *Wild at Heart* are dazzling; but there's nothing much inside and what one ultimately remembers is style, not substances.' But he also wrote, 'As Sailor and Lula, Nicolas Cage and Laura Dern turn in the best performances of their careers, making their characters' mutual attraction, tender feelings and fiery love-making utterly believable. Cage makes Sailor's central contradiction — the warmth with which he treats Lula and the violence with which he sometimes explodes — pieces of a convincing whole, and Dern brings a blind passion and commitment to lines like, "You move me, Sail, you really do. You mark me the deepest." '

Newsweek's David Ansen agreed, writing, 'For all its gory sensationalism, *Wild at Heart* is more silly than scary. As the movie threatens to become David Lynch's Wild Kingdom you may understandably lose track of just where the story is heading or exactly why you're supposed to care. Which is a shame because the performances of Cage and Dern are the movie's one real triumph.'

Terrence Rafferty in the *New Yorker* hated it. He wrote, 'Right from the start, just about everything is wrong with David Lynch's new movie and the wrongness has an escalating, vertiginous quality. Every false move seems to lead to another, more disastrous than the one before. The ride lasts just over two hours and when it's all over all you can do is stagger away in relief.'

So did David Denby in *New York* magazine. '*Wild at Heart* is full of self-mocking trash as well as perfervid excitement and the trash is not redeemed by the jokes,' he said. 'It seems almost a malignant work — an instant fetish object, an appalling, self-destroying voodoo doll.'

Phillip Lopate in *Esquire* found it childish and said, 'Whatever its merits, *Wild at Heart* hasn't much to say to adults. It is the sensation. The virtue is, you never know what's coming next; the drawback is, you may not care. Roller-coasters get monotonous.'

In *The New Republic*, Stanley Kauffman did not even like Nick and was unsure about Dern: 'Dern's performance is more a triumph of casting than of acting. As a wanton, passionate 20-year-old, she seems, most of the time, an early teenager pretending to be grown-up. This isn't a bad effect for the role. Cage is dreadful. He is unbelievable both as a cause of passion in others or a source of it in himself. His outbursts of violence simply mark the pages of the script where he was ordered to be violent.'

Nick was unmoved by the criticism. Three years later, he told journalist John Stanley of the *San Francisco Examiner* it was still his favourite film. 'It's my only movie which I can still watch and get lost in without thinking about what I had done in playing the character,' he said. 'I attribute that to David Lynch being a superior director.'

The film opened in the United Kingdom in August, in September in Germany and October in France, where it was renamed *Sailor and Lula*. British distributor Daniel Battsek was convinced the Cannes win would boost it. He told Oscar Moore of the British-based movie industry magazine *Screen International*, 'The Palme d'Or is simply a guarantee of quality. There is already interest because this is a David Lynch film and because he is pushing back the boundaries of sex and violence. But the Palme d'Or means that a jury, led by Bernardo Bertolucci, has said it works.'

The French distributor, Jean Labadie, who paid $960,000 for rights to France and Belgium, sight unseen, was astonished and delighted by its win at Cannes and did not foresee any problems with French censors. He said, 'The script was enough. There are few *auteurs* around with David's qualities. Americans are more scared of the censors than the censors are scared of the film. The X problem in America — Willem Dafoe's exploding head — is just a gag! The other violence is nothing compared with *Nightmare on Elm Street* or French TV every night. A Cannes winner is always more important in France than other territories. The win took me by surprise. My head exploded like Dafoe's but fortunately it landed back on my shoulders.'

Before he headed to Cannes, Nick had another taste of a different kind of French culture, heading back to New Orleans to make yet another small, quirky film, *Zandalee*. It co-starred Judge Reinhold, who had played Nick's friend in *Fast Times at Ridgemont High*. This time they play childhood chums who become far from friends as the story unfolds with tragic results. Nick plays Johnny Collins, an artist who falls madly in love with the Zandalee of the title, the wife of Thierry Martin, Reinhold's character. Zandalee is played by newcomer Erika Anderson, a model and radio disc jockey in Tulsa, Oklahoma.

The low-budget ($7 million) picture was shot in six weeks in The Big Easy and employed a host of local talent, including blues singer Aaron Neville.

In the film, Thierry is a burned-out poet who has inherited his father's business but cannot run it as well. His sexy young wife owns a vintage clothes shop. When Johnny returns to town and pals up with Thierry again, Thierry asks him to paint his wife. Johnny and Zandalee embark on a passionate affair, having wild sex all over the place, including a church confessional and in the kitchen at Zandalee's apartment, while her husband and friends sit at a dinner table in the adjacent room. At first Thierry tries to ignore what is going on, but eventually takes Zandalee off to the bayou to try to recapture the spark in their marriage. But Johnny turns up to stake his claim on Zandalee and the story ends tragically with Thierry's death in a boating accident that might be a suicide and Zandalee dying in Johnny's arms after being accidentally gunned down by an angry drug dealer seeking revenge on her lover.

The sex was so graphic that there were fears the film would get the new NC-17 rating that had replaced X in a bid to distance mainstream adult-content movies from straight porn. Director Sam Pillsbury, a New Zealander, was adamant that it was not pornographic. He said, 'I felt very strongly that it was very important in the making of this movie for nudity not to be the issue, but for it to be the intensity of what was going on between the people. I don't think this movie is pornographic. I mean, pornography is ugliness; it's dehumanised and this is the exact opposite.'

Nick found the sex even more overwhelming than the steamy scenes he had had with Dern in *Wild at Heart*. He admitted, 'There are the most sex scenes in a movie that I've ever seen. It's just chock full of sex. I think the director doesn't want it to have the lyrical edge to it that most sex scenes have. I think he wants it to look like reality. He almost shot it in a way that was documentary at times. Sex is a good memory. People don't take Polaroids ... or maybe some people do. But, you know, real love-making exists, and instead of lacing it with saccharine bullshit, he would rather do the movie in a literal way, in a real way, where the sex is a celebration of the life and not hidden under a lot of fancy lighting and everything.

'I think Johnny is a sort of vampire of innocence. He wants to corrupt innocence because it is very seductive to him. He's almost like a messenger of temptation. It was a different kind of role than I'd played before, and it's exciting for me to portray a character who is not out there, not evil, but immoral.

'*Wild at Heart* was a celebration of sex. David Lynch conveyed this aspect without compromising it. But *Zandalee* was about how sex can get out of hand, go out of control and destroy someone's spirit. It was a pretty dark exploitation of sex. Sex has always been a taboo subject in the movies because, with the exception of very few, nobody's really figured out how to record it on film and not make it seem distasteful. But why should it be? After all, it's something that everyone experiences in real life. To me, erotic art is some of the most valid artwork, and why not extend this to films? It's just unfortunate that pornography has turned sexuality into exploitation and jacking-off material. I think there's yet to be a movie made where sex can be celebrated in a way that is meaningful as it is in life. Then again, I don't know how you'd do it. I mean, it's not as if you can give people a sense of what it actually feels like.'

A writer in *Premiere* said that after Nick and Anderson finished an hours-long sex session on a closed set, 'both of them are smiling'. Ironically, however, Anderson said Nick was embarrassed doing the sex scenes.

She said, 'It was my first film but some of the sex scenes were really difficult even for someone with a lot of experience. When Nicolas had to peel off his jeans and tee-shirt and stand in front of me totally naked, he was more uptight than I was. He was incredibly nervous. It's a very explicit film but I don't think it's pornographic. Pornography is sex for the sake of it. There's too much going on in our film to call it porn.'

Zandalee opened in London in 1991 but went straight to video in the United States. *Daily Variety* commented, 'An overheated New Orleans sex triangle let down by a laughable script, *Zandalee* is about par with other romps like *Two Moon Junction* and *Wild Orchid*. Everyone concerned seems to think the picture is some kind of *9 ½ Weeks* Louisiana-style, but strip out the nudity and sack sessions and all that's left is a script that pulls its punches and seems to have been pasted together from subtitles on French movies.'

By the time *Wild at Heart* came out, Nick was being talked about for heavyweight roles, despite the débâcle of *Fire Birds*. Elia Kazan, the legendary director who made *A Streetcar Named Desire* and *On the Waterfront*, but who'd been scorned in Hollywood for years, was interested in him for a movie called *The Anatolian Smile*, which has not yet been made. Nick also considered another film which did not come to fruition, *Investigation*, in a role originally intended for Al Pacino. The film was to have been an English-language adaptation of the Italian movie *Investigation of a Citizen Above Suspicion*, which won the Best Foreign Film Oscar in 1970.

'I'd like to do a movie that was politically oriented next,' Nick said while he was promoting *Wild at Heart*. 'I'd like to rip the mask off American politics.'

He also discussed the failure of *Fire Birds* and speculated on why he had such a dry spell after *Moonstruck*. 'I think if there is a lesson there it's to stay true to your instincts,' he said. 'Working with David is a luxury in that you trust him and you go places with him. So I went into *Fire Birds* spoiled and everything felt so much different. I don't think people cared as much. I think it was more about money than it was about doing something that meant something.

'I don't try to be underground. I'm not against commercial films. I think they're great. If you can do something you care about and have it become commercial, then that's the best of both worlds. Mainly I want to do things that I care about that turn me on. And my tastes are a little left field. It could be the choices I have made in the past have been way out. Sometimes I feel that someone else is driving the car. I'm in the car but the car is being driven by somebody else, so I can't really say why I make the decisions I make or how I come about doing them. If I read something and like it, I do it. A lot of times it's something really wacky.'

On another occasion, he reflected on the impact becoming an actor had had on him, and speculated that, like Sailor, he could have turned to crime without the creative outlet. He said, 'It has been my ticket to freedom so I can't ever bad-mouth acting. It gave me a way out both financially and psychologically. I think if it wasn't for acting, I would probably be dead because I would ... I mean, it has been a tremendous outlet for anger and feelings. It's been an escape process. All my life I have generated these intense feelings. It's in my nature to use extreme terms. I'm always black or white. It's very hard for me to be grey. I carried a great deal of anger. I was an angry young man and somewhat rebellious and I dunno what I would have done. Who knows? But I felt that if I didn't have a proper channel to release my anger, it could have backfired on me. I would probably have turned to crime. I guess I should be careful what I say, but I have at times felt criminal tendencies but because of the work I have been able to release it. I've kept it on film. I'm attracted to outlaw figures, some kind of sociopath who can get through the problem and the circumstances and rise above it and reach a place of dignity and morality. These are the kind of characters I dig.'

Nick may have turned away from a life of crime but he remained a rebel. When he flew to England to promote *Vampire's Kiss* — which, thanks to the vagaries of film scheduling opened 18 months after its American launch — he stayed in five-star luxury at the prestigious the Brown's Hotel. It was hardly the trendiest spot in town, but Nick managed to spice up his stay by being banned from the tea lounge because his black T-shirt and battered leather jacket did not meet the dress code requirements.

He explained, 'I always stay here. I enjoy the strictness because it gives me a chance to improve my manners!'

CHAPTER NINE
DOTING DAD, RAMBLING ROMEO

As he drove through the streets of Los Angeles, Nick popped the lighter out of its socket and sucked a cigarette, one of the 30 to 40 Marlboro Reds he smoked every day, into life. Then he looked round at his month-old son, Weston, lying contentedly strapped into his safety crib on the back seat and disgustedly threw the cigarette out of the window. His relationship with Christina may have been rocky, he may have been unhappy at the prospect of becoming a premature dad, but once the baby arrived, Nick took to fatherhood instantly. Christina has always had primary custody, but Nick has always been a hands-on dad. Wordlessly persuading him to kick the cigarette habit — something Nick had been contemplating for a while — was just one of the ways in which Weston changed his life from the moment he was born.

'One of the amazing things about children is that they automatically cut out any debauchery or decadence left over from your youth,' he recalled later. 'As soon as Weston was born, I stopped smoking and started buckling my seat-belt. A lot of things had been gearing toward stopping smoking but it was the straw that broke the camel's back.'

Weston's birth also put a definite end to Nick's brief flirtation with marijuana. He revealed, 'There'd been a time before — it was like a three-month phase — where I was very upset. So I was trying to find answers elsewhere and experimented with smoking pot. I really liked it. But then it got to a point where I became paranoid and it started giving me anxiety attacks. So I stopped and I don't really like to smoke any more.' He added, 'One of the reasons why I felt connected to Francis Coppola was because he and I were the only two people in the family who had smoked pot.'

Nick may have given up smoking cigarettes but over the years he developed a taste for fine cigars. In addition, most of his screen characters have continued to light up. Smoking in movies has become a hot Hollywood topic because of the perception that more, and younger, characters indulge, and the anti-tobacco lobby want to see the trend reversed. But when Vice-President Al Gore invited Nick to sit on a committee to discuss the subject, he declined.

With the birth of his son, Nick started getting up earlier, turning his back on the days of lounging in bed until noon, and began working out more regularly and taking vitamins. He even admitted he might like to settle down, but ruled out Christina by saying he was looking for a stable, nurturing schoolteacher type.

'As yet, I've only met actresses and models and there's been an instability there,' he said. 'There is a distance in relationships. It's the business I am in. You're away a lot. It's hard to not hurt or be hurt. It's just one of the brutal facts. Originally, I wanted the homecoming queen that I could never get in high school. Then I grew out of that. And now, quite honestly, I think about someone who would be very nurturing and supportive of children and good with kids and who has their own identity and life. I'm actually looking forward to meeting some schoolteachers!'

While he and his ex were thrashing out the details over custody and child support, Nick became very vocal about how biased the American system was in favour of mothers and against fathers. He said, 'The system in America doesn't really accept that men are potentially good parents or that a single father can be warm and nurturing. The odds are against him in terms of a lot of things, you know, custody. The majority of family rights, and the right of parenting, are automatically given to the mother, and I find that aggravating. You have to go up against a wall to get your rights. That's what I'm doing. A single father does have rights but there are nefarious ways of convoluting that.'

By the end of 1992, he was saying, 'Every move I make now is determined by the impact it will have on my child. Fulton and I are in the middle of working out a formal agreement.'

Two years later, he was still convinced that fathers, all too often, got a raw deal. 'Men are going through a very weird time right now, especially single fathers,' he told Paul Young of the now defunct Los Angeles-area magazine *Buzz*. 'I remember one time when I was sitting in a custody evaluations office waiting to see my son, and this woman came up to me and said, "What are you doing here?" And I said, "Well, I want to see my kid." She said, "Why?" "Because it's good for us." "Good for you or for him?" "For both of us." And then she said, "Well, there must be a full moon tonight because there's a lot of single fathers coming in here who want to see their kids and I don't know what's going on. Do you want to be the mother? Is that it?" And I thought, OK, there's something really archaic going on here. There's a whole new attitude, a new gender bias happening against men. Much in the same way that women used to be, and still are, in some cases, victims of sexism when they weren't considered "good enough" to be a part of the workforce, men are seen today as being "not good enough" to raise children.

'I think part of the problem is the media. I saw a bus ad the other day with a picture of a cute little baby on it with the slogan "It's amazing how many men disappear when one of these turns up". I think the people who put out these messages actually *want* men to disappear. They want to continue the stereotype of the irresponsible, careless, alcoholic father. And the movies don't help much either. I saw Bruce Willis in *The Last Boy Scout* put a gun to his little girl's head to get her out of a bad situation. He was pretending to take her hostage, but you don't put a gun to a little girl's head. You don't make that image and put it out there. What we need is an action hero who has sensitive values, who's not just a robot, who's not a muscle man, but just a guy trying to save his relationship with his child. We could do with more images like that, images of men as nurturing personas, because there's a shift going on. More and more women are becoming profession-oriented and more and more men are becoming child-oriented. But we still don't have a concept of a nurturing male persona.'

Once the custody issue was sorted out, and Nick won the right to see the baby several days a week, he and Christina soon found themselves back on good terms. He raved about fatherhood and confessed he would love to be a full-time dad.

'Weston's changed the way I see things,' he admitted, coming up to the boy's second birthday. 'Family life is the road to happiness and contentment. I can't wait to have more children. I would be totally content being a house-husband and having a wife be the professional. I'd like to play with the kids' toys and fire trucks and wipe the pizza dough off their hands and make them laugh. I've learned more from Weston than from analysing my own depths. Babies, for whatever reason, are good luck, and when Weston was born, I became hyper-motivated. I think about Weston and he gives me strength. It's OK to be mushy. Otherwise there wouldn't be opera. Children are a way to pure joy. The only time that I've ever felt pure joy, pure happiness, I think, is when I've held my son. I don't know why that is, instinct or just the honesty that comes from him. You can't lie to children; you can't fool them.

'Of course, you worry about everything. You find yourself thinking, oh no, he's gonna bang his head or get a scratch or fall off his bike, and everything becomes a big issue. You just have to try to understand these things are gonna happen and not be overly protective. If I can say one thing about becoming a father, it is that it's made me look at life differently and value life a lot more. I used to be far more reckless, but now I realise that every action that I take will somehow, indirectly or directly, affect my child. That's quite a responsibility.'

And, perhaps remembering his own childhood longing for a 'girl's' toy, in his case an oven, he did not hesitate when an interviewer asked how he would react if his son wanted to play with dolls. 'If he wants to play with dolls, you let him play with dolls,' Nick replied.

He also felt much more mature, and admitted he was embarrassed by throwaway remarks he had made when he was younger, including the one about deciding to become an actor for sex. 'I said that when I was 17, when sex and money were big factors,' he pointed out. 'It's a hard habit to break, especially if women feel that they have to act a certain way to be attractive.' He confessed to Richard Natale of *Cosmopolitan* magazine that, at 28, he would rather have dinner and a conversation with a woman than leap into bed with her. 'I don't know where my libido's gone,' he laughed. 'A relationship is the one thing I haven't been able to crack yet. But I'm looking forward to it.'

Surprisingly, it looked as if that relationship could be with Christina after all, with John Stanley of the *San Francisco Examiner* reporting in early 1993 that she was living with him in his house in Pacific Heights.

Then, in July 1993, a Hollywood gossip column revealed that he was secretly engaged to Michigan-born Kristen Zang, a 19-year-old swimsuit model he had been dating for several months. Columnist Janet Charlton said, 'Now he's given her a pink diamond ring and Kristen tells pals her guy wants to wait a year before tying the knot.' They had been together for several months, and Kristen was actually only 18 when she visited Nick on the set of *Guarding Tess*. Kristen confirmed the engagement at a New York party to celebrate the start of *It Could Happen to You*. She flashed her ring at Melina Gerosa of *Entertainment Weekly* magazine and laughed, 'He doesn't want me to tell anyone but I'm sick of keeping it to myself.'

Nick's libido appeared to be back with a vengeance. Hollywood madam Heidi Fleiss had just been arrested for supplying high-class prostitutes to the rich and famous, and the film industry was full of rumours about the names found in her little black book. *Globe* magazine identified one of the celebrities as '*Hot Shots* hunk Charlie Sheen, who reportedly ordered up to 10 girls at a time to party with acting pals Nicolas Cage and Sean Penn.'

However, when Heidi was eventually brought to trial on pandering charges and later for tax evasion and money laundering, Sheen was the only celebrity named. He admitted paying more than $50,000 for hookers on at least 27 occasions, paying by cheque seven times and in cash at other times. Even though prostitution is illegal for the customer as well as the call-girl in California, he was never charged. Heidi was sentenced to three years for pandering but the conviction was overthrown for juror misconduct. She served 20 months for tax evasion before being released to a halfway house.

Nick's relationship with Kristen was volatile and before the end of the year he had called off their engagement. Janet Charlton, who had broken the news in the first place, revealed, 'Seems the 19-year-old swimsuit model couldn't keep from blabbing all their personal business in public — including the announcement of their engagement.'

A few months later, however, she wrote, 'Just when we thought that Nicolas Cage and Kristen Zang were about to settle down, he's acting like a single guy again. In New York he avoided her calls from LA, saying she was "a pain in the neck", and hung out at Scores topless bar. When he returned to Los Angeles, he was seen carousing and smooching with his ex (the mother of his child) Christina Fulton at Martini. But by the end of the same week, he was seen slow dancing to "Sexual Healing" at Martini with Zang once again!'

Nick himself admitted to Mark Marvel of trendy *Interview* magazine in the summer of 1994 that he was still with Kristen, although he seemed to be becoming concerned about the difference in their ages. He said, 'I've been with my girlfriend for two years. She's 20 and I'm 30. We were with Crispin Glover the other day — he's 30 too — and she said to us, "Generation X is not for you." And it really bothered Crispin. He said, "What does she mean, Generation X is not for me? If anything I'm a progenitor of Generation X." And what is Generation X anyway? I don't know. I can't put things into compartments like that. But I know why it made him a little upset and it kind of bothered me, too. It's about coming to terms with being 30 and not being part of the youth culture any more. Although the fact of the matter is we still have tremendous years ahead of us.'

The age difference may have been a factor in an unpleasant scene at a nightclub when Nick got into a confrontation with an old boyfriend of Kristen's. Nick was talking to British musician Julian Lennon when he suddenly took a punch in the face from her friend, who was only a year or so older than Kristen. At first he thought it was a joke, but then realised the younger man really was looking for a fight and became furious. Still, he made an effort to control his temper. He said, 'I started to get up and he walked away. He's a kid, basically. I felt bad for him, actually. I know if I do fight, I fight to kill. My motto has always been Maximum Violence Immediately. That means pushing the nose into the face, or whatever you've got to do. So I didn't want to get into a fight.'

Within a matter of months, the affair was over, in part because of the age gap. Nick went off to Las Vegas to film what was to become his tour de force, *Leaving Las*

Vegas, and during the brief shoot they parted, only to get back together again briefly before splitting up for good. It was a painful time for Nick, but just as he had used his emotion over parting from Jenny Wright to inspire his performance in *Moonstruck,* he incorporated the pain into his role as a tragic alcoholic in *Leaving Las Vegas.*

Yet the following March, Kristen was his date at the Academy Award ceremonies, only a few days before his surprise marriage to actress Patricia Arquette.

Nick later recalled their time together and their parting, telling *Playboy* magazine contributing editor David Sheff, 'The split-up was a difficult one; it had been a tumultuous relationship. But it was also a sweet relationship. We just weren't right for each other. I was a lot older than she was. I had to get up early and she liked to sleep in like you do when you're 18. She wanted to go to nightclubs. So there was a sadness when we had to split up and that sadness went into the movie, because the break-up came around the same time. A lot of the time when I was saying, "I love you" I was just heartbroken.'

He revealed that the parting also drove him to seek counselling. He said, 'I was going through a difficult break-up. I loved the person and although the relationship wasn't working, I couldn't leave. I knew it wasn't right for me. I knew we were both unhappy. It was like we kept clinging to each other and it had to come to an end. So I went to therapy.'

Kristen was sad about the split and felt betrayed by Nick's abrupt and unexpected wedding. But she soon found consolation in the arms of another superstar, Leonardo DiCaprio. She said, 'When Nicolas ran off to marry another woman, I was at the lowest point in my life. Leo was a knight in shining armour at a very difficult period in my life. Soon, Leo was there for me every step of the way.'

Nick's worries did not diminish as Weston developed into a bright, inquisitive child with a mop of reddish-blond hair and piercing blue eyes. Nick continued to take stock of his ever-increasing responsibilities to him — and to himself. He started looking back at some of the bizarre stunts he had carried out in his films, and ahead to roles which would present a positive image to the world.

He admitted, 'I've slowed down. I'm a "worrywort" now. It brings a new kind of emotion, a depth that wasn't there before. I'm always aware that what I do could affect my son. Being a father has had more of an impact on my life than anything else before or since. There's been a lot of press about how strange and bizarre I am. I used to feel great about being described as having strange and bizarre tastes. I tried to cultivate that image for a long time but then I became a father and that changed my outlook on everything. I think the most positive thing a person can do is have children. It made me look at my life in a completely new perspective; it humbled me quite a bit. You might even say it tamed me, because why would I want my son to think that his father is a maniac? My son, Weston, is the most important thing in the world to me. He's three now, and every time I make a wish on a birthday cake or whatever, it's always about him. I just wish everything for my son. There's nothing more important than that. Not my career, acting or anything else.

'I know this sounds like a cliché, and kind of romantic, but I'm 30 now and a parent. I suddenly became worried about my community. I don't want anything to happen to people I love. I used to feel like an irritant, or almost like an anarchist, or someone who really didn't care about his brethren. But now, more than ever, I feel like I am one of us. That's probably about the biggest change that I've gone through and I think it has to do with becoming a father.

'Making the transition into parenthood has given me this wealth of emotion that has really changed me, even in terms of acting. And my son's really made me aware that the weight of everything I do can directly affect him. Even things in my past. I'm aware people will say to him, "Your dad was a wild man," or "How come he ate a bug?" It gives you a tremendous responsibility and makes you think, do I need to be a role model?'

For years, Nick had nightmares about one incident that happened when he was with Weston as a toddler, when he was trying to protect him from anything bad. He recalled the incident in 1995, saying, 'I accidentally ran over a black cat once in my truck, and my boy was with me, and, you know, I didn't want him to see it. The cat lurched in front of my wheel and from the rear-view mirror I could see it jumping in the street and, like, doing all kinds of flips and stuff and I thought, I don't want Weston to see a mangled cat. He was only two. It's too much, it's too violent. That image came back to me last night. I was sleeping and there was that cat jumping in the rear-view mirror again.'

Although Weston gradually learned what his father did for a living, Nick did not let him see any of his films when he was little. He said, 'I just wanted him to have as normal a life as I could provide, considering I'm no longer with his mother. I didn't want the film image confusing things with the real person. I have friends who are children of actors who have said, "I saw my father get shot off a horse when I was five and I remember being really upset and thinking Daddy's dead." So I just don't want to take any chances. I'll wait till he's a little older.' He expected the first of his movies the child would watch to be *Raising Arizona*.

Perhaps it was because of his self-proclaimed new maturity that he wrote to *Playboy* magazine protesting that they had used unauthorised nude pictures of actress Uma Thurman, taken when she was on holiday in the Caribbean.

He said he was delighted by his recent *Playboy* interview with David Sheff, but added, 'It is therefore extremely upsetting to me that *Playboy* chose to run unauthorised photos of Uma Thurman. Your pictorials have always been presented with quality and taste. As you stated in the layout, you are not fans of this type of photography, which leads me to wonder why the magazine chose to be so blatantly hypocritical.'

The editors replied, 'Here's our thinking about Uma: when someone so celebrated and camera-worthy puts herself on display in public, it's disingenuous for her to be shocked that there were interested photographers in place. Didn't she give up her privacy when she chose a public beach in St Barts instead of a zillion cosier spots that were available to her?'

When Nick married Patricia, he also acquired a stepson, Enzo, who was two years older than Weston. Patricia had custody, and he treated them both the same way, calling them both his 'sons' and not making any distinction between them. As if to emphasise that the four of them were a family, he wore next to his wedding band a gold ring set with three coloured stones, one for Patricia, one for Weston and one for Enzo.

Nick could be an indulgent parent. He was photographed taking the boys on a shopping spree at a Toys 'R' Us near the castle, driving up in a pick-up truck. 'You guys in the mood to shop?' he was overheard asking as he pushed them into the store in a trolley. 'You can have anything you want. Anything. I'll roll the cart and you do the shopping.' A little while later they had spent $1,000 of his money on assorted goodies.

At times, having four parents involved in bringing up the two boys led to some complicated living arrangements. For many years, after they were married Patricia still kept her own home in Laurel Canyon, about five miles from the castle, which she shared with Enzo, and she and Nick did not live together full time, although they seemed to be very happy when they were with each other. A friend told *Globe* magazine, 'Patricia spends the night at Nick's house two nights a week. The next morning she goes home to her own house. Nicolas visits Patricia and her son several times a week at her house, but then drives to his place. They seem more like soul-mates than husband and wife. It seems like Hollywood's oddest marriage but something seems to be working for them. When they go out together they talk a lot, seem interested in what the other has to say and appear to appreciate being together.'

Wherever Nick was laying his head at night, he took Patricia to the 1997 Oscars, where he presented the Best Actress Academy Award to Frances McDormand for her role in *Fargo*. 'Christina was pleased that Nick and Patricia, who still love each other very much, were able to share the big night as a couple,' said one source. Nick told a friend, 'I love Patty and Christina in different ways. One is my wife and the other is the mother of my child. My son needs me and I'm going to be there for him 100 per cent. This may look strange to other people, but this is my life and I don't care what they think.'

Nick and Patricia were also spotted hanging out at The Nest, a trendy shop on the corner of Clay and Fillmore in San Francisco, which sells exclusive linens. But at the same time, *Globe* claimed they were consulting a mystic for help with their relationship.

A few weeks after the Oscars, Nick whisked Christina and Weston to Paris for a spring vacation. 'As Nick, Christina and Weston cavorted on the steps of the City of Science and Industry museum, they looked like the happiest family in the world,' an onlooker told the *National Enquirer*. Nick also made sure the family spent the weekend in style. They stayed at the city's lavish and legendary Ritz Hotel, which only a few months later would be the site for Diana, Princess of Wales' fateful last dinner with her lover, Dodi Fayed, whose father owns the fabled establishment on the Place Vendôme.

While in Paris, Nick appeared to be the epitome of the faithful and dutiful father. He eventually explained what was behind the rumours about Patricia and him splitting up.

'I tend to be at times more sensitive than a lot of fathers,' he told Ruthe Stein of the *San Francisco Chronicle*. 'I worry a lot. I'm always concerned that Weston's OK — phoning to make sure he's come home. All I can say is that some people want to take a good thing and turn it into a bad thing. Sometimes I'm working late, and Weston has to go to bed, so it's easier for me to just go over there and have dinner and say, "Hi, how was your day?" than to keep him up all night and bring him over to my house.' Glossing over the initial animosity surrounding Christina's paternity suit and his early reluctance to be a father, he insisted, 'We felt it was important to maintain a friendly relationship. Patricia and I understand that there are other people in each of our children's lives.'

Both the women in his life, as well as Enzo, joined him to cheer for Weston when he was entered in a martial arts competition at Beverly Hills High School in 1999. By then, Weston was a blue belt. His proud father, who videotaped the event, held up his hand in a victory salute when Weston won a medal. Other parents at the event were astonished at how friendly and relaxed all three adults were. 'Not many wives like their husband's former flames, let alone spend the day with them,' an astonished onlooker said.

As Nick and Weston both grew older, Nick admitted that his son — both his sons — had begun to influence his career choices, both in terms of the scripts he considered and how he approached his roles. Weston, beginning to understand what his father did for a living, also visited him on film sets from time to time. During one visit, when Christina escorted him to the set of *Face/Off* while he was in the middle of an interview with Larissa MacFarquhar for *Premiere* magazine, Nick said simply, 'He's my sunshine.' At one point, Weston was up for a role in the film, but Nick changed his mind because of the dangers of having so many guns on the set. Even though they were fakes, he was always acutely aware of the tragic death of martial arts actor Brandon Lee, son of kung-fu legend Bruce Lee, one of Nick's idols, because of a blast from a blank bullet. Although he recognised the need for weaponry in action films, he refused to pose for publicity posters carrying a gun. MacFarquhar described Weston as, 'A shaggy-haired little blond boy who looks like he's stepped out of some baroque cherub painting, or like one of those naked kids climbing rocks on the cover of the Led Zeppelin album *House of the Holy*.' She also noted that Nick addressed Christina as 'Honey'.

When Nick made *City of Angels*, playing an angel who becomes human because he falls in love with a heart surgeon, he said he drew on Weston's sense of wonder and innocence at all the new things children experience to help him portray himself as someone who had become human as a grown man and had to discover all at once the everyday experiences the people around him had learned over a lifetime. Even choosing to make the dark and threatening film *8MM*, a chilling descent into the depths of pornography and snuff movies, he said was partly inspired by the terror he felt as a father about the dangers and evils facing people in the modern world.

'Any parent knows it opens up huge doors of feeling. I became a responsible citizen when I became a father,' he reiterated. 'I became a member of the community. I care more about people than I ever did before becoming a father. The differences between my philosophies before and after I became a father are immense. Literally, I was like, "What do you mean, they're putting razor blades in apples on Hallowe'en?" Before, I couldn't care less. Now I'm a wreck about it. When I became a father, I started watching the news and getting really outraged by some of the things I heard — young people getting kidnapped, brutalised, mutilated and murdered. Again and again. And I would get angry and frustrated. I was powerless but I felt like I wanted to do something.'

Being a dad also made him aware of the risks he might face, and reinforced his conviction that he did not need to do his own stunts. 'I'm a dad and I want to be around to see my kid grow up.'

He confessed, 'I've slowed down since I got into this business. I'm not as mischievous as I used to be. The parenting aspect of my life has matured me to play more people-orientated roles. Now I'm looking to other roles that will give me the chance to project greater dignity. I've become less obsessed with my work and I'm less analytic than I was in the days of *Rumble Fish* and *Birdy*, when I was 19 and had raw nerve endings and I was spewing out all this emotion without much thought. Becoming a father made me interested in scripts where I could present a positive image. I've learned a lot from watching my kid. He's given me a whole new library of feelings internally. I've never felt that kind of love before and his birth has, by some definition, given me the feeling of love.

'He makes me worry a lot and I try not to obsess about the myriad of things that can go wrong when you're away working and you're not there at all times to watch and supervise. At the same time, he has given me so much. I've felt a whole new level of love which, frankly, was non-existent until he came along. I have two kids to take care of.'

By the time Nick was first talked about for the off-and-on project of *Superman,* the boys were old enough to have very firm opinions about the idea. They were not keen, but said that if he went ahead with it he had to be a strictly traditional Man of Steel, right down to the trademark red underpants worn over blue tights.

'The boys are not too happy with the prospect of Dad becoming Superman,' he admitted in 1998 to Canadian journalist Louis B Hobson of the *Calgary Sun.* 'They want to be Superman and have been playing superheroes for months now. I'm grateful to my sons because without them I wouldn't have had the vision to choose this project. Being a father has mellowed me in real life. Now it's time to mellow on screen, too.'

He laughed, 'You know, we Coppolas are very competitive! Weston wears his own Superman costume and thinks he could do it himself.'

Weston insisted that if he was going to do *Superman,* he had to wear the traditional outfit. 'I was afraid of wearing the red underwear because I could never understand why he wears the underwear on the outside,' he told Lawrence Grobel of *Movieline* magazine. 'I took some pictures without the underwear and showed them to my son and he said, "Where's the underwear on the outside?" I said, "I'm not going to wear it." "Why — are you embarrassed?" "Yeah." "No, Superman has to have that." '

Shortly after Nick and Patricia were married, there were false rumours that she was pregnant. In fact, they had both decided that they already had enough on their plates and put off plans to increase their brood. When a television interviewer asked him about plans for children in 1997, he replied, 'Not right away. Our hands are pretty full and it's as important to be as devoted as we can be to the kids that are here now.'

He also explained that as his career blossomed, he was finding it more difficult to spare enough time for Weston. 'I'm away on location, which has been a lot recently,' he said in 1998. 'I can't be there as a father and our relationship has lost some closeness because of that. It's just something that I can only hope to rekindle later in life.'

Unlike many actors, who try to keep their children away from the business, he said he would support the boys if they wanted to follow in his footsteps. He said, 'It's actually a secret dream of mine that my sons will go into the business, but I would never impose the business on them. I don't understand why actors keep saying they don't want their children in the business. It's been so exciting and rewarding for me. I think those people who try to discourage their children from becoming actors are afraid of being upstaged by them.'

A couple of weeks later, the *National Enquirer* reported that his marriage was on the rocks again. 'It's all over bar the fighting between Nick and Patricia — and he's heartbroken,' a friend said. 'Nick and Patricia have never even lived under the same roof. Patricia is sick and tired of the sham marriage and she's told Nick that.' Another insider said the couple had had a blazing row at the Château Marmont hotel near Sunset Strip when they went for a weekend getaway to air their problems. 'Patty wanted a total change in the marriage. Her ultimatum was either move in with me and have a normal relationship or call the whole thing quits. But the weekend turned into a horrible shouting match.'

Anita Talbot, gossip columnist for *The Beverly Hills Chronicle*, also reported their marriage to be in trouble, with Patricia wanting them to live together and have a baby.

Nevertheless, the couple did attend the Long Beach Grand Prix together, as guests of the PacWest racing team, who had a luxurious 53-foot, gleaming silver mobile home instead of a traditional hospitality tent. Young country singing sensation LeAnn Rimes was another guest. During the afternoon, Nick was relaxed and happy to mix with the crowds. He threw an autographed T-shirt to one fan, Victoria Peters. Her friend, Phyllis Forshay, retreated to a toilet, took her own shirt off and gave it to Peters, who got Nick to autograph it, too.

Less than a month later, Janet Charlton claimed in the *Star* that Patricia was hinting to friends that she might, indeed, be pregnant.

CHAPTER TEN

BASKING IN THE SUNSHINE TRILOGY

Fists flying, Nick laid into young actor Pat O'Bryan until his party pal Charlie Sheen dragged him away. New father Nick had been celebrating with friends, including Cary Elwes and James Wilder, in the exclusive Bar One club all evening, when O'Bryan, who had appeared in *976-Evil* and *Relentless*, arrived with a brunette on his arm. When the grinning girl pulled up her blouse to show off her assets, Nick was not amused and made some snide comments, according to witnesses, prompting O'Bryan to spring to her defence.

The spat briefly erupted into a free-for-all until Sheen dragged Nick away. Even then he and O'Bryan exchanged more punches as he headed for the door, and the row only stopped when Nick was bundled into a limousine and sent home.

Nick was going through a time of transition in early 1991. He and Christina had had a tumultuous relationship after the birth of Weston; although he already loved the boy, he was not ready to settle down. And despite the cult success of *Wild at Heart*, once again there were no great movie-makers hammering on his door.

Perhaps it was to ease the tension that he agreed to accept a different type of job — to take a road trip into the heart of America, à la Jack Kerouac, and write about it for *Details* magazine. He was accompanied by an old friend, Jeff Levine, whom he described as 'about 36, part dog, part bank robber, part 15-year-old man', and who would become Nick's partner when he created his own production company a few years later.

He explained the rationale behind his decision to take off in Jeff's white Ford Taurus — an utterly middle-aged, middle-class car totally unlike the sporty performance vehicles he preferred — on the journey from Los Angeles to New Orleans.

'I've been in one place for two long,' he wrote. 'I'm just sitting here in Los Angeles getting soft. Twenty-seven years old, balding, and without a shred of inspiration. My representatives tell me to stay in town so I can meet people for jobs. I've been doing that for a year. Petting my cat, thinking about exercise, never reading a good script. I haven't even had a decent dream in months. I keep flashing on *Easy Rider*. That movie made me go out and buy a motorcycle. I keep thinking about Kerouac's *On the Road*. That book made me want to discover America. I keep humming the Beatles' "Why Don't We Do It in the Road?". That song made me once have sex in the centre of La Brea and Melrose. The road compels me to escape, to listen to Lynard Skynard's "Freebird" and fly. New people. Adventure. Change. I've never driven cross country before and I could die without ever doing it. It's time to go.'

The trip got off to an inauspicious start. They had driven only a few miles and were still in Los Angeles' congested freeway system when the car's transmission blew. They had it towed to a garage and rented a gold Lincoln Town Car, even more middle-aged and middle-class, to replace it.

They headed eastbound on the Interstate 10 freeway, grandly named 'The Christopher Columbus Transcontinental Highway', which stretches from the Pacific Ocean at Santa Monica, California, to the Atlantic at Jacksonville, Florida, stopping first at Cabazon near Palm Springs, where giant models of dinosaurs, a green brontosaurus and a grey tyrannosaurus rex are landmarks at a truck stop. They checked out a bizarre museum inside the belly of the brontosaurus, before pulling over at a bar called Gabby's.

Here, Nick experienced the downside of fame and described how he deals with it. He wrote in his diary, 'I was getting spotted left and right. It turned into a blur for me and I went into tunnel vision. This is something I do when I know there will be a lot of people asking questions. The only way to get through a night of talking about yourself without getting irate is to mentally brace for it. Fame is not normal and it is not always fun. This was a shit-kicker bar. Jeff was growing nervous about one guy who kept shouting how ugly I was.'

However, the owner made them welcome and gave them free drinks, and Nick ended up giving her the purple velvet jacket he was wearing. Nick was already more mellow than when he had left LA; when women started showing more than their bras in the bar, he was unconcerned.

This was at the time of Desert Storm and Nick wrote, 'The troops coming home is a big event in the desert. The local women have been taking their shirts off and showing the soldiers their tits and the men have been giving them cases of beer. Is this an American phenomenon or does it happen everywhere? I think most men admire tits. Therefore the craving is international. However, the display, I imagine, is strictly American.'

Nick and Jeff left the Interstate 10 for the famed Route 66 further north and the following evening found themselves in another bar, this time The Kingman Club in Kingman, Arizona. Once again he was recognised, but by someone who recognised a character, not an actor, and seemed to have difficulty telling them apart.

Nick was sipping on a bourbon when he noticed a tough-looking customer staring at him, and said, 'Hi.' The man responded, 'You look like that guy in *Raising Arizona*.'

Nick wrote, 'I didn't want to lie to those eyes that looked like black steel. "I am him." I overheard the bartender mutter, "Bullshit." I held out my hand to Black Eyes and introduced myself, but he wouldn't shake. He refused to tell me his name. Maybe he was running from something.

' "What happened to the baby? What was his name?" "Nathan Arizona." "Yeah, what happened to Nathan?" "After kidnapping him? I gave him back." "Then you married a cop?" "Yeah, Holly Hunter." "Why'd you marry a cop? I hate cops. Cops are assholes." "I didn't really marry a cop. It was a movie, you know — make believe." '

The man, a Mexican, said he had been beaten up twice by police, then suddenly added, 'Hey, I don't care if you're a movie star. I dig ditches. Been shovelling shit for 20 years and I'm proud.' He then warmed to Nick, bought him a drink and said, 'I got a four-year-old son. He laughs a lot when he seen your movie.' 'I'm glad,' said Nick.

The next day, approaching Seligman, Arizona, at an altitude of about 7,000 feet, they ran into a spring blizzard in the middle of the desert and had to slow to 25mph because of bad visibility. They found yet another bar, the Black Cat, for a brief pause. Back on the road, they were slowed to 10mph but eventually made it safely to Camp Verde and Bowlers bar.

Nick revealed his secret for bar crawling. 'I know drinking is out of style,' he said. 'But I have learned that when I do drink, just saying to myself, "I am sleek and self-contained," spares me many problems. If you can function like a tiger on a hunt while indulging, you deserve the utmost respect. I can't stand a sloppy drunk.'

On to Socorro, New Mexico — El Camino Motel — then to the White Sands National Monument, near Alamogordo, site of the first ever thermonuclear explosion, the Trinity Device in 1945. Here the trip became weird. Both men felt claustrophobic because they had been alone together for so long and decided to let their emotions spill over in a fist-fight.

'We hiked to the top of a dune overlooking this white world,' wrote Nick.

Great place for a fight, I thought. The wind was whistling. We were alone. Before I could turn around, Jeff clocked me. It was a cheap shot. He caught me flush on the cheekbone under my eye but I didn't go down. I have always prided myself on my ability to take pain. I staggered back and smiled. "Why not?" I muttered. We went at it. I slugged Jeff in the stomach and he fell like a sack of potatoes. That was it. He was winded and the fight was over. I half-wished he had a little more in him but it was just as well. I didn't really want to hurt him. I tasted blood in my mouth.'

Back on the road with Nick at the wheel they drove past a number of prisons, with road signs warning against picking up hitch-hikers. Nick fell into a dreamlike stupor and fantasised about being pulled over by convict killers who wanted to hijack the car.

After the loneliness of the desert, they welcomed their arrival in Austin, the capital of Texas, on a Saturday night. They were ready to party and hit Maggie Mae's, which Nick had discovered shooting *Fire Birds*, and where he hoped to meet up with the pilot friends he had made back then. He sank several drinks bought by fans before leaving the club and bumping into his pals, EJ Mikeska and Bill Lee.

'We were all pretty astonished to see each other,' he said. 'They were throwing a going away party for some of their fellow soldiers. Somehow I find myself in a limousine and wind up at the Yellow Rose. If ever you want to see the finest burlesque, it's here. At the end of the night, I bring the party back to my hotel and find myself paying for every room on my credit card. That was not very sleek and self-contained of me.'

Finally, Nick returned to another old haunt, New Orleans, where they went on an all-night pub crawl, drinking 'hand grenades' — made from 190-proof grain alcohol — in the Tropical Isle Bar before hitting The Dungeon, 'a bar that looks like Aleister Crowley's inner sanctum', according to Nick. The next morning saw them downing chicory coffee and beignets at the Café du Monde before dumping the car and flying home.

A few months later, Nick's steady drinking practice stood him in good stead when he became involved in a drinking contest with actor Kiefer Sutherland, who was then on the rebound after his *Pretty Woman* star fiancée Julia Roberts dumped him virtually at the altar, fleeing to Ireland with his best friend Jason Patric just days before they were due to wed. Nick and Sutherland threw back tequila shots in Trinity restaurant while other customers cheered them on, according to *Star* magazine. Nick declared himself the winner after Sutherland staggered out after downing a dozen drinks.

Once back from his road trip, Nick finally found a script that appealed to him, *Honeymoon in Vegas,* about a New York private eye who flies to Las Vegas with his fiancée, only to lose her at the poker table to a playboy. Sarah Jessica Parker played the fiancée, and James Caan the older gambler with Mafia connections who won her.

Getting the part was far from plain sailing. Despite his long and varied career, and the fact that, on the face of it, *Honeymoon* was another oddball film, Nick did not automatically fit the bill.

Writer/director Andrew Bergman asked for — and got — a screen test. He said, 'Well, Nick wasn't exactly what I had pictured for it. I'd never met him; my image of him was from these movies, that he'd be a very "out there" sort of guy. But he had a passion about it. He came in and read and he was this guy.'

Nick himself recalled, 'When I decided I wanted to be in comedies, I had to screen test to get into *Honeymoon in Vegas* because people thought, here's the guy in the snake jacket with the wooden hand. He's crazy, he's not going to be funny. It was a bit of a sell. My agent even said it was a long-shot. Rick Moranis would've fit better. There wasn't a whole lot in my work that would suggest I could play this everyday, ordinary guy. People have told me they were expecting someone who's really way out there. I like to read a lot. And look at paintings. I don't have any athletic abilities. I really sit at home and scribble in my notebook. It's important for people not to know the actor so they can still imagine what the character can be like. You can stop being interesting.'

In *Honeymoon*, Nick plays Jack Singer, a New York private detective who specialises in divorce cases. He is madly in love with teacher Betsy Nolan, but does not want to marry her because of a death-bed promise that he will never tie the knot that his mother — a crusty cameo role by Ann Bancroft — had extracted four years earlier. When Betsy gives him an ultimatum he finally plucks up the courage to propose and suggests flying off to Las Vegas to do the deed. Their arrival coincides with a convention of sky-diving Elvis impersonators, whose antics add a surreal touch to the already outré gambling mecca. Caan's Tommy Korman character believes Betsy is the reincarnation of his beloved wife and is determined to have her. He sets up a 'friendly' poker game, takes Jack for $60,000 — and accepts Betsy for a platonic weekend on the lush Hawaiian island of Kauai as payment of the debt. Jack gives chase and after a series of mishaps ends up winning his love back when he accidentally finds himself wearing an Elvis outfit and reluctantly jumping out of a plane.

Nick enjoyed the unusual, for him, opportunity of playing someone who was relatively normal. He said, 'The film is the closest I've been to playing the real me. In fact, this is one of the only times I've worked with my own voice. I also related to the romance in the story — and the fear of commitment. My character must try to get his fiancée back and he's forced to do things that no amount of charm by his rival is going to top. I mean, this guy would die for his girlfriend. He nearly does. I would do the same.'

Parker admitted being nervous before she started working with Nick, because of his wild-man reputation. She said, 'I was very intimidated at the prospect of working with him because I had made all these assumptions about him based on his work. I though he was going to be very odd and inaccessible. But I found that he was really warm and funny and easy to work with. After they yell "Action", that's when you get this raving lunatic. Nick's choices were so funny that one take was basically wasted because I'd be laughing at what he was doing. You don't understand where he comes from, because when you meet him, he's a fairly normal person. But something happens in the work environment for him, I guess, that is a catalyst for letting us into the deep recesses of his peculiarities.'

She added, 'The presence he creates on the screen is so different from his personality. I think his true nature is really different from his roles. Before I worked with him, I was expecting someone rather eccentric and dark and brooding and perhaps dangerous. There are so many normal qualities to him, but he does care a lot about his work, which also defies that bad-boy image. You wouldn't think that someone who had that image would be that cultured and analytical and so well-read. He has a great aesthetic sensibility. I would imagine that a lot of people think he's strange and maybe not particularly social. But in fact I found him to be quite the opposite — very accessible, very normal and a loving and devoted father. He's very warm, very lovable, like he is in the movie. He's playing normal in extraordinary circumstances, as opposed to extraordinary in ordinary circumstances. Nick is more of an Everyman. Nick is very secure in his sexuality and manliness. I don't think he has to prove anything as a man. He doesn't use that bravado some people use. That's appealing. And it's not calculated on his part.'

Nick being Nic, of course, could not resist playing even a 'normal' character in an extreme way.

Bergman explained, 'I have a tendency to italicise words in the script for emphasis and there were times when Nick would take the italicised words and just knock them over the fence in ways I never expected. Then he'd say, "Was that too far over the top?" And I'd say, "If it's over the top I'll let you know. There's a lot of room at the top here."

Nick also acknowledged his appreciation of the italics, saying: 'That was my first chance to bring the wacky behaviour that I developed in *Vampire's Kiss* to a commercial form. I like the scene at the airport where I'm trying to get to the ticket counter and I can't do it quickly enough and I sort of go off. Andrew Bergman uses italics and I really got in synch with his italics — when to pound, when not to pound and when to go for it.'

The film was shot on location in Las Vegas before moving to New York and then Hawaii. Although he did not know it at the time, the Nevada city was going to have a major impact on his film career. During this shoot, however, he hated the place, especially when he fell into the temptation of gambling. About a month into the Vegas shoot, journalists were invited on to the set and Nick told one of them, 'When I first came here, it was kind of novel. By the second week, I was climbing the walls wanting to get out. It's a 24-hour circus and there's no escape. The hotels are designed so you get lost trying to get to the elevator, just so you have to gamble. It's all about manipulation. There's a fascinating understanding of human psychology. Did I win or lose? I actually did OK — I lost about $600 in one month of living here. So it could have been a lot worse. Of course, if I told you what I had to do to get back my $600 ... I was playing roulette. And I was betting on red. Isn't that wimpy?'

He had not learned his lesson, however, and continued to buy chips for a while, sticking with simple bets on red. This was because there was a rainbow over the desert one day and a friend of his decided it was an omen — red for rainbow. They stood at the table chanting: 'Rainbow, rainbow,' superstitiously hoping to boost their odds.

The ploy did not work. Years later, Nick admitted, 'When you're living in Las Vegas for a couple of months, it's impossible to walk by the tables and not throw something down to see what happens. The whole casino is geared up so you do that. You can't find where you want to go, you can't find exits easily, the rooms are pumped with oxygen so you can't sleep. You're always up and you go downstairs and you gamble. I was making small bets — $50 on red or black — but wasn't getting off on them. So I started going for the bigger numbers. It made Sarah Jessica Parker a little nervous. But I wasn't the guy at the baccarat table betting a million dollars. At one point, it got up to about $10,000. She was getting ill. I lost 10 grand and I couldn't get it back. I went up to my room and ran on the treadmill for about an hour so I could feel better about myself. Then I set my alarm for half an hour before the set call. I went down to the table and bet 20 grand and got all my money back. Then I stopped. I never bet again. I didn't like the way it made me feel. The only thing that's more poignant than being a winner is the feeling of being a loser.' If he had lost the 20, he went on, 'I would have gone to 40, 80, 160 — until I got it back. I was going to get my money back.'

Parker vividly remembered that evening as well, saying, 'I stood there and he lost such an enormous amount of money that it made me ill. My hands were shaking. I had to leave.'

Nick's other vivid memory of that stay in Las Vegas was hanging out with the Elvis imitators. He said, 'It was a little scary because they never dropped the accent. I think they saw me as one of their own, and I'm not sure whether I like that or not. No offence, but I can't really see myself being another person for my entire life. I mean, there was a guy there, a very sweet guy named Dave Elvis. We had a nice cigar when we finished working and liked him, but he never dropped the accent. "Helll-ooo, Nicky, you did a hell of a mean Elvis in *Wild at Heart*. When you finish here today, whaddya say we talk a little bit about E." I'm really gonna wrap here and go have a beer and talk about Elvis with these guys? I mean, it would have been interesting, but wrong movie.'

He found it ironic that Elvis should have been such an icon in two films as different as *Wild at Heart* and *Honeymoon in Vegas*, and laughed, 'Yeah, Elvis. He's haunting me. Just lately, I seem to have become the reluctant authority on Elvis Presley, because these two movies in a row are both connected to him.'

One sight-gag that Bergman was keen to include did not work out — probably for the best. One of private detective Singer's clients in New York was a man who was convinced his wife was having an affair with former heavyweight boxing champion Mike Tyson. Although the client was obviously deluded, the original script included a scene at the end in which Tyson walked through a Las Vegas hotel lobby with the woman. Tyson, however, was not interested and the idea was dropped. Bergman must have breathed a sigh of gratitude at that when, days before the film started shooting, Miss Black Rhode Island, Desiree Washington, accused Tyson of raping her in a Minneapolis hotel room. Tyson has always insisted the sex was consensual, but he was convicted of rape and served three years of a six-year prison sentence.

The cast and crew were on good terms and there were rumours that Nick and Parker had become more than friends. She had been dating John F Kennedy Jr, and was said to have set her cap at Nick and hoped to make the late President's handsome son jealous. Nick was certainly available; he and Christina finally split up during the filming of *Honeymoon*, though they have always remained close for Weston's sake.

A friend of Parker's later told the *National Enquirer* that Parker and Kennedy, who died in a tragic plane crash in 1999, had a brief romance before filming started, but that although he had promised to keep in touch he did not.

'She was shooting in Vegas with Nicolas Cage,' said the friend. 'She thought she could regain JFK's affection if she started a romance with Cage. Nicolas fell for Sarah.' When filming moved to New York, she met Kennedy again. The friend added, 'Although John had heard the rumours, he never asked about Nicolas.'

Once the cast and crew escaped to Kauai, where it was so hot that Caan fainted one day, Nick felt the urge to party. It was Hallowe'en and he watched *The Exorcist* on television, after which he decided he needed a less gruesome experience.

'For some reason the word *luau* came to mind,' he said. 'And I just thought, I gotta have a *luau*. I don't know why — maybe to lighten up the vibe I was getting from the movie. We'd been shooting out there for a month and nobody'd really seen any grass skirts or hula dancers.'

So he organised the traditional Hawaiian-style feast, which customarily features a whole roasted pig, cooked on a spit or in a pit dug in the sand. He continued, 'Originally, I wanted the pig on a spit turning around, but for some reason they don't do that — which to me is a crime against the whole spirit of the *luau*. So I said, "Put him on a surfboard and rush him in." And he was surfin'. He was hanging 20.'

Honeymoon in Vegas was the first of what Nick was later to call his 'Sunshine Trilogy'. He was inspired to turn to comedy in part by his maternal grandmother, Louise Vogelsang. She saw him in *Zandalee* and asked, 'Nicky, why don't you make something that me and my friends can go to and laugh?'

Nick recalled, 'My grandmother told me I needed to do a romantic comedy and not play a crazy man for a change. Normally if someone told me that, I'd have said, "Ahh, you don't know what you're talking about." But it was my grandmother and I thought about it and I realised she was right.'

His other influence was very different — Jim Morrison, lead singer of The Doors, who died of heart failure in the bath in 1971, aged just 27.

Nick said, 'I remember I saw Jim Morrison in an old TV interview once and he was really drugged up on something, but he said, "I haven't done a song yet that conveyed pure happiness." And I looked at him and thought, you know what? You were great, but you hadn't done that — and you could be really pretentious. And then I thought, am I being pretentious? I knew I could be funny but I didn't want to be funny. I wanted to be James Dean.

'I started to think about my own career. I love the films I've been in but they weren't what you'd call happy films. And I thought maybe I'd better learn from this and try to do something a bit more sunny, and get out of that complex, angst-ridden state that I had been in so many movies that I've played in. I didn't want to be a comedian. I was always avoiding the comedy side of my nature. Now I think, well, wait a minute. There's nothing wrong with making people laugh. So right now I feel like I'd like to do more comedies. I feel like I've done the dark side of things for ten years now. Sure I've made comedies in the past but they've been about things like kidnapping children. So I'm about to step into a new suit and try something a little funnier and lighter. I think I'd like to do more sunny movies from now on.'

When he made *Honeymoon,* Nick began reflecting on the image he had created for himself, and realised that some people could not see past the roles he had played. To some extent, he blamed the shortsightedness of audiences who forgot that actors are supposed to play characters which are convincing, however contrived they may be, but he also acknowledged his own role in cultivating their opinions.

'I'm fascinated by what people expect me to be like,' he said. 'I guess it's because if you play a far-out character and you really commit to it sometimes, people can't see past the snakeskin jacket or the wooden hand. Doesn't anybody remember there's such a thing as acting? That isn't me. I don't go home with plastic fangs in my mouth; I don't go home with my snakeskin jacket on; I leave my wooden hand on the set. I kept thinking, you don't know me. Those are characters. Those are things I like to create. I don't have a wooden hand, I'm absolutely terrified of bugs. Do you really think I play myself all the time?

'I never thought that the things I did were going to become stories that people would talk about for ever. I suppose I did cultivate the outlaw image and I admit I did work hard at it; it wasn't an accident. I'm calming down now. The image is one thing but the man is another. I've done an undoable thing; I've painted myself into a corner with these crazy, outlaw characters and it's become a nuisance. I've given myself a label that gets in the way when a producer or a director is casting a part. I was in some ways a wild man, yes, I admit it, but I'm a lot of other things, too, and I can't just throw water on the wild orchid all the time, I gotta feed the other plants in my garden as well. I realised I'd better play in a romantic comedy and show them this is acting, that I'm not this person. I'm trying to create different characters, because that's what I think an actor should do.

'I've always tried to change the characters I've played. But it seems to have backfired, creating this mysterious identity, so people don't really understand who I am. I guess they want to promote the wild-guy image because people want to be wild but they can't because they have to come home after work and watch TV and drink a beer — and wish they could hijack an aircraft or do an Elvis number or go to jail and get out and be a wild-man character ... I'm trying to let go of that now.'

He also later confessed that he had a much more mundane reason for wanting to make a big, mainstream studio film — money. *Wild at Heart* had won him artistic respect but no big roles to pay the bills. He said, 'It was only when I almost went bankrupt that I decided I had better do something. Let's say I came close to bankruptcy. I needed to pay the mortgage.' Later, he confirmed to the *Knight Ridder* news service, 'I'd ask myself, why is this person making it happen when I can't make it happen? I hadn't gone bankrupt — OK, I was only three weeks away from it, maybe, when I basically made the decision to go with the big studios.'

Ironically, a couple of years earlier he had laughed off the notion of worrying about cash-flow. He told *Playboy* magazine, 'I don't look at my bills. I try not to worry or think about money. I just keep spending until I get a phone call from my business manager telling me to stop. Even then, I have difficulty doing that. I like to purchase things and not worry about it. I find that money problems are too big a headache for me to think about so I wait until that phone call comes.'

Nick acknowledged his increasing maturity, facing up to his financial responsibilities and the pleasures and problems of fatherhood, and believed it was reflected in his new movie. But he could not resist moments of his old madness, throwing the occasional outrageous comment into conversations while laughing at himself.

He jokingly told Steve Pond of *Us* magazine in 1992, 'I feel like I'm cultivating a kind of calm and wisdom in my older age. I'm turning into more of a traditionalist and less of a deluded romantic, if you will, and I'm looking toward a functional family structure. I am not looking toward squalour and squander, I am not looking towards felonious assault with meat ... I don't know what that means.

'I think this movie is more accessible than some of the other movies I've made, but it's still a good balance,' he added. 'It maintains an off-beat charm that I like. The difference in *Vegas* is that I'm the sort of normal anchor surrounded by all this craziness. Usually, I'm the crazy guy surrounded by all the normal people. You can be extreme because what's happening is so frustrating and so alarming. That kind of jealous, paranoid frustration is a gas to play. I think with those other movies I made in the past, I was still very angry, still a rebellious spirit. I started in films when I was 17 and I wanted to get in touch with the younger, angrier audience. I remember when I saw *Moonstruck* for the first time I felt bad about myself. I felt I had sold out somehow. Now I see the movie and I think it's beautiful. I think I've actually matured into it. *Moonstruck* and *Honeymoon in Vegas* were made for an older, wiser audience. I needed to grow into understanding those characters. Directly after *Moonstruck* I made *Vampire's Kiss* to get back to that younger, angrier audience again. Not too many people saw it. I'm not angry any more and I guess I've mellowed with age.'

By the time he was 28 and publicising *Honeymoon in Vegas*, he had also matured enough to respect London dress codes, unlike when he was promoting *Vampire's Kiss*. *Time Out* writer Julia Maloof almost swooned when she met him in the River Room Restaurant at the Savoy. She gushed, 'Over 6ft tall, he projects that potentially fatal combination of appealing little-boy-lost quality and a disquieting magnetism. His classy herring-bone suit covers shoulders broad enough to chew on, his eyes are a dreamy blue and he flashes a slow-burning smile that could break hearts at 20 paces. Yes, girls, he is definitely very, very sexy.'

Although everyone concerned with the film was delighted with the finished product, especially as it cost only $20 million, well under the then-average of $26 million, and considering it was shot in expensive locations, Castle Rock Entertainment went to great pains to market it because they were concerned that the potential audience did not know much about it. They released the soundtrack album, featuring new interpretations of Elvis songs by artists including Billy Joel, Willie Nelson, Bono, Jeff Beck and John Mellencamp, three weeks before the movie, to build audience awareness. And they gave it a 'sneak' preview the Saturday before the official opening in August 1992. Sneak previews, surprise showings advertised at the last moment, are aimed at attracting a small but trend-setting audience who will brag about seeing a movie before it is open, and hopefully spread good reports of it in advance of the formal reviews. Castle Rock partner Martin Shafer explained, 'For me, the formula for sneaking a film is relatively simple. When the reality of the film exceeds the perception of it, you should sneak it. If the perception is greater than the reality, don't.'

The week before it opened, all three stars appeared on *The Tonight Show*, hosted by Jay Leno, who had just taken over from legendary presenter Johnny Carson. It is unusual for more than one star to appear on the same show to promote a film.

The film had a charity première at Mann's Chinese Theater in Hollywood, where a parking lot was transformed into a tacky vision of Las Vegas, with fake Greek statues, a wedding chapel and an Elvis shrine for the bar. Some 1,200 guests, including loud-mouthed comedy star Roseanne and her then-husband Tom Arnold, Billy Crystal, Kathleen Turner — who must have forgiven Nick for *Peggy Sue* — and Rob Reiner, joined the film's stars to dine on a buffet of spare ribs, calzone and crab wontons. A clutch of Elvis impersonators from the film were there, as was El Vez, a renowned Mexican Elvis wannabe, who wore a gold lamé suit. Waiters wore white, rhinestone-studded bell-bottomed jumpsuits. The event raised $20,000 for the Coalition for Clean Air. Nick was overheard saying, tongue-in-cheek, that he was 'thinking about moving on to Liberace'.

The Elvis impersonators — or 'Elvi' — were a great success, offering advice to fans of The King who fancied themselves in rhinestones, such as remembering to curl the left side of the lip, never the right, hold the microphone in the left hand, and choose Clairol blue-black hair dye. One of the impersonators, Johnny Baron, disclosed, 'Elvis used to put Band-Aids on his fingers in front of his rings because when he reached out, his fans would try to pull them off. We Elvi don't have to do that.'

A bemused James Caan confessed, 'When I first read the script, quite honestly I didn't believe Elvis impersonators existed.'

And Andrew Bergman said, 'They're ridiculous on one level, but then they strike me as being very brave people. There's something semi-religious about the whole Elvis thing. He's alive. He didn't die. Dare I say it? He's like a Christ symbol. People put on these garments and they become him.'

Most of the critics enjoyed the romp, though some of them seemed surprised at their own reactions. Duane Byrge in *The Hollywood Reporter* liked it almost in spite of himself. He called it a 'generic romance' but added, 'Crafty writer-director and film historian Andrew Bergman has spun out a madcap romantic comedy. While the plotting is disappointingly rudimentary, Bergman's sub-plots and asides are deliciously loony and spruced with hilarious slapstick. Cage's performance, alternately myopic and frenetic, captures the commitment contradictions of many modern males. Parker's bubbly, good-natured performance as the neglected girlfriend is positively winning.'

In *Daily Variety*, Joseph McBride wrote, 'Writer-director Andrew Bergman has a rare talent for intelligently conceived farce. Bergman brings out a goofy "Everyman" appeal in Cage that never lets him alienate the audience even in the character's most obnoxious moments.'

The *Village Voice*'s Daniel Schweiger wrote, 'Bergman's *Honeymoon* is made in escapist heaven, having all the exhilaration of a straight flush with a bodacious babe or hunk at one's side. Cage wins our sympathy while he loses everything, showing a great sense of timing that's been missing since *Valley Girl*. His Singer is a ball of hilarious hysteria, always trying to keep his head and never failing to blow his top.'

'*Honeymoon in Vegas* is a virtually non-stop scream of benign delirium, pop entertainment as revivifying as anything you're likely to see this year,' wrote the reviewer in *The New York Times*. 'Mr Cage is usually an actor who tries to demonstrate that more is more. Not this time. He plays Jack straight, without mannerisms. It's a beautifully disciplined performance that makes possible all of the film's peripheral dividends.'

Influential syndicated critic Roger Ebert wrote, 'There is a cheerfully rising tide of goofiness in Andrew Bergman's *Honeymoon in Vegas* that is typical of his work. Nicolas Cage is one of those actors some people like and others find excessive. I tend to like him, especially when he is consumed by love, as he was in *Moonstruck* and is again here.'

Desson Howe said in the *Washington Post*, 'If *Honeymoon in Vegas* is funny — and it is — it doesn't exactly ring with structural perfection. But with wonderfully bizarre Nicolas Cage scrambling and screaming his way through the proceedings, *Honeymoon* never attempts anything greater than goofy.'

The *Los Angeles Reader*, on the other hand, hated it, saying, 'Vegas never establishes a focus for the broad-stroked farce and, despite the gameness of the players and Bergman's audacious depiction of the glitzy gambling haven, there's too much *d'être* and not enough *raison*.'

The film opened number one at the American box office, taking a respectable $7.3 million over its first weekend and pulling in the $20 million it cost to make by the middle of September. Chat-show host Leno took out a full-page advert in *Daily Variety* congratulating the film — unfortunately misspelling Nick's name as Nicholas!

The *Los Angeles Times* professed to be astonished at the film's success, pointing out, 'Nicolas Cage, Sarah Jessica Parker and James Caan star, but they aren't known as dead-bang openers.'

They sent a reporter to do a wholly unscientific survey at a cinema on Sunset Boulevard, trying to gauge why people went to see it, and decided that the Elvis impersonators were the biggest attraction, followed by Nick.

'I think Nick Cage is a great actor,' said *Flatliners* star Kiefer Sutherland, Nick's sometime drinking rival, who had caught the afternoon screening. 'I just wanted to watch him.'

'I wanted to see Nicolas Cage,' agreed Kathy Striegel.

Michael Owen commented, 'Trailers, of course — and Nicolas Cage.'

The knowledge that he could carry off a more mainstream film, combined with growing older and enjoying the responsibilities of fatherhood, gave Nick a more relaxed approach to work but at the same time made him more aware of the world around him

He said, 'I worked hard at that outlaw image for a while. It was something I desperately wanted 'cause I thought that was so cool when I was watching movies. I always liked the outsider. I never liked the clean-cut superstar. For a long time I was feeling like an anarchist, wanting to destroy everything that seemed to be in the way. But that's a hard label to live up to. I don't want to be wild every day. I want to sit at home and play fire-truck with my son. Part of it was testosterone. Now that I'm approaching 30, my testosterone is balancing out. I don't feel a need to feed into the wild-man image any more, though it was fun while it lasted.

'I haven't been a political person in the past but I'm becoming more aware of being part of a community. And I've always felt that if we could just take care of the community we live in, that might be a better way to think than trying to be cop of the world — which America likes to do sometimes. I drive around in LA and see all the homeless ... it really starts to get me down and it's getting worse.'

With age and laughter also came social conscience and awareness.

CHAPTER ELEVEN

ROGUES GALLERY

Nick had no idea that enjoying a meal with his Uncle Francis would lead to him making a quirky little film that would become one of his personal favourites. As they were chatting about films they had seen and people they would like to work with, Coppola dropped into the conversation the unfamiliar name of John Dahl.

Nick recalled, 'I was having turkey dinner with my uncle, Francis Ford Coppola, and he said, "I saw this great film, *Kill Me Again*, with Val Kilmer." Well, when Francis Ford Coppola says something, you listen.'

The offbeat, noir, 1989 film, which also starred Kilmer's then-wife, British-born actress Joanne Whalley Kilmer, had been written and directed by John Dahl. Nick went on, 'I met with John and his brother, Rick Dahl, and I looked at the script for *Red Rock West* and I thought it would be fun to get in a brawl with Dennis Hopper.'

Nick, who had worked with Hopper much earlier in his career, in *Rumble Fish*, was also intrigued by the story of a stranger drifting into a small town and becoming entangled in misadventure, because of his road trip with Jeff Levine a few months earlier.

In *Red Rock West,* Nick plays Michael, a down-on-his-luck ex-Marine who fails to get a promised job on an oil rig and, after running out of cash as he drives home, heads into the local bar in Red Rock, Wyoming. His battered old Cadillac parked outside has Texas number plates, and bar-owner Wayne, played by JT Walsh, mistakes him for a contract killer from Texas he has hired to murder his wife. Smelling money, Michael readily assumes the killer's name, Lyle, and heads off to Wayne's ranch with a $5,000 down-payment to meet the wife, Suzanne, played by Lara Flynn Boyle. Michael tells her that Wayne has paid him to kill her. She has other ideas, however, and gives him $10,000 as a counter-offer to change his mind and kill her husband instead. Michael, who has no intention of killing anyone, accepts the cash, writes a letter to the local sheriff explaining what is going on, and heads out of town. But Red Rock proves to be the town he can't leave. Driving through a thunderstorm on his way out of town, he hits a pedestrian trying to flag him down and takes him to the local hospital. When doctors find a couple of bullets in his body they call in the sheriff

— who turns out to be Wayne, who arrests Michael. He escapes and runs off through the woods with Wayne giving chase with his gun. He manages to get away, only narrowly to avoid being run over himself. The driver offers him a lift and takes him straight to Wayne's bar. Naturally, the newcomer turns out to be the real Lyle, played by Hopper. Michael manages to escape again and goes to warn Suzanne, with Lyle in hot pursuit. Michael and Suzanne, who are sexually attracted to each other, go on the run. Suzanne, a cold-hearted money-grabber, gets her come-uppance; Michael, a decent chap at heart, proves that nice guys sometimes do finish first.

'While on the road, I became very aware of the romantic image of the wanderer,' Nick said, explaining his attraction to the role. 'In *Red Rock West*, I saw the guy as being like that — the idea of just stumbling into a small town and having the most subversive experiences with people. Nobody is who they say they are, everybody has an ulterior motive, a different name. The film is quite dark, it's about how money contorts people into doing things that aren't very nice. It's cowboy noir with a black-comedy edge. It's a smaller movie than most of those I've been making. It's a way of getting back to my roots, to find another style. So much happens to this guy in a period of two days that it borders on the comical. It's primarily entertainment, but hopefully it will have some thought to it. *Red Rock West* is a noir movie, a lot edgier than *Honeymoon in Vegas*. It's sort of a down-and-dirty, blue-collar, anti-hero picture of the kind that I'd like to see making a comeback. We're in a recession, and I think more and more people will relate to characters who are up against the wall, worrying where they're going to get their money from. This is the age of the blue-collar hero.'

With an initial budget of just $6.5 million, it was a much smaller film than *Honeymoon in Vegas*, which he had already shot but which had not yet been released, and he enjoyed making it. Despite his comments about the romance of the road, however, aspects of his role were far from romantic. He matter-of-factly told *Premiere* from the Arizona set, 'Last night I was being shot with a rifle while running through the forest. Tonight, I'm going to run someone over with my car. It involves a couple of guns, $500,000, a black Buick Riviera and a white Cadillac. He's a blue-collar guy who wants to work in construction on an oil well but his leg is screwed up. It's two days in his life that turn into total hell. He's in the wrong place at the wrong time. He's the kind of guy, if the world blew up, he'd be the last guy alive. Who would want to be that?'

In 1992, Nick moved into high gear making movies and started the pattern of virtual non-stop work he has followed ever since. He moved straight from *Honeymoon in Vegas* to a comedy called *Amos & Andrew*, once again playing an out-of-luck blue-collar worker sucked into a life of crime almost by accident.

Samuel L Jackson plays Andrew Sterling, a Pulitzer Prize- winning writer who buys a mansion on a luxury resort island off the coast of New England. Neighbours Judy and Phil Gilman, played by Michael Lerner and Margaret Colin, spot him through the window putting together his new stereo. They assume he is a burglar because he is black and call in the police, who besiege the house. When Police Chief Cecil Tolliver, played by Dabney Coleman, realises what the truth is, he does a deal with Nick's character, Amos O'Dell, a petty criminal he has in his cells, to take responsibility for the non-existent crime. He has to sneak into the house and take Andrew 'hostage', then surrender. In return, he will get a bus ticket out of town and Tolliver, who is running for re-election, will be covered with glory. Once Amos gets into the house he and Andrew, an upper-middle-class man with almost as many prejudices as his new white neighbours, strike up an unlikely alliance. The siege turns into a media circus with a fiery black preacher using it as an excuse to organise a race demonstration.

As it happened, the demonstration scenes were shot in early May, when Los Angeles had erupted into riots after the acquittal of four white policemen accused of the videotaped beating of motorist Rodney King. Streets were burned out, shops were looted, 60 people died and more than 2,000 were injured. The disturbances focused Americans on issues of racial tension.

'It's very topical,' director E Max Frye said while filming was in progress. 'The night they were burning LA to the ground we were kind of doing that here in North Carolina. It was a complete coincidence. It was sobering. We were looking at news accounts of the riots and we had 150, 200 extras enacting the same thing.

'Nick Cage plays a kind of down-and-out blue-collar guy who lost his job and who ends up by mistake in the island jail. He's used as a scapegoat by the local police to extricate themselves from this horrible blunder they made by responding to the panicked phone call. It has a tone more of *Catch 22* than of broad comedy. Everybody is playing their roles in a very serious manner. It's the way people overreact to certain things. There are no particularly bad people in this movie; it's about everybody else and confronting stereotypes.'

Frye was also full of praise for Nick. He said, 'He's a total pro, especially given his reputation as a lunatic. He's on time, knows his lines, works very hard and doesn't complain. Just the kind of guy you want to work with.'

Nick was also complimentary about first-time director Frye. He said, 'After *Honeymoon in Vegas* I wanted to do another comedy that made a point as well as entertained. Frye had only written *Something Wild* before selling this idea and although he was unproven as a director, I liked his approach. He had a vision of the story and that helped me to find the right style in which to play Amos.

'This is one time that I was able to play an off-beat character in a light-hearted way, because beneath the tough exterior he's the kind of guy who'd never willingly harm anyone. That's the paradox and the challenge — he looks one way but behaves another — a devil wearing a halo. He's the latest addition to my rogues' gallery of characters. He's a victim of the current recession. When hard times hit, he lost his job and since then he's been a scam artist, stealing cars, little stuff like that, forced by society to live outside the law but wishing he could return to normal life.'

Jackson was dubious about his role at first; in fact, he refused even to read the script because of the title, a play on a 1950s radio and television series called *Amos and Andy* which was about two black men. It was the first television show featuring an entirely black cast, but was perceived as perpetuating racial stereotypes. When his agent finally persuaded him to read it he was enthusiastic — but anticipated that some viewers would not be.

'There will be people who think we did treat something very seriously too lightly,' he said. 'You can't please all of the people all of the time. The fact that they use laughter to deal with issues of racism, issues of class struggle — because there's some élitism in there also — defuses the situation to the extent that people can sit there and enjoy the film and not be bludgeoned.'

Nick kept up his breakneck pace by going from *Amos & Andrew* to *Deadfall*, which was being directed by his brother, Christopher. Originally, it was scarcely a bigger project than the Super-8 home movies Christopher used to shoot, with Nick starring, in their garden at Long Beach when they were kids. But once Nick became involved, the film grew.

Christopher explained, 'It stared off as a teensy little $300,000 movie I was going to do in hopes it would lead to a bigger film. My brother wanted to be in it, and his friend Charlie Sheen wanted to be in it.' Their addition to the cast — Sheen had a cameo role — led to James Coburn and Peter Fonda coming on board, and to make it still more of a family film, Marc Coppola, Christopher's and Nick's brother had a role and their aunt, Talia Shire, also made a cameo appearance. Former Monkee Mickey Dolenz joined the cast as well.

The film, seen as a Nick Cage project, was picked up by Trimark Films for worldwide distribution, and the budget was said to be $10 million for a six-week shoot in Los Angeles. 'We've been working on the acquisition of this film for about six months,' Trimark President Roger Burlage told *The Hollywood Reporter* in early September 1992. 'We're very excited about the project.'

Deadfall is a story of deceit and intrigue, which opens with Joe Dolan, played by Michael Biehn, accidentally killing his confidence trickster father, Mike, played by James Coburn, when a con game goes badly wrong. His father's dying words send him to Santa Monica, to look up his Uncle Lou — Coburn again — Mike's twin brother, whom Joe did not know existed until then. Lou is another conman, working on a scam involving $2 million in diamonds with the aid of his sidekick and heavy, Eddie, played by Nick as a shuffling cokehead in a bad wig and shades. Joe and Eddie quickly start vying for Lou's favours, and Eddie's sexy girlfriend, Diane, played by Sarah Trigger, falls instantly for Joe. Nobody in this den of thieves can be trusted; even Joe's father has tricked him and is still alive. Eddie meets a grisly death, plunging head-first into a deep-fat fryer.

Christopher let his kid brother make up his own character, and Nick went back to his old, over-the-top ways. 'Bad wig,' he laughed, recalling making the film. 'Really bad wig. Like, two-dollar wig that you get on Hollywood Boulevard. That was a chance to work with Christopher and he let me go for it in the regard that I could have fun with the make-up and disguise myself so I could really take advantage of the opportunity.'

Red Rock West was screened at the Munich Film Festival in April 1993 and had already been released in the UK and Germany when it had its North American première at Canada's Toronto Film Festival in September. It was then seen at the Hamptons International Film Festival on New York's Long Island, followed by a screening on the cable channel Home Box Office in October. But it took months to filter into American consciousness and was due to be released on video before it found a home on the art-film circuit.

The Hollywood trade newspapers reviewed it at Toronto, with mixed opinions. Leonard Klady wrote in *Daily Variety*, 'A wry thriller with a keen edge, *Red Rock West* is a sprightly, likeable, noirish yarn with very definite specialised appeal. Centred on a case of mistaken identity, the internecine plot becomes progressively more complex without losing its sense of fun. Cage plays his dumb-guy role with aplomb. He's virtually as thick-headedly resilient as a cartoon character but manages not to lose audience sympathy. Modest only in budget, *Red Rock West* has upbeat prospects if it can secure the type of niche that propelled *One False Move* to cult status last year.'

The Hollywood Reporter's David Kronke was less enthusiastic but still said, '*Red Rock West* is a diverting little piece of yahoo-noir, a cleverly plotted game of cat-and-mouse where you can't tell the cats from the mice. Given that Cage and Hopper headline, perfomances are surprisingly muted. With the sort of narrative gymnastics this film undertakes, more of their crazed, wired energy would only have helped things along. Overall, though, the cast performs admirably.'

Despite the praise, and critical acclaim at other, smaller, film festivals, Propaganda Films, which produced it, could not find an American distributor. Test audiences simply did not know how to categorise it. Columbia TriStar Home Video had put up $3.5 million of the budget in return for US distribution rights, and they sold it to HBO to try and recoup some of their costs.

Behind the scenes, however, San Francisco cinema owner and head of Roxie Releasing, Bill Banning, was determined to give the film a wider audience. He called John Dahl, who told him that Columbia TriStar Home Video owned the United States rights. They said they were happy to let him release the film — but that they did not own a single 35mm version of the movie. Eventually, he won permission to get a print from the Canadian distributors and he released it at his Roxie Theater in San Francisco and the Oaks in Berkeley, on the other side of the San Francisco Bay in February 1994. It grossed $17,000, in its first weekend, not a fortune but a very respectable sum for an art house. It ran for a record six weeks and within a month it had broken the Roxie's all-time box-office take, and Banning had 20 prints struck for distribution around the country.

He said, 'It's unbelievable that such a great little film should slip through the cracks. It's got classic written all over it. "Cowboy noir" isn't a big hook, but it's a great hook to certain people.'

Everyone connected with the film was delighted, including, naturally, Nick. He was particularly pleased that the picture had its breakthrough in San Francisco, which he has always affectionately regarded as his adopted home town. He told the *San Francisco Chronicle* that one problem was that the budget had been raised without any more money actually being put into the pot, so there was nothing left to promote it.

'*Red Rock West* is exactly the kind of movie I love to do,' he told *Chronicle* journalist Peter Stack. 'It's outside the Hollywood studio machinery, a real alternative for people who like different things. But it also has that almost old-fashioned style of the '40s thriller. I'm really glad San Francisco people are going to see it. It was beefed up to $9 million and therefore ate up all the marketing and promotion and advertising money. It's such a shame. The thing would have gotten completely lost if the Roxie hadn't picked it up. I wanted the character to be minimal and contained. The movie has such an old-time suspense feeling to it. The fact that audiences are enjoying it is very gratifying because that's just the kind of film I'm most attracted to, away from the studio system, the machine. Gotta hand it to my home town for picking up on something cool.'

Ironically, because of the timing, he was able to get extra plugs in for *Red Rock West* while he was promoting *It Could Happen to You*, the third of his big-budget comedies that would form part of his 'Sunshine Trilogy'. He told Bruce Britt of the *San Francisco Examiner*, '*Red Rock West* meant something to me because I was dealing with money in my own life. At the time, I was trying to avoid selling out, or accepting roles I didn't want just because large amounts of money were being offered. Money can be tempting and it can make you think about things that aren't exactly healthy. The dignity in that movie was that the character surpassed the money question — in the end he basically says, "Screw the money." It's blood money and it's hard to spend cash that was gained dishonestly.

'I was so happy it happened in San Francisco because of my love for the city. It would have been nice if it had been released nationally but I'm happy it's had its own life. I think the cult movies are the ones that stay around longest. The big studio movies are cogent and important — they make people happy. But the problem is that the studios are very business-oriented and therefore they have to rely on formulas. The smaller movies are the breeding ground for creativity. That's where the chances are being taken and where people can do things without moguls breathing down their backs. That's why I'll always be making independent movies. I feel like I am really learning about my craft when I do those movies.'

The film's producer, Joni Sighvatsson, praised Banning highly. 'I can't say enough about his determination,' he said. 'The picture always had an audience and needed a small indie to take it on and give it a lot of care and nurturing. I would never have thought it could have a life after cable. But I was wrong and Banning was right and that's very encouraging.'

The film was gradually released in art houses across America, a very different process from the usual 'wide' opening of studio films, when the film is shown on thousands of screens for the first weekend to maximise takings. Along with great word of mouth which helped persuade people to see it, it also got generally good reviews and a few raves.

Syndicated columnist Roger Ebert admitted, 'When I saw it at the Toronto Film Festival I assumed it would be arriving in theatres in a few weeks. Instead, it almost missed theatrical release altogether. *Red Rock West* is a diabolical movie that exists sneakily between a western and a thriller, between a film noir and a black comedy. This kind of lovingly contrived melodrama requires juicy actors, who can luxuriate in the ironies of a scene, and the movie has them: Nicolas Cage, JT Walsh, Dennis Hopper and Lara Flynn Boyle. They must have had a lot of fun with this material.'

Richard Harrington wrote bluntly in the *Washington Post*, '*Red Rock West* would probably have been on a lot of film critics' best-of lists last year — if any of them had seen it. It is a treasure waiting to be discovered. The acting is solid throughout, from Cage's subdued but fuming Michael and Hopper's familiarly psychotic Lyle, to Walsh's weasely Wayne and Boyle's fatal femme.'

In the *Los Angeles Times* Kevin Thomas called it 'terrific', saying, 'It's also got an admirable something more; a concern for decency, embodied by Nicolas Cage's entirely likeable Michael. Cage's naturalness as a nice guy in trouble lends the film considerable substance while Hopper's wily foil, Boyle's tough dame and Walsh's minor-league baddie provide much amusement.'

'*Red Rock West* is a terrifically enjoyable, smartly acted, over-the-top thriller,' wrote Caryn James in *The New York Times*. 'Mr Cage, once an over-the-top actor himself, has become more restrained, funnier and appealing in the last few years. He gives the film an intelligent edge, playing Michael with the slightest Elvis drawl and the trace of a dim-witted expression.'

David Denby in *New York* magazine called it, 'The best American movie released so far in the Year of Our Lord 1994.'

Bob Strauss in the *Los Angeles Daily News* disagreed with his fellow critics, however. He wrote, 'A superior cast makes the mediocre, redneck noir thriller *Red Rock West* watchable, if not quite worth the time it takes to watch it. Cage, playing it straight for a change, and Hopper, doing his signature loon impression, provide some interest. But for the most part, *Red Rock West*, which has already been on cable TV, could just as easily have been called Blue Stone East, it's so generic and indistinctive a slice of country cut-throat pie.'

Nick was set to team up again with Dahl the following year, when he was announced as the $4 million star of *A Simple Plan*, based on a best-selling novel by

Scott Smith. The film went through several directors, cast members and studios — Ben Stiller was due to direct when Nick first became interested, with Ray Liotta and, ironically, Patricia Arquette, Nick's future wife, being discussed as his co-stars. Savoy films dropped the project because they thought the $20 million budget was too high; it became clear that the fledgling company was actually going broke and it eventually sold off all its films. The film was a dark comedy about two brothers who stumbled across $4 million in the wreck of a small plane, and who decided to keep the cash and ended up running foul of both the law and the bad guys. It was eventually made with Billy Bob Thornton, Bill Paxton and Nick's *It Could Happen to You* co-star Bridget Fonda, and was released in 1998.

At the same time as *Red Rock West* was trickling slowly into cinemas and finding a cult audience, *Amos & Andrew* was released — disastrously. Despite the film-makers' insistence that it was meant as a gentle satire, making fun of prejudices of every colour, most people agreed that it simply did not work.

Nick did his best to boost it, saying, 'The important thing is that we didn't cross over into offensiveness. The film digs at the behaviour of blacks and whites and points a finger at both sides. The police have their stereotypical impressions, as does the black Reverend, a militant, who incites his followers to march on the island for the sake of publicity. I think comedy is a good format to make statements on social issues.'

It was released in early March 1993 and not only was it hated by most of the critics but it was almost entirely overlooked; by April — even though the publication had reviewed it two months before — *Hollywood Reporter*, saying Nick was in final talks to star in what was then called *Cop Gives Waitress $2 Million Tip*, said he was last seen in *Honeymoon in Vegas*, ignoring both *Amos & Andrew* and *Red Rock West*.

Perhaps surprisingly, Mick LaSalle of the *San Francisco Chronicle* actually loved it; San Franciscans are notoriously politically correct. He wrote, '*Amos & Andrew* is a buddy-movie comedy about the state of race relations in the United States — a description that offhand might make it sound akin to a slap-happy picture about brain surgery. It's a light-hearted movie that, at times, strains under the weight of its heavy subject, but it has good actors, imaginative bits, and it works as entertainment. Jackson and Cage make a strong screen pair — Jackson with his stern authority and presence, Cage with his disarming quirkiness.'

At least Jeff Menell of *The Hollywood Reporter* enjoyed Nick's performance if nothing else about the film in his February review. 'Nicolas Cage adds another enjoyably quirky character to his portfolio and in so doing saves this film from its own intolerable contrivances,' he said. 'Aside from Cage, the clever title and Bobby Darin's catchy "Beyond the Sea", *Amos & Andrew* is an improbable tale that unfairly asks the viewer to stretch his or her credibility acceptance level way beyond the norm.'

In the *New Yorker*, Terrence Rafferty wrote, 'Cage takes over the movie — snatches it clean away from Jackson, Coleman and the rest of the large and gifted cast. (In a few scenes, the Gilmans' dog, a beautiful and personable white German shepherd, engages him in a fierce tug of war for the audience's attention but Cage prevails.) Cage is reason enough to see *Amos & Andrew*, but he can't quite save it from the stubborn inconsequentiality that sets in about halfway through.'

Daily Variety reviewer Lawrence Cohen, on the other hand, complained, 'Cage uses overdone physical shtick for momentary amusement and gets to recite an endless shaggy dog story about sea monkeys that some folks might find amusing. A one-joke sketch that doesn't work as a feature, Castle Rock's *Amos & Andrew* raises the question: "How did this film ever get made?" Few audience members will sit through its entirety to ponder that issue.'

Vincent Canby of *The New York Times* was equally scathing, writing, '*Amos & Andrew* is less breathless than emphysemic, a handicapped satirical farce whose roots are not in life but in other, better movies and sitcoms.'

'*Amos & Andrew* starts out with a promising premise but everything in it is off — the timing, the tone, the performances,' wrote Peter Rainer in the *Los Angeles Times*. 'It's the kind of film that makes you wonder from moment to moment just what E Max Frye, the writer-director, had in mind. Maybe nothing?' He did, however, add, 'Cage is pretty funny in his scenes with Jackson, who plays most of the movie in a grim funk.'

Critic Roger Ebert commented, 'The movie is not bad so much as misguided. It contains a lot of funny moments and some good performances but all the same ... It portrays an unpleasant situation and then treats it with sitcom tactics.'

Steven Rea of *Knight-Ridder Newspapers* called it 'wincingly bad' and complained, '*Amos & Andrew* is guilty of the same social and racial stereotyping it purports to lampoon.'

'Unfortunate title. Unfortunate movie,' was the summing up from Susan Wloszczyna in *USA Today*, America's only truly national newspaper. Jem Axelrod, in *Box Office* magazine, summed it up saying, 'Every so often there comes by an otherwise terrible movie that has one redeeming characteristic — perhaps a great performance, good direction, a provocative idea — that saves it. Unfortunately, *Amos & Andrew* is not such a movie. It is completely and homogeneously bad.'

While the critics were passing judgement on *Red Rock West* and *Amos & Andrew*, *Deadfall* was locked in a courtroom drama of its own. Christopher Coppola had met the short, 21-day shooting schedule and even brought the film in $240,000 under the budget, which was now revealed to be a modest $3.4 million, not the $10 million of speculation. Normally, this would be a feather in the cap for a first-time director.

However, Trimark were not happy with the finished film and demanded that some scenes be reshot and extra footage added. Christopher and Executive Producer Ted Fox agreed to do the work but asked Trimark to put up extra money; Trimark, in turn, said they should use the $240,000 budget surplus. Fox had taken out a completion bond — a standard film 'insurance policy' that the movie is completed on time and up to standard. The Completion Bond Company became involved, backing Trimark and threatening to wrest the end of the production from Fox. He went to court seeking an injunction to keep CBC out of the matter because his company, Deadfall Productions, had fulfilled its contractual obligations. CBC countered with a request for a restraining order to let them take control of the film without interference from Fox.

It was an unusual case because normally the completion bond organisation steps in when a film is over budget or running behind schedule. Although neither of these had actually happened, because of the dispute over financing the additional work, CBC were afraid that the extra scenes would not be done on time for the agreed date for delivery of the completed film. Trimark were financing it as a 'negative pickup', meaning they only had to pay for the picture when the finished negative was delivered.

'There were some scenes Trimark wanted to improve the film creatively, and it was their nickel,' said CBC lawyer Steven Fayne. 'Some scenes were missing that needed to be cleaned up. In one, an actor walks over and looks out the window. Normally, you would shoot out the window to see what he's looking at. That wasn't the case. This is the first time we've been in court over this particular issue. This film has become a tempest in a teapot. We're talking about a pittance, really, since what's required to fix it is three days of shooting. And this is certainly no *Gone With the Wind* in terms of budget.

'We had a delivery date of 8 March. The conversations between the producer and the distributor over how the scenes would be done never seemed to go anywhere. This was one-and-a-half weeks before the delivery deadline. The grounds for a guarantor is not only to make sure a picture comes in on budget, but on time. So we took over the picture and backed spending the additional costs. The risk from a guarantor's point of view is that the distributor could walk off the picture and the exposure is far more costly than spending that extra little bit fixing those shots.'

In the end, Los Angeles Superior Court Judge Robert O'Brien appointed producer John Hyde, a finance and bankruptcy expert usually called in to advise showbusiness firms facing bankruptcy, to take control of the film as a receiver, finish it and deliver it to Trimark.

The dispute did not delay the release of the film in the end, but the case was not actually settled until June 1994, with none of the parties disclosing who actually footed the bill for the extra scenes.

The additional shooting was not enough to save the movie, however. It opened at the Vancouver International Film Festival in October 1993, and was briefly released across the border in the United States the following spring, but sank without trace.

Ken Eisner, reviewing it in Canada for *Weekly Variety*, commented, 'Watchable only for camp value, *Deadfall* is at its best when cameo-laden anarchy reigns. As a tribute to film noir, it won't make it to *The Late Late Show*. Unfortunately, when Cage's character dies, so does the film.' Ironically, in view of the fact that Trimark wanted the film lengthened, he added, 'Losing a few minutes of dead wood might help block the bloated pic's free fall from limited theatrical run, but it's likely to end its days as a video oddity, saved for at-home Nicolas Cage retrospectives.'

The *Los Angeles Times*' Kevin Thomas was even more scathing when it opened at a solitary cinema in the LA suburb of Highland Park. He wrote, '*Deadfall*, a hopelessly callow, leaden-paced attempt at film-making is of interest only because it was directed and co-written by Francis Coppola's nephew, Christopher, and because it has a far more stellar cast than is usual for low-budget B pictures.' He describes Eddie as, 'A way-over-the-top Nicolas Cage, the director's brother, a cokehead given to shades, flashy clothes and a bad wig. On its posters, *Deadfall* is all-too-aptly billed as "the ultimate con".'

Nick was not around to read this review, but bad though it was he would probably have preferred to be in Los Angeles rather than on his latest set. He found himself trapped in hell when he agreed to make the light-hearted comedy *Trapped in Paradise*. It was shot in Canada during the coldest winter on record and Nick's comedy career basically got buried under the snow that covered the North American landscape during the freezing months spent filming there. After making the movie, he vowed to return to the more serious, and frequently offbeat, roles that had marked his earlier career.

He was set to star in *Kiss of Death,* but what really helped him come to terms with his unhappy situation was the knowledge that, after that, he would go on to make *Leaving Las Vegas*, a low-budget movie based on a critically applauded semi-autobiographical novel by John O'Brien, who killed himself soon after signing the deal for British-born director Mike Figgis to turn the book into a film.

Mid-way through the *Trapped in Paradise* shoot, Nick said to himself, 'I don't want to do this any more.' He recalled, 'I didn't want to do another big fluffy studio movie that was not going to work. And I just got angry with myself. I said, "I can't hold myself with dignity if I do this again." I was frustrated in the middle of the snow and the shoot. I was thinking I just don't want to make movies like *Trapped* any more. I can't do it any more.'

He went to his then agent Ed Limato and more or less put him on notice that doing comedy was no longer a laughing matter and he wanted a role 'I can invest my soul in'. Little did he know his salvation was just one script away. Figgis had sent his adaptation of O'Brien's book to Limato, admitting that there was no serious money to pay the Hollywood agent's client. Nevertheless, Limato read the script and in March 1994 forwarded it on to Nick with a note that read, 'This is the answer to all your prayers.'

Nick remembered, 'I got lucky with *Honeymoon in Vegas* and *It Could Happen to You*, and I thought I was on a roll. The script for *Trapped in Paradise* played well on paper, and with Dana Carvey and Jon Lovitz on board, I couldn't see how it could go wrong. Then, about halfway through the shoot, everything just exploded. I'm not into assessing blame and, frankly, I don't know who was at fault. All I knew was that I couldn't go through something like that again. I wanted to return to the movies I started out with, movies like *Vampire's Kiss* and *Raising Arizona*. I needed to get away from these comedies. Then this script for *Leaving Las Vegas* came in and it was the answer to my prayers. It's the only reason I got through that experience in Canada alive and sane.'

He also read the book, which he said affected him more than anything he had read since *A Clockwork Orange* or *Brave New World*. He remembered his Uncle Francis once telling him, 'Novels are beautiful but they're like old trains, and movies are the art form of our time.' Nick considered his uncle's sentiment too harsh. Nick, whose father always wanted him to be a writer, said, 'I think that writing's the root, and that a great novel tells the story in a way that movies are unable to tell. There's the imagination and the pleasure of lying in bed, reading a chapter and visualising it any way you want to hear them and not having them blasted into your brains or your eyes.'

Nevertheless, he knew that Figgis had done a superb job of translating the novel for the big screen. It helped to keep his spirits warm during the rest of that cold Canadian shoot.

In *Trapped*, originally called *It Happened in Paradise*, Nick plays Bill Firpo, the eldest and relatively most honest of a trio of incompetently crooked brothers; Dave, played by Lovitz, and Alvin, played by Carvey. Dave, a compulsive liar, and Alvin, a kleptomaniac, have just been released from a jail term for robbing a car wash, and under the terms of their parole they cannot leave New York State. Bill, who is trying to go straight and has found a job in a restaurant in New York City, takes charge of them. They con him into driving them to the town of Paradise, Pennsylvania, where they had heard from fellow jailbirds there is a poorly-guarded bank virtually begging to be robbed. The robbery is easy — but getting away proves impossible. A blizzard and a car crash trap them in the town and they discover to their horror that the people of Paradise are so nice, so generous, so innocent that they cannot escape their hospitality, ending up having Christmas Eve dinner at the house of the bank president they have just cleaned out of $275,000.

Much of the shoot, near Niagara Falls, was in temperatures of -30°F and by February 1994, while exulting over the success of *Red Rock West* after its belated release in San Francisco, Nick moaned to Peter Stack of the *San Francisco Chronicle*, 'It's so cold up here I can't wait to get back to California.'

Mid-way through the shoot, director George Gallo wrote in a part for a new character, a three-legged dog nicknamed Tripod. The German shepherd cross had been hit by a car when he was a puppy and his left front leg was badly injured. At the time, the mutt, then named Laddie, belonged to a family whose religion banned them seeking medical treatment, even for their pets. Gangrene developed in the leg and his owners were going to shoot him to put him out of his misery. Then a neighbour stepped in and offered to take the pooch off their hands. He took the dog to a vet, who amputated the leg. The neighbour could not keep Laddie but a friend, Lorne Kerr, offered him a permanent home.

In the chilly early hours of a February morning six years later, Lorne was walking Laddie through a neighbourhood in Elora, Ontario, where Nick and co were shooting a car chase scene. Gallo took one look at the pair and knew he had to include the dog. He said, 'I just saw this silhouette from the street light of this man with a cap on walking this three-legged dog in the snow. It was poetic. I thought, wow, this guy really loves this dog. And then I just said, "I've got to put this dog in the movie." '

Despite his unhappiness during the shooting of *Trapped*, Nick was professional enough not to knock it publicly before it was released. He enthused to Elias Stimac of *Drama-Logue* magazine, '*It Happened in Paradise* is the comedy to end all comedies. It's with Jon Lovitz and Dana Carvey, and I really went for that sort of *Around the World in 80 Days* madcap kind of performance.'

But once he escaped from Canada, he was happy to move on without a pause. Not only was he working on *Kiss of Death* but he was heavily committed to promoting *It Could Happen to You*. He told the *San Francisco Examiner*'s Britt, 'The analogy I use is that I can't seem to get off the grill. It's like I'm still on the grill and I have to keep it sizzling. I really haven't had a chance to catch my breath and take a look at what I've done. On the other hand, there's something to be said for continuous work. I've noticed that everything gets easier and things happen more fluidly. It feels like I'm not acting sometimes. One of the main goals in any kind of expression is to try and make it look easy. I would hope that to some degree, I'm making it seem easy.'

The $30 million *Trapped in Paradise* was originally due to be released in October but was pushed back to early December to capitalise on the Christmas theme. But Nick's bad run of critical luck continued and there was little Christmas cheer in reports about the movie.

'*Trapped in Paradise* may well be the worst Christmas movie since 1964's *Santa Claus Conquers the Martians*,' Kevin Thomas wrote bluntly in the *Los Angeles Times*. 'It holds its audience hostage for an unconscionable 111 minutes with a rambling, unfunny, thickly sentimental comedy that plays like third-rate Frank Capra. As bad as it is, it's understandable that players of the calibre of Nicolas Cage, Jon Lovitz and Dana Carvey became involved because, by and large, their parts are well written and because at the film's core is a viable idea. Unfortunately, writer-director George Gallo allows his essentially simple story to wander quite literally all over the countryside, piling it on with needless digressions and failing to make any of them more than faintly amusing.'

Janet Maslin of *The New York Times* wrote, 'Since *Trapped in Paradise* assembles three actors as amusing as Nicolas Cage, Dana Carvey and Jon Lovitz, it's a minor holiday miracle that this homey comedy barely elicits even a chuckle. As the fall guy who is crazily roped into his brothers' troubles, Mr Cage behaves with the looney chagrin he brought to a gleefully improbable comedy like Andrew Bergman's *Honeymoon in Vegas*. But this situation isn't sufficiently Bergmanesque.'

Rebecca Krause wrote in *Entertainment Today*, 'With a Christmas theme and winter scenery thrown in for good measure, this film takes a recycled, albeit sweet, storyline and throws it at you in the hopes of making you laugh. That in itself is not contemptible. Nor is the effort put forward by three acclaimed comedic actors. What is disappointing is that the laughs don't surface when they are supposed to.'

Syndicated columnist Roger Ebert, who gave the film a derisory half-star out of a possible four, said, 'I knew the movie was in trouble by the end of the second scene. The first scene had Nicolas Cage in it, which is a hopeful sign.'

Duane Byrge in *The Hollywood Reporter* called it, 'A fruitcake of a mix that is completely unappealing and uninspired. *Trapped in Paradise* is neither funny nor heart warming.'

His counterpart at the other showbusiness industry trade newspaper, Todd McCarthy at *Daily Variety*, found it a perfectly acceptable stocking-stuffer. He said, 'Whatever else one can say about it, *Trapped in Paradise* is undoubtedly the first movie in which a horse-drawn sleigh is chased by a cop car on Christmas Eve. An agreeable Middle American comedy intent upon reviving old-fashioned virtues in both film-making and real life, George Gallo's second feature doesn't serve up the big yucks needed to make it a breakout sleeper hit, but has enough in the way of sentiment and goofy situational predicaments to put it over as a serviceable holiday attraction. Cage is eternally split between his desire to keep the loot and determination to do the right thing.'

Desson Howe in the *Washington Post* bucked the trend completely. He acknowledged Gallo overloaded unnecessary extra characters to the cast but thought the individual funny moments were worth the clutter. He wrote, 'The question is, can a trio of amiable goofballs take you though a movie that's, well, not so great? *Trapped in Paradise*, a heist caper starring Nicolas Cage, Jon Lovitz and Dana Carvey, gets lost in a snow flurry of subplots and formulaic run-and-chase — right around the time you've settled in for a good comedy. But these three noodleheads are so endearing, it seems wrong to dismiss the whole thing. That, my friends, is what video rentals are for; *Trapped in Paradise* is the kind of movie you want to watch, fast-forward button at hand. You never know when something funny is coming along.'

It was no laughing matter for Nick, but his career was about to take another turn, one that would lead to critical and financial rewards he had never even dreamed of.

CHAPTER TWELVE

THE WINNING TICKET

Nick was in fine form when he, co-star Shirley MacLaine, director Hugh Wilson and a film crew did the rounds of Kernan Hospital. In breaks from filming at the orthopaedic rehabilitation centre, he happily signed autographs on anything from scraps of paper to the left side of X-Ray technician Laura Smith's starched white lab coat.

'I'm saving this side for Shirley MacLaine,' gushed an excited Smith. 'But she seems very guarded.'

The veteran Oscar-winning actress was indeed guarded, for the film they were shooting was *Guarding Tess*, the second of what Nick was to dub his 'Sunshine Trilogy', in which he played a Secret Service agent reluctantly assigned to the protection squad of a former US President's widow.

The hospital visit caused genial havoc, with the Hollywood invaders pursued by local media, hospital staff taking time away from their medical duties to watch actors playing doctors and nurses, and photographers snapping away at still more actors playing photographers taking pictures of the make-believe First Lady.

But nobody there was complaining. The two-month shoot, almost entirely on location in and around Baltimore, brought jobs for more than 1,000 local actors, extras and crew, including scores recruited at an open casting call and one extra who bid for the role at a charity auction.

Most locals welcomed the shoot, which showcased the city and the state of Maryland — nicknamed 'America in Miniature' because of its geographical and architectural variety — even though the film was actually set in Ohio. It featured local landmarks such as the mansion where MacLaine's character, Tess Carlisle, lived, an early 19th-century house named Laboroere in the historic Mount Washington suburb, which the film-makers renovated for its role. An early 20th-century landmark, the 2,500-seat Maryland Theater in nearby Hagerstown, was also redecorated.

However, the minister of a Hagerstown church refused to allow its doors to be filmed, because of Shirley MacLaine's well-publicised spiritual beliefs. The Rev

Robert Ridenour, pastor of the then 83-year-old Faith Chapel, said, 'Given the fact that Shirley MacLaine is a guru for the New Age Religion, which is contrary to Christian truth, we certainly would not want to give her our endorsement.'

After the success of *Honeymoon in Vegas,* Nick was cast in *Guarding Tess* as Doug Chesnic, a straight-arrow agent charged with the safety of beloved but crotchety former First Lady Tess Carlisle. He plays life by the rules but longs to return to the thick of things in Washington, and possible promotion. Tess, chafing at her virtual imprisonment because of her position, deliberately breaks every rule she can, driving dedicated Doug to distraction in his attempts to guarantee her safety. She delights in playing mind games with him and the story centres on their clash of wills. When Tess is kidnapped — because she breaks the rules by going out without her Secret Service detail — Doug is absorbed with guilt and works tirelessly to find her. When she is rescued, she finally realises why she needed protection, and the two at last recognise that they have a genuine affection and respect for each other, despite their constant bickering.

Nick admitted he was surprised to be offered the part because it was so different from his earlier roles, and said frankly, 'I think *Honeymoon in Vegas* clicked so the studios were excited and they wanted to work with me again.'

The film was originally developed by producer Scott Rudin for Paramount Pictures. However, studio boss Brandon Tartikoff, who had approved a budget of $18 to $20 million for the project, left Paramount unexpectedly after his daughter Calla suffered serious head injuries in a car crash and needed to spend months in rehabilitation in New Orleans. Tartikoff was replaced by Sherry Lansing. Lansing, of course, had been largely instrumental in getting *Racing with the Moon* made because she loved the script so much that she took it over from 20th Century Fox when she moved to Paramount, but she was not impressed by *Guarding Tess.* She gave director Hugh Wilson two choices — make the film for her with a much-reduced budget, no more than the low teens, or take it elsewhere. Rudin dropped out of the film, and Wilson took it to TriStar at a budget of $20 million.

Between finishing *Honeymoon in Vegas* and signing on for *Guarding Tess,* Nick had made three, yet-unreleased films which were destined not to cause much of a stir: *Red Rock West, Amos & Andrew* and *Deadfall.* So he was looking forward to capitalising on his *Honeymoon* success with the new film. He said, 'I've had an interesting common denominator in my career in that I've had the opportunity to work with the most creative, powerful women in movies. Kathleen Turner in *Peggy Sue Got Married,* Cher in *Moonstruck* and I'm about to start filming *Guarding Tess* with Shirley MacLaine.' He was also intrigued by the character of Tess, who reminded him of his own strong-minded and occasionally cantankerous grandmother, Divi Vogelsang.

Filming started in February 1993 and finished on time despite running into a series of setbacks. Co-producer Nancy Graham Tanen explained, 'We are making the movie in Baltimore and got caught in the worst storm of the century there. When it wasn't snowing it was raining and when it wasn't raining it was so cold that in one instance the boom arm of a very costly piece of camera equipment froze and cracked.'

The bad weather also caused a bulldozer being used in the scenes where Tess was dug out of her underground prison to sink into the mud up to its seat. Tanen went on, 'We had to rent a tractor with a huge winch to pull it free, and that took nearly a day.'

In addition, MacLaine had to take two days away from the production because her mother, Kathlyn MacLean Beaty, a former drama teacher and one-time actress, died in the middle of the shoot.

The stars did not let these problems get in the way of becoming firm friends and having a good time at work. Nick said one of the biggest attractions of the movie for him was the opportunity to work with MacLaine.

'I had seen her movies and I think she's a great actress,' he said. 'She put me right at ease. She's a very playful personality. She doesn't dwell on her own greatness. She's more fascinated in other people and wanting to know the scoop on things ... she likes to get the dirt.'

He went on, 'She's very outspoken. If she thinks something, she'll say it. She'll tease you, point it out with a frank attitude, but always in good humour. She always loves to mimic people and she'd imitate me just before my take. So I would joke with her about her magic powers.'

MacLaine responded, 'He's great on the receiving end of calamity. I saw that in the *Vegas* picture. I never expected that. I thought he was a weird guy who ate spiders and belonged to a cult that even I had never heard of. He asked me for advice about everything — child rearing, comedy, what he should do after this. After all, I've lived 3,000 years longer than him!' She also said that he was very intense, but added, 'Nick winks at his own intensity!'

She continued, 'He wasn't that intimidated by me. I put him right at ease by telling him to just be himself. He was just great. He would work out and do all that macho stuff, trying to get thin. Thin is not my type. I kept telling him that and he had this fantasy that I had a crush on him. So, I just let him think it, because, you never know, you could get lucky!'

MacLaine was also amused by the May-December romance between Nick, then 29, and 18-year-old Kristen Zang, which was in full swing during filming. Nick recalled that one day his co-star 'used her psychic powers and told me, "The girl you're with now is going to go away. When you're 35, you're going to meet a dark-haired woman who will be a social worker of some kind and she will be your wife." '

The following year, while he was promoting the film, he told *Drama-Logue* magazine he was still with Kristen and laughed, 'Check back with me in five years and I'll tell you if it came true. She's 19 now. Nobody thought we'd still be together and it's been a year-and-a-half. And that surprises Shirley.'

By the time he was 35, of course, Nick was married to someone entirely different — blonde actress Patricia Arquette.

Director Hugh Wilson, the creator of long-running television sitcom *WKRP in Cincinnati*, also loved working with Nick. He said, 'When I first started *Guarding Tess* with Nick, I was just knocked out by how good he is. And he's a terrific guy. You couldn't ask for an easier person to work with.'

Wilson spoke at length to real Secret Service agents to learn how the protection details work, and to understand the dilemma faced by the guards and the guarded. There were then more former Presidents and First Ladies alive than at any previous point in history, all entitled to protection for the rest of their lives. It has always been a serious business, but since the assassination attempt on President Ronald Reagan in 1981, it has been treated as a matter of life and death, 24 hours a day.

'At this very moment, there could be a whole contingent of Secret Service people sitting around Lady Bird Johnson's house or driving down Rodeo Drive with

Nancy Reagan,' said Wilson. 'The agent in the front seat would have a sawn-off shotgun between his knees. This is an invasion of privacy, no matter how it's handled.'

Both stars saw something of themselves in their roles; Nick his growing maturity, and MacLaine the frustrations of living under a spotlight for the best part of 40 years.

'Doug is straightforward, very focused, very direct,' said Nick who went to the White House to meet Secret Service officers as part of his research. 'But he is also one of those guys who joined the Secret Service because he likes the adrenalin rush that comes from a high-action job. In some ways, he embodies a classic hero essence, which I think is very appealing and something I have avoided in the past because I have opted to play more flawed kinds of characters in terms of their behaviour and personality traits. I'm like ready now to play a role like Doug Chesnic in my own life. Maybe it has something to do with turning 29, about to be 30, and the responsibilities that come with a later age. The problem is, in the service of Mrs Carlisle, he is basically a waiter or a butler. Doug's predicament is that if anything goes wrong, he's done a major disservice to the country. But his frustration is more with the situation than with Tess Carlisle.'

Said MacLaine, 'I understand Tess' plight; no privacy, surrounded by people who are at her beck and call when she'd rather be left alone. I think it rankles her that the taxpayers are paying for protection that she doesn't really want. Only because the President and the country want Tess to have protection does she go along with it.'

She told Dan Yakir of the *San Francisco Examiner*, 'She is lonely and restricted and desperately unhappy. They both have legitimate reasons for acting the way they do. It's more than mother and son. It's a companionship and a total dependency on each other. I don't see any sexual overtones to it — although Nick does because he's young. I mean, yes, this is the son she never had and she says so to the President. But he is her protector. She completely depends on him.'

In fact, screenwriter Peter Torkvei did see sexual elements in her portrayal. He said, 'Shirley brought a real sexiness to the character that hadn't been there before. That introduced a whole new element in her relationship with Nick — a flirtatiousness.'

Nick had to fight to play Doug quite so self-contained — or as he put it, 'In this movie I'm anal-retentive to the point of being too normal.' He admitted, 'I find that, generally speaking, if you're in a comedy, if you play it straight and serious, it's more interesting. If you're in a drama, if you play it with a little bit of comedic edge, it's more interesting. They felt I didn't smile enough. So they wrote a scene in the movie for me where we had to point out, "How come you never smile?"

'I think my own sensibilities are to enjoy the pictures that are more alternative, like *Raising Arizona* and *Wild at Heart*. But there was a need for me to make movies like *Guarding Tess*, which are about people you can kind of relate to in some regard and identify and get something from.'

The original version of the film opens with a state funeral for Tess after she dies from a brain tumour, with Doug contemplating their time together and the story being told in flashback. Test audiences hated her dying, however and, in December 1993, a new ending was shot and the opening scene and flashback sequences were re-edited. Tess still has a brain tumour, a fact she tosses casually into conversation during the movie, but which is not played up sufficiently to turn the film into a tear-jerker.

After the first tests, the movie was carefully marketed, with a trailer released for the Christmas 1993 season and scores of sneak previews before its March opening. Despite appalling weather, so many people flocked to see the movie that some had to be turned away. TriStar's Senior Vice-President for publicity, Ed Russell, said, 'We felt we had a film that appealed to people across the country. We had more than 150 word-of-mouth screenings that we began about a month before the film opened. We really went after a more sophisticated, upscale audience, knowing that this would be the audience that would come out enjoying the film most. What we found was that those early screenings were turn-away audiences in really bad weather back East in February.'

The ploy worked, both in terms of mainly favourable reviews and the box office, with the film opening in the number-one position and taking $7.1 million on its first weekend of release.

Los Angeles *Village View* writer Sean O'Neill watched it with low expectations but gave it high praise. 'The film stars Shirley MacLaine as a crusty ex-First Lady and Nicolas Cage as her harried Secret Service agent, roles through which either actor could sleepwalk,' he wrote. 'So it comes as something of a surprise that *Guarding Tess* works at all, and it's a real shocker that it works as well as it does. Cage's stock in trade is exasperation. He's a disaster as a leading man and he would be laughable in a straight romance but when he's running around tearing his hair out the guy is hard to beat.'

'In the new TriStar release *Guarding Tess,* the everyday hassles of protecting important public figures is the setting for a highly enjoyable character-driven comedy that features terrific lead performances by Shirley MacLaine and Nicolas Cage,' David Hunter wrote in *The Hollywood Reporter*. 'Cage is on top form again, able to get laughs from simple things like hauling around a wayward folding chair, while digging into one of his best roles to make use of his tight-lipped, blank-faced, slow-burning fuse.'

Daily Variety's Leonard Klady commented, 'There's a little gem of an idea in the film. MacLaine's not asked to do much more than the shrill, iron-willed matron. She does it well, if obviously. Cage has more fun with his part, delineating his character right down to the way he gingerly sips alcohol or absolutely never fails to buckle his seat belt.'

Syndicated columnist Roger Ebert wrote, 'As the story unfolds, we begin to sense a deep current of feeling between Tess and Agent Chesnic. It isn't love, God forbid, but a certain respect for a tough opponent and even some grudging affection. MacLaine and Cage are really very good. Cage, who can cheerfully go over the top (see *Wild at Heart* and *Honeymoon in Vegas*) is restrained here, yet very likeable. We feel for this man who has no life of his own except to guard a woman who has no life of *her* own.'

A self-confessed major fan of Nick's, Yadena Arar of the *Los Angeles Daily News* — she appealed to *People* magazine to name him as the Sexiest Man Alive in their annual ratings — raved, 'If they gave an Academy Award for casting, *Guarding Tess* would be this year's front runner. That's how good Shirley MacLaine and Nicolas Cage are. Not too much happens in *Guarding Tess,* but the little that does is exploited fully by the blue-chip cast. The on-screen chemistry between Cage and MacLaine is as good as chemistry gets without romance.'

Washington Post writer Richard Harrington agreed, 'The President calls Tess either "a national treasure or a pain in the butt" and MacLaine plays her both ways. As for the usually over-the-edge Cage, his stoic, beleaguered Chesnic is all tight-lipped, monotone servility. Cage does get a chance to cut loose when the film takes a wrong turn at the end with a bizarre kidnapping plot, a bitter medical diagnosis and a tension-filled rescue, but he also draws on a quiet stubbornness familiar from *Raising Arizona* and *Moonstruck*. Like the role itself, Cage is clearly in service here to a fabled but fading star, and he seldom slips on that second banana.'

Kenneth Turan in the *Los Angeles Times* thought the kidnap plot spoiled the film but loved the set-up and the acting. 'Though his work is problematic at times, there is perhaps no better actor of his generation who does better in ridiculous situations than Cage,' he said. 'Neither he nor the equally adept MacLaine forces or flaunts their characterisations.'

In the *New York Times*, Janet Maslin agreed, saying, 'This promising set-up introduces *Guarding Tess* as a tug of war between a grande dame and her resentful young aide and as such it has lively potential. Mr Wilson ultimately drums up an absurd intrigue plot and even throws in a bit of maudlin medical news.' But she added, 'Mr Cage, once again sounding mock-suave and Elvis, makes the most of his character's fragile cool.'

The *San Francisco Chronicle*'s Edward Guthmann dismissed it as 'a moderately funny comedy', and added, 'It's not dreadful, though, thanks to Nicolas Cage, who plays his scenes in a relatively moderate key (for him, anyway), and MacLaine, who brings nuance and intelligence to a part that's steeped in clichés.'

'Nicolas Cage as Doug is the embodiment of contained fury, reined in so tightly he seems on the verge of inhaling his own teeth to stop himself from biting Tess,' wrote Abbie Bernstein in *Drama-Logue*. 'It is a performance that is at once hilariously oversized and absolutely truthful. Shirley MacLaine as the redoubtable Tess is his match in every way, sweet noblesse oblige in her tone and industrial-strength steel in her eyes. It is a treat to watch Cage and MacLaine duke it out, nuance by nuance.'

Not surprisingly, Nick was delighted to have another number-one film, although he admitted he had not been sure how the first few days would go. 'I thought the picture could have legs but I didn't know if it would open well,' he said.

After *Guarding Tess* had opened, he speculated about his future work, saying, 'I'm trying to find some kind of trademark. I'm trying to find movies that I can be strong in, something to do with human struggles that can, in some way, act as a medicine to people, where people can identify and relate and not feel alone.'

Before then, however, he was looking forward to the opening of the third of his 'Sunshine Trilogy', a heart-warming tale of honour and honesty then called *Cop Tips Waitress*.

Nick once again wore a badge and carried a gun when he was reunited with his *Honeymoon in Vegas* producer and director, Mike Lobell and Andrew Bergman, this time playing a kindly cop on the beat in New York City, who does not have enough cash to tip a waitress but promises her half of his winnings if his lottery ticket comes up. Naturally enough it does, and he finds himself $4 million richer. Equally naturally, he does the decent thing and signs over half to the waitress — the day she was declared bankrupt. Most naturally of all, his spitfire of a wife is furious. She is so obnoxious and intent on lavishing money on herself, while the cop and the waitress spend their windfall helping other people, that it is inevitable that the marriage will end and the winners will get together.

Top: A young Cage, with Matt Dillon in the 1983 release, *Rumblefish*.

Below: With Matthew Modine in Alan Parker's highly-acclaimed film, *Birdy*, about a Vietnam veteran.

Nick as wannabe rock and roll star, Charlie Bodell, in *Peggy Sue Got Married*.

With Cher in *Moonstruck*.

Top: Playing Sailor in *Wild at Heart*

Below: *Honeymoon in Vegas*, with Sarah Jessica Parker. Cage plays a New York private eye who loses his fiancée in a poker game in Las Vegas.

Guarding Tess, with
Shirley Maclaine.

Cage with Patricia Arquette at the premiere of *Snake Eyes*.

Top: Cage with David Caruso and Barbet Schroeder at the 1995 Cannes Film Festival.

Below: With his parents, August Coppola and Joy Vogelsang.

The story sounds far-fetched but the first part actually happened. It was just a normal day on the streets of Yonkers, a comfortable suburb on the Hudson River within commuting distance of Manhattan, for 55-year-old detective Bob Cunningham. He chatted to waitress Phyllis Penza as he tucked into a plate of linguini at Sal's Restaurant, a regular hang-out. Then he was horrified to discover he was short of cash. He had just bought a blank lottery ticket and asked Phyllis to fill in three numbers, while he filled in the other three. The next night the numbers came up and Bob, the legal owner of the ticket, was $6 million richer. He told Gina, his wife of 20 years, what he had done and she instantly agreed that he must give Phyllis the half she had been promised.

Here, the fiction deviates from truth for dramatic and comedic effect. Robert and Phyllis remained good friends, but both their marriages stayed sound. 'We knew we were just friends,' said Phyllis, who left her job in 1986 because she was harassed by people asking for hand-outs. She and her husband, also Robert, a retired builder, moved from a modest flat to a three-bedroom, brick-built house in Yonkers. Gina Cunningham retired from her book-keeping job in 1986 but Robert did not retire until 1992. They bought a house from Gina's father, where they had lived for years in a top-floor apartment, and Robert treated himself to a new Cadillac every three years.

American lotteries in those days — 1984 — were paid out over 20 years, so Robert and Phyllis had to look forward to $142,857.50 each a year, before tax.

In the film version, which went through several name changes before being released as *It Could Happen to You*, Nick plays Charlie Lang, married to Muriel, a shrewish hairdresser, played by Rosie Perez. Charlie is the kind of old-fashioned cop who knows the kids and dogs on his beat and is a father figure people turn to for help, rather than shy away from. The waitress, Yvonne Biasi, who works at a small coffee shop in the trendy TriBeCa district of Manhattan, was played by Bridget Fonda.

Nick actually put Bergman and the script together, but he never expected to end up playing Charlie. He explained, 'I read the script before him and I told him about it. Then it went through the various channels that be at the studio. Then it finally came back to me, but originally I had read it and liked it, and I thought there was potential here to do a really sweet and romantic movie. I felt Andy had a lot of faith in me, more faith than I had in me in this role. I wasn't sure how I would do it but the thing that's great about working with Andy is that I've worked with him before, he knows what I'm capable of doing and where I can go, and when it doesn't work and when it does work. So we have a good rapport and a trust factor that sort of saves time. But his experience with me before in *Honeymoon in Vegas* was one where I was really encouraged to be quite flashy and large, and this one was all the way in the other direction. So I thought it was interesting that he would think of me for this.'

Nick was delighted to team up with Lobell and Bergman again, though at first he thought Charlie was simply too good to be true, even though the film was based on a true story. Although he had enjoyed playing more 'normal' characters in *Honeymoon* and *Tess*, he still felt more at home looking on the darker side of life. So he opted to play Charlie as a fairytale prince, and he and Bergman decided to base him on America's all-time favourite good guy, James Stewart.

'I was a little "shiver-me-timbers" at first when I knew I was going to be doing this,' he admitted to Elias Stimac of *Drama-Logue* magazine. 'I wasn't sure if I could make Charlie interesting enough, being that good and that nice. It's like when you go to the museums and see paintings of the devil, they're always so imaginative and bizarre. And then you see the angel, it's always so boring and sitting on a cloud and nothing's going on. But I had reached a point in my work where I felt I'd neglected the sunnier side of film. So that was the challenge with this film.

'A lot of people have asked me, "How could this be so? How could somebody promise a stranger two million and then give it to her?" But the question probably these days should really be, "How could you break your promise?" The fact that this actually happened helped. In real life, the person knew the waitress as a friend, so how could he not share it with her? The difference here is that this is a perfect stranger. So what I did was I formed a kind of fairytale reality to play this part. I like things that are a little larger than life anyway, things that stretch the realm of believability in real time. So I took this as a New York fable.

'Luckily, Andrew Bergman saw it the same way I did and, in fact, the way he shot the movie with cinematographer Caleb Deschanel is extremely loving. It had the nostalgia of some of the old New York love stories of the '40s and, indeed, of James Stewart films, which was Bergman's recurring direction to me, "Make him more Jimmy!" That's what I tried to do — although I wasn't exactly sure what it meant to be "more Jimmy". So I had to think about It's a Wonderful Life and I'd get an image of Jimmy Stewart in my head. I think the one line in the movie that I really felt like Jimmy Stewart was in the diner when Yvonne says, "Go do whatever it is you do. Well, go get a cat out of a tree or something!" and Charlie says, "No. That'd be the Fire Department." That came out like Jimmy Stewart. In the rhythm of that line I very specifically tried to sell Jimmy Stewart. Yes, this is the Jimmy Stewart movie, but I'm such a huge admirer that I'd hesitate to say I was impersonating him. It was really more of a tip of the hat, kind of a homage, you know. I do think he had what seemed to be a pure American innocence which trembled on the screen in a way that gave people hope. And there isn't a lot of that right now in the movies.'

Nick was also intrigued by the idea of playing a policeman because he was ambivalent about the force. While the screen image of New York policemen has historically been of jovial Irish-Americans, the reality of southern California cops was very different. Nick went on, 'I do think my sensibilities are better as an actor in the outlaw mode than the good cop mode. So I was a little nervous about this role. And again, I had to look at this persona like a prince from a fairytale or something. I couldn't play the reality of it, so to speak, because I grew up in LA and my relationship with the cops has always been a little bizarre. They've changed now here, they've cleaned up their act, but there were times when I didn't like the cops. I grew up not liking the police. So to play a cop like this was a real stretch for me. And the thing that really made it OK was that he was a New York cop and he was walking the beat, and these cops — I'm generalising but I spoke to a great number of them — are really into their neighbourhood, and they really become like a father figure almost. They're protectors, they look at it like parents. They speak with the neighbours, they play with the kids. They're really like heroes on their beat and that's a very different thing from the Adam 12 cops driving around and busting — that's a whole other kind of thing.'

Bergman, on the other hand, had no problems visualising Nick as a cop. He said, 'He's a funny, charming and real man. He has a wonderful ear and he's a real actor. When you see him in a cop's uniform at the start of the movie you believe him. It's not like, "Oh, here's Jack Nicholson or Tom Hanks in a cop uniform." He has a wonderful ability to become the guy. Nick makes ordinary guys so interesting. There's nothing white bread about anything he does.

'In *It Could Happen to You,* you have a wonderful, simple character in the cop and he is flanked by two women who are absolutely day and night. Rosie Perez and Bridget Fonda could not be more different. And that's what's funny — to see Nick go from Bridget, in the coffee shop, to Rosie, this harridan that he's married to, who's just killing him day and night, and that's the fun.'

He was also delighted to have Fonda on board, and thought her family connections — she's the daughter of *Easy Rider* star Peter Fonda, her aunt is actress, former political activist and exercise video queen Jane Fonda, and her grandfather, Henry Fonda, was one of the grand old men of American cinema with films like *Grapes of Wrath* and *Twelve Angry Men* — suited her perfectly to a romance with a twist of Capra. He said, 'Bridget has a real understanding of the kinds of films that were made in the '30s and '40s. Then again, if you had a grandfather who starred in *The Lady Eve,* it's not hard to understand the connection. She's incredibly smart and she has an amazing gift for comedy and for being completely real.'

Fonda was equally pleased to be there. She said, 'I sat alone and cried when I finished reading the script and that's rare for me. But it just hit such a nerve.'

Perez' role as the greedy, tasteless Muriel was the most difficult. It was essential for the audience to hate her so much that they approved of Charlie breaking his marriage vows. Producer Lobell said, 'We were worried because we think she's adorable. But the audience loves to hate her.'

Perez believed Muriel could not help the way she acted. 'I found that Muriel was innocent and naïve in a way,' she said. 'She didn't understand she has no taste, she didn't know that she was tacky, and that's funny.' She also praised Nick's approach to his role, saying, 'As an actor, you're always concerned about how you look. But Nicolas will risk looking ridiculous for the sake of the character and the film.'

One of the biggest stars of the film was New York City itself. Shooting took place in more than 100 locations around the city, though ironically the set that is the heart of the film, the Ideal Coffee Shop, was purpose-built.

'We built it from scratch on a piece of ground that was a parking lot,' said Lobell. 'It is a luxury, but we can really do what we want.'

The shop had a moveable ceiling and walls for ease of shooting, but it was so realistic that genuine customers wandered in off the street in search of coffee, and some even looking for jobs. The real coffee shop over the road, LeRoy's Coffee Shop, had its name changed to LeRoy's Tavern for the duration of the shoot, for a price. Owner Herb David was delighted to co-operate, and made extra money by supplying the set with provisions to cool them down during the sweltering New York summer.

'They're big *kibbitzers*, there's a lot of joking going on and we're feeding them all day long,' he joked. 'We're sending them buckets and buckets of ice, and buckets and buckets of sodas, and all kinds of cold drinks, so besides the breakfast and the lunch and the coffee breaks, we're getting a lot of extra business. And they're spending a mint.'

They also built the apartment where Nick and Muriel lived on a set, but Yvonne's home was a tiny apartment in Greenwich Village. Bergman said, 'I hate it when I see a movie about young, struggling characters in an apartment that I know must cost $9,000 a month!'

A few days before filming started in August 1993, the coffee shop was the centre of a street party for the cast, crew and guests, hosted by a tourism campain group, New York, It Ain't Over. Kristen Zang was there with Nick, flashing her brand-new pink engagement ring, and Bridget Fonda's steady, Eric Stoltz, was also on hand. The couple shared an apartment in Manhattan and Stoltz laughed, 'While Bridget was taking ballroom dancing lessons this afternoon, I was washing the floor at home.' Then New York Mayor David Dinkins attended, as did crooner Tony Bennet, who sang the movie's theme tune, *Young at Heart*, in a duet with Shawn Colvin.

The city's famed Central Park was another location, one which was difficult for both Nick and Fonda. They both suffer from acrophobia, a morbid fear of heights, so it was traumatic for them to do a balloon sequence flying over Central Park. 'And being suspended by a crane high up in the air,' added Nick.

The *New York Post* also features in the movie, with Isaac Hayes playing a photographer for the newspaper who chronicles the adventures and exploits of the prize-winners, and the paper joined in the fun by printing dummy front pages about them.

One of Charlie's endearing features is his habit of playing 'stickball', or rudimentary street baseball, with the kids he encounters on the beat. So he and Yvonne — who by this time has bought the coffee shop and instituted the 'Charlie Lang Table' which provides free food for the homeless — rent the legendary baseball shrine Yankee Stadium for the youngsters to live out their dreams. The Yankee Stadium scenes were shot on 7 September 1993, just 72 hours after a historic game between the New York Yankees and the Cleveland Indians in which Yankee pitcher Jim Abbott threw a no-hitter — a game in which none of the opposing batters were able to hit one of his pitches — only the third in the history of the stadium. True to the Frank Capraesque nature of the film, the producers recruited the youngsters from one of the toughest suburbs of the city.

The cast, crew and kids had a wonderful time, with the possible exception of Fonda, whose character Yvonne tried ineffectually to pitch balls. They bounced long before they reached the plate, the point where the batter is supposed to hit, prompting cinematographer Caleb Deschanel to yell, 'She's killing worms!'

Fonda admitted, 'I've always been petrified by these kind of sports. I'm so glad nobody asked me to hit. I'm not a baseball fan at all but I can't bear to say anything to Andy and Mike because it means so much to them.' But she gave the pitching a game try — so game she ended up hurting her arm and had to pack it in ice.

Nick and Bridget palled up making the film, and Nick played Charlie for real — almost — when he took her to the trendy Russian Tea Rooms and left a $60 tip. On another occasion, he was said to have been even more generous even though the waiter did not deserve it. According to the now-defunct British newspaper *Today*, he took his mother to a 24-hour diner where the service was terrible. The waiter snapped at Joy to hurry up and place her order. Nick then gave him the shock of his life. He said, 'I didn't want him to forget how incredibly rude he's been to my mother. So I pulled out a crisp $100 bill and gave it to him as a tip, and wrote on the back of my bill, "This might make you think twice before you treat somebody so badly again." '

While Charlie and Yvonne spend their money on good deeds, including buying subway tickets for homebound commuters, Muriel goes on a spend-spend-

spend spree, decorating the apartment in garish bad taste and splashing out on a fur coat, only to walk straight into a bunch of animal rights demonstrators who did some splashing out of their own — with paint.

The spending was fun, though unrealistic, given that the prize money would have been paid out over 20 years. Charlie and Yvonne would have earned $59,000 a year between them, but *Us* magazine priced their initial spree at $507,833: half a million dollars for the coffee shop; $2,400 to rent Yankee Stadium; $2,200 for two suites at the Plaza Hotel; $1,483 for two season tickets for the New York Knicks basketball team; $1,250 for 1,000 subway tokens; and $500 for a balloon ride.

Bergman was full of praise for Nick's work in the finished product. Asked by Sean O'Neil of the *Los Angeles Village Voice* if Nick worked best when he — or at least his character — was under pressure, he said, 'That's what you would think until you see this picture. For me, he works great not pulling his hair out. He has tremendous strength as a leading man. These circumstances are less insane than in other movies, where he's driven crazy by basically everybody he meets, but I think it's true that he reacts well to pressure, reacts in a way that's fun and compelling. I think there's a great vulnerability to him. He always describes himself as the guy who couldn't get a date in high school, and since I couldn't either I guess we work well together.'

The film showed well to test audiences apart from one detail — the title. Bergman said, 'Every time we screened the picture the audience just hated the name. So we thought maybe we should change it.' It became successively *Cop Gives Waitress $2 Million*, *Cop Gives Waitress $2 Million Tip*, which remained for some time before evolving into *The $2 Million Tip*, and finally making an abrupt change to *It Could Happen to You*.

The film opened with a gala première at the Paris Theater in Manhattan, with celebrities like Martin Scorsese, Illeana Douglas and television talk-show host Conan O'Brien among the guests being transported by bus from the cinema to a party at the trendy Boathouse in Central Park. Nick, who had gone on to film the disastrous *Trapped in Paradise* after *It Could Happen to You* had wrapped, was very different from his Charlie persona; he had grown a goatee for his latest role, playing the heavy in *Kiss of Death*, which was also set and being filmed in New York.

Once again, Nick came off well in the eyes of the critics, winning more praise for himself than did the film as a whole.

'What really make the film are Bergman's general restraint, despite the nature of the material, and the strong central performances,' wrote Brian Lowry in *Daily Variety*. 'Cage and Fonda are extremely natural as the good-hearted lug and the goodbye girl, while the squawking, raging Perez only needs to be fitted for a broomstick.'

Peter Rainer of the *Los Angeles Times* called the film 'slight but sweet,' but raved about Nick — and perceptively summed up Nick's approach to his 'sunny' films. He said, 'Is there any other actor who can play zigzag dementia as well as he can — in films like *Wild at Heart* and *Vampire's Kiss* — and then turn around and play zigzag normality — as in *Moonstruck* and Bergman's *Honeymoon in Vegas* and now *It Could Happen to You*? It could be that, for Cage, these ordinary guys are the weirdest of incarnations — normality as the ultimate masquerade. But he doesn't condescend to these characters or turn them into schmoes. He respects their tiny dreams and so, of course, when the dreams pay off big, they don't seem so ordinary any more. These characters become figures in a fable.'

In *Drama-Logue*, Elias Stimac wrote, 'Director Bergman has beat the odds and come up with another winner in the same comedic vein as *Honeymoon in Vegas*. He and writer Jane Anderson have crafted a Capraesque, sweet but not sappy love story that literally covers all bases. They are aided by a tremendous cast. Cage continues to impress as an Everyman leading man, comically conflicted all the way through, and Fonda is touchingly tender as his new friend. Perez is charmingly caustic.'

Influential syndicated columnist Roger Ebert pointed out, 'The story is not so much about romance as about good-heartedness, which is a rarer quality and not so selfish. And Cage has certain gentleness that brings out nice soft smiles on Fonda's face.'

Entertainment Weekly loved the chemistry but not the movie. Reviewer Owen Gleiberman wrote, 'Is there another contemporary actor with the gentleness, the yearning ardour, of Nicolas Cage? With his lost-puppy eyes and slightly gawky grin, he's like a poster boy for true romance. Cage flirts adorably with Fonda, who gets to exploit her best feature, the razor-sharp smile that cuts surprisingly far back into her pale, anxious face. As winning as these two are, however, their aw-shucks chemistry isn't supported by enough of a plot.'

In *The New York Times*, Caryn James agreed, 'Two good-hearted people find each other in New York City. Now that's a miracle. The other miracle is that the two stars of *It Could Happen to You* keep it sailing over a script that is often as predictable and flat as the movie's new title. The toughest trick in the film is to keep them human and likeable in the middle of all this fairy dust. Mr Cage and Ms Fonda manage to do that with winning simplicity.'

David Hunter wrote in *The Hollywood Reporter*, 'Two normal folks, too honest and too selfless, are the unlikely recipients of a few cool millions in this romantic fable that predictably goes through its paces. A more sluggish-than-usual performance from Nicolas Cage, a shriller-than-usual-turn from Rosie Perez and a numbingly sentimental tone are the down-sides.'

Robert Cunningham, the cop who had started it all, and who met up with Penzo once a year to split the winnings, said, 'It was funny. You're not seeing some guy get his head blown off.'

The film was not without controversy. A group of Asian-Americans complained that it was racist because of a scene including a Korean grocery store. Media Action Network for Asian-Americans complained to TriStar that the scene portrayed Koreans as 'unfriendly, overcharging workaholics', and objected to a policeman referring to the grocer's wife as 'that bitch'. Group President Guy Aoki asked TriStar to remove the word 'bitch'. He wrote, 'We believe in film-makers' rights to their own visions. But we feel they must be balanced with social responsibility.' TriStar said they had not intended to insult Koreans or other Asians.

Nick was relaxed and reflective as he promoted the film and looked back on the past couple of years and his non-stop schedule.

'The majority of my life has been in public and with the work,' he said. 'I've been on the road working non-stop for the last two years. I'm not really comfortable unless I'm working. I'm not very comfortable in life. I do feel at ease when I'm working. It's like I've chosen a life on the road and it's made certain parts of home life very difficult — because I haven't been able to see people I love, but that's the path I've chosen.

'I admit I'm not normally normal. I can't explain why that is and it's not something I can help. It's who I am and I was worried at first that I wouldn't be able to act normal in this movie. But I tried real hard and though Andrew had to talk me down a few times, I think I pulled it off. I think I come across normal, although I'm not sure what normal is. This is a real New York fable and I guess my character is the Prince Charming of this fairytale. That's not an easy part to play because it's not easy to make someone that goody-goody be interesting. I've always felt we have a little bit of good and bad in us — and that's what makes us complicated and all that. But Charlie is good, good, good, so I wanted to play him a little larger than life. Naturalism is a style that can be really effective but it can be really boring.'

Once again he invoked the spirit of Jim Morrison, telling Barry Koltnow of the *Orange County Register*, 'Most of my characters are filled with this weird internal angst and I thought it might be time for a change. I turned 30, I have a kid, and I remembered an old clip of Jim Morrison of The Doors talking about how he never made happy songs. He was right and I started to think about my own career. I love the films I've been in but they weren't what you'd call happy films. I wanted to make a film that was pure happiness and *It Could Happen to You* was it. It's like a '40s romantic comedy with a Capra touch; a romantic comedy with an emphasis on the sweet side of things. I felt it was time to do a character that was happier and lighter. I've done all this weird, internal angst stuff. That's good and valid but this afforded me the opportunity to play sunshine and happiness. Even I had a hard time feeling that this guy exists. That's part of why the role was so interesting to me. Frankly, I didn't know if I could be interesting as a nice person.'

And he told Mark Marvel of *Interview* magazine, 'I don't really pretend to know much about the socio-political import of *It Could Happen To You*, but I do think that it's good to have role models who mean what they say. The one code that I live my life by is to do unto others as I would have done unto myself. I try to have a certain amount of respect for people. I think people can see that with all the violence and homelessness there is, the world's beginning to rot. And so a movie like this might be a good return to the nostalgia of the '40s and '50s. I don't want to compare it to a Frank Capra film too much, but it does have a Capra-like fairytale aspect to it and that's how I played it. When I first read the script I had some difficulty believing this cop actually gives $2 million to a complete stranger. But the fact is, it really happened.'

Nick knew exactly what he would do if it happened to him in real life and he won a lottery. When asked by *Drama-Logue*'s Elias Stimac, he replied, 'Me, personally, right now in my life — it's easy for me to say this because I've chosen a path in my work which fortunately has been lucrative. I can say I'm fine. I've been paid well. So if $4 million came to me from something like a lottery, because I didn't earn it I might feel a little odd about it. And I can honestly tell you — and it sounds like some high-falutin' bullshit — but I'm a good believer in taking care of your own city and I'm very depressed about the whole homeless situation. So I would give it to the homeless. I would try to do something, maybe build a big house or a care structure where a lot of these people could go.'

Nick was delighted to know that he could, indeed, play happy and normal. But he was also sure that he would continue to look for alternative roles and takes risk. 'I had to prove I could move into the mainstream,' he said. 'But now that I'm there, I want to get back to doing independent movies again, because I believe the only way to keep any creative integrity is either to work with a powerful director who can get what he or she wants from a studio, or to do smaller, independent films.

'I understand the business of movie-making and I know that because of the huge budgets big studios can't afford to take risks. I accept that and I enjoy being in them once in a while. But that financial situation only increased the importance of the small films. Those are the films we do for art's sake. Those are the films where the new ideas come from.'

He was fleetingly tempted to do theatre. Family friend Bernard Gerston of the Lincoln Center had expressed an interest and Nick, who has always suffered from stage-fright, briefly contemplated doing Eugene O'Neill. But in the end he said, echoing comments made by Kathleen Turner in *Peggy Sue Got Married*, 'I'm really a film actor. I want a permanent record. I want to be there for ever.'

In a way, at this stage of his career he believed he had made his mark and was no longer overshadowed by his famous relatives, even though interviewers constantly pointed out his family connections. He acknowledged that, despite his fears at the beginning of his career, being a Coppola had not been a drawback — but neither was it the source of his success. When Stimac raised Nick's family connection to Francis Coppola, he replied, 'In some ways it motivated me. I got lucky that I had worked with him on *Rumble Fish* which was early on. But I have no reason to believe that if he weren't in my life, that I would not be doing what I'm doing now. I really don't think *Moonstruck* made $100 million because Francis Coppola is my uncle. I think if anything, it gave me motivation to go out there and try to really prove that I can do this myself.'

In fact, Nick had proved he was his own man — as well as Everyman.

CHAPTER THIRTEEN
WILD AND WEIRD AT HEART

Perhaps it was the impetuousness of youth or maybe he was just moon-struck, but, either way, it took less than a New York minute for young and romantic Nick to realise he had met the girl of his dreams. By chance, he set eyes on aspiring teenage actress Patricia Arquette one fateful day in 1987 as they happened upon each other in the world-famous Canter's 24-hour Jewish delicatessen on North Fairfax Avenue just down the road from the heart of Hollywood.

For 23-year-old Nick, there was no doubt that it was love at first sight. His puppy-dog eyes must have looked even more mournful than usual as he stood mesmerised, staring at her. Nick admits he knew he loved her 'the minute I met her'. She walked past him and for some reason said that she'd just eaten liver and onions. He was immediately smitten by this natural blonde's summer-blue eyes, lily-white skin — a rarity in California where most girls are deeply tanned, even now, despite the warnings from doctors about the dangers of contracting skin cancer — and sensuously-rounded, well-endowed body, all contained in a petite 5ft 2in frame. He made his move within seconds, shamelessly chatting her up with the bizarre and enigmatic opening remark, 'I'm an American,' and following it with an immediate proposal of marriage.

He had already established himself as an up-and-coming actor with star quality with films such as *Peggy Sue Got Married*, *The Cotton Club* and *Valley Girl* under his belt.

Patricia, on the other hand, was just getting started. A friend accompanying Nick in Canter's knew the few things she had appeared in and started to rattle off her restricted résumé: a TV special, a cheap sex romp called *Pretty Smart* and the horror movie *A Nightmare on Elm Street III*. 'I was horrified, exposed in my B-ishness,' she confessed.

Patricia was just 19 and, like Nick with his strong showbusiness family connections, she also had greasepaint flowing through her veins. She came from a long line of actors and entertainers. Her great-grandparents were vaudeville performers; her grandfather, comedian Cliff Arquette, played a well-known

163

character — country bumpkin Charlie Weaver — on a popular television game show in the United States, *Hollywood Squares*; her father, Lewis, who died in February 2001, was an actor on Broadway and was in the cast of the long-running TV drama *The Waltons*, which was seen around the world, playing mill boss JD Pickett; her older sister Rosanna had already starred in *Desperately Seeking Susan* with Madonna; and her brothers, Richmond, Alexis and David, were all destined to become actors.

Nick's friend flatteringly told pretty Patricia how much he loved her work and Nick immediately agreed saying, 'I'm a big fan of yours, too. I'm going to marry you.' He added, 'Listen, you don't believe me but I want you to marry me.' Nick remembered, 'The second thing I said to her was, "You're gonna be my wife." '

She was totally taken aback and turned him down flat. Sceptical Patricia thought Nick was crazy and wished that he and his friend would go to hell. But he persisted, begging her to go out with him and demanding that she send him 'on a mission' to prove his love. He asked her to set him a quest worthy of a medieval knight, to give him a list of chivalrous deeds that he must complete to win her hand. Although Nick's pestering made her feel uncomfortable, she was also enjoying the flirtatious conversation.

She remembered, 'I thought he was tricking me or something, I thought he was teasing me; he kept trying to go out with me and I thought, it's like a bet he has with his friends or something, I'm not the kind of girl he would chase like that. I don't understand. To be asking me for requests to win his love, like ten things, and when he finds them I'm supposed to marry him and I thought, that's kinda fun, I'll write this little list, you know, but he'll go away.'

Nick recalled, 'I said, "Put me on a quest. Let me prove I mean this." '

Patricia, who had been a wild child herself, was not lacking in imagination. She picked up a paper napkin and wrote out her wish list of almost impossible things to find and bring her. That catalogue included a black orchid; a genuine autograph of notoriously reclusive writer JD Salinger, author of *Catcher in the Rye*; a wedding dress from the Lisu tribe in northern Thailand; a portable toilet; and a Bob's Big Boy statue, a fibreglass mannequin that stood outside a chain of popular down-market American diners.

She said, 'So I said I wanted JD Salinger's autograph, he's like a hermit basically, and I want a black orchid from a jungle in Brazil and I want a Thai wedding outfit and I want this giant statue of a little boy and I want all these things, you know.'

Nick has often admitted he has always been attracted to crazy women and that he wanted a woman who could really 'kick my ass'. He confessed to Lawrence Grobel of *Movieline* magazine, 'With a crazy woman you're floating in space, so it's an infinity. Space and time break down in a way that you don't really know where you are.' He added, 'I guess I'm attracted to people who have bad stories to tell — I feel *simpatico* with them.'

In Patricia, he had certainly found more than he had bargained for. The daughter of free-spirited parents who eventually split up, she had grown up in a commune and says of her childhood, 'During those troubled oestrogen-explosion periods, I went from being an angel to a scathing, fire-breathing lunatic.' At 12 she was arrested for shoplifting and at 14 she shaved her head and ran away to live with her older sister. When she met Nick, she was already independent-minded and forging her own career and way in the world.

Right from the start it was a mission ... impossible. He recalled, 'First I had to find out where she lived. She wouldn't tell me. She said the street she lived on rhymed with "flower". I found out where it was.'

The following morning he really discovered just how difficult the tasks he had so willingly agreed to undertake would be to accomplish when a florist informed him that there was no such thing as a black orchid. Nick said, 'I went to a flower store and asked for a black orchid. The guy said they don't exist.' He later admitted, 'I quickly became aware many of them didn't exist.'

Not to be beaten, he bought a deep purple orchid instead and, with the aid of a tin of black spray paint, achieved the required colour, only to have Patricia witness him doing the deed when she peered out of her bedroom window at her mother's house as he sat astride his black Harley-Davidson FLH motorbike in the street outside, spraying away.

He remembered, 'I went to the art store and got a can of black spray paint. I got on my motorcycle with the orchid in one pocket and the spray paint in the other and drove to her house. And rang the doorbell. She wouldn't come down from the top floor. In my very showy way, I whipped the orchid out of my pocket. Then I whipped out the paint can and started spray-painting the orchid black. She was freaked out. I rang the doorbell again and she came down. I just gave it to her and got back on my motorcycle and left.' Nick recalled she said, 'Thank you' to him in a falsetto voice. He said, 'She was terrified.'

He had better luck getting the elusive Salinger signature. He found a Los Angeles memorabilia shop on Beverly Boulevard which miraculously actually had a letter written by Salinger, who hardly ever put his name to anything, to a woman, and signed by the elusive writer. 'I called an autograph store and asked if they had anything by JD Salinger — any kind of handwriting or autograph,' Nick said. 'The guy said that, as a matter of fact, he had a letter Salinger had written to a woman who I think had taken care of him at a boarding house or something.'

The next day, Nick drove back to her home again, this time in his silver-coloured Peugeot. Patricia was outside in the street playing hopscotch with some girlfriends. Nick pulled up and placed a cigar box on the street outside her front door and drove off. Inside the box, Patricia found the precious correspondence, which had cost him $2,500 to buy, accompanied by a sweet Dominican cigar and an apricot. Nick remembered, 'I got a call from her. She was off the Richter scale. She said, "OK, all right, just stop. Stop now." '

Day three found him not exactly defeated but definitely delayed. He arrived at her home to apologise for not turning up with one of the designated gifts. He explained that he and his friends had been out the previous night to acquire the requested Bob's Big Boy statue but they had lacked the necessary tools to unbolt it from the pavement outside the restaurant. He assured her that in a few hours he would be returning to the diner to complete the task; the monster-sized mannequin would be hers before the night was over.

'I'd already gotten the chain-saw,' Nick said, explaining his plans to liberate the statue from the pavement. 'I was gonna steal one and put it in a truck and leave it on her front lawn. But she freaked out and said, "No more." '

Patricia remembered, 'It was really panicking me. I had never been on a date with him and here I was going to have to marry him. I thought, oh my God, I'm gonna have to marry him and I don't even know him, I don't even know what his last name is.'

She immediately quashed the quest but agreed to a date as a consolation prize. Nick recalled, 'She started to freak out at that point. She said, "I don't know if I can marry you, but I'll go away with you."'

The actress, who in only a few years would firmly establish herself and her career by starring opposite Christian Slater in the 1993 cult hit movie *True Romance*, had set her new-found aspiring knight in shining armour some truly romantic modern-day tasks. Although the course of true love was definitely not going to run smoothly for the young couple, their chance meeting would have a lasting effect on both their lives.

Nick invited Patricia to go with him on a three-week trip to Mexico and she agreed. Actually, he did not intend them to remain in Mexico but, unbeknown to her, wanted to use it as a stop-over point on their way to Cuba, to see his grandfather Carmine Coppola conduct *Napoleon*, still hoping to convince her to marry him while they were away and turn the Caribbean excursion into a family occasion.

Carmine Coppola was a noted musician who had won Oscars for his scores for *The Godfather* and *The Godfather Part II*. But probably his greatest triumph was that, as a young man, he had written the original score for Abel Gance's silent 1920s' classic movie *Napoleon*, starring Albert Dieudonne. The score was more than three-and-a-half hours long.

Nick said, 'My grandfather was conducting his score for *Napoleon* in Cuba, and I knew the whole family would be there. I had a plan: I would get her to go with me to Mexico City, then I would abduct her, take her to Cuba and marry her while my family was there.'

Due to the tense political situation between the United States and Cuba in those days — and which still exists today — American citizens could not fly directly from the United States to Cuba, so Nick and Patricia flew to Mexico City, where Nick planned to collect their tickets at the airport for the rest of their journey on to Fidel Castro's Communist stronghold.

His subterfuge failed because, unfortunately, the tickets had been misplaced and his hot temper quickly got the better of him. By the time the situation had been resolved, he had thrown such a fit he was told by airport officials, 'You don't have the kind of attitude we want going to Cuba.' As a result, Nick and Patricia were refused permission to continue with their journey. Nick remembered, 'We got derailed at the Mexican airport. My tickets weren't there and I threw a temper tantrum. When the tickets arrived, they didn't want me on the plane.' They wandered round the streets of Mexico City, getting lost and watching a Mexican band playing Beatles songs, before cancelling the trip and flying back to the United States.

Their relationship was so complex that Nick had not even had sex with her — he couldn't. He later confessed that he was so deeply in love with her 'I wasn't able to have sex, because I was paralysed. I couldn't perform on that level.'

Even so, Patricia admitted that their weeks together were very intense. She remembered that on their first date 'we were kissing and kissing and kissing'.

However, Patricia had been so turned off by Nick's explosive outburst of rage that she decided to return to her old boyfriend. It would be a further eight years before the young lovers would eventually salvage their relationship.

'She didn't like how I was yelling at everybody,' Nick said. 'She went back to her boyfriend, and that was that. She broke my heart for many years.'

Patricia moved in with musician Paul Rossi and soon became pregnant, giving birth to a baby boy she named Enzo, after a minor character in *The Godfather*, while Nick later became a father himself with son Weston Coppola Cage by model and actress Christina Fulton. Nick said, 'We went on with our lives. I became a dad, she became a mother.' Nevertheless, Nick and Patricia kept in touch occasionally. He said, 'I maintained peripheral contact with her — she's a good person who is a doting, nurturing friend.' He remembered, 'We saw each other maybe four times. It was never a physical thing.'

Said Patricia, 'I had a child, then he had a child. We talked on the phone, ran into each other a few times. We were always very connected.' In hindsight, she confessed that part of the reason for their original romance hitting the rocks was that she was intimidated by his success and doubted his sincerity. She said, 'We had all of these similarities, but when we first got together I was a little intimidated by him. If I was to be with him when I was that young, I would have never known who I could have been on my own.' In some of their sporadic telephone calls, Patricia would tease Nick by asking him, 'Still wanna marry me?'

Over that period, the passion that Nick felt for Patricia had somehow also turned into a true friendship. She broke up with Rossi and both she and Nick dated a string of other people. On one occasion, the night she moved into a new house in the suburban Silverlake district of LA, she asked Nick to come over to keep her company and stay the night. But she was insistent that there would be 'no fooling around'. Even so, he was happy to spend time with her.

She was always in his thoughts, an old memory he could not shake off. Then history repeated itself and they bumped into each other at Canter's again one night when Patricia had popped in for a bowl of soup. Nick said, 'I'd been thinking a lot about her. Her face kept coming to me. I would meditate on her face. I went back to Canter's. I ran into her again. This time there was a change. Maybe because we were back at the place where we had met.' He remembered that on that second encounter in Canter's, she was wearing tight-fitting, silver-coloured trousers.

One day in January 1995, they were talking on the telephone. Nick was in a panic. He said, 'So I heard you have a boyfriend.' Patricia replied, 'Yeah.' He told her that he had had a premonition that she was going to marry her current boyfriend and he said, 'Well, I'm going to Egypt for a week. Don't get married while I'm gone.' Patricia told him, 'You don't have to worry about anybody else.'

She said, 'And when I said it, I just knew in my heart he didn't have to worry about me marrying somebody else. So that worked on my mind for a few months.' Her spontaneous assurance that she was not about to marry the man she was dating preyed on her mind. It dawned on her that Nick meant more to her than she had ever understood. She said, 'I realised I was ready. I didn't need any more notches in my lipstick case.'

Patricia had often described her ideal man as 'someone who looked like Jesus but was kind of like a magician, a clown, and a pirate all mixed together; someone confident enough to write his own moral code.' Throughout her dating life, she had been searching for 'an honourable, truthful, brave man', and now she had finally come to the realisation that Nick was indeed that man of her dreams — her knight in shining armour.

After that conversation, she confessed, 'He was on my mind. I needed to be reassured that the depth of his love would be as brave as before.' Nick had once told her that if ever she wanted to marry him to call him. One night in late March, she was sitting at home with a girlfriend and the woman's fiancé, when she abruptly announced, 'I'm gonna call Nick, and I'm gonna ask him to marry me.'

She confessed, 'Finally, I just got up the nerve and I called him and asked him to marry me over the phone.' Luckily for them, as it was to turn out, Nick was at home reading a comic book as the telephone rang. When she spoke to him, this time she didn't teasingly ask if he still wanted to marry her. She was deadly serious as she proposed to him. She started the conversation, 'Listen, I'm gonna ask you something.' Then she popped the question. Without having to think about it, he accepted. 'Well, OK, I'll do it,' replied the *Wild at Heart* star. 'Something inside me just said yes.' His affirmative response was so immediate, she had to point out she was serious. 'No, I'm really serious. I'm not joking,' she said.

'Yeah, I know,' he replied, 'I'm serious, too.'

Despite being so positive in his acceptance of her proposal, Nick still suggested that they shouldn't rush into it. He said, 'Originally, I said, "Let's take six months," but she didn't see it that way. She just felt that she didn't want to give us any reason to back out. So I said, "Fine, I love you, let's do it." ' He later recalled, 'It was almost like an arranged marriage, where we rushed into it. We didn't have a natural courtship, we just did it. It was a romantic gesture to marry as quickly as we did. But it was not a frivolous decision. I was genuinely aware of the work it takes to make a marriage work.'

Nick went on, 'I think for a woman to propose to a man in our society is a very brave thing to do. It's bad form for a man to say no to a woman who proposes, he will have to pay karmically, he will go up in flames.' But he admitted, 'I wouldn't have said yes if she were not my soulmate.'

Patricia promised to get back in touch within seven days to give him details of their wedding plans. 'Well, goodbye, husband,' she said. He had only one question before she hung up. 'Wait,' he said and then asked, 'Can I have your phone number?'

Nick need not have worried about not being in contact with her. Patricia soon arrived at his home, dressed in a figure-hugging black vinyl outfit and presented him with a purple — then his favourite colour — wedding cake. He said, 'When she showed up at my house dressed head to toe in black vinyl, carrying a big purple wedding cake, I knew I was with the right woman.' The thoughts of her that had haunted him throughout those eight years they were apart had gone from being a distant dream to reality. Finally, they were destined to be together. Nick concluded, 'It pays to wait.'

Trying to explain how their tortured relationship finally led to her making the proposal of marriage to Nick, Patricia said, 'It's like we both got on the same train. And we looked at each other, and we knew. But we were immature. So he had to go run on top of the train, and I went to go dance around in the diner car. And then we both got off the train at separate stops. And eight years later we both got back on, and we sat next to each other and smiled. Suddenly, things didn't feel chaotic any more. I felt ... calm.'

She consulted only one member of her family about her whirlwind decision to marry — Enzo, who by this time was eight years old. She said, 'He's very honest. He would have said, "I don't like that guy." Needless to say, Enzo didn't. The rest of her family learned of the nuptials via messages left on their telephone answering machines after the deed was done.

As a token of their new love, Nick bought them both rings. His was a large gold ring with the Greek God Zeus' head etched into a large ruby set in the middle. Hers was a Byzantine ring bearing a Greek Goddess. Nick said, 'Seeing that our love, in my estimation, had a kind of mythic feeling to it, I found her a Byzantine ring of the Goddess Diana, who was the archer, the hunter, queen of the witches, but not witches in the bad sense. And I thought, if she's going to be Diana, I'm going to be Zeus.'

Two weeks after the proposal, Nick and Patricia eloped. They drove up the Californian coast in Nick's blue Ferrari sports car to the picturesque beach town of Carmel, where Clint Eastwood had once been mayor, and married on the morning of Saturday, 8 April 1995, standing on a cliff overlooking the ocean, with only the town's former Chief of Police Donald McFarland as a witness and his wife, Kathee, a preacher who performed the ceremony, present.

'It was important to Patricia that the Chief of Police of Carmel would be a witness,' Nick said. 'I thought that was interesting. She wasn't messing around.'

During the service, which took only ten minutes, Patricia wore a leopard-print jacket and held a bunch of orchids spray-painted black and her precious Salinger letter. Sadly, years later, Nick's housekeeper, thinking the rare piece of paper was just rubbish, threw it away.

Patricia recalled, 'Stormy skies, crashing waves, dark woods — and everything out of focus except Nick in the centre with this light all around him.'

It has been said that as they exchanged their vows, sea otters bobbed up and down watching in the Pacific Ocean just yards away, but this is just another piece of the Nick Cage mythology that has built up around this charismatic individual. Nick admitted, 'I don't know where the sea otter story came in, because there were no sea otters, to my recollection. But it's a good story.'

Nick was soberly dressed in a dark suit, which seemed to match his sombre mood, for the occasion. Kathee McFarland recalled, 'He was real quiet. Patty giggled a lot.' The couple exchanged plain gold rings. They posed for a few photographs before heading for Nick's adopted home town of San Francisco, where he has a house in the upmarket Pacific Heights neighbourhood. They later lunched at The Cliffhouse restaurant.

Nick remembered, 'It was like a romantic hallucination. It was loaded, because we had spent no time together and all of a sudden we were married, so there was an incredible pressure.' He said later, 'It sounds speedy, but there was an eight-year history to the relationship. I married a woman who is my friend.'

Realising the pressures that both of them having careers as actors would cause to their attempts to lead a normal married life, they made a very special promise to each other. Nick revealed, 'We vowed we wouldn't go two weeks without seeing each other.' Nick was sure he had made the right decision when he married Patricia. 'There was no doubt in my mind that this woman was my equal,' he confessed. 'She is the person I would want to be if I were a woman.'

They made another pact although, thankfully for their co-stars, it didn't last over the years. They pledged that they would each eat garlic before filming a sex scene. Nick said, 'It was a way of sort of making sure that each of us was thinking about the other during a love scene. But we've since declared a cease-fire on the garlic.' They decided that they did not need to do it any more because they trusted each other.

Nick just knew that marrying Patricia was the right thing to do. He said a person knows it is love 'when you feel that something is very unique and you can't have it with anybody else and you want that person in your life and would do anything for them.' He knew.

But he also had a practical element that overrode the romance. He continued, 'It's a combination of that and the more scientific approach in that you choose the problems you want to live with. And you make a decision. Marriage is not a walk in the park. It's a lotta work and has to be treated with respect and nurtured.'

For her part, Patricia, who described Nick as 'my own private Atticus', referring to the kindly father and dedicated lawyer in Harper Lee's classic story *To Kill a Mockingbird*, and immortalised by Gregory Peck in his Oscar-winning performance in the 1962 movie version of the story, said, 'I know the marriage sounds really weird, incredibly abrupt but we married out of a deep love for each other. Not out of sexuality. We hadn't slept together in eight years. You go through life trying to explain your moral code to whomever your partner is at the time. Half the time they think you're insane. But we're both from the same tribe. We have the same moral code. There's no arguing about it.' She added, 'We have the same kind of eccentricities.'

Neither of them had really taken in the true impact of what they had done at the time. Patricia admitted, 'We woke up the next morning and I said, "Don't you feel like you grew in the night? Like suddenly you woke up six inches taller? And none of your clothes are gonna fit any more?" It's like a brand new Earth was born.' Later, she said of her new husband, 'He is the only man I have ever really, really respected ... I believe in him in this greater sort of for ever, dignity and nobility way.'

Getting married also had a deep impact on Nick. He said, 'Once I married Patricia, I knew my life made sense. It didn't make sense before. I was like I was a half-moon and I met the other half and everything became circular.'

The marriage also brought about a slight thaw in the relationship between Nick and his estranged father. 'He wrote me a nice letter when we got married,' Nick admitted. However, it did not mean that they had patched up their differences, which had blown up the previous year while on a flight to Ireland for a holiday.

Nick's hasty wedding came only two weeks before the opening of his latest movie, *Kiss of Death* — in which he played a ruthless killer opposite David Caruso's reformed crook seeking revenge for the killing of his wife — and it could, indeed, have meant the Kiss of Death to Nick's career as far as his legion of female fans were concerned, because they may not have liked the Hollywood hunk they idolised now being a married man. In fact, that did not happen. For the most part, fans of both Nick and Patricia were supportive of their rush to put rings on each other's wedding fingers. Patricia admitted: 'Girls come up to me and say, "It's sooooo romantic", and that's true. It is sooooo romantic.'

Kiss of Death was Caruso's first movie role since his controversial and very acrimonious split from starring in the popular television cops and robbers show *NYPD Blue*, and it was the first time in more than two years and five movies that Nick had played a bad guy in a picture. As a result, there was no time for a real honeymoon. Nick and Patricia decided to postpone that for a few weeks until the Cannes Film Festival in France where they were both starring in movies — he in *Kiss of Death* and she in *Beyond Rangoon*.

They did, however, take a short break in New York where they experienced the less-than-romantic adventure of taking a ride on the notorious Cyclone roller-coaster at the world-famous Coney Island fairground. Nick said later, 'I've always enjoyed speed but I'm not reckless any more. There's a time to go fast and a time to go slow, and I'm aware of the difference.'

The role of homicidal criminal Junior in *Kiss of Death* was a gamble for Nick but he had deliberately chosen the part because, he said, 'As a cop who gave away half a winning lottery ticket in *It Could Happen to You* I played nice, nice, nice. This was a chance to do bad, bad, bad.'

Nick won critical praise for his performance and, although it got mixed reviews despite many critics liking it, unfortunately for him and Caruso, *Kiss of Death* did no good for either of their careers. It bombed at the box office and soon sank without trace, earning less than $15 million from domestic box-office takings.

It was not just his family and fans who were taken by surprise by Nick's sudden marriage. Only a week before the wedding, his then long-time girlfriend, sometime fiancée and constant companion, stunningly beautiful model Kristen Zang, had been on his arm in a revealing, scoop-necked evening gown attending the Academy Awards ceremony. Kristen only learned from Nick that she was his 'ex' hours before he married Patricia. Their sometimes troubled two-and-a-half year relationship came to an abrupt end in a curt telephone call.

'Kristen was devastated,' a friend confessed. 'Nick called and told her, "I've met someone else and we're getting married." He didn't even say who he was marrying. Kristen believed she and Nick had patched up their problems and had a stronger bond than ever before.'

Kristen, who was just 20 and had been walking around wearing a stunning ring which Nick had given her in 1993, while telling friends they 'planned to wait a while to wed', was said to be 'numb and very hurt' at Nick's news. But, as is often the way in Tinseltown, she soon got over her heartache and by September that year was seeing then up-and-coming young Hollywood heart-throb Leonardo DiCaprio. Her love affair with Nick had sunk without trace but she found a life-raft in the form of Leo, and dated him on and off for several years.

Immediately after Nick and Patricia's marriage became public knowledge, totally phoney rumours that she was pregnant started to circulate but time soon proved them to be wrong. However, she has since said that she would like to have one child with Nick and maybe adopt others.

Although *Kiss of Death* was a financial failure, it did grant Nick and Patricia the opportunity of a romantic late Spring honeymoon on the French Riviera, albeit they were both under public scrutiny for most of the time promoting their new movies at Cannes' prestigious film gala. Their French getaway, in a suite at the luxurious Carlton Hotel, was often interrupted by the interviews they were committed to give to the journalists who dropped by. On one occasion, they even found themselves giving competing press conferences. While Patricia was seated, wearing a smart powder-blue suit and sunglasses, her golden locks slicked back in a flip, talking to a group of Japanese journalists in the ritzy Carlton Beach Restaurant, her new husband, nattily outfitted in a bright red jacket, and his co-star Caruso were just a short distance away at the end of the beach club's wooden pier, giving interviews and being photographed by jostling paparazzi precariously positioned on an overlooking bluff.

Drawing on her cigarette, Patricia cheerfully explained to the politely bowing, oriental reporters questioning her, 'I'm on my honeymoon.' As she sipped on her iced coffee and attempted to discuss the message of the political drama in which she was starring, all she was being asked was, 'Do you have a lot of fun together?' Giggling, she replied, 'We stay home and talk a lot. Laugh a lot. Jump on the bed.

Bark at each other.' The Japanese appeared embarrassed so she quickly launched into her anecdotes about making the movie, including telling the encircled hacks about the day that a 12ft-long King Cobra fell into the lap of her stunt double as she sat in a bamboo raft. 'Nobody dies,' she confessed.

As the two press conferences continued, she and Nick were dispatching love letters back and forth like school kids. Patricia asked the reporters for pen and paper and then told them, 'I want you to write, "I love you more than Godzilla," in Japanese. It will be like secret code.' The monstrous message written, Patricia maintained her movie star smile and happily posed for pictures with each of the assembled gathering, who had all brought pocket cameras to immortalise the moment.

Although Nick was the bigger star, during the eight years they had been apart Patricia had established herself as a worthy talent in her own right, having played such roles as the wife of cross-dressing movie director *Ed Wood* in Tim Burton's picture of the same title, an unmarried mother-to-be in Sean Penn's *The Indian Runner* and the housekeeper who steals Liam Neeson from his sickly wife in *Ethan Frame*.

In addition to their celebrity status at Cannes, Nick and Patricia were really enjoying playing husband and wife. When *Vogue*'s James Ryan called at their suite on the pretext of dropping off a bow-tie for Patricia's hair-and-make-up man Chris, who was allegedly being paid $1,500 a day to make her look even more fabulous than she already did, he was greeted at the bedroom door by Patricia wearing a dressing gown. She immediately asked him, 'Why are you acting all embarrassed? Come in.' Patricia summoned Nick from the other room. He strode in fully dressed — much to the relief of the stunned reporter — in leather trousers, a T-shirt and cowboy boots.

Patricia, who had the disconcerting habit of introducing people to everyone in the room and describing even slight acquaintances as 'my friend so-and-so', insisted on introducing Ryan to a cherubic blonde 'friend' called Suna. Then she announced that she had sent Nick's dinner suit to be steamed. Her doting husband responded in his familiar drone, 'That's a very wifely thing to do,' as Patricia beamed with delight.

Nick does not only play the hero in many of his movies; while in Cannes he had the opportunity to be one in real life. One night he was surprised in their suite by a prowler and, despite being naked, he proceeded to give pursuit. Wearing nothing more than an angry expression, he chased the trespasser into the hallway where the man fled at high speed before disappearing into the night.

By the next night, when the newlyweds attended a midnight screening of Gus Van Sant's black comedy *To Die For*, Nick was already dismissing the incident. Even Patricia, who had been shaken by the intrusion, had recovered and was more interested in discussing other adventures she had got up to. Ryan said, 'She had recovered from that but not from a tacky French television variety show she taped earlier in the evening with a cheesy magician and a Claudia Schiffer impersonator. As she and Cage related the day's escapades, there seemed to be a somewhat revolting competition to see who could utter the sobriquet "my husband" or "my wife" more often.'

The night they attended the *Beyond Rangoon* première, all Patricia wanted to do was hold Nick's hand as they walked up the lavish red-carpeted staircase into the theatre, but the horde of cameramen present were more concerned with getting photographs of her and the movie's director John Boorman. Ryan recalled the paparazzi being so aggressive that they actually prised Nick and Patricia apart. He said, 'Before they knew what hit them, they'd separated so paparazzi could get a clear shot of Arquette and Boorman.'

The memories of the crush in the lobby were quickly forgotten once the show was over and Nick told Patricia he liked her movie. His approval was all-important to her. They were almost carried into the formal dinner at the Hotel Majestic by the crowds of people pushing their way through the foyer as they made their way in after the screening. Ryan recalled, 'At the entrance, she let the air out of her lungs in a single, long "whewww".' She was so relieved that Nick liked the film.

Inside the dining room, the coosome twosome sat quietly with Patricia's hand resting on her Nick's. They occasionally exchanged bemused glances as two of Patricia's Burmese-born *Beyond Rangoon* co-stars performed a tediously long folk dance. Before the performance was finished, the newlyweds made their escape through a rear exit door without saying goodnight to those around them. The next morning, Patricia made their excuses saying, 'We just went back to the hotel to talk.'

During their first few months of married life, Nick and Patricia were totally wrapped up in one another, leading their family and friends to complain about them being elusive. When Nick's Uncle Francis planned a charity event that August at his massive 22-room Victorian house, which sits in the middle of the family winery, Niebaum-Coppola, in the Napa Valley, to raise funds for the region's homeless, he literally had to track his nephew down to ask him to attend as one of the celebrity guests. Once the movie mogul had finally made contact, Nick was happy to accommodate his uncle and even agreed to help cook the meal at the Hands Across the Valley event.

Six-hundred paying guests, volunteers and celebrities attended the Italian feast, served in the gardens outside Coppola's farmhouse with its impressive wrap-around porch that balmy Friday night. Ten local restaurants donated the services of their executive chefs to create designer pizzas with big-name luminary food presenters such as Nick as the bait to attract the big spenders to the $125-a-plate bash. Nick was accompanied by Patricia. He was thoroughly at ease and on good form throughout the party and had the crowd chuckling as he told them, 'It's important to eat, isn't it?'

Ironically, Nick kept his promise to make an appearance but the one person missing was Uncle Francis himself, who had been so insistent on his nephew's attendance. Unfortunately for the film-maker, he had encountered travel problems flying back to the United States from Belize, where he has a Central American estate. Throughout the evening, guests were assured that the director of the *Godfather* trilogy and *Apocalypse Now* would be arriving by helicopter at any minute, but he never showed up.

Nonetheless, the élite of Napa Valley were perfectly happy to be entertained by the likes of Nick and Patricia, Californian Senator Barbara Boxer and the San Francisco 49ers football team's former kicker Ray Wersching, who had the crowd falling about laughing when he threw a pizza high into the air only to drop it. The night's MC, Mike Schuman, a member of the 1981 49er Super Bowl team, joked, 'Good thing he's a kicker.'

Although Nick's career and private life were both on a roll that summer, he also found himself coming under fire for his bizarre dress sense. *People* magazine voted him one of the Worst Dressed men that September. 'He looks like a bandleader off duty,' costume designer Ringwood told the magazine. Another celebrity fashion critic, Rolonda, pleaded, 'Open your Cage, Nicolas, and go shopping.' And outrageous cross-dressing entertainer RuPaul told *People*, 'Nicolas Cage has his own personal style and it's bad.'

It wasn't long before tongues started wagging about whether the marriage was going to stay the course. Just because they were married, it did not mean that Nick and Patricia's life together after tying the knot would be any more conventional than their relationship had been before their wedding. It was soon discovered that despite being man and wife, they still preferred to live apart. For them, the key to happiness was having separate front door keys to homes several miles apart. They firmly believed that living separately added strength to their marriage and allowed them the freedom they both craved. A friend admitted, 'It seems like Hollywood's oddest marriage but something seems to work for them.'

However, living apart most of the time fuelled persistent rumours that there were problems with their relationship. Speculation about them was further heightened when they arrived separately for the LA première of *Beyond Rangoon* and acquaintances were advised not to bring up the subject of their marriage.

Although they admitted to arguing occasionally, witnesses who had observed them out and about during the early years of their marriage insisted that whenever they were in public, they appeared to be happy. An observer said that when they were out together, they talked a lot, seemed interested in what the other had to say and appeared to appreciate being together.

Nick preferred to spend most of the time living like a king alone in his 11-room Los Feliz castle, where he stored part of his fleet of fabulous cars. His son Weston was also a frequent visitor.

Meanwhile, Patricia enjoyed sharing her more modest home on the San Fernando Valley side of mountainous and more rural Laurel Canyon with her son. She said, 'It's nice to hear coyotes when they kill at night. It feels very safe.'

In the early days of their marriage, Patricia would spend two nights a week at Nick's house and return to her own home the next morning. Several times a week, Nick would drive over to visit her and Enzo but then return home. However, their schedule altered as their commitments and careers became more hectic.

But Nick and Patricia did not care what other people think about their unconventional living arrangements. He said, 'We intend to have a normal life — our idea of normal anyway.' And Patricia insisted, 'Neither of us entered marriage thinking it wouldn't be a strain. Life has strains in it, and he's the person I want to strain with.'

CHAPTER FOURTEEN
KISS OF SUCCESS

The drunken lorry driver was lying on the ground as the booted foot viciously kicked his body and head again and again. Every blow did more and more damage to the helpless soul wrapping himself up as tightly as he could in a fruitless effort to protect his body from injury. But as he lay there bleeding with his attacker standing over him, the tears started to pour down the assailant's cheeks. Nick had got so deeply into his character that he had become the violent thug he was portraying in *Kiss of Death* and, as a result, the movie nearly ended in disaster on the first day of filming.

What have I done? Nick thought, filled with sudden anguish. How could this have happened? Nick was more muscular and in better shape than he had ever been to portray madman Little Junior Brown in the Barbet Schroeder-directed movie, which was a remake of a 1947 classic film noir. He had been diligently working out for many weeks. There was not an ounce of fat on him. He had turned himself into the ultimate killing machine, which was the role he was playing.

He said, 'It was nauseating to me. I started crying, thinking I had killed somebody on my first day of shooting. And Barbet knew that we had only one take, one shot of it, and he said, "Well, we're going to have to use it." He said, "Unfortunately, but perhaps fortunately, it will have all the messiness of reality." '

During shooting the movie's violent opening scene, Nick had been so carried away that he had split open the stuntman's head, sending him to hospital for stitches and medical care. It quickly dawned on him how deeply immersed in the character of Little Junior Brown he had already become. It was a memory that would stay with him and make him acutely aware that when he was playing violent characters and got involved in fight scenes, he needed to be properly supervised and kept in check.

Despite his satisfaction with the 'Sunshine Trilogy', it was not until Nick made *Kiss of Death* that he finally felt he was achieving some of the main goals of his career. The range of characters he had played, in such a wide variety of film from art house to commercial studio productions, meant he was no longer typecast in the minds of film-makers and the public as a way-out weirdo. But when he embarked on the film, neither he nor anyone else could have realised what a giant leap it would mean to his career. He admitted, 'I did *Kiss of Death* and then I did *Leaving Las Vegas,* and then after that everything changed. But up until then, I was always frustrated by the roles I got.'

Although *Kiss of Death* never found a major box-office audience, earning just under $15 million in the United States, it certainly won Nick respect for his portrayal of the brutal, asthmatic mobster, a night-and-day switch from the loveable oddballs he'd portrayed in previous recent films. *Kiss of Death* was to become yet another turning point in opening up his options in his ever-changing and evolving pursuit of professional excellence. The way he was able to wheeze life into the character meant Nick easily overshadowed his co-star David Caruso, the heartthrob hero of *NYPD Blue,* who was making the transfer from TV to movie stardom for the first time. Although Nick's part was significant, Caruso was supposed to be the star and leading man.

Nick's then agent had actually advised him against making *Kiss of Death,* because that would mean an established Hollywood leading man playing second fiddle to a television star so-far unproven on the big screen. He told him, 'You can't support David Caruso in a movie.' But Nick, who was in Canada and not enjoying the experience of making *Trapped in Paradise,* said, 'I thought, well, you're wrong, because I think David's a good actor, Barbet Schroeder is one of my favourite directors, and I really want to play this part. To me it was like, finally, I was going to be able to get the stink off me of that last experience, to blow out of this state of schmaltz that I can't stand.'

While it turned out to be a wise career move for Nick to agree to play a second lead, leaving *NYPD Blue* was to prove a disastrous decision for Caruso, who had become an instant star playing battle-weary New York detective John Kelly on the hit show. Caruso would long live to regret his hot-headed decision to leave the security of the series, despite his $1 million fee for making the film.

Caruso, who had done film work early in his acting career before making the transition to television, had only made one season of *NYPD Blue* when he made *Kiss of Death* during the summer hiatus, and then announced he was leaving the top-rated show unless they upped his salary from $30,000 to $100,000 an episode.

For Nick, taking the part was a hunch that, certainly as far as critical praise was concerned, was to pay off. His character dominated the film. Without him in a scene the movie appeared flat, but whenever he appeared the film came alive. And there was also an extra bonus for Nick, which he was unaware of when signing to make *Kiss of Death* — a working honeymoon with Patricia on the French Riviera, where the film was first screened and where Schroeder was nominated for the prestigious Palme d'Or Award at the 1995 Cannes Film Festival. The only other nomination the movie got was an insulting Razzie — the tongue-in-cheek alternative Hollywood awards dished out for the worst movies and performances — when Caruso made it into the final five for Worst New Star in 1996.

Long before the picture was premièred at Cannes, Iranian-born Schroeder, who had directed Jeremy Irons and Glenn Close in *Reversal of Fortune,* the true story of socialite Claus von Bulow, accused of trying to murder his wife, and Nick's *It Could Happen to You* co-star Bridget Fonda in *Single White Female,* was predicting that Nick would steal the show. He said, 'For three months before production started, he was building his muscles. He must have spent hours and hours each day pumping iron. By the time he came to shoot the picture, he was a giant pack of muscles.'

No one could belittle Nick's dedication to his craft. The muscle build-up was especially impressive considering he would have to 'de-tone' quickly as soon as filming was over as he already knew that he would immediately be moving on to playing suicidal drunk Ben Sanderson in the next project he had lined up, *Leaving Las Vegas*. This was a complete contrast to a decade earlier when he had had to make the transition from playing an emaciated soldier recovering from the Vietnam war in *Birdy* to be ready only ten days later, having packed on 15 pounds of muscle, to play a super-fit rower in *The Boy in Blue*.

Nick adamantly refused to take steroids in his preparation for his role as Little Junior. Instead, he preferred to build up his muscle mass by relying on a rigorous weight-lifting exercise programme, working out two hours each day in the gym and eating a high-calorie, high-protein, eight-meals-a-day diet supplemented with amino acids. By the time filming began, he was so fit that he was easily able to handle one scene in which Little Junior is seen bench-pressing a stripper 40 times just for fun in the seedy Babycakes erotic club he manages.

In addition, he got part of his inspiration for his character's health problems from his own young son, Weston, who, like Little Junior, is an asthma sufferer. He said, 'My son had to deal with asthma, and I wanted to play an asthmatic character who was physically strong. In no way would I want my child to model Little Junior as something to be. But it was part of being able to play the dichotomy of the man who had asthma yet was this very strong, albeit nightmarish, character. He needs to be violent to survive. It's not unlike the jungle.'

After playing a string of nice guys in *Honeymoon in Las Vegas*, *Guarding Tess* and *It Could Happen to You*, and enduring anything but a sunshine period working on the comedy *Trapped in Paradise*, Nick had been delighted to move away from portraying those kind of loveable good guys with his performance as the maniacally evil Little Junior, one of the darkest characters he has ever played. Car-collecting fanatic Nick put it this way: 'I wanted to try and go back to that darker corner of my mind and come up with something. I liken it to a carbon clean-out, which is when you take a race car and blow the engine out, drive it over 100mph. I felt that I was getting gummed up and I needed to return to explosive, wild behaviour.'

Only just 30, Nick was at a point in his life where, he said, 'I don't want to feel homogenised. I don't want to sell pancakes. I want to stay pure to myself and my instincts.' As a result, he had decided to concentrate on making small movies for a while. He said, 'The stuff that blows my shirt up is the stuff that provides me an opportunity to change and to keep growing.'

For Nick, *Kiss of Death* was certainly all that. The movie was a remake of a film of the same title which had made Richard Widmark a star in his first film, playing the bad guy, and had matinée idol Victor Mature — the star of such classics as the 1942 *Song of the Islands*, the 1946 *My Darling Clementine* and later the 1949 *Samson and Delilah* — in the role now taken by Caruso. Widmark, who went on to star in such movies as *The Alamo*, *How the West Was Won* and *Murder on the Orient Express*, was nominated for a Best Supporting Actor Oscar for his *Kiss of Death* performance.

In addition to Nick and Caruso, the new version had an impressive cast that included Samuel L Jackson, Stanley Tucci, Ving Rhames, Michael Rapaport, Philip Baker Hall, Kathryn Erbe and Helen Hunt, who was also starring in the hit television comedy show *Mad About You* at the time, and who went on to win an Oscar in 1998 for her performance in *As Good As It Gets* opposite Jack Nicholson and Greg Kinnear.

Although *Kiss of Death* was described as a remake, in fact it was only very loosely based on the original. The title and the theme of a bad guy versus a good guy were basically all that were left of the original. The plot had been drastically changed. Caruso's role as ex-con Jimmy Kilmartin, a man trying to reassemble his life but who is unwittingly drawn back to the elements that put him behind bars in the first place, even had a name change; in the forerunner, Mature's character was called Nick Bianco. Susan Hoffman, who co-produced the movie, said, 'The whole idea of right and wrong had vastly changed since 1947. There was a naïve notion then about people in authority; everything was black and white.'

Schroeder saw his version of *Kiss of Death* featuring complex, multi-dimensional characters. He insisted that roles representing both sides of the law extend beyond straightforward black-and-white characters, as had been common in film noir classics. The way he directed the picture, he said, 'All the bad guys are grey and all our good guys are grey. The forces of good in Jimmy Kilmartin's world are as hard to read as the forces of evil, and this ambiguity is what I loved about the material.' He admitted that by the time he got round to shooting his version 'only the title and one plot point remained from the original', a claim that was disputed by some movie critics.

Despite Nick's protestations that he was deliberately darkening his screen image by playing Little Junior, he had in fact fallen into the project after an attempt to get a major salary hike for appearing in another project back-fired. He had been New Line Cinema's first choice to co-star with his old friend Jim Carrey in the movie *Dumb and Dumber*. It would have been a much more predictable role for Nick, with his growing list of comedic characters. But when he discovered that his *Ace Ventura* and *The Mask* pal was getting a ten-fold salary increase — to $7 million — for his part in *Dumb and Dumber*, he demanded a $2 million pay rise above his agreed fee. The studio baulked at that and the role of Carrey's sidekick finally went to Jeff Daniels, leaving Nick available for other work.

He could not have found a more different role from Harry in *Dumb and Dumber* than Little Junior. Yet, although Little Junior was without doubt a violent killer, Nick did not perceive him as being totally wicked, which was in keeping with Schroeder's view of his movie's characters being shades of grey. Nick said, 'Even though he's a very frightening and powerful human being. I don't think he's evil. He's doing what he has to do to survive in the urban jungle.'

The movie opens with ex-con Kilmartin trying to go straight but agreeing to one quick job to bail out his cousin, Ronnie, a seemingly pathetic petty crook involved with a professional car thieves ring, from the wrath of mobster Little Junior when a driver lets him down. When the scam goes wrong, Kilmartin is the only one who does not manage to escape from a convoy of car transporters carrying stolen vehicles. Rather than rat on his confederates and get a lighter sentence, he remains silent and goes to jail. Once he is incarcerated in Sing Sing, Kilmartin's wife is killed because of Ronnie and he is out for revenge. But in order to get that revenge and also be left alone once he is freed, Kilmartin eventually has to do a deal with the authorities, who are out to get Little Junior, the chief enforcer of his father's Mafia rackets.

'Although Little Junior is dangerous and volatile, he is desperately looking for his father's approval and not getting it,' Nick said in a sort of justification of his character's explosive nature. 'When his father dies, Little Junior experiences a catharsis.'

Despite its gritty storyline, Nick found working on *Kiss of Death* light relief after *Trapped in Paradise*. He said, 'I was excited by Barbet's hyper-realistic approach because, most of the time, I'm performing roles that are a bit larger than life.'

Not all of Nick's preparation for *Kiss of Death* was as strenuous as his gym workouts, although some of the other research may have induced just as much sweat. The movie started filming in early May 1994 in New York, and for several days in a row before shooting began, he was a regular visitor to the upscale Manhattan topless club Scores. Nick would sit there watching as curvaceous, semi-naked women gyrated and wiggled their sexy bodies in front of him for entertainment. His visits attracted the attention of the New York tabloid press, but his motivation for patronising the place, it was quickly explained, had nothing to do with the club's name. Scores club spokesman Lonnie Hanover kept a straight face as he said that, while initially everyone at the club had a hard time accepting Nick's claim that he was there for research — in the movie, Little Junior ran a strip club. He told them that was why he had to mix with the glamorous girls working in the club; he was soaking up the atmosphere and getting into his part. Everyone agreed that being an actor was a hard life!

Having to hang out with well-endowed strippers was not the only headache that would bother Nick or, come to that, his co-stars and the crew members, during making of the film. Although he and Helen Hunt had sizeable followings of fans who would turn up to watch scenes being filmed, it was fans of Caruso — because of his then TV star status — who created problems for the film-makers. The production team had to hire extra security guards as crowd co-ordinators to deal with the ever-growing number of admirers of local-boy-turned-actor Caruso, who had grown up in the New York borough of Queens. They showed up at every New York location. Kathryn Erbe, who played Kilmartin's love interest in the movie, remembered, 'We had screaming fans everywhere — literally hundreds of them. They were outside the buildings we were shooting in, outside our trailers. We had whole families hanging out waiting to see David until two o'clock in the morning.'

The movie seemed to have everything going for it. Lots of publicity because of Caruso, lots of fan interest and generally good reviews — especially for Nick, whom the critics overwhelmingly agreed stood out for his performance.

Nick was thrilled to have made the transition to movie villain. He said, 'I played nice, nice, nice. This was a chance to do bad, bad, bad.'

In one notable scene, Little Junior Brown tells Kilmartin, 'I got an acronym for myself: B-A-D; B-A-D — Balls, attitude, determination. You should get an acronym for yourself.' Kilmartin replies, 'How about F-A-B — Fucked at birth.' To which Little Junior responds, 'Nah. Too negative.' When the time came for the film reviewers to go to work, F-A-B was exactly what the critics felt about Caruso's decision to take the part.

Hal Hinson of *The Washington Post* wrote, 'Prior to its release, *Kiss of Death* was known as the movie that *NYPD* star David Caruso left television to make. And, for this erratic film's first few minutes, the small-screen phenom looks as if he might actually have what it takes to become a big-screen star. Then Nicolas Cage makes his entrance. Not to disrespect Caruso, who, it seems, is a passable if rather tedious actor, but Cage dominates the camera, stealing scenes by the sheer intensity of his inimitable strangeness.'

Todd McCarthy wrote in *Daily Variety*, 'A very loose and contemporised remake of one of the more celebrated late '40s films noir, *Kiss of Death* is a crackling thriller that feels unusually attuned to its low-life characters.' He commented that although the film would be the focus of media and public attention because it starred Caruso in his first role since leaving *NYPD Blue*, it was 'most noteworthy for Nicolas Cage's amazing turn as a colossally tough hood'. He went on, 'It is Cage who walks away with the picture, thanks to a stunning performance unlike anything he's done to date. With a goatee and bulked-up upper body, and seen early on bench-pressing a stripper in his club, Cage makes Little Junior a man of steely nerves constantly threatening to erupt into excruciating violence. Beyond this, Cage gives this despicable hood a depth and complexity, *vis-à-vis* his dying father, his asthmatic disability, his make-the-punishment-fit-the-crime sense of justice and his personal code of behaviour.'

The *Los Angeles Times* film critic Kenneth Turan concurred, writing, 'Cage, one of the few American actors who gets more interesting from film to film, comes close to kidnapping the picture as Little Junior.'

Caruso failed to get the critical acknowledgement he had hoped for. *The Hollywood Reporter*'s Duane Byrge summed it up, saying, 'While Caruso brings an apt real-life everyday weariness to his central role, it's not plugged with anything special that makes you want to follow this guy around for two hours. Among the cast members, Cage is the most dominating.'

Rod Lurie also had nothing but praise for Nick in *Los Angeles* magazine. He wrote, 'He has, with this film, become one of film's most unholy bastards since Hannibal the Cannibal.' He added, 'There is a moment of pure viciousness that simply cannot be topped. Before he begins his beating of one unlucky son of a gun, Junior puts on a raincoat. Cage's usually droopy eyes are alive and brimming. He's the ultimate schoolyard bully. It is easily his best performance.'

Added *New York* magazine, '*Kiss of Death* is the best crime movie since Scorsese's *GoodFellas*.' Owen Gleiberman wrote in *Entertainment Weekly*, 'The movie is a supremely smart and satisfying entertainment.' *San Francisco Chronicle* film critic Peter Stack raved about the movie and Bob Strauss, film critic of the *Los Angeles Daily News*, gave it three stars out of four. Abbie Bernstein wrote in *Drama-Logue* magazine, '*Kiss of Death* is shrewd, snappy and satisfying, a crime thriller rich with dimensional characters, sharp dialogue and engrossing plot developments.'

However, there were dissenters. Peter Berk wrote in *Entertainment Today*, '*Kiss of Death* is worse than a noble failure; it is a film which seems utterly pointless.' And syndicated columnist Marilyn Beck said, 'David Caruso's performance in *Kiss of Death* could prove to be the kiss of death to any dreams of big-screen stardom. In his first feature film since his much publicised exit from *NYPD Blue*, the actor exhibits none of the compelling presence or charisma that made him a star in the first season of his hit police drama.'

Reading such reviews may have made Caruso, who ironically shares the same birthday as Nick, although he is eight years older, wonder why he had decided to become an actor after seeing *The Godfather*.

Soon after *Kiss of Death* was released in April 1995, Nick was scheduled to start work on *The Funeral*, a 1930s family drama centred around three brothers involved in organised crime, again set in New York. But the production was thrown into turmoil when he suddenly dropped out and instead went on to make *The Rock* with Sean Connery. The makers of *The Funeral* quickly picked up the pieces and, after just a few days' delay, began filming with Christopher Walken replacing Nick, and Chris Penn and Calvin Klein model Vincent Gallo as the other brothers. The film came out to critical acclaim in November in 1996, with director Abel Ferrara insisting that he had always wanted Walken to play the part Nick had walked away from. Ironically, Walken happens to be one of Nick's favourite actors.

Nick said, 'I only made a verbal agreement with Abel Ferrara to star in *The Funeral*. Before I actually signed a contract, I got the offer to star opposite Sean Connery in *The Rock*. I'd done a few too many independent films. Even though *Leaving Las Vegas* turned out to be a box-office hit, it was a small film for which I was paid just a token salary. I needed a good-paying, commercial film, so I opted for *The Rock*. Before I could work out a deal with Abel to work on both films, he went ballistic.'

Certainly both Nick's personal and professional lives were on a roll in 1995, in spite of his decision not to appear in *The Funeral*. He had married Patricia, won rave reviews for his performance as Little Junior, *Leaving Las Vegas* was coming out in the autumn and he was set to earn his biggest fee to date, $4 million to co-star with Connery in *The Rock*.

Despite his keenness to get away from sympathetic characters, after playing the brutal Little Junior, he was anxious to escape that type of violence and was happy to be moving on to *Leaving Las Vegas*. After *Kiss of Death* had been released, Nick repeatedly expressed his desire to move away from such violent parts, although later he would later return to them even if he was playing the good guy rather than the thug.

He told *Rolling Stone*'s Fred Schruers, 'I'm just trying to get to the purity of the character, and it's much simpler now than it used to be. Now I'm kind of back to trying to be more truthful, not thinking so much that, oh, this will be shocking. But I realised on *Kiss of Death* that by the end of the day, you're nauseous with it — threatening one guy with a cigarette or punching somebody to death. I just thought, I don't want to go there any more — don't want to go to that shitty little corner of my mind where I could actually see myself contemplating this behaviour.'

Nevertheless, he did return to beating people to death in roles such as the detective character Tom Welles he would later play in the dark *8MM* and as the one-man army Cameron Poe in the adventure movie *Con Air*. They, however, had right on their side.

CHAPTER FIFTEEN

SOAKING UP THE SPIRITS

The full pints of Guinness stood next to empty glasses that needed washing on the top of the rickety wooden bar-room table. There were workmen arguing while playing darts, the floorboards creaked every time someone went up to the bar to order another round, and the air in the inn was thick with smoke. Nick and one of his closest friends, songwriter Phil Roy, were loving every minute of it. The old men in the pub were telling tales so eloquently that an eavesdropper would have thought they must have kissed the Blarney Stone that very morning. It was then that Nick was told about the haunted castle out in the country near Galway. He turned to Roy excitedly and said, 'We got to go, man. We got to go.'

Outside the pub stood the chauffeur, complete with monocle, Nick had hired along with a car so they could roam at will across the Irish countryside. 'Take us to Leap Castle, ancestral home of the O'Carroll family,' the driver was instructed. Nick had been told that the castle was famous because of the smelly apparition that dwelt there. Armed with a leg of lamb provided by the kindly innkeeper as a gift for the ghost, the intrepid pair lit candles in the darkened ruins and stayed all night waiting for the spirit to appear. At dawn, after spending the chilly night without success, they drove back to Dublin. Roy said, 'This is just a night with Nick.'

Their tour of Ireland was one escapade after another. They had even picked up a pretty Irish lass to accompany them for a while on their Irish adventure of a lifetime. They'd met the girl while staying at a manor, and she decided to tag along with them for three days.

Somewhere in the midst of playing darts and drinking Guinness, Nick began to capture a part of the character of Ben Sanderson, the alcoholic he was set to play in *Leaving Las Vegas*. He saw him as 'a man who was basically a great writer, who's drinking himself to death'.

Nick had planned his Irish excursion to complete his research into behaving like a drunk. In addition to Roy, he had invited his English professor father, August, on the holiday, telling him that it would be a literary and drinking expedition. But as they were flying over they became embroiled in a heated argument. Nick said,

'We landed and he went back and I stayed in Ireland and I found myself becoming fairly good friends with Dionysus, and going to pubs and having a tremendous amount of admiration for the Irish people in general because they all tell such great stories and they all have the command of the language, which is exactly what I wanted my father to see.'

So it was just Nick and Roy who ended up zig-zagging across the Irish countryside, from castle to country house, in their chauffeur-driven car. Roy recalled, 'Basically, we did Ireland by night.'

To prepare for his part, Nick, who was not a heavy drinker, had already spent weeks studying classic movies about drunks, including Jack Lemmon and Lee Remick in *Days of Wine and Roses*, Albert Finney in the big screen adaptation of *Under the Volcano*, Ray Milland in *The Lost Weekend* and *Arthur*, with Dudley Moore as the loveable playboy alcoholic. He said, 'I rented videos of every alcoholic performance I could get my hands on. I studied them and thought, what can I bring to the table that hasn't really been done yet?'

He said, 'I found Finney's the most powerful performance. But every one of those performances was great in its own way, including Dudley Moore's, and I took bits of each one and incorporated them into my character. They were all helpful. I thought Dudley Moore being funny yet tragic, that was something I could utilise, that concept. I wanted the character to be a guy who had this level of being positive even though he decided to kill himself. I needed to contrast that darkness with an upbeat attitude.'

He also drew further inspiration from watching Kris Kristofferson playing Barbra Streisand's alcoholic lover in the 1976 remake of *A Star Is Born*. He said, 'Even as he came down crashing, Kristofferson was always upbeat, always smiling and yet he was on this self-destructive kick. That is somehow more poignant than to be in the gutter crying all the time about how sad you are about how your life didn't work out.' He added, 'To me, it seems more real that if a person makes the decision to kill himself, he has let go of his troubles. He's no longer struggling to hold on. Consequently, during the filming I was having a blast. I mean, this guy was up — dancing, laughing! He was free.'

Nick admitted that the part of Ben, a scriptwriter who makes the conscious decision to go to Las Vegas and drink himself to death when his career is washed up, was difficult for him to grasp. He revealed, 'I've never felt self-destructive. I know when I was young my actions may have appeared self-destructive, but for me they were very alive. I want to live. I want to keep working. I want to smell the flowers. It was a creepy head space to get into.' In fact, Nick admitted that he was not the suicidal type. He said he would rather stick around and see what happens.

To help him find his character, he did a lot more than just watching videos and enjoying a summer holiday in Eire. He experimented with binge drinking and visited career alcoholics being treated in hospitals. He said, 'I also talked to drunks, studied their movements and read lots of literature on it. I couldn't find any film of someone experiencing delirium tremens, so I had to use my imagination for that. I thought this is a man who's jettisoned himself from his problems by hitting such an all-time low that he no longer feels pain. A man who's not afraid to die can do anything he wants, so I thought there should be a certain buoyancy to the performance, that he should be able to smile and be childlike — and that's how I tried to play him.'

Another part of his research was to make a videotape of himself getting drunk on one of his preferred drinks, gin martinis, to study and learn the sound of his own slurs. Afterwards, he erased the tape.

But he honestly admitted, 'I was completely intimidated by the role of Ben. I had never done anything like that before, and I didn't know if I could. It was really a leap off a cliff to have a go at this. I wasn't certain I could do it. I didn't have a relationship with alcohol myself. I read about the effects on the body. I tried to find film of people with DTs. I went to AA meetings. But I needed help.'

So Nick recruited the help of Tony Dingman, a long-time worker for the Coppola family, and a San Francisco poet and character who had known Nick since his childhood. Dingman was a man who insisted, 'I'm not an alcoholic, I'm a drunk.'

They started discussing boozing at Tosca, a San Francisco bar and popular hangout. Dingman recalled, 'Nick said, "I'm going to do this movie — it's beyond *Lost Weekend*." He sent me the script. We talked. I made some notes. He said, "Maybe you should come down to Vegas." It ended up a nice five-week gig. He didn't really need me, but I was supportive. And he's a very willing listener.' They shared martinis together although Dingman was adamant that Nick was not a drunk. In addition, Dingman said, 'I gave him things to read: Malcolm Lowry's *Under the Volcano*, stuff by Charles Bukowski and William Holden's life.'

Nick remembered, 'I just watched Tony. He would go on a bender and pass out, curled up in my trailer in a foetal position, underneath the make-up mirror. And he would go into these amazing diatribes — and I would put that in the movie. I wanted to give Ben a sort of crumbling elegance. He always takes on a British accent when he's most drunk. And I loved that clue to his flaw — because I love flawed characters.'

During a lunch break from filming some scenes on *Leaving Las Vegas* on a set in the Los Angeles' suburb of Burbank, Nick told leading showbusiness writer Bart Mills about his drinking coach. He said, 'He's a friend of mine who's a drunk. He makes no attempt to hide it. He's interesting to study. One day in my trailer here on the set, I was playing my bongos and he came in after tying one on and crashed into my make-up mirror. He looked like he'd crawled out of the abyss. That's the way I want to look in this movie.'

Nick found his drinking pal helpful on many levels and he was so grateful to his unconventional coach that Dingman actually got a 'thank you' acknowledgement at the end of the film's credits, quite an unusual honour for such bizarre services.

During that film break, Nick talked about his personal drinking habits and told Mills he had never had problems with the bottle. Years later, however, the actor would be photographed dishevelled and appearing tired after a night out at London's famous Stringfellow's nightclub. But at the time *Leaving Las Vegas* was released, he insisted, 'I like a glass of red wine with dinner and, from time to time, a martini. But I don't make a habit of it.'

Just as he had dedicated himself wholeheartedly to preparing for his role in *Kiss of Death,* so Nick meticulously familiarised himself with his character Ben and what he felt he would be like.

British-born movie maker Mike Figgis, who directed *Leaving Las Vegas*, said, 'The most impressive thing is the extent and depth of his preparations.' One evening while studying the script, Nick telephoned the director to ask why his character, a washed-up one-time movie executive, was described as driving a Jaguar. He passionately argued that like every other agent and director in Los Angeles, he would drive a black BMW. Figgis agreed and changed the make of car. After that, Nick carried on going through every other aspect of his character, including the clothes he wore and even the words he used when speaking.

Throughout filming, Nick persisted in putting his personal stamp on to Ben's personality. It was his idea that during his first, abortive oral sex escapade with the prostitute Sera, whom he meets and develops a tragic relationship with, Ben would sing a tune.

Elisabeth Shue, who played Sera, said, 'I go to change in the bathroom for this scene and he was out there singing this Batmobile song he'd made up. It was just so odd. I kept laughing and he really got my attention. He drew me in and kept me looking honest.' With hindsight, Figgis now believes that the singing concept was a pivotal moment. He said, 'It says this character has enough innate grace and humility that sex is not his sole agenda. And consequently made it a great sex scene.'

Strangely enough, the film was not automatically a movie built around Nick, even though usually the lead character is cast first. Although it was his performance that got the film its only Academy Award, the first person actually to be cast was Elisabeth Shue, a relatively unknown actress. Despite a history of lightweight roles, she was cast in the role of the hooker Sera in the dark love story long before Figgis ever thought of offering Nick the part of Ben, although he was the first and only actor the director seriously considered for the role.

When Figgis did decide to offer him the part, he thought he was going to have a big problem. By now, Nick was used to being paid salaries for one picture that were in the region of this film's entire budget. As it happened, however, Nick was very flexible and had decided that this was exactly the sort of small film he was happy to accept less to make. He regarded his higher pay-packets as subsidising the smaller ones so he could satisfy his artistic ambitions.

Figgis remembered the speech he made to win over his choice of leading man. He said, 'I told him, "I have to say, Nicolas, there is no money. When I say there is no money, I mean, you'll probably owe money by the end of the film." Which he did. I'm sure he blew the pathetic amount of money that we paid him very early on in one of his very generous bouts of hospitality. He said, "I make films where I do earn a lot of money so that I can do films like this." '

Once Nick — who was undoubtedly a bankable Hollywood name — had agreed to come on board, Figgis was in a position to get his financing guaranteed and get on with filming.

Happily for everyone, when Nick was brought in to star opposite Shue he did not pull the oh-so-familiar Hollywood stunt of saying, 'I'm the star and I'll have a say in who will be my co-star.' He immediately trusted that Figgis knew what he was doing. The director had wanted to work with Shue since 1989, when he had auditioned her for a film called *The Hot Spot*, a project that neither of them ended up working on. Figgis found in her a vulnerability and yet a strength that appealed to him. He felt so strongly that she was right for the part of Sera that he cast her after just three meetings without even giving her an audition — but he did warn her that he might have to drop her if the eventual backers insisted on a bigger name. As it was Figgis was not put in that invidious position.

Nick said, 'The only knowledge I had of Elisabeth was *Adventures in Babysitting*. I didn't quite understand how it would work. But when we started rehearsals, and I saw a little bit of footage on screen testing clothes and make-up, I saw what Mike had in mind and what she had in mind. It really wooed me.'

Although Shue had made a splash as the disaster-prone comic heroine in the 1987 *Adventures in Babysitting*, at the time *Leaving Las Vegas* was being cast she was best known for playing Tom Cruise's girlfriend in *Cocktail* and being the real-life sister of actor Andrew Shue, who was starring in the television series *Melrose Place*. After *Cocktail*, which was a 1988 box-office hit, she had kept a low profile, pursuing a degree from the prestigious Harvard University and doing legitimate theatre work in Los Angeles. Her other film work had included *The Karate Kid*; playing Michael J Fox's character Marty McFly's girlfriend, Jennifer, in the second and third instalments of *Back to the Future*; a supporting role in *Soapdish*; playing Robert Downey Jr's girlfriend in *Hearts and Souls;* and starring in the low-budget *Twenty Bucks*, a whimsical story that followed a $20 note as it passed from owner to owner.

The more he worked with her, the more Nick became impressed with his comparatively inexperienced co-star. He was so committed to making *Leaving Las Vegas* that in addition to agreeing to make the movie for around a tenth of his usual salary, he personally paid to rent a room at the famous Château Marmont hotel just off Sunset Boulevard — made infamous by the death of comedy star John Belushi there after a drugs binge — for two weeks so that he could rehearse with Shue under the supervision of Figgis. He said, 'I rented a room at the Château Marmont where Mike, Elisabeth and I rehearsed, and I saw how devoted she was to the part. There is a tremendous amount of pain inside Elisabeth Shue.'

One evening, he arranged for the three of them to be chauffeur-driven in his Bentley to a popular Los Angeles strip-club. Figgis said, 'It was a fascinating evening. He had gone to so much trouble. Nick knows I love Miles Davis and when I got into the car, "Kind of Blue" was playing.'

By the time filming began in September 1994, Nick recognised that his co-star was tapping into her own pain and was using it to produce a fine performance. He recalled, 'When we started shooting, she had developed this wonderful way of looking at the relationship, where she made it completely believable.' He had been worried that his own character was so hateful that no woman would want to spend five minutes with this man. So he was relieved that Shue 'somehow made it work, which is testimony to her ability. I guess nobody gave her a chance to act the way she can act. They just put her in these boxes of comedies that don't have much to offer and she obviously had this well of pain and depth inside her that Mike knew about.'

The pain inside her actually came from the tragic death of her oldest brother in a freak accident — he was impaled on the branch of a tree while larking about on a family outing and she had witnessed the tragedy. She was able to translate that into the way Sera desperately wanted Ben to cling to life even though he was so determined to die.

And it wasn't only Elisabeth who had been able to translate her grief at losing a loved one into the pain that her character felt. Nick also understood the sorrow experienced by the loss of someone close, when his own cousin, Francis Coppola's son Gian Carlo, had been killed in the boating accident in 1986. Nick admitted, 'Nothing prepared me for that.' They had known each other since they were boys and the Coppolas were a typically close Italian family. However, in retrospect, as far as Nick is concerned, this family togetherness seems to have weakened as the years have gone by.

He said, 'A lot of tragedies are looked down upon now because of the lack of commerciality, you know. But as Mike Figgis says, it's an essential part of our culture because it prepares us for the rites of passage. Maybe by some definition my cousin's death impacted my decision to do this movie, although it's an entirely different situation. It got me thinking about death at a very early age.'

For her part, Shue, who got her own recognition for her performance by being nominated for a Best Actress Academy Award, although in the end the Oscar went to Susan Sarandon for her performance as a nun opposed to the death penalty in *Dead Man Walking*, found it a joy working with Nick. She said, 'He is one of the most incredible actors I have ever worked with.'

Making *Leaving Las Vegas* was a hard shoot for her as she had only married director David Guggenheim two months before rehearsals began and had gone straight from wedded bliss to appearing topless and having to deal with one scene in which her character is raped and viciously beaten.

She remains eternally grateful to Nick for not pulling rank and demanding a more experienced actress as his co-star. She said, 'I owe him a lot in taking the chance of working with me, because obviously I was the most unknown factor in the mix. He fully embraced working with me, which I'm really thankful for.' When filming was over, she called Nick, 'By far the most brilliant actor I've ever worked with. He acts completely unselfishly; he's always creating in the moment so that when you're acting opposite him you're always drawn into what he's doing, because you never know what he's going to do next. He always allows you to create with him; he doesn't give a performance and you're over there. It's a performance that's created together. I owe a lot of what I did in the movie to him because of that kind of creativity that we shared. He's really incredible.'

Nick and Figgis only clashed once during the making of the movie. It happened when they were filming a scene in which Ben turns up at Sera's apartment covered in blood after being involved in a fight in a bar. He is behaving in a part-courtly, part-belligerent manner. Figgis said, 'I was not quite prepared for him to say he felt, "like the kling-klang king of the rim-ram room", which wasn't in the script. So I shouted as we rolled for the next take, "Good luck with the improvisation." Well, Nick got a look and said, "Oh, OK, I'll do a real straight one for ya then." I had made the mistake of thinking it was arbitrary, when in fact he'd worked it all out very carefully. He's still very sensitive about the perception that he's wacky, because his performance isn't that. It's all hard work. Nothing in it is arbitrary.' Nick said he had picked the 'kling-klang' expression from a line in a Frank Sinatra song.

'You can't believe how many lines in the movie are Nicolas — from "I'm a prickly pear" to "the kling-klang king of the rim-ram room" ', Shue added.

Even though he was playing a drunk, Nick could not actually drink alcohol while filming and perform his role on such a tight shooting schedule, so there is actually only one scene in the movie when Nick's performance is aided by booze, when Ben smashes up a blackjack table in a Las Vegas casino and is escorted out of the building by security guards, while screaming at the top of his voice. On that occasion, Nick allowed himself to experiment and the scene was filmed during a night shoot fuelled by him consuming sambucca and vodka.

The scene was actually filmed in Laughlin, a gambling resort on the Nevada–Arizona border about 90 miles south of Las Vegas. Figgis and his crew could not get permission to film the scene in Vegas because people there feared it would give the city a bad image, and in addition the film-makers could not find a stereotypical casino which would generate the right feel for the scene.

When Nick checked into the Laughlin's Gold River Resort, the staff expected to be greeting a Hollywood movie star. In fact, they found themselves looking after Ben Sanderson. Nick checked into the casino using his character's name and as soon as he got to his room, he telephoned room service for a bottle of vodka and some cranberry juice. Casino manager Brad Overfield said, 'He was really bizarre. A lot of people thought he had to be drunk or on drugs because he was so intense.'

Regardless of his lack of experience as a drinker, Nick put his own mark on his character rather than copying the actors he had studied in the videos he had watched. He said, 'Ben is self-destructive. The hard thing to do was to manifest the physical deterioration of an alcoholic to that acute a point. I guess John O'Brien, who wrote the book, had a very sad life; his father apparently felt that the book was a suicide note. One day his family all came to the set, and it was kind of a spooky day. I was wearing the exact same watch that John actually wore, which I had no idea of, and coincidences like that seemed to seep through the veil of what was real and what wasn't. It was a very emotional thing. They were crying.'

Just as Nick had meticulously picked a black BMW as his character's car of choice which, as it happened, was the make and colour that O'Brien actually drove, so Nick had decided that his character would have worn a Rolex Daytona watch, not knowing that O'Brien did indeed wear that as well.

If O'Brien's father was right, and it was a suicide note, it was a long one — 189 pages. O'Brien, an alcoholic, never saw his novel turned into a movie. He put a gun to his head at the age of 33 and blew his brains out just as filming was about to begin. He had written two other novels, *Better* and *Stripper Lessons*, and was working on a fourth, *Assault at Tony's*, at the time of his death. He did not leave an actual suicide note. Police who searched his apartment found among his few possessions a pizza box and an open vodka bottle. For weeks before his death, he had been jettisoning personal belongings. He had often travelled to Las Vegas alone researching his book.

One of the most painful aspects of his death as far as his widow Lisa, whom he had met at high school in Cleveland, Ohio, was concerned, was that she had no idea whether there actually was a Las Vegas prostitute whom her husband had fallen in love with. She said, 'John made frequent trips to Las Vegas alone to research the book, but we never talked about what went on there because I didn't want to know. As to whether there was a Sera, I think she was a composite of several people, and was essentially John's fantasy woman; someone who would love him and let him drink.'

Figgis considered cancelling the project when he learned of O'Brien's death. He said, 'Eventually I decided that John wrote a great book and the most I could do for him was to go ahead and make the film.'

The knowledge that O'Brien had taken his own life also weighed heavily on Nick.

'I think I was very cautious about the work because I was portraying sort of the echo of the soul of a dead man, and wanting to treat it with all the respect and humility that one has when you're saying the words of a dead man,' he said. 'I really felt the weight of portraying a dead man's suicide note. In order to do it, I knew I had to keep myself meditating on death. Believe me, I didn't like it because I'm a pro-life guy and I had to go to a crummy little corner of my head in order to deliver my lines with any authenticity. I knew I'd have to demand a lot of myself to play this character and that it would probably wreak havoc on my personal life, which it did.

By the end of the shoot, my girlfriend and I had broken up.'

Nick's dedication to being pro-life was a far cry from his attention-seeking early days when he would talk about wanting to die messily, in a punk version of hari-kiri.

It was true that in his private life Nick was experiencing his own emotional turmoil in 1994 as he struggled to film *Leaving Las Vegas*. As filming progressed, so Nick and then girlfriend Kristen Zang were moving ever closer to calling it a day. He later admitted, 'At the time I was going through the movie, I was also at the end of my relationship with my ex-girlfriend and so I was going through my own private wringer, anyway. In a lot of ways, that fuelled the performance. So I have Kristen to thank for that. She and I were not happy at that point, and it just went right into the character. Fortunately we managed to become friends after my getting married and all. At the time, I had become estranged from my father and my brother, and my girlfriend and I were in the long process of breaking up, so I was loaded with all this feeling.'

Although therapy, a route he often took, was a help, Nick found that the best treatment was his work. Even so, the emotional high price he was paying to play Ben was a drain on him.

Leaving Las Vegas was shot in just one month. Most movies take much longer to film but on this occasion the budget simply did not allow it. As it happened, that was good for Nick's mental health. He said, 'The fact that it was a 28-day shoot helped. On the set, I had that exhilarated joy, this feeling that the work was getting done and it was flowing. It was just happening, and I didn't have to think too much about it. I knew where I wanted to go. Mike, Elisabeth and I would all connect. At the end of the day, when I would go home, I would think about the character's head space and why he wanted to die. It started a thought process that became quite morose, and it made me miserable, because I am not that way. I do not want to die. So to try to understand that was creepy to me. And to live that for three months, or the normal length of a shoot, it could have gotten old really fast. There were some times I would go home from work, and I'd been trying to see the world through Ben's eyes, and then the street lights on the freeway just suddenly seemed like they were made of cardboard and the freeway itself was made of papier mâché, and it made me feel like nothing was real and this is all just so temporary.'

The relationship between Nick and Kristen did not actually come to an abrupt end when filming *Leaving Las Vegas* stopped. They tried to patch things up, even going to the 1995 Academy Awards together a few months after the filming of *Leaving Las Vegas* had been completed. Their romance limped along until it finally came to a screeching halt when Nick unexpectedly wed Patricia Arquette.

Although *Leaving Las Vegas* was a low-budget film, costing only $4.7 million to make, Figgis was able to attract a lot of talent to make cameo appearances. Among them were Julian Lennon, Richard Lewis, Lou Rawls, Mariska Hargitay, Laurie Metcalf, Steven Weber, Danny Huston and Bob Rafelson.

Even before *Leaving Las Vegas* was released, *Drama-Logue* wrote, 'Make no mistake about it: this is Nicolas Cage's year. He wiped David Caruso off the screen in *Kiss of Death* in a riveting performance as the vicious Little Junior Brown, and now he's nothing short of brilliant as the defiantly doomed Ben Sanderson in *Leaving Las Vegas*.'

Nick was seriously glad that his 'Sunshine Trilogy' was behind him. He said, 'I think I just wanted to get back to tragedies. I wanted to get back to darkness. I had been ignoring another side of myself. I felt that I was becoming typecast. Comedy at that point was not something I wanted to do again. I remember being struck on *Trapped in Paradise,* which was a miserable experience for me, and I just said to myself I don't want to do this mindless gobbledegook any more. Can't I just make a movie that I can be proud of again, and go back to my roots? No amount of money is important. I just want to do something I believe in. And then along came *Kiss of Death* and *Leaving Las Vegas.* So it was like an answer. I was very lucky. I had to get this off my shoulders. I just had to. *Leaving Las Vegas* is an opportunity to get back to a more sensitive style of acting, to fulfil some of my dramatic dreams. The kind of work I wasn't allowed to do in other genres.'

However, after he had left this film and the intensity that playing Ben generated within him, Nick admitted he felt he could go on to make another comedy after all. He considered several scripts with light-hearted plots, including *A New Leaf* and *Defective Detective,* but did not return to the genre for the next few years.

Although 1995 was proving to be a great year for Nick because of his marriage and the praise he was getting for his work, in fact all the rigours he had endured pumping up for *Kiss of Death* and then quickly transforming himself into a physical wreck for *Leaving Las Vegas* had actually been suffered the previous year. The reality of making movies is that there is usually a long gap between the time that a film is made and released. To make matters even more confusing, pictures are often not released in the order in which they are made.

Nick was back to a more comfortable physical state and entering a new trilogy period as the accolades for *Leaving* started pouring in. Nevertheless, the memory of forcing his physique through the transition from muscular punk to playing pathetic, puking, impotent Ben stayed with him. He said, 'I think my body went into a state of shock because one minute it was all pumped up and the next I was trying to look like a bloated alcoholic. I ate sugar, lived on fast food and stopped exercising. God, it was horrible. I got all lethargic and felt terrible. But I got the look I was going for. I wanted to look crummy and feel crummy, and I did.'

Obviously, the big question worrying Nick and the backers of *Leaving Las Vegas* was whether audiences would be left feeling uneasy after watching a movie that definitely would not have them rolling in the aisles. After all, it was the story of a Hollywood screenwriter determined to drink himself to death who has a sexless love affair with a prostitute who promises not to stand in his way.

Nick had a suspicion that a growing number of young Americans were tired of the 'baby food' that was being fed to them by the studios and he believed that they were ready for a return to a tougher, harder-edged type of film-making. He said, 'Everything goes in cycles, and maybe it's time again for movies like *Midnight Cowboy.* But I could be wrong.'

He was not wrong. Without doubt, as far as his professional life was concerned, the release of *Leaving Las Vegas* was the high point of the year.

Leaving Las Vegas premièred in Canada in September 1995 at the Toronto Film Festival. In the opening sequence, Nick is seen dancing down the aisle of a liquor store, sweeping bottles off the shelves and into a shopping cart, rhythmically swaying from side to side, obviously drunk but still able to function, as the viewer listens to grainy-voiced Michael MacDonald's version of the classic rock 'n' roll song 'Lonely Teardrops'.

Figgis recalled, 'Nick did his wonderful body improv stuff that he does. He's a dancer, a natural. It was meant to be seen much later in the picture, but we put it in as the opening shot because in one image it establishes that this man is charming, he's pretty energetic, and he's an alcoholic.'

But Nick stressed, 'And yet he's happy. A man who has made the decision to die is not really fighting any more. Ben had let go. It's like, "We're going down the river, and you can try to hold on, but if you just let go, you're riding, you're floating, you're up, you're smiling." And that seemed to be the way to do it and not have the lines become maudlin. I wanted Ben to be a sort of study in crumbled elegance; at one time probably the life of the party, a real star socially, great way with words, real command of the language, and a sense of style — the watch he wears, the way he dresses. And he's got to the point now where it's all starting to decay.'

Thoughtfully comparing the two roles, Little Junior Brown and Ben Sanderson, which had firmly taken him away from his sunshine period, he suggested, 'I think the main difference is that one character is destructive, whereas the other is self-destructive.' Remembering the two roles and his quick shift in gears from one film to the other, he added, 'The difficult thing about *Leaving Las Vegas* was that it happened so quickly after wrapping *Kiss of Death*. There was a complete shift in the headspace of the two people. Little Junior Brown is a character who will kill you if you, in some way, threaten his environment. Ben Sanderson is a man who's let go of his pain, his struggles and his life and has decided to do himself in. The one character is strong and the other is becoming very fragile, which was difficult on my body because I had to pump up and eat and gain weight for Little Junior Brown, and then a week afterwards be a person who was diminishing and becoming this thin wreck.'

For Nick there is a key to every part and he had to search for the means to open the door to Ben's soul. He said, 'I had to get into a certain attitude, a certain mode, where I could understand a man who wanted to drink himself to death. I could say the lines, "I don't remember why I'm drinking myself to death, I just know that I want to" and have some meaning to it, which was difficult. The main kernel that I could grasp was that he was not in pain, even though he was in the greatest sort of pain. Which is that once you let go of your struggles, and you're not holding on to your life, you can float.'

Drama-Logue noted, 'Cage infuses so much humanity in Ben Sanderson that you can't help but like the poor wretch and feel for him. You find yourself genuinely wanting him to live, yet admiring him for his extraordinary commitment to dying.'

Nick recalled, 'I really wanted Ben to be up, to be this guy who was charming, who was funny, and in that contrast to what he was doing to himself, more devastating in the end that he had given up his life. It's an irony, but Ben would not have found a true love if he was not a drunk. He would have probably put Elisabeth Shue's character in the same box as everybody else did, "You're a hooker, I can't take you seriously." But because of his state, even though he was going to die, he still died having the experience of a true love, because that's really what that relationship is. When I read the book, it was the coolest relationship I had ever seen between a man and a woman. The book crushed me. I cared so much for these people.'

Amazingly, movie audiences around the world and, more importantly as far as Nick's career was concerned, the members of the prestigious Academy of Motion Picture Arts and Sciences found that, despite Ben's relentless downward spiral, the film did indeed manage to be an inspiring love story, even if not a traditional one.

Nick said, 'I suppose every movie has a message of some sorts, but the message in this movie is not anti-drinking. I never wanted it to seem like I was getting up on a soapbox. If anything, I think that the message is that it is possible for anyone to find true love. These two people are at the lowest, both have been judged harshly by society, and yet they found love where neither judges the other. I'm not sure you could call this a hopeful movie. But I think it has something to say to people who maybe are at their lowest.'

The movie may not have been an anti-drinking film, but it was not a pro-alcohol one either. Nick said, 'If some people get encouraged not to, more power to them. But it's a love story from the word go.'

He did not expect droves of people to rush out to see his movie because it was a film that many people would find depressing and it was being released in the United States in the run-up to Christmas that year. He said, 'I wanted to do this film for my own reasons, not because I thought it would be a box-office smash. I wanted to explore a certain level of emotions that I was not allowed to reach in superficial comedy. I wanted to go to that place and examine it. It had been a while since I had been there.' He was happy with the outcome of the movie and confessed, 'I'm seldom happy with my work.'

For Nick, if other people got something out of watching the film that was great but, if they didn't, that was fine, too. He said, 'I understand that people don't want to be depressed by a movie. But just as comedy serves a purpose, which is to make people laugh and forget their problems, so does tragedy. Maybe tragedy helps us all deal with losses in our lives. For that reason, I think studios should make more tragedies, but they are afraid because it's not big business. But it was important enough for Shakespeare to write tragedies, and it's still important.'

When the giant MGM studios, which had acquired distribution rights for the United States, threw an intimate soirée at Hollywood's Muse restaurant, celebrating the rapturous reviews the movie achieved, Figgis, who was nominated for Best Director and Best Adapted Screenplay Oscars for his work on the film but lost out to Mel Gibson who won the Academy Award for directing *Braveheart*, and Emma Thompson who won for her reworking of Jane Austen's *Sense and Sensibility*, confessed that he owed a lot of people a lot of favours.

In addition to the artists doing cameos, Figgis was also deeply indebted to fellow Geordie Sting, the singer who had become a close friend since they worked together on an earlier movie. Before becoming a movie director, in his youth Figgis had been a member of the British rhythm and blues group Gas Board, which featured future pop star Bryan Ferry. He had also inherited his father's passion for traditional jazz. As a result he scored the music for *Leaving Las Vegas* himself, blending his own sexy jazz compositions with Sting singing standards like 'Come Rain or Come Shine' and 'Angel Eyes', to produce a highly melancholy soundtrack.

Figgis recalled, 'We recorded four songs in one day, with just a simple piano and bass, at Sting's beautiful old mansion house in England near Stonehenge.' He claimed that if someone listens closely to the soundtrack they can hear the sound of burning logs crackling in Sting's fireplace. He added, 'He just gave me his recording time and talent.' Referring to the going rates for paying such an artist at the time, he said, 'That's about $1.2 million worth of Sting if I were going shopping on the open market.'

Apart from his abilities as a director, Nick also admired Figgis for his musical capabilities. He said, 'I think Mike is a total artist. I felt like I had an opportunity to realise some of my musical dreams working with an artist like Mike Figgis. I've always approached acting from a musical standpoint, I think maybe because my grandfather was a composer. I remember him playing piano and tinkering and it not sounding like anything and all of a sudden it would sound like a melody. With acting, I try to do the same thing with the dialogue. I'll throw it against the wall and get a sound or a rhythm.'

After enjoying pay days in the millions, Nick earned just $240,000 for playing Ben. But agreeing to give such a bargain performance was a deal that he would never regret. He did not realise it, but the world would soon be toasting him. He was on the threshold of becoming one of the film industry's most prominent stars of the end of the twentieth century. The big movie studios were singing along to his tune now.

CHAPTER SIXTEEN

NOT GRIEVING LAS VEGAS

Tension filled the air as Nick paced back and forth across the floor of his downtown Los Angeles apartment. He was all alone, waiting for Patricia to join him. She was late and he was nervous, nervous like he had never been before. It was 25 March 1996, and as soon as she turned up they would be heading for the Academy Awards presentations. Dressed in a wide-lapelled Hugo Boss tuxedo, he was freaking out because she had not arrived. He admitted, 'I paced all day. I couldn't concentrate, so everything seemed like mush. I panicked about every piece of clothing I put on. Nothing seemed to fit or look right.'

When she finally did walk through the penthouse's front door, Patricia found him with nerves so frayed that she instantly realised something had to be done to calm him down. Placing a disc on the CD player, she asked him to dance. Like a scene from a movie, they locked arms and launched into a vigorous tango. As soon as it was over, Nick was relaxed enough to escort his wife downstairs and into the waiting limousine.

Despite the deafening clamour predicting a Cage win that night, Nick still could not hear it. He was not convinced he would win Hollywood's top honour. It was not until he read a downtown Los Angeles street sign as they were actually driving to the Oscar ceremonies that he finally believed he would indeed win.

Nick and Patricia were sitting in the back of the stretch limo winding its way through the streets near the Dorothy Chandler Pavilion. Nick was deep in thought, wondering about where his future would lie in light of what might or might not happen that night. Even though everyone kept telling him he was a guaranteed winner, he knew that being the front-runner meant nothing in the fickle world of Tinseltown. Then he looked out of the chauffeur-driven car's window and a large smile spread across his usually solemn face.

'I am very superstitious and, I don't know why, but seven has always been my lucky number,' Nick said. 'I was born on the seventh. *Leaving Las Vegas* was filmed in 16mm, which adds up to seven. You get the picture? I like the number seven. So I'm looking out the window and I see a street sign on a wall that says, in big red letters, "SPEED LIMIT: 7 MILES AN HOUR". Have you ever heard of a sign like that in your life? I hadn't. I don't even know what street we were on. But I knew that it meant something. I knew that it meant I was going to win. I know that sounds weird but I just knew.'

It was the second omen of the day. Earlier, he had spotted his *Moonstruck* co-star Cher out riding her Harley Fat Boy motorbike and that had made him feel lucky.

Still, as he sat there listening to actress Jessica Lange read out the list of contenders for the Best Actor award and then open the envelope, which finally revealed the winner to the billion television viewers around the world, Nick was still riddled with self-doubt. And that was despite the deafening Hollywood rumour-mill that he would win the Oscar, in a year when movies such as *Braveheart*, *Dead Man Walking*, *Sense and Sensibility*, *Babe* and *Apollo 13* were among those up for Academy consideration.

In some ways, that made it worse for Nick. What if I don't win? he thought. He was not one to assume. He was guarded and worried — so worried that he had not even written an acceptance speech for fear that it would be a jinx. He had made that mistake when the Independent Spirit Awards had been announced a few weeks earlier — and it became one of the few prizes he had not walked off with. He said, 'I didn't even want to prepare a speech. I had written one in case I won the Independent Spirit Award.' But that awards ceremony had named Sean Penn Best Actor for his performance in *Dead Man Walking*. Nick said, 'It was funny. Sean got up there and said, "Law of averages, Nick, law of averages." And I had my speech and I was driving home and I remember taking the speech, crumpling it and throwing it out of the window and going, like, "Wow, the independent movie market has forsaken me." But I was happy for Sean, we kind of came up together.'

At the time he added, 'Hopefully, we'll work together again.' It was a sentiment that not too many years later he would reject utterly.

Remembering how he had screwed up that speech made Nick think, 'It's not something you want to do to yourself. I was afraid that that would happen again.'

'I was a nervous wreck,' Nick recalled. 'I thought about taking something but I was afraid it might affect my timing, because I had to present as well. I had gone through this unusual series of festivals and award shows that had been a paper trail all the way up to the Oscar and people would say, "Why are you worried? Of course you're going to win, you've won everything else." But I did not know I was going to win. I'm very obsessive/compulsive, so things will stay in a loop with me. I'll keep saying, "But what if this happens?" and work myself into a state that is a force of nature. People around me have learned to deal with it. That night I was certain I was not going to win. So when it happened I was very relieved. I felt I could breathe. And a friend of mine said, "Be sure that you watch what's happening to you and accept it and feel good about it." Which was good advice. So when I got up there I took a deep breath and thought, Wow, this may never happen again, so I'm gonna enjoy this.

'When it comes down to the 11th hour, you're going to get caught up in the excitement of the moment. You try to relax, but then you start thinking about winning. And you start thinking about losing. And you realise that winning is better than losing. Then Jessica Lange opened the envelope and I could hear her utter the letter "N". When I heard the first consonant of my name, when I heard "Nnnn", I relaxed for the first time. She hadn't even gotten to the rest of my first name and I knew I was in. Surprisingly, my feet worked OK on the way up to the stage. I think it's because my good friend told me not to let the moment pass me by. And I didn't. I took it all in. I even remembered to breathe. It was a damn fine moment.'

Even so, for a few seconds his win did not fully register and Patricia had to yank him into action. He regarded the whole situation as 'a very dreamlike experience'. Nonetheless, Nick, who suffers from stage fright even on television, appeared tense as he took the podium to accept his Best Actor Oscar, even though he insists he was not at all nervous by then. He said, 'I've always had stage fright. That's why I've never done theatre. But for some reason I was relaxed that night. I remember thinking, I am not going to go up there and not enjoy this. I have to look at it and enjoy it. And I did. After all, it's not something that happens every day.'

He told the audience, 'Oh boy! Oh boy! Three-and-a-half-million-dollar budget, some 16mm film stock thrown in and I'm holding one of these. I have got to thank the members of the Academy for this, for including me in this group of super-talents and for helping me blur the line between art and commerce with this award. I know it's not hip to say it, but I just love acting, and I hope that there'll be more encouragement for alternative movies where we can experiment and fast-forward into the future of acting. Let me thank the awesome, multi-talented Mike Figgis. My incredible, amazing co-star Elisabeth Shue. I am going to share this award with both of you, and the late John O'Brien, whose spirit moved me so much. Tony Dingman, Annie Stewart; the producers Annie Stewart and Stuart Regen, everyone at MGM/UA and Lumière. I'd like to thank Ed Limato, my colleagues Gerry Harrington, Jeff Levine, Richard Lovett. Everyone in my family, my gorgeous wife Patricia. And I just finally want to say, "Hi, Weston. It's Daddy. I love you." Thank you.'

Nick, who says that he could not have created his complex character without experiencing 'the extremes of elation and worry' that come with fatherhood, said, 'It wasn't until I said I was never going to win an Oscar that it happened — whatever that means.'

When Nick signed on to make *Leaving Las Vegas,* his father, August Coppola, told him, 'You are making your epitaph.' August was, in fact, praising the project and was one of the few with the foresight to realise the film could be the making of his son as an actor. Although the comment was meant as a compliment, when Nick later related the story to the American newspaper *USA Today,* it was mistakenly presented as if his father had warned him that making the movie could be the death of his career. Nick said, 'It was misinterpreted. My father didn't mean I was ending my career. It was a big headline in *USA Today* and that really bothered him.' That misinterpretation led to a major falling out between father and son that caused them not to speak to each other and sadly had a bitter, long-lasting effect on their relationship.

However, many others in Hollywood felt the misunderstanding to be nearer the truth. Nick confessed, 'People told me, "This is not a good idea. Why do you want to do a drunk role? This will not be considered by the critics, by the Academy, because it's too dark for their liking." '

But no sooner had it been released than the picture abruptly emerged as the dark horse major contender to beat when film awards were being handed out that year. The highly influential New York Critics Circle gave it their best film award and they announced Nick as best actor of 1995. The film also won Nick another best actor award and director Mike Figgis a best director accolade at the prestigious

San Sebastian Film Festival.

Ironically, the picture had been shunned by every major Hollywood studio when Figgis had done the rounds pitching the script. Unbelievable though it now seems, it became such a hard sell that the film's domestic distribution rights were finally picked up for a mere $1.5 million by MGM/United Artists after three months of hard-bargaining negotiations with the producers.

Even when it was released to rapturous praise, many of the critics who fawned over the film were dubious that it would find commercial success. They doubted that there was an audience out there for such a dark film.

Leonard Klady wrote in *Daily Variety*, 'In *Leaving Las Vegas*, Nicolas Cage assays a character who's on a slide to touch bottom as he sinks deeper into depression and alcoholism. The film pulls no punches, takes no prisoners and flies in the face of feel-good pictures. And while highly laudable on an artistic level, the picture needs to attract top-flight critical response to make more than a modest dent at the box office. Commercially, its prospects are akin to that of a reformed tippler — not impossible, just precarious.' He added encouragingly, 'Cage is in top form as he purposefully stumbles through the movie. Apart from innate charm, he sidesteps any effort to make the character endearing. Shue is equally skilful.'

In the rival *Hollywood Reporter*, Michael Rechtshaffen said, 'Any similarities between the 1992 Nicolas Cage film *Honeymoon in Vegas*, and his latest release, *Leaving Las Vegas*, begin and end with the title. Stylish and strongly acted, *Leaving Las Vegas* is also a major downer and will likely be a tough sell for MGM/UA. To the ever-stretching Cage's credit, he manages to inject considerable pathos into a character who could have easily been dismissed as a worthless loser. Shue, meanwhile, admirably puts a serious dent in her wholesome screen reputation with her gritty portrayal of a tough survivor.'

Bob Strauss, film critic for the Los Angeles *Daily News*, described Nick's portrayal as 'arguably the best bottom-of-the-bottle performance ever filmed. It's wonderful work, if you can possibly stand it.' Mick LaSalle, movie critic for the *San Francisco Chronicle*, described Nick as 'extraordinary'. He added that Nick was 'an actor who is fast becoming a genre unto himself. If Cage is in it, it's often intelligent, offbeat, sly. *Leaving Las Vegas* is all those.'

Kevin Courrier of *Box Office* magazine, wrote, '*Leaving Las Vegas* is one of the most boldly original dramas of the year.' Wally Hammond of the London-based magazine *Time Out* described the film as 'highly compulsive viewing'. And Tom Shone in Britain's *Sunday Times* wrote, 'Despite its uncompromising depiction of a man determined to drink himself to death, *Leaving Las Vegas* is an extraordinarily beautiful film and Nicolas Cage gives the performance of his life as its alcoholic hero.'

New York magazine said, '*Leaving Las Vegas* is as close as we get to art in the American cinema of the Nineties.' And *Rolling Stone* magazine declared, 'Cage gives a blazing performance that cuts through Ben's alcoholic haze to reveal a startling sweetness and clarity. Is the film a metaphor for doomed romance in an age of AIDS and lethal addiction? Cage and Shue make it something more visceral and immediate: a cry from the heart.'

Meanwhile, Manohla Dargis proclaimed in *LA Weekly* magazine, 'That Cage is the most interesting if not necessarily the greatest lead actor in American film is in some measure due to his ability to infuse a character actor's idiosyncrasies into every performance. Ben isn't Cage's most brilliant creation, but it's an astonishing work nonetheless, a study in decay that's uncommonly free of vanity or vulgar appeals for compassion.'

And *The New York Times*' Janet Maslin lauded his 'devastating' performance, writing, 'Mr Cage digs deep to find his character's inner demons while also capturing the riotous energy of his outward charm.'

Figgis confessed to top showbusiness writer Bart Mills, 'Nicolas is the only actor around now who can carry such tragic material and make it watchable.' And soon after its release, he told the *Los Angeles Times* why he felt Nick had helped turn his screenplay into the critical hit it was quickly becoming. He said, 'He's the kind of actor who comes to the set having completely absorbed the script. He does a colossal amount of research beforehand and comes up with very, very intelligent alternatives to what's on the page. The bottom line is he's got a rather beautiful soul, like a great musician, and I think it shows in the way he expresses himself.'

Leaving Las Vegas had only been made into a film because Los Angeles art dealer-turned-first-time movie producer Stuart Regen, who also happened to be a friend of Figgis, believed so strongly in the project. Regen had found the 1990 novel in a second-hand book shop in 1991, by which time it was already out of print. Only 2,000 hardback copies of the book had been printed by an obscure Wichita-based publishing house, Watermark Press, which subsequently went out of business. Two hours after he'd finished reading it, he and author John O'Brien, who was living in Los Angeles, met to discuss turning it into a movie. Regen recalled, 'He didn't seem happy. He seemed wary of a stranger, and he was afraid that we'd put on a happy ending.' Finally, Regen optioned the film rights for just $2,000, giving O'Brien an assurance that it would not be turned into a tale with an uplifting ending. Regen could not even find backers in the United States to finance the rock-bottom budget and eventually he and Figgis had to get the French company Lumière Films to come up with the cash.

Lumière's Lila Cazes, who had previously produced *Bank Robber* starring Patrick Dempsey, Lisa Bonet and Forest Whitaker, *Fresh* featuring Samuel L Jackson and *Somebody in Love* starring Rosie Perez, Harvey Keitel, Anthony Quinn and Steve Buscemi, was happy to take over producing the film. Cazes, who personally financed the movie through Lumière, recalled how Figgis persuaded her to commit to the project. She said, 'I read the script and liked it. Then at the Cannes film festival, Mike Figgis came to our boat, and we had breakfast. There were other people at that breakfast, and they were trying to talk about different projects they wanted to do. I told him about *Leaving Las Vegas* and said I really liked it. He looked at me and said, "I can do it for $3.5 million." I said, "I don't believe you, but if you can do it for $5 million, I'll do it." He said, "You mean it?" I said, "I mean it." So he stood up and kissed me, and I made the film.'

By the time the movie was complete it actually cost $4.7 million, although movie mythology still has it that it did, in fact, come in as Figgis had predicted. Nevertheless, it was still a pretty staggering achievement, considering how many pictures go millions over estimated costs.

To save money, because of the minuscule budget, *Leaving Las Vegas* was shot on Super 16mm film stock instead of the standard 35mm, and had to be blown up for its release. The whole thing took just 28 days to film as scheduled, using only two cameras, and Figgis, who had previously directed five movies including *Internal Affairs* with Richard Gere and Andy Garcia, and *Stormy Monday* with Melanie Griffith, Tommy Lee Jones and Sting (who went on to work with him on the

Leaving Las Vegas soundtrack) was so short of cash he could not even afford to obtain the proper permits to allow him to film on Vegas' world-famous strip. Instead, he had to do it surreptitiously. In any case, the authorities in Las Vegas did not exactly welcome Figgis and his crew with open arms. They were concerned about the image such a dark movie would project to the world about their city, so they would only actually allow Figgis to film there for three days. As a result, much of the film was shot on a movie studio set in Burbank, a suburb of Los Angeles, and in the small, but nonetheless rival, Nevada gambling resort of Laughlin.

Money was so tight that the scene in which Nick's character Ben and Sera kiss underwater — a scene which is widely regarded by movie *aficionados* as one of the classic moments in the movie — almost never got filmed. Figgis explained, 'I'd written it in the script. When we came to looking at the reality of the schedule and the budget — it was written as an underwater lake scene — the production team said to me, "Look, you need housing for the camera. Shooting underwater is not easy. We're talking about a day to shoot this scene and it's going to cost you a lot of money. How valuable is this to you?" And I said, "OK. Reality. It's out of the script." '

But as luck would have it, when the cast and crew got to Las Vegas to start work, Annie Stewart, who was producing the movie along with Cazes, went on a tour of Nevada's gambling capital and came across something that would change the course of history, at least as far as *Leaving Las Vegas* was concerned. She walked up to Figgis and told him: 'I've just driven past a motel that has a swimming pool that's built up from the ground with little portholes in it. You could shoot the scene there.'

Figgis turned up at the motel with Nick, Shue, just one person to do hair and make-up and the cameraman, with the camera in a bag and a zoom lens. The director said, 'That was it. They valiantly dived into the pool. Thank God Elisabeth is an athlete who can control her movements underwater. They did the kiss. We just put a blanket over one of the portholes and shot it in daylight with no lighting. The entire sequence, which has now become such a pivotal image in the film, was the ability to spot the location, get there the next morning, shoot and be on your way.'

Cazes tried desperately to get $2.5 million for the US distribution rights but the only offer she got was from MGM/UA. Finally, she agreed to make the deal.

The next hurdle that had to be overcome was getting the movie an acceptable rating. Figgis was forced to trim some scenes and alter several others, amounting to about five minutes of changes in all, before the Motion Picture Association of America, the body that regulates film certification, would agree to give it an R rating, meaning that it could attract an audience and would not be stuck with a rating suggesting it was overly violent or pornographic. The alterations were not made to the version that was distributed outside the United States, which is now regarded as 'the director's cut'.

The distributor deliberately postponed opening the film until late October in the hope that it would stay in Academy members' minds as Oscar voting time came closer. MGM/UA marketing chief Gerry Rich said, 'By design, we held off the release until the end of the year anticipating year-end accolades. You can't count on anything, but we felt the film would be on a number of "Best Ten" lists.'

When Nick saw the final cut, he told Figgis, 'I think it's great. I don't know if anyone's going to see it.' Figgis' heart sank, hearing Nick echo the sentiments of so many studio bosses who had turned the movie down flat before MGM/UA had agreed to distribute it. It all came flooding back to him. He said, 'Studio people would be very moved, then I wouldn't hear from them again. Some would even watch it and cry. Everybody said, "We think it's a wonderful film, but we wouldn't know how to begin marketing a film like this." '

Others would tell him, 'Yeah, it's a great film, but it's so dark you oughta be crazy.'

Los Angeles Times writer Claudia Puig said, 'The task was indeed staggering. How does one go about selling a bleak drama that chronicles in grim detail a screenwriter's decision to drink himself to death?'

But MGM/UA set about marketing the movie gently, giving their promotional material a light touch. It was released in just a handful of cinemas in a few big cities. As the critical praise poured in, and the word-of-mouth was passed on by the exclusive few who had seen it, so its success grew.

Even though it was released to a limited number of cinemas in a handful of locations, it still managed to gross nearly $1 million in its first four weeks. Compared to movies such as *Titanic, Jurassic Park* and *Star Wars: Episode 1 — The Phantom Menace*, that was a mere bagatelle, but considering this was regarded as an art-house film with no wide appeal, it was an indication of great success. By the beginning of January 1996, the film ranked 20th among the 70 or so films being shown on cinema screens across the country and had earned $3.26 million. That week, it was only being shown in 48 cinemas across the entire United States.

In Tinseltown, there is nothing like Oscar speculation to give box-office life to a small struggling movie. Underdogs such as *Pulp Fiction, The Piano* and *The Crying Game* had all benefited from such speculation before and, as the critics raved on, so the buzz was growing that *Leaving Las Vegas* would be liked by the members of the all-powerful Academy of Motion Picture Arts and Sciences.

The speculation was right. The Academy members gave the movie the nod in four Oscar categories when the nominations were announced. Nick was nominated for Best Actor; Elisabeth Shue for Best Actress; and Figgis for both Best Director and Best Adapted Screenplay.

Nick's and Shue's nominations came as no surprise to legendary singer Lou Rawls, who had a cameo role playing a concerned taxi driver. He said, 'I knew the minute I walked on the set that there was a special chemistry between Elisabeth and Nicolas. There was a sense with all the crew and cast that we were doing something memorable.'

Figgis thought the worst when he woke too late to hear the Academy Award nominations actually being announced that Tuesday morning in February 1996. He said, 'I started frantically channel surfing and tuned in to the very end of a TV report, when they said, "The *Leaving Las Vegas* team must be disappointed." I didn't think we were nominated for anything.' It wasn't until several minutes later he discovered the truth — and disappointment did not come into it. He was delighted.

Coincidentally, the nominations were yet another chapter in Beverly Hills High School's long history of drama achievements. Two of its former students, Nick and Richard Dreyfuss, were among the five nominees that year competing for the Best Actor Academy Award. Dreyfuss was up for his portrayal of the dedicated music teacher in *Mr Holland's Opus*. John Ingle, who had taught both of them drama at school, was thrilled that his former students were competing for the top acting honour.

Once Nick had been nominated for an Oscar, his price tag as an actor immediately started sky-rocketing. He was already negotiating with producer Jerry

Bruckheimer, for whom he had just been working on *The Rock*, to star in a second action adventure movie, *Con Air*, and he was also talking to Paramount Pictures about starring opposite John Travolta in the bizarre *Face/Off*, to be directed by top Hong Kong movie-maker John Woo.

Nick's co-star in *The Rock*, Sean Connery, had given him some advice on how to escape the quagmire of fame after the young actor won his Golden Globe Award for Best Performance by an Actor in a Motion Picture Drama for *Leaving Las Vegas* earlier in 1996. Nick revealed, 'Sean Connery told me, "Just forget about it and let it go." What he was saying was, "Do not dwell on something like this; do not feel you can rest on your laurels and just get lazy." I knew that it could either be a great thing or it could be the kiss of death, because so many people get high on their own achievements and somehow they think they're superior, and that is really dangerous. They sort of snob themselves out of the business. So I thought the best thing for me to do was to do the absolute opposite of a movie like *Leaving Las Vegas*. I think I have to keep doing what I've been doing, following my heart.'

The prizes had been coming thick and fast in the build-up to the Academy Awards. When Nick accepted the Screen Actors Guild award for best actor, he told his colleagues, 'I didn't go to college. This is my university, and I'm gonna consider this award my degree.' His mother, long since recovered from her battle with depression, was in the audience and smiled broadly as her son spoke.

By winning an Oscar, Nick, at 32 years old, was following the family tradition. His grandfather Carmine Coppola, who had died in 1991, won an Oscar for Best Original Dramatic Score for *The Godfather, Part II* in 1974; his uncle Francis won for co-writing *Patton* in 1970, for co-writing *The Godfather* in 1972 and for producing, directing and co-writing *The Godfather, Part II* two years later.

Nick's father was not in the audience to watch his son become the latest member of the Coppola clan to receive an Oscar. There was still bad blood between father and son over Nick's *USA Today* 'epitaph' comment. Since the article had appeared, the two had not spoken. Nonetheless, after Nick's Oscar victory, August sent his son a congratulatory telegram and Uncle Francis, who had also had his differences with his nephew, sent him a basket of flowers.

For a long time, Nick and his father only communicated by leaving messages on each other's telephone answering machines. It took a long time for the rift to heal but, eventually, it did. For Christmas the following year, Nick bought his father a Bentley. He parked it in front of his father's house with a red ribbon on it.

'I said to him, "You've always been as good as a Bentley to me," ' Nick said. 'He really loved it. We're both extremely sensitive men. He accesses his talent to write, the same way I access my talent to act. We're both artists.'

The award gave Nick a sense of belonging, not just in Hollywood, but within his accomplished family. He said, 'I can hold my head up with dignity and know that I did it my way.' But he had no intention of returning to his true Coppola family name. He said, 'It's nice to have two names. One is me me, the other is an invention of me. Being Nicolas Cage, it's almost like an alter ego.'

It was Nick's night. But the best moment of the evening was not what people might imagine, but rather, he said, 'When Jessica Lange wiped Patricia's lipstick off my mouth in the elevator on the way to the press room after I'd won.'

He did not let his family arguments lessen the joy of winning the most precious statuette in Hollywood. He said, 'When you get an Oscar, you are being recognised by your peers and that was so important to me. The prejudice I experienced because of my name was like a pitchfork in my butt and it made me work twice as hard at everything I did. The Oscar took 15 years, but it took care of all the past hurts. But the Oscar had meaning way beyond resolving some pain. It told me that I wasn't crazy all those years when I picked the roles I did. There was a reason for what I did, and the Oscar said that my ideas weren't wrong.'

Nick, who, when he accepted the part of Ben Sanderson had told anyone who would listen that he felt America was ready for a change of movie back to the vein of films like *Midnight Cowboy*, confessed he actually never anticipated the impact *Leaving Las Vegas* would have on movie-goers or how successful it would make him. He said, 'I never expected anybody to go and see that film and I certainly didn't expect to win any awards for it. That was fine with me; that's not why I did it. I did it because it was a great role and it was different. The amazing thing is that, unbeknownst to me, the country was taking a new look at cinema. People were interested in different things and I wasn't even aware of it. For the first time in my life, my tastes were in sync with other people's. How weird is that? For once, my opinions about material became in sync with what other people thought. I hadn't changed. Other people just came around. You know, I suspected it would happen, oddly enough, while I was watching MTV and saw what was happening with music. Grunge was everywhere, and people were singing about some pretty dire stuff. And that's when I thought the movie might have a chance. From the most mundane places, sometimes you can spot a shift in the country's mood.'

The 1996 Oscar ceremony was one of the most memorable in the academy's history. Not because of Nick or even the other winners, including Mel Gibson's *Braveheart*, sweeping the board with awards for best picture, director, cinematography, sound editing and make-up; Susan Sarandon as Best Actress; Kevin Spacey as Best Supporting Actor in *The Usual Suspects;* or Mira Sorvino as Best Supporting Actress in *Mighty Aphrodite*. But rather for the appearances of Kirk Douglas, who at the time was 79 and recovering from a stroke, there to receive a lifetime achievement award, and Christopher Reeve, a quadriplegic after his tragic horse-riding accident, strapped into his wheelchair and utterly still but for his facial movements, painstakingly delivering a tribute to Hollywood's social conscience for making such films as *Silkwood*, *In the Heat of the Night* and the AIDS drama *Philadelphia*.

Before the Academy Awards, Patricia had gone the obligatory Hollywood route and visited the world-famous Harry Winston's jewellers to hire the necessary diamonds to wear for the occasion. Nick has often described his wife as 'the most anti-money person I know'. Nonetheless, he told her, 'Honey, if I win this award, the diamonds are yours.' He had had written into his *Face/Off* contract that if he did indeed win an Oscar, he would get a bonus. Nick recalled, 'It just so happened that the bonus they gave me for *Face/Off* was the exact amount of the diamonds that she was renting from Harry Winston.' When he won, Nick told her, 'Well, we're both taking something home.'

After the ceremony, Nick and Patricia headed to the Governors' Ball, one of the social highlights of the after-Oscar party scene. Los Angeles is usually an early town with most restaurants closing up long before midnight as people working in the movie and television business and the financial services industry have to be out of bed at the crack of dawn. However, on the night of the Academy Awards, all the rules go out of the window and the place rocks until the sun has long been up. Avid art collector Nick had, out of all the parties he could have gone to, especially wanted to go to the Governors' Ball because one of his favourite glass makers was also attending the bash, but after he thought Dale Chihuly cut him dead, preferring to talk to Donald Trump, he moved on. He said, 'The night got amazing. We went into this restaurant and there was Stevie Wonder. And I said to him, "Mr Wonder, this is my wife, Patricia. She's my golden lady." Which is his great song. And he took her hand and sang "Golden Lady" to her, which was heartbreakingly beautiful ... so my night became terrific then.'

Nick and Patricia headed home to their Gothic-style castle in the Hollywood Hills where they were joined by friends including Jim Carrey, his partner on the Irish adventure, Phil Roy, and loads of others. Nick recalled, 'My cousin Roman showed up. And the Cassavetes sisters came by. And my cousin Sophia. My agent Richard Lovett, and my manager, Gerry Harrington. I got some caviar out of the refrigerator and we had a little soirée.'

Roman Coppola said, 'What struck me about the evening was that it reminded me of the pictures you used to see of Howard Hughes and Gary Cooper hanging out at Chasen's. I was thinking that someday we'll be looking at a picture of Nick and Patricia and Jim and Phil from that night.'

Despite his late night, Nick still managed to get up in the morning and go back downtown. He recalled what becoming an Oscar winner felt like. He said, 'The next morning, I'm downtown, and I'm walking by the news-stand, and it was the first time I'd been on the front page of the newspaper, which was ... interesting. Then I went to this old coffee shop to have a cup of coffee and some pancakes, and the cook and chef come out and clap, and it was a great feeling. Then I get in my car and put my Beatles song on that I play when I'm feeling proud, which is 'Baby, You're a Rich Man'. So I'm listening to that in my Lamborghini, and I'm driving to the beach, feeling pretty good, when a cop pulls me over. And I think I'm going to get a ticket, which is what normally happens in that car, but they say, "We just want to say congratulations." And that was cool. And I'm walking on the beach, and surfers, like, hundreds of yards away are going, "Hey, Nick, congratulations!" And it was just a wild day. For one second, Los Angeles felt like a small town. It took about 80 hours after I won the Oscar to determine when I was dreaming and when I was awake. Patricia wrote me a note, a sweet note, about a week after the Oscars. It said, "Before, women wanted you. But when you went up there you had my lipstick on your face. It was a win for every married couple and a celebration of marriage." '

By the time the 1995–96 awards season was over, *Leaving Las Vegas* had won an Oscar and been nominated for three more, as well as having been nominated for three BAFTA awards, the British equivalent of the Academy Awards. It won one Golden Globe and had been nominated for three more, and won four Independent Spirit Awards with two more nominations. The film also won four awards from the Los Angeles Film Critics Association, one from the USA National Board of Review Awards, three USA National Society of Film Critics Awards, and two New York Film Critics Circle Awards. In addition, Nick won a Screen Actors Guild Award and Shue was nominated. Internationally, the film won two prizes at the San Sebastian International Film Festival in Spain and was nominated for a third, and Nick became the youngest actor ever to receive a Lifetime Achievement Award at the Montreal World Film Festival.

All in all, it was a phenomenal success for such a bleak topic and a movie produced on such a shoestring budget. It was also sweet revenge for Figgis, who recalled, 'The word went around when we started shooting that Nick Cage and

Mike Figgis were making the most unreleasable film in the history of Hollywood.'

Nick was surprised that he was finally being recognised for his acting in what had seemed to be such a fringe picture, a movie that appeared unlikely to receive accolades. He echoed Figgis' sentiments and said, 'If I thought about awards, I would not have been able to do a movie like *Leaving Las Vegas*, because the word around town was that Mike and I were making the most unreleasable movie in Hollywood. I had some fear that the movie would not get released.'

Thanks to Figgis' perseverance, his fear was unfulfilled, although not without foundation.

Nick and Figgis enjoyed working together so much that they were gung-ho about teaming up together again as soon as possible. They discussed joining forces on Figgis' next project *One Night Stand*, which was due to start filming in May 1996, by which time Nick would have finished his commitment to *The Rock* and *Miss Julie*, a film version of August Strindberg's 1888 play about sexual repression and class schisms. Nick said, 'We are both interested in carrying on this relationship. When Scorsese found De Niro — that is how I feel.'

But as things were to turn out, Figgis went ahead to make *One Night Stand* with Wesley Snipes, Nastassja Kinski and Robert Downey Jr after Nick decided to drop out of the project. The movie was about a successful, married director of commercials who has a passionate one-night affair with a beautiful married woman while on a trip to New York, and the ramifications it has on his life. Nick had been married for less than a year and decided that he did not want to play an unfaithful husband. He said, 'I was not in a place in my world at that time, right after I'd just gotten married, where I wanted to play a man who was cheating on his wife. It just wasn't somewhere I wanted to go. I just didn't want to go there.' When Figgis finally decided to go ahead with Snipes in the lead he added the extra element of it being an inter-racial affair.

As for *Miss Julie*, in which Figgis had hoped to have Nick starring opposite *The English Patient* co-star Juliette Binoche, that film finally began production in London in March 1999 with Saffron Burrows as Julie and Maria Doyle Kennedy and Peter Mullan in the other starring roles.

Nick admitted that winning an Oscar had changed him. He said, 'There's less to rebel against when people are listening to you. The Oscar has given me a chance to have my ideas accepted instead of stomped all over as they were in the past. People in power in Hollywood will think twice before shutting doors on me these days.'

Oh, how right he was. All of a sudden, the major studios were standing in line, waiting to heap money on an actor they had always considered to be a substantial commercial risk.

Jerry Bruckheimer, the producer of many huge Hollywood hits, was first in line to snap him up even before the precious envelope had been opened. He said, 'There are too many actors who kind of blend together. Nick stands out. He's got a God-given talent that's all his own.'

Finally, that talent had been recognised.

CHAPTER SEVENTEEN

SOLID AS THE ROCK

Nick was the first to admit he was a hesitant hero as he struggled to adapt to becoming an adventure movie heart-throb. He did not automatically take to this new genre, co-starring in the explosion-filled epic *The Rock* with veteran action superstar Sean Connery, produced by legendary maestros of mayhem Jerry Bruckheimer and Don Simpson (who sadly died from a heart-attack shortly after filming began), and directed by Michael Bay. He had some very practical and simple concerns which appeared to conflict with the ready-for-anything reputation of his early days. As he became involved in a series of dangerous stunts, mostly shot on infamous Alcatraz Island, Nick learned that war games were not child's play.

He explained, 'I enjoyed working with Sean Connery but I was concerned about the safety because it was the first real experience of this genre for me. Alcatraz, if you are not there with a guide, is a very dangerous place. There are cliffs that appear out of nowhere that drop many hundreds of feet into a bed of rusty pipes and nails. I used to joke and call it Tetanus World. There's metal corroding there, there's lead paint on the walls. Fortunately, nobody got hurt. But I had to be kind of a bore about it, where if there's a rusty nail over there and an explosion over there, I want to know where everything is. You really have to look out for yourself when you make this kind of movie.'

Doing the unexpected and casting Nick in an action movie appealed to producers Jerry Bruckheimer and his then partner Don Simpson, who had had a string of hits with movies such as *Beverly Hills Cop* starring Eddie Murphy, *Crimson Tide* with Denzel Washington and Tom Cruise's *Top Gun*. Explaining the reasoning behind the choice of Nick, Bruckheimer said, 'We like to take characters that maybe you haven't seen in the action genre. Eddie was new at it, and Tom Cruise definitely wasn't considered an action star when we put him in *Top Gun*. Nick is a very physical guy, he works out every day. What you have in Nick is the physicality that the audience doesn't know about — that and the fact he's funny.'

In *The Rock*, Nick plays mild-mannered FBI chemical weapons specialist Dr Stanley Goodspeed, who has to save millions of lives by infiltrating the notorious

Alcatraz Prison. With the aid of Connery's character, mysterious, imprisoned British agent John Patrick Mason, reputedly the only man to have escaped from Alcatraz Island, Goodspeed is charged with stopping a band of renegade soldiers. They have taken hostages on the Rock, now a national park, and their commander, played by Ed Harris, is threatening to launch a deadly nerve-gas attack that would wipe out part of San Francisco unless the US Government pays reparation to the families of soldiers killed on secret missions. To complicate matters further, Goodspeed has just learned he is about to become a reluctant father as his girlfriend is pregnant. Added to all this, there is no love lost between Mason and the Americans. A former SAS officer, he had been thrown into the slammer without trial for stealing the FBI's most sensitive files in the early 1960s.

Although Connery had senior status, Nick was nevertheless accommodated with star power and was allowed creative input to his unwilling hero's character, such as writing his own dialogue. In the initial drafts, Goodspeed was frustrated with his job and wanted to be a field agent. But Nick did not like the idea. He explained, 'I said, "I can't play Stanley with any dignity if you make him that way." I wanted to make him very positive, a character who liked his job and wanted to save people, not hurt people, sort of a non-violent man. A man who is afraid and is not afraid to cry. I could never play the FBI agent as a guy who is working in the lab out of frustration because he really wants to be out in the field killing people. I can't do that with dignity. I told them we have to make this guy someone who loves being in the lab and then he's out in the field because he can't help it.'

Nor did he see his clean-cut character as a ranter and raver, in-your-face kind of guy. He said, 'I'm not going to lose my cool and debase myself and start swearing and say, "Fuck this, fuck that ..." I didn't want that kind of attitude. I thought that would be unusual. I wanted him to be into God; I wanted Stanley to be a somewhat religious man, which I thought would be somewhat unusual in an action movie.'

But Nick acknowledges that without his Academy recognition he would not have had the clout to have Goodspeed altered so drastically. He confessed, 'Stanley was written as just another gung-ho action hero, but I didn't want to play him that macho. I wanted to turn him into a neurotic action hero. I wanted to tweak the action genre a little. Without all the hoopla surrounding my Oscar nomination, I don't think they'd have let me play him that way.'

Even Goodspeed's first name was changed. Originally, Nick was playing Dr Bill Goodspeed but he said, 'My dentist is Stanley Golden. His manner is interesting and some of it was right for the role.'

Goodspeed was not the only role to get a complete make-over. Connery disliked his one-dimensional character and had the script redeveloped to make his British agent much more complex, with a personal history as a sub-plot.

The two actors quickly became a team, taking over the storyline and changing it as they thought fit. They spent hours reworking the script and on occasion they simply improvised. Nick recalled, 'Sean and I got into a mode that seemed really to click. We developed a rapport, and it just went into a kind of synchronicity where we actually got a kick out of what each of us was doing ... I mean, he's not hiding off in a corner meditating and becoming a teardrop, and I'm not becoming a raindrop. I think we've figured out how to act without getting too Method.'

When Nick had his first meeting with 007 star Connery to rehearse, he recalled, 'I remember I was singing "Let's Go Surfing Now", which is a line from the classic 1960s California-sound hit "Surfin' Safari". Sean says, "Who's that by?"

and I said, "The Beach Boys." He says, "I haven't heard of them." I said, "But you guys both got big at the same time." And he said, "They must be dead." '

Technically, the two actors had met before — on stage. When Connery won his only Oscar, an Academy Award for Best Supporting Actor in 1987 for his performance as the grizzled older policeman in *The Untouchables*, Nick presented him with the prestigious statuette. However, Connery did not regard that as a meeting. He said, 'I liked him as an actor always. I saw quite a lot of his movies, but I never met him before *The Rock*. He certainly wasn't a disappointment, we got on terrifically.'

By the time filming was over, they were members of a mutual admiration society. Connery said, 'I found him totally professional, which is really something in this day and age.'

Nick was in awe of his older co-star. Even though he had made more than two-dozen pictures, Nick was just 31, compared to the legendary Scot, who had a vast body of work that set him apart as a far more experienced actor. Nick confessed to a confidante before that first rehearsal meeting, 'It's hard for a young actor to find a mentor in the business. I'm hoping to ask him questions, get some advice.' Nick had found Shirley MacLaine to be such a mentor when they had worked together on *Guarding Tess*. 'She's very giving,' he said.

Connery lived up to everything Nick had imagined. He said, 'He was a very straightforward man who cared a great deal about the work. He was open and available, and willing to step into the role of mentor, which is unusual these days.'

Nick had admired Connery since he was a young boy when his father took him to see *Dr No*. He always felt that Connery bore a remarkable physical resemblance to August Coppola. After seeing that film, he regarded his father as James Bond with a PhD and so, in Connery, he basically saw his dad every time he looked at him. 'I used that for *The Rock*,' he confessed. 'It helped me to see Sean as a father figure for my character.'

When Lawrence Grobel of *Movieline* magazine asked what it was like acting with someone who looked like his father, Nick replied, 'It gave me a mentor-like relationship, which is very difficult for actors to find. He likes actors and he doesn't like to be bullshitted or double-crossed. He validated some of my thoughts that I was concerned about. He's enjoying a career where he's at the top of his form at his age, which is remarkable. I mean, who gets to act that long and still be an event with every movie? I would ask him questions about determining image — you know, the movie star image. What about an actor who wants to change his voice or his look? He said, "Don't worry about that, don't concern yourself with image. Just do your work." '

There was no battle of egos between the two stars. Nick said, 'He has the coolest screen presence in the history of cinema. He inspired me to go the other direction and play Stanley more flawed and not completely confident. For me, Sean Connery is the grand master of this genre. He's one of the only superstars I know who can go from an action movie to a soul-searching, in-depth drama movie, and his is a career that I've modelled and emulated. So when I worked with him, it gave me an opportunity to pick his brain and ask him every question that I wanted to ask.'

Connery, who was paid $13 million — far in excess of Nick — to appear in the film, and who was credited as an executive producer, confirmed that Nick had sought his advice.

'Yeah, I offered him the benefit of my experience,' he admitted.

One day, they were sitting in the Scot's trailer when he gave Nick a poignant business lesson. Connery, whom Nick nicknamed The Master, picked up a dollar bill and ripped off a piece. 'That's for your agent,' he said. He tore off another piece, saying, 'That's for your manager.' A further rip was accompanied by, 'That's for your lawyer.' Another rip came with the comment, 'That's for the Inland Revenue,' and another with the words, 'That's for whatever other taxes.' He was finished and so was the dollar bill. Connery was left with just a fragment of the original bill. He said, 'This is what you have to work with, so figure out how to do it. Simplify everything. And for Christ's sake, if anybody tells you, 'You wouldn't understand this, it's too complicated,' then call them on it. Save your money. That way you don't have to do movies you don't want to do.' Again and again, Nick would return to the trailer for more down-to-earth lectures on life.

Luckily, Bay, who had been a fan of Nick's ever since *Raising Arizona*, was happy to accommodate his input to the film. The director loved idiosyncratic actors and had always felt that he wanted an actor with a twist to play the scientist. He said, 'Nick's got a quirky side to him. His character is the everyday guy on the mission from hell. He's not the typical stud hero going on a mission, and I think Nick's quirkiness really made it a charming thing. The role called for someone who could be believable as an Everyman. But not just any Everyman. What kind of a guy would like working in a place where he goes into a glassed-in gas chamber and works with deadly chemicals? Not a normal guy, but normal enough so that when we put him in an extraordinary situation, the audience can identify with him. Nick is perfect for the role and the fact that he is such an unpredictable actor makes it even more effective. We're not used to seeing him in this role. Nick is the real deal and people like that about him.'

By the time the movie was finished, the script had been rewritten so many times that a raging controversy developed over who should actually get the credit for writing it. 'There were a lot of cooks in the kitchen,' Nick admitted. 'Jerry Bruckheimer is very similar to my Uncle Francis in that way. Things are always being changed and tweaked.'

Nick was keen to emphasise his character's intelligence so, whenever he could, he had him referred to as Dr Goodspeed, not Stanley. He said, 'So instead of relying on macho, we run on smart.' His model was Richard Dreyfuss' shark expert in *Jaws*, who states that he became interested in sharks when one ate his boat. He said, 'In *The Rock,* there's a scene about chemistry. I say, "I got my first chemistry set when I was seven, I blew my eyebrows off and we never saw the cat again and I've been into chemistry ever since." '

He attributed his skills in honing dialogue to his father encouraging him to write short stories when he was a boy. He felt this early training helped him mould Goodspeed into the multi-dimensional character he became; a boisterous boffin who reluctantly assumes the mantle of a messiah. Even though this was an action movie, he was still able to add some humour to his character.

Ever-meticulous in his research, Nick got his chemical/biological expertise and jargon by hanging out with a real-life FBI agent. The Federal Bureau of Investigation co-operated with the movie even though in the film the FBI director is an untrustworthy, double-crossing, self-motivated political animal who comes across as a total sleazebag. Nick said, 'I met a real FBI person, and he is not a happy man. He looks very concerned. I sat in on a lecture that he gave. Most of it was classified, he wouldn't let me hear it. But he did tell me there was eight ounces of a chemical now in Russia that is so powerful it would exterminate the entire world if properly dispersed — and it's sitting there. I said, 'You're making this sound like it's inevitable.' And he said, 'I'm afraid it is.' Well, why would you want to have a kid, being a guy who knows that? Why would you want to do that to a kid? I felt really lousy after that, and I brought it up in rehearsals. I said, 'I don't think Stanley should want this child. He should emotionally think it's wonderful, but a guy with that kind of knowledge would not want to do that to a child.' But how do you touch upon that without dragging everybody down in the audience? So there was still that obligation, that responsibility.'

Although the FBI were willing to help, the US military were not, because they were unhappy that the villains are US Marines. Bruckheimer said, 'When we went to the government and said, "We'd like your co-operation to work with the military," they said, "No." But they came back to us and said, "If you make it the civilian militia instead of the Marines, we might co-operate," — and we said, "No." ' Bruckheimer and his partner were not prepared to give up the idea of the commander as a misguided man with honourable intentions. Ironically, in the original script the bad guys were terrorists.

The military may not have been helpful but the authorities running the island certainly were. During the shoot, the cast and crew could well have had problems getting on and off Alcatraz, which had been closed as a federal prison in 1963 by then US Attorney General Robert Kennedy because of spiralling upkeep costs and public outrage over the tough conditions. Alcatraz is run by the Golden Gate National Recreation Area — part of the US National Parks Service — and the US Coast Guard, and is normally a popular tourist attraction. However, a budget crisis in Washington DC during the shoot caused a government shut-down and parks like Alcatraz were closed to the public.

Disney put the Alcatraz park rangers on its payroll and handed over between $50,000 and $100,000 to clean up hazardous materials, including asbestos in two buildings, and shooting was allowed to continue. Even so, once the tourists were allowed back on the island at the end of the crisis, the visitors came first and filming had to be fitted in around them and could not interfere with regular park business.

Filming on Alcatraz was originally scheduled for three days but after Bay viewed the island and the script had been repeatedly revised, the crew ended up working there for nine weeks and The Rock became the largest movie ever filmed there. Alcatraz, America's most popular urban park, attracting up to 4,000 visitors a day, became the only national park that was not completely closed during the government emergency.

Unlike many others in the business, Nick's only addiction is working out. He has a two-hour session with a private trainer every day he can, and certainly several times a week. He is so into his exercise programme that he gets annoyed if anyone tries to talk to him while he is working out. He also prefers individual sports, such as running, to team activities. He admitted, 'It becomes almost a ritual in the day when you go through the pain, and break walls down, and get to clarity of some kind. That's what running is for me. For me it's always been about my sanity. It's always been, if I don't work out, I'm going to lose it. I work out so I can download the problems of the day, empty my mind and blow the stress out, and I feel great afterwards. It's really more about my mental health than anything else.' Without doubt, he needed to be fit to handle the rigours of starring in The Rock.

According to Bay, Nick was determined to show off his physique in the film. He recalled Nick telling him, 'Mike, I want to rip my shirt off and show my pecs, 'cause I've been working out.' Bay replied, 'But you're going to look silly, 'cause you're surrounded by Navy SEAL, the baddest of the bad, and you're just a lowly FBI agent.' Bay claimed in the end Nick got his way when they were shooting a scene in his character's apartment. He said, 'One day I show up to the set to shoot a scene, and Nick comes in with a robe on. Suddenly, he pulls it off, and he's wearing this little pinkish-purple Speedo-type underwear. And I said, "OK, let's just get it over with." ' As a result there is a scene in the movie where FBI scientist Stanley Goodspeed is seen lounging around in his home, playing his guitar and wearing underpants.

But Nick, who almost seems ashamed of his muscular figure despite the work he puts into it, disputes the story. He said, ' 'I want to rip my shirt off and show my pecs?' I didn't say that. I've never used the words "my pecs".' Nick has a completely different recollection of why the scene was shot that way. He did concede, 'It's a funny story, but ...' — while not looking at all amused. He explained he wanted the scene like that because it was an amusing follow-on from the previous scene, in which Goodspeed was locked in a glass chamber being contaminated by deadly chemicals. He said, 'The image of him alone in his socks and his underwear, with a guitar, strumming chords, and a glass of wine — that was funny. But it wasn't about, "Oh, God, you've got to see me nude." It's not that. I'm always trying to keep my clothes on.'

It was definitely true that since being embarrassed by his body in *The Boy in Blue*, while Nick had shed clothes on many occasions for love scenes, he had avoided doing so to prove he was a muscle-man.

He also finally got his way in adding the bizarre expression 'Zeus's butt-hole' into the script — as in 'How in the name of Zeus's butt-hole did you get out of your cell?' — although to this day many people don't understand why the expression needed to be added to the dialogue anyway.

Drama-Logue's Elias Stimac commented, 'The amazing thing about Cage on screen and off is that he is able to balance such delicate issues with an understated sense of humour — a trait that instantly allows viewers to relate to his characters.'

And so it was with Goodspeed. Although he was a chemical super-freak, a man torn by his contradictions and convictions, he was still amusing. Nick said, 'The humour has to be organic, it has to come out of the situation. Like life, there are some horrible situations that are funny in spite of themselves. So I always try to find the humour. I think it's more interesting to attack a dire mode with humour, because humour is a survival mechanism. When I'm dealing with a lot of pain in my life, I find that I'm more funny than I am when everything is at peace. I don't know why — I think perhaps when I was a child that was my way of escape, or my way of dealing with the world when I was unhappy. And if you look at most comedians, a lot of them say that they had unhappy childhoods.'

The Rock was only Michael Bay's second outing as a big screen director, having made his name making commercials. He first directed the Will Smith–Martin Lawrence action picture *Bad Boys*, for which he was hand-picked by Simpson and Bruckheimer after becoming the youngest-ever winner of the Directors' Guild of America's Commercial Director of the Year award in 1995.

Despite his relative inexperience, Bay takes the credit for *The Rock* having one of the most spectacular movie car chases of all time. Like so much else, the chase was a late addition. But Bay could not resist indulging himself and putting his own spin on the classic San Francisco car chase scenario, as first seen in the late Steve McQueen's classic 1968 picture, *Bullitt*.

He admitted, 'Our chase scene wasn't even in the script but I had to do it. Besides, I thought we needed more action scenes in the movie. We had a cool set-up with the story but we were a big summer action movie and we needed a lot of action. So I approached that car chase like I approach all my work; aggressive and in-your-face.'

In the scene, Mason, who has been held without trial for more than three decades for stealing sensitive, top-secret government material, makes a break for it and Goodspeed gives chase in a commandeered yellow Ferrari, only to write it off spectacularly in an explosive crash when one of San Francisco's world-famous cable cars rises 15 feet in the air, flips over on its side and slides down a street. In an age when virtually anything can be computer generated or enhanced, every contortion of the cable car was real. The only fabrication was constructing the stunt carriage with a hollow interior so that it weighed only 5 tons, compared to the real ones which weigh around 14. Steel cylinders were welded into the frame in a vertical position. Inside the cylinders, poles about 10in wide and 3ft long were inserted, and the rest of the cylinder was filled with nitrogen to send the cable car hurtling into the air.

Associate producer and stunt co-ordinator Ken Bates said, 'It was much like a bullet being fired. We used a large blast of nitrogen, which is just compressed clean air, to blow the pole out of the cylinders at a pressure of 600lb per square inch. That's what actually pushed the cable car into the air — spitting out those poles. I would say about 30,000lb of force flipped the cable car.'

Astonishingly for a movie in which money was no object — the budget was $70 million — the whole stunt only cost $150,000. The film's problem was time, not cash. The release date was brought forward, so Bay had to work round the clock editing the final cut.

Bay admitted to being a tough director, saying, 'I was in everyone's face. I came from commercials and music videos, a world where the money had to go on the screen and not into out-of-control spending, which happens on action films. Doing a movie this size was war.'

Surprisingly, most of the time filming was amicable. On one occasion, however, Nick objected to wearing a wetsuit for the underwater scenes. He told Bay, 'I can't wear this — I look like Bubble Man! Look at Sean — he looks cool.' Bay patiently talked him into wearing the outfit. As Goodspeed, Nick was supposed to look awkward and out-of-place, so just before the scene was to be shot, Bay craftily adjusted the mask, pushing it askew so that Goodspeed would look even goofier.

There was, of course, one major, sobering upset during the shoot — the death of Simpson. Bay remembered, 'One day Nick was screwing up and I asked what was wrong. He goes, 'Didn't you hear? Don is dead.' They kept it from me. They wanted me to finish the day. I don't think people knew how to deal with it, it was so shocking.' Bay finished the shot and went into Bruckheimer's trailer where he just sat for two hours. Nick confessed, 'Someone accidentally told me. It's difficult to concentrate when one of the conductors dies and you're still doing the piece.' Bruckheimer was also in shock. He said, 'For me, it was a great loss. He was like a brother to me.'

Harry Humphries, the former US Navy SEAL who trained the cast, revealed that it was easy to tell between Nick and Connery who was the 'action virgin'. Connery professed to hate water and guns, but according to Humphries, 'He was extremely proficient with a firearm. On the other hand, Nick was an obvious beginner, but as he got better he developed quite an interest in shooting recreationally.'

Nonetheless, when Nick was questioned about his new-found interest in firearms he became very cagey. He said, 'What I have is an interest in protection. I want to make sure everybody I know and love is safe. I can't really pretend to know what the right thing is, but I do see certain violence in the community accelerating.'

He quickly adapted to his new chosen genre and said, 'The funniest thing about it is, this is probably the most expensive movie I've ever made, and for some reason, I just got that Super 8 feeling that I used to have when I was a kid, when my brother and I would make movies. We'd be like, 'OK, let's put that over there and now you're going to fall down, and you pick the gun up.' Ironically, the bigger the movie and the more the action involved, the more you feel like a kid playing in the backyard. That's kind of a fun feeling, and an infectious feeling. And as long as you come from that good place, where you know that you're enjoying yourself, then I think the movie will be enjoyable.'

After Nick had finished making *Leaving Las Vegas,* he rejected a number of projects before agreeing to make *The Rock*, which was pitched as *Die Hard* — referring to Bruce Willis' hit action movie series — on Alcatraz. He said, 'I finished *Leaving Las Vegas* and I turned down quite a bit of stuff that came my way but didn't seem right. I worked out. I was running and just sort of taking care of myself and life, then this *Rock* project came along. And I thought, OK, this is a project where I can go completely in a different direction. Action is kind of the last frontier; I haven't mastered action. It's not something I'd done well before, and I wanted to try to learn to do it. See what's there, if there's anything I can bring to it. I think it's important that it's so widely received, and anything that powerful should be dealt with responsibly and morally.'

There was also an ulterior motive for making an action movie. Despite all the hype about it being Nick's first, any dedicated Nick Cage fan will recall another, completed in 1990. The difference was this time he wanted to get it right. It was as if Nick was trying to erase the memory of the military movie *Fire Birds*. In that film, he and Tommy Lee Jones had been criticised for being laughable playing US helicopter pilots battling South American drug barons. When confronted with the suggestion that he wanted to correct a previous failure, Nick confessed, 'Yeah ... that didn't work. That was another reason I wanted to try action again. I didn't know what I was doing back then. I just didn't have a clue.'

Nick, who admits to having made mistakes in his choice of some films such as *Fire Birds*, *The Boy in Blue* and *Trapped in Paradise*, adamantly defended his decision to go from a thought-provoking, philosophical movie to taking a testosterone-filled, high-adrenalin ride with more appeal to adolescent boys and macho men than lovers of fine performances.

He said, '*Leaving Las Vegas* was the answer to all my prayers. When it came along, I knew it would allow me to dig a little deeper than some other roles I'd played — to get back into that crummy old corner in my mind, dust off the cobwebs and see what I could come up with. Well, I've done that now. I did this small film and it gave me a chance to take a chance. Now I'm doing the complete opposite because I like to keep flipping the coin. I think there are a lot of different kinds of movies to make. I liken it to the bands I admire — they do all kinds of songs.

'I wanted to go completely in the opposite direction, and when *The Rock* came around, I thought, well, this would be unexpected, wouldn't it? It's the kind of movie that plays on the world stage. But for a long time I'd thought that action films had lacked characters. I saw a need to play people authentically. I think that people tend to get tired of the same old stagnating approach to that monosyllabic, stoic, macho steroid-head, which to me can offer very little at this point. I had been contemplating the notion of a sensitive action hero for some time.'

Besides, starring in action films would expose his work to a much wider audience. He said, 'I saw the action format as one of two that really translates worldwide — comedy being the other. I wanted to get on that stage. I wanted it to be something I could improve upon. *Leaving Las Vegas* was a movie that people were ready for. It's the opposite of *The Rock*. *The Rock* is the kind of movie which I consider valid and cogent, and I wouldn't have done it if I didn't think it had value in going to the cinema and getting your mind off your problems. But *Leaving Last Vegas* is a movie you go to when you want to look at your problems.'

Still, making *The Rock* was a far more demanding movie, physically, if not emotionally, than *Leaving Las Vegas* ever was. After shooting was over he confessed, 'Now, I feel like I'm in good shape and I can handle what's thrown at me, but you have to really be out for yourself on an action movie. I bored Michael Bay to death because I'm not one of those actors who does stunts. I did not want to get hurt, I didn't want a bomb going off in my face, or having to lose half my hearing or my eyesight. First of all, I'm a dad. I want to be around to see my son grow up. Second of all, the stunt guy needs the job, too, he's got to make some money. And third of all, I want to finish the movie. I don't want to be here any longer than I have to be, and if I get hurt we shut down production. So I just don't do it.' He honestly admitted, 'I'm just not one of those macho guys, I guess. I don't really get it.'

Not wanting to be there any longer than he had to included Nick's determination to escape Alcatraz each night when filming was over and head back to his Pacific Heights mansion. Meanwhile, Connery could not be bothered to travel every day and had a luxury cabin built on the island so he could stay overnight whenever he wanted and get more rest.

Nick's life had changed so drastically in just a few short months. He had got married and now he was beginning his transformation from oddball actor to major A-list Hollywood leading man. As well as going from being single to seriously committed in 1995, he did a complete about-face as far as the kind of movie roles he chose. The actor with a reputation for picking weird and way-out characters, and who had also dabbled with lightweight comedic parts, was totally and unexpectedly reinventing himself as an action movie hero. But this was Nick, so right from the beginning it was obvious he would not be playing the stereotypical action hero.

Embarking on this new journey, after the drastic pay cut he had taken to make *Leaving Las Vegas*, also meant he was on his way to becoming within a few short years one of Hollywood's highest paid stars. He had already signed for *The Rock* and started making it long before his Academy Award victory. But when he commenced on the first of what would become his trilogy of action movies — *The Rock*, *Con Air* and *Face/Off* — which he describes as 'my triple action album', he was on the path that would eventually escalate him into the $20-million-a-picture salary bracket, a stratosphere that only a handful of Hollywood actors have achieved.

Nevertheless, for most people the idea of Nick Cage in a typical Simpson–Bruckheimer fast-paced film full of car chases, explosions and shoot-outs was hard to imagine.

'When I did *Leaving Las Vegas,* then *The Rock* came out, everything sort of came into focus — the previous work that I had done,' he said. 'I'd always had a devoted but small fan base that got me, but by and large the majority never really did. When that happened with *Leaving Las Vegas,* the earlier part of my work came into focus, and suddenly scripts came to me that I didn't really get the opportunity to try before. So I became like a kid in a candy store, thinking, wow, this is great. Now I can finally work with the people I want to work with and make the movies I want to make.'

From a $240,000 cut-price pay day for *Leaving Las Vegas,* he had agreed to salaries of $4 million plus a percentage of the profits for *The Rock,* $6.5 million for *Con Air* and $7 million for *Face/Off,* all before he got the Oscar nomination, let alone the award itself. After the Academy Awards, he was firmly established in the $6–$7 million pay bracket and rising for future films. In addition to his salaries, there were clauses in his contracts for *The Rock* and *Con Air* that he would get a $250,000 bonus if the films broke the $100-million mark. *The Rock* went on to make more than $134 million from the United States domestic box-office earnings alone and *Con Air* took in excess of $101 million from American cinema ticket seat sales. Plus, with *Face/Off,* which made $112 million domestically, there was a clause that specified, should he win an Oscar that year, he would receive an extra $250,000 bonus.

Nick was laughing all the way to the bank but he has never made light of his new-found fortune. When *Playboy* magazine's David Sheff asked him if his pay rises made him chuckle, he said, 'I don't chuckle. I have respect for the dollar.'

In fact, free-spending Nick has always needed every penny he could earn. He confessed, 'There's one thing I have some difficulty with, and that's hanging on to money. I find ways of spending money that mystify everybody around me. They're amazed. They want to know how I do it.'

Things were really coming together for him. Looking back he said, 'That period seemed like a kind of harmonic convergence in my life. Everything just sort of happened at once. Things started to work more smoothly for me. Things just sort of shifted and I felt much more in control of my instrument.' Music-loving Nick often expresses himself in musical metaphors, comparing his acting style to a jazz musician improvising a riff around a melody.

But at the same time, he admitted that his eclectic choice of roles made it difficult for the public to pin him down. He said, 'One of the things I've tried to find over the years was an image. And I became aware that after 27 movies, I had no image. So I thought about how I've gone back and forth my whole career. I made three romantic comedies, I made three alternative movies. I'm doing three action movies in a row. And I decided, well that's the image — to consistently expect the unexpected. I want to have as many careers as I can possibly have in one career.'

Although Nick's career has involved playing such a diverse range of characters, one thing that movie-goers can expect is that each of them has some of Nick's unique comic sensibilities, which is partially the result of his fastidious script preparation. He said, 'I think there's an approach which I try to maintain, which I think is a musical approach. The fact of the matter is I rewrote most of my dialogue in *The Rock* — it just wasn't on the page. And in that, I can come up with melodies and rhythms that, since working on *Peggy Sue Got Married*, I have really explored. So if audiences are finding a similarity, then yes, that would be it. It's a stylistic thing, I think.'

For a while there was a chance that Nick would not be able to make *The Rock* because he had already committed to *A Simple Plan*, for which he had also negotiated a $4 million fee under a pay-or-play deal, meaning he got paid whether the movie got made or not, provided he did not back out. His wife Patricia Arquette was at one point talked about for the female lead. John Dahl, who had directed him in *Red Rock West*, was hired to direct. Filming was supposed to start at the beginning of 1996 so there was an obvious scheduling conflict as work on *The Rock* was due to begin in the autumn of 1995 and continue into early the following spring.

Nick had fallen in love with the plot of *The Rock*, even though he wanted to change the script, and told Bruckheimer he wanted to do it if he could get round this problem. Bruckheimer went to Savoy Pictures, who were making *A Simple Plan*, to see if they could resolve the situation. Bruckheimer said, 'We were working out a deal with Savoy to finish Nick as quickly as we could and give them a stop date so they could have Nick.' All too often, such scheduling problems are enough to torpedo a star's involvement in a project — but not this time. Bruckheimer added, 'We got very lucky — not for Savoy — but for us. They went out of business. And we had Nick Cage.' *A Simple Plan* was finally resurrected at Paramount studios three years later.

In fact, Nick's involvement in *The Rock* helped Connery agree to do the film. Bruckheimer told entertainment industry expert Martin A Grove that after Savoy pulled out of *A Simple Plan* and Nick was committed to *The Rock*, 'we sent the script to Connery. To be honest with you, Connery really wanted to work with Nick Cage. He thought he was a brilliant actor and wanted to be in a picture with him.'

Bruckheimer and scriptwriter Jonathan Hensleigh, who wrote *Jumanji* and *Die Hard with a Vengeance*, flew to London to meet Connery, who jetted in from Spain. Connery also wanted script changes but, after the discussions, he committed to the project.

Another problem Nick faced was nothing to do with the movie but something being conjured up in parts of the media. It was the early days of Nick and Patricia's marriage and, as filming progressed, so did the rumours that it was their relationship that was on the rocks. Whatever they did, the gossip persisted.

As if to give the gossip-mongers the lie, one day when Nick had a break from filming, he wandered into the trendy Krizia boutique on San Francisco's Grant Avenue with sexy Patricia, dressed in pink hot-pants and matching spike heels, on his arm. He splashed out thousands of dollars on numerous items including a see-through jacket and see-through raincoat. Jasmin Braslow, the store's owner, said, 'They were so young, so sexy.'

Thanks to *The Rock*, Nick and Patricia were able to spend a lot of time in late 1995 and early 1996 in San Francisco. At the time, the *San Francisco Chronicle*'s leading columnist was Herb Caen, one of the masters of American journalism who has since died. He missed nothing which affected personalities in San Francisco. As Nick and Patricia's first anniversary approached, he was pleased to report that their honeymoon certainly wasn't over after one of his sources spotted them in a restaurant. He wrote, 'Nicolas Cage and Patricia Arquette were all over each other at Enrico's last Friday noonish, coming up for air only long enough to ingest a few more oysters and graciously sign autographs. Then back to chewing ears.'

Just as Nick was wrapping up post-production work on the film in early May, the popular *Late Show*, a late-night television talk show hosted by comedian David Letterman, by coincidence went on location for a week to San Francisco, hoping to get as many local stars as possible to make guest appearances. Joanna Jordan, the show's British-born talent executive, chased Nick to make an appearance but he turned her down because he was too busy finishing work on his film.

He had actually been on the show before, but only after declining and then being pursued by Letterman himself. On that occasion, although Nick liked Letterman, he turned down his invitation because he found him intimidating. Letterman got so exasperated that he finally sent Nick a note with a simple five-word message: 'Stop being such a woman.' So Nick recanted and went on the show, but he kept the note in his back pocket when he appeared in case he needed to pull it out and use it as ammunition against Letterman if he was attacked. Nick said, 'I was going to whip it out and go, "What do you mean by this? Do you have something against women?" ' As it happened, he did not need his secret weapon.

San Francisco had happily adopted sometime resident Nick as a native son. So when Disney decided to hold the movie's première actually on Alcatraz Island the first Monday in June 1996, it quickly became one of the main social events of the year in the city.

Although city officials and park service officials were delighted to help, planning the party for 500 Hollywood and Bay Area celebrities was not without a few hiccups. For starters, there were the seagulls and black-crowned night-herons to think about. Disney executives wanted to show the movie in a tent on the western point of the island near the old prison laundry — a site that played a significant role in the film when the mismatched Dr Goodspeed and his armed force finally penetrate the impenetrable. But that was home to a major nesting colony for the birds. So before officials would allow Disney to host the largest gathering of rogues since Al Capone and Machine Gun Kelly resided there, the studio had to agree to move the screening to the recreation yard where the prisoners once played baseball.

Nevertheless, park officials were predisposed to accommodate Disney as the studio had forked out a small fortune to remove the hazardous materials and bankroll the rangers.

Getting a ticket to the star-studded event was like winning the lottery, even though the parks service insisted that all the guests had an educational experience and not just a party, a standard requirement for all people visiting Alcatraz. To fulfil this obligation, guests had to go on a 30-minute tour of the former maximum-security prison before seeing the movie. Life on the rock was described to them by their guide, convict-turned-author Jim Quillen, who had spent ten years on Alcatraz for kidnapping and was actually incarcerated there during the infamous 1946 riot in which two prison guards and three inmates were killed. He recalled, 'It was a bloody mess, and we all paid for it after it was over. Nobody deserved to be sent there. The place was inhuman. The rules were inhuman. The harsh conditions solved nothing.'

Security for the party was tight to make sure there were no gatecrashers — almost as tight as when it was a prison. Bob Gault, director of Walt Disney Entertainment attraction operations, who was overseeing the party arrangements, joked to Craig Marine of the *San Francisco Examiner*, 'It's going to be tougher to get into Alcatraz Monday night than it was for the prisoners to get out.'

By now, Nick was working on his next role as convict Cameron Poe in *Con Air*, so he was sporting a beard. He was escorted to the party by Patricia, decked out in a three-quarter-length, chocolate-brown satin coat with matching trousers from Dolce & Gabbana, an aqua silk blouse that reflected her aqua eye-shadow and a fringed platinum hairdo. As they mingled with guests, Patricia was asked about her outfit and cryptically said, 'I'm wearing underwear. I never go anywhere without my underwear.'

Connery and co-star Harris were also on hand to chat with guests, including San Francisco Mayor Willie Brown, up-and-coming star Jada Pinkett, who later married Will Smith, *Star Wars* mogul George Lucas, Rob Schneider, one of the stars of the cult American television show *Saturday Night Live*, and John Cusack, who was starring opposite Nick in his next movie. However, in *Con Air* it was Cusack who played the Federal agent and Nick who was the convict.

Nick, casually attired in a dark T-shirt and black trousers, also brought his cousins, Sofia and Roman Coppola, the children of his Uncle Francis, and his brother Christopher Coppola, who was not very complimentary about the movie or the party. He said, 'I thought Nicolas was excellent, and it was fun I suppose on some level. But it had no soul. There is rarely a message or a subtext in movies nowadays.' As for the star-studded party, he added, 'Not my cup of tea. I was hoping to see sharks in the water but I saw more in the audience.'

Guests were brought to the island by ferry as a bi-plane circled overhead with a banner reading: GET READY TO ROCK. Several hundred people had gathered at San Francisco's famous Pier 41 to watch Nick and the others board the ferry. Nick told the adoring fans he was looking forward to getting back to Alcatraz even though the weather had been miserable there during filming and a lot of people had complained. He said, 'So many people suffered on that little island that I'd be the last person to complain about the weather there.'

He need not have worried; the weather gods were smiling on the event that evening. June nights can be unpredictable in San Francisco but the air was balmy, the breeze was cool and the famous fog never made it under the Golden Gate. Before watching the movie, guests were given popcorn, licorice and M&M chocolates to chew on and afterwards they dined on fettucine, sesame-encrusted salmon, grilled tenderloin of beef, corn flan and asparagus tips.

San Francisco's flamboyant black mayor Brown, known for his love of stylish hats and often escorted by beautiful, well-dressed women, confessed later that, when he got the opportunity, he simply could not resist discussing the famous car-chase scene with Nick. He said, 'I hadda talk to Nick Cage about wrecking that Ferrari in this movie. What kind of bull is this? Blowing up a cable car with a Ferrari?'

Guests had been told to dress casually, but this was a Hollywood event, just moved 400 miles north. Brown, always a natty dresser, this time decked out in a nautical navy-blue blazer, yellow shirt and navy-and-yellow polka-dot tie, found himself apologising to Patricia for mispronouncing her name at a party. Patricia thought she had the last laugh when she told him that she wasn't at the party in question; it was her sister, actress Rosanna Arquette. But never one to be lost for words, Brown replied, 'I guess I'm off the hook.'

Despite Gault's boast that the real rock would be impenetrable, gatecrasher Jeff Bunch had already sipped a cocktail with Connery by the time park rangers working as security guards spotted him. The then 35-year-old daredevil windsurfer had landed his board on the north side of Alcatraz at around 4.30pm and shed his wetsuit, under which he was wearing a black tuxedo and trousers, complete with wing-collared shirt and hand-tied bow. As skilfully as any of the soldiers in action on the screen, he had made it up the side of the cliff and into the party. 'I thought I would take a look and be on my way,' admitted Bunch, who was charged with trespassing on federal land. 'Maybe they'll put windsurfers in the next movie.' Other onlookers bobbed around in a small armada of assorted crafts offshore.

It was possibly his smart attire that gave Bunch away as he talked to Connery, clad in a tan parka jacket and fisherman's sweater, with wife Michelle, dressed all in black and looking more like she was in Cannes than California.

Chatting to *Los Angeles Times* society writer Bill Higgins, Nick said, 'Alcatraz is interesting because it's a kind of perverse place. Usually, when you think of going to an island you think of escaping from the city. Here, you think of escaping into the city. To have a party on it is an odd dynamic.'

Nick and Patricia, Connery and his wife, Ed Harris and Michael Bay all departed Alcatraz on the midnight Red and White line tour ferry, but the evening was still young and they decamped to San Francisco's Tosca Café where the party continued until 5.00am.

His party mood lasted all week as Nick gave interviews to the world's press, flown into San Francisco to help promote the film. Later that week in a hotel suite on San Francisco's ritzy Nob Hill, David Eimer of *Time Out* questioned him about becoming an action hero after his performance in *Leaving Las Vegas*. Nick said, 'I think it's exactly what I want to do at exactly the right time. I'm the guy who came out of all the alternative movies, the weirdo, the freak, the guy who eats bugs, and I've got Simpson–Bruckheimer saying, "Please be in our movie." Nobody would have thought that — I wouldn't have thought that — so it's like, finally what I've been doing culminated into one moment and they're going to let me do what I want to do on my own terms. I can do a large-scale movie and still approach it in exactly the same way I did *Raising Arizona* or *Vampire's Kiss*.'

It is generally hard for most movie critics to speak kindly of action movies. But *The Rock*, which was dedicated to the late Don Simpson, opened four days after the Alcatraz bash to remarkably respectable reviews and Nick got high honours for his performance.

The hometown *San Francisco Chronicle* had nothing but praise for the film and, more importantly, its new action hero. Film critic Peter Stack wrote, '*The Rock* is a raucous, in-your-face, commando-style action thriller that makes provocative use of Alcatraz as a lunatic's lair and San Francisco as a sitting duck. Sean Connery, Nicolas Cage and Ed Harris star in this heavy-metal cinematic event — but Cage steals the show, adding a touch of wimpiness to the high-decibel bravado.'

Robert Ebert, one of America's most respected and popular critics, said, '*The Rock* is a first-rate, slam-bang action thriller with a lot of style and no little humour. And there are three skilful performances.'

Kenneth Turan, film critic for the *Los Angeles Times*, noted, 'The closing credits for *The Rock* include a dedication, 'in loving memory to Don Simpson', but this last film from the late producer and his partner Jerry Bruckheimer so perfectly encapsulates everything the pair have stood for that the actual words are superfluous.'

Daily Variety film critic Todd McCarthy said, '*The Rock* is inescapably entertaining, a high-octane, kick-butt actioner that dresses up a far-fetched premise straight out of a Steven Seagal movie with top-flight actors and an ultra-slick package. This final outing from the Simpson–Bruckheimer team has the strutting, souped-up, hardware-fetishising personality of their signature productions, and should rack up customarily muscular BO both here and abroad. Cage, in his first appearance since his Oscar win, proves equally engaging as a sort of goofy chemical-set geek who must rise to the occasion of proving he's a man among the he-men élite.'

And David Hunter in *The Hollywood Reporter* described *The Rock* as 'an above-average big-bucks action movie with enough macho behaviour and explosive thrills to please fans of the genre'. He added, '*The Rock* has the usual problems with credibility, but the ride is so fast and ferociously executed that one has fun with its excesses while admiring the solid performances from its trio of stars. Nicolas Cage and Sean Connery as the mismatched duo of good guys assigned to stop a terrorist attack by a rogue general, however, make this slick and often silly film a thoroughly entertaining rush of high-tech warfare and reverse-prison-breaking on the oft-used setting of Alcatraz Island.'

The Rock even managed to be nominated for an Oscar — in the Best Sound category! And it was nominated as Best Edited Feature Film for the American Cinema Editors awards. In addition, it won Nick and Connery some acting awards. Nick was voted Favourite Actor in an Action/Adventure movie at the 1997 Blockbuster Entertainment Awards and Connery was named Favourite Supporting Actor in an Action/Adventure movie. The two were also Best On-Screen Duo in the MTV Movie Awards. At those awards, the car crash was nominated as Best Action Sequence in a movie and the film was also nominated as Best Movie. The ShoWest Convention, USA, presented it with its Favourite Movie of the Year award.

More important than the critics, the movie-going public loved *The Rock*. It earned more than $331 million worldwide and, when it was released on video in the United States, it became the biggest pre-booked title ever, surpassing the previous record-holder, *Die Hard with a Vengeance*, with video stores ordering 830,000 copies. Subsequently, there has often been talk of pairing Nick and Connery in a sequel.

Nick could not have been happier. Sometimes he still liked to act like the class clown he was at school. To show his frivolous side, he occasionally liked to dress outrageously. Bruckheimer remembered, 'We were going to Tokyo to open *The Rock* and Nick shows up at the airport wearing a bright orange hat, an orange jumpsuit, chartreuse-green shoes, and reflecting blue sunglasses. That was the mood he was in that day.' Nick isn't sure what impression he made on the Japanese but when he recalled his outfit, he chuckled and said, 'I was feeling very Warhol-esque on that day.'

Despite his continuing success, Nick was still cautious about life. He told Canadian writer Louis B Hobson, 'Even though my life is good, I know everything is in transition. Life is full of surprises, so I can't get lazy. I know things are bound to change and that scares me a little. These days, I'm not a particularly good sleeper. Maybe I'm afraid to miss even a moment of these good times.'

If only Nick had had a crystal ball he might have rested more easily. He was firmly on his way to becoming one of the most influential and prolific actors in Hollywood and the good times would be staying a while.

CHAPTER EIGHTEEN
NO CON JOB

Nick had always been a prolific actor throughout his career, but after embarking on his self-proclaimed 'triple action album', his movies seemed to be coming out as fast as bullets from a gun. His fans were almost getting a surfeit of his films as his second and third adventure shoot-'em-ups, *Con Air* and *Face/Off*, were released just three weeks apart, although that was not the original intention. But, as fate would have it, they ended up competing for US box-office kudos in the summer of 1997.

By now Nick had made it on to *Entertainment Weekly* magazine's Most Powerful People in Hollywood list. Commenting on his rocketing salaries and status, the magazine stated, 'At these prices, he can't repeat indulgent performances of the past.' Asked how he felt about making the list and the magazine's comments, he pondered the question and looked wounded as he told *GQ* writer Lucy Kaylin, 'I understand what they're saying, which is that I'm in movies now that cost the studio $70 to $90 million, and I feel responsible that I have to sort of meet with them and make sure they're happy. But at the same time, I have to stay true to myself. I have to do the work that got me there, or I'm not doing anybody any good.' And reminiscing on his wild, early acting days when he would do anything for effect, even eat a bug, Nick went on, 'I never want to lose the ability to just go for it. But at the same time, it just seems like the stakes have gotten higher.'

As far as top producer Jerry Bruckheimer was concerned, the stakes for Nick had certainly got higher as he was prepared to cast him in two big-budget movies in a row.

The idea for *Con Air* — an action adventure film in the classic vein of such movies as *The Dirty Dozen*, *The Magnificent Seven* and *The Wild Bunch* — came from an article in the *Los Angeles Times* newspaper about the US Marshals Service, which transports around 150,000 prisoners every year between institutions around the United States. Disney studio executives brought in Bruckheimer as a possible producer. He discussed the idea with Joe Roth, then chairman of Walt Disney studios — where Bruckheimer had had a long-standing production deal with his late partner Don Simpson — and scriptwriter Scott Rosenberg, whom he knew and had previously written *Things to Do in Denver When You're Dead* and *Beautiful Girls*. Bruckheimer recalled, 'We thought it was an interesting venue for a movie, so we concocted the story about the prisoners taking over the airline.'

From that, *Con Air* was born. In the movie, Nick plays former US Army Ranger Cameron Poe, a decorated war hero unfairly jailed for manslaughter after protecting his wife from thugs. On his way home at the end of his sentence, Poe finds himself as a soon-to-be-paroled passenger on a prison service transport plane taking a bunch of the most violent convicts in America to a new maximum-security prison. During the journey, the prisoners take control of the aircraft and it is down to Poe to save the day. He is aided in his seemingly impossible endeavour by intuitive US Marshall Vince Larkin, played by John Cusack, who is monitoring the activities on the plane from the ground and guesses that the government has an ally on board.

During the journey, Poe has an opportunity to get off the plane and save himself. But despite his desire to get home to be with his wife and the little daughter he has never seen, he chooses to stay on board to save a dying buddy and a woman prison guard.

The cast of actors playing the bad guys — 'Somehow they managed to get every creep and freak in the universe on this plane,' states Poe — was any movie buff's dream come true. Topping the list was acclaimed stage and dramatic actor John Malkovich as vicious psychopath Cyrus 'the Virus' Grissom, Steve Buscemi as mad Garland 'The Marietta Mangler' Greene and Ving Rhames as deadly Nathan 'Diamond Dog' Jones. Add to that Bruckheimer's penchant and ability for on-screen spectaculars, and the explosive plot was sure to end up as movie mayhem.

'I wanted to make a movie that was really an odyssey,' Bruckheimer said. 'All Cage's character wants to do is to go home to his wife and child, and he's caught in this horrendous situation. To me, it's like classic Greek tragedy in literature, and I love that.'

While Bruckheimer was overseeing production of *The Rock*, he had begun developing *Con Air*. He said, 'I told Nick the idea, because we were having such a great experience working together. And he said, "When the script comes in, why don't you let me read it?" When the script came in and I was sort of pleased with it — it still needed more work — Nick persuaded me to show it to him. I did, and he said, "Look, I'd love to do it." And that's how it all started.'

Getting the lead in *Con Air* was all part of Nick's overall plan for his long-term career. He said, 'It was a decision that I made to move into action roles. I had been aware years ago of a certain strategy that I wanted to have. I have seen a lot of important actors get caught up in their own importance, and I've heard them say that an action movie is beneath them, and the next thing you know, they are making that kind of movie and supporting an action star because they had to keep their career going. And I didn't want that to happen. I wanted to determine that I would make these movies that are smaller, more thought-provoking, and I will be in charge of these movies that are bigger and more stimulating. I wanted to be able to do both. I didn't want to be a victim of my own pretence.'

After flexing his action muscles successfully in *The Rock*, he was happy to continue in the genre for a while, though he hoped he could add some characterisation to roles that could too easily become cartoonlike rather than realistic.

He admitted, 'At first, it was very daunting for me, because I didn't know whether I could fit into this genre. It was important for me to have some character development while, at the same time, be somewhat convincing. I try to forget about the Oscar and not dwell on that. I feel good about my choices. Some people might say I sold out. They have the right to say it. But I was just as committed to the action character in *Con Air* as I was to the complex guy in *Leaving Las Vegas*. In some ways, I feel more creatively satisfied working in the action genre than I have on almost anything else. Action films are a tremendous world stage; everyone goes to them. And generally, they're not getting good character acting — just a little dialogue before cutting to the explosions.'

Ironically, when his co-star Malkovich talked about his reasons for making the movie, he sounded more like one of those actors Nick was talking about who finds himself supporting an action star. When the film was released, Malkovich bluntly told a journalist why he did *Con Air*. 'Money,' he said. 'I have a production company and projects I would like to do. Also, I mostly lately have done these European art things that nobody sees. You have to do things people see or you don't get to do anything.'

Bruckheimer had already decided to give award-winning, British-born commercial director Simon West his first chance at helming a big-budget Hollywood film. Like *Rock* director Michael Bay, West, who had cut his teeth as a BBC film editor, was an unknown quantity as far as making the transition from commercials to movies was concerned. But just as the late Don Simpson and Bruckheimer team had trusted Bay, so now solo producer Bruckheimer was content to hand over a project budgeted at $75 million to yet another inexperienced and untested young director. West was best known in the United States at the time for introducing viewers to thirsty frogs and ants in a series of commercials promoting Budweiser beer. Bruckheimer liked directors who had established themselves making commercials because, he said, 'They can tell a story in 30 seconds. They're trained to move quickly.'

He told West, who admired Nick and wanted to work with him, that Nick was interested and the whole project just started coming together. Bruckheimer said, 'Nick had met Simon and liked him. And we were off to the races!'

As always, Nick immersed himself in his work and took it upon himself to get involved with rewriting the script and suggesting changes to the plot. It was his idea to change Poe from being a street fighter into a former Army Ranger and he gave the character his God-fearing Alabama background. Nick said, 'I had to make this man seem plausible as someone who could survive a situation that's incredibly dangerous. Also, I wanted to bring in a spiritual concept, which I hadn't seen in action movies. We needed a way for Poe to survive this group of bad guys without a gun. This way, we automatically understand his training. And the other thing is that the Rangers' motto is never to leave a fallen comrade behind. That's why he doesn't leave the plane when his best friend is down.'

Nick also wanted to play Poe wearing long hair and a beard. At first, his ideas met with resistance because it was perceived that the character's appearance and dialect — 'I didn't know how to play a man from Alabama without a southern accent,' said Nick — would turn audiences off. But he prevailed. He added, 'We had a few weeks of polite debate. At the end of the day, I gave up the beard and kept all the other stuff. I managed to stick to my guns. I'm proud of the character. I watch *Con Air* and I think, I made this guy. I got some clay together, and I built him.' Nick didn't even fully lose the battle over the beard, for Cameron Poe's chin is covered with stubble throughout the movie.

Another of his suggestions was to have one of the guards on the plane a woman so the character of Guard Sally Bishop — played by Rachel Ticotin, who had previously appeared in such films as *Don Juan DeMarco*, *Natural Born Killers* and *Total Recall* — was created.

'I wanted it to be a female because it raised the stakes of suspense on the plane,' Nick said. 'Because there were these sex-crazed, sex-starved convicts, and that would put her in jeopardy, which would put my character and his morals, his Southern morals, of putting women on a pedestal — which I admire — into the script. I had to find points in the screenplay to rewrite or play up to make it more clear that he would stay on the plane. By making him a Southern man and by making Guard Bishop a woman that's in his space, he would not leave her there to be dishonoured.'

Nick and screenwriter Rosenberg spent hours together, bouncing ideas off each other and writing until they were able to fine-tune the script to Nick's satisfaction. Nick said, 'We would get together, and Scott and I would talk it through and come up with ideas. Also, in investigating Poe's Southern aspect, I wanted to bring more of the spiritual beliefs of the character. He was a man who believed in God, and that's in a way how he survived the prison experience. I thought that would be an interesting thing to see in an action movie. My own religious beliefs aside, I had not seen that before in an American action hero, so why not try it?'

However, Nick never sought a writing credit for his work on the film. He said, 'I'm not the sort of actor that's gonna ask for writing credits. As long as I can do the acting the way I know I can do it to my fullest, then I'm happy.'

Rosenberg had actually hitched a ride on a plane used by the US Marshals Service so he could get a feel for the atmosphere on the aircraft. Prisoners are usually transported in Boeing 727s and sit in regular passenger seats, although they are handcuffed and shackled. To make it more dramatic, Rosenberg decided to change the plane to a much bigger C-123, so he could add the miniature cells where the more vicious convicts were placed in the movie.

To develop his character, Nick took inspiration from his childhood in Long Beach. He said, 'It was just a way for me to be able to realise a character that had been lurking around in the back of my mind that I wanted to see come to life. In my neighbourhood, when I was growing up, there were these guys who had the long hair and they were really ripped and they wore the tank-tops and worked on their Chevelles outside and drank beer. They looked like the kind of guys you did not want to get into a fight with. So I have a sort of affection for these characters, and I wanted to bring to life this man who may or may not exist — the pure essence of the trailer-park bad-ass who actually has a sensitive side, loves his family, and is just in the wrong place at the wrong time. I don't know if he exists, but I like to think he does. And when I see *Con Air*, I look at Cameron Poe, and I think, well, there's my new baby, I hope he has a good life. It was great inventing you, now I have to move on.'

Another reason Poe was so focused was because, said Nick, 'I was able to make my character a guy who wants to deliver a $4 stuffed pink bunny to his daughter. That's basically the driving force.'

This led to one of the funniest lines in any movie that summer, when Poe says to a ruthless killer, 'Put the bunny back in the box.' He is referring to the stuffed toy he wants to give his daughter for her birthday. Nick explained, 'I was trying to find a symbolic metaphor for the love Cameron has for his child in the middle of all this hell, and also a way to extract humour. By writing that scene, I wanted to have a straightforward, tough-guy attitude about the bunny rabbit.'

Nick felt he needed to understand what prison life was really like to prepare for his role as a convicted killer. So he managed to persuade the Californian prison authorities to allow him to visit Folsom Prison, one of the toughest jails in the state's penal system. It was an experience he found both scary and surreal.

He had only won his Oscar a few weeks before his visit. Now he went from hob-nobbing with Hollywood's most glamorous and wealthy people to rubbing shoulders with some of the most desperate and dangerous residents of California's prison system. He said, 'In order to go out into the yard, I had to sign a hostage release form.' This meant that he acknowledged that the authorities would not negotiate for his life should he be taken hostage. He went on, 'The inmates were polite, but it was intimidating all the same. Most of the guys in the yard had caught the Oscar telecast on TV. A lot of them asked for my autograph.'

Unlike a lot of stars who would be full of bravado and dismiss the whole experience as a bit of a jaunt, to his credit, Nick has never played down the seriousness of the whole episode. He admitted, 'It was very successful but very scary. I got some good ideas talking to them but your mind starts to trip out to the fact that you're talking to someone who's killed people. It's like you enter a black hole of sorts, where you don't really know where you are. It's quite terrifying.'

But in the midst of all this pleasantness and apparent normality, as he was signing autographs and chatting, the situation suddenly turned dangerous and Nick had to be rushed to safety. He said, 'There was an attempted stabbing. The yard is segregated by gangs. I'd spent too much time talking with one group. A rival gang got jealous and sent a guy in with a knife to break up my visit.'

Nick was so freaked, he claims to have gone home and 'stayed in the bath for about two days ... to relax'.

Despite his wild ways as a young actor, Nick has, in fact, never spent as much as a night in jail. He said, 'My record is really clean, off as that may seem. There are a few pranks I wish I hadn't committed, but fortunately none of them landed me behind bars.'

Nick was accompanied on his prison visit by West and Bruckheimer. In the end, they decided not to film at Folsom and instead shot the movie's prison scenes in an unused jail in downtown Los Angeles.

'He talked to the guys there,' Bruckheimer recalled. 'He picked up on the accents, the hair. Then he said to me, "I'm going to be a cross between Elvis and Gregg Allman."'

Playing a role like Elvis was hardly a new experience for Nick, who had invoked The King in *Wild at Heart* and *Honeymoon in Vegas*, but now he planned to add elements of Gregg Allman, the long-haired member of the Southern rock band the Allman Brothers who was briefly married to pop diva Cher, Nick's Oscar-winning co-star from *Moonstruck*.

West was astonished by Nick's enthusiasm. He revealed, 'Nick would come to the set every morning with new lines for the scenes we were shooting. He gets so involved with the characters he's playing that he begins to think like them. He was very good at coming up with one-liners. It wasn't a question of turning them down; it was a question of working them in.'

The director had very definite opinions as to how he saw Nick's character. Luckily, Nick wanted to develop Poe along the same lines. West said, 'I saw him as such a hero, such an honourable man — he's Gary Cooper in *High Noon*. He's so much better than the rest of us. I saw this movie as a modern-day western, and Nick Cage is John Wayne.'

To play a man who had spent eight years in prison, Nick once again altered his physical appearance, putting himself on a strict eating and exercise regime which he nicknamed the 'Con Air diet'. He eliminated butter and oil, switched to skimmed milk and increased his usual work-outs, lifting weights, doing a lot of aerobic conditioning and running six miles a day. He kept up his exercise routine whenever he was not on camera. Instead of sitting around the set relaxing between takes, he would run on a treadmill installed in his trailer. He said, 'I cut out all fat from my diet. I practically lived on canned tuna and fat-free pretzels. The body type I wanted was modelled on Ken Norton, the boxer. I wanted to look really ripped but not bulky. In my own life, I prefer to run and stay lean.' Dedicated as always, he added, 'It had nothing to do with vanity. I had to convince people that my character could have survived in a prison.'

At one point, Disney executives were worried that Nick was getting too big and looking too scary. Nick said, 'I thought, well, that's a new one — too many muscles for an action movie.' They wanted him to make Cameron Poe more like his nerdy Stanley Goodspeed character from *The Rock*. He told them, 'No way. This is what I do; this is what you hired me for, my instincts.'

Defending his highly muscular physique, he told *Drama-Logue*'s Elias Stimac, 'I think there's an appropriate time to show it, and an inappropriate time. I think Cameron Poe is somebody who would be at a level of physical fitness, because he has to survive, he has been in jail and it's the survival of the fittest. So I think he's the type of guy who works out to stay focused mentally and physically. In my own life, I don't work out that hard, I don't want to be that big. It's more for me — I like to stay balanced by working out. I use working out as a means to calm myself. Endorphins are real chemicals that exist in your body that you can access just by working out — you don't have to be on Valium. If you work out, you can cool yourself out. And that, more than anything, is my reason for exercise. But I had to work out to get in shape for this role. That was an intense regimen.'

In preparation for his role, he also watched a lot of other action movies. He said, 'I watched a lot of Harrison Ford and Clint Eastwood movies, because they seem to have found that perfect balance.' From Ford he learned 'you can create a character, like in *The Fugitive*, who's overwhelmed with emotion, or you can play a character who's a little insecure in a giant action situation and then rise to the occasion. People laugh at me and say I didn't work as hard on *Con Air* as I did on *Leaving Las Vegas*. The truth is they're just very different. I had to find ways to be convincing in an action film. Action only gives you a certain amount of time to convey a point as an actor, so it teaches you to be succinct. That was a learning experience — finding exactly what's required for the character in each moment. The other thing I like about action is that it's pure cinema, an experience you can only get from the movies.'

Nick has always tried to approach his roles from both a physical and psychological point of view and that was certainly what he was doing on this occasion. In getting into Poe's mind-set, he certainly both amused and amazed the cast and crew with his on-set antics. West remembered, 'Before certain scenes, he would howl like a banshee and leap on to a wall. We thought he was rehearsing for *Spiderman* or something.' Nick explained that he was just 'blowing off steam'. He said, 'In order to prepare, I internalise so much that I need to release the emotional build-up that entails.'

But not all his antics were quite so off-the-wall; he also showed his gentle, romantic, almost ladies'-man side. West recalled, 'Nick's very, very charming. One day, one of the girls on the camera crew sneezed and he said, in character, in his Southern drawl, "A man could fall in love with you just for the way you sneeze." She just melted, and all the women on the set went weak at the knees.'

Just as Nick and West had their definitive ideas on what Poe should be like, so the producer had his defined line on what he expected from the characters in his movie. Bruckheimer said, 'I like to make villains very smart. It enhances your heroes.' So he saw Malkovich's Cyrus character as 'a complete product of the prison system'.

Nick was delighted to be working with such an acclaimed actor but he saw the irony that they were co-starring in a movie where the special effects were equally important as their acting abilities and that the audience that *Con Air* would attract would not be going to see the film because they were both regarded by the critics and their peers as fine actors. He recalled, 'I had to laugh at one moment because here's one of the most revered actors of stage and film for the last 20 years and I finally get to work with him, and what are we doing but standing on top of a fire truck, and he's coming at me with an axe and I'm hitting him with a pole. I thought, I guess we're not doing Steinbeck or Eugene O'Neill. We're going to be kids again, aren't we?'

The irony that the final scenes of *Con Air* took Nick back to Las Vegas for the third time in a movie did not escape writer Rosenberg. He said, 'It wasn't intentional. I wrote that in before Nick came along.' But he did want to cash in on the coincidence. He had the idea that the trailers for the movie that were to be aired in cinemas months before the film was released should proclaim: 'The first time you saw him, he was honeymooning in Vegas. The next time he was leaving Las Vegas. Well, he's back!' The screenwriter laughed, 'I thought it would have been great.'

He may have been back in Las Vegas, but Nick had learned his lesson making *Honeymoon in Vegas*. There was no way he was going to lose money at the tables again — even if he had won it all back the last time. Nor did he think he was gambling on his reputation by moving into the action movie genre. He said frankly, 'I'm a bit of a hot property right now. That's not going to last, so I'm going to capitalise on my popularity. There will be lots of time and opportunity in the future to go back to doing small, low-budget independent films.'

The film-makers had had an unexpected bit of luck which enabled them to make the last few minutes of the movie even more spectacular than the original screenplay had intended. As the plane loaded with convicts crashes into Nevada's gambling capital, the fuselage ploughs through the main foyer of the world-famous Sands Hotel and Casino demolishing the entertainment complex's main tower.

The scene was not in the original script but was quickly written in when the producers discovered that the casino was to be torn down to make way for the construction of the new $2 billion Venetian Hotel — an Italian-themed resort complete with its own replica of the Venice canals and Roman piazzas. In the final planning stages as the movie was going into production, it would be the world's largest gaming complex, with 6,000 hotel rooms and a 200,000sq ft casino.

Bruckheimer and his team realised it was an opportunity too good to be missed. They could develop the ending into a mind-boggling, unforgettable, phenomenal film finale.

As if Las Vegas was not already Neon Nirvana, the makers of Con Air did all they could to give the city in the sand an extra boost of brightness by adding a further 10,000 light bulbs to the foyer of the legendary casino, which was once the playground of Rat Pack members Frank Sinatra, Dean Martin, Sammy Davis Jr, Peter Lawford and Joey Bishop.

Carol Cling of the Las Vegas Review-Journal was on the set on one of the nights the stunt was being filmed. It was an unusually cold October evening, cold as only nights in the desert can get. She recalled, 'Cast and crew huddled against the suddenly unseasonable October chill, setting up a shot adjacent to the shattered fuselage of the make-believe plane. Most of them wore parkas or jackets to ward off the chill. But Cage braved the cold in ragged jeans and a tattered undershirt, one bearing fake dirt smudges and bloodstains that made him look as though he'd just been through a harrowing, and highly perilous attempt to thwart the Con Air hijacking. Between takes, an assistant draped a parka over the actor, who gingerly slid his arms into the sleeves, being careful not to dislodge a bandage on one bulging bicep, or the fake blood smeared on it. Almost as soon as Cage shrugged into the jacket, however, it was time for his next take. So he slipped out of the parka and returned to his take.'

The scene was supposed to take place in the sweltering heat of summer so crew members hovered around Nick, spraying his face and body with water to simulate sweat.

Before Bruckheimer and West learned about the demise of the Sands, they had considered the movie ending with the plane crashing into a variety of locations including the capital of the United States, Washington, DC, but ended up with the lucky fluke of the gambling capital of the world. Bruckheimer said, 'Initially, it was going to crash into the White House, but I just didn't believe it — it made it too absurd.'

But Las Vegas made sense, not just because the south-western location worked as far as the hijacked plane's fictional flight path was concerned, but also as far as Bruckheimer was concerned. He said, 'It's a worldwide icon. It attracts a lot of interest — and it's exciting.'

Always the practical producer and businessman with his eye firmly focused on the bottom line as far as the dollars he was spending were concerned, he admitted, 'The Sands became the perfect thing to crash the plane into. Otherwise, we would have had to build something else to destroy.'

In true Bruckheimer style, the movie is packed with amazing special effects. Before the C-123 attempts to land on the world-renowned Las Vegas Strip, it is seen crashing through the signature guitar-shaped neon sign of the Hard Rock Hotel. To create this astonishing stunt, an 18-ft replica of the sign was built and used for the crash. The special effect became the most extensive and expensive use of miniature neon in a film ever, with the lights made as thin as spaghetti.

Not surprisingly, not all stunts go as planned. That was certainly the case when they were filming the dramatic last few minutes of *Con Air* and the movie almost came to a rather more abrupt ending than expected. The crew built a fake front on to the hotel and filled the abandoned casino with working slot machines, loads of additional neon lights and hordes of extras posing as gamblers. A rail track was laid out of shot beneath the 15 cameras to be used to capture this footage, which was a one-time-only opportunity. A real C-123 cargo plane was supposed to be towed by cable along the track, through the façade of the foyer and across the casino floor at around 50 miles per hour.

West said, 'It had taken so long to set it all up through the night. The cable ran all the way through the casino on all of these pulleys, then was tied to a huge truck parked out back. I think the driver had fallen asleep in the cab because it had taken so long to rig it. The sun was coming up, the sky was turning blue and I was screaming, "Let's go, let's go!" They called the driver on his radio, I think they woke him up, and, startled, he put his foot on the accelerator and gunned it. The cable snapped because he went away so fast.'

As a result, 15 tons of aeroplane crashed through the casino at an entirely undramatic, yet still unstoppable, 2mph. Worse still, the plane was slowly heading towards a 10ft drop that had been built at the end of the rail tracks.

West confessed, 'This was "The Plane" and if it went over the edge at this totally unusable speed, it was destroyed. Everyone was holding their breath as it reached the edge, there was this awful creaking sound and it stopped. So the sun came up, we went home and, luckily, the next night the cable worked.'

Unfortunately, not all the things that went wrong during filming had such a happy ending. Earlier in the shoot the production was on location at Wendover, in the desert on the border between Utah and Nevada, where the plane was supposed to have landed to drop off an escaping South American drug baron. Tragically, a member of the special effects team, Phil Swartz, was killed when a rigged plane accidentally fell, crushing him underneath. Luckily, none of the leading actors was on the set at the time of the accident.

A lot of *Con Air* was a physically hard shoot for the cast and crew. In all, they spent around six weeks in Wendover, which had previously been used as one of the major locations for filming the science fiction blockbuster *Independence Day* for the scenes where Will Smith's character pulled an alien across the desert. Bruckheimer said, 'It was the middle of summer, so it was well over 100°F every day. Sometimes it got up to 120°F. Even though it was dry, it was very difficult to work. And you have these very long days because the sun doesn't go down until about nine. That's why you shoot later in the day. We had to start early because it was so hot. It was very tough on the crew and the actors.'

West admitted, 'We were working 16-hour days. And, stupidly, I decided to shoot in the desert in the summer. Then we ended up in Las Vegas in November during a freak cold snap and we were doing night shooting in 10-below weather, with Nick having to run around in a little T-shirt in the rain. Every day there was a different disaster, and I'd go around saying, "How are we ever going to finish this thing?"'

In addition, the actors were physically hard on themselves and each other. There was a lot of macho tension between them during down time because they were all playing hard convict characters. Actress Rachel Ticotin witnessed it first hand. She said, 'There were a lot of push-ups, pull-ups, a lot of physical competitions. At one point, we were sitting around and it got into this serious discussion of who would be the last man standing if they all got into a brawl.'

West had to use all his management skills to keep his cast in line. Luckily he had a daughter, who was three years old at the time, so he applied the same discipline techniques to the actors as he did to her. He joked, 'You have to be quite strict when you have 20 of them on the set together because all they want to do is have fun. That's why they're actors, they didn't want to get a proper job. Other times, it was just a matter of creating the proper environment so they could do their best work.'

While making Con Air, Nick met ruggedly handsome young actor Pete Antico, who sadly suffered from Tourette's Syndrome, a mysterious neurological disorder that causes physical convulsions and inappropriate, often vulgar, vocal explosions. Astonishingly, Antico, who had a part in the film, was able to control his symptoms when he acted.

Nick was fascinated by the condition and Antico's brave battle, which had allowed him to get several other movie roles. For a while, he considered developing a film based on Antico's life story. He and his old buddy Jeff Levine had set up Saturn Productions and Jeff was actively searching for projects that would be 'movies with morality and characters with a conscience'.

Nick said, 'I'd like to see less cynicism in the movies, more passion and chivalry and a sense of what it means to be honourable. Movies like High Noon were once acceptable — that sort of code of honour that makes a man stop his wedding day and do the right thing.' His idea was for Saturn to develop a film that would focus on self-control and focus.

Antico told him his philosophy was 'A man is truly the master of his own universe.' Before breaking into acting, Antico had been a fight trainer and stuntman and had doubled for such stars as Sylvester Stallone, Don Johnson and Robert De Niro. Antico was also the founder of a charity fighting racial, ethnic and social prejudice called We Care About Kids.

However, the project never got off the ground. It was one of so many that fell by the wayside in Nick's unbelievably busy schedule.

Antico wasn't the only interesting character who had overcome the odds to act in Con Air. Danny Trejo, who played serial rapist Johnny 'Johnny 23' Baca, was a veteran of several movies — Anaconda and From Dusk Till Dawn — and TV shows, as well as many of California's toughest prisons. In his early life, Trejo had been jailed for armed robbery and drug offences. An admitted addict, he finally overcame his problems and turned his life around. However, after surviving many years in prison, he had more sense than to get involved in any of the physical competitions that sometimes develop between actors.

He said, 'I've watched so many of those kind of things turn bad and, being in prison, the last thing you want to do is compete with somebody because he might be a sore loser.' He added, 'Simon was able to, like, put the fantasy and the reality together, and that's what makes a good movie. But this is a make-believe kind of thing. I mean, they're all killers, and you're not going to disrespect another killer like these characters do. The reality is, in prison, you find the politest people in the world. If I know you're a killer, I'm going to say, "Excuse me," a lot.'

Throughout the making of Con Air, Nick and Patricia were once again dogged by rumours that their marriage was in trouble. Gossip was flying around the Internet that they were having big problems. Patricia confessed to journalist

Louis B Hobson, 'When Nick and I attended the Golden Globes in January, I snuck out for a cigarette. A couple of friends followed me out, essentially to commiserate. I assured them everything was fine, but I could see they weren't buying it. A couple of weeks later, someone confided they'd read the rumours on the Internet. We've just bought a new home that's much too big for a bachelor pad.'

Patricia quickly got on-line and surfed the net to read the stories about their marital discord for herself. She told Hobson of their formula for keeping the marriage on track. She said, 'We sleep together every night we can. The only exception is when one of us is on location and even then the other person tries to be there whenever possible.'

Nick took a break from filming *Con Air* to fly up to Canada from Los Angeles to attend the 1996 Montreal World Film Festival, where, at 32, he became the youngest actor ever to receive the gala's Lifetime Achievement Award. Previous recipients had included Anthony Hopkins, Michael Caine and Max von Sydow. He laughed, 'Yeah, well, it feels like a lifetime. I think I've prematurely aged since I started acting.'

Putting another dampener on the rumours, he was accompanied by Patricia. He received a tumultuous ovation as he took the podium to receive his accolade. In accepting his award, Nick told the audience that receiving the honour softened the memory of days when he thought he would never work again. He said, 'I hope it encourages young actors to not be discouraged by bad reviews and unemployment, no matter how wild their artistic dreams may be.'

Journalist Judy Stone noted, 'His sense of humour and modest demeanour added a likeable human dimension to the often shaggy characters he has played in his films.' Nick talked to her about making *Con Air* and said it was his third prison role. He asked her jokingly, 'Is it because of my name?'

Once production was well under way, first-time director West began to feel that he may have a commercial hit on his hands. He admitted, 'About half-way through, it started to feel as if we had something. Also, because we were cutting at the same time, by the last day of principal photography we had the entire film cut — a two-and-a-half-hour cut. When you do that, you can pretty much see the film as it's going to be. It ended up two hours, actually just under. So it started to feel good.' The final cut was 115 minutes, and audiences tend to like films that are under two hours. West said, 'I think that under two hours' running time really does help the action movie because of the level of visceral bombardment you're being given. The body can only take it for so long!'

Originally, *Con Air* was supposed to be released in March 1997 but executives at Disney's Touchstone Pictures decided to push it back for a 6 June release. They made the decision to release the movie then because it was precisely a year after the opening of *The Rock*. Dick Cook, Walt Disney motion picture group's Chairman, said, 'It worked very well for us before.'

But there was more to it than superstition. Bruckheimer had shown a few of the studio executives some early footage and they suddenly realised it might not be just a success but a huge hit. They perceived it as being different and unique which generally generates a lot of box-office interest in America, especially during the high-profit summer months.

When the film opened, the reviews were mixed, although generally favourable towards Nick. It is rarely fashionable or chic for critics to rave about action-adventure pictures, and likewise, comedies customarily fare badly when it comes to awards like the Oscars. The critics like to distance themselves from the general public and be seen to enjoy something more 'deep and meaningful'.

Todd McCarthy of the *Daily Variety* wrote, 'Unlikely action star Cage, very buff, walks the fine line between self-preservation and selfless heroics with great aplomb, keeping the audience with him at all times.' While Duane Byrge of *The Hollywood Reporter* said, 'As the parolee who risks his life to thwart the cons, Cage exudes bravery of the decent Everyman who rises to the occasion. With his flowing locks, scraggy beard and beatific gaze, Cage exudes a Jesus-on-the-cross sacrificial persona, albeit a Christ who pumped iron.'

Abbie Bernstein wrote in *Drama-Logue*, 'Nicolas Cage makes Cameron suitably tough, ornery and noble in about equal portions; we like the guy and believe he can take care of himself in his dangerous environment.' Of the movie itself, he said, '*Con Air* is a quintessential popcorn, relatively entertaining despite plot improbabilities that a 747 could fly through.'

Los Angeles Daily News film writer Bob Strauss commented in one article, '*Con Air* is distinguished from the pack of cinematic thrill rides by the unusual high calibre of its cast.' But in another — even though he gave the movie a rating of three stars — he dug the knife in, saying, 'Lots of really smart actors do lots of dumb action-movie posturing in *Con Air*. To say there's not a believable moment in *Con Air* is to overstate the obvious. To acknowledge that things reach entire new thresholds of absurd overkill in the last 20 minutes is, actually, something of a tribute to the talented actors who keep this wacko thing flying for as long as they do.'

Meanwhile, some reviewers were baffled by Nick's decision to become an action hero. Mick LaSalle, movie critic for the *San Francisco Chronicle*, wrote, 'Whether *Con Air* will determine if Cage can make it as an action star isn't the question here. The real question is: why on earth should Cage want to be Sylvester Stallone?' And *Newsweek* magazine's David Ansen asked, 'If you can't take *Con Air* as a big, noisy joke, why would you want to take it at all?'

But as far as Bruckheimer and the studio were concerned, the critics that matter are the moviegoers, the people who buy cinema tickets, and they gave it two thumbs up. In the first weekend alone it made $24.1 million in the USA, meaning it was definitely a high-flying hit. *Con Air* earned more than $100 million from American box-office revenues during its run, making it a bona fide blockbuster.

It even managed to garner some award honours, although not for Nick. It was nominated for Best Sound at the 1998 Academy Awards and also for Best Song for 'How Do I Live?' In fact, there was a controversy over the song because red-hot LeAnn Rimes recorded a version of it but the film-makers finally decided that, at 14 years old, she was too young to sing such a love song so it was recorded again by Trisha Yearwood, who appears on the movie's soundtrack. The song won its category at the ASCAP Film and Television Music Awards, was nominated for a Grammy but also got a Razzie nomination, the tongue-in-cheek, alternative Oscars given out for the worst movies of the year. But John Cusack won a Blockbuster Entertainment Award for Favourite Supporting Actor in an action-adventure movie and Rachel Ticotin was nominated for the female counterpart.

And like *The Rock*, an unforgettable party was laid on for revellers attending the première. Close to 600 guests were flown in on two chartered aircraft to Las

Vegas' McCarran Airport, where they were met on the tarmac by dozens of baton-wielding guards and waiting prison buses. Helicopters circled overhead, as motorcycle cops escorted the cavalcade to the nearby Hard Rock Hotel and Casino. The red carpet was laid out for the guests, and the casino was filled with metal detectors and barbed wire to make it feel a bit like a federal penitentiary. They watched the movie seated on aeroplane seats and were given packets of *Con Air* peanuts to snack on. The foyer was done out like a jail cell.

Nick, casually dressed in a leather jacket and white T-shirt and by now clean-shaven with a neat, short haircut once again, was all smiles with Patricia clinging to his arm. A star-studded guest list included most of the movie's stars, except John Malkovich who was in France and John Cusack who was on location filming *Midnight in the Garden of Good and Evil* for director Clint Eastwood. Other guests included Jon Lovitz, Pauly Shore, Joely Fisher and Penn Jillette, of the comedy duo Penn and Teller.

A huge, purple-ceilinged tent was erected in the hotel car park for the party after the première. Done out like a Las Vegas casino lounge, it was filled with chandeliers, vintage neon and seafood buffets. The centrepiece of the decoration was a one-fifth-size scale model of the film's C-120 aeroplane crashing into the Hard Rock's signature guitar sign.

One thing that Nick was quickly coming to realise about the new genre he was mastering was the amount of time it takes to make an action movie. He discovered it meant he no longer had the time to make small movies like *Leaving Las Vegas*. He said, 'What I did not know was that the average action movie takes about six months to shoot, so that's something I've learned. These action movies take longer than I thought they would. So I haven't really been able to find the time right now to do the smaller movies, but I am going to.'

It was not the time it took to make an action movie that producer Bruckheimer was concerned about. There was an uncertainty about Nick's appeal as an action star that he could not predict. He said, 'We don't know if he can open a picture by himself in foreign markets because *The Rock* had Sean Connery. So this will tell the story.'

Asked Nick, 'Do I feel the pressure? Sure, because you know people spent a lot of money on Con Air. There's a sense that I need to really make this movie perform well. But at the end of the day I'm an actor, and what I'm mostly responsible for is whether or not my acting comes through.'

He was certainly aware of the new pressures he was under, and with the different kind of success he was achieving came a new Nick. He was not only reinventing his career, but also himself.

When Ruthe Stein interviewed him for the *San Francisco Chronicle* to promote *Con Air*, she found him much more serious than in the past. He refused to take off his jacket for a photograph, a refusal which offended the *Chronicle*'s Entertainment Editor Liz Lufkin, who felt he was not in a sunny mood that summer. She said, 'Only last year, Cage was posing for photographs with his shirt unbuttoned, showing off lots of body hair. Now he is insisting on wearing grown-up clothes when he meets the press, such as the expensive dark sports coat, worn with a fashionable lavender shirt, in our pictures.' Half-heartedly defending her interviewee, Stein explained, 'His whole new pitch is that he's matured — he's a father and a star, no longer a rebel. The feeling was, this is all part of the new image, the new Nicolas Cage, the buttoned-down, mature Nicolas Cage.' Stein's conclusion was that he had been more fun before. She said, 'He seems very serious. Then again, he has a lot to be serious about. He's got this $70 million movie resting on his shoulders.'

Nick need not have worried about carrying an action movie by himself. *The Rock*, which also starred Sean Connery, had finally grossed $330 million worldwide. *Con Air*, which was being carried by Nick alone, went on to make more than $223 million worldwide, making it the 125th biggest-grossing movie of the 20th century — and that was before video sales. Without doubt, it was a more than respectable showing for the young actor, who was still only 33 years old, while the action actors he was competing against were heading towards old age: Arnold Schwarzenegger was turning 50 that summer; Sylvester Stallone was 51 and Harrison Ford was 55!

Stallone had the grace to admit, 'Nick brings a more character-driven sense to the action hero, a little darker, more complicated and conversational.'

CHAPTER NINETEEN
TRIPLE ACTION ALBUM PLAYS ON

Nick gazed in disbelief at the full-length mirrors in front of him. A bemused grin flashed briefly across his features before contorting into anguish. He leapt to his feet, grabbed a hat-stand and smashed the mirrors to smithereens, before turning on his astonished friends and screaming obscenities at them. They leapt back, stunned and appalled. But John Woo, the Chinese film director who had achieved world-wide cult status for the way he could portray the most brutal screen violence through deft, almost balletic, choreography, was delighted.

'I was so surprised,' said Woo. 'It was great. And I felt great about it.'

The scene was the first take of a pivotal scene in the third of Nick's action trilogy, *Face/Off*, when, for the first time, his character of Sean Archer appreciates the extent of his actions in the interests of justice. Thanks to the miracle of medical science, his face has been transformed into his arch-enemy, a terrorist who is threatening Los Angeles with a bomb, and who had also killed Archer's son six years earlier. He has literally had his face removed and replaced, so he is gazing at his own reflection and seeing the image of the man who almost destroyed his life.

Woo recalled, 'In the rehearsal, Nick looked in the mirror and got up and laughed and got mad and grabbed the stand and smashed the mirror; that was it, and it was great. But when we were shooting, he got up and laughed and got mad and smashed the mirror and suddenly he turned, yelling and screaming at his friends, "Fuck you, fuck you, fuck you!" That part came from his instincts at that moment, and he went off camera yelling at the people and changing his lines. Of course, then I had to say, "Nick, sorry about that, but none of the cameras caught it. How about we do it again?" That kind of happening really excites me.'

That spontaneous understanding of how his character would act marked Nick's growing ease as an action star. His own knowledge that he had mastered the genre, however, made him start thinking about his next move.

Nick had suddenly emerged as the leading figure of the younger, artistically accomplished new action-adventure movie heroes. Bob Strauss, film writer for the *Los Angeles Daily News*, called him, 'One of the most inventive and daring actors of his generation. There isn't a more daring, honest actor working today, nor one more respected, witty and entertaining away from the camera.'

Nonetheless, Nick himself was anxious to shrug off his mantle as the 'thinking man's action hero'. At the première of *Face/Off*, he admitted, 'I don't know about labels and compartmentalising. I've tried hard to continue growing and trying different things. I think I'm still the same actor I was when I made a comedy or a drama as an action picture. They all require the same amount of detail and attention.' Strauss countered, 'We know how much pain and torment mean to Cage.'

There was a lot of history to *Face/Off* before Nick, with Patricia at his side, arrived for the première at the world-famous Mann's Chinese Theater on Hollywood Boulevard on a balmy June evening in 1997. The script had been knocking around Hollywood since 1991 and had gone through several incarnations over the years with different production teams and studios before finally getting under way with Chinese-born director John Woo, the most celebrated of the great Hong Kong film-makers — once dubbed the 'Mozart of mayhem' — at the helm. Established action superstars Arnold Schwarzenegger and Sylvester Stallone had even been considered as the most likely leading men in the early days of the screenplay's history.

Woo, who had established himself making action movies in the former British colony before hitting the big time in Tinseltown, was picked as the ideal director after writers Mike Werb and Michael Colleary caught a late-night showing of his classic action movie *The Killer*. But, initially, Woo had turned the project down. It landed on his desk after he had just arrived in Los Angeles to make a name for himself as a director of mainstream movies. He rejected it then because he did not want to open his account in Hollywood by making what was perceived at the time as a science-fiction film. Woo said, 'I never liked to make science fiction because no matter how great those films are, they still seem fake to me.'

Initially, *Face/Off* had been set 200 years in the future, which meant including many computer-generated special effects which Woo didn't like, but after several rewrites, and some input from the director, it became a modern-day thriller, while retaining a sci-fi premise. Woo said, 'I always want my work to be driven by the characters and not the action. When this script was first brought to me, it was set well into the future and was really a science-fiction piece.'

The plot kept some of the original elements but, as it developed, it became much more the story of two diametrically opposed characters — one good, one evil — who literally walk a mile in each other's shoes. Through the various stages of development, it grew into much more of a story about two competing men and their interaction, rather than just another action movie.

The script finally appealed to Woo once it had been developed significantly beyond its original inception. It was good versus evil but the lines between the two were blurred, which was another twist that appealed to Woo.

He said, 'In my mind, everyone is equal. The bad guy sometimes has a good quality; the good guy sometimes has a weakness. My theory is there are no really good guys or bad guys in this world, so good and bad is always like a mirror. I always believe that all the very good guys have some kind of warts, so that's reflected in the characters.'

Woo had just completed directing another action thriller, *Broken Arrow*, with John Travolta and Christian Slater, when he finally committed to the *Face/Off* project, which was to become his third US movie. He said, 'After I finished directing *Broken Arrow*, it came around to me again and the script was now set in the present time which meant it was somehow more real and could be more emotional.'

Terence Chang, Woo's business partner, explained that his colleague had changed his mind because in its current form 'it meant we needed two really good actors, because they both had to play both parts'.

Never was a truer word spoken about this complicated tale of face-swapping. As the plot unfolded, the actor playing good-guy cop Sean Archer suddenly became evil Castor Troy and vice versa. So the body of the good guy became bad and the evil terrorist became Mr Nice Guy and, as a result, the two actors not only had to play both parts but also had to be able to adopt each other's mannerisms.

Woo had had such a good experience working with Travolta, and the two had become such good friends, that he decided he would like to work with him again in one of the leading roles for *Face/Off*. Woo said, 'John and I are both a bit old-fashioned. We both long for days gone by of honour and loyalty, a world where people really care about each other. I look for actors with heart, and when you carry this humanity on to the movie set, it makes for the best working environment.'

Travolta admitted, 'With someone as gifted as John Woo, someone who understands your heart, it's difficult not to want to work with him.' Unfortunately he was already committed to making the ironically titled movie, *The Double*, which meant filming could not get under way until the late summer or early autumn of 1996 — and even then the right deal had to be struck.

Another problem was finding the right 'double' for Travolta, as the two main characters swap faces on to what were supposed to be similar bodies. When the quest for a talented actor with a similar physique failed, Woo felt the only route to take was to find an outstanding actor who could match Travolta's performance skills. Nick then became a front-runner for both Woo and for former *Saturday Night Fever* and *Grease* star Travolta.

Woo recalled, 'After we got John, we tried to figure out who we could get to match John — the body and the face, but, more important, an equal actor so they could play against each other. John suggested Nick Cage. And I had also dreamed for a long time of working with Nick Cage; on *Tears of the Sun*, a project that fell apart after nearly a year's work, I suggested using Nick. John and Nick admire each other so much; they had both wanted to work together in a film for a long time. After we met, we all felt this cast was going to be unbelievable.'

The director felt Nick was right for the film because he thought he was witnessing changes in what movie audiences expected from their movie heros. He explained, 'Some American audiences like a traditional hero, who never cries, never dies, but I thought that kind of hero was getting less popular, and they were starting to want someone more real. Audiences were responding to Nicolas Cage as the new hero, because he was so human, and so elegant as well, and was just like a real person. Nick Cage is an amazing actor.'

As luck would have it, both Nick and Travolta were presenters at the Hollywood Foreign Press Association's Golden Globes awards ceremony that January in 1996. From the early stages, the production team had been convinced that a Nick/Travolta teaming would work for the film. However, their opinion was confirmed when they saw the two actors together on television. Steven Reuther, who, along with actor-turned-movie-mogul Michael Douglas, was one of the executive producers, said, 'We got to see them standing right next to each other and said, "Yeah, this is perfect. This is gonna work." It became a long process of making the deal with these guys. Both of them said they would do it — if the other guy does it. Deal-making is about details. So it took a long time to advance the deal so that everybody had the security they needed to know that if the picture got made, it would get made with both these guys.'

Whenever there is a movie with two enormous film stars it is only natural that egos have to be massaged. In the case of *Face/Off*, the sticking point ended up being over the movie credits, often a bone of contention in the entertainment business. Both Nick and Travolta wanted top billing. Travolta pointed out that he was an Academy Award nominee but, by the time this problem developed, Nick had won his Best Actor Oscar for *Leaving Las Vegas* and was quickly able to point this out. Finally, Travolta's advisers added up his huge box-office takings, which far outstripped Nick's, and his name did indeed come first — although Nick's was also above the title.

Where an actor's name is placed in the credits is a big deal in the movie industry. Years before *Face/Off*, in 1992, Nick had agreed to take a pay cut to star with John Cusack and Daryl Hannah in the movie *Pure Heart*, which was to be filmed in Bombay, India. Nick and Cusack were to play two feuding brothers fighting for the love of the same woman. But Nick pulled out just two weeks before the filming was due to start when his representatives at the giant ICM agency were given a deal memo stating that their client's name was to come after Cusack's in the credits. The idea that Nick would be playing second banana to Cusack was abhorrent to the movers and shakers at ICM and, as a result, the deal was no deal. That meant the end of an $8 million movie that was never made.

But that was not the case with *Face/Off*. Less than three weeks after *Pulp Fiction* star Travolta was confirmed as joining the cast as FBI agent Archer, Nick came on board in the other lead as Castor Troy — although for much of the movie they (sort of!) played each other's character. As cinema audiences eventually discovered, the film was as much *About/Face* as *Face/Off*. When the cameras started rolling, Travolta played Archer for only about the first 20 minutes until he infiltrated the terrorist operations of his loathsome adversary. Once Troy's face had been removed by lasers and grafted on to Archer's skull, it was Nick's turn to be 'Archer' for most of the rest of the film. And once Troy had, amazingly, recovered from a coma, appropriated 'Archer's preserved face and taken over his identity, job and even moved in with his family, it was Travolta's turn to be the bad guy.

At the time the movie contract deal was going through, Nick was wrapping up work on *The Rock*. The plan had been that once *The Rock* was out of the way, he would then start work on *Face/Off* before rejoining Jerry Bruckheimer to film *Con Air*. But in the end it was another kind of swap, this time of the filming schedules and *Con Air* ended up going before the cameras first.

Executives at Paramount Studios, which was releasing *Face/Off*, were overjoyed to have signed up Nick, as it meant they had secured deals with both *Leaving Las Vegas* actor Oscar nominees. A week earlier, Elisabeth Shue had signed to star opposite Val Kilmer in their big-screen version of *The Saint*.

And Nick was delighted to be working with Travolta. He regarded it as fate that they were in the same movie. While filming *Moonstruck*, his co-star Julie Bovasso, who had previously played Travolta's mother in the disco-hit *Saturday Night Fever*, had told Nick, 'You're the dark side of John,' which he took as a sign that they were destined to work together some day.

Said Woo, 'If you put serious actors in an action movie, they'll make the movie totally different. It's more convincing and touching and intelligent than what we're used to in these things.'

As often happens with movies, things did not go as planned. Travolta, who was to be paid $17 million for starring in *The Double*, ended up storming out of rehearsals in Paris in early June that year after a row with the movie's controversial director, Roman Polanski, and the whole thing ended up in a messy legal battle that dragged on for more than a year before an out-of-court settlement was finally reached just as the case was due to go to trial.

Filming of *Face/Off*, which cost $90 million to make, was postponed, finally got under way at the end of 1996, after Nick had completed shooting *Con Air*, and continued into early spring 1997. There was a slight cross-over in the film schedules and, as a result, Nick could not start his *Face/Off* scenes until three weeks after Travolta had begun filming. However, the two actors had been exchanging ideas about their characters for months.

Travolta, a natural mimic, quickly became the driving force behind getting some 'Nickisms' into the character of Castor Troy, although he was the soul of deference when the two began trading suggestions about the movie. Travolta said, 'I'd absorbed a lot of Nick watching him over the years. But it was all things I wanted permission to use.' For example, Travolta had a certain idea for the way Troy should walk. He said, 'It's a very low-slung, sweeping kind of thing. A saunter almost. It's very specific to Nick's natural gait. And I said if you don't mind, maybe we could use that Nick Cage cadence for the bad guy's voice, too, and I could just adapt that. You know, the way Nick slows down and enunciates and "pronunciates". He's almost poetic in his talking.'

Watching Travolta impersonate him actually had a lasting effect in helping Nick become a little more secure about his own presence as an actor. He said, 'Part of why I have changed my voice in so many roles, and have been on this quest to transform myself in many of my earlier characters was because I didn't feel I had a voice or behaviour that was interesting enough to imitate. And I've always taken note that some of the greatest stars have been ones with imitable voices: James Cagney, Humphrey Bogart, Clint Eastwood. And I've never felt that I had that. So when I started to watch John do me, hearing what it was that he picked up on in my voice, which was a sort of elongating of words and the enunciation of things, I suddenly got it: "Oh, OK, there's something I have that can be imitated." It sort of made me feel like I had gotten to a point where I didn't need to hide behind characters all that time.'

There was no doubt that Travolta was a fan of Nick's. He said, 'Nick is the definition of the spirit of play. He lives with his creativity in high gear. He's gracious, genuine and artistic. He's good at pushing the limits of a character in a very creative way. And he actually invites you to do the same. By nature, I'm similar, so maybe I'm just being an egotist here. It's freeing. Exploring barriers. If you do it well, it pays off. And if you don't do it well, it still pays off, because you dared to go somewhere.'

For his part, Nick had equal praise for his co-star. He said, 'John's a great actor and mimic. He can mime anybody. He really had me down. His delivery is more subtle than my personality, so for me it was much harder to get in synch with his vocal rhythms. I had a joy of a time working with John. I felt a kindred spirit with him, a sense of play and fun that's important to making a performance exciting.'

Nick also had to impersonate Travolta's mannerisms to develop the transformation of his character. To achieve that he tried to observe as many of Travolta's characteristics as possible. He said, 'John has a vocal rhythm where it's kind of like an endearing little boy; you can almost see, "Don't hurt me," in quotations. And he has an innate politeness.'

His intention was to take a relatively straightforward bad guy like Troy and turn him into a complete lunatic. He explained, 'I felt like this character was someone who would have a Chihuahua stuck in the basal ganglia part of his brain. He's a song-and-dance kind of bad guy. So one time when John Travolta was holding a gun to my head and I was saying, "I think you better pull the trigger because I'm ready" — then all of a sudden I started singing, to freak John's character out. So I started singing like a bad '70s rock star.' Putting on an Air Supply-style falsetto voice, he sang out loudly, 'I'm ready! Ready for the big ride, baby!' The director was a little startled at first by this departure from the script but he soon came round to Nick's way of thinking.

Due to his arrival on the set after filming began, the first dailies that Nick watched were of Travolta as Archer on a fairground roundabout being shot at and witnessing his young son cut down by the sniper's bullet and dying before his eyes. Travolta remembered, 'He called me up and he said, "John, the gauntlet has fallen. I saw your scene, and I wept." Well, when he saw it in dailies it had Louis Armstrong singing "What a Wonderful World" on the soundtrack, so it really pointed it up. Nick said, "I'm sobbing, watching these dailies. I can't thank you enough. You've made the decision for us about the level of acting we're going to do for this movie. Now I've really got to work." '

Also in the cast were double Oscar nominee — for *Nixon* and *The Crucible* — Joan Allen, who was cast as Archer's long-suffering doctor wife; Gina Gershon, who had previously appeared in *Showgirls* and *Bound*, as Troy's girlfriend; and up-and-coming actor Alessandro Nivola as Troy's brother Pollux.

To ensure his two superstars made the transition from one character to the other, Woo said, 'I had John and Nick work together to practise each other's walk, manner, gestures. Both guys were very serious. They were in the same room with me and I had them watch each other and imitate each other, how they'd smile and cry and express anger — all the different expressions on their faces. It was very funny.

'Nick and John and I spent some time having a long discussion about the characters. They both created the characters and then talked to each other and imitated each other. For instance, John threw out some ideas for when he was playing the good guy, then Nick would make some suggestions for John as the good guy. Then during the shooting, I did some experimenting. Most of their scenes were separate, so whenever I finished shooting one of them, I'd cut his scene together fast and show the scene to the other one so he could see how he was playing the character. Working with these two actors was the most wonderful experience I've ever had. They have no jealousy. They were so polite and humble and respectful of each other. Every day, whenever they came to the set, all they talked about was the character and the scene. Even if one of them wasn't in the scene, he'd often be on the set, talking to the other to see how he worked, to learn from him. They were like two brothers — actually better than brothers, because there were no fights or jealousy. They were just happy to be working together.'

Veteran character actor Harve Presnell, who played the FBI boss in the movie, was completely in awe of Travolta and Nick because of the lack of competition and ego playing between them. He remembered that they both came in, did their jobs and left 'all the crap to others'.

Despite his stars' undeniable talents, Woo did, however, have to get his actors to loosen up to get the performances he wanted out of them. He said, 'At first, they were playing the emotional scenes a little more subtle — the traditional American way. But they really wanted to do something a little more real. So, after the first day, I said, "Let's try it another way — my way. You want to cry, just cry. You want to laugh, just laugh. You want to hit the wall, do it. You want to smash the table, smash the table. You want to sit down, just sit down. Just do it exactly how you feel." Wow! That opened everyone up. It made John and Joan Allen and Nick Cage very happy, so we tried it that way. Some people think that's maybe too over-the-top, but it gives the actors a lot of room to explore themselves. So we did only one or two takes for each set-up. And then that was it. And everyone felt great, because all the emotions were real. And it kept things interesting for me.'

Woo enjoys the unexpected. He said, 'I've already seen the whole movie in my mind, so I like to have new things happening every day. I usually see the actors move first, then I set up the cameras. But sometimes, after I've set up all those cameras and we're shooting, suddenly they'll come up with something from their instinct. They'll just do it, usually something that wasn't in the script or in the rehearsal. That really excites me. Like the scene in the clinic, when Sean Archer wakes up, having become Castor Troy.'

There was plenty of confusion on the set caused by the switched identities of the characters. Woo said, 'I would mess up their names, and call Nick "John" and John "Nick". Even the crew messed up their names.'

Always a movie *aficionado*, Nick had not only admired Woo for years, he also admired Chinese actor Chow Yun Fat, the star of many of Woo's Hong Kong-made movies. Nick took time out from working on *Face/Off* to turn his admiration into a joke. Woo recalled, 'Nick always wanted to do the same thing as Chow Yun Fat. During one session of shooting, he emerged looking dapper, put on a small moustache and asked, "John, do I look like Chow Yun Fat?" '

Nick was not the only one having fun making *Face/Off*. The scriptwriters played their own practical jokes on the audience. In Greek mythology, Castor and Pollux, whose namesake stars make up the constellation Gemini, were the twins of Leda by the God Zeus. The brothers were said to have fought together in the Trojan War. Also, the name of the floating prison in the film is Erewhon, which is an anagram of 'nowhere' and the name of a satirical novel by Victorian author Samuel Butler.

When Woo asked Nick to work on top of the 200ft-tall oil rig which was supposed to be Erewhon prison, anchored in the pitching Pacific Ocean during filming of an escape scene, he remembered, 'Nick was a little nervous. We're both scared of heights.' Of course, Nick agreed, knowing that Woo did not want to rely on special effects or stunt doubles. Nick recalled, 'The ocean was two feet in front of me and there was a helicopter shooting blanks ten feet behind me. It was a bit windy that day so I was aware that if I didn't do it just right, anything could happen.' As it was, nothing untoward did happen. Travolta agreed to similarly dangerous feats. Woo said, 'If a character is supposed to be scared, I want to see the actor really scared.'

Another in-joke was that once Nick, as Archer, escaped from Erewhon, he stole a beige Volvo as his getaway car. In *The Rock*, his character Stanley Goodspeed drove a beige Volvo.

Although there were some humorous lines in the script and some more subtle jokes were included in the action, Nick did not feel the comedic aspects were being over-done. He said, 'I saw elements of it being very funny but I also saw it as a sci-fi horror film.'

Unlike some actors who find playing with guns fun, just as he'd been cautious when doing stunts for *The Rock*, Nick also treated the 'shoot-em-up' scenes, and those in which he was wielding a sub-machine-gun, with the greatest respect. He confessed, 'I wouldn't say it was fun. Ever since the Brandon Lee thing, I'm very nervous about guns on the set. It's something you have to treat with respect and be careful around. It makes me more on edge. Plus they're extremely loud and you have to wear stuff in your ears or you will lose your hearing.'

Rising star Brandon Lee, the son of martial arts actor Bruce Lee, died in a tragic on-set accident while making *The Crow*, when he was shot and killed by a faulty stunt gun.

Woo was still dubbing the final sound mixes just three weeks before *Face/Off* was due to be released in the USA on 27 June, only 21 days after Nick's *Con Air* had gone into the cinemas.

Originally, *Face/Off* had wrapped on 1 April, but after it was shown to a test audience in Los Angeles the cast and crew were brought back together for an additional half-day of filming, at a cost of $300,000, to add an ending that would settle the fate more conclusively of an orphaned little boy who became a central character in the plot. At that secret screening, 65 per cent of the audience had questioned why the movie did not end with the boy's fate resolved. It was an issue that Woo had wanted to deal with when he was doing the original shooting and the audience's reaction gave him and his writers the opportunity to correct the situation.

'It was the ending we always wanted,' insisted Woo, who had argued with Paramount executives to film the ending two ways, but time and money ran short and he was originally forced to film a more restrained wrap-up scene with the Archer character.

The fact that Woo was able to get Paramount executives to agree to the new ending after the test screening was a sign of how far he had come in the few years he had been working in America. Although he had had two decades of experience making movies in Asia, he watched his first mainstream movie, the 1993 Jean-Claude Van Damme vehicle *Hard Target*, suffer heavy recutting by studio bosses at Universal who disagreed with his idea that even action films should have pathos and that heroes needed feelings. The bitter experience of *Hard Target* had actually made him consider returning to Hong Kong.

Ironically, as it turned out, Woo was able to use a scenario in *Face/Off* that he had originally dreamed up for *Hard Target* — a spectacular boat chase.

Nick was highly complimentary about Woo's technique in filming his fight scenes. The director choreographed every movement to perfection giving his action sequences a balletic feel. 'The way I'd be moving, I felt that I was more like a ballet dancer than in an action film,' he said. 'The first time I saw a couple of John Woo movies, it was like an epiphany went off in my mind. This man had taken violence and turned it into a ballet. I know we've all heard Sam Peckinpah movies called "ballet-like" before, but John Woo approaches a level of operatic emotion. And somehow he did it in a way that I didn't think body-count. I didn't feel exploitation. I almost felt it was comedy, it's so over-the-top.'

Nick was anxious to take tired, old action conventions and 'breathe a sense of being out of control' into them. He said, 'I wanted Castor Troy to have a more "mod" look than the usual way we see gangsters in movies.' As a result, at the beginning of the movie, Nick had Castor Troy clad in an Armani suit and he got him carrying gold guns and wearing gold cuff links. 'He's sort of the Liberace of crime.'

When the film was released, medical experts lambasted it for its ridiculous plot. Dr Steven M Hoefflin, a Santa Monica, California-based plastic surgeon with a long list of celebrity clients including Elizabeth Taylor, Michael Jackson, Don Johnson and Ivana Trump, said, 'An operation like that would be completely impossible. It would be like picking up the Empire State building and switching it with the Plaza Hotel. There are all these underground connections that you'd have to make — water pipes and telephone lines and electrical connections. It couldn't be done.'

Nevertheless, the movie critics almost universally loved it. 'It's a pleasure to report that Face/Off is packed with more ideas than it knows what to do with,' said the LA Daily News' Bob Strauss. 'It's pretty much the only action movie you need to see this summer.'

Todd McCarthy of Daily Variety wrote, 'Action audiences and the actors' many fans will relish this one, making for big box office here and overseas.' Duane Byrge of The Hollywood Reporter said, 'A mesmerising, pulsating blast, Face/Off is brainy and brawny, traits that are wonderfully exhibited by its two stars, whose deliciously ripe performances are highly entertaining. As the stolid crime-fighter, Travolta smartly conveys not only his character's flat-footed virtues but demonstrates his light-footed capabilities when the situation calls for more. As the megalomaniacal Castor, summer action man Cage is deliriously evil, a Luficer as loony and deadly as there is. Most wondrous about their performances is that both Travolta and Cage, when put behind the other's face, can pull off stunningly deft approximations of the other's character and style. And that's when the fun erupts. The switched-identity scenes are at once chilling, hilarious and utterly amazing. Hats off to the Face/Off production team.'

Drama-Logue's Abbie Bernstein was yet another critic to heap praise on the movie. He wrote, 'John Travolta starts out as the grieving, guilt-wracked real Archer, then swaggers into his Troy pretending to be Archer; Nicolas Cage is positively diabolical when he introduces the real Troy, showing us a man wracked by undiluted despair as the Archer trapped beneath Troy's face. The two singularly and together give virtuoso performances, acutely aware of one another's mannerisms and able to duplicate them, ever reminding us of who started out as whom.'

The film even got unexpected praise from one of the world's most renowned financial newspapers. Joe Morgenstern of the Wall Street Journal wrote, 'Watching good actors do their stuff is always a pleasure, but watching the two extraordinary stars in Face/Off do each other's stuff turns out to be a crazy thrill of amazing intensity. I couldn't take my eyes off John Travolta and Nicolas Cage, and I could barely keep track of the delicious complexities that flow from the movie's premise: mortal enemies who appropriate each other's faces in the course of a final confrontation.'

USA Today reviewer Andy Seller gave the film three stars out of a possible four. He said, 'The best scenes in Face/Off are when things quiet down and Travolta and Cage get to explore the grim, up-tight agent and the lusty, vibrant terrorist.

They both play both. It's a pleasure to watch them aping each other's mannerisms.' Roger Ebert, one of America's leading film critics, concluded, 'The two actors, working together, have devised a very entertaining way of being each other while being themselves.' Leah Rozen summed it up in *People* magazine, 'Its premise is so nutso, so patently ridiculous, that this movie would seem destined to fall on its titular face. But *Face/Off*, in which Travolta's and Cage's characters literally trade faces (and the actors swap styles), is a complete and total blast. In addition to stunning action sequences — its climactic speedboat scene puts the lumbering *Speed 2* to shame — *Face/Off* has what *The Lost World: Jurassic Park*, *Con Air*, *Batman & Robin* and the summer's other big movies are missing: characters with intellect enough to reflect on their actions.'

Only a few critics, such as Britain's *Sunday Times* reviewer Tom Shone, did not like it. Highly critical of Woo's skills as a director, he wrote, '*Face/Off* starts promisingly enough, with jets and Jeeps, blitzing it out in a runway shoot-out, and ends with nothing more high-tech than fisticuffs on a beach. As with much else in this film, he's got things arse-about-face.'

But it was Shone who had to do an about-face as far as the people who really matter were concerned — the cinema-going public. The film earned more than $112 million in the US alone and became one of the ten most popular films of the year. Worldwide, it took more than $241 million at the box office.

In a survey of the top 50 coolest moments in movie history conducted by Britain's *Empire* magazine, *Face/Off* came in sixth for the scene in which a freak gust of wind caused Nick's full-length coat to flap in the blast as he walked to a private jet. Nick admitted the moment was not planned. 'It was all luck,' he said.

Nick was pleased with the end result. He said, 'I felt really proud of it because I was able to go back to what I had learned on *Vampire's Kiss*, which was sort of my experimental laboratory where I tried things out, facial expressions and attitudes. I was able to utilise that kind of acting in some of the scenes in *Face/Off*. John Woo just let me go for it.'

Face/Off debuted in top spot at the American box office the weekend it opened, firmly knocking Disney's *Hercules* cartoon adventure into second place. It earned more than $22 million and would have done better had it not been for the heavyweight boxing match between Evander Holyfield and Mike Tyson — in which Iron Mike bit a chunk from his opponent's ear — which was shown on television that Saturday night.

Nick was on a roll because *Con Air*, which had already been open three weeks, still made it to number five at the box office.

Face/Off was also a hit on the awards circuit. It was nominated for an Oscar for Best Sound Effects at the 1998 Academy Awards, won the Rembrandt Awards' Audience Award for Best Foreign Motion Picture and Nick and Travolta won the MTV Movie Award for Best On-Screen Duo. At the same ceremony, they were both nominated for Best Male Performance and also Best Villain and the film was nominated for Best Movie. And at the Blockbuster Entertainment Awards, Travolta was nominated as Favourite Actor in an Action/Adventure and both Joan Allen and Alessandro Nivola were tipped for their supporting performances. But the Blockbuster Awards was probably Nick's biggest triumph of the year; he won the Favourite Actor category for his performances in his two summer hits, *Face/Off* and *Con Air*.

Nick said, 'I've learned, making these last three films, that it's entirely possible to do sound character work in the action genre.'

Travolta and Nick had worked well together and become friends making *Face/Off*, but a year later they would be in a face-off of a very different kind when Paramount tried to pit them against each other to conclude a movie deal. Travolta had been negotiating for months with the studio to star in the thriller *The General's Daughter*, which was to be directed by Simon West. The discussions nearly came to an abrupt end in early 1998 when the tired actor, who had made ten movies in three years, demanded that the studio either pay him $25 million for the role or cast his wife, actress Kelly Preston, whom he rarely saw because of their hectic schedules, as his co-star. Studio executives balked and started chasing Nick, who had worked with West on *Con Air*, and Sharon Stone, for the roles. However, three weeks later, Paramount rereleased Travolta's hit movie *Grease*. It earned $13 million over its first weekend. Suddenly, Travolta was the blue-eyed boy once again and Paramount were prepared to give him whatever he wanted. The film went ahead with West directing Travolta, Madeleine Stowe, James Cromwell and Timothy Hutton, while Nick went on to make *8 Millimeters*, which was later released as *8MM*, with director Joel Schumacher. Nick then went on to co-star with his own wife Patricia in the Martin Scorsese-directed *Bringing out the Dead*.

Although they looked like an ideal couple as they arrived for the *Face/Off* première, Nick and his wife of two years were still being dogged by rumours that their marriage was in trouble.

Despite the rumours of marital woes, the pair maintained their dignity and weathered the storm. Without ever acknowledging the legitimacy of any of the rumours, Nick said later, 'I am more in love now than when I married. We all know that marriage takes work; you don't just throw in the towel when there's any kind of problem, you work through it.'

As the triple action album was on its final track, it was becoming increasingly obvious that even though Nick was a devoted father and husband, he was occasionally uneasy at the thought that his life had drastically changed. He said, 'There's not enough eccentricity in my life now. It's pretty much about family and work at the moment. But it's important to keep that eccentric spirit alive, because when that goes, I think the work will go. So when I have a day to myself, I like to try to find ways of doing something unique with it. One of the things I like to do is go downtown — to Little Tokyo and Chinatown and Olvera Street — and pretend like I've gone to different parts of the world without having left LA.'

Olvera Street is the heart of the old Mexican hamlet which gave birth to modern-day Los Angeles, and is flanked by the two Asian communities.

Nick confessed, 'I cry a lot. My emotions are very close to my surface. I don't want to hold anything in or it festers and turns into pus — a pustule of emotion that explodes into a festering cesspool of depression.'

The bond between Nick and Travolta lasted long after they had returned to being themselves and *Face/Off* was far behind them. Travolta said, 'The one thing that Nick said, as a person, that he learned from me was that he admired that I was not embarrassed to live life like an art. That I saw that art wasn't just on a screen or the stage, it was also in the way you ate dinner, in the way you travelled, in the vehicle that you drove, in the plane that you flew, in the way you read a book, in what cup you chose to drink coffee out of. Nick said, "If John can do it, I can do it." And he's taken what I do as a basic idea and he's elaborated on it, and I admire his full-bodied approach to it. And I said, "Nick, that makes me happy, because I feel very alone sometimes in this way of thinking, and the idea that someone as gifted as you is joining me in the world of life-as-an-art, it makes me not feel peculiar." '

Nick was serious about emulating Travolta. He said, 'I have to work at playing life as an art, which is a term I like. Organising my life like an art; knowing how to get the right amount of sleep, the right amount of exercise, to not eat something that's going to make me feel bad, so I can feel balanced. I'm always staving off despondency and gloom, because I don't like it. I'd rather be more in control of my emotions, because I function better on many different levels if I take care of myself. John was the one who actually coined that phrase. I thought that was so well put.'

Although Nick had embraced his new genre and undoubtedly proved that he had mastered it, there was something that did not sit comfortably with him. This was reflected in some of his decisions, such as refusing to pose with a gun in movie posters. Perhaps that is why in the middle of his career as an action star, he had set up his own production company with long-time friend and road-trip partner Jeff Levine, an associate producer on *Face/Off*.

After *Con Air* and *Face/Off*, Nick felt that, for now at least, his action series had played itself out. He declared that working with Woo, a master of the genre, 'gave me a chance to sharpen my instincts with that style of acting. And it is a style, because you have to propel the story with a minimum amount of dialogue and compete with the explosions going off. But after that I did say to myself, "OK, let's move on." '

He was next set to star opposite *Sleepless in Seattle* leading lady Meg Ryan in the tragic love story *City of Angels*. Although *Sleepless* was definitely one that had cinema-goers reaching for the Kleenex, Nick did not see it that way. He regarded the film as 'more of a celebration of life'. It was more the direction he felt he now wanted to go with his acting. He said, 'I just want to do something pure, without trying to show off.'

Hollywood's most talented chameleon was about to undergo another colour change — yet again.

CHAPTER TWENTY

WINGING IT

The camera swept from ground level, up the side of an unfinished skyscraper to a narrow girder high above the lights of downtown Los Angeles. Two figures were perched on the metal bar, 40ft above the roof, deep in conversation. Nick and his co-star Dennis Franz were paralysed with fear as the chill night wind whipped around them. This was not a stunt, with Nick and Franz's faces being superimposed in close-ups while highly-trained doubles did the dangerous stuff. True, they were both wearing safety harnesses in case of an accident, and to demonstrate how safe the situation was, both the film's director and producer had sat on the narrow steel bar first. But neither actor was altogether convinced, and once back on solid ground they needed a stiff Scotch or several to stop their legs trembling.

In *City of Angels*, Nick plays Seth, an angel sent to this world to escort souls to heaven. He stares at cardiologist Maggie Rice (played by Meg Ryan) as she struggles to save a patient's life, and he ends up feeling that she is more heavenly than heaven itself. As a result, Seth yearns to swap eternal life for life with Maggie and searches for a way to become human and experience love. This celestial being becomes willing to trade eternity for mortality and the woman he loves. As the story unfolds, it turns into a tear-jerking, stairway-to-heaven love story, for not long after Seth achieves his wish, Maggie is killed, leaving him on earth while she heads for the life hereafter.

In a pivotal scene, Seth seeks the advice of Nathaniel Messinger, played by *NYPD Blue* star Dennis Franz, a former angel who has successfully made the transition to becoming a human being. The two characters chat 40 storeys above Los Angeles seated on the girder, above a skyscraper under construction. These were the moments — or rather, hours — that caused them both such anguish, both feeling they were far too close to heaven for comfort. Nick has never overcome his fear of heights and he was forced to combat his phobia again, just as he had done in *Face/Off*.

He said, 'It was no special effect. Dennis and I were actually sitting on the top of a building under construction. I was terrified at the prospect of going up there so both the director, Brad Silberling, and the producer, Charles Roven, went up first to show us it was safe.'

When Nick, who is usually prepared to do whatever it takes to immerse himself in the character, still appeared to be nervous and a little reluctant to climb the lofty heights, some of the crew rather cheekily started reminding him that he had just been picked to replace tragically injured Christopher Reeve as the new Superman. 'Because of the teasing that day, I have an idea of what's in store for me as soon as I put on the costume,' he later admitted. But it was not just the crew who were poking fun at Nick; so did his co-star, despite his own, very real reservations. Nick said, 'I was having some real trepidation about it. And Dennis was saying, "Come on, Superman!" So I have a good idea of what my future holds ... '

The jokes did not help to ease Nick's fear. To keep his mind off his precarious situation, he said, 'I had to keep looking at the horizon and sort of hum a little tune in my head to calm myself. I never could look down. We were both horrified. When we finally came down, I said, "What do you say we have a glass of Scotch and never do that again?" '

Franz was just as nervous. He recalled, 'We were filming the scene on the roof of a 40-storey building in downtown Los Angeles at about 2.00am on a windy night. So, that was no blue screen. We were on a grid 40 storeys high. But we were completely safe because it was recessed in from the edge of the building. Still, when you're that high ... So to encourage us, Brad and Chuck both got up there and sat for ten minutes to show us they could do it. So that was our last out. Now we were sunk. We had to get up there. You could see the terror in our faces. I came within an inch of saying, "Please let me down from here." I kept waiting for Nick to say something. But he just stared at me the whole time. "Just look at me," he'd say. So, I'm looking, and he's got these big old eyes running through me. I'm thinking, man, this is really crazy. Let's just get it finished. The shoot took five hours and then we went downstairs to Nick's trailer and shared a bottle of Scotch.'

Bottle? Glass? What's the difference? Franz insists it was a bottle but Nick claims it was a glass. Then he laughed and said, 'Well, it might have been a couple!'

The girder that Nick and Franz sat on was actually 42ft above the top storey of the building and all they had to protect them were safety harnesses that could not be seen by the cameras.

That was not the only high-level feat Nick had to confront. During the course of filming, he also found himself perched on top of billboards, aeroplane wings and traffic signals. He said, 'I guess I felt like then maybe I could really act because when I saw the movie, I didn't seem scared. But, I tell you — I was terrified.'

Co-star Andre Braugher, best known as Detective Frank Pembleton on the hit television series *Homicide: Life on the Street*, who had also appeared in *The Tuskegee Airmen*, *Primal Fear* and Spike Lee's *Get on the Bus*, played Seth's angel friend Cassiel. In one scene, he is seen sitting on top of a road sign above a busy Los Angeles freeway with the traffic rushing by below. He remembered, 'We were actually up there. For me, it was just like sitting on a park bench after you're strapped in. After a while, just to keep your legs from falling asleep is the big chore. But Nick has an aversion to heights and part of the task was keeping his mind off the fact that we could at any instant be plunging to our deaths.'

The trailer Nick and Franz retreated to after their high-rise ordeal was a measure of Nick's status by 1997. In Hollywood, it is said that the true worth of a star can be measured not by his or her salary nor box-office receipts, but by the size of trailer the studio provides for them while they are making a movie. By the time Nick went on to make *City of Angels*, he wasn't so much occupying a trailer as a luxury liner on wheels.

Barry Koltnow went to interview him on the set for the *Orange County Register*. He recalled, 'Standing alone was a trailer — no, that doesn't quite cut it. It was more than a trailer. It was a converted luxury bus, like the kind those country singers ride around in when they're on tour. It was sleek, seductive and designed so that outsiders could not see in or get in. There was no name printed on the door. There was, however, an intercom, and I was buzzed in. The inside of the trailer was even more plush than anything I had imagined. It was all done in leather with low, lounge-like lighting, and I came across Cage sitting behind a small dining-room table about to enjoy a gourmet meal prepared by a personal chef who was still standing by his stainless-steel kitchen.'

Koltnow congratulated Nick on his continued success since winning the Oscar and going on to enjoy a string of box-office mega-hits. He pointed out that success does not go unnoticed in Tinseltown, heavily hinting at the opulent trailer. Appearing slightly embarrassed by his surroundings, Nick replied, 'Yeah, this is pretty nice, isn't it? But it's only rented for this movie. It's not like I drive around town in this thing. But I figured that I'm practically living on the set these days, so I might as well be comfortable.'

Nick was sitting more than comfortably. After the successes of *The Rock*, *Con Air* and *Face/Off*, which were among the top-grossing movies worldwide of all time, he was indisputably a commercially viable force to be reckoned with. In just one year, the combined worldwide grosses of his three films was more than $530 million and they still had plenty of earning power in reserve since the last two had only been recently released. In fact, when the receipts were in, the three films earned more than $795 million around the globe.

Although *City of Angels* was set in Los Angeles and was perceived as a full-blown love story, it was actually loosely based on German film director Wim Wenders' cult classic 1988 movie *Wings of Desire*, a story that unfolded in post-World War II Germany. It was one of the most intelligent and admired art-house films of the 1980s.

However, there were more to the changes than just moving the location and period from post-war Berlin to late-1990s California. 'Outside of the concept of there being angels observing people and hearing their thoughts, it's a completely different story,' Nick insisted. 'Wenders' film is a masterpiece but it's primarily about what's going on in the minds of the citizens of Berlin after the war. There are elements of great romance in *Wings of Desire*, but *City of Angels* is about nothing but a romance so it's a very different story.

'I was a big fan of *Wings of Desire* and loved the reworking of the script. Also, I saw an opportunity to make a film that had a lot of levels to it, a film that would make people think and feel. It's hard to find those these days. *City of Angels* is a fantasy in the tradition of *It's a Wonderful Life*.'

Whatever anyone might say or whatever parallels they might draw, Nick would never see *City of Angels* as a remake. He said, 'I didn't feel like we were remaking the movie. I knew we were borrowing from the movie but it was more like a homage to the film.'

He said, 'Like *Leaving Las Vegas*, this is essentially a love story, but because it involves angels and the afterlife, it's not as grounded in reality and is more of a fantasy. The script did remind me, though, of what it was I was trying to achieve with *Leaving Las Vegas*. Surprisingly enough, that film was about the celebration of life for me, of not taking things for granted and looking at life through the eyes of a child. Our ability to feel awe over the myriad experiences of life seems to fade as we get older, and without being precious, I wanted to examine that with this film. The challenge, of course, is to find a way of expressing this idea that won't come off as cute but as purely joyful. Whether I'm doing an action movie or a love story, my approach to the work remains the same. It's all about trying to do something original with material that's been done before, fitting the needs of the genre, and still maintaining your own concept of things.'

Compared with *Wings of Desire*, Nick strongly believes that *City of Angels* 'asks more questions about the nature of what it means to pass away, and is there any solace in passing away? And what does it mean to be alive? It examines a little more, if I dare say, the issues of passing away ... and really amplifies the notion of celebrating life and the little things in life a little more. So it's a different movie.'

He was pleased the story was set in Los Angeles, which was the idea of scriptwriter Dana Stevens, who had previously written Michael Apted's *Blink*, and Dawn Steel, who produced the film with her husband and long-time partner Charles Roven. Nick said, 'This film is also a postcard for LA, which is a character in the movie.' In fact, many of the locations around Los Angeles were parts of the city where he had once lived. He said, 'Since this is my home, I'm happy we showed LA in a way that's very romantic.'

After his action trilogy, Nick felt *City of Angels* was the right direction for him to take. He said, 'This film conveys simple and pure feelings of peace and happiness without sounding like a Hallmark card. I had been thinking about doing a film like this when the script came in. It was important to me to get back to a more personal point of view with the acting. I'd been thinking a lot about with acting, what is it I want to say? What's the next level I want to go to? It sounds trite, but it occurred to me that I'd like to be able to get back to that place when I was a child, when I was awe-struck by something as simple as a raindrop, or sunshine on my face, or the way it felt to go swimming in the ocean. I know that I've worked hard and used quite a bit of willpower myself not to become cynical and jaded. It takes work. Somebody once said that a cynic is a disillusioned romantic. What I want is to keep the romantic and the passionate alive in me. *City of Angels* was a script that provided that for me, because I'm playing a character who is in awe of people. He loves people — he thinks they're God's greatest creation, because we have flesh and spirit and light, whereas he is only light. I don't think life would be worth living if I didn't take a moment to appreciate, in almost a gullible way, the value of something as simple as the smell of a tree in Lake Tahoe. That's what this movie is, I think, trying to say. That's sort of the way I've always been and I know I wouldn't be able to act if I became too cynical. I know it would damage my instrument. I wouldn't be able to express feelings the way I do if I suddenly became jaded and cynical.'

Director Brad Silberling, who had previously made the children's ghost story *Casper*, explained the reasoning behind casting Nick. He said, 'We needed an actor with the presence of a silent-film star, because a good deal of this character is articulated through the expression in his eyes. Nick is this huge, hulking, handsome person with an exquisite set of eyes, and I'd noticed that even when he wasn't cast for his vulnerability, he comes across on screen as completely open. So he was perfect for Seth.'

However, Nick did not quite see it that way. He said, 'You have no idea how impossible it is to play an angel. Do angels blink? Do they have shadows? Reflections? It can drive you nuts.'

It was ironic therefore that Nick, who resorted to the notion that the eyes were the window to the soul, decided to make the fact that Seth did not blink during the early scenes of the movie an important part of his character's mannerisms. He said, 'Hollywood had turned out quite a few angel movies around that time, and I didn't want to do anything that had already been done. If there's anything unusual in how I approached this part, it would be that I find angels somewhat terrifying. So rather than playing Seth sweet and lovely, I tried to inject something a bit spooky into him, in order to convey some sense of other-ness. For instance, I don't blink in certain scenes.'

The films he was referring to were *Michael*, starring John Travolta, and *The Preacher's Wife*, starring Denzel Washington and Whitney Houston. But although *City of Angels* was dealing with heavenly creatures, these cherubim were not the kind of cheerful busybodies with white bodies and feathered wings usually pictured. Instead, they were cold, aloof creatures in black overcoats, lurking in libraries and on beaches at sunrise. At best they appeared to be moody eavesdroppers; at worst, stalkers.

Nick said, 'My natural inclination is to express emotions physically and violently. For the first half of *City of Angels*, Seth just observes and his reactions are so subtle. I really had to trust the old adage that the eyes are the windows of the soul — and I believe that — because that was all I was working with for the beginning of the movie. It's something that I've also been thinking about, can you be interesting as an actor without doing very much? Can you just use your eyes? I think you can say a lot with your eyes. I've often thought, wouldn't it be interesting if you could hypnotise the camera? I wanted to take a hypnosis class to see if I could learn how to use hypnosis in movies. It's just a goofy experiment, but it's a fun idea. This was maybe a chance to play with the Svengali aspect of the hypnotic gaze.'

It was Nick's intention that Seth would not blink at all until he became more human and started behaving more like one. However, Nick did not always win his battle to avoid batting his eyelids. Some blinks beat him and as a result made it on to the screen which annoyed him when he saw the finished product. He said, 'They could have cut it out or digitally removed it.' As he strove to put his personal stamp on his character, Nick found it quite a struggle to ensure he never blinked in the relevant takes. He admitted, 'I sort of put that on myself.'

He also found playing Seth quite restricting in the early scenes. He said, 'I felt constricted for the first 20 minutes,' which is the period when his character mostly observes what was going on in the world. 'It was hard to just have faith that it would be enough, because my natural inclination is to move and to get wild. You have to think about something that is meaningful to you — a purity, a memory of love — and just have faith that you can tell it through the eyes.'

Relying on his eyes to convey his feelings after starring in a string of action movies where he could be far more physical was a real challenge for him. He explained, 'It made me nervous because my tendency is to act, to take it out there. But you forget that with your eyes you can tell so many things, especially if you conjure up some memories that are especially meaningful. I wanted Seth to have the eyes of a child, to show the love and the excitement of discovery. How could I convey that without seeming silly and goofy?'

As the movie progressed, he recalled, 'I really wanted to convey the joy of life and the simple things in life, like when I was a kid discovering sparkles in the sidewalk or the way the ocean feels on your skin. These are little things we all take for granted, and we become jaded. But these are the little things that pull you back. Those of us who live long enough to go through the pain and grief, we need to remind ourselves of the simple pleasures that bring us out of our funk. That's what *City of Angels* is all about. That's what Seth was all about. He didn't take anything for granted, he was not jaded or cynical.'

Unlike *Leaving Las Vegas*, where Nick was able to do his research by boozing with buddies, or *Con Air*, where he visited a top-security prison, preparing for Seth and getting the character to a position he felt was correct was slightly more of a problem. He said, 'It took a while to figure out. It wasn't like I could just call up an angel and ask, "What's it like?" '

In the film, Seth finally swaps his wings — although he doesn't actually have literal wings in the picture — for life, by literally falling to earth by plunging off a building. That's the way they do it, according to the movie.

Nick preferred Seth once he was less angelic and more human. He admitted, 'It was delightful to be able to fall to earth and wake up human. One reason I made the movie was because of that great acting exercise: what would it be like if you woke up and you were experiencing life for the first time? How do you convey that? I wanted Seth to be borderline-psychotic, just feeling all this stuff for the first time, adrenalised like he was high with life. Slowly, some of the harshness of life enters. But I never wanted him to lose the spirit of awe, the child-like spirit of still being bewildered by and beholden to rain, or of the way a pear tastes.'

Talking about the change from action movies to romance with religious overtones, Nick said, 'With the action films I am to a degree standing outside and laughing at the whole spectacle. My sense of irony is a big part of my personality so it's hard for me to suppress it, but I have to for *City of Angels*. Ironic distance wouldn't work for Seth, because he's primarily driven by a sense of awe.

'I hoped to give some comfort about the fears we have about dying — and living,' he said. 'It was important for me to get back to a more personal point of view with the acting. I make movies that I'd want to see; I've always liked action movies and I just made three of them. But I had 15 years of movies behind me and I've tried to make every kind of movie there is. When I'm 70, I hope to look back on my career and see that I kept changing and the kinds of movies kept changing, and that's why I stayed interested. The idea of playing Seth was exciting to me. I never want to get comfortable with what I'm doing. I don't think I can grow. So I want to push myself further. And, frankly, that's dangerous because you can fall on your face and look very silly.'

He confessed, 'When you're playing something as far out as an angel you can pretty much write your own rules. In preparing for the part, I read a book called *The Physics of Angels* that made fascinating correlations between Albert Einstein's theory of relativity and St Thomas Aquinas' hierarchy of angels. One point they made is that we now use scientific terminology to deal with things that were formerly the province of theology — for example, a photon is not unlike the popular conception of an angel, in that both are entities of light capable of travelling. In the end, these things remain ultimately mysterious, but there's no denying that science and theology intersect at various points. One of the things that emerged from the book was that people in science are just using different words to describe the same things they were talking about in medieval times. For example, we say things like "magnetic field". The book says that's the same thing as a "spirit" or the "soul". If you lose the conception of angels having wings and bugles, and you think of them as life particles with a certain charge that might have a protective energy that might turn you in a certain direction, or that might keep you from getting into a car accident — that's an interesting thought.'

Throughout his work on *City of Angels*, Nick carried a copy of *The Physics of Angels* with him so he could refer to the book if necessary and he shared the content of the book with his co-star Braugher so he could get a better feel for playing an angel. Nick said, 'Another thing they say in the book, which I find very poetic, is that the sun has consciousness and the stars can think. People say miracles don't exist — well, look around. I see miracles every day. Flying in an airplane when I was making this film I saw the Northern Lights dancing purple and green in the sky and no one could explain them and that was enough for me.'

Despite having done such thorough research, Nick was still evasive about his own opinions on the existence of angels. A stubborn sceptic, he describes himself as a man of science rather than metaphysical mumbo-jumbo. He said, 'I'm not gonna be so narrow-minded as to say angels don't exist. I don't know. I've never seen an angel. But if they do, I somehow doubt that they have wings, live on clouds and blow bugles. As is probably true for most people, there have been times in my life when I felt something else was driving the car in a benign and positive way. Was it an angel? Like everyone else, I like to think so. And maybe it's here on earth.

'I believe in energies. I really believe that energy continues even after we die and that angels are a protective energy. It's possible that there's light that has a heaven-protective charge to it. I was on the freeway once and accidentally shifted into reverse. I spun around and went into a 180 and faced the oncoming traffic. I ended up manoeuvring backwards, down a crowded, busy freeway. I should have crashed and died but something protected me. I should have been dead. Somebody else was steering the boat. I was aware of a force protecting me at that very moment. I guess you can say I was touched by an angel.'

That incident happened when Nick bought an Austin Healey with a V8 engine, which he decided to convert from a manual transmission into an automatic gearbox, and his guardian angel could actually have been a down-to-earth truck driver. Nick recalled, 'I had taken it to a mechanic to put an automatic shifter in it. The mechanic did a really sloppy job. If you barely knocked the shifter it would go into separate gears. I was driving on the Hollywood Freeway and I accidentally bumped it into park. I was doing 80mph at 10.00pm. I wound up facing traffic and then a Mack truck was coming at me. I thought, this is it, I'm dead. The truck driver had a CB radio and said, "Put the car in reverse." I did and drove backwards until I got off at the exit, backwards! I was going to meet a girl for a date — this was a few years ago, I was around twenty, twenty-one — and I went to her home and said, "Look, I'm going to need a drink, right now." '

Despite his ambivalence about angels, Nick was excited by the spiritual aspects of the screenplay. He said, 'I feel like we're moving into very spiritual times and people are finding the need to have faith in something other than themselves. People want to believe there's something we can move on to when we die.' Nick professes to believe in God and added, 'That's been very helpful to me. It's nothing to do with my career, just the process of living and things going wrong for people you love.'

Nick used the bizarre 1997 death of his friend, INXS singer Michael Hutchence, as an example of what he meant. Whenever Australian Hutchence, who hanged himself in a Sydney hotel room, visited Los Angeles, he and Nick used to go riding Harley-Davidson motorbikes together. After finishing *City of Angels*, Nick went to Canada to film *Snake Eyes* and, while there, he had caught an INXS concert. He said, 'We all went out afterwards. A month or so later, he [Michael] died and it's just weird. That's what I mean about having faith when this sort of stuff starts happening and it's people you know.'

As he grew older, Nick, who was not brought up to be religious despite his Italian heritage, became increasingly reflective about spirituality. He said, 'I've always had this sense, this faith that there was something there for me, guiding me. I started thinking that way when I was seven, and I still get comfort knowing there's electricity in our bodies and little sparks going off in our brains. That's pure energy and it's got to go somewhere, hasn't it? I feel there might be some kind of continuation and I enjoy believing that it doesn't just stop.' But he admitted that as he got older, 'I really want to savour the miracle of life. I find I'm becoming rejuvenated by the little things we all take for granted, the things that cynicism can make us lose sight of.'

He once flirted with Buddhism and explored Eastern religion further by reading *Zen Mind, Beginner's Mind* by Shunryu Suzuki.

And talking about reaching a milestone birthday, he told Mark Marvel of *Interview*, 'I felt mortality. I don't really think metaphysically and I'm not religious but when I turned 30 I became aware of how transient this is. I really want to know what happens next but if you contemplate your existence too much it can drive you crazy. I have a certain amount of faith that it's not gonna be all that bad because everybody does it — dies, I mean — and, if anything, it's just nothing rather than something. This is something — what we're doing right now. I do think there's an electrical current of energy that surrounds all living things, and you have to wonder where that goes when somebody dies. It doesn't seem like it would just stop. It's been said we return to the primordial swamp of life, whatever that is. Maybe part of us will come back as a grasshopper, and part will be a cow.'

When he was asked if he thought he would come back as a higher or lower species he responded, 'The question is, how do we know what's lower? Let's put it this way — I just don't want to come back as a dashboard. But I have a feeling that could be more likely than not.'

Just as Nick had adopted a wild, weird way when he was younger, as he mellowed he was developing new habits to help him deal with his celebrity status. He said, 'I work out for an hour to balance myself out. I've handled my pressure with the celebrity thing because of the little rituals I do to get through the day. I try to find six hours a week to take a moment to do something that rejuvenates my spirit, whether it's playing with my son on the beach or something like that ... something like really stopping to breathe the air. I can really feel reactivated. I do a better job at work when I have that time. It sounds trite but it's important. It's so easy to become jaded. Life for me is like an art, too; you have to play your life, you have to say, "You know what? I'm not feeling so hot tonight. I'm going to bed early." You have to take advantage of that and learn when things are too much.'

The fact that, in the end, *City of Angels* is full of angst and tears, genuinely appealed to Nick. He said, 'I think any true love involves sacrifice, you have to give something up for true love to prosper. Take the simple concept that marriage is two parties giving something up, their freedom, if you will, to be together."

Nick hoped that ultimately people would find the movie uplifting. He hoped they would leave the cinema with 'some sense of solace — maybe that death isn't that bad. But stick around, because life is really a miracle.'

Although Meg Ryan was the producers' first choice to play Maggie, Nick was only brought in to play Seth after his old protégé Johnny Depp was involved in initial negotiations for the role which led nowhere. Nick originally asked $17 million to star in the film but eventually, after two weeks of discussions in July 1996, settled for $12 million plus a sizeable cut of the profits, while Ryan was also enjoying her biggest pay day to date, $8.5 million against 10 per cent of first dollar gross, which meant she would get a bonus once box-office takings exceeded $85 million. A lot of money was being spent on just two salaries when the film's entire budget was little more than $50 million.

Andre Braugher was supposed to be co-starring opposite Dustin Hoffman and Sharon Stone in the sci-fi movie *Sphere*, which was being shot in the San Francisco area in 1997, but he dropped out to take a less demanding role in *City of Angels*, because it meant he would be able to spend more time with his family. The cast was complete when Dennis Franz, who played Detective Andy Sipowicz in *NYPD Blue*, also agreed to a major role and the cameras were ready to roll by April 1997. So a film about angels co-starred two of the best-known TV detectives in America at the time.

Just as Nick always does his research thoroughly for all his roles, so does Meg Ryan. She spent weeks in operating rooms preparing for her role as the cardiologist with a heart of gold. She admitted, 'It's so great to watch a surgery. You're right there, looking at the heart, staring inside the chest cavity into this smooth pink space. And inside is this heart that just wants to beat, like a happy dog. It's a miracle. It's been one of the greatest moments in my life.'

Nick hit it off with her immediately. He said, 'Meg's really a serious actress. A pro. She's all about work, which I like.' Although he found that there was an ease to her approach to acting, he also believed that she had a fine sense of what was required and knew exactly the amount of emotion to give to make a scene work.

Ryan was equally flattering about her co-star. She said, 'There's something very normal about Nick and also some things that are very unconventional. Until now, I don't think his films have really shown his Everyman qualities, but they're there. He's a lovely person, very generous and very assured. And he has a great sense of humour. But he can also be abstract, obtuse and absurd. There's this fantastical quality that's perfect for an angel.'

Playing romantic leads was nothing new for either Nick or Meg Ryan. He'd starred in *Moonstruck*, *Peggy Sue Got Married*, *It Could Happen to You*, *Honeymoon in Vegas* and *Leaving Las Vegas*, while she'd done *Sleepless in Seattle*, *When Harry Met Sally*, *When a Man Loves a Woman*, *Joe Versus the Volcano* and *French Kiss*.

Nick was particularly pleased with Seth once he had fallen to earth. He felt that his love scene with Meg Ryan, which took two days to film, did light up the screen. He said, 'I think it worked because of the nature of the two characters. Seth is the ultimate virgin and sex is a miracle of life, so I liked the idea of him being curious about that. Experiencing touch and lovemaking for the first time — imagine what that would feel like? He has never even had flesh and now he is going to have sex! What is that like? So I wanted to make it seem like it was the most amazing sensation ever.'

Nick also liked the idea of Seth having a dark side. Besides flying around in a dark designer overcoat rather than white wings, Seth is interested in other visceral pleasures, not just sex. Nick said, 'This angel even wants to know what smoking a cigarette is like. He wants it all!'

Just as Nick had discovered the movie-going public's opinions had changed and had come closer to his point of view as far as *Leaving Las Vegas* was concerned, so he felt people were becoming more emotionally honest, something he felt he had always been, even at the risk of making himself appear slightly off-balance and out of step with the times. He said, 'I lived through the '80s, when cynicism was hip and it was cool to be sarcastic, and I looked pretty silly as a romantic always talking about passionate things. But people are a lot more open now and I feel more like I fit in.'

The English-language adaptation of Wenders' film had been a labour of love for veteran producer Dawn Steel ever since she had seen *Wings of Desire*, which had won several film festival awards. Steel, a pioneering movie executive who produced such films as *Flashdance* and became one of the first women to run a major studio, had bought the rights to Wenders' film in 1989 and it had taken her almost a decade to get the movie made. So there was a tragic irony attached to her project, for it was to be her last film. Steel, who was married to co-producer Charles Roven, died of a brain tumour before the picture was released.

The fact that his wife died while making the film made it even more poignant to Roven, given the emotional subject-matter. He said, 'The film is not really about an angel; it's about life and death and love. We had many projects in the development pipeline, but this was the one that was closest to Dawn's heart.'

Nick understood why it had meant so much to Steel. He said, 'I think a movie like this has the power to affect people's thoughts and conversations, make us ponder the deeper meaning of existence. And I hope it might give some comfort.'

Generally, entertainment journalists are a pretty hardened and cynical bunch who have witnessed just about everything the silver screen can offer and as a rule sceptically manage not to become caught up in any of it. So *San Francisco Examiner* journalist Jane Ganahl found herself in an unexpected predicament when she went to a special press preview of the movie one Saturday afternoon in early Spring 1998.

Ganahl, who had wept while watching the movie, recalled, 'After the film, the 20 or so entertainment journalists on my bus, who spend their lives going from movie junket to movie junket, were uncharacteristically silent. "What did you think?" whispered one critic from Chicago. I told him my reaction and he seemed to breathe easier. "I thought I was the only one!" he said. "I thought it was good entertainment, but it touched me pretty deeply." ' Ganahl, whose mother and sister had both died of cancer in the previous two years, pointed out, 'Baby-boomers like us are getting older, losing our parents — and each other — so films and books that deal with dying might be the wave of the future. After all, we're all seeking to make sense of it all.' Ganahl was amazed that the film had had such a profound effect on many of the movie pros who had seen the film.

But it was not quite the same when those critics sat down to write their reviews. Although some were highly flattering, an equal number felt sitting through the heavenly story was pure hell.

Emanuel Levy wrote in *Daily Variety*, '*City of Angels* is a superlatively crafted romantic drama that solidly stands on its own merits. The endlessly resourceful Nicolas Cage, as a celestial angel, and a terrifically engaging Meg Ryan, as a pragmatic surgeon, create such blissful chemistry that they elevate the drama to a poetic level seldom reached in a mainstream movie.'

Mick LaSalle, film critic for the *San Francisco Chronicle*, was equally complimentary. He said, '*City of Angels* is an odd hybrid but a successful one. It marries the lyricism and heavy atmosphere of a European art film with the soaring spirit of a Hollywood love story. As an angel experiencing human sensation for the first time, Nicolas Cage's power of concentration is such that he can convince an audience it's witnessing his first touch, his first kiss. There's no doubting his tenderness, his elation or his innocence. It's Cage's most Jimmy Stewart-like performance. As Seth, the unsophisticated angel, he moves gently but unrelentlessly in the direction his pure heart takes him. In one scene, waking and finding himself human, Seth runs through the street beaming and hailing strangers like George Bailey in *It's a Wonderful Life*.'

And Mike Goodridge wrote for Britain's *Screen International* magazine, 'Art-house snobs may dismiss *City of Angels* as a second-rate imitation of its source movie *Wings of Desire*. However, mainstream studio movies are rarely this artfully composed or as achingly ethereal ... It's a film full of surprises.'

But just as Nick's character spent time sitting on top of freeway signs with the traffic roaring by beneath, chatting with Cassiel, so other critics sat on the fence with their opinions. Kenneth Turan, film critic for the *Los Angeles Times*, commented, 'Attractive as well as off-putting, it manages to leave a pleasant afterglow for those in the mood for its kind of loving.' And David Ansen for *Newsweek* commented, 'Meg Ryan might not be the first person you'd cast as a heart surgeon, and Nicolas Cage is far from the wispy, ethereal types usually drafted to play angels, yet here they are as the surprisingly convincing lovers — one mortal, the other celestial — in *City of Angels*.' While *Entertainment Weekly* critic Owen Gleiberman wrote, 'This syrupy fable about becoming human is too cloyingly abstract to divine much difference between our world and the next one. All the difference finally comes down to is feeling water on your skin — or, in a pinch, having to take public transportation.'

Other critics were even less enamoured. Joe Morgenstern wrote in the *Wall Street Journal*, 'It's the movie's solemnity that will either enchant or repel you, and I can't pretend to have been enchanted.'

Stephen Holden of the *New York Times* appeared to be saying he liked it when he wrote, 'All the elements of a blockbuster Hollywood sobfest are sumptuously laid out in *City of Angels*, a film that wants desperately to outdo *Ghost* and *Titanic* in the love-from-beyond-the-grave movie sweepstakes.' But then he asked, 'So why don't the ingredients gel into a melt-in-your-mouth, tear-drenched pudding of palpitating heart and flowers? Miscast as Seth, Mr Cage looks more like a serial killer than an angel, and in the scenes when he steals up behind people and lays invisible hands on their bodies, it often looks as though he were contemplating slitting their throats. Even when he's making cow eyes at his beloved and wearing the insipid little smile of a lovesick puppy, there is something deeply creepy in Mr Cage's celestial vibrations. Most of his dialogue is intoned in a hushed semi-whisper that's meant to convey profundity but that, given the banality of what he says, sounds like the shadow come-on of a cult leader recruiting candidates for brainwashing. Mr Cage and Ms Ryan gaze and gaze and gaze into each other's eyes, but the most feeling they are able to generate is a mixture of vague yearnings and icky sympathy.'

However, when the film was released, Wenders was pleased with the way his original had been converted into a Hollywood production. He said, 'The number of music videos and commercials that have used *Wings of Desire* as a model is astonishing. With this film, I feel much less violated. It's done with respect, with a sense of discovery all its own. It's not just, "Look, Ma, no subtitles!" I feel quite proud that a film shot without a script was considered worth redoing by a major studio. *Wings of Desire* could never be remade in a conventional sense; it could only be used as a point of departure, and that's exactly what Dana and Brad did.

'The two films reflect on each other in interesting ways. I was a little anxious when I got the script. But with every page, I felt Dana had done something intelligent and respectful, translating my "poem" into an American story. It's still a film about love, but a very, very different one.'

Silberling was pleased to hear that the version he directed had met with Wenders' approval. He said, 'We'd be fools to remake *Wings of Desire*. My film tries to recapture the spirit of his film, but it's praise from a distance, not hero worship.'

Nick now appeared to be at peace with himself and his career. He said, 'There's a touching message to this film that I wanted to be a part of. I needed to play Seth because I feel I've been acting as weird individuals for too long. I look back at my past, in my films and my life, and wonder why I needed to express myself in such a tortured way. I'm more at peace with myself, and playing an angel who tries to impart his serenity to the world is something I feel in my own life. I don't need to be outrageous, that part of me is gone.'

The film première was held at Mann's Village and Bruin Theaters, in the Los Angeles district of Westwood, home of the University of California, Los Angeles, with 'angels' clad in black trenchcoats sitting on top of the cinema billboards. After the show, they mingled with guests at the party held in the Mondrian Hotel's ultra-chic Sky Bar, which was chosen because of its sweeping view over the city. Nick was with Patricia, who was also celebrating her birthday. He noted, 'Somehow we manage to mix our social lives with business.' The event raised nearly $400,000 for the Dawn Steel Putting Girls in the Picture Fund, aimed at helping underprivileged youngsters achieve their ambitions.

The film may not have gone down well with a lot of the critics but music lovers certainly appreciated its theme song 'Iris', which turned the Goo Goo Dolls into a red-hot band that year.

This was supposed to be the beginning of Nick's fantasy trilogy, which would have also consisted of *Superman Lives* and *The Defective Detective*, to be directed by Monty Python comic-turned-movie maker Terry Gilliam. But Nick's dream of being in fantasyland for a while quickly turned into a nightmare when *Superman Lives* was suddenly put on indefinite hold only weeks before the cameras were set to roll when a row over the movie's escalating budget — it was estimated it was going to cost a staggering $150 million — led to executives at Warner Bros rejecting actor-director Kevin Smith's script, and quirky director Tim Burton quitting the project.

Soon after *City of Angels* was released, Nick added yet another accolade to his ever-increasing collection of medals. At the 1998 San Francisco International Film Festival that April, Nick was presented with the Peter J Owens Award. Named after a long-time San Francisco arts benefactor, the award is given each year to 'an actor whose work exemplifies brilliance, independence and integrity'.

Nick was delighted to be receiving the award in the city which has for many years been his home-away-from-Los Angeles and which he has described as the 'city that has played host to my best fantasies'. At a black-tie, fund-raising dinner-dance for AIDS charities to launch the festival, guest of honour Nick was accompanied, as usual, by Patricia, dressed in a low-cut, pink satin Felicia Farrar gown and pearl necklace. Nick chatted with fellow guests Sharon Stone, her journalist husband Phil Bronstein, and Robin Williams, who all have homes around the city. Stone told Nick that since she had married Bronstein, then a senior editor on the *San Francisco Examiner*, she had spent most of her time living in San Francisco. Nick replied, 'You're lucky. I wish we could live here.'

Among the 450 other guests, who had paid as much as $1,000 a ticket to attend the star-studded event, was choreographer Michael Smuin, who had directed some of the fight scenes in one of Nick's early movies, *Rumble Fish*. He confessed, 'I thought he was a really good actor, but I never dreamed all this would happen to him, and it couldn't happen to a nicer guy.'

Unfortunately for Nick, two of his former leading ladies who were supposed to be on hand cancelled at the last minute. Cher had to drop out only the day before due to a scheduling conflict and Rosie Perez pulled out after the organisers refused to supply her with first-class air tickets.

Nick was happiest at the celebrity-packed gala dinner held at San Francisco's ANA Hotel when he was discussing his new movie. But when someone described *City of Angels* as a 'chick flick' he took grave exception. He took offence and said sharply, 'That's not a term I like. I took my kids to see it.'

He actually received the award four nights later at San Francisco's Kabuki theatre. He was with his son Weston but not Patricia, because she had been forced to fly back to Los Angeles early as Enzo was sick. The tongue-waggers would have liked to have read something into her departure but Nick said later, 'Things are incredible between us today and I've so much love for her that I can almost make myself cry over the fact that I've needed someone like her for so long. I think a lot of people hurt inside if they feel unloved or they don't have the right person in their life. I need to feel loved and supported. That's been part of my problem in the past and being with Patricia has definitely filled that void in my life.'

Because he was not with Patricia that night, usually low-key Nick had two private security guards to watch over Weston, as well as two San Francisco police officers, so he could accept the award with peace of mind, knowing that his beloved son was being watched over. The audience and organisers alike were most impressed that he had bothered to write an acceptance speech even though it was for an audience of 400 rather than the millions who watched him get his Oscar. But then, Nick is a strong supporter of the festival.

Ruthe Stein of the *San Francisco Chronicle* commented, 'Whatever the reason for his allegiance, Cage has become a big booster of the San Francisco International Film Festival, one movie star who can be counted on to show up when he says he will and be unfailingly charming — even to a woman who, under the guise of asking him a question, demanded his autograph.'

After receiving his award, Nick took part in an on-stage discussion with film writer Stephen Farber about his career. The event wound up with a screening of Nick's 1984 movie *Birdy*, which he had personally picked from all his movies as an example of his body of work. He admitted, 'I used not to be able to watch it. I sometimes call what I did in it emotional vomit. I was just emoting and emoting.'

Nick was supposed to stay for the screening but once again he could not watch it. However, it had nothing to do with his emoting but with Weston playing up. The youngster, who was seven at the time, developed a serious case of boredom and wanted to leave. Ever the doting dad, Nick agreed and they disappeared into the night with Weston doing kung-fu kicks on the pavement outside as father and son waited for their limousine. They were engaged in a serious conversation on whether to go for pizza or Chinese. Maybe because Weston was in a martial arts mood they decided on Chinese.

That evening, Nick's career was on yet another high but at the back of his mind he was worried because for a few months at least it looked like he was going to be out of work. *City of Angels* had just been knocked off a two-week run occupying the top slot at the American box office by *The Big Hit*, starring Mark Wahlberg and Lou Diamond Phillips, but showed every sign of becoming a huge hit. In fact, it went on to earn very respectably more than $78 million in the USA alone. But Nick had just learned of Warner Bros' decision, temporarily at least, to pull the plug on *Superman Lives*, which had been delayed again and again.

'The picture's on hold,' Nick confessed to Stein at the ceremony. 'I don't know what I'm doing — I'm wide open.'

Not for long.

CHAPTER TWENTY-ONE
SUMMER OF DISCONTENT

Almost a year before he learned that *Superman Lives* — which at the time was called *Superman Reborn* — had been placed on hold, Nick found himself at the centre of a nasty legal wrangle over his commitments to that movie and another he was set to make, *Snake Eyes*. The furore erupted in late May 1997 when furious executives at Paramount Pictures and Creative Artists Agency swapped angry legal letters over Nick's obligations and availability to star in both — *Snake Eyes* for Paramount and the *Superman* movie for rival studio Warner Bros. *Snake Eyes*, a craps term referring to two ones on a pair of dice, was a thriller about a corrupt detective who sees something strange during a heavyweight prize fight at a casino in New Jersey's Atlantic City.

At the centre of the dispute were agreements Nick's representatives at the giant and influential talent agency CAA, and his management company, Brillstein-Grey, had made with both studios for their client to star in the two films, which were seen as extremely high-profile summer releases for the following year. The protracted row, which had the potential of costing everybody involved millions of dollars and doing immense damage to their reputations, quickly developed into what one CAA agent described as 'the ugliest situation I've ever been involved in'.

Each studio believed that once he had finished *City of Angels*, they had Nick committed to their particular project. But that appeared not to be the case because there was an overlap in the shooting schedules and Nick could not be in two places at once. He could not film them simultaneously because the locations were thousands of miles apart.

The situation escalated into such a problem that the Chairman of Paramount's parent company, Viacom Entertainment Group, Jonathan Dolgen, Warner Bros co-chairmen Bob Daly and Terry Semel, CAA President Richard Lovett and Brillstein-Grey's Brad Grey had all became personally involved in an attempt to reach an amicable agreement, which at the time did not seem very likely.

Although Nick had had the same manager, Gerry Harrington, for several years, he had only recently signed on with CAA and he was so important to the agency that his affairs were being personally handled by the company's president.

The problem hinged on the timing of the two films. *Snake Eyes* was scheduled for a 12-week shoot in Montreal, starting at the beginning of August, and *Superman Reborn* was due to start on the west coast on 1 October. Warners had offered Nick the chance to play the nerd with the nerves of steel as early as February that year, and he appeared keen to suit up. He had even joked to friends that his wife would get a kick out of telling people she had slept with Superman. Warners' understanding was that when he signed with Paramount to make *Snake Eyes*, it was on the condition that he would be available to start work on the *Superman* film on time, and they believed they had documents to support their opinion.

Paramount, on the other hand, believed that CAA had waived that contingency agreement when another of their clients, Will Smith, dropped out of *Snake Eyes* over a pay dispute when he rejected a $9 million offer earlier in the year. Smith had wanted $12.5 million but he insisted that he pulled out of the movie over creative differences rather than money.

His representatives at CAA had been trying to work out the schedules for both pictures and had held separate discussions with each studio when Nick had shown interest in making *Superman Reborn*.

After talking to Paramount, CAA executives tried to get Warners to push back their start date by a month, a suggestion that did not go down well with the Warners suits sitting in their air-conditioned offices in the Los Angeles suburb of Burbank. In the meantime, agency representatives were also in discussions with Paramount about another of their clients, Al Pacino, replacing Smith as the bent cop's old buddy Navy Commander Kevin Dunne, now a highly-placed Department of Defence staff member working with the US Secretary of Defence in *Snake Eyes*.

The bitterness between Warners and Paramount was further complicated because they had both been involved in a heated bidding war along with MGM, 20th Century Fox and Universal to secure the rights to Snake Eyes, which was to be director Brian De Palma's first project after he finished *Mission: Impossible* with Tom Cruise. *Snake Eyes* was a story that De Palma had helped writer David Koepp develop. Paramount won the bidding war at the end of 1996 when executives agreed to pay a staggering $10 million, one of the largest up-front package commitments ever, for the various rights to the script and De Palma's services. Koepp's and De Palma's *Mission: Impossible* had grossed more than $180 million from US box-office receipts alone in the summer of 1996 and the duo had previously teamed up on the Al Pacino film *Carlito's Way*. De Palma had also directed Kevin Costner, Sean Connery and Robert De Niro in the Prohibition-era detectives-versus-the-mob movie *The Untouchables* for Paramount.

'The combination of Brian and David was too exciting to pass up,' said Paramount's President of Production, John Goldwyn. 'We loved the script. It really explored this character who is tested by the circumstances to become a hero, which he does and earns it legitimately and compellingly. It also has great smash sequences.'

To complicate the high-level competition for his services still further, CAA represented both Nick and De Palma, and Nick had films in the works at both studios. For Paramount he had *Face/Off*, which was due to be released just a month after the row erupted, and he was in the middle of making *City of Angels* for Warners when the legal letters were flying about. Paramount suggested that the *Superman* production team could get the job done by pushing the start date back and also filming six days a week instead of five, while Warners suggested the situation would be resolved if work on *Snake Eyes* started earlier.

At a top-secret summit one evening at Grey's home De Palma and Paramount studio chief Sherry Lansing, herself a former producer who had worked with Nick on *Racing with the Moon*, worked out a way to film Nick's scenes in *Snake Eyes* early in the shoot. It seemed that a resolution had been reached following more legal letters between Paramount, CAA, Grey and Nick's lawyer Jake Bloom. Nick would start filming *Snake Eyes* for Paramount on 21 July, as soon as he had wrapped *City of Angels*, and he would then move on to *Superman Reborn*, which Warner Bros had agreed to push back by one week to 6 October. The agreement was that if Nick had not finished his work on *Snake Eyes* in time, he would have to return to that project once *Superman Reborn* had finished filming.

However, it was felt that Nick had ample time to complete his work as the Atlantic City detective Rick Santoro, who finds his redemption by becoming a hero. Another source told *Daily Variety*, 'Neither studio was happy with how it was handled. But the problem is resolved now and we can go on from here.' Throughout it all, CAA maintained that the agency had never dropped the contingency clause and that the communications problem fell at the feet of Paramount executives. Nevertheless, the constant finger-pointing and accusations that had surrounded the whole messy situation left a trail of bad blood between the participants that would linger on for some time to come.

Nick was not made fully aware of the details until much later and so he managed to remain unfazed throughout the whole débâcle. He was just glad it had all been resolved. However, when he did learn the full extent of the dispute, he was not happy about being embroiled in such a bitter and public battle between the two studios. He said, 'That didn't feel great. I've always tried to do my business in an honest, straightforward manner, and it's frustrating when you hear that something was said that wasn't said and you feel a little out of the loop. My word is important to me, so that was a very unpleasant episode.'

As it happened it was all irrelevant because, as the year progressed, *Superman Reborn* did not take flight that year or the next.

The dispute between the two studios was not the only ugly quarrel Nick found himself involved in that summer. After an absence of many years, one of the most elusive directors in Hollywood let it be known in 1995 that he was preparing a comeback. Terrence Malick — whose movies *Badlands* in 1973 and *Days of Heaven* five years later made him one of the most critically acclaimed film-makers in the business — was planning to shoot a new big-screen version of *The Thin Red Line*. The script was his own adaptation of James Jones' World War II novel about America's bloody defeat of the Japanese at Guadalcanal. *The Thin Red Line*, the sequel to Jones' *From Here to Eternity* and hailed as one of the most realistic war novels ever, had been filmed once before, in 1964, with a cast led by Keir Dullea and Jack Warden.

When a secret reading of Malick's screenplay was held at the Los Angeles home of Phoenix Pictures boss Mike Medavoy, an A-list of Hollywood stars turned up to take part, including Kevin Costner, Martin Sheen, Peter Berg, Ethan

Hawke, Neil Patrick Harris and Dermot Mulroney. Malick had turned his back on Hollywood for 17 years, living in self-imposed exile in Austin, Texas, and now everyone in Tinseltown wanted to work with him. Along with Costner, Johnny Depp and Brad Pitt hoped to snag parts in the movie and multi-million-dollar earners such as John Travolta, Woody Harrelson and George Clooney all took massive pay cuts to do bit parts for scale, just to be in the cast. The final movie line-up also included Sean Penn, John Cusack, John Savage, Jared Leto, Ben Chaplin and Nick Nolte. But Nick's name was nowhere to be found in the cast. In movie industry circles, Nick's exclusion from the film quickly became one of the most gossiped about examples of the temperamental director's strange behaviour.

Malick and Nick had lunch together at Musso and Frank's in Hollywood on 17 February 1996, shortly after Nick's Oscar nomination was announced, and they appeared to hit it off tremendously. The director then took off for Australia where he was scouting for locations. He returned by the middle of the summer and tried to call Nick to tell him about the trip but his telephone number had been disconnected. One of the production team involved in casting said, 'Terry felt it was an act of rudeness, if not betrayal and irresponsibility, and Terry's reaction was, "Fuck him." '

The reason he was ignored for a part remained a mystery to Nick until a year later when Malick was back in Australia making the picture and once he knew, he was outraged. He only discovered what had happened after journalists visited *The Thin Red Line*'s location on a publicity trip and were told the background to his exclusion. He was deeply hurt once the story appeared in print. He wrote to *Entertainment Weekly* magazine, saying, 'When Mr Malick returned to the US he would have been able to locate me by contacting any of my representatives. Naturally, I would have been available to Mr Malick and would have welcomed further conversations, but my phone number had been disconnected due to a number of harassing calls following its leak to the public. I was saddened and disappointed by the statements, especially since they were attributed to a man whose own privacy is so fiercely guarded. In any event, I am sure *The Thin Red Line* will be excellent, and I eagerly await its release.' However, despite being nominated for a Best Picture Oscar, *The Thin Red Line* was ignored in the 1999 Academy Awards while its rival war film, Steven Spielberg's *Saving Private Ryan*, picked up four.

Nick was a great fan of Brian De Palma's work and was especially fond of *Scarface*. So it was to be expected that when they and scriptwriter Koepp got together to discuss the project, he and the director quickly hit it off and became firm friends.

Nick recalled, 'I was a fan of Brian's movies, obviously. And I read the David Koepp script, which was very good. But when I had dinner with both Brian and David, it became clear to me that much of what was in Brian's mind, visually, wasn't really on the page in the script, and that what David had written was a structure that enabled Brian to work his wizardry. The two had formed a symbiosis that seemed very exciting, and it occurred to me that this would be pure cinema. So I wanted to participate. My own take on things is to try to experiment and switch things around and look for something more unique than is necessarily on the page. And Brian is very encouraging of that, and I feel he does the same with the camera. So the two of us really hit it off. We have similar sensibilities. We

The Oscar-winner, with his Academy Award for best actor, for his role in *Leaving Las Vegas.*

Stills from *Leaving Las Vegas*, the role for which Cage deservedly won an Oscar for best actor. His co-star was Elisabeth Shue.

Top: *Trapped in Paradise*.

Below: With Sean Connery in *The Rock*.

Top: A dramatic still from the action-packed *Con Air*, in which Cage plays a wrongly-imprisoned man. The film also starred John Malkovich.

Below: With Meg Ryan in *City of Angels*.

8mm. Top: with Joaquin Phoenix and, *below*, with Peter Stormare.

Top: *Gone in 60 Seconds*, with Angelina Jolie.

Below: Brian de Palma's *Snake Eyes*.

Top: Cage with Martin Scorsese, director of *Bringing out the Dead*.

Below left: With Patricia Arquette on the Hollywood Walk of Fame.

Below right: Oscar night celebrations, with Kevin Spacey and
Patricia Arquette.

Top: With Penelope Cruz in *Captain Corelli's Mandolin*.

Below: Taking a break from filming on Cephallonia.

are, in some ways, very similar as people, and I came out of it with a new friendship. So it was a good marriage for us.'

Ironically, Nick was not the first choice to play flamboyant but corrupt detective Santoro. De Palma had wanted Nick's *Face/Off* co-star John Travolta, whom he had worked with before in the 1981 movie *Blow Out*, for the part. Mel Gibson was also briefly considered.

Finally, the cameras began to roll on *Snake Eyes* at the beginning of August 1997, with Gary Sinise, who had previously appeared in *Forest Gump*, for which he was nominated for a Best Supporting Actor Oscar, *Apollo 13* and *The Quick and the Dead*, co-starring, in the role passed over by Smith and Pacino, as Kevin Dunne.

The movie was actually filmed mainly in the French Canadian city of Montreal, with the Forum, formerly the home of the legendary Canadiens ice hockey team, doubling for the Atlantic City casino and auditorium. De Palma had hoped to film at the Arena in Atlantic City, but it was not available at the right dates because the Miss America pageant was being held there. It was also far more cost-effective and simple to film in the Canadian province of Quebec than to use the genuine location. For the purposes of the film, the Arena was transformed from a stand-alone venue to the auditorium of a hotel-casino.

The thriller, which cost $65 million to make, was not what had become Nick's standard kind of shoot-'em-up action adventure. He said, 'It wasn't your typical macho thriller. There was no sex and not all that much action, but it was really tense and suspenseful.' There was talk of it being Hitchcockian in style, a word which De Palma had used before in his movies *Dressed to Kill* and *Obsession*.

Although Nick was pleased with his work on *City of Angels*, he felt that *Snake Eyes* was a release valve for his emotions, once again giving him an opportunity to push the boundaries. He said, 'After being so controlled and internal for *City of Angels*, this one allowed me to get wild again. For me, it was a chance to work with an auteur film-maker and just fit into his very stylistic world. In *City of Angels*, I felt very straight-jacketed by the role; I couldn't move much. It was all about looking and trying to hypnotise and connect. Do everything with the eyes. Rick Santoro is movement and jazz — he wishes he was Dean Martin. There was a lot of fun playing the part. A lot of mischief. I was always trying to find the most far-out choice and then, "Let's see if I can make it work." I do that because it keeps me interested. Maybe it comes from the need to still surprise.'

The classic suspense film involves a lot of dialogue for fast-talking corrupt cop Santoro, which presented a new challenge for Nick. He said, 'I had to get used to talking fast because I'm not a fast talker. My internal metronome, my cadence, is much slower. So I had to adopt the old movie style of speaking. I had to step up to Fred MacMurray speed. All the great actors in the old days, like Cagney, talked really fast. They were good at it. When I first started doing it, it felt false. Talking fast has something to do with brain chemistry — a lot of fast talkers are incredibly smart.'

For the role, Nick chose to have the flawed Santoro, a loud man with a penchant for gambling and its associated vices, dressed in a flashy Hawaiian shirt. He said, 'They had a series of leather jackets they wanted me to wear, but I felt it was old news. I wanted this guy not to be your typical image of a New York detective, with a cigarette and a leather jacket. I wanted him to be more of a *bon vivant* in attitude and attire. Even if they are rogues, people are attractive if they are happy to be alive. I fell in love with this rust-coloured suit, and I thought the Hawaiian shirt worked well with it. He's a man of questionable taste. He's a cop on the take, so he's a hypocrite. He's a little tarnished, his clothes connote a man who's spending his money in very flashy ways. He's got a gold cell phone. He's not somebody you really want to hang with. He's an anti-hero who's done the wrong thing all his life but when push comes to shove, he discovers who he really is. He's a little bit lousy. But the thing is, he transforms, and what I like about that is that the guy you would least expect to do the right thing does it. And to me, that's a more interesting type of hero, the anti-hero. The whole movie is really kind of like that, nothing is what it seems to be. Rick is symbolic of that.'

At the beginning of *Snake Eyes*, the US Defence Secretary is assassinated during a boxing match only inches from his seat, given to him by his old buddy Dunne (Gary Sinise). Dunne's boyhood friend and now a well-placed local detective, Santoro (Nick), reluctantly takes charge of the murder investigation, and the problem of the 14,000 suspects being held in the casino's auditorium.

The movie opens with a 20-minute sequence following the detective through a fast-paced series of encounters with supporting players just before the fight is about to begin. It begins with a TV news report on the stormy boardwalk, then shifts inside the packed arena, following Santoro as he weaves through the throng, bets with bookies, roughs up gangsters, talks to his wife on one mobile telephone and his girlfriend on another and generally reveals his entire character while leading viewers on a tour of the sports facility. The scene was particularly significant because De Palma had the entire opening scene shot on a Steadicam camera and it was done in an exceptional single take, making it the longest and most complicated Steadicam shot in movie history. After that, the rest of the sequence was filmed in highly choreographed, five-minute intervals.

Nick said, 'We shot the first 26 pages of the script continuously, from A to Z, without a cut. Normally I like taking my time with dialogue and punctuating lines with pauses. But Brian wanted a rapid-fire pace, like the style of the films in the '30s. Gary and I had to speak a lot of lines and hit the end mark as the camera followed us. At the same time we were trying to make certain, in this one scene, that the audience would be clear about our relationship. It was a high-pressure, but liberating, acting experience.

'These extremely long takes would go on and on and on, with mountains of dialogue. There was so much adrenalin going on in these takes; we knew we were doing something exciting. But when you're moving and talking that fast and the camera's going with you and all of those people are there, you get into this buzz that's undeniable. You can't really think, you're like an animal moving and talking on instinct. That does create a certain mania. Good thing I trusted Brian to use material that would not embarrass me.

'It was definitely more challenging working with Brian than some of the other, more visual directors I have worked with. The fact that he wanted to do those long takes at the beginning of the movie. I'd never done anything like that before. He'd call it "No Net Productions" because it was like we were all on a high wire. I had mountains of dialogue, and I knew I had to talk fast to get it all out. And if I dropped a line or fluffed a word, we had to go all the way back to the beginning again. And sometimes that was frustrating because something special would happen in a take but it would be lost because we were going for this continuous thing. And then the Steadicam people were working their butts off trying to make sure that everything looked right. It was the most intense symbiosis I've ever had with a camera in that all the moves with the camera were choreographed together. It was a thrilling rush, but at the same time quite scary because you felt the pressure. We'd rehearse it and rehearse it all day, and then we had one hour to get it at the end, sometimes. So we'd just go for it knowing that the chips were up and that we had to do it.'

Gary Sinise said, 'It was like theatre in a way. Everything was going on at once. There was a lot of happening in the big shots and it all had to work together. If one element was missed, the whole shot was blown. Performing in the arena filled with thousands of screaming extras was a big adrenalin rush. Everyone had to stay focused. There was no net, you just jump and go. It was very exciting to work this way with Brian. He was well prepared and very clear on how the shots were going to be pieced together.'

De Palma himself felt the opening set *Snake Eyes* apart from other suspense thrillers. He said, 'I think it has a very interesting way of telling the story, when you're brought into it through one character in a very complicated Steadicam shot. You sort of see everything happening so fast, you don't really know exactly what happened and you're sort of intrigued to go back to the various points of view to figure out who shot who and why. It has a wonderful kind of development of a character relationship between the three principals that gets even more dramatic as the film goes on. It's kind of surprising, and that's what you want in movies, you want to be surprised and entertained. Any time you feel like you're going down a very familiar road, you can sort of get your eyes glazed very quickly.

'Shooting the opening shot was exhilarating and tough because it's very complicated and you need really good actors. They have to be like ballet dancers. They have to be able to hit marks and they've got to do walking and talking. You've got a huge crowd of thousands of people who will be moving around, and you've got to make sure that everybody doesn't trip over each other, and you've got to keep moving. If you make a mistake you've got to go back to the beginning. Working with all those extras looks a lot madder than it was.'

Many of the arena scenes involved working with 14,000 local extras making up the fight crowd. But as the story unfolds, the 14,000 fight fans become suspects or accomplices because somewhere among their number are the killers. Nick recalled, 'The tough part was that, after the first few hours, the novelty of being in a movie really wears off and we had to keep them going, because the crowd is a major force in the film.'

The whole opening was broken up into four sections and took almost ten days to film. As the scene progresses a stunning blonde carrying a card with the numbers of each round is often seen. The round girl was played by actress Christina Fulton, the mother of Nick's son, Weston. She flirts with Santoro, and gives him her mobile phone number.

De Palma was highly complimentary of the way Nick handled the scene. He said, 'Nick is a very skilled actor who can do practically anything. Plus, he's a real gentleman, is very professional and takes the work seriously. He can effectively deal with aesthetic problems. You never have to wait for Nick, he's always there, willing to experiment. He has a sense of humour and style of outrageousness that's very much his own and that he brings to the character of Rick Santoro. It makes him exciting to watch.

'Nick is a very exciting actor. He's funny. He can be big. He can be very sensitive. He has a tremendous amount of experience and training. He's not afraid to look any way, or try anything; it's all you ask from any really good actor. Working with Gary, who's one of the really fine character actors, was great. Together they created this sort of relationship that was very moving ultimately.'

Sinise, who was an accomplished Chicago area theatre actor long before he made the transition to the big screen, was equally complimentary. He said, 'Nick has a unique approach to acting. He's constantly looking for something to shift the scene from one that's ordinary to something with more flair, more edge, to spin the scene in a not-usual direction. We had a good time bouncing off each other. Nick is not afraid in his work, unafraid to try something outrageous. That's what has given him his staying power, that fearlessness that he has.'

Most Hollywood stars would have resisted playing a hero like Santoro because in many ways he does not come across as being heroic, but then Nick never has been one to stick to convention. He said, 'It's always more interesting to me when the guy you think of as the louse does something that saves the day because it's more unexpected, it's surprising. And it says something that fits in with this whole piece, which is that nothing is really what it seems to be, that there's a conspiracy. And Rick himself is the guy who's wearing the black hat. But then you discover he's the guy who, when push comes to shove, knows what he's going to do. I think characters that are more complex, generally are more interesting than the cut-and-dried, black-and-white. I'm not interested in that as much. I like flawed character, I like characters with problems who try to overcome their problems.'

Nick found Santoro to be a fun but truly authentic character. He said, 'Usually, movies don't depict the hero behaving the way most men actually do. But Brian's not afraid to be honest in that way and he puts it on film. Rick is a paradox.'

Apart from the opportunity to play a flawed character, Nick also wanted to make *Snake Eyes* because it was a chance to work with De Palma, widely regarded as one of the great directors of his generation. He went on, 'He's very intuitive and insightful with actors. He doesn't say much, but he knows what he wants. He lets the actors find it without micro-managing. A lot of young directors tend to get in there and micro-manage a performance, which comes from an insecure place. Brian's a secure film-maker. Once he said to me, "We got that, let's go to lunch." When we came back he wanted to do the scene again. I hadn't had time to think about it, but it felt much better, like I could hit it out of the park. I asked if that was intentional and he said, "Yeah." That's a man with almost a Zen way of directing.'

Nick always believed De Palma would allow him to push himself and his character to the limit. He said, 'I watch *Scarface* yearly. I loved that he let Al Pacino have such range as an actor. I knew Brian would give me the same latitude and would encourage me to be out there as I wished. I saw my detective as this sleazy, wild, manic guy. It felt great to be totally irreverent again. My friends who saw the dailies from *Snake Eyes* say the old Nick is back.'

He joked that he wanted to put on the snakeskin jacket from *Wild at Heart* again, but of course he had given that to Laura Dern at the end of the shoot. But when the film was released, he confessed, 'Yesterday, I actually wore a black snakeskin jacket.'

He added, 'I always knew Brian would print the right takes, and I wouldn't be embarrassed.' That was important because Nick had made quite extreme choices in the picture. Nick said, 'I did sort of push it to another level. I had just finished *City of Angels*, which was a reserved and introverted performance. So I knew I wanted to play the *Snake Eyes* cop in a liberating way. I said, "Come on. This guy is on the take. He feels good. And in his opinion, he's the king of the city." '

A few scenes were actually filmed in Atlantic City with its famous boardwalk lined with casinos, the mecca for gambling on the east coast of the USA, but Nick had learned his lesson making *Honeymoon in Vegas* and stayed well away from the tables. He said, 'Mostly I stayed in the hotel. I liked the boardwalk. But I didn't gamble at all. I gamble too much in my work.'

In the 1970s and 1980s the explicit violence and erotic scenes in many of De Palma's movies frequently ran the director foul of the Motion Picture Association of America, the body which decides what rating a movie will receive. So no one should have been surprised that he found himself once again battling with the MPAA over *Snake Eyes*, except that his latest thriller contained no nudity and none of the level of savagery, such as people being hacked to death with power saws or cut to pieces with a bloody straight-edged razor, on which the director had built his reputation.

De Palma, who was contractually obligated to deliver *Snake Eyes* as a film that would get a PG-13 rating, giving the movie better access to the lucrative teenage market, was furious because the MPAA rated his movie R. In the past, his films had been routinely threatened with X ratings and he would often have been delighted to breeze through the process with an R.

'This is outrageous!' ranted De Palma, complaining that the cuts required for a PG-13 rating would damage the film. De Palma, who refused to make the cuts, was also annoyed because he felt that he was not being supported by executives at Paramount in his attempt to appeal the rating *Snake Eyes* had been given. The top brass at Paramount thought that it was a fuss about nothing and De Palma should make the changes. Robert Friedman, Vice-Chairman of Paramount's motion picture group, said, 'The film was on the borderline. We're really talking about nothing — we're talking about a punch and one use of a four-letter expletive.' But he denied that he had not supported the director.

In the end, De Palma won his battle with Paramount but not with the MPAA. *Snake Eyes* was released uncut but with an R rating, meaning that, in the United States, people under 17 could only be admitted if they were accompanied by an adult.

Nick was not on top form the week that *Snake Eyes* was due to open in August 1998. It had nothing to do with the movie, however; he was suffering from a serious bout of sinus problems and had not been able to exercise for days. He had been forced to swap his routine of pumping up with weights for constantly blowing his nose.

At the party to celebrate the première, Sherry Lansing championed Nick by saying, 'He chooses challenging roles that always put him at risk.' After the screening, the Paramount lot had been given a gambling theme for the party. Guests could try their luck playing casino games while dining on boardwalk-inspired foods such as soft-shell crab sandwiches, sundaes and pizza. A sign that the rift between Nick and his father was definitely behind them was that August Coppola was among the guests who also attended the ritzy buffet dinner after the screening. Nick, as always, was escorted by Patricia, who also had her sister Rosanna and brother David, accompanied by his then girlfriend and future wife, *Friends* actress Courtney Cox. Also present were Gary Sinise, stunning *Spin City* TV series actress Carla Gugino (who played the leading lady, Julia Costello, in *Snake Eyes*), actor Stan Shaw (who played heavyweight champion Lincoln Tyler in the movie) and Nick's old friend, *Leaving Las Vegas* director Mike Figgis.

Nick thought that De Palma had made the movie work. He said, 'It's one of Brian's best movies, if not his best. I'm not given to hyperbole, so I mean it when I say that.'

Before *Snake Eyes* was seen by the public or film critics, its ending went through a radical change. In the original ending, Detective Santoro and Julia Costello, the woman whose discovery of corruption leads to the Defence Secretary being killed, race out of a crowded elevator at the fictional Arena in Atlantic City as an enormous tidal wave crashes over the boardwalk and washes them away under thousands of gallons of water. It was a physically demanding scene for the actors that ultimately ended up on the cutting-room floor when De Palma decided it added nothing to his story after getting feedback from a test screening.

'We had to remove it because people kept on thinking it was some kind of disaster picture,' De Palma said. 'We did the sequence with a big wave, and it just took people out of the movie. It was too big for the story.'

However, in the final cut Santoro still tells Julia, 'I keep dreaming I'm back in that tunnel, under water, only in my dream I drowned.'

Just as thousands of gallons of cold water had been poured over Nick and Gugino, so the majority of film critics, who totally disagreed with Nick's opinion of *Snake Eyes*, dumped cold water all over the movie in their reviews.

Daily Variety critic Todd McCarthy said, '*Snake Eyes* is snake-bit. After a razzle-dazzle opening, this hyperactive thriller about a corrupt cop's investigation of a political assassination devolves into a mere excuse for a stylistic exercise by director Brian De Palma, one whose wispy threads of dramatic plausibility and character involvement unravel completely by the time of the incredibly silly final reel. This late-summer Paramount release will offer a true test of Nicolas Cage's star status and ability to open a picture single-handedly; opening roll of a dice will likely be a winner, followed by a quick loss of luck.'

Michael Rechtshaffen of *The Hollywood Reporter* wrote, 'All the visual dazzle in the world can't gloss over the spoken drivel that pours from the picture's hackneyed script, even with actors as good as Nicolas Cage and Gary Sinise attempting to breathe some life into the tired clichés.'

Rod Dreher wrote in the *New York Post*, 'Nicolas Cage is an immensely talented but notoriously erratic actor, and each one of his movies is a roll of the dice. He craps out in *Snake Eyes*, a dreadful suspense thriller that wastes what's best about Cage and the most interesting about the story.'

And Kenneth Turan in the *Los Angeles Times* said, 'Brian De Palma is a superb technician in search of a great film. Regrettably *Snake Eyes* is not it, not even close.' David Denby said in *New York* magazine, 'I can't think of another movie that starts so brilliantly and ends so miserably as this one.' And the doyen of American critics, Roger Ebert, condemned it with, 'It's the worst kind of bad film. The kind that gets you all worked up and then lets you down, instead of just being lousy from the first shot,' although he did concede, when talking about the opening scene, 'Cage is wonderful.'

Only a few critics liked the film. One of the handful to give it glowing praise was Peter Rainer, of the Los Angeles-based *New Times*, who wrote, 'Nicolas Cage has never seemed more dazzling than he does in the new Brian De Palma thriller *Snake Eyes*. Playing Rick Santoro, a corrupt Atlantic City cop who likes to think he's "everybody's friend", Cage for almost two continuous hours is boogeying to his own inner beat. It's like watching a great jazz musician give a fantastically extended riff. The entire film takes its cue from Cage's spritzes and jags; it's a delirious performance in a delirious landscape.'

Another was Andy Seller of *USA Today*, who wrote, 'If you love bravura film-making for its own sake, bet on *Snake Eyes* and win big.' Joe Morgenstern of the *Wall Street Journal* also found a few good things to say about *Snake Eyes*, especially Nick and Sinise. He wrote, 'They're a fascinating pair in a film that richly deserves them. *Snake Eyes* tickles the brain by exciting the optic nerve.'

Just before *Snake Eyes* was released, Nick received yet another honour; being inducted into the world-renowned Hollywood Walk of Fame. More than 1,000 fans packed on to Hollywood Boulevard, a mecca for tourists visiting Los Angeles, to watch the Friday morning ceremony under a blazing sun that last day of July 1998. Casually dressed in a light suit and open-necked shirt, Nick, who was accompanied by Patricia, walked up and down the boulevard — oblivious to the dangers that dog all celebrities — chatting to the crowd before stepping up for the presentation outside the Galaxy Theater Complex at 7201 Hollywood Boulevard.

As his fans cheered, clapped and screamed, their idol said, 'This is the most amazing day of my life. You stuck by me from the very beginning. I'm an LA boy. This is my city. I used to live around the corner from here. I used to walk around here and ask myself if I could only have my name on one of these stars.'

Johnny Grant, Honorary Mayor of Hollywood and Chairman of the Walk of Fame, presided over the event. In addition to Patricia, on hand to watch him enthusiastically receive his award were Courteney Cox and David Arquette, *Leaving Las Vegas* director Mike Figgis and *Snake Eyes* co-stars Gary Sinise, Stan Shaw and Carla Gugino. Nick's aunt, actress Talia Shire, and Paramount boss, Sherry Lansing, the wife of Oscar-winning director William Friedkin, were also there. Nick was the 2,112th celebrity to receive a star on the Walk of Fame.

A few days later, Nick and *Titanic* director James Cameron, who was still basking in the glory of his mega-hit movie, were spotted lunching together at sunny Santa Monica's Locanda del Lago restaurant. They were deep in conversation. Army Archerd, the undisputed king of the Hollywood gossip columnists, revealed, 'While both men said they want to work together, no specific property was decided upon.'

Although Nick had travelled extensively during his career, in his own mind he still regarded himself as an average guy from Long Beach, the suburban city just south of Los Angeles where he was born and brought up for the first 12 years of his life.

So it seemed like a good gimmick for the American magazine *Esquire* to persuade Nick to return to his old neighbourhood in Hackett Avenue, Long Beach, to reminisce about his childhood for an article to be published at the time *Snake Eyes* was being released. However, the trip down memory lane turned into a far more emotional experience for him than anyone could have realised. Nick was escorted on the visit by *Esquire* journalist Scott Raab, whom he picked up at his production office on Sunset Boulevard one morning. Complaining that smoke was pouring from his 1967 yellow Ferrari in which they were to make the 30-mile trip to Long Beach, he told Raab, 'On the way down, I noticed smoke so I guess it'll be even more of an adventure.'

Raab said, 'The smoke turned out to be nothing more than the oily residue of two months sitting idle while Cage was on location.'

Even though it was not far, Nick had forgotten the way and had to rely on the journalist to give him directions from a huge map book Nick tossed into his lap. Raab said, 'No sooner had I squeezed into the '67 Ferrari than Cage says, "I brought us a Thomas Guide," and thrust into my hands a binder of maps as thick as the Pentateuch.'

Thomas Guides are large-scale road maps that all Californians rely upon to find their way around the ever-expanding cities in the Golden State.

When they finally arrived outside his old home, Nick didn't recognise it and was so apprehensive he had to be coaxed into knocking on the front door. Raab recalled, 'He seemed genuinely nervous, ready to bolt. At the door, he knocked twice, quickly. A woman from the next house opened her door and came toward us, yowling her delight. She stopped in her tracks a few feet away, staring. "I'm Maggie," she called out. "You're a big star." Nick replied, "I guess, yeah. That's me. I grew up here." '

Maggie explained that her neighbour was probably nervous about opening the door because there were two strange men standing on her porch. Finally, after Maggie called out that it was OK, a woman in her 40s came to the door and opened it.

'Hi,' Nick said shyly. 'Hi. I used to live here.'

The woman, whose name was Ellen, replied, 'I know.' There was some confusion as both women were convinced that Nick had visited the neighbourhood before and he had to explain that it had not been him but one of his brothers. The women did not seem to grasp this as they chattered away excitedly.

'Well, I just wanted to say hi,' Nick continued, looking for an excuse to retreat. 'I, uh, wanted to come back. I love it here. There used to be a big tree, a big jacaranda tree, in the front of the house, that had periwinkle blossoms on it. Do you remember that?'

This caused more confusion as Ellen, shaking her head, said, 'It wasn't here. Our neighbour had one, and I used to love it. I remember they cut theirs down.'

Nick attempted to make his apologies and leave but Ellen insisted that before he went he must come into the house and 'sign a wall'. Surprised, Nick said, 'If you ... if you ... if you want me to ... I will. Yes.'

After a tour around the house and the back garden, which brought childhood memories flooding back, Nick asked Ellen, 'Which wall would you like me to sign?' She pointed high up the kitchen wall to a small overhang where the living room and kitchen met.

'I hate to mar your house up,' Nick told her. 'Is there a paper or something I can sign? You seriously want me to write up there?' Pulling out a chair for him to stand on, she replied adamantly, 'I seriously want you to, yes.'

At her insistence, he wrote, 'To Eric, Shannan, Steve and Ellen — I love this house.' Then he signed it.

'So you have good memories here?' asked Ellen.

'Yeah,' he replied. 'Well, I have memories, yeah. Well, that was very kind of you to let us come by. All right. God bless you.'

He edged out the door but before leaving altogether, he walked up the street and back down an alley that ran behind the house. As they prepared to leave Hackett Avenue, Nick appeared pensive and distant. He told Raab, 'It's kinda sad. It's hard. It's draining. I mean, just, you know, you know, there's an overwhelming kind of combination of things I'm feeling right now. Sort of a melancholia and sort of release, a freedom. It looks better than I thought it was gonna look. I'm not talking about the house — the whole area, the whole neighbourhood, everything. It looks charming. All this stuff that I've tried to do, this drive, the desire to make it — when I see what my life could have been, the simplicity of it, the charm of just not trying so hard. And I wonder — if I'd just stayed here, somehow.'

Raab concluded, 'This is the danger of wading too deep into nostalgia, into that ocean of a child's feeling-memory; to be swept under and out of sight by the tow of illusion, of what-might-have-been.'

For Nick there was no going back. His snake eyes were firmly focused on the future.

CHAPTER TWENTY-TWO

CLOCK STARTS TICKING ON THE MIDNIGHT TRILOGY

'Now I'm in my Midnight Trilogy,' Nick declared as he started work on the dark drama *Eight Millimeter*, which was set in the seedy world of pornography and particularly the extreme depths of sado-masochism where few people venture. The film would later be retitled *8MM*. His role was a far cry from the celestial character he had played just two movies before in *City of Angels*. This time he was playing an avenging angel who finds himself in hell on earth. Nick saw his new character as the beginning of yet another trilogy phase in his career, for after *8MM* he was to join director Martin Scorsese in another bleak tale. Nick said, '*Eight Millimeter* is a very, very grim, scary movie, and then I'm going darker still with *Bringing out the Dead*.' At the time, he was not sure what would be the third dark movie of this new predicted series of three, but in hindsight he decided that the midnight trilogy had actually started with *Snake Eyes*.

The other thing he did not know at the time, but certainly discovered later, was the public and critical outcry against *8MM* once it was released, simply because of its subject matter. When the film finally hit the cinemas, viewers strongly objected to it, because it was seen as exploiting pornography and the victims of pornography to cash in on a grubby and offensive world.

Nick agreed to star in the twisted thriller, which was about as dark and cold as mid-winter at the North Pole, because 'it became clear to me after reading the script that you don't have to go to the jungle or go to war to deal with extreme horrors. They can be right in your own backyard. It's a cautionary tale of what can happen if you don't keep an eye on your children. The nightmare exists, and it's right around the corner from you.'

Unfortunately, after such a phenomenal run of success that had begun to peter out with *Snake Eyes*, *8MM* was to turn into a real-life nightmare for his career.

After Warner Bros had grounded the *Superman* project, he found a soulmate in similar circumstances with whom to embark on his trip to the dark side. Director Joel Schumacher — responsible for *St Elmo's Fire*, *Falling Down*, *Flatliners*, *The Client*, *A Time to Kill*, *Batman Forever* and *Batman and Robin* — had also just had another movie about a comic book hero, the next instalment of *Batman*, put on indefinite hold by Warner executives, making him available to helm the $40 million-budgeted *8MM*.

In the movie, Nick stars as Tom Welles, a family man detective hired to investigate the authenticity of what appears to be a snuff movie found by a wealthy widow in the safe of her late tycoon husband. He justified accepting the grim subject matter because of Welles' personality. He said, 'What attracted me was the character. As an actor, I have to find new ways of being interested in my work so it stays interesting for the audience. And sometimes it means I have to look in places that push the envelope or are more risky so that I can either fall on my face in this experiment or grow from it or do something new. And with *8MM*, I found a script which seemed very risky, which appealed to me. It wasn't your standard studio movie.'

The script was written by Andrew Kevin Walker, who had previously enjoyed a hit with his screenplay for the grim Brad Pitt thriller *Seven*, which involved seven killings, each a macabre illustration of one of the seven deadly sins. Schumacher said, 'In *8MM*, we don't have seven deadly sins, we have about 507 and they're the real thing.'

Without doubt, *8MM* was far from the usual fodder for a big-budget Hollywood studio movie. As Nick's straight-laced Pennsylvania private eye delves deeper into his assignment to learn the truth about the reel of film which seems to contain the indescribably brutal murder of a young girl, he becomes more and more embroiled in the underground world of pornography in Los Angeles and later New York. He is exposed to illegal and barely-legal material showing every conceivable — and inconceivable — fetish and deviant sexual activity including bondage, S&M, bestiality, rape videos, child pornography and the ultimate depravity — 'snuff' movies, in which killing the victim on screen is the climax. Snuff movies have been the subject of discussion for many years, though whether they actually exist is hotly debated.

Schumacher himself said, 'I hope they don't exist. I've never seen one. I don't know anyone who's ever seen one. When you get pretty deep into the illegal pornography research, the rumour is there's some fake snuff. And we tried to show that in the film. The question I have then is, yeah, but who's the audience for that? I mean, isn't watching fake snuff the same as watching real snuff? That doesn't make it better. There's only one thing I know, having lived for a while on the planet earth. There is no atrocity that you can dream of that someone hasn't done, and done worse than you ever dreamed. There is violence in us. We like to think that it's just an aberrant person here and there, but we know deep down that it isn't. What's the difference between ethnic cleansing and the Holocaust? Nothing. It's not unusual for you to turn on your television and some adult has raped and murdered a child again. And we say, "How could a human being do this?" Because they wanted to. There are lots of movies about serial killers, but that's too easy because a serial killer is a crazy person and we can chalk them off. This is about deeper evil than that. It's about people who just don't care; human life just is not of any concern to them.'

The director had resigned himself to the fact some people saw his movie as sexploitation. He said, 'That was my biggest fear. Strangely enough, my fear wasn't to go there, my fear was to glamorise it. That I would in one second glamorise it so it seemed erotic, titillating or seductive.' He hoped that most people would not think he and Nick were taking advantage of people victimised by criminal pornographers but then, referring to the popular children's television show, he pointed out, 'Some people think one of the Teletubbies is gay!'

Nevertheless, Schumacher wondered whether in post-Monica Lewinsky America anything in his picture would truly be found to be shocking. He said, 'I always make films on the theory that the audience is as sophisticated as we are. In a lot of the media, and in a lot of the Hollywood film industry, there's this attitude that the audience is like children. "Don't tell them that! They can't handle that." But just think of what everyone in the United States has had to deal with in the last two years — and on television; oral sex and DNA and ethnic cleansing ... I mean, what is it, in this day and age, that anyone thinks they don't know about out there? It's all out there. There were billions spent last year in the United States sex trade, so let's not kid ourselves. You know that if you wanted to look at illegal pornography, it would only take you two or three hours before you tracked someone down who would show you something. All of this is on the Internet, including kiddie porn.'

Schumacher may have speculated that nothing could shock the general public but with vicious S&M he was to touch more of a raw nerve than he had realised.

Nick was attracted to the character because of his own feelings of helplessness that such terrifying acts as described in the movie can and do take place. As a protective father, he personally felt vulnerable. He said, 'I found a character which seemed to be in synch, on a much grander scale, with some of the feelings I have had in my own life — just being an American citizen, being a parent, watching the news and hearing about these horrible things that sometimes can happen to young people in our country. Young people who get kidnapped, who get murdered, who get brutalised, mutilated. And feeling angry about it, feeling powerless about it, and feeling hopeless. And Tom Welles is that. He's the metaphor of that man. On a realistic level, he's just a guy who's a detective living his life and being on a case. On a symbolic level, I think he's the amalgamation of a lot of people in America who are angry and frustrated by the horrors that they hear on the news. I know I get angry when I hear about a horrible thing that happened to a child.'

Nevertheless, Nick was not prepared to condemn all of the mainstream adult movie industry as being in the same league as the perverted criminal activity shown in this film. He said, 'I don't think it's fair, and I don't think the movie is suggesting that the entire porno industry is this sort of subculture of S&M. The porn industry is an $11 billion-a-year industry. I think there are different factions of the pornography audience. There are a lot of lonely people out there and it provides a release. I don't see anything wrong with that. I don't think that's what's going on in *8MM*. I think this is more of an examination of the horrors that can happen to young people who run away. Is it sexual? I think it's just sick. It's disturbed. It's a chemical imbalance. I don't think it would be fair to say that this is what sex is.'

However, Nick appeared to be a bit naïve when it came to the most dubious end of the porno business, especially 'snuff'. He confessed, 'I was kind of aware that this stuff was out there, although I hadn't really seen any. A friend of mine said he had one, and he was certain it was real. He was so revolted, he sent it to the police. But the police determined it was fake.'

Throughout the publicity for the film, it was stressed that 'snuff' movies were a modern urban myth and that no one had actually ever found an authentic one. Still, Nick believed in their existence. He said, 'If you consider the Roman Empire and the Colosseum and the gladiators — there is a blood thirst that people have.' He was right to hold that belief. For even though the FBI were quoted extensively in interviews about the movie, basically dismissing the idea of such films existing, not long after *8MM* was released two Germans were jailed for making the real thing.

Nick's idea was to portray Welles with the utmost steadiness and simplicity, really underplaying his character. He said, 'It was an experiment. I like guys like Steve McQueen, who seem to be able to resonate or be larger than life doing, well, nothing. I think the power in that was the power of interpretation. So I said to Joel, "Can I try going the other way, like the old maxim of less is more, and see if this works? I'm just curious. I haven't really done it." And he said, "Yeah, we should both grow from this movie in some way. You and I have both been given to flash — let's try to go in the other direction." Which is what we did, and I'm pretty pleased with the results.' He may have been but very few others were.

Schumacher, a former costume designer-turned-movie-maker and self-confessed reformed serious drug user, had established a reputation for a flamboyant style but he found the idea of toning things down as refreshing as Nick did. He said, 'We had both had luck with more theatrical, show-offy work, if you will. It was time for us, individually, to work on a more restrained, more internalised, more inwardly developed level.'

Nick got on well working with Schumacher. They seemed to be in tune with their ideas. He said, 'Joel is a very positive personality. He's a fun person to be around. He's upbeat; he inspires a great deal of trust in his actors. He certainly did with me.'

Part of Nick's reasoning for playing his character so coolly and controlled through as much of the movie as he did was that he genuinely did not trust himself when it came to act out Welles' anger. It is only towards the end that Welles truly loses his grip and lets the dark side he has been polluted by take over for a while. Nick had learned his lesson about playing intensively violent characters years before making *Kiss of Death*, when on the first day he became a little too enthusiastic and sent someone to the hospital when a fight scene got out of control. Nick admitted, 'I said to Joel early on that violent scenes are a little difficult for me because as an actor I try to trick my mind into thinking I'm really there so I can do the lines with some authenticity. And lately, over the years, I've noticed that you can go so far there that it's a little scary. He said, "Don't worry about it. We'll make sure the set is cool and that no one crosses the line, that we don't lose control and that nobody hurts themselves." That was very helpful.'

Nick's wife was also worried that he might find his part tough and get too carried away in his role. He said, 'She knows how upset I can get. I may appear cool, but the truth is different. I went into *8MM* with my eyes wide open, aware of how dark and intense it could be. I would get back home and put on a silly movie to try and get my mind off it. But I would be haunted during sleep and wake up dreading to have to go through it again.'

Working as hard as he does, obviously Nick doesn't get much time to relax, especially as he has worked virtually non-stop for the last few years. But when he does get time to kick back and let his intense mind wander, he admits that he is no different from millions of other people around the world. He likes to relax in front of the television and admits that he is guilty of 'mindless channel-surfing. I know, it's awful. But nothing else relaxes me the way that does. It's like having a giant video jukebox, a slide show.'

The shows that really get Nick's attention and stop him endlessly surfing are often found on the American cable network the Discovery Channel, which specialises in wildlife and educational programmes and other documentaries. He also enjoys catching up with old movies on one of the many cable channels dedicated to the Golden Age of cinema.

He rarely goes to the cinema because he finds it a bit of a hassle. But as a diligent member of the Academy of Motion Picture Arts and Sciences, he feels it is his duty to watch as many new films as possible because he wishes to cast his Oscar vote fairly and accurately. Like other actors, he takes part in two ballots, to nominate five people in each of the four acting categories and then to choose a winner. All Academy members, no matter which branch of the industry they are in, vote for Best Picture. He said, 'I have to vote for the Oscars so I really try to see everything on tape.'

As he was preparing for the role of Tom Welles, Nick wrestled with questions about his character. Should his private eye, a clean-cut conservative with a wife and child and a simple lifestyle, be tempted on his journey into Hades, and therefore become tainted? Or should he be a white knight, a hero who maintains his virtue manfully against all the odds? In the old days of movie-making, the second route would have been the way he had to go, but Nick knew that the truth of his dilemma was that in modern-day America, people would tend towards temptation.

Nick recalled once asking British-born pop superstar-turned-sometime movie actor David Bowie how he continued to be so pure in his work. Nick said, 'He said he'd never got comfortable. It struck me then that I never want to get comfortable. When I made the decision to be in action movies, that wasn't comfortable. With *8MM*, I'm very uncomfortable.'

In the movie, Nick's character has to watch a series of porno movies, depicting various perversions, as he hunts for the ultimate 'snuff' films that will help him reach his conclusion about the authenticity of the reel he is investigating.

Although the movie business is about fantasy, some of the fantasies in *8MM* had a certain realism about them that Hollywood actors might have found difficult to do. To shoot one of the torture-and-bondage films Nick's character watches, two professional dominatrixes — one blonde, one brunette — were hired. They turned up on the set with their own slave, a fairly attractive, middle-aged man who earned his living as a respectable, well-paid Beverly Hills doctor.

'They brought him on to the set, naked, except for a leather G-string, barefoot on the cold cement,' Schumacher remembered. 'They hog-tied him, put a ball gag in his mouth and a blindfold on his face, and wrapped his head in plastic wrap, leaving one tiny hole near a nostril for him to breathe through. They threw him down on the floor like an animal and proceeded to whip him — mercilessly. Welts were all over his body. It would have been fine by me if they had faked the whipping.' But what astonished Schumacher most was when he discovered the good doctor had paid his torturers $250 for the privilege. An incredulous Schumacher added, 'And he thanked them. And he thanked us!'

As has become his personal style over the years, to prepare for his part Nick did his own individual investigation into the porn industry. He said, 'I researched and learned a lot about it, and saw some pretty raw bondage films. The whole porn industry isn't sick and corrupt and depraved as the people depicted in this movie.' However, he deliberately did not research this particular subject matter as deeply as he has on many of his other movies. He explained, 'My character is an outsider to the world of hardcore porn. He's shocked and disturbed by what he sees. For this reason, I didn't want to see much of the real stuff. I would have been too informed.

I let other people do the research for me.' He happily admitted that he did not view a 'snuff' movie in the course of his research, and he added, 'And I don't want to either.'

Despite his enthusiasm for the project, Nick found this film one of the most disturbing he had ever worked on. He was very troubled by the sex scenes simulated in the movie so, in contrast to his usual way of working, he stayed away from the set unless he was actually needed there. On previous films he had always been happy to hang around the set, even when he wasn't working, so that he could bounce ideas off other actors, watch and learn from their performances and generally interact so that he and they could benefit from each other and turn in more rounded performances for the overall good of the movie.

In *8MM*, Welles has to visit a film set where an S&M video is being shot, because he believes it might be where the footage he is investigating was filmed. Nick found those scenes, of all the work, the most difficult week of filming of the entire picture. He said, 'The imagery in that set was very spooky and the action in the scenes was very disturbing. It was like a nightmare you couldn't escape from.'

He was often asked what the message was supposed to be in *8MM* and whether it was likely to alter people's opinions of the porn industry. He said, 'I don't know about having any beliefs or ideas changed. I want people to feel that they saw a very complicated character study that they understood, that they relate on some level to the frustration that many Americans feel about what happens to young people in our country. A lot of young people. Not everyone, but the ones who get abducted and hurt, and that frustration which they can relate to in Tom Welles.'

Due to the violent ending, in which Welles metes out his own justice to the killers, there was concern that one message the film might project is that the justice system is failing in the United States and people must therefore seek their own retribution. Nick said, 'I don't know that I agree with it, but I certainly understand it. You know sometimes the law just doesn't work.'

Referring to one of the most infamous cases in modern American history, when athlete-turned-movie actor and TV presenter OJ Simpson was acquitted of criminal charges of murdering his ex-wife and her friend, Nick went on, 'I don't think it worked with OJ Simpson. So you can understand where somebody would go that far. What's unusual about Tom Welles is that he's going that far with somebody he's not even related to and whom he's never met. He's pushed over the edge and I think it's fairly obvious that this man is a complicated character who has problems in his own right. What's interesting to me and what I think gives any character an interesting shelf life is when it raises more questions than answers. And you get in step with this guy. By all appearances, he's a normal, conservative man, wearing a suit, very serious about his job. He has a very mundane, although loving, relationship with his wife and has a little baby girl who is the pride and joy of his life. Well, that's something we can all relate to. We are him as the audience. Then something starts to change and he starts to become violent and it's too late. We don't want to be him any more, and we're already into the ride with him.'

Along for the ride with Tom Welles, at least part of the way, is an unlikely sidekick, a sex shop assistant called Max California, who harbours ambitions to be a punk rock star and becomes the detective's guide on his tour of human grotesquerie. California is played by up-and-coming actor Joaquin Phoenix, the brother of teen idol River Phoenix, who died tragically from a drugs overdose on the pavement outside a Hollywood nightclub just as he was enjoying superstardom. Phoenix gave one of the few memorable performances in *8MM* and generally escaped the critics' wrath unscathed.

Nick found that working with the young actor reminded him of his own youth. He said, 'Phoenix had all the energy and intensity and excitement of the Method, and it brought me back to when I was 19 and doing *Birdy* and feeling the need to really live the part.' At one point in their journey through the human jungle, California gives the detective some advice which became one of the few immortal lines from the movie: 'There are things you'll see that you can't ever unsee.' That line from the script would come back to haunt the movie-makers because many critics wished they could 'unsee' *8MM*.

On the set, Nick worked out at lunchtime. His routine was three miles on the treadmill, some sit-ups and then back on the treadmill for another two miles. It is the ultimate escape for him as he finds that he doesn't think much when he is exercising, which he tries to do five days a week. He said, 'It's meditation of sorts.'

Nick received an unexpected compliment soon after finishing work on *8MM*. Usually recognised for his acting abilities, he was proclaimed to have the best body in Hollywood in a poll published in early autumn 1998. He was voted in first place of the Top Ten of today's muscular movie stars by the body-building magazine *Flex*, beating *Blade* star Wesley Snipes, who came in second. In third place was *Boogie Nights* star Mark Wahlberg, followed by *Jerry Maguire* Oscar-winner Cuba Gooding Jr, and heart-throb Brad Pitt in fifth place. Following them were Kurt Russell, Denzel Washington, Brendan Fraser, Daniel Day-Lewis and finally Russell Crowe. A spokesman for the magazine said, 'Cage caught the attention of the judges due to the physique changes he brings to his different roles. He was buffed for *Kiss of Death*, then downscaled to look like a chronic alcoholic for *Leaving Las Vegas*. By the time he shot the action flick *Con Air*, Cage was super-buffed, complete with bulging biceps and triceps. He is dedicated to working out.'

Nick admitted, 'I work out so I can download the problems of the day, empty my mind and blow the stress out, and I feel great afterwards. It's really more about mental health than anything else.' Never did he need that release valve more than when he was making *8MM*.

In the original script, which neither Nick nor Schumacher read, Welles is so profoundly disturbed by what happens to him during the course of his investigations that at the end he drives head-on into a brick wall, committing suicide. Early on it was decided that audiences would hate the hero dying — even if he had become jaded and corrupted from his experiences — and the script was altered. In addition, in Walker's script the character was older, more tired, more of a burned-out soul. In the writer's mind, Welles was more of a character that an actor like Gene Hackman would portray. But Schumacher made Welles younger, with more to lose and more to learn about life. Then Nick, as always, added his own input. He said, 'The only thing I said to Joel was that we should find a way to end this movie with some sense of hope.' Nick was also worried about clichéd detective scenes such as sitting in cars and going through files. He said, 'It concerned me that it might take too long to get to the suspense.'

The end result was that Walker was among those who were unhappy with the movie. Once changes had been made, the writer distanced himself from the project and ended up not speaking to the director. He even refused to give face-to-face interviews, conducting one back and forth by fax!

Nick said, 'I like horror movies and, to me, *8MM* was as close to a horror film as I could get and maintain my dignity as an actor.'

Nick and his wife were a little surprised one morning when the doorbell rang a couple of months before *8MM* was due to be released in the United States and a special delivery package addressed to him was presented to them. Inside the box was a selection of outrageous sex toys. Nick stood there stunned as Patricia demanded an explanation. It turned out they were from the producers of the movie, a practical joke thank-you gift for his performance.

Even before the film made it into American cinemas, it sparked outrage across the United States from right-wing groups, Christian lobbyists and parents' organisations who all objected to the movie's topic. Even the tycoon regarded as America's biggest 'smutmeister', Larry Flynt, the controversial pornography publisher who has been wheelchair-bound since a would-be assassin cut him down, was indignant about the film. He said, 'If you've got a script that's pure fiction based on a "snuff" film, it's very inappropriate for any film-maker to take it on. It's disturbing that Hollywood would make a film that panders to a small percentage of society. Sex for the most part is a very sensual, fun thing. Believe me, anything on the fringe — severe bondage, bestiality, necrophilia — you're dealing with less than 10 per cent of society.' He saw films such as *8MM* as handing the religious right and radical feminists more ammunition with which to attack the sex industry.

The film was originally set for release in early February 1999 in the United States but the date was pushed back to the end of the month to avoid Valentine's Day. The weekends around 14 February are traditionally good for the box office, but mainly for romantic films, and this was not, by any stretch of the imagination, a date movie. The studio bosses at Sony, who were releasing the film, felt that if they did not alter the opening date, *8MM* would, without doubt, fail at the box office because of what people decide to watch on a given day.

Instead, it premièred at the Berlin Film Festival that February but did not go down well. Patrick McGavin, who covered the festival for *The Hollywood Reporter*, described it as, 'adequate movie-making but highly questionable entertainment'. He added, 'It's unlikely the film will outlive the controversy likely generated by its grim subject matter. Women particularly will be turned off by the material.' Derek Elley of *Daily Variety* said *8MM* was an 'overly dark and often gratuitously nasty film'. He found Nick's performance 'not up to the job'. He added that his character 'could most kindly be described as one-dimensional'.

Janet Maslin of the *New York Times* felt Nick was 'seriously miscast in the role of a straight-arrow family man'. Describing the scene in which his detective character watches the 'snuff' movie, she wrote, 'While watching this film, the star winces and cringes like someone who has never even seen Nicolas Cage strut through *Face/Off* or *Leaving Las Vegas* or *Wild at Heart* with worldly swagger.' Bob Strauss of the *Los Angeles Daily News* commented, 'Cage plays it so grave and depressive that our attention repeatedly drifts away from him.'

The *Los Angeles Times* film critic Kenneth Turan was one of the most outspoken in his attacks on the film. He said, 'Those foolhardy enough to place themselves at the mercy of *8MM* can expect the following emotions: disgust and revulsion, then anger, followed by a profound and disheartening sadness. There are some films whose existence makes the world a worse place to live, and this is one of them.'

Schumacher could not understand the outrage his film had prompted. He said, 'What's wrong with a story about someone who, through his own repulsion and indignation over this, takes action? Why not? Because it might make some people uncomfortable? Well, so what? Does film only exist as medication? When you make a movie like *Patch Adams* you're hoping you're going to leave people with a heartfelt, warm, inspired feeling. You make *8MM*, you're hoping to disturb. And if you disturb the audience, you've done your job.'

Nick was very protective of his director, rejecting comments that he was the wrong man for the job. Nick said, 'First of all, I think that Joel is a visual genius. I think a lot of people share that view, especially people who understand film-making. Secondly, I feel that Joel had really reached kind of the dead end of the blockbuster stuff. I think he was fried, fed up with it. I sensed in him something similar to what I sensed in Mike Figgis when we did *Leaving Las Vegas*. It was after they took the cut away from him on the movie he did with Richard Gere, *Mr Jones*. It was a very good film and they took the cut away from him and re-edited it. And I could tell that Mike was extremely angry about it and wanted to move on. Well, I sensed kind of that attitude in Joel. He was very happy that he got to work with Warner Bros and to make these films but he was really ready to get a little more personal with his expression. I think he really wanted to say, "I'm also this guy and can make this kind of movie and watch out." I'd seen this work in *Falling Down* and also to a degree in *A Time to Kill*. He's almost like two different film-makers. He's the guy who can do the movie with flair and panache — almost like a musical — and he's the guy who can do the vigilante film to the most terrible degree.'

Although he had been panned in the past, Nick seemed sincerely baffled by the reaction. He said, 'I think this movie and *Leaving Las Vegas* were the two that have pushed me to my limits. I went further this time, certainly in terms of the violent aspects of my personality, than I've ever gone before.'

Apart from just its content prompting hostility and offending people, the film also caused a controversy over the American system of rating movies. The Motion Picture Association of America had slapped *8MM* with an NC-17 rating, but after some sex and violence had been minimally trimmed by the director, the board agreed to revise that to an R category. However, it was widely felt that by giving *8MM* an R rating, the MPAA had sold out to the major studios.

Among the scenes Schumacher had to trim was one in which Nick's character was in a sex club and a man can be seen in the background, from behind, having sex with someone up against a wall. The director said, 'We had to cut it because you see his buttocks thrusting eight times. And you're only allowed three.'

But film critic Turan of the *LA Times* was not in the mood to make light of such issues. He angrily said that the MPAA rating system had become 'bankrupt'. He went on to blast it as 'a system that's gotten used to making deals and changing ratings for a cut here and a cut there. The ratings board has become so compliant with the major studios that it can't see the forest for the trees; it no longer has the stomach to insist that a film that graphically investigates the dehumanising ultra-violent world of "snuff" films ought to have an NC-17 placed on it no matter what nips and tucks the studio coyly agrees to make.'

At least some people could make light of the controversy. One comedian said, 'It was originally called *35 Millimeter*, but they had to make a lot of cuts.'

In Europe, the movie also got restricted ratings which impeded its potential box-office revenues as so many potential movie-goers were unable to buy tickets to see it.

Nevertheless, despite being roughed up by the reviewers, it did manage to snuff out its competition to top the American box office during its opening weekend, earning a respectable $14.3 million over the three-day period, which was more than twice what the film in second place earned, although that movie, Mel Gibson's *Payback*, was in its fourth week in cinemas. Equally importantly for Nick himself, it was his sixth consecutive movie in a row to earn more than $14 million in its opening weekend in the United States, proving that he had become virtually critic-proof. Andrew Hindes, a box-office expert for the *Daily Variety* newspaper, said, 'Given the picture's murderous critical reception and grim subject matter, credit for the solid showing probably goes to the enduring appeal of star Nicolas Cage.'

Despite bad reviews, not just in the United States but by critics around the world, film fans in Italy, Spain, Mexico and Argentina flocked to see it, while Australian cinema-lovers took the advice of the reviewers. It grossed more than $36 million in a 12-week domestic run and more than $46 million overseas.

Nick said, 'I don't think it's a commercial film by any stretch of the imagination. I didn't make it to be box office. I thought it was very brave of the studio to make a movie like this. But I don't think we're setting a precedent. Movies like *Seven* and *Silence of the Lambs* have also been very dark and there's a sensibility out there for it. If you make everything happy and cheery, all you get is mush. Life isn't like that. My favourite period for movies was the '70s and I think a lot of people would agree with that. Film-makers of the time were not quite so interested in box office. Whoever made the best movie was the film-maker to watch. So I like to think of *8MM* as sort of an exercise in that style.'

Nick was able to score a few points from the controversy over the movie. He took the opportunity to point out that he might be getting older but, despite having settled down from his wild and wacky past, he wasn't mellowing into middle-aged complacency. He said, 'I don't think anyone could look at *8MM* and suggest that I was making safer films. I want the community to be safer for my kids, and yes, I like the idea of a cosy domestic life. All of that is very appealing. But that's where it ends. With my work, it's going to be just as dangerous and confronting as it ever was.'

He pledged, 'I will continue to play characters that force me to really deeply analyse various aspects of the human psyche, both positive and negative. For a long time, I was so flamboyant, and I was acting in much more of a grand style, that I became really intrigued by the possibility of expressing myself in this other, more contained manner.' But, almost as if he was covering himself for the future, he added, 'I guess what I'm trying to say is I want to do a little of everything, and experience whatever range I have. I've done the larger-than-life stuff, I've been there. And I've set up this potential for risk, so hopefully people won't be too alienated by whatever I choose to do next.'

Next was *Bringing out the Dead*, which he had already made as he tried to suppress the furore over *8MM*. He already knew he would again be wearing a cloak of darkness, but that there would be a chink of light thanks to his old friend and movie mentor Jerry Bruckheimer.

CHAPTER TWENTY-THREE

RINGING OUT THE DEAD FRIENDSHIP

Nick and Patricia were delighted to welcome one of Nick's oldest friends and two-time co-star Sean Penn on to the set while they were filming *Bringing out the Dead* in Manhattan in the depths of the New York winter in December 1998. Most of the movie was shot at night and this was one of the rare occasions they could actually get away. Nick and Penn, who was awaiting the release of *The Thin Red Line* and *Hurlyburly* that month, reminisced about the adventures of their youth when they had worked together in *Fast Times at Ridgemont High* and *Racing with the Moon* and hung out chasing girls. They laughed, joked and, full of bonhomie, headed off to a restaurant for drinks and dinner — good friends, good company, good food. The conversation carried on long into the evening with Penn calling Nick and Patricia his 'family'. When they finally called it a night, as they parted, they all agreed that they should get together again soon.

It was not until the next morning when Nick saw the prestigious American magazine *Newsweek* that he discovered that Penn had already stepped over the thin line of friendship to attack his acting in an interview. Penn, long hailed in Hollywood as one of the best actors of his generation, despite starring in a series of flops including *Taps, Shanghai Surprise* and *We're No Angels*, told the publication's Karen Schoemer that he felt most big, commercial movies were abominable and that he was appalled when talented actors debased themselves by starring in them.

Petulant Penn had told her over breakfast in a Marin County coffee shop, 'I saw *Snake Eyes* last night. It's not just that movie, it's most movies. As damaged as I am, as reckless as I've been, I never murdered my own voice. I think actors shit on their profession all the time. They can't do a pure movie again because they carry so much baggage.' Strangely, *Snake Eyes* was a Brian De Palma film. Only five years before, Penn had starred with Al Pacino in the big-budget Mafia movie *Carlito's Way*, which was directed by De Palma.

It was one of a string of insults Penn had hurled within a few weeks, but the one which, above all, he could not ignore. In an interview he gave to the *New York Times*, Penn got in a dig at Nick for starring in such mainstream movies as *Con Air*

287

and *Face/Off*. Penn lectured, 'Nick Cage is not an actor. He could be again but now he's more like a ... performer.' And he told *Entertainment Weekly* magazine that it is impossible to do 'the kind of movies I want to do' if you accept a $20 million fee, which was exactly the salary Nick commands.

Nick had chosen to turn the other cheek about the other remarks but, after the *Newsweek* interview, he had reached boiling point. He said, 'I was particularly upset because the day before he made his hurtful remarks, Sean visited me and my wife on the set. We all went out for drinks and supper and he kept calling us his family and then the next day he stabs me in the back. The door to our friendship is now closed. In this business, you get enough negativity from the press without having your friend dump on you in public.'

Until that moment, Nick had considered Penn to be like a brother. But he was furious that the actor and sometime director was suggesting he had ditched his principles to cash in on Hollywood fame. He added, 'He's worked several times with my wife and I consider him *mi famiglia*. There are a lot of my fellow actors who are jealous of my success. We don't have to put each other down in the press. Now I'm aware of his true colours.'

He was sick of the obvious resentment harboured against him in Hollywood. Nick Nolte told *USA Today*, 'Nick's gone. Nick was a marvellous actor. Then, bam! You know, he's got to turn down the $20 million.' And in a radio interview, Stephen Baldwin described Nick as 'ugly'. And he later commented, 'I just don't enjoy his movies.'

But Penn was the straw that broke this camel's back. Nick felt he did not need to prove himself to any of them. He had established a long track record of making art-house movies including *Wild at Heart*, *Red Rock West* and *Rumble Fish*. He considered his credentials to be impeccable, especially as he had dropped the name Coppola in favour of Cage to avoid cashing in on his uncle's fame. And he was talented enough to parlay all that way-out stuff into winning an Oscar — for the far-from-mainstream *Leaving Las Vegas* — and having a string of box-office blockbusters.

Penn's comments still rankled Nick a few months later, when he defended his choice of roles to *Detour* magazine, saying, 'My opinion is that I have always wanted to be exactly where I am. I have always wanted to be able to make action moves, to be able to make art films, be able to make comedies, and to go from one genre to another, and to never be trapped in a specific type of character or a specific type of movie. I'm not going to say that I'm too complicated for that, but I have more than one side to my needs of expression. I think any actor ultimately would get tired of playing the same role over and over again.'

Coincidentally, the day after Nick declared their friendship dead, Penn, Nick's Oscar rival in 1996 when he was nominated for his role as the convicted killer in *Dead Man Walking*, was named as the 1999 recipient of the Peter J Owen Award at the San Francisco International Film Festival. The previous year, Nick had been honoured with the same award, given to an actor whose career 'exemplifies brilliance, independence and integrity'.

As Nick had left the film festival and ventured into the cool San Francisco air after being presented with the award that Sunday evening in late April 1998, he had been concerned about what the future might hold. But he need not have worried. Although his dance card was wide open once *Snake Eyes* was completed as a result of *Superman* being grounded, he was firmly established as that rare kind of leading man whom Hollywood considers a good fit for just about any role. Within a few days, he was being inundated with invitations to tango.

Among the numerous parts that were being suggested to him were the lead in Woody Allen's then untitled new project, which later became *Sweet and Lowdown* — a part that eventually, and ironically, went to Penn — and the chance to co-star with *The English Patient* Oscar-winner Juliette Binoche in *Miss Julie*, a project being worked on by his old friend, *Leaving Las Vegas* director Mike Figgis, which they had discussed after Nick had won his Oscar. He was also offered the Gulf War drama *Three Kings*, which eventually went to George Clooney; *I Am Legend*, which was an on-again, off-again science-fiction vehicle for Arnold Schwarzenegger; and *Pathfinder*, to be directed by Jan De Bont.

However, Nick soon accepted an offer from Martin Scorsese, the director of such movies as *Raging Bull*, *GoodFellas* and *Casino*, to star in *Bringing Out the Dead*, which, as it was to unfold, would for the first time give him an opportunity to work with his wife, although Patricia was not cast until several months later. Once Scorsese had made the approach, Nick was happy to trade the cape and tights he had longed to wear in *Superman* for a pair of rubber gloves and a stethoscope in the legendary film-maker's gritty, darkly humorous drama.

Ever since they had married, there had been talk of Nick and Patricia working together. For a long time they had considered playing suave and sophisticated amateur detectives Nick and Nora Charles in a remake of the classic 1934 movie *The Thin Man*, which had originally starred Myrna Loy and William Powell. There had been strong rumours that that would be their first joint project immediately after Nick had won his Academy Award for playing a drunk, which would have been an ironic choice as the Charleses were confirmed cocktail-swigging, socialite sleuths.

Nick was interested in playing Nick Charles because he wanted to 'lighten up', while Patricia said, 'We've done heavy roles, and now it's just time for some fun.' The crime-fighting Charleses were always accompanied on their escapades by their very astute fox terrier Asta. Patricia joked, 'I wonder what Babe is doing,' referring to the pig with ambitions of being a dog whose namesake film was up for Oscars the same year as Nick.

However, Nick and Pat were not destined to play Nick and Nora in the foreseeable future. They soon discovered that Hollywood studios are reluctant to cast a husband–and–wife team, especially when someone as bankable as Nick was one of them. He admitted, 'A lot of studios won't hire married couples. They think it takes the magic out of it.'

So when they were eventually cast together, it was strange that it was on a project that was nowhere near as frothy as a *Thin Man* romp would have been. It was also against Patricia's wishes, even though they had often talked about working together, because she feared she would be accused of nepotism. She even kept the fact that she was up for the co-starring role a secret from her husband until after she had been cast. Patricia said, 'I didn't want to be hired because of Nick. My agent mentioned me to Marty [Scorsese]. I told him not to call Marty again, but he did. So I read for the part, and Marty wanted me. I had to have my own process because of my incredible pride. Then they told Nick.'

Patricia was not completely unknown to the director. She had just finished work on the Stephen Frears-directed *The Hi-Lo Country*, which also starred Woody Harrelson and Billy Crudup, and was produced by Scorsese.

Bringing Out the Dead was a big-screen adaptation of first-time novelist Joseph Connelly's book about a burned-out paramedic. It was not even due to be published until the following year when producer Scott Rubin learned about it in 1997, bought the rights to turn it into a film and pitched it to executives at Paramount Pictures.

'*Bringing Out the Dead* had this little voice that said, "Pay attention to me now," ' said Eric Steel, an executive with Rubin's production company who had actually discovered the project through a contact in the publishing business.

Author Connelly was no stranger to the subject he was writing about, having worked as a paramedic in New York. Assigned to the graveyard shift, he attended writing classes during the day as he struggled to establish himself as an author before successfully selling his harrowing novel. The big-screen adaptation was by Paul Schrader, who had first collaborated with Scorsese on the gritty 1976 drama *Taxi Driver*, and they followed up that working relationship on 1980's *Raging Bull* and *The Last Temptation of Christ* in 1988.

Connelly, who worked as a technical consultant on the set, was impressed with Nick from their first meeting, and was astonished by his technical skills once filming started. He told Esquire, 'I met Nicolas Cage a month before shooting started. We sat in a restaurant like two people having dinner — ordering food, then eating it. He brought out his copy of my book, with passages underlined, margins crammed with notes. He said that the role of Frank Pierce was the hardest he'd ever taken. We ordered Scotch and talked about "my character" until it became impossible to tell which one of us we were talking about. I noticed that Cage seemed to be stooping a little more than when he'd come in. Ever since I quit being a paramedic, I'd been trying to straighten my perpetual stoop, and I could see from Cage I hadn't succeeded.'

The minute the producer read the story, he knew it had 'A Martin Scorsese Picture' written all over it. Rubin said, 'I told Eric when he bought it in, if we don't get Marty to do this, this won't be a movie. Marty was the obvious and only choice for this book. These are the themes he's explored his entire career.'

Before the film could come together, executives at the giant Creative Artists Agency once again found themselves in the middle of delicate negotiations between rival studios, Paramount and Warner Bros, not just because of one but two highly-talented people they looked after — both Nick and Scorsese were clients. *Bringing Out the Dead* was a Paramount Picture but at the time, even though they were the people who had put *Superman* on hold yet again, Warner Bros still had a $20 million pay-or-play deal with Nick, meaning they could hold him to his contract and delay the start of *Bringing Out the Dead*. Both *Three Kings* and *I Am Legend* were Warner projects, so the studio could theoretically have switched Nick's deal to one of those rather than just hand him the cash for starring in nothing. As it was, by Hollywood standards, Nick made an incredible business decision. He told Warner executives that he would be prepared to be loyal to the *Superman* project but he would not hold them to the deal! He was willing to take a gamble. He handed them back a guaranteed $20 million on a possibility that some time in the future they might get their act together and make the movie and might still want him as the star.

Scorsese was also committed to a deal with Warner Bros on the biographical picture *Dino*, about the legendary singer Dean Martin, with Tom Hanks set for the title role. However, that project was bogged down with problems, not least of which was trying to work out the schedules for the ideal dream team of stars thought to be the perfect choices for Dino's Rat Pack buddies Frank Sinatra, Sammy Davis Jr, Peter Lawford and Joey Bishop, and his long-time on-screen partner and off-screen adversary Jerry Lewis. The front-runners for the ideal cast were Jim Carrey as Lewis, John Travolta as Sinatra, Wesley Snipes as Davis, Hugh Grant as Lawford and Adam Sandler as Bishop, making it a nightmare to put the film together. All of them were committed to a string of other projects for the coming year and beyond.

Barbara De Fina, who has produced nine Scorsese movies including *Bringing Out the Dead*, remembered, 'Marty has all these projects that he's been developing for years and years, and often we go through these long, painful development processes. But as *Dino* hit snags, *Bringing Out the Dead* seemed a good alternative.'

Not only was Scorsese free and the script ready but Nick, whom the director envisioned as his ultimate choice for the leading role of Frank Pierce, was also available. Diplomacy ruled and Warner Bros executives freed up the time to allow *Bringing Out the Dead* to be made, which meant favours and goodwill could be called in at a later date.

In the movie, Nick plays Frank Pierce, a veteran ambulanceman in New York's Hell's Kitchen, who cannot escape from the horror and suffering he witnesses on the streets. He is haunted by the visions and gore of the people he saves — or more particularly, those he cannot save. As a result, the troubled paramedic's psychological condition reaches a critical point. Pierce starts to become unhinged after he accidentally kills a teenage asthma victim called Rose, whose ghost then follows him everywhere. In an effort to redeem himself over her death, he heroically saves the life of an elderly patient, only to realise that he should have let him die. The role was particularly poignant for Nick as his own son Weston is asthmatic.

Patricia, who plays Mary Burke, the daughter of the man whose life Pierce had saved when he suffered a devastating heart attack, only to regret his heroic measures later, was not the only cast member familiar to Nick. In addition to his wife, he was teaming up again with Ving Rhames, who had co-starred with him in *Con Air* and *Kiss of Death* and who plays the paramedic's partner Marcus. Tom Sizemore was cast as the paramedic's old partner Tom Walls and John Goodman played another paramedic called Larry. Rhames, Goodman and Sizemore coped with the horrors of the job very differently from Frank, respectively seeking solace in religion, food and brutality.

Playing the daughter of a man being kept alive in hospital only by frequent CPR was also poignant for Patricia, whose mother had died of breast cancer the previous year and whose father was in hospital during the filming.

In the years between marrying and starting to work together on *Bringing Out the Dead*, Nick and Patricia had both been working virtually non-stop. Although they had wanted to work together they had not influenced each other's decisions on which parts they chose. Nick said, 'Generally speaking, we don't really help each other with our decision-making process. We don't read each other's scripts.'

Not without some anxiety and plenty of misgivings, to prepare for his role Nick hitched rides with paramedics in the wild and dangerous South Central area of Los Angeles and also in New York. He admitted, 'It can get rough out there.' He was permitted to spend a week with the paramedics in Los Angeles. When he went out with them he put on a disguise so that people would not recognise him. *City of Angels* had just been released at the time he was doing his research. He said, 'I didn't want to compound the grief and confusion people were feeling by having Nicolas Cage turn up at their door. I'd just played an angel and I didn't want to walk into a room with this family that's in a state of grief and shock and be like, "Hi! Here I am!" I was a little bit conflicted about it.'

Nick quickly discovered that the streets of Los Angeles were far more dangerous than the madness of Manhattan. He went on, 'I went on real-life runs with ambulance drivers in both New York and LA. I can tell you there is a lot more violence in LA. In three days in New York, I didn't see anything that terrified me, but then I came back to LA to do some research. In one night we were called out to drive-by shootings, stabbings and slashings. In LA we wore bullet- proof vests. My heart was really pumping. I realised quickly this was no movie, it was the real thing. I saw things I never expected or ever wanted to see. Those ambulance guys are true heroes.

'Most of us don't think twice about the ambulance driver who comes into our lives to take Grandpa out. In fact, paramedics are probably victims of more lawsuits than any other profession. It's this horrible reality of people who are actually like saints, who are trying to save people's lives, and then getting shat on for it. And when I examined that world I became kind of depressed by it. I saw people who were shot and slashed in an effort to save someone and I thought, How can these people do this every day for years? So for me, it was a chance to play a character in depth, and go further into the actual dismantling of a heroic person and almost see it as a chemical imbalance or a condition: when helping you is killing me. *In Bringing Out the Dead* you go into the anatomy of a heroic personality and see that it is disturbed.'

His hands-on research obviously paid off. While Connelly found Goodman's efforts at performing CPR hilarious, he was struck by Nick's abilities.

'There was little advice I could give Nicolas Cage,' he said. 'He was so good it frightened me. Over the summer he'd ridden with medics and his skills were better than those of some people I knew working the street. Nick was so good at being Frank Pierce that I decided he didn't need a paramedic consultant. I deflected questions about Frank back to Nick. Believe me, he would have made a hell of a technical adviser if he didn't look so depressed all the time.'

Nick found his character to be 'much more crazy' than his last role of Tom Welles in *8MM*. He said, 'This guy is burned out. It's a post-traumatic stress disorder situation. He's going through hallucinations and being haunted by ghosts of people he was unable to save.'

Despite the stress of his latest character, Nick believed that he was actually mellowing and that his wild-man days were behind him. He told *Detour*, 'I don't know where my anger went but I rarely yell, if ever. I don't call people names, I don't hit people. I don't have any urge to do any of those things. I don't know how that happened that I got to this point but I'm glad I did. I guess ultimately I felt that it didn't do any good. When people get really angry they kind of make fools of themselves and they're kind of silly to watch.'

Singer-actor Marc Antony, who co-starred as a dreadlocked street sleeper, agreed with Nick's assessment of his more laid-back persona. He said, 'Nick had a wonderful calming effect. My first day I was completely nervous because I had a big scene and I went up to Nick and I said, "Man, everything is so overwhelming, I don't know if I can remember my lines." And Nick said, "If it makes you feel any better, I don't know my lines either." That was my first 10 minutes on the set and it just set a tone of comfort.'

Scorsese felt he understood Pierce. He said, 'I really responded to the material.

Basically, Frank's emotional conflict and his search fascinated me. He needs some meaning in his life, and really a sense of contentment of some kind, not happiness, but a rest.'

It was an easy decision for Nick to sign on for the movie. He said, 'I wanted to work with Scorsese, and I felt that what paramedics do is so important to the community, and people don't really know what they do. When they get there, it's like, "You're late!" or "Couldn't you come any faster?" or "It's about time!" or "Don't take me to the hospital!" and all that. But Marty would say that they're saints. And I think it's important that people know what these people go through.'

He saw *Bringing Out the Dead* as 'a return to *Taxi Driver* territory, what with Paul Schrader writing the script and all. But whereas *Taxi Driver* was about going into the darkness, confronting your demons and losing yourself in the process, this one is much more about coming out into the light. It's more a spiritual journey than anything.'

Ironically, while Nick ended a friendship while making *Bringing Out the Dead* so the project had patched up the friendship between Scorsese and Schrader.

After making three movies together, Scorsese and Schrader had been discussing collaborating on a fourth when, in the late 1980s, a clash of personalities sent them off in different directions. Schrader said, 'I think it became clear to us that it was time to back off a bit. Our two egos had gotten too big for the size of the room. As I said at the time, "We've made three great films together. Let's be happy with that." I never expected to work with him again.' So Schrader was taken aback when Scorsese telephoned him out of the blue to suggest he write the screenplay for *Bringing Out the Dead*. He went on, 'As soon as I read it, I understood why he thought I was the guy to do it. It's material I'm very comfortable with. I know exactly how Scorsese thinks when it comes to this kind of subject matter. We're kind of two souls in a creative lock step. We know how to do this particular kind of thing.'

Nick enjoyed working with Scorsese. He said, 'Working with Marty was a terrific experience for me. Scorsese is a master film-maker but he's also still a student and that's what I like about him. He's still fascinated with learning every aspect of film-making. I've never met anybody who loves film more than Martin Scorsese. I mean his whole life is devoted to it. He has a tremendous library of films that he was kind enough to show me. I would go to his screening room and watch beautiful prints of films like *Phantom of the Opera*. I was very stimulated by the experience.'

But he especially enjoyed having his wife in the cast. He went on, 'Working with Patricia was great because I could see her process. To know that she's one of the most generous actresses is a great thing. I've worked with a lot of actresses and some are great and some are not so great and she's one of the great ones. You can tell what someone is like when you live with someone but you don't know what they're like on the set until you actually work with them. You can hear about it. You can observe it, but when you're in the moment with them, it's a very intimate place to be. Are you going to be supportive or not, and she is supportive. And I was supportive with her. There's a little bit of a trick because we know each other so well we can kind of see that we were acting, so we have to act very well in order not to be found out.'

Nick admitted to a few butterflies working with Patricia for the first time. 'I was really nervous during the first scenes we did together,' he said. 'You can't fake it when you're intimate with somebody. You're very familiar with each other and there are no surprises. We sort of became mutual truth barometers because we knew we'd detect anything phony in each other's performances. We don't even have a love scene. All I get is one little kiss on the cheek from her. But I guess, since everyone knows we're married, it sort of brings the love scene to it without having to film it.'

Even though they were husband and wife, they kept their distance during filming. Patricia revealed, 'We went to work in separate cars and had separate trailers on the set. We tried not to talk much when we were working because we didn't want to influence each other or make each other feel awkward. Your husband can throw you off like nobody else.'

Working together also disrupted the family's equilibrium because the entire film was shot in New York. Nick said, 'We flew home every weekend because we really didn't want to take the kids out of school.'

The weekly trip back to California was written in to Nick's contract, and during the five-month shoot he did not miss a single visit. The coast-to-coast commuting also helped him play a character who was losing control. He quipped, 'The constant jet lag sure helped!'

Even though they were working together, Nick was still dogged by rumours that he had a wandering eye. Late one night, or rather early one morning, just before Christmas 1998, he stopped by at the twentieth birthday party thrown for Mia Tyler, daughter of Aerosmith rock star Steven Tyler. It was at the ritzy Limelight club, in the trendy Chelsea area of Manhattan. He remained at the party with a stunning young woman until 4.00am, and made a point of letting top New York gossip columnist Mitchell Fink know that the woman was his 'female assistant' and that her fiancé was also attending the party.

Despite the continuing chit-chat about marital woes and infidelity, and their insistence on separate cars and trailers, Nick and Patricia presented a united public face to the world. After more than four years together, Nick said, 'There is a lot of gift-giving. And in the gift-giving process on both sides there is a lot of thoughtfulness, and a deep understanding of each other. Patricia knew that my grandfather was Toscanini's first-chair flautist, and so on my birthday she bought all of Toscanini's recordings and gave me this great turn-table so that I could listen to my grandfather play flute. So I thought that was very thoughtful. And conversely, she's always struck me as something of a Joan of Arc personality — she'd look great in armour. She's got the knight's sort of *corazón*, that courage, and so I bought her a painting of a Joan of Arc-like woman riding a horse, a white stallion. And it's her.'

Bringing Out the Dead was not due to be released in the United States until the end of October 1999, with releases in the rest of the world coming in the following months. However, in late June a rough cut of the film was shown to a test audience in New York and the response was very favourable, especially as the viewers knew they were not seeing the completed picture. One of the select audience revealed, 'Nick Cage's acting is far better than that of his recent movies such as *8MM*.' The reviewer added, 'After having seen this early version of the film, I am truly excited about the possibilities of how the final version can turn out. I can't wait to see it again.' However, another amateur critic at the screening felt that Nick was miscast and the movie too slow. The reviewers were surprised to note that he had grown his hair and had it dyed slightly grey to give his character a battle-weary appearance.

The film's première was held at New York's Ziegfield Theater, to benefit the Coalition for the Homeless, and a special preview for 25 real New York Emergency Medical Service paramedics, who were said to be left 'speechless with admiration' for Nick's performance, was also held. Nick and Patricia turned up for the première hand in hand, laughing off the latest reports that their marriage was on the rocks, this time from Fox News' respected showbusiness writer Roger Friedman.

Given the setting — the mean streets of New York — and the dark, brooding protagonist who spends his nights driving them, the film inevitably drew comparison to Scorcese's 1976 film *Taxi Driver*, which won Oscar nominations for stars Robert De Niro and Jodie Foster, as Best Actor and Best Supporting Actress, as well as Best Picture and Best Original Score.

Rolling Stone loved the film. Its reviewer wrote, 'What director Martin Scorcese and actor Nicolas Cage have created in *Bringing Out the Dead* — it's an extraordinary first collaboration — is a ghost story. Oh, there's action, romance and a gallows humour to ease the burden carried by Cage's character, EMS paramedic Frank Pierce, but the film is a ghost story nonetheless. Far more clearly than the child in *The Sixth Sense*, Frank sees the dead and feels their pain.

'Cage, who gives a blazing, implosive performance, uses his haunted eyes to reveal the emotional scars that Frank can't heal.

'In advance of the inevitable comparisons, it needs stating that *Bringing Out the Dead* is not *Taxi Driver* in an ambulance. Frank is not out for a cathartic bloodbath — he means to do good and play guardian to these lost souls; that is, if the job doesn't kill him first.'

In *Daily Variety* Emanuel Levy said, 'Based on Joe Connelly's pulp novel, it's a quintessential New York nocturnal tale of the occupational hazards, joys and sorrows of a paramedic, splendidly played by Nicolas Cage, as he "routinely" goes about his job of saving lives.

'Though this is a more mature work, critics will likely perceive it as *Taxi Driver* a generation later, and not only because of the protagonists' similar professions. Like the earlier film's Travis Bickle, Frank Pierce (Cage) is a man on the edge, an insomniac loner who works the graveyard shift and, in the midst of his work's hustle and bustle, undergoes a severe spiritual crisis that may lead to either self-destruction or redemption, two motifs that run through Scorcese's three-decade œuvre.

'In his best role since the Oscar-winning *Leaving Las Vegas*, Cage is suitably cast as a tormented, empathic man in desperate need of salvation and sleep; pic's closing image of him achieves a poetic, quasi-religious tone.'

David Hunter of *The Hollywood Reporter* was equally enthusiastic, though he noted — correctly — that the film would not be a box-office success.

He wrote it was, 'probably not headed for a big pay day at the box office or with critics, but in the seriousness of its artistic purpose and level of craftsmanship it easily stands out in the crowd of current releases. *Dead* is dark but not bleak, clever but not jaded, weird but not distastefully so.

'A lot of it works and keeps one glued to the screen, with Cage no disappointment as a soul tortured by the awfulness of his job and thrust into bizarre scenes of human misery.

'There's a mission to this movie, and the theme of compassion leads to a powerful, subtly stated epiphany for Frank in a merciful gesture for someone more miserable than himself.'

Respected syndicated columnist Roger Ebert also loved the film, and Nick, again comparing it to *Taxi Driver*.

'Like Travis Bickle, the hero of Scorcese's *Taxi Driver*, Frank travels the night streets like a boatman on the River Styx, while steam rises from manholes as if from the fires below,' he wrote. 'Travis wanted to save those who did not want saving. Frank finds those who desperately want help, but usually he is powerless.

'The film wisely has no real plot, because the paramedic's days have no beginning or goal, but are a limbo of extended horror. At one point Frank hallucinates that he is helping pull people's bodies up out of the pavement, freeing them.

'Nicolas Cage is an actor of great style and heedless emotional availability. He will go anywhere for a role, and this film is his best since *Leaving Las Vegas*. I like the subtle way he and Scorcese embody what Frank has learned on the job, the little verbal formulas and quiet asides that help the bystanders at suffering. He embodies the tragedy of a man who has necessary work and is good at it, but in a job that is never, ever over.'

The *London Evening Standard* also invoked the spirit of Travis Bickle, but with less enthusiasm. Critic Alexander Walker wrote, 'Instead of Robert De Niro in a cab, Nicolas Cage is behind the wheel of an ambulance, a paramedic in the rat-run of Hell's Kitchen. His trade is ministering to the body, but his divine impulse compels him to seek the souls of those he saves.

'Patricia Arquette plays an ex-junkie and the daughter of a heart-attack patient. She catches Cage's eye the way that Jodie Foster's pubertal prostitute in *Taxi Driver* caught De Niro's.

'*Bringing Out the Dead* is an anguished film: a masterly one but not one to threaten *Taxi Driver*'s iconic status. In spite of Cage's expressively self-lacerating performance, achieving the look of sainthood that Old Testament prophets sought by a sojourn in the desert and even experiencing a hallucinogenic ecstasy that's given the works by Scorcese's wild camera, Cage's missionary loner lacks the psychotic power of De Niro's tribal outcast. It's like someone revving the throttle: impressive noise, but never involving.'

Los Angeles Times film critic Kenneth Turan was even less enthusiastic. He wrote, '*Bringing Out the Dead* is at its best capturing the crazed cacophony of lives sustained by adrenaline and caffeine, as feckless ambulance personnel fling themselves into the maw of the city at night in a whirl of sirens, anxiety and blinking lights. Though there's no denying that this is beautiful film-making, *Bringing Out the Dead* is a film you admire rather than warm up to.'

He described Nick as 'spaced out' and found Frank's co-dependent relationship with recovering junkie Mary unconvincing, adding, 'Despite the virtuosity with which it's made and the way it's enlivened by the periodic use of black humour, *Bringing Out the Dead* has the same kind of difficulty connecting with the audience that Frank has with Mary.'

Nick had been considering the lighthearted *The Family Man*, then set to be directed by Curtis Hanson as his follow-up to *LA Confidential*, as his next movie after *Bringing Out the Dead* but he dropped out of that project to rejoin his action-adventure movie mentor Jerry Bruckheimer in the high-speed drama *Gone in 60 Seconds*, a remake of a critically panned 1974 drive-in genre movie of the same title which starred and was directed by HB Halicki. He had been looking to return to the big action-adventure epic format ever since starting work on *Bringing Out the Dead*, and had toyed with the idea of joining director Ron Howard on *The Sea Wolf*, an adaptation of Jack London's famous novel. The book had been filmed several times, including a notable 1941 version starring Edward G Robinson as the blood-thirsty sea captain who rescues the survivors of a commercial shipwreck. But *The*

Sea Wolf ran into problems over the budget and finding the right location for a drama set on the ocean, so he opted for the new version of *Gone in 60 Seconds*, which was scripted by Scott Rosenberg, who had previously written *Con Air* and *Beautiful Girls*. Besides, a Bruckheimer eardrum-destroying action movie was a tried and trusted route for him. The film was originally set in Boston and around Massachusetts but the location was switched to Southern California so that Nick could be close to home and Patricia.

The movie tells the story of a reformed auto thief who must assemble a crew of car thieves and steal 50 specific vehicles during one night in a bid to save his troubled brother (played by Giovanni Ribisi, who was Medic Wade in *Saving Private Ryan* and also had a recurring role on the TV series *Friends*.) Also in the cast are veteran actor Robert Duvall, British soccer superstar-turned-actor Vinnie Jones, *Unforgiven* and *Titanic* actress Frances Fisher, rapper Master P and James Duval, who had previously appeared in *The Weekend*, *Independence Day* and *SLC Punk*.

Critics hated the original film but admitted it contained a memorable 40-minute car chase so it was ripe fodder on to which Bruckheimer could put his memorable stamp, especially with Rosenberg's screenplay. The tall tale really appealed to car fanatic Nick, who had an opportunity to do his own driving stunts despite objections from his studio bosses, who were worried that their insurance budget would be busted if he got injured.

Hot new actress Angelina Jolie played his love interest. Bruckheimer said, 'I had just worked with her father. I worked with Jon Voight on *Enemy of the State* and I thought it was appropriate to hire his daughter. He was such a gentleman. She's hot in more ways than one.

'In the film, she and Nick are an item. They were an item six years ago before he left town to straighten out his life, and he comes back and one of the first people he calls is his ex-flame. Nick's character is somebody that used to be on the other side of the law and he's changed his ways and now is on the right side of the law. But really he has to get his brother out of a problem that he's in. There's a strong romance between them. It pulls at the heart-strings. Nick is a romantic guy and she is amazing.'

One day while working, Jolie asked a 'gofer' to fetch her a cup of coffee. To her horror, when the pretty blonde returned — coffee in hand — Jolie discovered it was Patricia, who was on the set visiting her husband. Embarrassed Jolie apologised profusely but good-natured Patricia shrugged it off. She told her, 'Don't worry about it, I do it all the time at home.'

Although Nick was working relentlessly, he took a break during the filming of *Gone in 60 Seconds* to fly to San Francisco with Patricia and Enzo for the wedding of her brother David and *Friends* star Courteney Cox. Pat danced with Enzo at the reception at the trendy prohibition-style Bimbo's 365 club near Fisherman's Wharf, while Nick looked on with a smile.

After having made *Snake Eyes*, *8MM* and *Bringing Out the Dead*, Nick admitted, 'My last three movies have been pretty dark. They've made me far more quiet, reflective and introspective.' So he decided to repeat the game plan he had used after winning his Oscar. He said, 'I got so many offers to play dark, self-destructive characters after *Leaving Las Vegas*. Instead, I did a series of popcorn movies that I felt would make me more accessible to mainstream audiences. You can't be successful in this business unless you're embraced by a mass audience.'

His popcorn movies, of course, were his action trilogy: *The Rock*, *Con Air* (both produced by Bruckheimer) and *Face/Off*. Now Nick was ready to record some more sweet music for his self-proclaimed action album. So what better choice than a noisy Bruckheimer car-chase epic? After all the heat Nick had taken over *8MM*, it was ironic that London's *Time Out* magazine had once described the original movie as 'a rousing exercise in auto-snuff'.

Nick said, 'It's pure action. I owe a lot to Jerry. As a young man, I lived the fast life. I drove motorcycles. I collect cars, but nobody would cast me in those kind of action films until Jerry cast me in *The Rock*. There's kind of an adrenalin when we work together. There's a process. You're sort of under the gun and you have to make things work and develop the material as you go along. And that's both exciting and terrifying. But something in that "no net" style of working, where there's nothing underneath you, sparks the activity. So you just sort of go with it. But it's fun. It actually allows a lot of the actors to become more of a part of the great process. I know Jerry likes to collaborate.' He casually explained he was returning to mainstream action movies 'because I'm an action kind of guy'.

That was not his only motivation; he enjoyed the combination of fast cars and a reformed character returning to crime for a worthy cause. He told *Los Angeles Daily News* writer Bob Strauss, 'I am a car freak and that did have a lot to do with my decision to make the movie. They built up the backstory of the two brothers and his needing to go back into a life of crime to, ultimately, do good. That to me was interesting, because that's not your standard, politically correct action hero. I thought the idea of having people root for a car thief would be unique.'

Bruckheimer was pleased to be teaming up with Nick again. He said, 'He's a wonderful actor. I'm lucky to be with him and to be able to make a third movie together, which is very exciting. The first two, *The Rock* and *Con Air*, did phenomenally, so hopefully we'll follow in those footsteps and do it all over again.' Bruckheimer regarded joining forces with Nick as almost a family reunion. He said, 'It's like going to camp. You go to camp and then you go to school, and then you come back to camp again. It's the same thing. It's a reunion. Nick's a friend and we talk all through the year, whether we're working on a picture or not. He's such a gracious individual and so friendly, warm and giving that it's just great to be with him.'

It was also the most lucrative deal of Nick's career up to that point. After accepting just $1 million for his role in *Bringing Out the Dead*, which had a budget of only $32 million, he was joining the exclusive $20 million club, whose members included Tom Cruise, Mel Gibson, Harrison Ford and his old friend Jim Carrey. On top of that staggering salary he was also to receive 15 per cent of every dollar the movie grossed at the box office, not just on the designated profit. He seemed embarrassed about his phenomenal deal. He confessed, 'I wish that actors' contracts were not public domain. These contracts are far more intricate than they seem. What this proves to me is that I got very lucky in my ability to do so many different kinds of roles. It didn't always look as if things would turn out this way for me.

'It's kind of a tricky subject to talk about because money tends to evoke all kinds of emotions, and it can get in the way of the movie itself and the work itself. I don't think any actor likes to have their salary publicised. It wasn't something I ever imagined would get out so fast. It was like the second I signed the deal it was in the trades. If it's an action-based vehicle or a large studio movie and that's the going rate for that kind of film, then I'm all for it, get paid. But I wouldn't want a film-maker with a lower-budget movie to think, well, I'm not going to Nick because he has to be paid that much. I've equally made a point in my career that I will do pictures for a fraction of my salary, and I want to keep that message out there. Sometimes it's important to cut my price.'

Nick is a realist when it comes to the movie business, which he recognises is all about 'commerce'. He accepts that it is in part thanks to the success of his action trilogy that he has become a force to be reckoned with in the movie industry. He said, 'The success of *The Rock*, *Con Air* and *Face/Off* all at the same time really did put me in this position.' And on top of having three blockbuster hits, winning an Oscar around the same time added to his bankability.

Whatever Nick does, it constantly appears that there are critics out there who want to pick fault with him. Now he was being accused of copping out. Shane Danielson of the British newspaper *The Independent* asked, 'If, as he claims, the real challenge now is to act, rather than to perform — to command a film, rather than simply to dominate it — then his decision to make another mindless action flick seems faintly perverse, a comprehensive waste of time and talent. Why bother?'

This kind of attitude infuriates Nick. He said, 'Look, it's just a big, dumb, popcorn movie. Pure escapism. And sure, critics might not appreciate that, but I feel like I'm ready for it now. I've just done some very intense, very dark character studies in a row, and now I just want to enjoy myself. And I think I'm allowed to do that. Fundamentally, I think a good performance has a kind of resonance about it, a truth and honesty or whatever — and that holds true whether it's a comedy or a drama or some big-budget action movie. Working within a particular genre doesn't stop you from trying to do interesting work. Often it's what you can do within the boundaries of that style, how you can subvert it a little, or what you can bring to it, that makes for something really powerful.'

Nick even wrote an article for the London *Evening Standard* defending his decision to make different kinds of films. He wrote, 'When I won the Oscar for *Leaving Las Vegas* I made a conscious decision that I would do smaller films as well as big, action blockbusters. I was in the middle of making *The Rock* when I won the Oscar. Afterwards I thought it was best to forget about the award, not get high on myself — and not risk becoming pretentious as an actor.

'I hope I'll continue to make movies that are thought-provoking and emotionally challenging — but I don't want to start smoking Gitanes and saying I will only do that. Because I also have a love for popcorn movies like *Gone In 60 Seconds*. The real challenge as an actor in action roles like this — while there is a formula to it — is that you have to be very concise. You can do what you want with the character, but make sure it serves the structure because you have to keep this big engine rolling. But the real attraction is that ever since a kid I wanted to be Charles Bronson or Steve McQueen.

'Audiences are smart and when they go to action movies they want credible performances, to make the illusion more real. I want to believe that this guy can drive this car that fast. A lot of great actors are following suit, they're not worried about expressing themselves in a genre picture like this. They're doing it very well, it's been great for them in return.'

On another occasion he repeated his praise for McQueen, saying that he modelled his Memphis Raines character on him. He said, 'I was trying to copy a certain mode where you try to do as little as possible and see if it's still interesting. Steve McQueen has always been my model for that, because he seemed like he did nothing but still it was interesting to watch.'

He was under no illusions that the film would be great art, and had no apologies for that. 'Gone in 60 Seconds is the type of movie you go to in order not to think about anything,' he said. 'It's like putting on a certain kind of music where you're not concentrating. I go there, I get the popcorn, I get my mind off my problems.'

Of all the exotic and vintage cars earmarked for theft, the star was a 1967 Shelby GT 500 Ford Mustang, a fastback designed by auto legend Carroll Shelby, which was nicknamed Eleanor. Twelve Mustangs were used for her scenes, which involved Nick driving in a hair-raising car chase and leaping the car over a traffic jam — leaving her badly battered in the process. Only one was a genuine Shelby, and that was actually a 350 with a body modified to look like the more powerful model.

Production designer Jeff Mann explained, 'The 1967 fastback embodies the best of the Shelby Mustang's brutish but sexy qualities.' But he added, 'There's no reason to sacrifice the real thing.'

Carroll Shelby, who won the Le Mans 24 hour race in 1959, produced his Mustangs from 1965 to 1970, when they were killed off by rising insurance costs and stricter car safety standards. Only 2,048 were built in 1967, at an original price of $4,200. A model in excellent condition today would go for more than $45,000. Shelby, who married British-born Cleo Shelby in 1967, kept one of each models of Mustang he designed and has had only one stolen — and that, ironically, was a 1967 GT 500 fastback. 'I went out to lunch and it was gone,' he told USA Today.

By another irony, presumably not lost on Nick, Steve McQueen drove a 1968 fastback in another classic car-chase movie, Bullitt.

The cars were not the only stylish elements of the film. Nick had a jacket specially designed, one into which he could put all the tools he needed for his character to steal cars. It was suggested that once the movie came out it might be a hot new fashion item. Nick said, 'I hope not.'

One accessory likely to become a sought-after item, at least for people who could afford it, was his wrist watch. While he was working on Gone in 60 Seconds, luxury lifestyle magazine The Robb Report named him in their Best of the Best list in 1999 for the Patek Philippe timepiece he favours wearing.

Nick, who loves cars, thoroughly enjoyed making Gone in 60 Seconds, which was a real relief valve for him.

In preparation for the role he had extended his passion for driving to include racing cars and said, 'Whenever I feel I'm losing my sense of freedom and need to replenish myself, I get into a very fast car and zoom around a track. It sort of blows away the pressure. It's a very fast way of getting your mind off your troubles, because you're focused on staying alive driving round that track.'

Ironically, though, when Nick was involved in an accident in one of his luxury cars, he was not even driving. In October 1999 his chauffeur-driven Bentley was in a crash when a teenager driving a Toyota turned in front of the car on Hollywood Way in Burbank. He was on his way to the NBC television studios to tape an interview for the Tonight Show with Jay Leno.

Lt Joe Latta said, 'She cut in front of him and it went crunch.' The car suffered only moderate damage, according to Lt Don Brown, but the repair bills were expected to run into the thousands because of the make.

Nick also learned about stunt driving for the role, although, perhaps surprisingly, he did not enjoy that. He told Rolling Stone, 'That takes a lot of concentration, because you never know when you can shoot past a mark or spin out or hit something or somebody. They put me in stunt-driving school for a couple of days, which, to be honest, I didn't enjoy. I don't like peeling out, burning rubber, doing 360s and 180s. But I do like race-car driving — what happens when you hit an apex and come out of the apex of a curve.'

He could also drive 'virtual' cars pretty well. A few weeks before *Gone* opened, he and a group of friends sneaked through the back door of the NASCAR Silicon Motor Speedway at Universal City Walk, a lifestyle theme park next to Universal Studios in Hollywood. He played for about 30 minutes, coming in sixth of 21 racers, before leaving, again through the back door. He did not leave empty-handed; a sales assistant recognised him and gave him a matching Dale Earnhart tee-shirt and cap. Tragically Earnhart himself was later gone in less than 60 seconds, dying in a crash while taking part in a NASCAR race in 2001.

During filming of *Gone in 60 Seconds*, the cars to be 'stolen', many of them one-of-a-kind models borrowed from serious collectors and worth hundreds of thousands of dollars, were watched over carefully to avoid any possibility of damage. The cars' minders must have kept an equally careful eye on one of the film's technical consultants — a convicted car thief Nick and Bruckheimer had met during research for *Con Air* at Folsom Prison. He turned up on the set each day accompanied by a prison guard.

Thanks to the movie Nick learned a new profession. If ever he could no longer get work as an actor he was by now an expert at stealing cars — although he confessed that he would not be Gone in 60 Seconds. He said, 'I might need a brick to do it in 60 seconds. Usually you do it with a butter knife but I don't want to explain how to steal a car.' The police must have breathed a sigh of relief that Nick was being such a responsible citizen.

Bruckheimer also said the team did learn quite a lot about stealing cars but they did not show many technical details on screen. He said, 'We have one little bit with Lo-Jack. What we're showing is pulling these cars into containers with copper wires around them that interferes with the signals.'

Lo-Jack is an automated system which uses a homing device to track stolen cars.

However, some police forces were worried about the possible impact of the film. In Maryland, Baltimore County Police stepped up patrols near cinemas and car parks when the film opened. Corporal Vicki Wareheim said, 'It's a direct response to the movie. It's a pro-active stance.'

Detective Sergeant Bob Jagoe of Baltimore Regional Auto Theft Team added, 'This is a sport to a lot of kids who are impressionable. Kids who steal cars tell me they think they're in a movie when they do it. It's thrill-seeking and recreational. The movie reinforces the idea that it's a sexy thing to do. The possibility is there. You know, monkey see, monkey do. If they're already stealing cars they might try a new technique.'

And in Canada the Royal Canadian Mounted Police blamed the film for a dramatic rise of car thefts in Burnaby, a working-class suburb of Vancouver with a population of 180,000. Normally car thefts ran at an average of 20 a week; the weekend *Gone in 60 Seconds* opened the figure jumped to 31.

Constable Phil Reid said, 'It would be silly for us not to think it is a factor. It does raise an eyebrow.'

The film was launched at a première at the National Theater in the Los

Angeles suburb of Westwood, home to the University of California, Los Angeles. Guests who attended the screening and went on to a party at the Peterson Automotive Museum included Bruckheimer, director Dominic Sena, stars Nick, Angelina Jolie — with her brand new husband Billy Bob Thornton — Vinnie Jones, Robert Duvall, Giovanni Ribisi and Delroy Lindo, as well as Nick's *The Rock* director Michael Bay, his *Gone In 60 Seconds* co-star Tom Sizemore, James Coburn, who appeared with him in *Deadfall*, and his cousins Sofia and Roman Coppola. Other luminaries were Disney boss Michael Eisner, who was accompanied by former car company boss Lee Iacocca — who took Carroll Shelby with him when he moved from Ford to Chrysler — Ben Affleck, Melanie Griffith and Antonio Banderas, Robert Towne, Juliette Lewis, Joel Silver, Anthony Edwards, Rupert Everett, Andy Garcia and Jon Lovitz.

The party was the first major public outing for Jolie and Thornton after their surprise nuptials a few weeks earlier. But when pictures of the event were published, Patricia was nowhere to be seen.

Despite the star power of three Oscar-winners, Nick, Duvall and Jolie, critics pretty much dismissed the film as too much talk and not enough action — especially not enough car action.

Daily Variety went straight to the point, opening its review, 'Big scenes at the beginning and end of *Gone in 60 Seconds* prominently feature an auto compactor, which is exactly what should be used on this lemon. Perfectly dreadful in every respect, this big-budget remake of the late HB Halicki's 1974 indie hit may well rep the nadir of the Bruckheimer (and Simpson) franchise, and doesn't even rate on the most basic level as a good car-chase picture.'

The reviewer went on, 'Director Dominic Sena makes no attempt to build suspense from the thefts and getaways; it's only the spectacle of crunching metal, crashing glass and squealing rubber that interests him. But pic is a bore even on the level of a demolition derby, which is surprising given the importance given to hot cars in the Simpson/Bruckheimer œuvre.

The other trade paper, *The Hollywood Reporter*, was just as scathing and direct. Kirk Honeycutt wrote, 'Like a stolen car driven into a chop shop during the dead of night, *Gone in 60 Seconds* has seen all of its major components stripped away. Gone are logic, character development and nuance; this is movie-making pared to the bare essential of movement. But having streamlined this admittedly commercial vehicle for a fast box office payoff, its producers have astonishingly failed to deliver the anticipated jolts and thrills. How can a movie about an auto-theft ring contain so few car chases?

'Starring no fewer than three Academy Award winning actors and directed by video and commercial director Dominic Sena, Gone is an action movie without much action. So much footage is devoted to the design of the "boosts" — the recruitment of thieves, tracking down of cars and establishment of their exact locations — that there is time for only one substantial car chase during the final reel.'

Jack Mathews in the Los Angeles Daily News was equally unforgiving. He wrote, 'Whether it's a compliment or an insult to say that Dominic Sena's *Gone in 60 Seconds* is the ultimate popcorn movie depends on what it is about popcorn you like, eating it or hearing it explode.

'Certainly there's nothing here to chew on.

'*Gone in 60 Seconds* is a mindless, cliché-ridden action-cartoon, a blur of metal and fire and screeching tyres with bad dialogue, cardboard characters and a volume set so high it makes the Indianapolis 500 sound like chamber music.'

Los Angeles Times critic Kenneth Turan commented, 'The most regrettable thing about *Gone in 60 Seconds* is that it doesn't rise to the level of its excellent trailer. That pump-up piece of business has focus, pacing, concision and wall-to-wall action — all the things the full-scale version does without.

'Acting would only get in the way of all this frantic activity so *60* doesn't bother to offer much, instead allowing us to watch capable performers struggling with weak material. Cage lets his sunglasses do the work for him, Jolie has little outlet for her trademark charisma and Vinnie Jones comes off best by having the least to say.'

Entertainment Weekly's Lisa Schwarzbaum, grading it a D, said, 'Even hard-core escapists are bound to be defeated by the generic tough-guy twaddle and the impersonal race/crash/explode sequences. In revving up auto-eroticism for a young generation, the producer and his by-the-numbers director ought to be able to make grand auto theft at least look sharp, cool, hip, dangerous — anything but humdrum. They don't

'"This guy can drive!" a cop admiringly says of Memphis, while Cage steers madly like his really fat paycheck depends on it. Drive? Drive? This gentleman can't even start his engine.'

Randy Dotinga wrote in APB, a website devoted to crime, 'There is an even greater crime than grand-theft auto going on here. Somebody has pilfered the personalities of all these actors.

'Cage sleepwalks through his performance, one of the worst of his career. But it's not his fault that he has to spout lines like his inane advice to his fellow thieves, "Think slow, think real."

'After many tedious scenes of people standing around talking, *Gone in 60 Seconds* finally gains some momentum in the second half when the car thefts begin. But there's very little tension and any moviegoers on the edge of their seats will be there because they're getting up to leave.'

The *San Francisco Chronicle* was equally dismissive of the film as a whole but had faint praise for Nick. Critic Mick LaSalle said, 'It has real-live actors — Oscar winners, in fact, in the three main roles — but they're just working for a living this time out. The characters are clichéd. The story is unbelievable and phenomenally silly, not a good combination.

'Cage doesn't bring his patented intensity to the role of Raines. But as always, he's fun to watch. It could be anyone in the role but it might as well be Cage.'

People magazine summed it up succinctly, 'Bottom Line: Forgotten even faster.'

Who cared what the critics said? Teenage boys and young men led the rush to cinemas, and *Gone* made $25.5 million in its first three days of release, knocking the Tom Cruise blockbuster *Mission: Impossible 2* from the number one place after three weeks. When it came out on video people rushed to rent and buy it.

'In our business the public votes,' said Chuck Viane, president of distribution at Buena Vista Pictures. 'No one else.'

Nick, never one to worry about the critics' comments, would have agreed.

CHAPTER TWENTY-FOUR

FROM DRACULA TO DOMESTICITY

Bald and emaciated, with fangs and clicking, claw-like fingernails, pointed ears and rolling eyes, the creature flickering in black-and-white images was a long way from the scarily sexy Dracula epitomised by Christopher Lee and spoofed by George Hamilton. As Nick has often said, the 1922 silent horror film *Nosferatu*, was one of his earliest and deepest influences.

But the grotesque, overgrown gnome on the screen was not the German actor Max Schrek in his first — and most memorable — role as the bloodsucking vampire. Rather, it was actor Willem Dafoe, Oscar-nominated for his role in *Platoon*, playing Schrek, in turn playing Nosferatu. And it was a triumph for Nick — his first film as a fully-fledged producer bringing one of his most treasured films back to the screen — with a twist. In this film, *Shadow of the Vampire*, Schrek was portrayed not as an actor playing a vampire, but as a vampire playing an actor; his reward, not mere money, but the swan-like neck of his leading lady.

While Nick and his partner Jeff Levine had already set up Saturn Films and had a number of movies in the pipeline at various film studios, their long-term ambition was to establish themselves as an independent company taking care of every aspect of film-making. They were determined that this would not simply be a 'vanity' outfit concentrating on vehicles for Nick to star in, but an opportunity to make different material.

Shadow of the Vampire, which had been knocking around Hollywood for a decade, fitted the bill in every way when it found its way on to Nick's desk in 1998. Written by Steven Katz, who shared Nick's childhood fascination with the silent picture made by German director FW Murnau, it was a fictionalised account of the making of *Nosferatu* posing the question: who is the biggest leech — the vampire who cannot help his nature or the film-maker prepared to sacrifice, literally, his cast and crew to make a movie which will immortalise him?

Announcing the film in early 1999, between finishing work on *Bringing Out the Dead* and starting *Gone in 60 Seconds*, Nick said, 'With *Shadow of the Vampire* as Saturn's début, our goal is to establish ourselves as a long-term player in the international film business.'

His partner Levine added, 'We are fascinated by the enigmatic question Steven asked, "What if, in Murnau's pursuit of cinematic authenticity, he went beyond the accepted moral limits imposed by society?"'

Willem Dafoe had already been cast as Schrek, with John Malkovich as Murnau — a role Nick had originally envisaged for David Bowie. Like screenwriter Katz, the director, E Elias Merhige, was a virtual unknown with just one artsy, silent film to his credit. The film was to be shot in Luxembourg with a largely European crew, and BBC Films had UK rights to the finished product.

If the film was a perfect choice for Nick's first credit as producer, it was also a labour of love for Steven Katz, whose only previous credit was for writing a Tom Hanks-directed episode of the 1998 TV miniseries *From the Earth to the Moon*. He recalled, 'I was writing plays, experimental theatre in New York. I had a little company called Mission Theater and I just had this idea for a vampire movie. This was in 1988, around then. I happened to be in LA and I met an agent at CAA and I asked her, "If ever I write a screenplay, will you read it?" and she said sure. About a year later I wrote *Shadow of the Vampire*, which was my first screenplay, and I haven't written a play since.

'I think *Nosferatu* is the film that defined the vocabulary for horror movies, so you kind of see the blood of *Nosferatu* pumping through a whole century of spooky movies.

'On the other hand, I think the film itself is incredibly evocative. It's got the weirdest vampire ever put in a movie. Especially weird considering when the movie was made. The people's image of vampires at that time was this late romantic image of the very erotic, sexy vampire. The vampires you saw in Stoker's *Dracula* and LeFanu's *Carmilla*.

'He set this incredibly weird vampire against this incredibly realistic backdrop. Murnau was a very architectural director. He used a lot of realistic locations in all of his films.'

Ironically, Katz was one of the many writers who worked on various drafts of the movie *Interview with the Vampire*, based on the novel by Ann Rice and starring Tom Cruise, Brad Pitt, Antonio Banderas and Christian Slater.

Because of that 1994 film, he found his own difficult to place. He explained, 'Vampire movies have a very weird sort of relationship with Hollywood studios. They only like to make one every decade, pretty much, and I guess mine was just ill-timed. They decided not to make it. They also love making really bad vampire movies.

'So a few other directors had been attached to it and nothing had happened with it. Finally, my agent at the time was Nick Cage's agent and Nick had founded his own production company, Saturn Films. My agent gave Nick this script, knowing, as I do now, Nick's incredible love for the movie *Nosferatu*. Nick told me Max Schrek was one of his principal inspirations for actually becoming an actor. If you remember his movie *Vampire's Kiss*, he did an homage to Schrek in it.

'That was the first script that went into Nick's company and he agreed to do it. It took several years, because it was an independent film, to raise the money and get it all set up. That was basically the process.'

Katz even cast Dafoe as Schrek in his mind, having seen him on the stage in fringe productions in New York, before he had launched his film career. He suggested him to Jeff Levine. He added, 'That was kind of a dream come true. It was really funky to have the writing experience where you sit in a room and concoct an idea out of whole cloth and then see it happen. Then, like actually walk on to the set and there's the actor you always imagined playing the part getting the rubber ears put on.

'I was partially in awe of Dafoe just because he's such an incredible and professional actor. He's just so bloody good-natured. The guy had to sit in a make-up chair for four or five hours and he would trot out on to the set. He'd wait around, then they'd haul him out, then film him for 15 minutes and then the day was over and he would have to trot back to the chair and spend an hour-and-a-half as they peeled the crap off. And he was so nice about it!

'You know, it was an independent film. It wasn't an expensive film. It took about a month to shoot. There was no reason to get involved in it if you're very into the whole prima donna stuff. This was a true labour of love.'

In *Vampire*, the film within the film, *Nosferatu* is shot on location in the former Czechoslovakia, with Eddie Izzard playing actor Gustav von Wangerheim and Catherine McCormack as Greta Schroeder, the leading lady who is literally sticking her neck out for the role. Other cast members include Cary Elwes and Udo Kier, who, coincidentally, played Dracula in the 1974 film *The Blood of Dracula*.

It is based on the Bram Stoker Dracula story, but Murnau had to change the name because the Stoker family would not give him the rights to use it.

Malkovich, as Murnau, tells his film crew that the actor he has hired to play Count Orlok, the unknown Max Schrek, has immersed himself in the study of vampirism in general and this role in particular, and will only ever appear in full costume and make-up. He is a subscriber to the Stanislavski approach so beloved of Nick himself.

Schrek's first appearance — in a scene in the film within the film — is shocking, with Dafoe made up hideously as a rail-thin, bald freak with pointed ears, prominent teeth and long fingernails.

With the cast and crew unaware that Schrek is a real vampire, they treat him warily but not with fear, and for a while Murnau can control him. But he becomes increasingly more powerful, eventually attacking the 'cinematographer', who dies. On another occasion, he snatches a flying bat and casually starts eating it.

As the vampire becomes more out of control, the script includes bizarre exchanges between Murnau and Schrek; when Schrek casts a hungry eye over the cinematographer, Murnau asks, 'Why him? Why not the script girl?' only to be told, 'The script girl — I'll eat her later.' Murnau takes to his bed, dosed on laudanum, as his film continues towards the all-important final scene, in which Schrek is to sink his all-too-real fangs into Greta's neck.

In reality, Schrek — the name means 'scream' in German — was a mystery man who shot only at night. There were mysterious deaths and disappearance during the real shoot of *Nosferatu*, including the disappearance of the original cinematographer.

Director Merhige got the job, despite his lack of experience, thanks to Nick's old schoolfriend Crispin Glover. His one previous film, *Begotten*, a silent fantasy about God killing himself, thus prompting the emergence of Mother Earth and Son of Earth, was highly regarded on the festival circuit when it was released in 1991, but was seen by very few people apart from that. One of them, however, was Glover, who thought its quirky elements would appeal to Nick.

Merhige explained how the script for *Shadow* made the rounds of various studios. He said, 'Finally, it made its way to Saturn Films, which is Nick Cage's production company. Nick had a desire to get the film made, but he was in a quandary to find the right director for the project.

'What happened was that Crispin Glover — before Nick had ever started his production company — had given him a copy of *Begotten* as a present. Nick saw *Begotten* and said that he couldn't think about anything for two days except for that film and that it really affected him. So when he opened up the doors to Saturn Films' production company he decided, "OK, let's get hold of this guy because these are the kind of people I want to work with."

'Then we met and talked about everything from Nicola Tesla to Leonardo Da Vinci. We have very similar passions in art history, the history of ideas and all of that. Three days later, he sent me the script to *Shadow of the Vampire* and I knew that in that script there was a great movie to be made. I made a few passes on the script myself to get the script up to speed as a shooting script.'

He said Nick was a wonderful producer, a professional who left his director to direct but was always on hand to offer help, advice or support.

'He left it to me to make the film,' he went on. 'At the same time, he was there when I needed him — in terms of bouncing an idea off him. Or having him look at a cut of the film with a fresh pair of eyes. It's rare to find producers who make a film much better. In this case, Nick helped make the film great. First of all, he is an artist. Second of all, you can bounce ideas off him. A lot of producers want to take control of a film — like, "Oh, I'm the producer, I'm in control of the picture." There was a great deal of deference to me from him.'

Nick also helped promote the picture in the run-up to its release by narrating a daily comic-strip version of *Shadow of the Vampire* on the Internet to promote it.

Directing *Shadow* also gave Merhige a bonus — because of the stir over the vampire movie, *Begotten* was released on DVD.

From a practical point of view, the film was largely put together by two Britons, executive producer Paul Brooks and co-producer Richard Johns, who had executive-produced and produced the 1998 film *Killing Time*. Brooks met Jeff Levine on a trip to Hollywood and convinced him that with his experience of making low-budget films outside the studio system he was the man for the job, and that Luxembourg, with a friendly tax climate for film-making and castles for atmosphere, was the place to do it. He brought Johns on board and, with a budget of just $8.5 million, the pair of them started assembling the crew and some of the cast, including Eddie Izzard at Johns' suggestion. Johns was on the set the first time Nick visited and said, 'He was really sweet, really intrigued. This was his first moment as a producer.'

Thanks to its content and the film technique, which included recreating scenes from the black-and-white original as well as including some footage from the 1922 movie, but shooting the rest in colour, this was clearly a film to be launched at festivals where it would attract an audience looking for something different, rather than be sold as a mainstream movie.

It was presented at the Cannes Film Festival during Directors' Fortnight at the beginning of May 2000 and won its first rave review. Top Internet webmaster Harry Knowles, whose irreverent *Ain't It Cool News* has become one of the most influential opinion-makers in the film industry, flew from his home in Austin, Texas, to Cannes for the day to see it.

He reported, 'In *Shadow of the Vampire* we have ... what is without a doubt in my mind one of the greatest renditions of a vampire ever.

'This movie should be marketed seriously, playing up the mythology of the film and the history and reality of the mysterious circumstances surrounding the alleged Max Schrek.

'First and foremost, the credit of this film falls completely and without trepidation upon the brow of the director, E Elias Merhige. This is his sophomore film, and it is not only not a slump, but a complete and utter success. This movie isn't simply about making a movie. The film is a story about making a deal with the devil. It's a creepy friggin' nightmare of a film that makes you laugh and get real, real, real quiet. The perfect mix of the recreated scenes with vintage footage, the irising into black-and-white and the irising out into colour. While sounding extremely simple ... it's dazzling. Breathtaking.

'Merhige also directs Dafoe to the single best performance of his career. In *Shadow of the Vampire*, Dafoe melts away and all we are left with is a centuries-old vampire. A once noble human transformed so long ago into a blood-consuming monster that he can no longer recall his origins. He's gone so long that he can't remember how to turn others into creatures like him. His goblets are gone, no longer does he have servants. Instead he's a vulture, a rat, living on scraps of blood.

'What else besides Dafoe worked? EVERYTHING. John Malkovich as a determined film-maker. Also ... finally Eddie Izzard has a great film under his belt. Cary Elwes is also great, as is Udo Kier. And Catherine McCormack as the lead actress of the production.'

It was also entered in the prestigious Avignon Film Festival in June 2000 and won one of the three prizes, the Prix Tournage, or Best Picture award in the section for American films. Then it went to Toronto in September, Sitges in Spain in October and Hawaii in November.

It was finally released at the end of December 2000, only in New York and Los Angeles, to qualify it for Oscar consideration, before a wider release in January 2001.

Nick was all smiles at the première party at the Egyptian Theater, which was a benefit for American Cinematheque, an organisation which lovingly restored the historic Egyptian on Hollywood Boulevard, which was built in 1922 and hosted Hollywood's first-ever première, *Robin Hood*, starring Douglas Fairbanks. Willem Dafoe, Udo Kier and E Elias Merhige also attended the bash.

It was Nick's second new release in a week. *The Family Man* had opened only four days earlier, making $15.2 million to rank third in the box office ratings that weekend, behind the new Tom Hanks film *Cast Away* and the Mel Gibson/Helen Hunt picture *What Women Want*.

Critics raved about *Shadow of the Vampire* for the most part, praising every aspect of the cast and the production.

Todd McCarthy of *Daily Variety* wrote, 'The first and arguably the greatest vampire film, FR Murnau's 1922 *Nosferatu*, is the subject of a much-belated and stimulatingly warped "making of" in *Shadow of the Vampire*. Wholly absorbing and inspired in parts, this carefully crafted curio dares to suggest that Murnau made a Faustian pact with an actual vampire to play the title role in exchange for the neck of the film's leading lady at production's end.

'Director E Elias Merhige's first professional feature is not nearly as weird as his strikingly original student thesis film, *Begotten*, a fest and cult hit in 1991. The highly æstheticised approach to film-making espoused by Murnau, the "difficult actor" syndrome seen in the extreme and the injection of vampirism into a historical undertaking involving prominent figures all provide intriguing grist for the mill. Add to that one of the more successful representations of the making of a classic film — a considerable feat in itself — and Merhige & Co can be said to have mostly pulled off a daunting exercise.'

In *The Hollywood Reporter*, Kirk Honeycutt was equally enthusiastic, writing, '*Shadow of the Vampire* rummages through a dark and hallowed portion of early silent-movie history to create a fanciful concoction certain to please cinema buffs and lovers of vampire lore. Bravura performances by John Malkovich and Willem Dafoe spice up a savoury cinematic stew that is alternately funny, clever and a touch perverse.

'*Shadow* is one of those movies in which the actors appear to be having great fun. Udo Kier puts sweaty anxiety into his role as put-upon producer Albin Grau, and Cary Elwes revels in self-confidence as flamboyant cameraman Fritz Wagner. John Aden Gillet brings aristocratic impudence to the writer, Henrick Galeen. McCormack is the temperamental, morphine-addicted stage actress distressed at even being on a movie set and Eddie Izzard is quite good at playing the role of a man who can barely act.'

Associated Press reviewer David German wrote, 'Darkly comic and creepier than many straightforward horror flicks, *Shadow of the Vampire* is a bright and original homage to pre-talkie days. The movie simultaneously spoofs and honours the overarching conventions of the silent era, when make-up was spread with a shovel and every gesture was a Victorian stage flourish.

'Malkovich is excellent as the imperious Murnau, who is so caught up in his conceits that he believes his film can give eternal life to an already immortal vampire. There's fine support from Catherine McCormack as the haughty leading lady, Cary Elwes as a flamboyant cameraman and Udo Kier as the money-conscious producer.

'But as with Murnau and his real vampire, director E Elias Merhige's film draws its true life from a remarkable, Oscar-worthy performance by Dafoe. Though done up as Schrek's pointy-eared, emaciated Nosferatu for the entire movie, he projects himself miles beyond the make-up.'

Glenn Whipp in the Los Angeles *Daily News* also loved it, pointing out that it was the ultimate example of Method acting, in which the performer lives the character, on and off set. He wrote, 'Of course, the Method comes with its drawbacks, too, as bitingly illustrated in *Shadow of the Vampire*, which just happens to be one of the year's funniest, spookiest and most audaciously conceived movies. In the re-imagining of the silent vampire classic *Nosferatu*, we see what happens when a director goes a little too far in his quest for film immortality and casts the ultimate Method man in the title role of the blood-sucking count.

'This is a smart, sophisticated, hilarious horror-comedy that college students could enjoy alongside film buffs. And it contains a mind-bending performance from Willem Dafoe, an actor who, it should be noted, doesn't believe in the Method.'

In *The Buffalo News* critic Jeff Simon praised the film and actors — but had a special word for Nick. '*Shadow of the Vampire* is utterly and wonderfully nuts — daft, exhilarating, hilarious and poetic all at the same time,' he wrote. 'It is the truly sublime notion of *Shadow of the Vampire* that this strange actor (Schrek) who, in life, did indeed creep out those on the *Nosferatu* set by always appearing to them in full make-up and costume, was no Method actor but, in fact, a real vampire who sucked his way through the film set.

'Not least of Shadow of the Vampire's pleasure is that director Elias Merhige has done an extraordinary job of simulating the black-and-white scenes from Nosferatu in the middle of a film that is, otherwise, photographed in gorgeous colour. Merhige's only other film, Begotten, was entirely silent.

'That's how Merhige got the job here. As wild a talent as he is, this film is really Nicolas Cage's baby. A lifelong devotee of the silent film, Cage spent many of his nutso early days modelling his performances on the great silent actors (see Vampire's Kiss for Cage, the young actor, doing his best to be a sort of modern Max Schrek).

'As his first official act as a film producer, Cage plucked Steven Katz's delicious script out of Hollywood's deep freeze, shoved Merhige into the director's chair and got John Malkovich and Willem Dafoe to play the damnedest comedy team you've seen in movies in a very long time.

'I don't know about you, but the way I see it, Nicolas Cage, as a producer, is Hollywood rookie of the year.'

Internet magazine Salon, on the other hand, hated the film and hinting at a case of The Emperor's New Clothes, decided it was pretentious fare to be fawned over by pretentious lovers of art for art's sake. Andrew O'Hehir wrote, 'In Shadow of the Vampire, Malkovich stars as legendary silent-film director FW Murnau; Dafoe, in ghoulish make-up, plays a genuine vampire hired to impersonate one in Murnau's 1922 classic Nosferatu. The combination certainly sounds like the ultimate in '90s hipsterism, but all this glum and slight entertainment manages to prove is that the '90s are over.

'An art-up-the-butt avatar such as RW Fassbinder or Wim Wenders would have revelled in the archness and overripeness of this whole enterprise; who is the real vampire — the honest bloodsucker or the ruthless artist? As it is, Steven Katz's screenplay feels choppy and uncertain, but in hands like those its morphine-fuelled pace and grandiose pronouncements about aesthetics might have been rendered into a languorous, decadent delight, chocolate with an absinthe centre. E Elias Merhige, an American director known for the underground film Begotten and his music videos for Marilyn Manson, can only manage a mildly amusing spoof with some striking images, a Saturday Night Live for film students.'

As the Hollywood awards season rolled around, Dafoe was the big winner, picking up a Golden Globe award and top honours from the Los Angeles Film Critics Association. He also won the President's Award for an Outstanding Creative Performance at the Fort Lauderdale International Film Festival and a Golden Satellite award.

And he was nominated for the Best Supporting Actor Academy Award, one of two nods for the films, the other being for Best Make-up.

This was not a film that anyone expected to make a fortune, but going into the Oscar weekend it had grossed nearly $8 million, so was destined to make its production costs before going to video.

While Willem Dafoe played two roles — Schrek and Schrek playing Orlok — in Shadow of the Vampire, Nick was seen as two sides of the same character in his next starring role.

In The Family Man, he plays Jack Campbell, a powerful Manhattan money man with all the trappings of life in the fast lane — Ferrari, high-rise luxury apartment, a walk-in wardrobe where colour-coded bespoke suits await his daily choice. As a new graduate, he has headed for work experience in London, leaving behind Kate, the love of his life, played by Téa Leoni, with promises that he would return — promises that he broke.

Then one fateful Christmas Eve 13 years later, outside a New York convenience store, he brags to a would-be thief that he has no regrets in the world, not realising that the 'thief', played by Don Cheadle, is actually an angel who knows his past.

He wakes up on Christmas Day to find himself in bed with Leoni, living the life he had passed up on, the family man of the title. This means coping with a wife, two children, in-laws and friends — not to mention a humble job as manager of his father-in-law's tyre sales store. When he drives from his new suburban house in New Jersey — wearing a tatty track suit instead of his usual haute couture — the doorman at his Manhattan home will not let him in, a neighbour with whom he has shared a joking flirtation for years denies all knowledge of him and when he heads for his office, he is equally unrecognised. Worse, watching financial news on television he sees an old rival at his financial firm, bearing his title and taking credit for a major deal which he had actually put together.

As he stumbles through his new life, not knowing his best friends' names, striking out at the bowling alley when he is supposed to be a champion and — worst of all — having to change his 'son's' nappies, only his six-year-old daughter realises he is not who he seems to be.

Director Brett Ratner originally refused to read the script, partly because he was too busy working on the Jackie Chan/Chris Rush film *Rush Hour* and partly because he had no interest in doing a romantic comedy. Then the day he finished the *Rush Hour* shoot, his agent called and begged him to read it, and he loved it so much he was in tears by the end. Unfortunately for him, by this time *LA Confidential* director Curtis Hanson was attached, along with Nick. They both dropped out of the project and the script was sent to John Travolta. Ratner had been calling Beacon Productions asking for the movie and, as it happened, Travolta wanted him to direct. Ratner got the job, but Travolta ultimately passed on the role.

Ratner then went after Nick, who had not played a comedy since *It Could Happen to You* in 1994, only to have Nick turn him down five times before he was happy with the script and the direction the film was taking.

'Any movie he's in with a woman — *Raising Arizona*, *Moonstruck* — there is a chemistry,' Ratner told the *Los Angeles Times*. 'He's like an underdog, because he's not the most handsome or automatically gorgeous. And he's able to express the frustrating moments everyone has. If you watch those old movies with Jimmy Stewart – there was a bigness there. Cage has that same old-fashioned quality.

'Nick was the guy I really had to convince and it was such a difficult process to get him to agree because it's just like when you read *Fargo*, it reads like a TV movie but the Coen brothers' vision of it is so interesting. What I tried to explain to him was, "Look, Nick, I'm not making *Mr Mom* here. I'm making *Kramer v Kramer* but with humour." I gave him specific examples of scenes from those movies so he could understand the tone of what I was going after. Like in *Kramer v Kramer*, the French toast scene.'

While wincing at many aspects of his new life and desperately trying to recapture his old one by gestures like trying on a $2,500 Ermenigildo Zegna suit —

only to wince even more when Kate buys him a Zegna knock-off and cannot understand his pained reaction — he gradually starts falling in love all over again, and even finds himself admitting that there is something to be said for family life, though he is not quite sure what it is.

Nick believes the turning point for the unhappily transplanted Manhattanite comes when he watches a video of his New Jersey counterpart unembarrassedly singing the Delfonics' song 'La, La, La, La, I Love You' to his wife at a birthday party, in front of a crowd of friends.

'To be that open, to be that free, to just sing to your wife on her birthday — diamonds aren't going to be more meaningful than that, you know what I mean?' he explained. 'That's what he has to understand; that Manhattan Jack, with his obsession with money, is missing the boat. He's chased the wrong muse.'

At the end of the film, inevitably, he is restored to his real life and tracks down Kate, whom he discovers as a driven, high-powered single lawyer — as opposed to a socially conscious attorney taking on cases for poor people at cut rates in her New Jersey existence — living in Manhattan but about to move to France. Grieving for the family life he now knows he has missed out on, he asks her to give them a second chance. Just as she had pleaded with him at the airport all those years ago to tear up his ticket, it was his turn to beg her to stay. 'I like the idea of running through the airport and trying to get the girl back,' he said. 'That's a character I find easy to play.'

When he agreed to make the film, he worried at first that his New Jersey character would be too bland, but Ratner convinced him not to go overboard with the performance. Nick said, 'I resisted the temptation to be crazy or wild, which was difficult because that is where I feel most comfortable. There was a tension there in the character which was fine because I was trying to be more subtle. And we both agreed that the movie should be a throwback to the Capra-esque style of film-making and I was definitely tipping my hat to Jimmy Stewart.'

Inevitably, given the theme that a relatively poor but happy family life beats living for nothing but money and material things — and the all-important presence of an angel — the film was compared Frank Capra's classic Jimmy Stewart picture *It's a Wonderful Life*.

Nick also saw other elements in the film that appealed. He said, 'We were going for the feel of *Heaven Can Wait* with *A Christmas Carol* and *Kramer v Kramer*. I had done a few films in a row which were intense, dark, dramatic portraits of unhappy people. I thought it would be a nice change of pace to be in a movie that's a little more life-affirming.'

Ratner revealed that when Nick saw the completed film for the first time, he wept.

'I am soft that way,' Nick, the devoted father, admitted. 'Though it can't be corny. It can't just be *manipulato*. It has to have just the right amount of edge to make it feel real enough for me to get misty-eyed. I like love stories. I always have.

'I've always felt comfortable in romantic films. There's something that occurs in the chemistry with an actress where you feel like you can go places, emotionally, a lot easier than in, say, a war picture. The love story, in every case, evokes myriad emotions because that's the way love is. So I have a lot of fun with it and I feel comfortable in it, and I guess I was excited to get back into that mode.' His statement gave a clue to his strong admiration for his Captain Corelli character in *Captain Corelli's Mandolin*.

Ironically, given the final disintegration of his marriage, which ended little more than a month before the release of *The Family Man*, Nick admitted the enormous appeal of New Jersey Jack's lifestyle — though he had no ambitions to give up the movie world to work in a garage. He said, 'The ideal thing for me would be to have a home, kids, a family, make one movie a year and live in a neighbourhood where kids can ride their bikes and have friends down the street. That would be nice.'

He added, 'I think both characters have been similar to me in my own life. I'm probably more Manhattan Jack than New Jersey Jack but I don't think either one is necessarily better than the other. I think both could learn from one another.'

Recalling his visit to his old neighbourhood in Long Beach, he described it as his own moment of reflecting on what might have been. He said, 'I remember thinking to myself that if I hadn't really forced myself to kind of make it in the movie industry and come to Los Angeles and Hollywood, things probably would have been so much less complicated. So I think I had a "what if" period there.'

Like Nick, Ratner was at pains to point out that the film was not judging one lifestyle to be superior to the other. He said, 'We never thought we're going to make a judgement in this movie that it's better to be poorer and have a family and you'll be happy, or it's better to be rich. The idea is that it's not judgemental. We're not saying that Nick's life as an investment banker with an enormous amount of money is a bad life. It's a good life and Nick has made it a good life. What we're saying is, this is a situation where you look and you say, "What if?" And that's why the movie ends with a certain amount of ambiguity.'

Nick's seven-year gap from comedy and success in big-budget, fast-paced action movies left some people unprepared for his approach to Jack, though once again he was at pains to point out he had always enjoyed moving through different kinds of films and characters.

Even Marc Abraham, producer of the $60 million film, said, 'Nick is a really complicated guy. I never met any actor who's more of an artist than Nick. He can't stop working. He's comfortable in a world that's moving pretty fast, but he's also a sensitive guy. It surprised me that he'd be sensitive. My image of him is a tough guy.'

Nick understood his impression, telling the New York *Daily News*, 'That's the perception of me in the past five years. But action is just one part of a larger package. The public who have been with me for some time remember *Guarding Tess*, *Moonstruck* and *It Could Happen To You* — movies that signal that this role was in my library. It just took me seven years to get back to it.

'I can go from comedy to action to drama. That way I stay fresh and can keep working as much as I want. That's been my plan from the beginning and I'm pretty stubborn. I think I won "Most Stubborn" in my high-school yearbook. That was really the worst. Others had "Most Charming" and "Most Exciting". But maybe stubborn's not so bad.'

Abraham eventually realised how right Nick was for the role — but he admitted that during the wrangling over the final script there were times he wished Nick would just go away.

'Movies like this are made by the casting,' he told the Los Angeles *Daily News*. 'If you don't have the right star, someone with a certain amount of power, in the role, they can be slight. But if you have a great actor in the role, they can definitely rise to a different zone.

'And we had to have a guy who could believably play a titan of industry and be a fish out of water. Other comedic actors out there could mug their way through the life they were thrust into, but not easily be believed as an individual who could have been a really serious king of arbitrage.

'It was a very painful process. And there were times, before I knew Nick, when I really disliked him. That was because all I kept getting from his agents was, "Well, he's in … No, he's out … Now he's in … Now he's out." So I thought, the hell with this guy. Even though I think he's great, I'm not gonna be tortured by him every day.

'But now that I know him and had such a wonderful experience working with him, I so understand it because he's such an artist. Nick is an extremely sensitive person. I mean, he's played tough guys and done broad comedy, but actually he's one of the most vulnerable people. He is an organism which absorbs the universe, almost, without any kind of shield around him. And I think that's why he's such a wonderful actor.'

Shooting the movie, which started in November 1999, had moments of hilarity and drama. In one key scene — in which Jack chases Kate through their suburban house as they fight over the last piece of chocolate cake, only to end up having passionate sex on the stairs with cake and creamed smeared all over their faces and clothes — Nick got a crumb lodged in his throat, reducing him to a coughing fit while the crew called for glasses of water and volunteers to perform the Heimlich manœuvre.

A much more threatening medical drama shut down production for ten days, when Leoni's baby daughter, Madelaine, developed double pneumonia and had to go into hospital.

The Family Man was the first film for Leoni, who is married to *X Files* star David Duchovny, after the birth of Madelaine and she was delighted to be doing a comedy. Leoni, who starred in the hit television series *The Naked Truth* and was cast in *Jurassic Park III*, said, 'Her illness was one of the most emotionally and physically altering events of my life. It was extremely scary and painful. Something like this does give you perspective. I was a different person after I came back to the set. It made me feel more deeply about everything. More than anything else, it's the gloriousness of my family I appreciate now.'

Despite her devotion to David and Madelaine, just as Nick said he identified more with Manhattan Jack than New Jersey Jack, Leoni said she was far removed from her suburban Kate character. 'We don't have a mini-van and I don't bowl,' she joked.

Dutifully promoting the film when it was released in Christmas 2000, knowing that interviewers were itching to ask him about the divorce was difficult for Nick, given that the movie was about choices and regrets. He repeatedly insisted he would not discuss his personal life, but he was clearly choosing his words carefully. He told one interviewer, 'I'm happy with the choices I made. I have to be. That's the only way to keep walking forward in your life. You can't live your life fully if you live with remorse and regret.' To another he said, 'I think that all the choices I have made — I'm not going to go into detail about my family life — in terms of family and things have been some of the best choices I have made.'

On yet another occasion he said, 'I'm really happy with my life, but I also know everything can be transitory. Life is always full of surprises and I'm not going to let myself get lazy and say it's always going to be this way.'

The post-première party for *The Family Man* was held at the Palladium club in Hollywood, where Seal sang *This Could Be Heaven* to an audience which included Nick, co-stars Don Cheadle and Jeremy Piven, along with Hollywood heavyweights including Stacey Snider, Irving Azoff, Jerry Bruckheimer, Robert Evans, Joel Silver and Russell Simmons.

Critics generally liked the film, while agreeing it does not match up to its Capra predecessor, though not all of them bought the line that the film does not make judgements between the two lifestyles.

Michael Rechtshaffen of *The Hollywood Reporter* wrote, 'Its "what if?" hook might be pure, undistilled *It's a Wonderful Life*, but what *The Family Man* lacks in original concept it more than compensates for in skilled execution.

'A fantasy/romantic comedy about a driven Wall Street exec who is offered a valuable glimpse of the path not taken, the picture is an unexpectedly introspective surprise.

'With Nicolas Cage (making a welcome return from action-movie purgatory) and Téa Leoni (in by far her best performance to date) on hand to bring it all home, Universal appears to have found the sleeper capper to a remarkable year.'

CNN reviewer Paul Clinton said, 'This is a story about second chances, and yes, it is a homage to those 1930s and '40s films made by the legendary Frank Capra — especially *It's a Wonderful Life*, his crowd-pleaser starring Jimmy Stewart about the man who got a look at how different the world could have been. Many cynics called that overly sentimental 1946 film and others he directed "Capracorn". Some doubtless will make similar claims about *The Family Man*.

'Sure, this film wears its heart on its sleeve, and director Brett Ratner and scriptwriters David Diamond and David Weissman have manipulated this story to tug at your emotions shamelessly. But so what? It works. Tug away!

'It's been a while since Cage has starred in a flat-out romantic comedy. Thankfully, this time he's dropped most of his quirky mannerisms and strange speech patterns and gives a straightforward, heartfelt performance.

'Another nice touch is that this film makes no judgements about the two different lifestyles lived by Cage's character. There are no bad choices or good choices, the film implies, but only choices.

'Yes, this movie is schmaltzy — but again, so what? It's also heartfelt, a great date movie and perfect for the holidays.'

Jack Mathews, critic for the New York *Daily News*, agreed. 'On no level does *The Family Man* approximate the wonder and emotional depth of Frank Capra's Christmas evergreen. In fact, its logical lapses fly in the face of that film. We're asked to believe that a man with no memory of his last 13 years, and no desire to remember it, can move among people he has never met and not be immediately throttled and transported to Bellevue [a large New York psychiatric hospital].

'But for those who pay their money and suspend their disbelief, there are rewards. Cage is a wonderful light comedian.

'There's a sweetness, and sense of inevitability, to the relationship between Jack and Kate, and the actors live it with an almost defiant earnestness. She looks at him in a way that confirms that love, indeed, is blind, and as Jack falls in love all over again, only an *American Psycho* would say that Manhattan bachelorhood has more to offer.'

And the *San Francisco Chronicle*'s Bob Graham said, 'In *The Family Man*, Nicolas Cage gives a performance that invites audiences to lay cynicism aside in a romantic fable about a rich Wall Street wheeler-dealer bachelor who learns to love the life he might have had as an ordinary suburban family man.

'Actually, *The Family Man* is not just a fable about what might have been. It is a story about someone who learns to love his own life. Anyone can do it.'

Despite the protestations from Nick and Ratner that the film made no judgements, *Los Angeles Times* critic Kevin Thomas profoundly disagreed. Pointing out that Leoni's Kate is a nag who has clearly killed Jack's ambitions once and does so again when, in a cunning bit of plot contrivance, he is offered a job at his Manhattan firm, he wrote, 'It all makes you wonder. Kate is presented as the perfect wife, but if so, why can't she understand that someone of Jack's obvious brilliance might not be fulfilled selling tyres? For that matter, what if it had been Kate who had wanted to go off to London? If Jack had tried to stop her, he would have been labelled a male chauvinist pig.

'There's a false dichotomy running through this film, making career and family an either-or choice, and Kate, for all Leoni's radiance, is more killjoy than dream girl. Cage is a protean actor of wide range and authority, and the film's cast is large and substantial. But in terms the corporate Jack would understand, it's still no deal.'

Nevertheless, he added, '*The Family Man* is an ambitious, carefully crafted Christmas movie that tries to be *It's a Wonderful Life* for the new millennium but lacks the honesty to pull it off. Not even a sincere and heroic effort by Nicolas Cage can redeem the film's essential phoniness. Still, Cage's charisma and a lot of shameless heart-tugging will surely prove a potent lure with many moviegoers.'

Joe Leydon of *Daily Variety* found the plot derivative but praised Nick and Leoni. He called the film, 'A slickly-produced slice of sentimental hokum that borrows freely from a half-dozen or so other, better feel-good movies.

'Once again taking full advantage of slightly against-the-grain casting, Cage is improbably but impressively adept at playing a high-powered Wall Street warrior who's magically granted a brief glimpse of the simple life he could have lived on the road not taken.

'For more than half its length, *Family Man* wrings easy laughs from Jack's not-so-quiet desperation in lower middle-class discontent. (Cage conveys Jack's mounting horror with just the right degree of darkly comic edginess.) After an hour or so, however, Ratner and his writers attempt a jarring about-face, to show Jack falling in love with his wife, his children and his low-profile life as a salt-of-the-earth Joe Average. The switch is, to put it charitably, a great deal less than persuasive.'

In the Internet magazine *Salon*, Andrew O'Hehir agreed. He said, 'Nicolas Cage provides a positively delightful razor's-edge performance as Jack Campbell, a filthy rich, swinging, single investment banker who wakes up one morning as a New Jersey tyre salesman with a wife and two kids. Jack is such an unredeemed rascal, and his reaction to his new life in suburbia so histrionic, that we hardly notice the movie painting itself into a narrative corner where it finally dies of neglect.

'Cage can do more by simply exhaling than any actor in movie history; with one nearly silent expulsion of breath he can express all the existential disappointment of European philosophy. When he opens suburban Jack's closet for the first time to view the baby blue sweater vests and Hawaiian shirts, he heaves a heavy sigh, "This is just *subpar*." On his first attempt to change his infant son's soiled diaper, his eyes roll back in his head as if he's about to lose consciousness, "Oh! Holy Mother of God!'

Nick, who had in a way been leading a double life of his own for months with the pretence that he and Patricia were back together while they were actually hammering out a divorce deal, was now established in a dual professional life, as producer of a critically acclaimed film as well as an actor. And if the reviews for *The Family Man* were mixed, his performance was popular and audiences enjoyed the film enough to push it past the $75 million box office mark after 12 weeks of release in America alone.

His marriage may have ended but his career was getting back into step after a series of box office and professional stumbles as he marched towards his next projects, two World War II films which could hardly have been more different.

CHAPTER TWENTY-FIVE

BATTLE FRONTS: AT HOME AND ABROAD

When Nick agreed to rejoin the Italian Army to play the lead in a big-budget version of British author Louis de Bernières' highly popular romantic novel *Captain Corelli's Mandolin*, he could have had no idea that the movie would become a love story both on and off screen. And neither could he have realised that, between the time he signed the contract to star in the film and its first screening, his love life would become publicly scrutinised and his marriage exposed as being as dramatic, complex and fictional as any of the parts he has played.

As events unfolded during 2000, it became apparent that if Nick and actress wife Patricia Arquette's marriage were a movie, no one would have believed the plot. But the true background is even more fascinating than the newspapers reported at the time. Despite their fairytale romance, their public show of affection when Nick won his Oscar, their cooing at premières and often talking about their bizarre marriage which involved them living apart in separate homes in Los Angeles for several days a week, the whole thing was destined for failure.

Nevertheless, they had maintained an eccentric and seemingly friendly relationship for more than five years. That relationship became strained when Patricia started lobbying Nick to move in with him and have a normal husband-and-wife relationship. An acquaintance revealed, 'Nick had grown used to having his own space and living the life of a married bachelor.'

Patricia was completely oblivious to what had been going through Nick's mind and was absolutely flabbergasted when process servers handed her the divorce papers while she was on the set of the movie *Little Nicky*. The unexpected turn of events certainly stopped Patricia from laughing that morning as she worked on the comedy in which she co-starred with Adam Sandler. A friend said, 'She had no idea it was coming. It was a stupid, chance remark that meant nothing to her. She was just making conversation over dinner.'

According to Nick's divorce petition, which was filed with the Los Angeles Superior Court on 24 February 2000, the two had not lived together since 10 January 1996, just nine months after their cliff-top wedding overlooking the Pacific

Ocean at Carmel, California. Citing 'irreconcilable differences' — the only grounds for divorce in no-fault California — for the break-up of the marriage, Nick asked the court to honour a 16 March 1996 agreement stating how their assets and property should be divided, and further asking the court not to order him to pay spousal support, then or at any time in the future, and the determine that he and Patricia did not have any community property. The agreement was made long before he started commanding US$20 million per picture. In March 2000, the prestigious *Forbes* business magazine rated Nick as one of the top-earning stars in Hollywood. The divorce papers appeared to confirm the long-standing rumours that while Patricia had continued to live at her modest house in Studio City, Nick had divided his time between homes in Bel Air, Malibu and the Hollywood Hills.

While he was making his movie *The Family Man*, no one on the set had had a clue that Nick was anything other than what the film title suggested. Patricia and her son and Nick's son Weston had often visited him. A crew member said, 'The cast and crew had no idea anything was going on. It seemed everything was cordial between them.'

However, those who had worked on *Gone in 60 Seconds* were not so surprised. A crew member said, 'Patricia visited the set once and they had a huge argument. He'd be on his cell phone with Patricia and he'd walk around screaming into the phone.'

Patricia was greatly upset by Nick's behaviour on the set of the high-speed movie, which was filmed in Los Angeles and his home town of Long Beach, according to crew members. One said, 'He loves danger. He loved to take his motorcycle out for a ride during lunch and when he'd come back sometimes there would be a pretty young girl on the back. He'd want to show off his driving skills and drive fast on the bike, which made everybody on the set a bit nervous. Sometimes, he'd be spotted driving down Melrose Avenue on his bike, looking at the girls. Patricia was nowhere in sight.'

Still to most people, Nick and Patricia appeared a perfectly happy married couple. They had been at a dinner party at a Los Angeles steak house only a month before the divorce shock. A waiter said, 'They seemed absolutely fine, talking together and being very attentive to each other.'

But there were others to whom the bust-up came as no surprise. If anyone had really been listening to what Patricia had been saying, they might have picked up on clues that all was not as it seemed. Just before the divorce proceedings began, Patricia hinted that all was not well when she told an interviewer, 'You can love somebody to death but it's difficult. My little girl idea of being married is quite different than it really is.' While in another interview she said, 'I think marriage is harder than being a parent.'

In an even more bizarre and unexpected turn of events, just five days after he filed for divorce, Nick withdrew his petition. Full of remorse, he instructed his lawyers to issue a request for dismissal of the case and he set about winning her back. A confidante said, 'Nick felt he'd been pushed into a corner by his advisers. He feared that unless they divorced, she would take him to the cleaners.'

Nick found himself having to eat humble pie, telling Patricia that he had made a mistake, that he still loved her and wanted her back. In his bid to make amends, Nick skipped the wrap party for *The Family Man*, which to keep in with the theme of the movie was held in a bowling alley in Los Angeles on Sunday, 2 April 2000, so he could spend more time with Patricia. The newly-reunited couple were said to be making up for lost time. Nick's absence from the party was because, according to *New York Daily News* columnist Mitchell Fink, 'They were getting reacquainted.'

Briefly, Nick and Patricia and the boys started playing house together. One astonished movie industry observer said, 'Just when everyone thought Hollywood's strangest relationship was over, it's back on — and weirder than ever.'

Before he left for Greece to start filming *Captain Corelli's Mandolin*, Nick and Patricia jetted by private plane to the Bahamas on what was supposed to be a second honeymoon in the Cayman Islands. They had been encouraged to take the trip by Weston and Enzo, who had lobbied them not to split up. They stayed for several days — going deep-sea fishing, visiting a local theme park and sightseeing. They even went house-hunting, viewing the spacious beach house of Bear Sterns financial institution's managing director emeritus Paul Hallingby, as a possible paradise retreat.

However, Nick would not remain the family man he now appeared, as, deep down, his wife had realised. Less than a month after Nick skipped his bowling alley party, Patricia was spotted alone attending the opening night of Karen Finley's one-woman fringe theatre show *Shut Up and Love Me*, in which the actress told tales of egregious sex and rolled her naked body in honey. Patricia got so engrossed in the show that she even got on stage in her platform-shoes, white-fringe jacket, studded bell-bottoms and halter top, and helped the star of the show pour the honey on to the theatre floor.

Well-known Hollywood gossip columnist Ted Casablanca also attended the event, which was staged in a theatre on trendy Santa Monica Boulevard in West Hollywood. He went outside to have a cigarette as smoking is banned in theatres, restaurants and bars in Los Angeles, and found Patricia standing on the pavement doing the same.

'At first, I thought, leave the woman alone,' said Casablanca. The openly camp columnist added, 'But that was before I had my nicotine fix out on the street, right where Pat-doll was getting hers.' Stubbing out his Marlboro, Casablanca approached her and started chatting about her *Little Nicky* movie and what it was like working with Sandler. 'I hear he's a wild man on the set. Is that true?' Casablanca asked. He went on, 'Patricia was so charming and fetching up close I kept thinking Nick Cage was a fool.' Talking about Sandler, Patricia replied, 'Oh, no. You should see how nice he is to people on the set. And not just the actors — everybody. He's very sweet.'

Deciding he would not be doing his journalistic duty if he did not ask her about her troubled relationship with Nick, Casablanca asked if she was going to give her marriage another try. Casablanca said, 'If ever I thought a human face wasn't capable of going from Mary Pickford to Medusa in a millisecond, I was quite wrong. My question was followed by some lovely conversation-killing silence. She finally offered, "I haven't decided. And even if I had, I wouldn't be telling a gossip column." At this point, the star's smile returned. Barely. I explained I'd had numerous queries from readers, which I had, wanting to know her romantic status. Patricia snapped, "They'll just have to wonder." '

The fans did not have to wonder very much longer. Nick and Patricia were drifting further and further apart. And it was more than just the miles that would come between them as Nick shot movies in Greece and then Hawaii. When Patricia visited the set of *Captain Corelli's Mandolin*, she stayed in a house on one side of Sami, the Greek harbour on the island of Cephalonia where de Bernières' story was set and the film shot, while Nick remained in his villa on the other side of town.

It had been more than a decade since Nick had played an Italian soldier. The last time he was an Army lieutenant in the less-than-successful, quirky *Time to Kill*. Nevertheless, he was happy to get back into uniform and rejoin Italy's military in occupation, this time portraying the sophisticated, musically-minded officer in a big screen telling of the *Captain Corelli* story.

Whereas *Time to Kill*'s young Lieutenant Enrico was a man riddled with guilt over what he had done to a young woman in Ethiopia in 1936, Captain Corelli is a jovial and honorable romantic who strives to do the right thing by the girl he falls in love with while serving on a Greek Island during World War II. Apart from the fact that *Time to Kill* and *Captain Corelli's Mandolin* were both period movies about Italian army officers serving overseas, the two films could not have been more different. While *Time to Kill* was a low-budget, foreign-made movie which disappeared into obscurity, *Captain Corelli's Mandolin* was a big-budget, largely British-produced film. It was intended to be an epic blockbuster, and partly backed by a Hollywood studio. The Tinseltown influence meant *Captain Corelli* was destined to attract massive publicity, on top of the enormous following for de Bernières' 1994 book, which has sold more than a million-and-a-half copies. It is a book which has enjoyed a phenomenal run in the bestsellers lists since its publication.

The Working Title Films — the company behind *Four Weddings and a Funeral*, *Billy Elliot* and Britain's most successful movie to date, *Notting Hill* — joint production had the benefit of financial support from Universal Pictures. Universal's publicity machine swung into operation early on, generating huge interest long before the film had even found its way into cinemas. The film would also later benefit from involvement by Miramax, the film company behind many critically-acclaimed smash hits, and the French company Canal Plus.

In what was probably a brilliant marketing move, Hugh Grant's London book shop owner character is seen in the final scene of *Notting Hill* sitting on a park bench with his pregnant wife, played by Julia Roberts, her head resting on his lap, as he leisurely reads a copy of *Captain Corelli's Mandolin*.

Right from the start, *Captain Corelli*, which was published in the United States under the title *Corelli's Mandolin*, generated interest. In fact, interest in the film reached such an early fever pitch that months before its release Cephalonia reported a British tourism boom.

'Greece is very much in fashion this year and the "in" place is the *Captain Corelli* island of Cephalonia,' a spokesman for specialist Greek tour company Kosmar Holidays said early in 2001. The previous year, Cephalonia had welcomed nearly 95,000 visitors, of whom 85 per cent were from the United Kingdom but, thanks to Nick and his movie, tourist officials were bracing themselves for far more during the first summer of the new millennium.

Captain Corelli's Mandolin was given the Hollywood treatment because film executives saw it as a *Doctor Zhivago*-like love story. It had all the benefits of being a drama set on an idyllic and picturesque island during Mussolini's ill-fated occupation of Greece. It therefore gave the cinematographer plenty of opportunities for wide-screen panoramic shots showing off the beauty of the Greek island. The film could be mistaken for a giant come-to-scenic-Greece commercial.

Tim Bevan, one of the producers, said, 'It's like *Doctor Zhivago*, an amazing love story set against an epic backdrop. The book isn't cinematic, but I think emotion is what makes epics. If you have big emotions, you can construct a movie.

It's a big, epic romance. The war is the backdrop to the movie and politics gears things up, because it's about life and death. But the argument over the politics and the civil war is as dull as ditch water as far as we're concerned. What this is about is maintaining an emotional through-line for 100 minutes and making them cry a lot.'

Captain Corelli certainly turned into a big movie in every sense of the word once Nick agreed to star. He had briefly flirted with the idea of starring in the film, which was originally budgeted at just US$25 million, in the summer of 1999 but dropped out that July because of scheduling conflicts. However, he had a change of heart after his schedule was rearranged and the following month rejoined as the film's leading man again.

Ironically, the producers were determined not to go the standard Hollywood route in bringing the book to the big screen. Bevan's partner Kevin Loader first became aware of the book in 1996 and loved it. Loader said, 'When I first read Louis de Bernières' novel, I thought it would make a fantastic film, although it's a very difficult book to adapt. It's written in a magical and peculiarly individual style which endeared it to readers everywhere. But dramatically it has several problems. Commercially it has one fantastic asset, which is a love story, which everybody wants to make movies of.'

Loader showed the book to a director he had worked closely with previously, Roger Michell, who had made *Notting Hill*. The producer went on, 'We didn't want to take the book to Hollywood, they would never understand it. In fact, I phoned friends in Hollywood and got them to sneak me out the Hollywood readers' reports on the book and it was pretty clear to us that no Hollywood executive had got past page 100, and neither had their bright graduate readers. So we ended up with Working Title Films in London, who had a reputation for doing good, ambitious, high-budget films in England.'

Once the producers had secured film rights to the movie, Nick was at the top of the list to play Corelli right from the start. Bevan admitted, 'We wrote down a list of actors around the world who mean something and who can play Corelli. Nick was at the top of an extremely short list.'

For his part, Nick loved the character from the start. He said, 'When I first read the script, I was very emotional. I don't know why, I was moved by the story's romantic aspects. It seemed to me to be unlike anything I'd done before. I've normally avoided period pictures. I've felt inherently I was a contemporary personality. So I didn't know if I would be anachronistic or not. That had something to do with it, the challenge of wanting to try it.'

He recognised that *Captain Corelli's Mandolin* might redefine the scope of his acting abilities. He said, 'I felt I was missing the experience of working in a romantic, period film and even doing a movie where I was not an American.' Admitting to a new-found preference for working on projects based on books, he added, 'You're using your own imagination but it's being guided by the novel itself, the writing itself, which can stimulate you. It can give you great ideas.'

Once he was on board, the film attracted other named actors and the budget mushroomed, eventually ending up at around US$50 million, although there was wild speculation that it went up as high as US$90 million. However, Nick cannot be blamed for the escalation in costs. He turned his back on his usual US$20 million salary and agreed to take a big cut because he was so impressed by the project. Bevan said, 'He and his agents were great. He took a cut. He realised this wasn't an action picture and cut his cloth fee accordingly.'

But there were other costs involved. As the film expanded into what it was to become, hundreds of extras were hired, entire Greek villages were given a going over to transform them into the picturesque Venetian-style architecture of the period and the Greek government even loaned the movie-makers two minesweepers and two landing craft as well as military personnel.

Loader explained, 'We always knew we had to find a star for this role and as the budget and the ambition of the film drifted upwards, the star had to become more and more bankable. Nicolas Cage has a very interesting career. He can play romantic heroes, he can play moody, dark, introspective characters, and he's an action hero who takes his shirt off, greases his torso and jumps out of aeroplanes. Corelli has to have a little of all these traits, and also has to have incredible charm but the spiritual inner quality that Corelli has. And I think Cage has those things brilliantly. The key issue if you cast an American in the role of Corelli is the accent problem. How are you going to create this world in which there are Italians, Germans and Greeks? There is not an American character in either the book or the film.'

Both Nick and the producers were determined that he would play Corelli as an Italian. He has always thrown himself into his characters in ways such as building up his body to play Little Junior Brown in *Kiss of Death* or shedding all his muscles just weeks later to play suicidal Ben Sanderson in *Leaving Las Vegas*. To play Corelli, he had an army of voice coaches to help him work on his accent and even mandolin teachers so he could actually learn to play the instrument.

Nick admitted that learning to play was a disconcerting experience. He said, 'That was incredibly daunting because I'm not a musician, even though my grandfather was a conductor.' Nevertheless, the consummate professional learned his way round the mandolin so well that some of his playing is actually included on the soundtrack of the movie. He said, 'Hearing some of my playing — that's pretty scary. But I feel like it worked out.'

In the movie, Nick talks with a strong Italian accent thanks to his coaches. One of his Italian teachers got so into the movie that she actually sent Loader two scenes of herself on tape reading the script urging him to give it to the casting director so she might be considered for the role of Nick's love interest.

An enormous problem confronting the producers was that the actual island of Cephalonia had suffered a devastating earthquake (7.2 on the Richter scale) in 1953, which claimed the lives of 476 inhabitants and had destroyed much of the original architecture, which unlike most of Greece had a heavy Italian influence. Cephalonia is one of the Ionian islands, which are situated between Italy and Greece. They were controlled by the Venetians for about 300 years and subsequently the towns and villages had a completely different appearance from the more familiar white cubist Greek villages, which are the ones usually seen in tourist brochures for the islands.

For a long time, the producers thought that they would not actually be able to film on the island where the story was set. However, thanks to the confidence of one of the original set designers, Stuart Craig, who was scouting locations, that all changed. Craig convinced Loader that it was feasible to make the movie there despite all the problems. Loader recalled, 'The ferry we were on had just docked in the port of Sami to take on more passengers. Stuart Craig got off and looked at its completely new construction of concrete buildings. He came back on the boat as it was leaving to go to the Greek mainland and said, "You know, I may be going mad, but I think we might be able to do the film here."'

The result was that the movie was shot where the story was set. The movie-makers ambitiously rebuilt parts of the town and constructed completely new sets in the island's countryside to create the original beauty of the old Cephalonia prior to the earthquake.

Film-maker John Madden, who ended up directing *Captain Corelli*, said, 'The advantages of filming there hugely outweighed the legion of disadvantages. It was a kamikaze choice by Universal, since we were filming outside and there was nothing to do if the weather didn't participate.' Studio executives need not have worried. The Greek gods smiled on the production and the weather stayed perfect.

In the film, Nick plays Captain Antonio Corelli, a decent and suave Italian officer who commands the isle's garrison after Italy defeats Greece. He soon embarks on a heated affair with the beautiful daughter of the local doctor, Iannis. Spanish stunner Penélope Cruz plays the daughter Pelagia, while veteran British actor John Hurt plays her father. Corelli has a love rival in Pelagia's fiancé, a local fisherman-turned-freedom fighter, Mandras, played by Welsh actor Christian Bale. Obviously, the course of true love does not run smoothly. Despite their feelings for one another, Corelli and Pelagia are forced to deal with their political and personal allegiances together with all the consequences that the war throws at them.

Although the film sticks basically with the theme of de Bernières' book, there were some major changes made to the story to enable it to make the transition from print to film. For example, the movie concentrates on the World War II love story and does not span the six decades of the book.

De Bernières original had been embroiled in controversy from soon after its publication and the producers wanted to avoid getting involved in any further confrontations. *Captain Corelli's Mandolin* had been criticised for being historically inaccurate and deeply unfair in the way it portrayed the behaviour of the Communist partisans. The story opened old wounds that had still not healed after 60 years. The controversy was not just because de Bernières painted a picture of the partisans as sheep-stealing brigands and the Italian occupiers as amiable buffoons. Despite many real-life Corelli–Pelagia romances having taken place during that period in the island's history, the Italians were still an occupying Army and for a long time were the islanders' enemies. In an ironically tragic turn of events, thousands of Italian troops were slaughtered there by their former German allies once Mussolini was overthrown and the Italians capitulated. The Germans treated them like traitors rather than prisoners of war or former allies. The story hit many raw nerves and nothing was simple about the tangled web the events of that period had woven.

De Bernières had at first brushed aside the criticisms of his historical accuracy. The author, who had briefly pursued a military career with the British Army, was staunchly anti-Communist. In response to an attack by the British pro-Communist newspaper the *Morning Star*, he wrote in 1999, 'Your ship has sunk, brothers. How long are you people going to sit in the dark in an air pocket, wanking each other off?' But by the time the movie was being made, de Bernières admitted he might have been wrong about some of his assumptions. He even agreed to changes when the book was published in Greece to avoid causing offence.

Many locals at first resisted having the film made at all, let alone on the island where the actual historical events that form the backdrop to the tale had unfolded. But after assurances from the producers that the story had been tempered and changed, their fears were alleviated and the production team even enjoyed a great deal of co-operation from the islanders. Shopkeepers in the fishing village of Sami happily accepted payment to shut down to allow sets to be built over their storefronts, while many of the 1,800 residents were hired as extras, being paid 17,000 drachmas a day ($47) or 20,000 drachmas ($56) if they brought a donkey.

De Bernières said, 'It was never part of the purpose of *Corelli* to stir up bad blood. *Corelli* is about other themes and I wouldn't want the book distorted for Greek readers. Which is why I agreed with my publishers and my translator that some of my language and opinions should be moderated.'

One of de Bernières' most vocal critics was, ironically, the movie's scriptwriter, Shawn Slovo, who was raised in South Africa where her father Joe was head of the banned Communist Party in the apartheid era, and was the only white African National Congress executive member. She said, 'The big problem I had with the book was its politics. I found the portrayal of the Greek partisans quite offensive and inaccurate.' Others had concerns that the central character of the story is a soldier fighting for Mussolini's fascist regime so it might be difficult to see him as a hero. However, Slovo did not see that as a problem. She said, 'Corelli is a man whose country goes to war and is conscripted. He's not a fascist, he's not a Communist. When your country declares war, you don't not fight.' Nick felt exactly the same way. He said, 'My feeling is, Corelli's conscripted, he's not a fascist. He's an intelligent man.'

As Nick comes from a half-Italian American family — and had played an Italian American successfully opposite Cher in *Moonstruck* — it might seem that the role of Corelli would have come easy for him. But he does not think that was the case. He said, 'I'm also half-German-American and the film deals with an unfortunate period when Germans were under Hitler's reign and thousands of Italian solders were assassinated on this island. But I do feel a connection with Corelli because he is so musical. There are two conductors in my family, my grandfather Carmine and his brother Anton. Carmine was also a composer, so I feel that he is in me. Though I've never been musically trained, I felt that came naturally to me.'

The concern over the political correctness of the book was one of the reasons why the story was changed to focus on a World War II love story. Out went scenes of Communist atrocities, characters were dropped altogether and some of the relationships between principal characters were changed.

Filming generated a lot of interest as it was the first major movie to be filmed in Greece since the 1991 Italian–Spanish hit *Mediterraneo*.

Long before shooting began, the film's original director, Roger Michell, was forced to drop out of *Captain Corelli* for health reasons after suffering a mild heart-attack. He was replaced by John Madden, who had previously made *Shakespeare in Love*. Luckily for the producers, Madden was very similar in temperament and working method to Michell.

Madden said, 'One of the attractive things about this book and story is it's about World War II, though not from a perspective that anyone's seen before. It manages to encompass humour, romance, almost farce on occasions, with very dark material indeed. That's the strength of the original material. I like to go into a film that has its own world.'

With Madden's input, Slovo even added scenes that were not in the book. The film sees Corelli and Mandras meet, an encounter which never occurred in the novel. Madden said, 'Everything that is in the film is implicitly there in the book. It's just a matter of how you distill it and how you lift certain things to the surface.'

The director focused his attentions on Corelli's character. Corelli is, according to Madden, 'An irresistible man; irreverent, funny, hedonistic, utterly spontaneous, less interested in the mechanics of war than in the melodic intricacies of his mandolin, preferring to train his men to sing Puccini than to fire weapons.'

The film-makers faced more problems than just the initial hostility of the locals. The environment was just as hostile as the people had originally been. Madden and his team quickly discovered that filming on such a remote paradise as Cephalonia had its drawbacks. He confessed, 'It's a fantastic place with richness of landscape. But it's entirely without cinematic infrastructure. It's a tough place to set up a film of this magnitude.'

Despite the problems the movie-makers were finding making the film on the remote island, Nick quickly adapted to life there. He moved into a rented villa, enjoyed a good social life — hosting parties — and appreciated the food. Before long, he developed a taste for the local delicacy, grilled octopus. He said, 'It's the Greek dish of choice and when I go somewhere new I like to try the food.'

While some other members of the cast, such as John Hurt, were regular visitors to the local tavernas, Nick tended to stay at home and entertain in the fortress villa he called home. Among his visitors were Madonna and her daughter Lourdes, who dropped in to see him while sailing on a friend's yacht with then-boyfriend Guy Ritchie, whom she married in Christmas 2000. Robert De Niro also dropped by to visit the set.

Principal photography began on the island on 18 May 2000. The summer that year was especially hot in Greece and took its toll on the cast and crew. The heat was stifling. Nick's co-star Christian Bale confessed, 'The only thing moving on the set were the goats.'

The Mediterranean heat that had sparked flames in the hearts of fictional Corelli and Pelagia was also having a real-life effect on Nick and his leading lady. Spanish beauty Penélope Cruz had first gained American art-house exposure for her sultry role in Bigas Lunas' *Jamon Jamon*, which she followed with roles in Fernando Trueba's Oscar-winning *Belle Epoque*, Pedro Almodóvar's *Live Flesh* and Alejandro Amenabar's *Open Your Eyes*. She had also won Spain's Goya award for best actress for her role in Trueba's comedy *The Girl of Your Dreams* and gained international recognition starring in Almodóvar's Oscar-winning *All About My Mother*, in which she played a pregnant nun with AIDS.

Even though movie studio executives regarded her as a woman on the edge of international stardom — the greatest European import to Hollywood since Brigitte Bardot — she was not the first choice to play Pelagia. She had previously only featured in a handful of English-language movies, her first being the Stephen Frears-directed 1998 *The Hi-Lo Country*, which was also for a Working Title film. She had donated her salary from that film to Mother Teresa's children's sanctuary in Calcutta, where she had worked as a volunteer. Ironically, one of her co-stars was Patricia Arquette, soon to be Nick's ex-wife.

The *Corelli* producers had been wooing *Phantom Menace* star Natalie Portman for the role of Pelagia but she was forced to withdraw from negotiations because she was contracted to start shooting *Star Wars II* in Australia that summer. After Portman's withdrawal, it took only two meetings between Madden and Penélope, who had just wrapped a co-starring role opposite Matt Damon in the Billy Bob Thornton-directed *All the Pretty Horses*, for the director to decide she was ideally suited to tackle the part of the fiery Greek goddess. The stunning enchantress had the ideal dark complexion to play a Greek, even though she had actually been born into a humble family on the outskirts of the Spanish capital of Madrid in 1974.

Actor Mark Feuerstein, who co-starred with her in *Woman on Top*, was not surprised that movie-makers and co-stars fell for the former ballet dancer's charms. He said, 'You'll never find someone as beautiful, smart and funny.'

It certainly did not take long for Nick to notice Penélope's sultry brown eyes, kissable lips and silky black hair. He had nothing but compliments for her and her acting abilities. He said, 'She is very free. You don't see the acting, you just see a person being. I saw pure emotion and someone who has a great heart, which she conveys on film. That just makes you a better actor.'

The actress had been spending her free time on the Greek island reading in cafés by the harbour, swimming in deserted coves and dancing at a seaside disco, until Nick invited her for a ride on the back of his motorbike. Everybody loved the easy-going and affable actress. Associate producer Susie Tasios said, 'She would talk to kids, she would talk to old ladies. Someone would come with a bunch of flowers and she'd give them back one. She absolutely knew how to win their hearts.' Certainly Nick was no exception.

He was not the first American co-star to fall for her charms and, if rumours were to be believed, Nick would not be the last. Matt Damon had developed a close relationship with her while they had been making *All the Pretty Horses*, although they both insist it was not a romance but a deep friendship. Whichever, their closeness seemed to have fizzled out by the time she started work on *Corelli*. Penélope, whose past loves have included a Spanish singer and a Czech assistant director, was soon attracted to Nick. Their attraction for each other promptly became an open secret on the film set.

Despite the pretence that Nick and his wife Patricia had overcome their earlier problems, their marriage was in tatters, as had been blatantly obvious by the distance between them when she had visited him on Cephalonia. It would not be long after filming *Corelli* finished that Patricia would decide that she had had enough and return to court to make her own petition to end the marriage.

When filming finished in Greece, Nick was only briefly back in California before heading to Hawaii to start his next movie, *Windtalkers*. But while making that movie, he still found time to jet back to New York to dine with Penélope in the fashionable Nobu restaurant, while she was in the Big Apple filming *Vanilla Sky* with Tom Cruise.

Unfortunately for the coy couple, members of New York's infamous paparazzi were outside the restaurant, which is a favourite hang-out of the rich and famous. They left separately, Nick, wearing a grey sweatshirt, black leather trousers and a brown leather bomber-jacket, and Penélope in jeans and a sexy, figure-hugging black blouse, but were both caught on film and the gossip machine quickly swung into action.

While he was making *Windtalkers*, Patricia turned the tables on Nick and instructed her lawyers to file her divorce. The papers were filed with the Los Angeles Superior Court on 17 November 2000. The timing could not have been worse as far as Hollywood publicists were concerned. Nick's feel-good Christmas movie, *The Family Man*, about family values and relationships, was about to be released the following month to cash in on the season of goodwill, a time of year which tends to bring out a lot of American sentimentality.

However, there was little goodwill in Nick and Patricia's relationship. One of her friends said, 'Patricia had finally grown tired of trying to make Nick fit into the role of a husband and father. This time she was the one throwing in the towel.'

While Nick had claimed that they had separated on 10 January 1996, Patricia maintained in her court papers that they had been together as man and wife until 1 November 2000. The discrepancy could have made a big difference if a judge and jury had to decide how to divide their assets. Nick maintained they had only actually lived as man and wife for nine months, while Patricia insisted they had had a relationship that was man and wife for five years and six months. In her petition to the court, Patricia's lawyers stated that 'there have arisen unhappy differences and irreconcilable disputes' between their client and Nick. Hollywood braced itself for yet another headline-grabbing, public and messy divorce battle.

But that was not to be. There was so much knowledge that the marriage had long been on-again and off-again that no one had bothered to look closely at the legal paperwork the couple had filed. If they had, they would have discovered that by the day the papers were filed, everything had been thrashed out between Patricia and Nick. The couple had carefully dotted the Is and crossed the Ts to conclude their relationship with the minimum of fuss. There would be no divorce battle. There would be no mud-throwing in court. The marriage was over. All their financial affairs had been settled. Divorce case BD334861 was just a formality. It was one of the quickest divorces in Hollywood history and no one, apart from Nick and Patricia and their lawyers, had realised it.

Their relationship was destined to end in disaster right from the start because it was too intense. Besides, she could never compete with the great love of his life — his son Weston. Nick describes his relationship with Weston as, 'The most important relationship of my life.' For him, it is a relationship that opened up many other emotions that he had not felt before and completely altered his outlook on life.

For months after Patricia filed for divorce, there would be silly speculation that Nick was trapped in a love triangle between Patricia and Penélope; that after the death of Patricia's actor father Lewis in early 2001, Nick had telephoned her to give condolences.

If he saw any irony in the fact he was committed to promoting a movie about a ruthless workaholic financier who learns to be happy with family life over the Christmas holidays, just as he had personally come through a divorce, he did not let on. Always dedicated to his craft that December, he threw himself into a round of interviews to help hype *The Family Man* while trying to avoid questions about his personal life. He neatly side-stepped questions and failed to mention that the divorce was a done deal.

Nevertheless, it was not an easy time for him. The divorce had taken its toll on him, even if it did not show. Just before Christmas, while promoting *The Family Man*, he told old acquaintance, Bob Strauss, the film writer for the Los Angeles *Daily News*, 'I am in therapy, if that's what you're asking. I do think about things and try to, sort of, self-analyse, what it is that I'm doing or why am I doing it. But I have to say that, at this time in my life, I feel very good. I feel pretty calm. But I am passionate about the work. If my name's on a movie, I want people to know that they can trust me and I'm not going to sell them out.'

Penélope tried to play down her romance with Nick and suggestions she was responsible for his bust-up from Patricia. She said, 'I like Nick very much. He's one of the best actors. I think he's always good.'

It would not be the only time in the winter of 2000–2001 that Penélope would have to profess her innocence. When Tom Cruise broke up with Nicole Kidman it was suggested that Penélope was partly to blame because the *Mission Impossible* superstar had become smitten with her. Penélope insisted, 'I am not a man-eater or someone who is even very confident about their sexuality.'

Long after *Corelli* had finished shooting, Nick and Penélope were still together despite speculation over her relationship with Cruise. In fact, it was speculation that Penélope was at the centre of a love triangle involving her, Nick and Cruise that finally forced her to admit she was having a relationship with her Corelli co-star. After being branded 'the other woman' in Cruise's life, a friend of the actress revealed to newspapers that Penélope had admitted, 'There's nothing going on between us. I can't believe what everyone's saying about me and Tom. It's very upsetting. We've just been working on a movie together, that's all. Yet it's all over the papers that I'm the other woman — that it's my fault. It's embarrassing and very hurtful to me and to Tom. It's upset my boyfriend, too. Nick knows it's only rumours but it's not nice to read in the papers about your girlfriend seeing another man.'

Nick and Penélope were rarely seen in public together during the run-up to Christmas 2000. They tried to avoid the prying eyes of the media. But by the end of the year, their relationship had blossomed into a red hot romance. Penélope jetted into San Francisco, where Nick still maintained a home, to spend a weekend with him over the Christmas and New Year holiday season. If Nick felt any angst over his break-up from Patricia, he certainly did not show it when he picked Penélope up from the airport and whisked her off to trendy Tomasso's restaurant for lunch before retiring to his home in the afternoon. Later that evening, they emerged to dine on oysters at another up-market San Francisco hang-out named Zuni. An eyewitness said at the time, 'They're obviously very much in love.'

As the world eagerly awaited the release of the movie version of *Captain Corelli's Mandolin*, Nick was happy with his life and his work on the film. He believed that fans of the book would be happy despite the drastic changes to the story. He said, 'A film is a different expression or form of art and you have to make changes to make it work. The book is very long, too, so you have to find ways of condensing the material or creating new scenes to convey the same sentiment but in a faster way.'

He was very pleased with the way the film turned out. He said, 'It's tremendous. I'm really pleased with John Madden's work, with Penélope's work. John Hurt is fantastic in it. I would love to work with all of them again. My character goes through a big transformation. He begins his life in the film as a *bon vivant* soldier who loves music, wine and women and then realises there's a war going on and it's now affecting him in a major way. He has to pick up the pieces from there. And John really develops all of that with his draft of the screenplay. It's a wonderful love story. Before I had to do the conducting scenes, I'd think of my grandfather and I'd say to myself, "I've got to call out your name now and you've got to help me." It took a lot of conviction to be believable in that.' And just as Corelli's on-screen life had gone through a big transformation in 2000, so had Nick's.

Corelli was the first film Madden, whose other movie credits include *Mrs Brown*, had directed since he had made *Shakespeare in Love*. He was delighted to have worked with Nick. The director said, 'Nick is an actor who defines himself by the risks he takes. He's brave. He's disciplined. And he's really on top of his skills. He's thought around the part and comes to the set with a cupboardful of ideas to try. He sees how narrow the neck of the bottle is and he knows exactly how to aim the liquid to fill it. I love the fact that he won't settle. Almost unique among American A-list actors, he's pushing himself across boundaries he hasn't yet crossed. Whether or not all of them are advisable he doesn't concern himself with, which is terrific because he wants to keep fresh. He's somehow retained his sense of mischief, of humour, of freedom to work without a safety net.'

Just as *Shakespeare in Love* had won over the hearts of members of the Academy of Motion Pictures Arts and Sciences, who vote for the Oscars, early word had it that *Captain Corelli's Mandolin* was also a film which could be a major contender for top honours. Nick could once again be a Best Actor Oscar nominee, with John Hurt strongly favoured for a Best Supporting Actor nomination in 2002. That was good news for the islanders of Cephalonia who enthusiastically compared it to the 1964 movie *Zorba*, starring Anthony Quinn, that was filmed in Crete and won three Oscars and was nominated for four more, and the 1961 Greek-set *Guns of Navarone*, which won one Oscar, was nominated for six more, as well as being voted Best Picture at the Golden Globes awards.

Madden was aware that, in Hollywood, his movie was being compared to *The English Patient*, which won the 1996 Best Picture Oscar. He was confident that his *Captain Corelli's Mandolin* would play a sweeter tune and find a wider audience than *Patient*. He said, 'Its strength is its uniqueness, and with Nick Cage and Penélope Cruz playing the leads we think the movie can reach across the demographic boundaries of male and female, of art-house and wide audience appeal.'

Talking about Nick's performance, Brad Schreiber wrote in *Daily Variety*, trade newspaper of the movie industry, in March 2001, 'While the actor has stretched his range with diverse performances, perhaps his greatest career leap is shortly to come in the romantic period epic *Captain Corelli's Mandolin*.'

Only time would tell whether the film would establish Nick in yet another movie genre; whether Nick would be a family man again; and whether Penélope would be the one to help him achieve that. Nonetheless, Nick remained a romantic at heart. He confessed, 'Definitely my dream is to have more children, a family, and all that. There's time.'

CHAPTER TWENTY-SIX

ISLAND HOPPING

Turning 37 on 7 January 2001 presented Nick with a milestone. He had been a professional movie actor for 20 years. In those two decades, he had gone from being a struggling bit part player to becoming a member of the Hollywood super league and one of the most recognisable faces in the world. He agonised over what he should do to celebrate both his birthday and reaching 20 years as a movie actor. As the date approached, he confessed it presented him with a dilemma. He said, 'I've been thinking about it a lot. I've been wondering whether to celebrate it somehow, as 20 years is a benchmark. If you are a shirt-maker and had been in business 20 years, you might throw a party. So I'm thinking of doing that.'

Nick did not ponder the question too long. He held his party at the Sky Bar, a penthouse nightclub that is one of the trendiest hotspots in Los Angeles and a favourite celebrity hang-out. He ordered a giant stuffed pig with an apple in its mouth for his guests to dine on. By his side that Sunday night was his lovely *Captain Corelli* co-star and lover Penélope Cruz. Nick's uncle Francis Coppola, his cousin Sofia Coppola and friends Ed Norton, Salma Hayek, Lucy Lui, David Spade, Michael Bay, Jerry Bruckheimer, Spike Jonze and Playboy boss Hugh Hefner were also there to help him celebrate. Revelling in his reputation as a hellraiser, aging lothario Hef playfully offered his seven buxom girlfriends to Nick as a 'birthday gift.' However, the birthday boy thought better of it and politely and diplomatically declined the generous offer. Pop star Kid Rock gate-crashed the lavish bash but made up for his uninvited appearance by buying Nick a $600 bottle of 25-year-old Macallan single malt Scotch.

Still broodingly handsome, Nick had reached the prime of his career. But he was also aware that he was getting older. More and more he talked about his hectic schedule and that he wanted to pack in as much as possible because one day he would be forced to slow down a bit. Nick said, 'Someone once asked Humphrey Bogart how he made so many great films, and he said, "I just kept working. I never stopped working." I'm driven to get things done. I feel like I'm in my prime, and I'm not always going to be able to be, so I'd like to make an abundance of films now.

I'm hoping if I keep doing it, one of them's going to be really great.'

Workaholic Nick was certainly pushing himself with a hectic schedule and has shown no signs of letting up. He continues to churn out movie after movie and has expanded his business empire to take on other projects, such as producing and developing movies.

As the years have passed by, so his soulful boyish looks have matured into approaching middle age. His hairline has receded drastically over the years and top San Francisco dermatologist Vail Reese revealed in 2000 that Nick has some acne scars that are now showing. However, getting older did not seem to bother Nick as he celebrated his birthday and 20 years in show business.

His choice of a stuffed pig was a throwback to the previous few months when he had been working in Hawaii, where the local delicacy is slow-cooked suckling pig. After filming *Captain Corelli's Mandolin,* Nick went almost immediately from the Greek Ionian isles over to the middle of the Pacific Ocean to start work on another World War II drama, filming on the Hawaiian island of Oahu. *Windtalkers* was supposed to start shooting in the middle of August but director John Woo, with whom Nick had worked on the highly successful *Face/Off,* ran into some pre-production problems which meant that the start date had to be pushed back until the end of the month.

On the face of it, the brief delay should not have proved too much of a problem. However, foreseeing further delays, Woo anticipated that he would not now finish filming until the end of January 2001, which meant Nick had to scrap another movie. Woo's foresight was well justified. Unlike *Captain Corelli,* which enjoyed the benefit of glorious, if hot, weather, the Hawaiian weather Kevin Costner discovered when he made the disastrous *Waterworld* there — can be unpredictable and Woo's filming schedule was hampered by heavy rains. In the end, *Windtalkers* turned into a six-month shoot.

Comic-book fan Nick, who had long harboured a desire to play Superman in a movie, also had ambitions to appear in another superhero film based on *Marvel* comic characters. He had agreed to play the Green Goblin in the movie version of *Spider Man* opposite Tobey Maguire in the title role. But that film was due to start shooting in November 2000, which meant Nick had to pass on the opportunity of wearing green tights. He contented himself with simply swapping his Italian army uniform for US military combat gear. The role went instead to Willem Dafoe, star of Nick's producing début, *Shadow of the Vampire.*

Windtalkers, which had a $100 million budget, is a World War II epic, based on the true story of a group of Navajo Indians who were Marines and used their ancient language as a military code that the Japanese were never able to crack. It co-stars Christian Slater, Noah Emmerich, Brian Van Holt and Frances O'Connor. The code-talkers helped defeat the Japanese in the battles of Saipan and Iwo Jima in the South Pacific.

Woo claims to have toned down the carnage that is a familiar part of his movies for *Windtalkers* although his sound team claim it was they who had to tone down the noise of the battlefield scenes. Woo's fans need not worry. There were still plenty of battle scenes shot to satisfy them. Even though Woo was cutting down on his usual diet of violence, the film still appealed to the famous action director. He said, 'It's a movie about friendship, patriotism and honour. It's a very serious movie. Drama and action ... real action, you know, not that kung fu type. I intend to make the movie look very real, and touching.'

So instead of being a shoot-'em-up, *Windtalkers* focuses on the relationship between Nick's US Marine character, who has been assigned to protect the Indian encryption experts, and one of the Navajos. As Joe Enders, Nick is a Marine sergeant who has been shattered, both physically and psychologically, by war. Enders develops a friendship with Private Carl Yahzee, who is played by Canadian actor Adam Beach, and through his new-found friendship the sergeant struggles to find peace, even though he has deadly orders to carry out if all goes wrong. His job is to prevent his young charge's capture from the Japanese at all costs — even if that means killing the encoder himself.

It had taken years to develop the story of the code-talkers far enough along for it to become a movie. Originally, co-producer Alison Rosenzweig had seen the story of the Navajos' role in the war as a documentary. Her brother kept trying to persuade her that it would make a terrific film. But it was only when she discovered that each Navajo had a white bodyguard with orders to kill the man he was protecting if capture appeared imminent that she saw its potential as a movie. Rosenzweig said, 'The moment I read that, I knew this could be a feature film.'

Screenwriter John Rice, who is married to Rosenzweig's co-producing partner Tracie Graham, was not enthusiastic about the film at first. He said, 'I thought it was a hard sell; though I loved the moral dilemma from the get-go.'

The major obstacle was the audience appeal problem; the large number of World War II films being released by Hollywood and having Native Americans in lead roles. Rice asked, 'Could we have come up with any more strikes against us?' However, after more than 13 drafts, the screenplay came together although there were plenty of hurdles to overcome before the movie-makers reached that point. Rice went on, 'I liked the idea of having a war as a background for "red man–white man" issues. The more I thought about it, the more intrigued I became.'

Rosenzweig's passion for the project was fuelled by the theme and the characters. She said that the genre was 'far less important to me' than the relationship between two men with diverse backgrounds. She said, 'It's a story of their growing friendship; basically a heterosexual love story. Nicolas' character is psychologically wounded, emotionally unavailable and he finds a new appreciation for life through Beach.'

After months of perfecting the movie pitch, the writers began meeting potential directors. Rice said, 'We did every dramatic beat; it was a live staging. We became the characters, reciting 25 lines of the strongest dialogue.' When Woo saw them do it, he loved the project. Tracie Graham said, 'He stood up in the room and clapped and said, "That's my kind of movie."'

Getting Nick to play the lead was important for the film, not just for his commercial value but also his ability to portray a tortured soul. Rosenzweig added, 'He's perfect. He was always the number-one choice; the only actor we actually talked about doing this film.' Rice said, 'We had to have someone who can show he needs to work through something, in this case, his own redemption story.' Nick liked the story so much he committed after only seeing the first draft of the script.

Before filming had even begun, Nick found himself embroiled in a controversy over the film. Just as the Greeks were unhappy before filming started on *Captain Corelli's Mandolin*, so the Navajo Indians were unhappy about *Windtalkers* when they learned the film was in development in 1999. They accused Nick of 'dishonouring' them. Sam Billison, the then 74-year-old president of the dwindling Navajo Code-Talkers' Association, claimed Hollywood was demoting the Native

Americans to a secondary role.

Like *Captain Corelli*, *Windtalkers* was set against a real-life backdrop. Scores of heroic Navajo radio operators, who sent messages that Japanese could not understand, died at Saipan and Iwo Jima, even though there is no evidence of any being killed by the guards assigned to protect them. Billison had spent a year in hospital recovering from wounds he received in the conflict.

The Navajo language is one of the most complex in the world, with four tones, glottalised consonants, a 'click' like the South African Xhosa tribe and a 35-letter alphabet. Fewer than 80,000 people spoke Navajo so it was ideal for use as a way of transmitting information the Japanese could not decipher. Many of the 450 code-talkers were just out of school, but even the teenagers were not spared the potential death penalty if they faced capture.

Billison, who sat on the Indian Tribal Council, was furious that Nick and not a Native American was the hero of the film. He accused Hollywood of perpetuating the stereotype of Tonto as the loyal sidekick to the Lone Ranger. He personally wrote to Nick. He said, 'For too long in Hollywood, our people's stories have been told only through others' eyes and in inaccurate and dishonourable ways. Even more disturbing is that it appears that this movie is going to tell our story with a white actor as a hero.' He demanded that his association be given script approval to 'set the record straight on the Navajo gift of our sacred language to save our country'. A Tribal Council spokesman said, 'They should tell the story of the coders the way it was, from the Navajo point of view, not Hollywood's.' Just as the Greek issue blew over, so the Indians' outraged smoke signals diffused into thin air.

As is usual, Nick had tremendous input in developing his character. He pushed Woo to let him appear, in the beginning at least, totally broken. Just as he had done many times in the past, Nick came up with the defining trait that would sum up Enders' character for the audience. He decided that the sergeant would chew aspirin all the time, trying to numb his pain with pill after pill.

Woo said, 'Nick always finds some interesting thing to make the character more rich, more touching. He's dedicated. He's precise. On-screen and off-screen, when you talk to him, he's real. He's never hiding anything.' When the Chinese-born director and Nick worked together on *Face/Off*, the actor decided to give his psychopathic villain, Castor Troy, a regal presence. He took inspiration from Elvis Presley, who always had an aide carry a cigar box full of his personal effects. Nick told the movie's prop man to fill a box with Chiclets, an extra pair of sunglasses, a jack-knife and some illicit-looking hand-rolled cigarettes. In one classic *Face/Off* scene, Troy is handed the box and he ostentatiously changes sunglasses as an underling assists him to change overcoats.

Nick may have been playing a broken man but his character was still a Marine. So the exercise-loving actor worked out as hard as ever with a trainer who incorporated additional weights to his daily routine. As a result he was looking especially buffed up in late 2000. he admitted, 'I told my trainer I wanted to look like a hardened Marine.'

He may have worked hard to get into shape for his character, but Nick had ducked out on going to a special boot camp that the other actors had had to endure to get into shape for their *Windtalkers* roles. He had been unable to attend the intense week of training because he had been busy at the time wrapping *Captain Corelli*. Co-star Van Holt admitted, 'We've been heckling him about that ever since.'

In other preparation for the part, Nick researched extensively, reading historical accounts of the Pacific campaign and watching war movies. He became so obsessed with kamikaze pilots, even though they are not a significant part of the *Windtalkers* story, that he decided to develop a film about them through his Saturn Films production company. He said, 'The Japanese had a *bushido* code, which was to live with death, live constantly reminded of death, and earn the right to die. You have to work hard to earn the right to deserve your rest.'

The work ethic is certainly something Nick adheres to. Unlike so many of today's stars, who pace themselves and take long breaks between films, he works as hard as the actors from the old studio system of Hollywood's golden era. He also relates to the Japanese pilots' fixation with death. Strangely aware of his own mortality, he is also motivated by death and thinks about it a lot, even though he is still a relatively young man. He said, 'When I was 15, I used to meditate on it and say, "OK, I'm going to take the samurai approach. I've got a lot I've got to get done in my life and I know I'm going to die, so I better start working hard now." I used to read Miyamoto Musashi's *Book of Five Rings*. So in a way, death has always been something that I've kind of embraced and confronted.'

Death is not the only thing that connects Nick to the Japanese. He is not seen doing commercials in the United States, but in Japan he does boost his earnings by doing advertising promotions. There, he appears on television for a Japanese *pachinko*-parlour chain. *Pachinko* is a pinball-type game that is a tremendously popular form of gambling with the Japanese. In English, Nick says, 'I love all Japan. I love sushi, Mount Fuji,' while a voice translates his statement into Japanese.

While he was making *Windtalkers*, Nick feared that his break-up from Patricia might affect his acting abilities. He was greatly relieved to discover that this was not the case. He told British journalist Martyn Palmer during an interview, 'I had a great experience the other night. I was on the set of my new movie, *Windtalkers*, with John Woo. Without getting personal, I've been going through some things and I was concerned that I wouldn't be able to access my craft, that I wouldn't be in the right frame of mind. I did this monologue and I surprised myself. I was at home and I knew what I was doing, what was required of me. And I felt free, free as an actor, and that really excited me. Like I still feel good about me, I'm not losing my enjoyment of what I do.'

He felt much the same when he talked to Bob Strauss of the Los Angeles *Daily News*. He told the journalist, whom he had spoken to many times previously, 'I feel very comfortable working. I feel that acting is my friend, and whatever it is I'm going through in my life, I still have that to make me feel like I belong in some way. I feel very satisfied. The other night, I did this scene with John Woo and I felt very like it's still there for me, it still is my friend.'

Despite the early morning calls and long days filming, Nick quickly adapted to the Honolulu nightlife, acting more like the bachelor he was about to become than a man worried about a crumbling marriage. The seemingly tireless actor made the rounds of the clubs around Waikiki Beach. One of the Hawaiian islands' most famous celebrity residents is Don Ho, a Polynesian-style Dean Martin. Tourists to those exotic islands flock to see him perform. Nick often popped in to Ho's Island Grill nightspot but his favourite hangout instantly became the Pipeline Café on Pohukaina Street in Honolulu. One week he stopped in three times, dancing the night away and sipping on his new favourite cocktail, the intriguingly named Sex on the Beach.

Known for his often outlandish fashion sense, Nick also indulged his taste for collectors-item vintage *aloha* Hawaiian shirts. *Aloha* shirts are the traditional dress of the Hawaiian islands for men. He dropped by Bailey's Antiques and Aloha Shirts twice, astonishingly spending more than $13,000 on seven of the shirts. On his first visit, he spent $8,000 for five shirts. On his second visit, Nick and his trainer roared up on new Harley Davison motorbikes and he paid more than $5,000 for just two shirts. The shop's owner, David Bailey, revealed that the shirts were early 1950s vintage made of DuPont rayon. Nick posed for photographs before leaving. Bailey said, 'They departed looking good in the shirts he bought.'

Back on the mainland, nightlife-loving Nick returned to the Sky Bar the month after his birthday to celebrate completing *Windtalkers*. He and Woo hosted a lavish $40,000 party for the cast and crew. As usual by now, Penélope was with him. Among the guests were Nick's co-star Adam Beach and dozens of other revellers. The guests drank Dom Perignon champagne and nibbled on calamari, salmon and other delicacies. Nick and Woo happily endured some good-natured ribbing in a 15-minute movie that the crew had put together which parodied Woo's over-the-top action style. The short film was filled with non-stop explosions and balletic, carefully-choreographed gunplay as witnessed in one of the classic action scenes in *Face/Off*.

Nick and Penélope had been the main attraction when they turned up together for Lisa Marie Presley's thirty-third birthday party at Smashbox Studios in Los Angeles on 2 February 2001, just a few days before the *Windtalkers* bash. They slowly made their way through the crowd holding hands and cuddling as they headed in to congratulate Elvis' daughter, who was briefly married to the other King of pop Michael Jackson. As Presley's former sister-in-law Janet Jackson and Kelly Preston, the wife of Nick's *Face/Off* co-star John Travolta, boogied to the sound of the soul band performing on stage, Nick and Penélope stopped to chat with actor Jason Lee.

The summer of 2000 may have seen Nick's marriage crumble quicker than feta cheese in a Greek salad, but his relationship with Penélope had grown strong and his professional life boomed. His movie projects were stacking up and his own production company, Saturn Films, was going from strength to strength. In the same month that Nick had headed for Hawaii to start *Windtalkers*, he and Saturn's then Vice-President of Creative Affairs, Norman Golightly, had struck a deal with Intermedia films, moving their allegiance away from Walt Disney, where they had been based, to produce two $30m – $60m pictures a year.

Nick was pleased to be doing business with Intermedia. He said, 'Intermedia has not lost sight of their desire to make quality films despite their substantial financial resources. They are very talent-friendly, and Norm and I are very excited about developing and packaging a wide range of material in conjunction with them.'

Intermedia co-chairman Nigel Sinclair was equally pleased with the deal. He said, 'Nicolas is an enormously talented actor whose career has spanned the spectrum — from David Lynch's indie road movie *Wild at Heart* to *Leaving Las Vegas*, to huge mainstream blockbusters such as *The Rock*. We feel fortunate to be able to participate in building Saturn as a great production company and we look forward to being in business with Nicolas and Norm for many, many years.'

Saturn CEO Nick and Golightly worked well together. In February 2001, Nick promoted his friend and colleague to President of Production, after Saturn's success with its inaugural feature film *Shadow of the Vampire*, which had earned two

Oscar nominations, a best supporting actor nomination for Willem Dafoe and one for best make-up. He admitted, 'Norm is a tremendous asset to Saturn Films, and the contribution he has made to our company has been instrumental in our success and growth. He is a loyal and dedicated colleague who has proven his capacity to bring quality work to Saturn.'

Golightly was equally complimentary as he discussed his promotion. He said, 'Nicolas has an unbelievable passion for film and a relentless commitment to producing exciting and uncompromising pictures. Quite simply, Nicolas is Saturn, and I am thrilled to be taking this next stage with him as well as with the company.'

With 20 years' experience as an actor behind him, Nick was anxious to expand his horizons, which is why he had committed himself to expanding Saturn, which he founded in 1997. He said, 'I saw Saturn Films as a safe haven for actors. It's an actor-driven company, where performers can find material that's a little bit unusual, that studios might be wary of. It's a laboratory for actors, really.'

In the future he hopes to act in, produce and some day direct all kinds of projects, from no-frills art films to big-budget blockbusters. His big paydays now allow him the luxury to take risks occasionally.

He said, 'I always felt that I had an eye for talent, and as an actor I really couldn't access that, I was responsible for managing by own abilities. I was interested in finding ways to put talented people together.' He had worked with both Willem Dafoe and John Malkovich. He admired Malkovich so much that he actually turned down the starring role in *Con Air* several times until Malkovich agreed to co-star in the movie. Dafoe, who appeared with Nick in *Wild at Heart*, and Malkovich had never worked together but Nick felt they would be ideally suited for *Shadow of the Vampire*. He said, 'It's a little like inviting people to a party, finding who would be interesting together.'

Although he does not intend to appear in every Saturn-produced movie, the company is also a vehicle to find acting projects for him. It enables him to be involved with a project from the very beginning rather than being brought into films that have already been developed by major studio executives who have their own view on how a story should be presented. Golightly said, 'It gives us a chance to start from square one and say, "Let's make this happen." I think this company is born out of Nick's love of film. We're striving to find films that are a combination of good entertainment, thought-provoking and entertaining films. We see ourselves as a cutting-edge company, working with both established film-makers and cutting-edge, new film-makers. We pride ourselves on thinking out of the box. We choose our projects first and only decide later whether Nick will act in them.'

Even though everything was going well for him, Nick did, however, have one major career disappointment. For many years he had longed to play Superman in a movie. It seemed he was destined to be cast in that role right from the opening moments of his first leading role. When the audience catches sight of his character in the opening minutes of the straights-meet-oddballs teen flick *Valley Girl*, Nick is seen walking on the beach with his chest shaved to leave a V-shaped carpet of hair which was sculpted as a tribute to the Man of Steel, whom he worships. However, it was another 14 years before he was actually first considered to replace tragic, wheelchair-bound actor Christopher Reeve as the DC comic books superhero in *Superman Reborn*, which later became *Superman Lives*. After a long on-off history, the movie was eventually scrapped. Nick was the first to admit he was deeply disappointed when executives at Warner Bros decided there was not enough

Kryptonite in the studio's coffers to get the fifth in the current series of *Superman* movies in front of the cameras.

He said, 'To me *Superman* is an American myth. The English have Shakespeare, the Greeks had Zeus and the Americans have Superman and Batman, so I see this as an opportunity to use a very powerful voice and try and do something responsible and positive and different with it.'

There was so much hype about a new Superman film and the character is such a money-spinning franchise for Warner Bros that fans were flabbergasted that the studio put the movie on indefinite hold in 1998. After such expensive disasters as Kevin Costner's *The Postman* and *Sphere*, which starred Dustin Hoffman and Sharon Stone, the studio decided to scale back on big event movies. The fact that *Batman and Robin* — also perceived as a sure-fire franchise money maker — under-achieved at the box office in 1997, helped to undermine the studio's confidence in their prospective movie.

The headline in the *Los Angeles Times* announced, IT'S A BIRD! IT'S A PLANE! SUPERMAN ON HOLD AGAIN. The story had gone through many incarnations before it seemed like a definite go with Nick as Superman being directed by Tim Burton, who helmed the first two Batman movies, *Batman* and *Batman Returns*, and produced the third in the series, *Batman Forever*. It had seemed set to go months earlier but, after a long slog of toiling with the screenplay, Burton finally rejected the first version of the script, by writer-director Kevin Smith, who had previously worked on *Clerks* and *Mallrats*. His story was based on a series of comic book episodes about the death of *Superman*, including his loss of special powers, his subsequent rebirth and the restoration of his super-abilities.

Smith had run into problems with Warner executives long before Burton took the helm. He complained to *Buzz* magazine, 'You'll never meet a more anxious bunch of motherfuckers in your life. They're calling you every day, "What have you done for me lately? What's going on? When are we getting pages?" I'll think twice before signing on to a studio film again.'

Nick was looking forward to working with Burton, whom he regarded as 'a real artist', so that was an added disappointment for him. He said, 'Tim is to me the champion of the outsider. I loved what he did with *Ed Wood* and *Edward Scissorhands*. To me, Superman is the greatest example of the ultimate freak outsider from another planet who is trying to fit in with a world where these sort of do-good heroics are more or less a compulsion to be loved.'

They had had several meetings to discuss the project before it was shelved. Nick told *Drama-Logue*'s Elias Stimac, 'When I scratched the surface of Superman, I looked at the American pop myth of the character and saw the incredible effect that it's had on our society. For example, I think the Lois Lane character liberated a lot of women. She was an independent, professional journalist who was the object of Superman's desires. So I don't look at Superman as being beneath me. I look at it as an important project even though it doesn't fall into that *Leaving Las Vegas* category of independent art film. In my opinion, it's about what you consider to be important.'

He added, 'I plan to utilise the wide-reaching audience of *Superman*, and be very responsible with that stage. I think Superman is a character that will affect children and adults all around the world, so I want to try to say something with that character, and I've got very specific ideas about what that is. So I want to say some things with the character, and play up certain aspects of his condition, if you will —

his feelings of being different, or being an alien and trying to fit into a world of which he's really not a member.'

An escalating budget, which peaked at $180 million, finally made the money men at Warners worry that it would be difficult to get a decent return on their investment. Even with powerhouse producer Jon Peters behind the project, they decided to put it on the shelf for a while. Once they had put it on hold, Burton decided to walk away from the project although Nick remained loyal, even letting the studio off their guaranteed payment of $20 million until they could sort out a satisfactory script. 'I could have, but I didn't collect on it,' he admitted. 'What can I say? To be honest, I've got my whole career ahead of me, and I believe in maintaining a relationship in this industry. And Warner Bros is one of only five studios, and I don't want to create any problems.'

He explained, 'The main problem was that the script came in very expensively. And to me it was worth the gamble because if you love the *Superman* character and the Superman universe, especially with a guy like Tim Burton, you're going to create a fantasy that's going to be a visual feast, and people are going to go see it. But the studio felt that this was their most important franchise, and they wanted the script to be great. And they felt that it was good but not great, so they're going to keep working on it.'

The choice of Nick to play an American icon, albeit a cartoon one, was controversial to say the least. The fact that he announced his intention was to put a new spin on the familiar character and make him more human-like as far as his feelings were concerned only helped to fuel the controversy.

During the early days of discussing the role, he said, 'I would make Superman a freak, but a beautiful freak in that he really cares about people. I wouldn't be afraid to talk about his loneliness and his feeling like an alien, never fitting in and so always compulsively needing to do heroic acts so people would like him and he would feel loved. But that part's still up in the air. No pun intended.'

Nick did not stop there in expressing his desire to play a different kind of Clark Kent. He went on, 'I hope to bring a new take to the screen. I have very specific ideas for Superman, very different ideas. I have different ideas of what super is, and what it isn't.' And he repeated to *Time* magazine's Richard Corliss, 'I want to show how his heroic deeds come from a need to be accepted. He's an alien, he's been adopted, he senses he's different — all the feelings of being weird and insecure.'

Expanding on his theme he went on, 'I am interested in the idea of Superman as the ultimate outsider. And I want to bring out a little more what it would be like to be an alien living on Earth. And all those heroic deeds — might they not be a compulsion to make sure I am loved? If I do these deeds will I be acceptable?'

At that point Nick was already considering repeating the role if it should become a continuing series, 'as long as the nature of the character continues to deliver positive values.'

One of the reasons why Nick wanted to play the Man of Steel was his own son Weston. He said, 'I don't know if I would have had the vision to say, "Superman would be a good role for me" if I had not been a father. Superman speaks to all ages but he comes from a child's universe. And I remember what I felt like as a child being teased. And if there's one kid out there being called a weirdo or a freak, he can look at Superman and think, "Wow, if he's different like me, maybe I can be Superman!" I see it as an opportunity to reach a lot of kids around the world and say something positive.'

Nick was at the time prepared for the fallout from purists who did not consider him Superman material. He said, 'I like that, actually. I like that I have always played "Everyman" because each and every man can be Superman.'

Despite his previous track record for changing his physical appearance to his parts, Nick had no plans to bulk up to play *Superman*. He said, 'I'll just do the maintenance training I always do to maintain my sanity. It's a great way to blow out stress, and with the schedule I'm on now, I definitely need it.'

Although he was enthusiastic about sporting Spandex, Nick admitted that one of the many challenges to playing Superman would be putting on the costume. He said, 'That's the biggest challenge for me. Committing to the costume. Unlike the look of Batman, which is inherently sexy because he's all in dark colours, the Superman costume can go into silliness very easily.'

Nick even experimented with the look but he said, 'It's an icon that's been around at least 50 years and I don't want to mess with it.' He had considered not wearing the red underpants on the outside but that idea got the thumbs down from Weston and Patricia's son Enzo.

After the boys had had their say, Nick conceded, 'We have to stay true to the classic image of Superman. It would be wrong to reinvent him entirely.'

But he admitted, 'I just want to go a little further with the concept. He's definitely going to be an alien. What Christopher Reeve did was perfect, so what else can we do with it? It's a simple, but perfect, story. Because it has so many levels and layers to it, it has become the great myth of pop American culture. There's the whole question of adoption — he was adopted by these ordinary but kind people in Smallville. It's a story of father and son unlike any I can think of in pop culture. It's also a great story of nurture versus nature; what is his genetic encoding versus the way he was brought up? You could get very scientific about it. It's going to be a great acting challenge, because I've got to commit to conveying when he's Superman that he's a warrior from the future, and not be embarrassed by that suit.'

Also, Nick would have had to deal with the challenge of making his audience believe he is a totally different person when Clark Kent puts his glasses on. He said, 'On a subliminal level, that's a beautiful metaphor — you can be a wallflower who's very shy and uncomfortable, but all you have to do is take off your glasses and you're totally beautiful. There's something quite magical about it.'

In late June 1999, William Wisher, the screenwriter best known for his long-time collaboration with *Titanic* director James Cameron — they worked together on the *Terminator* movies — was appointed by Warner Bros to write a new *Superman* script. He had previously delved into the comic book genre with the Sylvester Stallone vehicle *Judge Dredd*. His version of *Superman* was still going to revolve around the death and rebirth of Superman but he was said to be putting a different spin on it so the film could be brought in around the $100 million budget mark.

Even though a new script was being developed, Nick finally came to the realisation that his dream of playing Superman would never be fulfilled and he decided to pass on the project. He said, 'It was a great idea whose time came and went. After a certain point, it becomes diminishing returns. I've been answering questions about Superman for five years. Right now it's best that Warner Brothers and myself move on to something else. In a way, the fact that I was going to play Superman for so many years sort of ruined my chances to play any other hero. Now I can't be anything else. And I didn't even get to be Superman.'

Despite his disappointment over the Superman project, he has never lost his interest in reading comic books. He said, 'Well, I don't really read them. I sit there and hold them and look at them and lose myself in the covers, if that makes any sense. I like the old ones. I like the old *Marvel Mystery* covers back in the '30s and '40s, with the Human Touch and the Sub-Mariner, The Spectre, he was omnipotent, he could do anything. Which made him a very unsuccessful comic book character 'cause you need to have a weakness in order to be intriguing. If you can do anything, no one's going to feel any suspense. But I loved the character anyway. I like the horror comics — *EC, DC, Timely* — they just warm my heart. I don't know why. There's something nostalgic and childlike about them.'

He did not have time to harp on what might have been, as his dance card was full and he was enjoying working at fever pitch. He said, 'I feel that because I've worked as much as I have, I've really found a shorthand in approaching my work. I think I know how to hit the notes now because I have been doing it for so long. And I feel that I'm in my prime. Later on I'll probably slow down a little.'

Nick, who had passed on the opportunity to star in *The Perfect Storm*, which went on to be made in the summer of 1999 with George Clooney and Mark Wahlberg, is scheduled to co-star with Clooney in *The Life of David Gale*, which will be made by Nick's Saturn company. In the film, Clooney is expected to play Gale, a professor and opponent of capital punishment who is convicted of murdering another activist and is put on death row. Nick is said to play a small but pivotal role in the film, which is to be directed by Alan Parker, who directed Nick in *Birdy*.

The Hollywood A-list pretty much consisted of 'the C crew' in 2000 and 2001 — Cage, Cruise, Clooney and Crowe — so all the indications were that with two of them in the film it was destined, at the very least, to attract a lot of media interest and hype.

Through Saturn, Nick is also lined up to produce *Iron Man: The Lou Zamperini Story*, the remarkable, stranger-than-fiction true-life story of an athlete and war hero, which would follow him from his early days as a track star in Torrance, California, to appearing in the 1936 Olympics in Berlin and on to serving as a pilot with the US Air Force during World War II. When his plane crashed into the Pacific, Zamperini and a colleague were adrift without food and water for 47 days, only to land on a Japanese island. There, they were held captive for two years by Japanese sergeant Matsuhiro Watanabe, a vicious guard nicknamed 'The Bird', who tortured Zamperini throughout his internment. After the war, Watanabe avoided prosecution as a war criminal by hiding out in the remote mountains near Nagano until the statute of limitations ran out. In 1998, Zamperini was invited to carry a torch for the US in the Nagano winter Olympics, and while in Japan attempted a reconciliation with his former torturer, only to have their meeting barred by Watanabe's family. The movie is set to be made by Universal Pictures in conjunction with Nick's management team Brillstein-Grey. Nick will be one of the producers for his Saturn Films production company.

With Saturn, Nick also had *Tom Slick: Monster Hunter* under development for Fox. Slick was a Texas oil millionaire who in the 1950s squandered his fortune financing expeditions to search for mythical creatures like The Loch Ness Monster and Bigfoot, and Nick would play him as well as produce. Golightly said, 'It's Indiana Jones meets the Coen brothers.' When he first became interested in the eccentric explorer, the news prompted false rumours that he planned to launch his own Nessie-hunting expedition.

He is also expected to return to a family man role in a new version of the 1962 Glenn Ford and Shirley Jones film *The Courtship of Eddie's Father*, being written for Saturn by the prolific writing team of Dan Cohn and Jeremy Miller. Nick would play a warm, crotchety, young widowed father struggling to find a new wife who meets with his six-year-old son's approval as a stepmother. In the original, the boy was played by Ron Howard, who would go on to star in *Happy Days* and later to direct hit films like *Cocoon*, *Splash*, *Apollo 13* and *Liar, Liar*. The film went on to become a popular television series with *Incredible Hulk* star Bill Bixby, who died of prostate cancer, as the dad. It is expected that the film will be given a new title before its release.

In addition to his acting commitments, Nick is also committed to producing a host of other pictures including *Press Your Luck*, based on the true story of a down-on-his luck Ohio man who discovered how to beat a TV game show, which is expected to star Bill Murray; *Chain*, a revenge story about a man who comes back in a new persona to wreak revenge on a treacherous motorcycle gang; and a romantic comedy called *The Bitter End*.

Nick and Saturn also entered a production deal with Lions Gate Films International to make the dark romantic comedy *Heartbreaker, Inc*, based on a story created by Nick and again scripted by Cohn and Miller. The story is about a professional heartbreaker who is hired by rejected men to turn the tables on the women in their lives.

Saturn's offbeat slate and youthful energy has proved a pleasure for Nick. Talking about his production company, he said, 'Our goal is to establish ourselves as a long-term player in the international film business.' He noted, 'I've been allowed to surround myself with creative people even when I'm not acting. I get stimulated by exciting people who are passionate about their craft, passionate about film-making, have ideas and are free thinkers. That kind of keeps me sharp as an actor as well. I'm able to stay passionate because I'm around passionate people.'

Nick has come to realise that he cannot star in every movie he likes that comes his way. He said, 'It is important to maintain a balance by producing other people's work through my own company. Many times there are movies and genres of films that I enjoy, but I'm not ready to act in them or don't really know if I should act in them. For example, I like Hot Wheels toy cars. I liked them as a child, so I talked to Mattel and said, "What do you think about a Hot Wheels movie?" I've tried to get Jerry Bruckheimer involved in that. I'm probably not going to be in it, but I think it would be a lot of fun for children. Also, it enables me to make movies that are probably of smaller scale and that way I can have a little control over them.'

However, his future projects appear endless. There is also talk of *Speed Racer*, a $35 million, live-action, big-screen version of an animated television series that aired in the United States in the 1960s and 1970s, in which he is supposed to star with Johnny Depp under the direction of Gus Van Sant for Warner Bros. Plus the comedy *I Now Pronounce You Joe and Benny* (or possibly *I Now Pronounce You Chuck and Larry*) in which Nick and Will Smith would play a pair of heterosexual firemen who marry to get better insurance benefits. Nick would play a widowed firefighter worried about what will happen to his two young children if he dies. After he saves the life of his friend, a fast-talking ladies' man and fellow fireman, played by Smith, the pal promises to do anything to repay him. Nick's character calls in the favour by inviting him to have a same-sex marriage because of the family employment bonuses he would be entitled to. As the story unfolds, the two men's situation becomes a *cause célèbre*.

A new version of Roald Dahl's classic children's story *Charlie and the Chocolate Factory* for Warner Bros is also in the works with Nick the front-runner to play the loopy confectioner named Wonka. The story was first turned into a musical movie starring Gene Wilder in 1971, called *Willy Wonka and the Chocolate Factory*. The new movie is being written by *Out of Sight* screenwriter Scott Frank. Brad Grey, who is expected to produce the new film and is a partner in Nick's management company, said, 'Nicolas would be a wonderful choice. He can combine mystery, warmth, and darkness all at the same time.' Frank, however, would like to see Will Smith in the role. He said, 'I went back and read the Oompa-Loompa songs and they're very hip-hop.'

Nick also found himself in competition with *Mission: Impossible* and *Eyes Wide Shut* superstar Tom Cruise to play another comic book hero. Both high-powered Hollywood big-hitters were keen to play *Marvel* character *Iron-Man*. Nick just was not going to let go of his dream to play a cartoon character. Even with *Superman* out of the picture for him, Nick is still in the market to find another way to perform superhuman feats.

As Nick's career continues to go from strength to strength, so more and more accolades keep being heaped up on him. In January 2001, he was presented with the Charles A Crain Desert Palm achievement award at the twelfth annual Palm Springs Film Festival. Among others receiving awards at the same festival was Nick's old friend and co-star Sean Connery, who was given the gala's lifetime achievement award, and the director's achievement prize went to *Gladiator* and *Hannibal* movie-maker Ridley Scott. Nick's *Moonstruck* co-star and admirer, pop diva and Oscar-winning actress Cher, was to have presented him with his award but unfortunately she had to pull out a few days before the ceremony.

However, another admirer travelled thousands of miles to honour Nick in March when he became the first actor ever to receive the Distinguished Decade of Achievement in Film Award at ShoWest 2001, the annual gathering of cinema owners in Las Vegas. Nick's *Captain Corelli's Mandolin* director John Madden flew all the way from London to pay tribute to him and present him with the top award. Madden said, 'Nick Cage is an actor. He is also a star, but the order is significant, and the two terms do not always coexist. His choice of roles is a testament to his determination to live dangerously, to explore as many genres as he can and to test himself against unusual material.'

Robert Sunshine, the chairman of Sunshine Group Worldwide which operates the event, said, 'Over the course of a decade, Nicolas Cage has delivered some of the most memorable performances ever on screen. We are honoured to pay tribute to him at ShoWest 2001.' Brad Schreiber of *Daily Variety* wrote, 'Whether actually eating a cockroach for *Vampire's Kiss*, portraying the darkest recesses of alcoholism in *Leaving Las Vegas* or reinventing himself as a thinking, action hero in *The Rock*, throughout his career Nicolas Cage has shown an unflagging courage in his acting choices. It is for this risk-taking and commitment to character that Cage is honored with ShoWest's first ever Distinguished Decade of Achievement in Film Award.'

Nick confessed that he was still looking for roles to test himself. He said he was still seeking 'roles that would challenge me, roles that were unlike the previous roles, so I could push myself to grow in some way — anything that seemed unique to me'.

Over the years, Nick has mellowed. He admitted, 'I had a reckless period, but I'm done with that. I like red wine. Is that a vice? I don't drink coffee. I don't smoke. I like driving, but I'm not stupid about it. If I want to go fast, I go to the track. And I'm not an angry person. I'm amazed that I'm not. I sometimes wonder where my temper is. I used to have a temper. But I don't have a temper any more. It's weird.'

Part of his mellowing was brought about by his beloved son Weston. Nick said, 'Before I was a parent, I was more of an anarchist. I didn't care. You know, I wanted to shake things up. I was adamant that I rattle the cage, as it were. After I became a parent, I sort of calmed down a bit and became less interested in making a punk statement.'

He may have matured as both an actor and a man, but Nick can still surprise everyone with a new and outrageously wacky idea or performance. His fans have often been confused by his career going in so many different directions. They never know what to expect when they go to see one of his movies because his films are not stereotyped and he is not an actor who can be typecast. This might explain why he can go from having a blockbuster success to a revenue earning disaster, even though he may be happy with his performance.

So Nick has come up with a bizarre solution that shocked the entertainment industry. He wants on occasions to change his name for special projects. His idea is that, for certain films, instead of being known as Nick Cage he will go by the name of Miles Lovecraft. The name is inspired by jazz legend Miles Davis and the 1920s science fiction author HP Lovecraft. Nick said, 'Whenever you saw Miles Lovecraft in a movie, you'd know it was going to be dark subject matter, an independent film. It would be my own little internal protection device so people aren't going to *8MM* expecting to see *The Rock*.'

His vastly experienced team of talent agents and managers were horrified by the idea. So far, executives at his management company Brillstein-Grey and his talent agents at the giant Creative Artists Agency, have succeeded in talking him out of going through with his wacky plan. Nick admitted 'his team' have warned him that people would think he was nuts, not that that has ever stopped him in the past.

In many ways, the movie Nick started work on in March 2001 would probably be more suitable for his alter-ego Miles Lovecraft than action and romantic hero Nick Cage. He packed on around 20lb — his contract stated he had to put on 15 — to star opposite Meryl Streep in *Adaptation*, a film directed by Spike Jonze and written by Charlie Kaufman, the director and screenwriter team that made *Being John Malkovich*. In the film, Nick plays two roles, a Los Angeles scriptwriter named Charlie Kaufman — a joke by the eponymous scriptwriter — and his imaginary twin brother, Donald. They are sexually frustrated brothers who are overweight but suffer from a particular mental disorder, which means they may not actually be too heavy but that is how they see themselves. The film is loosely based on Susan Orlean's novel *The Orchid Thief*, and follows the scriptwriter's attempts to adapt Orlean's anecdotal novel for the screen. Streep, whom Nick has longed to work with, plays Orlean. In between suffering both love-sickness and writer's block, the central character enlists his imaginary twin, who is a fledgling screenwriter, to collaborate on the script which eventually becomes a huge hit. Nick admitted, 'I like flawed characters because somewhere in them I see more of the truth.'

The budget for the film was only in the region of $25 million, which Nick could command as his salary, but once again it was an interesting concept that appealed to him so he agreed to accept an up-front fee of around $5 million in exchange for a sizeable portion of the box-office gross. If the movie proved to be a major success, this would be a shrewd business move on Nick's part.

For the role, Nick became the heaviest he has ever been in his life, weighing more than 14 stone. The fitness fanatic that he has always been faced packing on the pounds with trepidation. He talked to doctors about how it might affect his desire to eat more in the future and he warned Jonze that he was not sure how he would behave after three months of forgoing his daily workout regime. For Nick, working out is not just for his physical health but also his mental well-being. Preparing for the role was not the most pleasant time for Nick. He said, 'Exercise is a huge stress release. I do it because if I don't, I start getting really paranoid.'

While Nick was working on *Adaptation*, he got word that the studio had decided to push back the release date for *Captain Corelli's Mandolin* in the United States. Originally it had been planned to release the movie in the USA on 27 April and a week later in the United Kingdom. However, studio executives decided to delay it until later in the year in America. Officially, the studio stated the reason was that post-production could not meet the release date.

Universal Pictures Distribution President Nikki Rocco said, 'We wanted to give the film-makers as much time as they needed to complete it and deliver the best cut of the film — that's our first and foremost priority.' It was also claimed more time was needed to market the movie to the public. Rocco said, 'Our experience indicates that adult films that are more serious and literate take more time to build awareness. We wanted to give our marketing team ample time to screen it for the press and opinion-makers.'

But if that was the case, why was the film still going to be opened in Britain on 4 May 2001? The reason — the British knew and loved the book while Americans were not so aware of the story. Plus, and this was an even bigger reason, studio executives wanted to place the film in the more Academy-award-friendly second half of the year in the United States. This would mean the film would be fresher in the minds of the members of the Academy of Motion Picture Arts and Sciences, who vote for the Oscars, and would therefore have more of a chance to walk off with awards.

Meanwhile, there seems to be no end to the diversity of characters in Nick's ever-growing body of work. He said, 'I want to have a career where I can look back when I'm 70 and I want to say I pretty well did everything.'

There seems little doubt that this versatile and prolific actor will do just that.

EPILOGUE

Nicolas Cage is the ultimate Everyman actor who can step from dark and thought-provoking roles to light comedy or action-packed adventures. So many actors make what they do look hard or, at the very least, claim it is hard. Yet Nick has always had the knack of making it look easy and enjoyable. He admits, 'I do have fun, and it's important to me to try to do that, 'cause I feel it will be fun for the audience as well.'

But a lot of thought and effort has gone into creating his superbly skilful performances. His choices of film may sometimes be surprising, but there has been nothing haphazard or erratic about the way he has charted his professional life.

'I've put a lot of focus and thought into managing my career,' he says. 'I haven't wanted to rely too much on other people. I've tried to be very specific about the choices I've made, knowing what it is I need to get a balance.'

His intriguing body of work, so varied that it verges on the schizophrenic, has had the uncommon effect of attracting a devoted following of both men and women. Yet he modestly plays down his popularity, joking, 'Generally, the thing that's emerging is that people enjoy seeing me go berserk.'

But this master of the craft of movie-making knows exactly what his audience wants and expects. He says, 'It's very important to me, though, that whatever I do, I'm giving people their money's worth. The death is if you don't do your job well. And I've always tried to do my job well.'

Nick handles his fame well. 'I don't have a bodyguard, I don't have an entourage and I don't wear disguises or anything like that,' he says. 'I move about pretty freely. I've been doing this since I was 17, so I had a slow build. I've been comfortable growing into a kind of star position where it's not such a double-whammy on you as if suddenly it happened overnight and you're trying to think, What the hell am I going to do with this new way of life? It was more of a slow build for me. So it's never really jumped out at me in such a way that I felt claustrophobic or under invasion.'

Always polite and patient to his fans even when being mobbed by autograph seekers, nonetheless he understands the strains facing actors who can't or won't react the same way. He says, 'They are the pressures of always having to be "on" when you meet people, always feeling watched or observed.' So if he doesn't think it is going to be a good day to go out, he says, 'I don't go out. I stay home. I'll eat at home. I find that the best thing to do is monitor myself when it comes to the public. I try to treat people with respect because I believe in doing unto others as I want done to me. So if I can't be polite or positive with somebody, then I just don't go out. The reason I do that is that I know how powerful it can be not to be polite with people. If I met somebody who I was fascinated with or enjoyed their work or what-not, and maybe I caught them on a wrong day, it would just ruin the whole thing for you if they weren't polite or gracious. That can really be damaging for both people. I want the public to view me in a positive light as much as I can help it, and I don't want to ever get in a situation where I view the public with distrust. I want to continue to see the public in a positive light and not as an entity that is trying to take something away from me.'

He is not simply concerned with presenting himself professionally in a good light. Although he does not have a formal religion, he lives by the simple rule of treating others as he would wish to be treated, and once said, 'I will never, ever park in a handicapped space. It's not my style and I think that people who do are inviting some kind of bad karma.'

Nick had no formal training and knows he was lucky to be so successful so young while maintaining his sanity despite the wild man reputation of his early career. He says, 'I don't act for fame. I act to become characters. Acting is a very grey area. How do you act? What's the method? What am I supposed to do? I think a lot of actors, when they start at a very young age, feel the pressure of the camera. That can also lead to the drugs and the alcohol.'

But for him it was the opposite. The camera freed him. It soaked up his anger and gave him a route to direct his energy. He said, 'I understand Laurence Olivier. He's become my favourite actor. I understand that need to never stop working because if you do, then you can see the mess that your life has become.'

He also knows he can't keep doing the same kind of movies he has done in the past. He says, 'Would I want a steady diet of action movies? Absolutely not. I've never wanted a steady diet of any kind of movie. I remember once I got sick of comedies, and that's all anybody would hire me for. Now I'm dying to do a comedy! And I want to do a musical.'

Nick admits that for the last few years he has worked non-stop and has probably taken on far too many projects, but he claims that will change. In future, he says, 'Instead of making three movies a year, I'm making one-and-a-half.' With the amount of work he has in development, however, no one around him is holding their breath to see whether he will keep his promise.

He justifies his dedication to his career by saying, 'I've been acting since I was 17 years old and I've always found a kind of surrogate-family experience through film-making. It's always a balancing act between my work and my family, but the problem is that acting comes out of a place of survival and need for me. Plus, I feel I'm a more balanced person when I'm working.'

Unlike so many people in whatever field they choose, he has never become jaded.

'Acting for me is this incredibly sacred hero that came in and saved my life. To me, it's been like a therapy — it's what's kept me balanced, kept me with a sense of purpose. I could get all the stuff out of me that I had, all that fire — anger, or love, or lust. Anything. All actors are wounded birds — we couldn't really be doing anything else. I've done scenes with five extremely talented actors all in the same room — one guy's barking, another's shouting profanity, the other's in a trance, one's asking to be hit. It looks like we're all in a nut-house. We all take our afflictions and we transform them into a place where they can be, be glorified. When the fact of the matter is, historically, we're all street urchins. Gypsies. We came out of the gutter. We've become so glorified in the movie-star system that it's become this artificial royalty, which, if you look at the roots of it, is completely preposterous. The truth is that we're circus clowns.'

Nicolas Cage is no circus clown. He is a true actor, who brings a humanity and a realism to his characters, and is able to make them believable even when they are totally unbelievable. He says, 'My characters are generally flawed — neither all bad, nor all good. So I always look for a little bit of humanity in them, it's irresponsible not to be.'

His father August Coppola once told him, 'Tom Cruise sells perfection, you sell imperfection.'

Maybe, but it is perfect imperfection.

FILMOGRAPHY

Fast Times at Ridgemont High (1982) Director: Amy Heckerling. Producers: Art Linson and Irving Azoff. Screenplay: Cameron Crowe, based on his book. Photography: Matthew R Leonetti. Editor: Eric Jenkins. Music: Joe Walsh and various recording artists. A Universal Pictures release of a Refugee Film production. Cast: Sean Penn, Jennifer Jason Leigh, Judge Reinhold, Robert Romanus, Brian Backer, Phoebe Cates, Ray Walston, Scott Thomson, Vincent Schiavelli, Amanda Wyss, DW Brown, Forest Whitaker and *Nicolas Coppola* (in a bit part). US Box Office: $27,092,880

Rumble Fish (1983) Director: Francis Ford Coppola. Producers: Fred Roos and Doug Claybourne. Screenplay: SE Hinton and Francis Ford Coppola, based on SE Hinton's novel *Rumble Fish*. Photography: Stephen H Burum. Editor: Barry Malkin. Music: Stewart Copeland. A Universal Pictures release. Cast: Matt Dillon, Mickey Rourke, Diane Lane, Dennis Hopper, Diana Scarwid, Vincent Spano, *Nicolas Cage*, Christopher Penn, Larry Fishburne, William Smith, Michael Higgins, Glenn Withrow, Tom Waits and Herb Rice. US Box Office: $2,494,480

Valley Girl also released under the title *Bad Boyz* and on video as *Rebel Dreams* (1983) Director: Martha Coolidge. Producers: Wayne Crawford and Andrew Lane. Screenplay: Wayne Crawford and Andrew Lane. Photography: Frederick Elmes. Editor: Eva Gardos. Music: Men at Work, Culture Club and others. An Atlantic Releasing Corp release of a Valley 9000 presentation. Cast: *Nicolas Cage*, Deborah Foreman, Frederick Forrest, Elizabeth Daily, Michael Bowen, Cameron Dye, Heidi Holicker, Michelle Meyrink, Colleen Camp, Tina Theberge, Richard Sanders and Lee Purcell. US Box Office: $16,797,122

Racing with the Moon (1984) Director: Richard Benjamin. Producers: Alain Bernheim and John Kohn. Screenplay: Steven Kloves. Photography: John Bailey. Editor:

Jacqueline Cambas. Music: Dave Grusin. A Paramount Pictures release of a Jaffe-Lansing production. Cast: Sean Penn, Elizabeth McGovern, *Nicolas Cage*, John Karlen, Rutanya Alda, Crispin Glover, Kate Williamson, Suzanne Adkinson, Shawn Schepps, Julie Philips, Michael Talbott and Carol Kane.
US Box Office: $5,384,756

The Cotton Club (1984) Director: Francis Ford Coppola. Producer: Robert Evans. Screenplay: William Kennedy and Francis Ford Coppola, based on a story by William Kennedy, Francis Ford Coppola and Mario Puzo, suggested by a pictorial history by James Haskins. Photography: Stephen Goldblatt. Editors: Barry Malkin and Robert Lovett. Music: John Barry. An Orion Pictures release of a Zoetrope Studio Production. Cast: Richard Gere, Gregory Hines, Diane Lane, Lonette McKee, Bob Hoskins, James Remar, *Nicolas Cage*, Allen Garfield, Fred Gwynne, Gwen Verdon, Lisa Jane Persky, Maurice Hines, Laurence Fishburne and Tom Waits.
US Box Office: $25,928,721

Birdy (1984) Director: Alan Parker. Producer: Alan Marshall. Screenplay: Sandy Kroopf and Jack Behr, based on the novel *Birdy* by William Wharton. Photography: Michael Seresin. Editor: Gerry Hambling. Music: Peter Gabriel. A TriStar Pictures release. Cast: Matthew Modine, *Nicolas Cage*, John Harkins, Sandy Barton, Karen Young, Bruno Kirby and Nancy Fish.
US Box Office: $1,494,883

The Boy in Blue (1986) Director: Charles Jarrott. Producer: John Kemeny. Screenplay: Douglas Bowie. Photography: Pierre Mignot. Editor: Rit Wallis. Music: Roger Webb. A 20th Century Fox release of an ICC-Denis Heroux-John Kemeny Production. Cast: *Nicolas Cage*, Cynthia Dale, Christopher Plummer, David Naughton, Sean Sullivan, Melody Anderson, James B Douglas, Walter Massey, Austin Willis, Philip Craig and Robert McCormick.
US Box Office: $94,621

Peggy Sue Got Married (1986) Director: Francis Ford Coppola. Producer: Paul R Gurian. Screenplay: Jerry Leichtling and Arlene Sarner. Photography: Jordan Cronenweth. Editor: Barry Malkin. Music: John Barry. A TriStar release from Rastar of a TriStar/Delphi IV and V Productions production. Cast: Kathleen Turner, *Nicolas Cage*, Barry Miller, Catherine Hicks, Joan Allen, Kevin J O'Connor, Jim Carrey, Lisa Jane Persky, Lucinda Jenney, Wil Shriner, Barbara Harris, Don Murray, Sofia Coppola, Maureen O'Sullivan, Leon Ames, Randy Bourne, Helen Hunt and John Carradine.
US Box Office: $37,848,832

Raising Arizona (1987) Director: Joel Coen. Producer: Ethan Coen. Screenplay: Ethan and Joel Coen. Photography: Barry Sonnenfeld. Editor: Michael R Miller. Music: Carter Burwell. A 20th Century Fox release of a Circle Films presentation of a Ted and Jim Pedas/Ben Berenholtz production. Cast: *Nicolas Cage*, Holly Hunter, Trey Wilson, John Goodman, William Forsythe, Sam Murrey, Frances McDormand, Randall 'Tex' Cobb, TJ Kuhn, Lynne Dumin Kitei and Peter Benedek.
US Box Office: $21,188,258

Moonstruck (1987) Director: Norman Jewison. Producers: Patrick Palmer and Norman Jewison. Screenplay: John Patrick Shanley. Photography: David Watkin. Editor: Lou Lombardo. Music: Dick Hyman. An MGM/UA Communications release of a Metro-Goldwyn-Mayer presentation of a Patrick Palmer-Norman Jewison production. Cast: Cher, *Nicolas Cage*, Vincent Gardenia, Olympia Dukakis, Danny Ailello, Julie Bovasso, John Mahoney and Louis Guss.
US Box Office: $79,198,828

Never on Tuesday (1987) Director: Adam Rifkin. Producers: Screenplay: Adam Rifkin. Photography: Alan Jones Editor: Ed Rothkowitz Music: Richard Stone A Palisades Entertainment Corp Picture. A Paramount Home Video release. Cast: Claudia Christian, Andrew Laeur, Peter Berg, Dave Anderson, Mark Garbarino, Melvyn Pearls and Brett Seals. Uncredited cast: *Nicolas Cage*, Cary Elwes, Emilio Estevez, Gilbert Gottfried, Judd Nelson and Charlie Sheen.
Straight to video in US

Vampire's Kiss (1989) Director: Robert Bierman. Producers: John Daley, Derek Gibson, Barbara Zitwer and Barry Shils. Screenplay: Joseph Minion. Photography: Stefan Czapsky. Editor: Angus Newton. Music: Colin Towns. A Hemdale release of a Magellan Pictures production. Cast: *Nicolas Cage*, Maria Conchita Alonso, Jennifer Beals, Elizabeth Ashley, Kasi Lemmons, Bob Lujan, Jessica Lundy, John Walker and David Pierce.
US Box Office: $600,804

Tempo di uccidere also released under the titles *The Short Cut* and *Time to Kill* (1989) Director: Giuliano Montaldo. Producers: Leo Pesoarolo and Guido De Laurentiis. Screenplay: Furio Scarpelli, Giacomo Scarpelli, Paolo Virzi and Giuliano Montaldo, based on the novel *Tempo di uccidere* by Ennio Flaiano and Rizzoli Editore. Photography: Blasco Giurato. Editor: Alfredo Muscietti. Music: Ennio Morricone. A Titanus release of an Ellepi Film/Dania Film/SURF Film/DMV Distribuzione/Italfrance co-production, in association with Reteitalia. Cast: *Nicolas Cage*, Ricky Tognazzi, Patrice-Flora Praxo, Giancarlo Giannini, Gianluca Favilla, Georges Claiese, Robert Liensol and Vittorio Amandola.
Straight to video in US

Fire Birds also released under the title *Wings of the Apache* (1990) Director: David Green. Producer: William Badalato. Screenplay: Nick Thiel and Paul F Edwards, based on a story by Step Tyner, John K Swensson and Dale Dye. Photography: Tony Imi. Editors: Jon Poll, Norman Buckley and Dennis O'Connor. Music: David Newman. A Buena Vista release from Touchstone Pictures of a Nova International Films presentation of a Keith Barish/Arnold Kopelson production. Cast: *Nicolas Cage*, Tommy Lee Jones, Sean Young, Bryan Kestner, Dale Dye, Mary Ellen Trainor and JA Preston.
US Box Office: $14,760,451

Wild at Heart (1990) Director: David Lynch. Producers: Monty Montgomery, Steve Golin and Joni Sighvatsson. Screenplay: David Lynch, based on the novel by Barry Gifford. Photography: Frederick Elmes. Editor: Duwayne Dunham. Music: Angelo Badalamenti. A Samuel Goldwyn Co release of a Polygram/Propaganda production.

Cast: *Nicolas Cage*, Laura Dern, Diane Ladd, Willem Dafoe, Harry Dean Stanton, Isabella Rossellini, Crispin Glover, W Morgan Sheppard and Sherilyn Fenn.
US Box Office: $14,535,649

Zandalee (1991) Director: Sam Pillsbury. Producers: William Blaylock and Eyal Rimmon. Screenplay: Mari Kornhauser. Photography: Walt Lloyd. Editor: Michael Horton. Music: Pray for Rain. An Electric Pictures-ITC Entertainment Group production. Cast: *Nicolas Cage*, Judge Reinhold, Erika Anderson, Viveca Lindfors, Joe Pantoliano, Marisa Tomei and Aaron Neville.
Straight to video in US

Honeymoon in Vegas (1992) Director: Andrew Bergman. Producer: Mike Lobell. Screenplay: Andrew Bergman. Photography: William A Fraker. Editor: Barry Malkin. Music: David Newman. A Columbia release of a Castle Rock Entertainment presentation in association with New Line Cinema of a Lobell/Bergman production. Cast: James Caan, *Nicolas Cage*, Sarah Jessica Parker, Pat Morita, Johnny Williams, John Capodice, Roberto Costanzo, Anne Bancroft, Peter Boyle and Burton Gilliam.
US Box Office: $35,222,000

Amos & Andrew (1993) Director: E Max Frye. Producer: Gary Goetzman. Screenplay: E Max Frye. Photography: Walt Lloyd. Editor: Jane Kurson. Music: Richard Gibbs. A Columbia Pictures release of a Castle Rock Entertainment Production, in association with New Line Cinema. Cast: *Nicolas Cage*, Samuel L Jackson, Dabney Coleman, Michael Lerner, Margaret Colin, Brad Dourif and Giancarlo Esposito.
US Box Office: $9,461,630

Red Rock West (1994) Director: John Dahl. Producers: Sigurjon Sighvatsson and Steve Golin. Screenplay: John and Rick Dahl. Photography: Mark Reshovsky. Editor: Scott Chestnut. Music: William Orlis. A Roxie Releasing release of a Polygram Filmed Entertainment presentation of a Propaganda Films production in association with Polygram Filmed Entertainment. Cast: *Nicolas Cage*, Dennis Hopper, Lara Flynn Boyle, JT Walsh, Timothy Carhart, Dan Shor, Dwight Yoakam and Bobby Joe McFadden.
US Box Office: N/A

Deadfall (1994) Director: Christopher Coppola. Producer: Ted Fox. Screenplay: Christopher Coppola and Nick Vallelonga. Photography: Maryse Alberti. Editor: Phillip Linson. Music: Jim Fox. A Trimark release of a Ted Fox Productions production. Cast: Michael Biehn, James Coburn, *Nicolas Cage*, Sarah Trigger, Peter Fonda, Charlie Sheen and Talia Shire.
US Box Office: N/A

A Century of Cinema (1994) Documentary. Director: Caroline Thomas. Producer: Caroline Thomas. Screenplay: Bob Thomas. Editor: William Cole. Cast: Richard Attenborough, Kim Basinger, Milton Berle, George Burns, *Nicolas Cage*, Kevin Costner, Billy Crystal, Tony Curtis, Kirk Douglas, Clint Eastwood, Jane Fonda, Harrison Ford, Morgan Freeman, Charlton Heston, Bob Hope, Anthony Hopkins,

Bob Hoskins, Shirley MacLaine, Bette Midler, Liza Minelli, Demi Moore, Maureen O'Hara, Sidney Poitier, Richard Pryor, Burt Reynolds, Julia Roberts, Mickey Rooney, Meg Ryan, Arnold Schwarzenegger, Steven Spielberg, Sylvester Stallone, James Stewart, Meryl Streep, Donald Sutherland, Jessica Tandy, Denzel Washington and Shelley Winters.
US Box Office: N/A

Guarding Tess (1994) Director: Hugh Wilson. Producers: Ned Tanen and Nancy Graham Tanen. Screenplay: Hugh Wilson and Peter Torokvei. Photography: Brian Reynolds. Editor: Sidney Levin. Music: Michael Convertino. A TriStar release of a Channel production. Cast: Shirley MacLaine, *Nicolas Cage*, Austin Pendleton, Edward Albert, James Rebhorn, Richard Griffiths, John Roselius, David Graf, Dale Dye, James Handy and Susan Blommaert.
US Box Office: $27,023,278

It Could Happen to You (1994) Director: Andrew Bergman. Producer: Mike Lobell. Screenplay: Jane Anderson. Photography: Caleb Deschanel. Editor: Barry Malkin. Music: Carter Burwell and Joe Mulherin. A TriStar Pictures release of an Adelson/Baumgarten and Lobell/Bergman production. Cast: *Nicolas Cage*, Bridget Fonda, Rosie Perez, Wendell Pierce, Isaac Hayes, Victor Rojas, Seymour Cassel, Stanley Tucci and Red Buttons.
US Box Office: $37,784,369

Trapped in Paradise (1994) Director: George Gallo. Producers: Jon Davison, George Gallo and David Permut. Screenplay: George Gallo. Photography: Jack N Green. Editor: Terry Rawlings. Music: Robert Folk. A 20th Century Fox release of a Jon Davison/George Gallo production. Cast: *Nicolas Cage*, Jon Lovitz, Dana Carvey, John Ashton, Madchen Amick, Donald Moffat, Richard Jenkins, Florence Stanley, Angela Paton, Vic Manni, Frank Pesce, Sean McCann, Paul Lazar, John Bergantine, Sean O'Bryan and Richard B Shull.
US Box Office: $5,845,551

Kiss of Death (1995) Director: Barbet Schroeder. Producers: Barbet Schroeder and Susan Hoffman. Screenplay: Richard Price, based on the 1947 screenplay by Ben Hecht and Charles Lederer from a story by Eleazar Lipsky. Photography: Luciano Tovoli. Editor: Lee Percy. Music: Trevor Jones. A 20th Century Fox release. Cast: David Caruso, Samuel L Jackson, *Nicolas Cage*, Helen Hunt, Kathryn Erbe, Stanley Tucci, Michael Rapaport, Ving Rhames, Philip Baker Hall and Anthony Heald.
US Box Office: $14,942,422

Leaving Las Vegas (1995) Director: Mike Figgis. Producers: Lila Cazès and Annie Stewart. Screenplay: Mike Figgis, based on the novel by John O'Brien. Photography: Declan Quinn. Editor: John Smith. Music: Mike Figgis. An MGM/UA release of a United Artists/Lumière Pictures production. Cast: *Nicolas Cage*, Elizabeth Shue, Julian Sands, Richard Lewis, Valeria Golino, Graham Beckel, R Lee Ermey, Laurie Metcalf, David Brisbin, Xander Berkeley, Julian Lennon and Lou Rawls.
US Box Office: $31,983,777

The Rock (1996) Director: Michael Bay. Producers: Don Simpson and Jerry Bruckheimer. Screenplay: David Weisberg, Douglas S Cook and Mark Rosner from

a story by David Weisberg and Douglas S Cook. Photography: John Schwartzman. Editor: Richard Francis-Bruce. Music: Nick Glennie-Smith, Harry Gregson-Williams and Hans Zimmer. A Buena Vista release of a Hollywood Pictures presentation of a Don Simpson and Jerry Bruckheimer production. Cast: Sean Connery, *Nicolas Cage*, Ed Harris, Michael Biehn, William Forsythe, David Morse, John Spencer, John C McGinley, Tony Todd, Bokeem Woodbine, Danny Nucci, Claire Forlaini, Vanessa Marcil and Gregory Sporleder.
US Box Office: $134,017,832

Con Air (1997) Director: Simon West. Producer: Jerry Bruckheimer. Screenplay: Scott Rosenberg. Photography: David Tattersall. Editors: Chris Lebenzon, Steve Mirkovich, Glen Scantlebury. Music: Mark Mancina and Trevor Rabin. A Buena Vista release of a Touchstone Pictures presentation of a Jerry Bruckheimer production. Cast: *Nicolas Cage*, John Cusack, John Malkovich, Steve Buscemi, Ving Rhames, Colm Meaney, Mykelti Williamson, Rachel Ticotin, Monica Potter, Dave Chappelle, MC Gainey and John Roselius.
US Box Office: $101,091,253

Face/Off (1997) Director: John Woo. Producers: David Permut, Barrie M Osborne, Terrence Chang and Christopher Godsick. Screenplay: Mike Werb and Michael Colleary. Photography: Oliver Wood. Editors: Christian Wagner and Steven Kemper. Music: John Powell. A Paramount Pictures release of a Douglas/Reuther-WCG Entertainment-David Permut production. Cast: John Travolta, *Nicolas Cage*, Joan Allen, Alessandro Nivola, Gina Gershon, Dominique Swain, Nick Cassavetes, Harve Presnell, Colm Feore, John Carroll Lynch, CCH Pounder, Robert Wisdom, Margaret Cho, Jamie Denton and Matt Ross.
US Box Office: $112,238,697

Welcome to Hollywood (1998) Director: Adam Rifkin and Tony Markes. Producer: Zachary Matz. Screenplay: Shawn Ryan and Tony Markes, from a story by Adam Rifkin. Photography: Kramer Morgenthau. Music: Justin Reinhardt. Cast: Tony Markes, Adam Rifkin, Angie Everhart, David Andriole, *Nicolas Cage*, Laurence Fishburne, Jeff Goldblum, Cuba Gooding Jr, David Hasselhoff, Mike Leigh, Ron Shelton, Will Smith, Bobbi Thompson and John Travolta.
US Box Office: N/A

City of Angels (1998) Director: Brad Silberling. Producers: Dawn Steel and Charles Roven. Screenplay: Dana Stevens. Based on the film *Wings of Desire*, directed by Wim Wenders and written by Wim Wenders and Richard Reitinger. Photography: John Seale. Editor: Lynzee Klingman. Music: Gabriel Yared. A Warner Bros release, in association with Regency Pictures, of an Atlas Entertainment production. Cast: *Nicolas Cage*, Meg Ryan, Andre Braugher, Dennis Franz, Colm Feore, Robin Bartlett, Joanna Merlin and Sarah Dampf.
US Box Office: $78,745,923

Snake Eyes (1998) Director: Brian De Palma. Producer: Brian De Palma. Screenplay: David Koepp based on a story by Brian De Palma and David Koepp. Photography: Stephen H Burum. Editor: Bill Pankow. Music: Ryuichi Sakamoto. A Paramount release of a DeBart production. Cast: *Nicolas Cage*, Gary Sinise, John

Heard, Carla Gugino, Stan Shaw, Kevin Dunn, Michael Rispoli, Joel Fabiani, Luis Guzmán, David Anthony Higgins, Mike Starr, Tamara Tunie and Chip Zien.
US Box Office: $55,591,409

8MM (1999) Director: Joel Schumacher. Producers: Gavin Polone, Judy Hofflund and Joel Schumacher. Screenplay: Andrew Kevin Walker. Photography: Robert Elswit. Editor: Mark Stevens. Music: Mychael Danna. A Sony Pictures Entertainment release of a Columbia Pictures presentation of a Hofflund/Polone production. Cast: *Nicolas Cage*, Joaquin Phoenix, James Gandolfini, Peter Stormare, Anthony Heald, Chris Bauer, Catherine Keener, Myra Carter and Amy Morton.
US Box Office: $36,360,923

Bringing Out the Dead (1999) Director: Martin Scorsese. Producers: Scott Rudin, Barbara De Fina. Screenplay: Paul Schrader from a book by Joseph Connelly. Photography: Robert Richardson. Editor: Thelma Schoonmaker. Music: Elmer Bernstein. A Paramount Pictures release. Cast: *Nicolas Cage*, Patricia Arquette, Marc Anthony, Cliff Curtis, John Goodman, Mary Beth Hurt, Ving Rhames, Tom Sizemore and Aida Turturro.
US Box Office: $16,642,210

Gone in 60 Seconds (2000) Director: Dominic Sena. Producers: Jerry Bruckheimer and Mike Stenson. Screenplay: Scott Rosenberg. Photography: Paul Cameron. Editors: Chris Lebenzon and Tom Muldoon. Music: Trevor Robin. A Buena Vista release of a Touchstone Pictures and Jerry Bruckheimer Films presentation. Cast: *Nicolas Cage*, Angelina Jolie, Giovanni Ribisi, Robert Duval, Frances Fisher, Master P, Vinnie Jones.

The Family Man (2000) Director: Brett Reiner. Producers: Marc Abraham, Tony Ludwig, Alan Riche and Howard Rosenman. Screenplay: David Diamond and David Welshman. Photography: Dante Spinotti. Editor: Mark Halftrack. Music: Danny Elman. A Universal Pictures Release of a Beacon Pictures Presentation of a Riche/Ludwig-Zvi Howard Rosenman Production. Cast: *Nicolas Cage*, Téa Leoni, Don Cheadle, Jeremy Piven, Saul Rubinek, Harve Presnell, Mary-Beth Hurt, Robert Downey Sr and Paul Sorvino.
US Box Office $74,679,430

Captain Corelli's Mandolin (2001) Director: John Madden. Producers: Tim Bevan, Eric Fellner, Mark Huffam and Kevin Loader. Screenplay: Shawn Slovo, based on a novel by Louis de Bernières. Photography: John Toll. Editor: Mick Audsley. Music: Stephen Warbeck. A Universal Pictures release of a Studio Canal Plus, Universal Pictures and Working Title Films production. Cast: *Nicolas Cage*, Christian Bale, Penélope Cruz, Martin Glyn Murray, John Hurt, David Morrisey and Irene Pappas.
US release summer 2001

Windtalkers (2001) Director: John Woo. Producers: Terence Chang, Tracie Graham, Alison R Rosenweig and John Woo. Screenplay: Joe Batteer and John Rice. Photography: Jeffrey L Kimball. Editor: Steven Kemper. An MGM/UA release of an MGM/UA production. Cast: *Nicolas Cage*, Adam Beach, Christian Slater, Peter Stormore, Noah Emmerich, Mark Ruffalo, Brian Van Holt, Martin Henderson,

Roger Willie, Frances O'Connor and James D Dever.
US release November 2001

Christmas Carol: The Movie (2001) Director: Jimmy T Murakami. Producer: Iain Harvey. Screenplay: Piet Kroon and Robert Llewellyn. Editor: Taylor Grant. Music: Julian Nott. A UIP release of an Illuminated Film Company, Medien-Beteilgungs-Gesellschaft MBH and The Film Consortium production. Cast (voices): *Nicolas Cage*, Simon Callow, Arthur Cox, Michael Gambon, Jane Horrocks, Rhys Ifans, Iain Jones, Robert Llewellyn, Juliet Stevenson and Kate Winslet.
No US release date.

Adaptation (2001). Director: Spike Jonze. Producers: Jonathan Demme, Vincent Landay and Ed Saxon. Screenplay: Charlie Kaufman and Donald Kaufman, based on the nonfiction novel *The Orchid Thief* by Susan Orlean. Photography: Lance Accord. A Columbia Pictures release of a Clinica Estetica production. Cast: *Nicolas Cage* Meryl Streep, Chris Cooper.
No US release date

Television

Best of Times (1981) Cast: *Nicolas Cage* and Jill Schoelen.

Industrial Symphony No. 1: The Dream of the Broken Hearted (1990) Director: David Lynch. Producer: David Lynch. Music: Angelo Badalamenti and David Lynch. Cast: Michael J Anderson, *Nicolas Cage*, Julee Cruise and Laura Dern.

American Heroes & Legends — (1992) — Series — *Nicolas Cage* narrated episode on Davy Crocket

Hi-Octane — (1995) — Series — *Nicolas Cage* guest-starred

Awards

1988, Golden Globes — Nominated Best Performance by an Actor in a Motion Picture — Comedy/Musical — *Moonstruck*

1989, Catalonian International Film Festival, Sitges, Spain — Best Actor — *Vampire's Kiss*
(Tied with Michael Gambon for *The Cook, the Thief, His Wife & Her Lover*)

1989, Independent Feature Project West — Nominated Best Actor — *Vampire's Kiss*

1993, Golden Globes — Nominated Best Performance by an Actor in a Motion Picture — Comedy/Musical — *Honeymoon in Vegas*

1995, San Sebastian International Film Festival's Silver Seashell Award — Best Actor — *Leaving Las Vegas*

1995, New York Critics Circle Award — Best Actor — *Leaving Las Vegas*

1995, National Society of Film Critics Award — Best Actor — *Leaving Las Vegas*

1995, National Board of Review Award — Best Actor — *Leaving Las Vegas*

1995, Los Angeles Film Critics Association Award — Best Actor — *Leaving Las Vegas*

1996, Screen Actors Guild Award — Outstanding Performance by a Male Actor in a Leading Role — *Leaving Las Vegas*

1996, Golden Globes — Best Performance by an Actor in a Motion Picture — Drama — *Leaving Las Vegas*

1996, Academy of Motion Picture Arts and Sciences (Oscars) — Best Actor — *Leaving Las Vegas*

1996, British Academy of Film & Television Arts — Nominated Best Performance by an Actor in a Leading Role — *Leaving Las Vegas*

1996, Independent Spirit Awards — Nominated Best Male Lead — *Leaving Las Vegas*

1996, Montreal World Film Festival, Canada — Lifetime Achievement Award (youngest ever actor to receive this award)

1997, MTV Movie Award — Best On-Screen Duo — Shared with Sean Connery — *The Rock*

1997, Blockbuster Entertainment Award — Favourite Actor, Action/Adventure — *The Rock*

1998, Blockbuster Entertainment Award — Favourite Actor, Action/Adventure — *Face/Off* and also for *Con Air*

1998, MTV Movie Award — Best On-Screen Duo — Shared with John Travolta — *Face/Off*

1998, MTV Movie Award — Nominated Best Male Performance — *Face/Off*

1998, MTV Movie Award — Nominated Best Villain — Shared with John Travolta — *Face/Off*
1998, Star on Hollywood's Walk of Fame (31 July 1998)

1999, Blockbuster Entertainment Awards — Favourite Actor — Drama/Romance — *City of Angels*

1999, Blockbuster Entertainment Awards — Favourite Actor — Suspense — *Snake Eyes*

1999, MTV Movie Awards — nominated — Best On-Screen Duo — shared with Meg Ryan — *City of Angels*

2001, Blockbuster Entertainment Awards – Favourite Actor – Drama/Romance – *Family Man*

2001, Blockbuster Entertainment Awards – Nominated Favourite Actor – Action – *Gone in 60 Seconds*

2001, California State University, Fullerton — Honorary Degree